PROFESSIONAL
TEAM FOUNDATION SERVER 2013

PROFESSIONAL

Team Foundation Server 2013

PROFESSIONAL

Team Foundation Server 2013

Steven St. Jean
Damian Brady
Ed Blankenship
Martin Woodward
Grant Holliday

wrox
A Wiley Brand

Professional Team Foundation Server 2013

Published by
John Wiley & Sons, Inc.
10475 Crosspoint Boulevard
Indianapolis, IN 46256
www.wiley.com

Copyright © 2014 by John Wiley & Sons, Inc., Indianapolis, Indiana

Published simultaneously in Canada

ISBN: 978-1-118-83634-7
ISBN: 978-1-118-83641-5 (ebk)
ISBN: 978-1-118-83631-6 (ebk)

Manufactured in the United States of America

10 9 8 7 6 5 4 3 2 1

For general information on our other products and services please contact our Customer Care Department within the United States at (877) 762-2974, outside the United States at (317) 572-3993 or fax (317) 572-4002.

Wiley publishes in a variety of print and electronic formats and by print-on-demand. Some material included with stan-dard print versions of this book may not be included in e-books or in print-on-demand. If this book refers to media such as a CD or DVD that is not included in the version you purchased, you may download this material at http://book-support.wiley.com. For more information about Wiley products, visit www.wiley.com.

Library of Congress Control Number: 2014930418

For Kim, Danielle, and Jessica, who keep me grounded. With all my love.

—Steven

For my amazing wife, Lisa—the best person I've ever met.

—Damian

To Mom, Dad, Tiffany, Zach, Daniel, Mike, and Grandma, and to all those on the product teams that make this an amazing product that positively impacts so many in the software engineering community.

—Ed

To Catherine.

—Martin

To my son, William Grant Holliday.

—Grant

ABOUT THE AUTHORS

STEVEN ST. JEAN is a Senior ALM Consultant with Microsoft's Premier Support for Developers team. Prior to that, he worked with Notion Solutions for six years as a Senior ALM Consultant. He has twenty years of industry experience, the past seven focused on assisting clients with maturing their development processes, including the use of the Microsoft tools stack. He is a former Microsoft MVP in Visual Studio ALM, a Microsoft Certified Solution Developer in Team Foundation Server (TFS), and an author and technical editor of a number of books pertaining to ALM and TFS. He speaks on various ALM process and tooling topics at user groups and code camps. In his free time, he enjoys spending time with his wife and daughters, traveling, and photography. You can find his technical blog at `http://sstjean.blogspot.com`, and his Twitter handle is @SteveStJean.

DAMIAN BRADY is a Solution Architect and State Manager for SSW in Brisbane, Australia, specializing in Application Lifecycle Management and ASP.NET development. He spends most of his time working with teams to mature their development process, but is never too far from a keyboard—cutting code and bringing projects to completion. Damian is an MVP in Visual Studio ALM and runs the Brisbane .NET User Group and the annual DeveloperDeveloperDeveloper Brisbane conference. He regularly presents at events in Australia and internationally, including Tech Ed Australia and New Zealand. You can find his blog at `http://blog.damianbrady.com.au`, and his Twitter handle is @damovisa.

ED BLANKENSHIP works at Microsoft as the Product Manager for Visual Studio Online, Team Foundation Server, and Application Lifecycle Management. Before becoming Product Manager, he was the Program Manager for the Lab and Environment Management scenarios of the Visual Studio ALM and Team Foundation Server product family. He began working with Team Foundation Server and Visual Studio ALM from its inception nearly eight years ago.

Before joining Microsoft, Ed was awarded as a Microsoft Most Valuable Professional (MVP) for five years. In 2010, he was voted the Microsoft MVP of the Year for Visual Studio ALM & TFS by his peers. Ed was also a TFS consultant and the ALM Practice Technical Lead at Imaginet (formerly Notion Solutions). Prior to consulting, Ed was the Release Engineering Manager at Infragistics, where he led a multi-year Team Foundation Server and Visual Studio Team System implementation globally to improve the development process life cycle.

Ed has authored and served as technical editor for several Wrox books. He has also authored numerous articles, and spoken at various user groups, events, radio shows, and conferences, including TechEd North America. You can find him sharing his experiences at his technical blog at `www.edsquared.com` and on Twitter with his handle @EdBlankenship.

MARTIN WOODWARD is a Principal Program Manager on the Visual Studio team at Microsoft. He frequently speaks about Application Lifecycle Management and Team Foundation Server at events internationally and has coauthored several books on the topic. Before joining Microsoft, Martin worked at Teamprise and was the Team System MVP of the Year. You can find more information at his blog at `http://woodwardweb.com`, reach him at @martinwoodward on Twitter, or listen to his podcast at `http://RadioTFS.com`.

GRANT HOLLIDAY is a Senior Service Engineer for Microsoft Visual Studio Online. Visual Studio Online offers Team Foundation Server and other developer services hosted in Windows Azure, accessible from anywhere using existing and familiar tools, and supporting all languages and platforms. As a Service Engineer, he works behind the scenes to keep the service up and running smoothly for customers around the world. Prior to this role, he traveled around Australia visiting customers and performing TFS and SQL health checks as a Premier Field Engineer. He also spent three years in Redmond, Washington as a Program Manager in the TFS product group. He was responsible for the internal TFS server deployments at Microsoft, including the largest and busiest TFS server in the world used by Developer Division. Grant shares his experiences managing TFS at his blog `http://blogs.msdn.com/granth/`.

ABOUT THE CONTRIBUTOR

EDWARD THOMSON is a Software Development Engineer for Microsoft Visual Studio, where he develops the core Git functionality for Visual Studio and Team Foundation Server. Prior to that, he developed Team Explorer Everywhere, Microsoft's set of cross-platform version control clients for Team Foundation Server. Before joining Microsoft, Edward developed version control tools at Teamprise and SourceGear. You can find Edward on Twitter as @ethomson and online at http://www.edwardthomson.com/.

ABOUT THE TECHNICAL EDITOR

ANTHONY BORTON is the lead ALM consultant for Enhance ALM Pty Ltd, an Australian consulting and training company specializing in Application Lifecycle Management. He delivers training on Microsoft's ALM products through Seattle-based training provider QuickLearn Training, and is the lead ALM trainer behind www.alm-training.com. Since passing Microsoft Exam 001 back in 1993, Anthony has completed over 58 exams including Microsoft Certified Solutions Developer: Application Lifecycle Management. Anthony is a sought-after trainer and has delivered technical training and consulting in the United States, Europe, and all across the Asia Pacific region. He is a Microsoft MVP (Visual Studio ALM) and a Microsoft Certified Trainer. In his spare time he enjoys traveling and spending time with his family.

CREDITS

EXECUTIVE EDITOR
Robert Elliott

PROJECT EDITOR
Christina Haviland

TECHNICAL EDITOR
Anthony Borton

SENIOR PRODUCTION EDITOR
Kathleen Wisor

COPY EDITOR
Nancy Rapoport

**MANAGER OF CONTENT
DEVELOPMENT AND ASSEMBLY**
Mary Beth Wakefield

DIRECTOR OF COMMUNITY MARKETING
David Mayhew

MARKETING MANAGER
Ashley Zurcher

BUSINESS MANAGER
Amy Knies

**VICE PRESIDENT AND EXECUTIVE
GROUP PUBLISHER**
Richard Swadley

ASSOCIATE PUBLISHER
Jim Minatel

PROJECT COORDINATOR, COVER
Todd Klemme

PROOFREADER
Nancy Carrasco

INDEXER
Robert Swanson

COVER DESIGNER
Wiley

COVER IMAGE
©iStockphoto.com/36clicks

ACKNOWLEDGMENTS

I'D LIKE TO THANK the entire team that worked to get this book out under an extremely tight deadline. To my coauthor, Damian Brady, it was a blast working with you. Thanks for your diligence on top of your day job, holidays, and all the other things that life throws at you. To my Contributing Author, Ed Thomson, a big thank you for jumping in at very late notice to make sure we did justice to the Git content. To Ed Blankenship, Martin Woodward, Brian Keller, and Grant Holliday, thank you for your work on the earlier versions of this book. You have provided us with a solid, comprehensive base to work from. A special thanks to our Tech Editor, Anthony Borton, whose deep technical knowledge kept us honest and made this a better book than we would have made on our own. To our Technical Proofreader, Anna Russo Vance, also a big thanks for stepping in late in the process and giving the text one last sweep to ensure we made the best book possible.

A big thanks to the Editorial team at Wiley, which kept us on track (cracked the whip)—Christina Haviland, Nancy Rapoport, and Robert Elliot—and to the Wiley Production team for making it all look so good.

Thanks to Brian Harry and the original Visual SourceSafe team members from OneTree Software. Visual SourceSafe was my "gateway drug" into the world of version control and Application Lifecycle Management. I've realized that I wouldn't have this level of passion for ALM if I had not worked with this tool early in my career.

Thanks also to the Visual Studio team at Microsoft for producing the most complete set of ALM tools on the market and for continuing to innovate into the cloud with Visual Studio Online. I'm looking forward to some great features in the coming releases.

Finally and most importantly, I want to thank my wife, Kimberly, and my daughters, Danielle and Jessica, for putting up with me during this whole process. I'm sure it wasn't easy. Your love and support made this possible.

—Steven St. Jean

I WANT TO THANK my coauthors, Steve, Ed, Martin, and Grant, for allowing me to be a part of this edition of the book, especially to Steve for his additional mentorship and advice along the way. Thanks also to Ed Thomson for your expert contribution as we crept closer to the final deadlines. The help from the MVP community as well as members of the product teams at Microsoft has been invaluable. I want to thank everyone who replied to e-mails and answered any questions I had, often with a ridiculously short turnaround.

This book would not have been possible without the support of the editors, reviewers, and all at Wiley who provided their support. A special thanks must go to Christina Haviland for her expert guidance as well as her understanding when I had to put the book on the backburner for a few weeks. Thanks also to Anthony for keeping us honest from a technical standpoint.

I want to thank the excellent and supportive team at SSW for pushing me to the high standards you set as consultants, and for reminding me I had work to do by all too frequently asking, "How's the book going?" In particular, thanks to SSW's illustrious leader Adam Cogan, whose influence and enthusiasm have helped me achieve some goals that once seemed a long way off. I also want to acknowledge the fantastic developer community in Australia and Brisbane, in particular. I'm privileged to work in an environment with so many smart and dedicated professionals.

Finally, I want to thank my family: Johnny, Ma, Pat, Sarah, and Roo. I'm very lucky to have one of those rare families you can always depend on when you need them. Most important, thank you to my amazing wife, Lisa. Marrying you will always be my greatest achievement. You have encouraged me, supported me through many a late night and weekend, and feigned interest in the book even though I might as well have been writing in Latin. I love you and I'm so proud to have you with me as we work toward our goal of being wealthy, unemployed, multilingual, professional surfers. Or something.

—DAMIAN BRADY

I REALLY WANT to thank everyone involved with putting this book together, including the author team, editors, reviewers, and everyone who was able to give us great feedback and help along the way! Thanks to my coauthors for the great teamwork and contributions that have made this book awesome. I have really appreciated their guidance along the way, as well as all of the new things that I have learned from each author's expertise. I truly enjoyed working with y'all.

The help from each of the product teams to put together such a great book can't be discounted! A personal thanks to Brian Harry, Sam Guckenheimer, Matt Mitrik, Mario Rodriguez, Anu, Muthu, Aseem, Nipun, Satinder, Gregg Boer, Jim Lamb, Jason Prickett, Chad Boles, Phillip Kelley, Christophe Fiessinger, and Chris Patterson on the product teams at Microsoft. I appreciate all of their contributions, advice, and, most of all, their in-depth insight into the product over the years to provide a better understanding of all the moving wheels of Team Foundation Server.

I also want to thank all of my former Microsoft MVP colleagues who have been a great group to be a part of as well as to work with now. A special thanks goes to Mike Fourie, Tiago Pascoal, Anthony Borton, Steve Godbold, Mickey Gousset, Steve St. Jean, Chris Menegay, Dave McKinstry, Joel Semeniuk, Adam Cogan, and Neno Loje for all of their help.

Thank you to everyone who has helped me throughout my career over the years! Thanks for pushing me to get better in my craft and fueling my enthusiasm. Thanks also to my family and friends for their guidance along the way and for always supporting me. I couldn't have done this without each of you.

—ED BLANKENSHIP

I WANT TO THANK my coauthors for allowing me to help them in putting this book together. You will struggle to meet a group of folks who know the breadth of Team Foundation Server better than they do, and it has been a pleasure to work with them all.

My colleagues in the entire Team Foundation Server group (past and present) have obviously been essential in the making of this book, but I would like to especially acknowledge the help, advice, and assistance from the following people both inside and outside Microsoft—Aaron Hallberg, Philip Kelley, Chad Boles, Buck Hodges, Matthew Mitrik, James Manning, Jason Prickett, Ed Holloway, Doug Neumann, Ed Thomson, Peter Provost, Terje Sandstrom, and William Bartholomew. I also want to thank the ALM Rangers and ALM MVPs that make the Team Foundation Server community such a vibrant community to be a part of.

Finally, I want to thank my wife, Catherine. I owe Catherine so much for so many things, both big and small. I know that she signed up for "in sickness and in health" on that wonderful day in Newcastle when she agreed to be my wife, but I'm pretty sure she'd have thought again if our vows had been "in sickness and in health, through the course of four books and through the countless nights apart or vacation days messed up due to my husband not understanding the term 'work/life balance.'" Lucky for me, she keeps her promises. And I promise to spend the rest of my days trying to make her understand how grateful I am. For everything.

—Martin Woodward

I'D LIKE TO THANK everyone who made this book possible. Once again, we formed the dream team of Team Foundation Server knowledge and experience.

Thank you to my co-authors, Steve, Damian, Ed, and Martin. Thank you to the Wiley project team for keeping us on track and helping with the polish and production effort that a technical book like this deserves.

Second, I'd like to thank the Microsoft Services team in Australia and the worldwide Premier Field Engineering team. I returned home after some time in Corp, and you welcomed me with open arms into your organizations—I am truly honored to call myself a PFE.

A big thank you to Brian Harry and the Team Foundation Server team in Redmond and Raleigh. The TFS team is truly world-class in its customer focus, and I am lucky to work with such great technical talent.

Finally, I want to thank my family for all the late nights and weekends it took to get this over the line.

—Grant Holliday

CONTENTS

PART III: PROJECT MANAGEMENT

CHAPTER 12: INTRODUCING WORK ITEM TRACKING   303

INTRODUCTION

Over the past decade, Microsoft has been creating development tools designed for the ever-growing engineering teams of software developers, testers, architects, project managers, designers, and database administrators. In the Visual Studio 2013 line of products, there are tools for each team member to use to contribute to a software release. However, it's not enough to allow for awesome individual contributions. You must also organize the collaboration of those contributions across the larger team, including the stakeholders for whom the software is being built.

Beginning in the Visual Studio 2005 release, Microsoft introduced a new server product named Team Foundation Server to complement its development products. Now in its fifth release, Team Foundation Server 2013 has grown with all of the investment from the past decade and fits nicely in the Visual Studio Application Lifecycle Management (ALM) family of products. Before the Visual Studio 2010 release, the Visual Studio ALM family of products was given the brand of Visual Studio Team System, which is no longer used in the latest releases.

In September 2011, Microsoft announced the availability of Team Foundation Service Preview. This service started by providing the base functionality of Team Foundation Server but built on the Microsoft Azure cloud platform. Over the next two and a half years, the teams at Microsoft worked to expand the feature set of the service from basic version control, work item tracking, agile project management, and builds to the current feature set, which adds an elastic build service, cloud-based load testing, better agile planning tools, and web-based test management. The Team Foundation Service was renamed to Visual Studio Online in November 2013 to better reflect the services provided to development teams.

As you will find out, Team Foundation Server and Visual Studio Online are very large products with lots of features for managing the software development life cycle of software projects and releases. The authors of this book collectively gathered, from their past experience since the first release of Team Foundation Server, to document some of the tips and tricks that they have learned along the way. The backgrounds of the authors are quite diverse—managing one of the largest Team Foundation Server environments, designing the collaboration pieces for non-.NET development teams, managing releases at a software development company, and a consulting background where customers are helped each week to solve real-world challenges by taking advantage of Team Foundation Server.

WHOM THIS BOOK IS FOR

If you have been looking to Team Foundation Server to meet some of your software development team's challenges for collaboration, then this book is for you. You may have seen the Team Foundation Server product in your MSDN subscription and decided to set up a new environment internally. You may now be wondering how to administer and configure the product. You may have also noticed the new, Visual Studio Online service offering by Microsoft and wondered where to get started.

This book is for everyone—from the developer using Team Foundation Server for day-to-day development, to the administrator who is ensuring that the environment is tuned to run well and who builds extensions to the product to meet the needs of their software development team. You may also be preparing for any of the Application Lifecycle Management (ALM) Microsoft certification exams for administering or using Team Foundation Server, and you will find many of the exam topics covered in this book.

This book does not require any knowledge of Team Foundation Server to be useful, but it is not meant for developers or testers who are just starting out their craft. Team Foundation Server can be used for teams as small as one to five team members to teams consisting of tens of thousands. Code samples in the book are presented in C#, but they could also be implemented in other .NET languages (such as Visual Basic.NET).

You can find a road map for the book based on your team role later in this Introduction in the section "How This Book Is Structured."

WHAT THIS BOOK COVERS

This book covers a complete overview of the Team Foundation Server 2013 product and provides hands-on examples for using the product throughout many of the chapters. This book only covers the latest version of Team Foundation Server 2013 and does not provide detailed information on how to use earlier versions of Team Foundation Server.

The book is divided into five main parts, with detailed chapters that will dive into each of the feature areas of Team Foundation Server 2013.

- ➤ Part I, "Getting Started"
- ➤ Part II, "Version Control"
- ➤ Part III, "Project Management"
- ➤ Part IV, "Team Foundation Build"
- ➤ Part V, "Administration"

HOW THIS BOOK IS STRUCTURED

You may have picked up this book and are wondering where to get started. This book has been written so that you can start reading in a particular chapter without needing to understand concepts introduced in previous chapters. Feel free to read the book from cover to cover, or, if you are in a hurry or need to reference a specific topic, jump to that particular chapter. The next sections describe where you might get started in the book based on your role and the topics that might be most relevant for you.

Developers

There are plenty of features that are available for developers who are using Team Foundation Server. You might begin by reading Chapter 4, "Connecting to Team Foundation Server," to get started with exploring the different options available for connecting to your server.

After that, you can begin your review of the version control features available in Part II of the book:

➤ Chapter 5, "Overview of Version Control"

➤ Chapter 6, "Using Centralized Team Foundation Version Control"

➤ Chapter 7, "Distributed Version Control with Git and Team Foundation Server"

➤ Chapter 8, "Version Control in Heterogeneous Teams"

➤ Chapter 10, "Branching and Merging"

➤ Chapter 11, "Common Version Control Scenarios"

Once you have a good grasp of the version control features, you may want to familiarize yourself with the work item tracking and reporting features in Part III of the book:

➤ Chapter 12, "Introducing Work Item Tracking"

➤ Chapter 14, "Managing Teams and Agile Planning Tools"

➤ Chapter 15, "Reporting and SharePoint Dashboards"

Finally, if you want to automate your build and release process, you can take advantage of reviewing those features in Part IV of the book:

➤ Chapter 17, "Overview of Build Automation"

➤ Chapter 18, "Using Team Foundation Build"

➤ Chapter 19, "Customizing the Build Process"

➤ Chapter 20, "Release Management"

Testers

Team Foundation Server and Visual Studio include a host of new features for testing. You might begin by reading Chapter 4, "Connecting to Team Foundation Server," to get started with exploring the different options available for connecting to your server.

After that, you will want to increase your understanding of the work item tracking features (which help track test cases, bugs, tasks, requirements, and so on), as well as the project reporting features in Part III of the book:

➤ Chapter 12, "Introducing Work Item Tracking"

➤ Chapter 14, "Managing Teams and Agile Planning Tools"

➤ Chapter 15, "Reporting and SharePoint Dashboards"

If you are a technical tester, and will be automating test cases using the numerous automated test capabilities, then you will want to familiarize yourself with the version control features (which is where you will store the source code for your automated tests) in Part II of the book:

➤ Chapter 5, "Overview of Version Control"

➤ Chapter 6, "Using Centralized Team Foundation Version Control"

➤ Chapter 7, "Distributed Version Control with Git and Team Foundation Version Server"

➤ Chapter 10, "Branching and Merging"

➤ Chapter 11, "Common Version Control Scenarios"

Finally, if you are interested in the testing and environment/lab management features available in Team Foundation Server, you can consult Part V of the book:

➤ Chapter 26, "Testing and Lab Management"

MICROSOFT TEST MANAGER

If you are using Microsoft Test Manager (available if you have acquired either Visual Studio 2013 Ultimate, Visual Studio 2013 Premium, or Visual Studio 2013 Test Professional), you may want to consult the companion to this book, *Professional Application Lifecycle Management with Visual Studio 2013* Mickey Gousset, Martin Hinshelwood, Brian A. Randell, Brian Keller, and Martin Woodward (Wiley, 2014). Several chapters in that book discuss the features available in Microsoft Test Manager for test case management, executing manual tests, starting exploratory test runs to generate test cases, filing rich actionable bugs, creating temporary environments for development and testing use, and automating user interface tests. For more information about this book, visit `http://aka.ms/ALM2013Book`.

Project Managers and Business Analysts

As a project manager or business analyst, you will want to ensure that you have insight into the software release or project, and be able to interact. You may also be interested in what customizations are possible with the process that Team Foundation Server uses for your teams. Project managers might also be interested in the capability to synchronize project data in Team Foundation Server with a Microsoft Office Project Server instance. Business analysts may want to create and track requirements, including the traceability options from inception to implementation. Additionally, project managers and business analysts may want to learn how to seek feedback from customers and stakeholders and turn that feedback into new requirements, change requests, or product backlog items.

You might begin by reading Chapter 4, "Connecting to Team Foundation Server," to get started with exploring the different options available for connecting to your server. All of the features that would be relevant for project managers and business analysts are discussed in Part III of the book:

- Chapter 12, "Introducing Work Item Tracking"
- Chapter 13, "Customizing Process Templates"
- Chapter 14, "Managing Teams and Agile Planning Tools"
- Chapter 15, "Reporting and SharePoint Dashboards"
- Chapter 16, "Project Server Integration"

Project managers and business analysts may also be introduced in the companion to this book, *Professional Application Lifecycle Management with Visual Studio 2013* Mickey Gousset, Martin Hinshelwood, Brian A. Randell, Brian Keller, and Martin Woodward (Wiley: 2014), which can be found at http://aka.ms/ALM2013Book for further reading.

Executive Stakeholders

Executive stakeholders find plenty of use for Team Foundation Server by gathering insight into how software releases and projects are progressing, and often want easily accessible dashboards with the information. The executive that leads the engineering organization may also be interested in planning a Team Foundation Server deployment, including who should administer the server. Additionally with Team Foundation Server 2013, development teams can request feedback from stakeholders who then can provide rich feedback using the Feedback Client.

You might begin with the following chapters in Part I of the book:

- Chapter 2, "Planning a Deployment"
- Chapter 4, "Connecting to Team Foundation Server"

After you have a good understanding of the concepts in those chapters, you can then explore the necessary work item tracking and reporting features available in Part III of the book:

- Chapter 12, "Introducing Work Item Tracking"
- Chapter 14, "Managing Teams and Agile Planning Tools"
- Chapter 15, "Reporting and SharePoint Dashboards"

Team Foundation Server Administrators

If you find yourself in the position of administering a Team Foundation Server instance, this book provides plenty of great information for performing that role. In Part I of the book, you might begin by reading Chapter 2, "Planning a Deployment," to understand what is required for setting up a Team Foundation Server environment. You can then install a new server by going through Chapter 3, "Installation and Configuration." If you are upgrading from a previous version of Team Foundation Server, you may want to begin by reading through Chapter 27, "Upgrading Team Foundation Server," before you get started with the upgrade process.

It is recommended that, as a Team Foundation Server administrator, you understand all of the aspects that end users will take advantage of, including version control, work item tracking, and automated builds. You can read all of the chapters in Parts I through IV for information about those aspects of Team Foundation Server.

Additionally, Part V is dedicated to topics that will be of interest to administrators:

➤ Chapter 21, "Introduction to Team Foundation Server Administration"

➤ Chapter 22, "Scalability and High Availability"

➤ Chapter 23, "Disaster Recovery"

➤ Chapter 24, "Security and Privileges"

➤ Chapter 25, "Monitoring Server Health and Performance"

➤ Chapter 26, "Testing and Lab Management"

➤ Chapter 27, "Upgrading Team Foundation Server"

➤ Chapter 28, "Working with Geographically Distributed Teams"

➤ Chapter 29, "Extending Team Foundation Server"

Extensibility Partner

If you are interested in extending the capabilities of Team Foundation Server 2013, you will find many opportunities and extensibility points throughout this book. You may want to begin by reading through Chapter 29, "Extending Team Foundation Server." You will also find extensibility options covered in several other chapters of the book:

➤ Chapter 13, "Customizing Process Templates"

➤ Chapter 15, "Reporting and SharePoint Dashboards"

➤ Chapter 19, "Customizing the Build Process"

WHAT YOU NEED TO USE THIS BOOK

To perform many of the hands-on examples in the book, it will be helpful to have a Team Foundation Server 2013 environment or Visual Studio Online account that you can use to test out the different features in the product. You do not necessarily need separate hardware because you can install Team Foundation Server 2013 on client operating systems such as Windows 8 and Windows 7. Don't worry about setting up and configuring a new Team Foundation Server 2013 environment yet; you learn about that in Chapters 2 and 3.

Chapter 1 discusses a few options for acquiring Team Foundation Server, including an entire virtual machine image for demonstration purposes. Chapter 4 also discusses the different tools that you can use to connect to your Team Foundation Server environment, which will be needed throughout the book.

The source code for the samples is available for download from the Wrox website at:

`http://www.wrox.com/go/proftfs2013`

FURTHER LEARNING

Each of the authors write technical articles about Team Foundation Server and other Visual Studio products from time to time that you may benefit from for further learning. Feel free to check out the authors' blog sites and subscribe to them in your favorite RSS reader.

> ➤ Steven St. Jean—`sstjean.blogspot.com`

> ➤ Damian Brady—`blog.damianbrady.com.au`

> ➤ Ed Blankenship—`www.edsquared.com`

> ➤ Martin Woodward—`www.woodwardweb.com`

> ➤ Grant Holliday—`http://blogs.msdn.com/b/granth`

Additionally, the two main blogs and RSS feeds we recommend you follow for all of the latest news and updates are:

> ➤ Brian Harry—`http://blogs.msdn.com/b/bharry`

> ➤ Visual Studio ALM Product Team—`http://blogs.msdn.com/b/visualstudioalm`

CONTINUOUS PRODUCT UPDATES AND RELEASE SCHEDULE

As you move forward with Visual Studio and Team Foundation Server, remember that the product teams are now shipping updates more frequently—roughly every three months. These updates will include a roll-up of performance and bug fixes as well as new features that are completed. For those that will be using Visual Studio Online, new updates and features are automatically deployed every three weeks.

You will want to make sure you are always up to date on both your development machine where Visual Studio products are installed and also your Team Foundation Server environment servers. This book was written for the released version of Team Foundation Server.

You can find out more information about this new release cadence for Visual Studio and Team Foundation Server at `http://aka.ms/TFSShippingCadence`.

CONVENTIONS

To help you get the most from the text and keep track of what's happening, we've used a number of conventions throughout the book.

> **WARNING** *Warnings hold important, not-to-be-forgotten information that is directly relevant to the surrounding text.*

> **NOTE** *Notes indicate notes, tips, hints, tricks, or asides to the current discussion.*

SIDEBAR

Asides to the current discussion are offset like this.

As for styles in the text:

➤ We highlight new terms and important words when we introduce them.

➤ We show keyboard strokes like this: Ctrl+A.

➤ We show file names, URLs, and code within the text like so: `persistence.properties`.

➤ We present code in two different ways:

```
We use a monofont type with no highlighting for most code examples.
We use bold to emphasize code that is particularly important in the present
   context or to show changes from a previous code snippet.
```

SOURCE CODE

As you work through the examples in this book, you may choose either to type in all the code manually or to use the source code files that accompany the book. All the source code used in this book is available for download at `www.wrox.com`. Specifically for this book, the code download is on the Download Code tab at:

```
http://www.wrox.com/go/proftfs2013
```

You can also search for the book at `www.wrox.com` by ISBN (the ISBN for this book is 978-1-118-83634-7) to find the code. And a complete list of code downloads for all current Wrox books is available at `www.wrox.com/dynamic/books/download.aspx`.

Most of the code on `www.wrox.com` is compressed in a .ZIP, .RAR, or similar archive format appropriate to the platform. Once you download the code, just decompress it with an appropriate compression tool.

Alternately, you can go to the main Wrox code download page at `www.wrox.com/dynamic/books/download.aspx` to see the code available for this book and all other Wrox books.

ERRATA

We make every effort to ensure that there are no errors in the text or in the code. However, no one is perfect, and mistakes do occur. If you find an error in one of our books, such as a spelling mistake or faulty piece of code, we would be very grateful for your feedback. By sending in errata, you may save another reader hours of frustration, and at the same time, you will be helping us provide even higher quality information.

To find the errata page for this book, go to `http://www.wrox.com/go/proftfs2013` and click Errata link. On this page, you can view all errata that has been submitted for this book and posted by Wrox editors.

If you don't spot "your" error on the Book Errata page, go to `www.wrox.com/contact/techsupport.shtml` and complete the form there to send us the error you have found. We'll check the information and, if appropriate, post a message to the book's errata page and fix the problem in subsequent editions of the book.

P2P.WROX.COM

For author and peer discussion, join the P2P forums at `http://p2p.wrox.com`. The forums are a web-based system for you to post messages relating to Wrox books and related technologies, and interact with other readers and technology users. The forums offer a subscription feature to e-mail you topics of interest of your choosing when new posts are made to the forums. Wrox authors, editors, other industry experts, and your fellow readers are present on these forums.

At `http://p2p.wrox.com`, you will find a number of different forums that will help you, not only as you read this book, but also as you develop your own applications. To join the forums, just follow these steps:

1. Go to `http://p2p.wrox.com` and click the Register link.

2. Read the terms of use and click Agree.

3. Complete the required information to join, as well as any optional information you wish to provide, and click Submit.

4. You will receive an e-mail with information describing how to verify your account and complete the joining process.

> **NOTE** *You can read messages in the forums without joining P2P, but in order to post your own messages, you must join.*

Once you join, you can post new messages and respond to messages other users post. You can read messages at any time on the web. If you would like to have new messages from a particular forum e-mailed to you, click the Subscribe to this Forum icon by the forum name in the forum listing.

For more information about how to use the Wrox P2P, be sure to read the P2P FAQs for answers to questions about how the forum software works, as well as many common questions specific to P2P and Wrox books. To read the FAQs, click the FAQ link on any P2P page.

PROFESSIONAL

Team Foundation Server 2013

PART I
Getting Started

1

Introducing Visual Studio Online and Team Foundation Server 2013

WHAT'S IN THIS CHAPTER?

➤ Getting to know Team Foundation Server 2013

➤ Understanding what's new in Team Foundation Server 2013

➤ Acquiring Team Foundation Server 2013

This chapter introduces you to Microsoft Visual Studio Team Foundation Server 2013. Here you learn what it is for, the key concepts needed when using it, and how to acquire it.

For those users already familiar with Team Foundation Server, the discussion in this chapter highlights areas that are new or have changed substantially. However, because understanding the legacy of a technology is always helpful, this chapter also includes some of the history of the Team Foundation Server product, which will help explain how it became what it is today.

This chapter also discusses the improved release model, including the ability to have Microsoft manage hosting, frequent upgrades, and backups by leveraging Visual Studio Online (formerly Team Foundation Service). Later chapters go into more depth with an examination of the architecture of the Team Foundation Server product.

WHAT IS TEAM FOUNDATION SERVER?

Developing software is difficult—a fact repeatedly proven by how many projects run overtime or over budget, or fail completely. An essential factor in the success of any software development team is how well the members of the team communicate with one another, as well as with the people who wanted the software developed in the first place.

Team Foundation Server provides the core collaboration functionality for your software development teams in a very tightly integrated product. The functionality provided by Team Foundation Server includes the following:

- Project management
- Work item tracking (WIT)
- Version control
- Test case management
- Build automation
- Reporting
- Release management
- Lab and environment management
- Feedback management
- Chat and team communication tools

Each of these topics is explored extensively in this book

Team Foundation Server is a separate server product designed specifically for software engineering teams with developers, testers, architects, project managers, business analysts, and anyone else contributing to software development releases and projects. Logically, Team Foundation Server is made up of the following two tiers, which can be physically deployed across one or many machines:

- **Application tier**—The *application tier* primarily consists of a set of web services with which the client machines communicate by using a highly optimized, web service-based protocol. It also includes a rich web access site to interact with a server without having to install a client such as Visual Studio.

- **Data tier**—The *data tier* utilizes SQL Server to house the databases that contain the database logic for the Team Foundation Server application, the data for your Team Foundation Server instance, as well as the data for your Team Project Collection. The data stored in the data warehouse database and Analysis Services cube are used by Team Foundation Server's reporting functionality. All the data stored in Team Foundation Server is stored in the SQL Server databases, thus making the system easy to back up.

Team Foundation Server was designed with extensibility in mind. It can integrate with a comprehensive .NET Application Programming Interface (API). It also has a set of events that allow it to integrate with outside tools as first-class citizens. The same .NET programming model and event system are used by Microsoft to construct Team Foundation Server, as well as the client integrations into Visual Studio.

Team Foundation Server has plenty of competitors, including other enterprise Application Lifecycle Management (ALM) systems and purpose-specific products (such as source control systems). The main benefit of having all the different systems available in one product is that Team Foundation Server fully integrates the different systems. This allows for true innovation in the development tools space, as you will notice with several of the new tools available in this latest release. Instead of worrying about integrating the separate systems yourself, you can take advantage of the work that

Microsoft has done for you. Jason Zander, currently Corporate Vice President of development for Windows Azure, makes this particular point well in a blog post originally about Team Foundation Server 2010. You can find the blog post at `http://aka.ms/IntegratedALMSolution`.

When you compare enterprise ALM products currently on the market, you will discover that Team Foundation Server was designed to be easily customized and extended. Team Foundation Server ensures that developers using any development platform can participate and easily use Team Foundation Server, including Visual Studio, Eclipse-based development, Xcode, and many more.

WHAT IS VISUAL STUDIO ONLINE?

Installing and configuring Team Foundation Server has traditionally meant a significant investment in time and infrastructure. In addition to the initial setup, maintenance of an on-premises Team Foundation Server instance required ongoing effort.

In October 2012, a hosted Team Foundation Server was released to the general public under the name *Team Foundation Service*. This hosted service meant that a team could make use of many of the features of Team Foundation Service without the significant investment in infrastructure and maintenance. Since its initial release, the product has been continuously extended and improved.

In November 2013, Team Foundation Service was rolled into a new product called *Visual Studio Online*, which incorporates a number of developer services, including most of the features of an on-premises Team Foundation Server installation as well as Visual Studio, collaboration tools, load testing and build services, a diagnostic service called *Application Insights*, and even an online code editor.

Visual Studio Online is free for teams up to five users, and is also available on a per-user per-month subscription basis. A number of plans are available that include various features. These features include access to a hosted Team Foundation Server with unlimited Team Projects and basic project planning tools, and either the Visual Studio Express or Visual Studio Professional IDE. The plans also include a certain amount of cloud build and load testing time.

WHAT'S NEW IN TEAM FOUNDATION SERVER 2013?

If you have used legacy versions of Team Foundation Server, you may be curious about what is new in the latest release. As this book demonstrates, it is a big release with considerable new functionality and improvements across the board. While many of these features are explained throughout this book, if you have used a previous version of Team Foundation Server, the features described in the following sections will be new to you. Some of the client-side topics are covered in more detail in the companion book to this volume, *Professional Application Lifecycle Management with Visual Studio 2013 by Mickey Gousset, Martin Hinshelwood, Brian A. Randell, Brian Keller, and Martin Woodward* (Wiley, 2014).

Version Control

One major change with this release was the addition of an alternative, distributed source control option within Team Foundation Server. While this was seen as a surprising move by many, it was really just addressing a common complaint many organizations had with source control in Team Foundation Server.

There are many powerful project management features provided by Team Foundation Server, but the primary reason for adopting a system like Team Foundation Server will always be source control. Developers have increasingly been moving to distributed version control products, such as Git or Mercurial, and the limitations of the centralized source control system provided by Team Foundation Server was a common reason cited by organizations choosing to use an alternative product. While support for disconnected workspaces was provided with the addition of Local Workspaces in the 2012 release of Team Foundation Server, team members were still limited to a single server-side repository for a workspace.

By adopting Git as a first-class version control alternative, Microsoft has added true distributed version control to the product. Developers can keep a full local repository, which allows them to work with multiple branches and commit locally before pushing their changes to the server.

We want to note two important points with respect to the distributed version control offering in Team Foundation Server. First, the Git implementation is a standard implementation of Git rather than one that has been specifically written for Team Foundation Server. This means you can work with a Git repository in Team Foundation Server in exactly the same way as you would with any other implementation. Second, despite the history of Team Foundation Server, both version control options are considered equals and are supported fully. The project management functions in Team Foundation Server are still available and code changes can still be linked to work items. Distributed version control is covered in detail in Chapter 7.

Team Collaboration

Team Foundation Server 2012 introduced a built-in set of experiences for requesting, responding, and managing code reviews. It uses the powerful work item tracking experiences behind the scenes as well as some specialized user experiences to help you discuss changes. This was a powerful way of formalizing collaboration between team members.

A new feature has been included in Team Foundation Server 2013 that allows team members to make comments directly against code, right from Team Web Access. You can make comments on an entire file, specific lines of code, or even a complete changeset, and just like code reviews, you can have threaded discussions. This provides a great way for team members to collaborate, directly against the code itself, without having to manage the complete code review process.

A new Team Room has also been added to Team Web Access in the 2013 release. This feature not only allows developers to chat in real time, but it notifies them of relevant events such as build completions and code changes.

Web Access

Team Web Access was completely redesigned in Team Foundation Server 2012 to provide an even better experience for those without any of the traditional clients available. It is friendly to modern browsers, including mobile browsers, and works well with both desktop and tablet devices.

Microsoft has further updated and improved Team Web Access in Team Foundation Server 2013. The agile management tools have also been improved and now have support for tags, backlog and board improvements, updated process templates, and support for Agile Portfolio Management. Some new features have been implemented for Team Web Access as well, including a new Test Hub, Team Rooms for live chat, and work item charts.

Agile Product Management

Additional new experiences added to Team Web Access are agile project management and product planning. The new Agile Planning tools are specifically designed for users practicing Agile development, but can actually be beneficial for those using any process.

The primary changes introduced in this release include Agile Portfolio Management and a set of improved process templates for managing projects.

The great thing about these changes is that they allow you to roll-up requirements so management can see just the level of detail they are interested in. Each team can have its own set of backlog items that contribute to a shared "feature" backlog.

Release Management

Release Management for Visual Studio 2013 is a powerful tool for automating the deployment pipeline for developed applications. Formerly known as InRelease, Microsoft acquired the product from a Canadian company called InCycle in June 2013.

The Release Management tool allows teams to deploy applications to multiple server environments and has strong integration with Team Foundation Service. Complex release workflows can be defined with a visual interface. Importantly, teams can define the promotion path of a single build through multiple environments and enforce a process of approval and promotion.

> **NOTE** *Release Management for Visual Studio 2013 is discussed in more detail in Chapter 20.*

ACQUISITION OPTIONS

Microsoft has also greatly improved how you may acquire Team Foundation Server. Several options are available to you, as discussed in the following sections.

Licensing can be somewhat confusing, but Team Foundation Server licensing follows the licensing pattern of other Microsoft server products. There is a server license. Additionally, with some notable exceptions, each user that connects to the server should have a Client Access License (CAL) for Team Foundation Server.

> **NOTE** *For more information about those potential exceptions, or questions about what you will need to purchase, you can seek help from a Microsoft Partner with the ALM Competency or your local Microsoft Developer Tools Specialist, or you can refer to the End-User License Agreement (EULA). A licensing white paper dedicated to Visual Studio, MSDN, and Team Foundation Server is also available at* http://aka.ms/VisualStudioLicensing.

Visual Studio Online

By far, the easiest way to get started with adopting Team Foundation Server is through a new hosted option available directly from Microsoft called Visual Studio Online (formerly Team Foundation Service). It shares a majority of the same code base as the same Team Foundation Server product used on-premises but modified to be hosted from Windows Azure for multiple tenants. It is available at `http://tfs.visualstudio.com`.

The best part of using Visual Studio Online is that your team need not worry about backups, high availability, upgrades, or other potentially time-consuming administration and maintenance tasks. Another nice thing is that Visual Studio Online customers will receive frequent updates that even include new features before on-premises customers.

> **NOTE** *Brian Harry, Product Unit Manager for Team Foundation Server, announced that the internal product teams improved their engineering process so well over the past two to three years that they are able to quickly provide more frequent updates. Starting with Team Foundation Server 2012, the product team has provided frequent updates that include the typical performance and bug fixes but also brand new features. The frequency of updates since this announcement has been significantly faster than in the past, with four post-RTM releases to Team Foundation Server 2012 and one Team Foundation Server 2013 release in the past 12 months.*
>
> *Team Foundation Service customers have seen updates made more frequently than the on-premises edition. Brian mentioned that his teams are able to deploy hotfixes daily, but full-featured updates have thus far been released every three weeks (with a small number of exceptions), which lines up with the internal sprint schedule. You can learn more about this topic from Brian Harry's blog post at* `http://aka.ms/TFSReleaseCadence`.
>
> *One thing to take away from this discussion is to make sure that your team always uses the latest update of Team Foundation Server if you choose to install it on-premises.*

Teams using Visual Studio Online are able to leverage an elastic set of standard build servers. This elastic build service provides standard build machines available and clean for each of your builds. Teams can even integrate their elastic builds with their Windows Azure accounts to provide continuous deployment to instances of their applications or sites hosted in Windows Azure. Teams can also take advantage of on-premises build servers connected to Visual Studio Online.

Microsoft released the Team Foundation Service as a free trial in late 2012 and rolled it into the commercial Visual Studio Online service in November 2013. They announced that the full feature set will be provided to teams of up to five at no cost. Additionally, MSDN subscribers will be able to leverage Visual Studio Online as an additional benefit to their MSDN subscription.

Visual Studio Online is offered under a subscription model. The Basic plan is free for five users, and subsequent users can be added on a per-user, per-month basis. In addition to the Basic plan, two other user plans are available with differing capabilities and inclusions.

To date, Visual Studio does not have full parity with the on-premises product. For example, the lab management, reporting, and process template customization capabilities are features not currently available. As Visual Studio Online evolves over time, there will be greater, if not full, parity with the on-premises edition.

In the meantime, for teams that would like the full set of features but still have someone else manage their Team Foundation Server instance, options are available through several third-party hosting companies.

Express

Small software engineering teams can leverage an Express version of Team Foundation Server 2013 that is available and free for up to five developers. Team Foundation Server Express is available at `http://aka.ms/TFS2013Express`. The Express edition includes, but is not limited to, the following core developer features:

- ➤ Version control
- ➤ Work item tracking
- ➤ Build automation

This is a perfect start for small teams that want an on-premises Team Foundation Server instance without any additional costs. If your team grows beyond five, you can always buy CALs for users six and beyond. The Express instance can even be upgraded at any time to take advantage of the full set of features without losing any data.

Trial

One of the easiest ways to acquire Team Foundation Server is on a 90-day trial basis. You can download the full version of Team Foundation Server and try out all of the features without having to purchase a full copy. The DVD ISO image for the trial edition is available at `http://aka.ms/TFS2013Downloads`.

If you install the trial edition of Team Foundation Server, you can easily apply a product key to activate the trial edition. You could even move the team project collection from the trial server to a different server instance once your team has decided to fully adopt Team Foundation Server.

Alternatively, if you need a 30-day extension, you can perform one extension using the Team Foundation Server Administration Console once you're near the end of the trial period. You can find out more information about extending the trial by visiting `http://aka.ms/ExtendTFSTrial`.

If you would rather have a virtual machine that is ready to use (including all of the software necessary to demo and evaluate Visual Studio 2013 and Team Foundation Server 2013), you can download the all-up Visual Studio 2013 virtual machine image. The virtual machine has a time limit that starts from the day that you first start the machine. You can always download a fresh copy of the machine to begin your demo experience over.

> **NOTE** *You can find the latest version of the virtual machine available at* `http://aka.ms/vs13almvm`.

Volume Licensing

Microsoft has plenty of options for volume licensing, including Enterprise, Select, Open Value, and Open License Agreements, that will help your company significantly reduce the overall cost of acquiring an on-premises edition of Team Foundation Server. Different options are available based on your company size and engineering team size. This option is by far the most popular choice for companies looking to acquire Team Foundation Server, MSDN subscriptions, and Visual Studio licenses.

If your company acquired an earlier version of Team Foundation Server through a volume licensing program, and also purchased Software Assurance (SA), you may be entitled to a license for Team Foundation Server 2013 without additional cost, if the SA was still active on the date that Team Foundation Server 2013 was released.

> **NOTE** *For more information about volume licensing, discuss your options with your Microsoft internal volume licensing administrator, your local Microsoft Developer Tools Specialist, or a Microsoft Partner with ALM Competency. You can find out more information from the Visual Studio Licensing white paper available at* `http://aka.ms/VisualStudioLicensing`.

MSDN Subscriptions

Beginning with the Visual Studio 2010 release, a full production-use license of Team Foundation Server 2013 is included with each license of Visual Studio that includes an MSDN subscription. Those MSDN subscribers also receive a Team Foundation Server 2013 CAL available for production use.

This now enables developers, testers, architects, and others with an active MSDN subscription to take advantage of Team Foundation Server without additional licensing costs.

> **NOTE** *For more information about MSDN subscriptions and for links to download Team Foundation Server 2013, visit the MSDN Subscriber Downloads website at* `http://msdn.microsoft.com/subscriptions`.

Microsoft Partner Network

Companies that are members of the Microsoft Partner Network and have achieved certain competencies can be entitled to development and test-use licenses of several of the products included with an MSDN subscription, including Team Foundation Server 2013.

> **NOTE** *For more information about the requirements and benefits available for Microsoft Partners, visit* `http://partner.microsoft.com`.

Retail

If you are not able to use any of the other acquisition methods, you can always acquire Team Foundation Server 2013 through retail channels, including the online Microsoft Store. You can purchase the product directly from Microsoft online at `http://aka.ms/TFS2013Retail`. It is also available from many other popular retail sites.

One of the nice benefits of purchasing a server license using the retail channel is that you also receive a CAL exclusion for up to five named users. This benefit is available only from licenses purchased through the retail channel, and it is not included with other acquisition avenues discussed in this chapter.

SUMMARY

As you learned in this chapter, Team Foundation Server is a product with lots of features and functionality. This chapter introduced the types of features available, including those new to the latest release. Additionally, you learned about the different acquisition methods for getting the software for Team Foundation Server.

The next few chapters will familiarize you with planning a Team Foundation Server deployment and installing a brand-new server. You will also learn about the different methods available for connecting to your new server. Chapter 2 begins that discussion with an examination of deploying Team Foundation Server.

Planning a Deployment

WHAT'S IN THIS CHAPTER?

➤ Organizing a plan for adoption

➤ Setting up timelines for adoption

➤ Structuring team projects and team project collections

➤ Hardware and software requirements

Before installing or configuring Team Foundation Server, it is helpful to lay out a plan and to identify the areas that need some preparation work to ensure a successful adoption. This chapter discusses methods for gaining consensus in your organization for the adoption. You will learn about some potential adoption timelines and strategies to ensure a smooth transition for your teams from legacy systems to Team Foundation Server 2013. Finally, the discussion walks you through some of the immediate preparation steps for gathering what you will need before you start the installation and configuration of your new Team Foundation Server environment.

In Chapter 1, you read about the high-level features available in Team Foundation Server 2013, including new features for this release. Now it's time to convince your boss and team that it would be worthwhile to adopt Team Foundation Server 2013. The following sections examine some of the ways you can prepare for your proposal to your team.

IDENTIFYING AND ADDRESSING SOFTWARE ENGINEERING PAIN

One key to selling the idea of an Application Lifecycle Management (ALM) solution is to identify the pain points that your organization and teams are experiencing, and to address those pain points with possible solutions. You may find that some of the common problems people are seeking solutions for are the same problems that plague your organization.

This section identifies some common problems that plague many development organizations, and it provides some helpful discussion about how Team Foundation Server and the ALM family of Visual Studio 2013 products attempt to address those pain points. You may have additional pain points that you would like to solve, and it is always good to flesh those out to ensure that you are identifying and solving them as part of your adoption of Team Foundation Server.

This book covers many of the ALM topics because Team Foundation Server is a part of the Visual Studio ALM family of products. You can find out more information about all of the different ALM tools available across the Visual Studio family in the companion book *Professional Application Lifecycle Management with Visual Studio 2013* available at `http://www.wiley.com/WileyCDA/WileyTitle/productCd-1118836588.html`.

Transparency of the Release or Project

Does your team have difficulty understanding any of the following questions during the release cycle?

➤ Are we on track to release at the end of the month?

➤ How much implementation has been accomplished on the requirements in this release?

➤ How are our testers doing in authoring and executing their test cases?

➤ What changed in last night's build?

➤ Why did this set of files change in this recent check-in? Was it used to implement a requirement or fix a bug?

➤ Which requirements are getting good test coverage versus requirements that are largely untested?

➤ Is the company investing in the right areas of our products based on feedback from stakeholders?

➤ How do you balance the capacity of team members against the priority of work you want to accomplish?

➤ How much work is your team capable of delivering for a given iteration?

➤ How can you be sure the release in production matches the release that was in a test environment?

Teams that have a problem getting visibility into their release process often want to start by finding a tool that will gather all of the data necessary to easily answer some of these questions. Team Foundation Server is one of the best products available for transparency because it allows you to store all of the different artifacts from the beginning to the end of the software development life cycle. Not only does it provide a way to capture that information, but it also allows you to make informed decisions using rich links between those artifacts and systems. Team Foundation Server provides rich information by exposing the end-to-end relationships that exist across artifacts.

Collaboration across Different Teams and Roles

Some teams have difficulty providing information and communicating across different functional groups. Testers may not feel that they have enough information about bugs returned to them as rejected, and developers may feel that they don't have enough information about the requirements they are supposed to implement or the bugs they are supposed to fix. Stakeholders and business users may not feel that they have an easy way to provide feedback about the applications they interact with so that the software development teams will be able to act appropriately.

If your team is experiencing some of these problems, you may benefit from being able to easily see information and notes about the different artifacts in the software process stored in Team Foundation Server.

Automated Compilation, Testing, Packaging, and Deployment

Teams may end up spending a lot of time at the end of release cycles completing manual steps to compile, package, and deploy their applications. They may be performing these actions on a developer machine, and manually copying to staging and production environments.

These manual steps are often error-prone and can result in unforeseen issues and failed deployments. By taking advantage of the automated build system in Team Foundation Server, your team can reduce the complexity of this process and turn it into a repeatable end-to-end solution that occurs at regular intervals or is triggered by changes introduced by your developers.

Additionally, you can leverage the automated build system to introduce a "gauntlet" of checks that each check-in may go through to verify the quality of those changes by using the gated check-in feature in the Team Foundation Build system. This can help your team reduce entropy by preventing defects from ever being introduced to the version control repository.

> **NOTE** *The new Release Management for Visual Studio 2013 product allows teams to define, configure, and automate deployments to multiple target environments. This tool can reduce risk and ensure repeatable deployments that support your organization's release pipeline and approval process.*
>
> *See Chapter 20 for more information about Release Management for Visual Studio 2013.*

Managing Test Plans

The testing or quality assurance departments may be organizing their test cases using Word or Excel documents, which can make it hard to organize your catalog of test cases. Additionally, tracking the execution progress of each test case may be extremely difficult; thus, it becomes difficult to gauge the progress of testing in your release.

Team Foundation Server allows you to manage your collection of test cases; it also allows you to manage the progress of test execution during the release cycle. This includes the ability to track tests across multiple configurations that your product or application needs to support.

Parallel Development

Development teams have notoriously experienced difficulty in managing changes across multiple lines of development that can occur concurrently. By supporting the previous release, while stabilizing the next release, and then also performing early work on a feature release, you can end up having trouble keeping each of those parallel lines of development organized. Integrating changes made between those releases is especially time-consuming and error-prone, especially if developers are manually applying fixes to each of those code lines.

Testers are often curious about how bug fixes and changes have been included in a particular release. And they might often need to figure out if fixes have been applied to other releases of the application.

The Team Foundation Version Control system in Team Foundation Server provides excellent branching and merging tools for easily managing parallel development, including the ability to track changes across branches. This helps you to easily see which branches have changes integrated into them as well as how and when those changes got there.

> **NOTE** *The new Distributed Version Control system gives developers more freedom to work on multiple parallel development tasks at once. Using Git, developers can work on multiple branches within local repositories before confidently committing changes to the server.*
>
> *See Chapter 7 for more information about Distributed Version Control with Git.*

ADOPTING TEAM FOUNDATION SERVER

The maximal value from Team Foundation Server is realized when it is used in a team. Therefore, ensuring a successful Team Foundation Server adoption requires alignment with many people in your organization. The following sections should help you avoid some common pitfalls and provide you with some suggestions on where to start with what may seem like a large and daunting product.

Adoption Timeline

In general, splitting up the adoption by team/application has proven to be a successful approach. Some of the effort may end up being the same for most teams, and lessons you learn from earlier transitions will help you become more successful in the following transitions. Table 2-1 presents a sample adoption timeline.

TABLE 2-1: Sample Adoption Timeline

ACTIVITY	ESTIMATED TIME
Planning for deploying Team Foundation Server	One week
Identifying the process to adopt and process template customizations	Two to four days
Designing the branching and merging strategy	One day
Customizing the process template (dependent on the level of customization of the process identified)	One to four weeks

Table 2-2 discusses the additional adoption steps for each team or application.

TABLE 2-2: Sample Adoption Timeline for Each Team

ACTIVITY	ESTIMATED TIME
Developing a custom migration tool (needed only if not using one commercially or freely available)	Two to four weeks
Testing the migration	One to two weeks
Initial training sessions for teams (occurs one week before transition)	Half a day for each team member
Migrating source code	One to two days
Migrating work items	One to two days
Follow-up training sessions for teams (occurs one week after transition)	Half a day for each team member

Phased Approach

Another approach that works well is adopting each piece of Team Foundation Server separately in different phases of a larger deployment project. This allows you to plan each phase, execute that adoption, and then train the teams on the new features and processes available in that particular phase.

Some find that teams are better able to absorb training for the new features when they are exposed to them incrementally. You may have a higher success rate by splitting up the adoption project, and then focusing your time and attention on making each part succeed. However, you'll eventually find some teams very eager to adopt future phases, so be sure you don't keep them waiting too long!

When introducing any new tooling into a large organization, it is important that you address the key pain points first. Many companies will identify traceability of work through the development life cycle, and this is often an area that is poorly addressed by existing tooling. For others, the version control system being used may be out-of-date (unsupported) and performing poorly. It is, therefore, usually the version control or work item tracking components that people begin using when adopting Team Foundation Server.

Luckily, Team Foundation Server is flexible enough that you can still get value from the product when using only one or two components of the system. Once you have adopted both version control and work item tracking, the next area to tackle to gain the most benefit is likely to be Team Foundation Build. By automating your build system and increasing the frequency of integration, you reduce the amount of unknown pain that always occurs when integrating components together to form a product. The key is to gradually remove the unknown and unpredictable elements from the software delivery process, and to always look for wasted effort that can be cut out. Using the new Release Management helps your team deploy the same build across multiple environments, no matter how complex the configuration.

Automating the builds not only means that the build and packaging process becomes less error-prone, but it also means that the feedback loop of requirement traceability is completed. You are now able to track work from the time that it is captured, all the way through to a change to the source code of the product, and into the build that contains those changes.

At this point, you may identify the need to document your test cases and track their execution throughout the release. With the traceability between test cases and requirements, you'll be able to better identify the requirements in your product that are covered appropriately by your testers.

After a period of time, you will have built up a repository of historical data in your Team Foundation Server data warehouse, and you can start to use the reporting features to predict if you will be finished when you expect (for example, is the amount of remaining work being completed at the required rate?). You will also be able to drill into the areas that you might want to improve—for example, which parts of the code are causing the most bugs.

To put all of this together, you will more than likely end up with the following adoption phases, but you will want to adopt them in the order that works for your organization:

- ➤ Phase I: Version Control
- ➤ Phase II: Work Item Tracking
- ➤ Phase III: Automated Builds
- ➤ Phase IV: Test Case Management
- ➤ Phase V: Reporting
- ➤ Phase VI: Virtual Environments and Lab Management

You'll notice that this book has generally been laid out in this order to help you address each area in order of typical adoption.

> **NOTE** *After getting used to the tooling, you should look at your overall process and adopted process templates to ensure that all of the necessary data is being captured—and that all the work item types and transitions are required. If there are unnecessary steps, consider removing them. If you notice problems because of a particular issue, consider modifying the process to add a safety net. It is important to adjust the process not only to fit the team and organization, but also to ensure that you adjust your processes when you need to, and not only because you can. See Chapter 12 for more information about process templates, work items, and other topics related to tracking work.*

Hosting Team Foundation Server

For the team to have trust in Team Foundation Server, you must ensure that it is there when they need it, and that it performs as well as possible. For organizations that depend on creating software, your version control and work item tracking repositories are critical to getting your work done. Therefore, those features should be treated on the same level as other mission-critical applications in the organization.

The Team Foundation Server infrastructure is a production environment for your company. Ideally, it should be hosted on a server or multiple servers with adequate resources (both physical memory and disk space). If hosted in a virtual environment, then you should ensure that the host machine has sufficient resources to handle the load of all guest machines, including superior disk I/O performance.

When planning upgrades, configuration changes, or when performing training, you should use a test Team Foundation Server environment. For some organizations, the test requirements justify the purchase of a hardware platform equivalent to the production environment.

However, for many scenarios, using a virtual Team Foundation environment will provide a suitable environment for testing. These virtual environments are especially useful when developing a new process template or testing work item process modifications. Microsoft provides an evaluation version of Team Foundation Server preconfigured as a virtual hard disk (VHD) file. This is frequently used as a test bed for work item modifications and new process templates.

> **NOTE** *Brian Keller, Microsoft's Principal Technical Evangelist for Visual Studio ALM, publishes frequently-updated virtual machines with Team Foundation already set up and populated with working projects. These can be extremely useful for demonstration purposes and for testing new work item templates and plug-ins. You can find the full list of Visual Studio ALM virtual machines at* `http://aka.ms/almvms`.

Identifying Affected Teams

One essential activity is to identify all of the different teams in your company that would be affected by deploying Team Foundation Server. Following are some examples of those types of affected teams:

➤ Developers

➤ Testers/Quality Assurance

➤ Product/Program Managers

➤ Project Managers

➤ Business Analysts

➤ Designers

➤ User Experience

➤ Change Management

➤ Release Management

➤ Technical Documentation/User Education

➤ Technical Support

➤ Information Technology

➤ Executives or other stakeholders

➤ Business Users

➤ Remote Teams

Generating Consensus

If anything, you should over-communicate any plans for rolling out Team Foundation Server and/or a new process. Change is difficult for some people, and this has been one technique that seems to ease those concerns.

Once you have identified all of the affected teams, it's helpful to generate consensus by suggesting that each team nominate a team member to represent the team as decisions are made about the deployment. This is generally a good way to ensure that everyone is involved, and that information ends up getting disseminated throughout the organization. You can have this "advisory" group help determine how to configure the server and the process that ends up being adopted. Going through this process allows those who are involved to have some buy-in to the deployment and, ultimately, champion the success of the change within their teams.

One word of caution, however, is that you should be sure to have an executive stakeholder in this group who is available to make final decisions when there are disagreements. It's important to ensure that decisions made by the group end up benefiting the business, so having this "final-authority" representative is helpful. The others in the group will feel better about giving their input and hearing why a particular decision is made, even if it's not the decision they supported.

Team Foundation Server Administrator

You will likely need to identify a resource who is responsible for managing the configuration and health of the Team Foundation Server environment. Your organization may not necessarily need a full-time resource for this task, but this will generally take a good amount of regular effort to ensure that this mission-critical environment is running smoothly for your company. This resource might fill several of the following example hats:

- ➤ Champion and lead the adoption in the organization.
- ➤ Implement process changes.
- ➤ Identify and write new reports.
- ➤ Manage permissions and administer the environment.
- ➤ Identify and implement maintenance windows.
- ➤ Design and implement branching and merging strategies.
- ➤ Architect build resources and build processes for use in the organization.
- ➤ Administer the virtual lab management assets.

Some larger organizations have even identified a team to manage each of the areas that Team Foundation Server may touch in the software development life cycle. This can be considered a *shared engineering* team that works with its "customers" in the organization to implement the needs of the company. Those customers are the teams using the Team Foundation Server environment internally. This team's work for managing the Team Foundation Server environment can even be prioritized by the advisory group mentioned previously, and often the team's leader serves as the chairperson of the advisory group.

A common question comes up about whether an IT or engineering organization should own the management of the Team Foundation Server environment. There are pros and cons to sole ownership by either team. IT organizations have had experience in managing corporate applications, but might not fully understand the needs of software development teams and departments. However, engineering departments might not have the expertise to manage hardware and disaster-recovery concerns that keep the servers running in optimal health.

A shared responsibility approach has proven to be successful. For example, the IT department may maintain the actual hardware; run regular backups; and take care of networking, power, and cooling needs. The engineering organization can own the application (Team Foundation Server) itself, which would include installing service packs or patches, configuring the team projects, and managing security. That shared management responsibility requires close collaboration across each department, which is essential for running a smoothly operating development environment.

Pilot Projects

A key way that your organization can learn what you might need to customize in Team Foundation Server is to identify a team, small project, or release willing to be the "guinea pig" to test Team Foundation Server. By setting up a pilot project, you can learn lots of information that might be helpful before rolling out to a larger audience in your organization.

Following is some of the information you will possibly discover:

➤ Custom reports you might need to provide that your business has been used to receiving from legacy applications

➤ Common pitfalls your pilot team has experienced that can be addressed when training other teams

➤ New features that might be more valuable to adopt ahead of other features in the products

Don't underestimate the amount of information you will learn from this pilot team and project. It can certainly give your organization more confidence in proving that the system will help you solve your organization's pain points.

MIGRATION STRATEGIES

Oftentimes, software development teams will have been using several different systems to track their source code, bugs, project management tasks, requirements, and even test cases. You might be in a situation where you want to migrate from those legacy systems to Team Foundation Server. Several different approaches and, thankfully, plenty of tools are available to assist you with your migration.

> **NOTE** *If you are upgrading from a previous version of Team Foundation Server, be sure to see Chapter 27 for information on planning the upgrade instead of following the migration techniques mentioned in this section.*

Version Control

Migrating from a legacy version control system to Team Foundation Server version control is one of the most common starting places for software development teams.

Visual SourceSafe

If your team is still using Visual SourceSafe (VSS), you should be aware that the product's support life cycle has ended. You should migrate to Team Foundation Server using the link to the VSS Upgrade Wizard in the Team Foundation Server Administration Console. This wizard will help you migrate source code from your VSS repositories to Team Foundation Server, keeping the change history during the migration.

Other Version Control Systems

If you aren't currently using VSS, then you have options as well. The Team Foundation Server product team at Microsoft has been working on a platform for migration and synchronization scenarios. This platform is freely available on CodePlex and is actively used internally at Microsoft. Out of the box, it contains adapters for Team Foundation Server 2008 and up, as well as Rational ClearCase, Rational ClearQuest, and file system-based version control systems.

The Team Foundation Server Integration Platform has been built on an extensible platform that allows for different adapters to be created to migrate source code from other systems. The CodePlex project has received numerous and regular contributions from the product team, and you can expect more adapters to come out in the future.

If you are feeling up to the challenge, you can also create a custom adapter for your version control system using the Team Foundation Server Integration Platform's extensibility hooks. You might consider contributing to the CodePlex project for others to take advantage of the custom adapter if they run into the same migration scenario that you faced!

> **NOTE** *You can get more information about the Team Foundation Server Integration Platform by visiting the CodePlex project's site at* `http://aka.ms/ TFSIntegrationPlatform`.

There is also a family of commercially available third-party migration solutions that will allow you to migrate your source code from popular legacy and third-party source control systems.

> **NOTE** *Chapter 9 discusses more about migrating from legacy version control systems, including Visual Source Safe.*

Work Item Tracking

In addition to migrating source code, most teams will want to think about migrating *work items* from their legacy systems. These may be bugs, requirements, test cases, tasks, and so on.

Thankfully, the Team Foundation Server Integration Platform mentioned previously was also designed to move work items in addition to source code. Currently, an adapter allows you to move your legacy artifacts over from IBM Rational ClearQuest into Team Foundation Server. Again, custom adapters can be built using the extensible architecture of the Team Foundation Server Integration Platform to migrate work items from other tracking systems.

There are several other methods that you could use to import your work item tracking data. You may use Microsoft Office Excel and the integration that Team Explorer adds to allow you to import spreadsheets of information. Commercial tools are also available for importing artifacts from HP Quality Center into Team Foundation Server.

> **NOTE** *Chapter 12 has more in-depth information and an introduction to Team Foundation Server work item tracking.*

STRUCTURING TEAM PROJECT COLLECTIONS AND TEAM PROJECTS

A common question that ultimately will come up after setting up Team Foundation Server is how you should go about structuring your team project collections and team projects. It's helpful to plan your strategy before installing and setting up the environment so that you make the right choices from the beginning. Changing the strategy can lead to a lot of effort in reorganizing, and you'll even find that some changes are downright impossible. Team Foundation Server supports creating a strategy that will be effective, flexible, and scalable to your organizations.

Ultimately, the strategy will be formed based on the isolation needs for your organization. Software development teams have traditionally described three constant concepts for how they managed their applications:

➤ **Projects**—These are the units of work centered on a given effort with a start and end date. You can easily map these to product releases, contracts, or initiatives. The projects and team within it usually follow a process such as Scrum, Capability Maturity Model Integration (CMMI), and so on.

➤ **Products/codebases**—These are described as the "source code" that makes up an application product, or group of products (suite/family). It is what the developers, designers, and other specialties work on, and its by-product (files such as `.exe`, `.dll`, and so on) is consumed by a *customer*.

➤ **Organizations**—These are the divisions, business units, departments, or teams that work on projects that deliver products to end customers.

Team project collections provide the ability to group a set of tightly related team projects. When you are thinking about them, you should focus on correlating them with products/codebases or application suites. For example, if your company makes four unique product lines that have almost no codesharing between them, it might be practical to create four team project collections. If, on the other hand, your company has several products that compose a solution or product suite with high code reuse, framework sharing, or even simultaneous release, then you will have a single team project collection.

Some organizations have multiple business units or departments that traditionally manage their own software configuration management servers/repositories. These organizations will find that team project collections also benefit them by isolating each business unit, but are still able to consolidate the management and maintenance of a single Team Foundation Server environment. This type of functionality would be described as *multi-tenancy*.

Ultimately, you will need to decide the isolation needs of the departments in your organization and how you might segregate certain resources, such as build and virtual lab resources based along those lines.

NOTE *Chapters 21 and 22 provide a more in-depth look at team project collections and scalability features.*

SCOPE OF A TEAM PROJECT

At its very core, a Team Project contains all of the artifacts such as source code, work items, builds, reports, and an associated SharePoint team portal site. In general, a team project is "bigger than you think." A good way of thinking about what must be grouped into a single team project is to think about the impact of a typical requirement for your software development project. If the requirement would affect the ASP.NET front end, Java middleware, and SQL database repository, then all these projects and teams of developers probably want to be working on the same team project.

Following are three general areas that are used when scoping a team project. But every organization is different, and yours might need to combine these aspects when deciding on your approach. For some organizations, it makes sense to have only a single team project in a single project collection. Others may have more than a hundred.

➤ **Team project per application**—In general, *team project per application* is the most common approach when scoping team projects, and probably the position you should first consider. Generally, requirements are addressed by the entire application, and several people are assigned to work on it. The applications typically have a long life cycle, going from inception, active development into the support, and then finally to end-of-life phases.

➤ **Team project per release**—The *team project per release* methodology is useful for very large teams working on long-running projects. After every major release, you create a new team project. At this point, you can carry out changes that might have come about from your post-release review. You might take the opportunity to reorganize your version control tree, improve process templates, and copy over work items from the previous release that didn't make it.

This methodology tends to be suited to large independent software vendors (ISVs) working with products with a very long lifetime. In fact, Microsoft itself uses this approach for many of its products. In these cases, it is generally safer to start as a team project per application, and then move to a team project

continues

continued

per release (if required) to make reporting easier. This is traditionally the case if the releases tend to span a long timeframe (such as a multiyear project or release cycle).

➤ **Team project per team**—For smaller teams (fewer than 50) where the number of people working on the team tends to stay fairly static, but the applications they work on are in a constant state of flux, the *team project per team* approach may be most suitable. This is most often seen in consulting-style organizations, where the same group of people may be responsible for delivering applications for clients with rapid turnaround. If your team members are often working on more than one project at a time, the same team or subset of the team works together on those projects over time, or if the project life cycle is measured in months rather than years, then you may want to consider this approach.

As an alternative, a single team project collection per customer could be used for the consulting-style organizations that must provide all of the artifacts (source code, work item history, and so on) to the client at the end of the project, because the team project collection contains the entire work. If you do not have to deliver all of the artifacts of the project to the customer as a requirement, however, you should not necessarily use the individual team project collections approach.

Considering Limitations in Team Foundation Server

When deciding the appropriate team project collection and team project structure for your organization, it is helpful to understand the limitations of the feature set in Team Foundation Server that may affect your desired strategy based on your team's goals with using the product.

Ultimately, you can use the knowledge of these limitations to arrive at the most appropriate scoping of team project collections and team projects for your organization. You will want to ensure that you think about possible changes to the products, application families, teams, and organizational structure, and how these limitations may impact those changes in the future.

Renaming a Team Project

At the time of this writing, you unfortunately are not able to rename a team project once you have created it. There is no workaround for this limitation. You should ensure that you have fully reviewed and arrived at your team project structuring strategy before creating any team projects.

Additionally, you should consider the names you give to team projects that represent products or product families whose names have not been determined. Once you pick a name for the team project (especially if it uses a code name or some other early project name), that name will be used for the entire lifetime of the team project.

If you are using a larger team project, then you can use area paths to differentiate among different product families, products, and ultimately the components in those products. Area paths can be renamed and reorganized at any time. Chapter 12 provides more information about area paths.

One key difference for a team project collection is that you can change the name of a team project collection at a later time, provided you have an on-premises installation.

Moving Work Items across Team Projects or Team Project Collections

Because you can choose to use completely different process templates for team projects, you are unable to move work items across the team project boundary. Ensure that you pick the appropriate scoping level for a team project. For example, if you want to create a bug in one application, and later find out that it is really for another application in another team project, you will find out that you cannot move the bug to the other team project. In this case, you will have to create a copy (because the "bug" artifact may not even be named the same in the other team project's process template) of the work item in the next team project.

Instead, you may consider scoping the team project larger to include multiple applications in the same application family. You can then organize the applications within the team projects by using the area path hierarchy. To move a bug between two applications stored in the same team project, you would then just change the area path to the one that represents the other application. However, all applications or teams that use a team project must use the same process template. Chapter 12 provides more information about area paths.

Managing Work Items from Multiple Team Projects in Office Excel, Project, or Project Server

Similar to the previous limitation, because team projects can have different process templates, the Microsoft Office Excel and Project add-ins for managing work items do not work with work items from multiple team projects. As mentioned, you will want to ensure that you scope the team project to be larger, and use the area path hierarchy to distinguish between applications or teams. Then use the iteration path hierarchy to distinguish between releases and iterations/sprints.

Additionally, now that you are able to set up two-way synchronization with Project Server, you will notice that an enterprise project plan in Project Server can be mapped only to a single team project. If you have an enterprise project that spans multiple applications that might exist in multiple team projects, then your team project strategy will need to be modified to have a team project that contains all of those applications. However, multiple enterprise project plans in Project Server can be mapped to a single team project in Team Foundation Server. Chapter 16 provides more information about integration with Project Server and Team Foundation Server.

Managing Teams and Capacity Planning

Team Foundation Server 2012 introduced new support for managing team artifacts and membership as well as Agile planning tools, including the ability to plan sprint/iteration/project/release resource capacities. Portfolio management tools were added in Team Foundation Server 2013. These concepts are scoped within a team project. That means that a "team" has members, and the work it performs is defined inside the same team project.

The capacity planning tools plan for work only inside the same team project. Therefore, if you have team resources that are shared among multiple product releases/projects, then you will want to contain the entire set of products team members work on in the same team project if you want a single view from a team and a capacity planning standpoint. Chapter 14 discusses defining teams and using the new Agile planning tools available in Team Web Access.

Tracking Merged Changes across Branches in Multiple Team Projects

You are unable to use the branch visualization and track merged changes visualization features for branches that span across the team project boundary. In general, your branching and merging strategy should avoid creating branches across team projects if you plan to use the visualization features introduced in Team Foundation Server 2010.

You are able to have multiple branch "families" inside the same team project. You can even have different security permissions defined for each of the branch families to prevent one team from having the same permissions as other teams. You can withhold read permissions for certain teams so that they do not see all of the version control content inside the team project's version control repository. Chapter 11 discusses more options for setting up a version control repository, including the ability to have multiple product families stored in the same team project.

Reports and Dashboards Scoped to Team Project

If you have larger team projects that encompass multiple applications in an application family, team, and so on, you will notice that the standard reports and dashboards will be scoped to use the data inside the entire team project. Each of the reports enables you to filter the data, including some by area path and iteration path fields for the work item data. This does not mean that you are unable to create reports with data across team projects. This only means that the default reports are scoped to a team project.

Additionally, the SharePoint dashboard features allow you to create multiple custom dashboards. Each custom dashboard can then include web parts that are scoped to a specific area path and iteration path as well.

Moving Team Projects between Team Project Collections

Once a team project is created in one team project collection, you are unable to move the team project to another existing team project collection because there may be a conflict between the IDs used for the different artifacts (such as changeset, work item, and build unique identifiers).

One option you do have is to split a team project collection, which allows you to create a clone, and then remove all of the unwanted team projects from each copy. This allows you to essentially move a team project to a *new* team project collection. There is no workaround available for moving a team project to an *existing* team project collection.

The key takeaway from this limitation is that it is possible to split a larger team project collection into multiple team project collections but impossible to consolidate or reorganize team projects among team project collections.

Artifacts Scoped to a Team Project Collection

One of the important features of team project collections is that all of the artifacts contained within a team project collection are isolated from other team project collections. For example, all of the different link types between version control files and changesets, work items, builds, test cases, test results, and so on, can be contained only within the team project collection.

Another example is that you will not be able to add a link between a test case that exists in one team project collection and a requirement that exists in another team project collection. If you need this type of traceability, you should include team projects that need to link between artifacts within the same team project collection.

Additionally, you are unable to branch and merge across team project collections, even though you are able to branch across multiple team projects within the same team project collection. There is no workaround available for this feature, so ensure that you scope the team project collection appropriately to account for this feature limitation.

Certain hardware within a broader Team Foundation Server environment is also scoped to team project collections. For example, build controllers and agents, as well as test controllers and agents, are scoped only to a single team project collection.

Finally, you are unable to create work item queries that need to pull work items from team projects across multiple team project collections. However, you can create a work item query to pull work items from multiple team projects inside the same team project collection. Also, the reporting warehouse contains information about artifacts stored in all team project collections and team projects, so you can create custom reports that pull that information together.

Server Limitations

Team Foundation Server is an extremely scalable product. However, you should understand its limitations so that you optimize the performance of the environment. It is also helpful to know that most of the limits are not enforced by the product, and are general best practices and recommendations from the product group to maintain a certain level of performance.

Team Foundation Server can support thousands of team project collections mainly because of the support for scale-out architecture. The limits are tied more to the SQL Server hardware used in your deployment. A SQL Server instance can support 30 to 100 *active* team project collections. This range is related to the physical memory available to SQL. *Active* team project collections are those being accessed daily by the team.

Given this, if your deployment structure requires hundreds of team project collections, you have essentially two choices:

➤ You may buy additional hardware and make available more SQL Server instances for use by the Team Foundation Server environment.

➤ You could consider grouping team projects more aggressively within existing team project collections.

To maintain high performance, you should limit the number of team projects stored within a team project collection. The actual number of team projects to include in a team project collection is limited by the complexity of the work item types defined within the process templates being used by each of those team projects. The work item types included in the standard process templates (for example, the Microsoft Solutions Framework for Agile Software Development 2013 process template) have been shown to support more than 500 team projects on a server on adequate hardware.

There is a linear relationship between performance degradation and the number of team projects within a team project collection. Make sure you keep this in mind as you develop your team project structuring strategy and that you appropriately plan for additional hardware resources if many team projects will be required.

PREPARATION FOR A TEAM FOUNDATION SERVER ENVIRONMENT

The following sections examine some of the preparation steps that are beneficial to take care of before you start to install a new Team Foundation Server.

> **NOTE** *If you are upgrading from earlier versions of Team Foundation Server, you will find the upcoming sections beneficial in understanding the necessary preparation steps. You can also consult Chapter 27, which is dedicated solely to upgrading.*

Understanding the Architecture and Scale-Out Options

You have multiple options when configuring your Team Foundation Server deployments. You can deploy all the components (Team Foundation Server application, SQL Server, SQL Analysis Services, SQL Reporting Services, and Windows SharePoint Services) onto one machine. This is called a *single-server installation* and should work fine for 500 users or fewer. In general, single-server installations are the easiest installations, as shown in Figure 2-1.

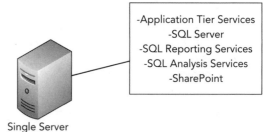

Single Server

FIGURE 2-1: Single-server installation

For more than 500 users, a *multiserver installation* should be considered. There are several flavors of multiserver installations. At its most basic, there are two servers. One server is the data tier, running SQL Server and SQL Analysis Services, and the other is the application tier, running Team Foundation Server, SQL Reporting Services, and SharePoint, as shown in Figure 2-2.

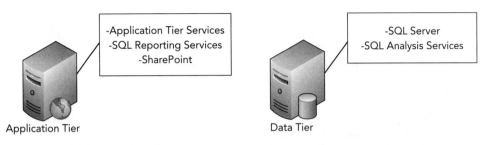

FIGURE 2-2: Multiserver installation

> **NOTE** *Notice that the SQL Reporting Services component is actually installed on the application tier server instead of the data tier server in a multiserver configuration. This is because the front-end SQL Reporting Services component is web-based and can be load balanced along with the other web-based components of Team Foundation Server. This will allow for easy and optimal scalability in the future if required by your environment.*

Your organization may have an existing SharePoint Portal Server and/or a SQL Server Reporting Services Server that it wants to use in conjunction with Team Foundation Server. For that scenario, you would then have a server for running the Team Foundation Server application tier, a server for running the SQL Server databases, and separate servers for running SharePoint Portal Server and/or Reporting Services. Figure 2-3 shows a sample topology using this particular scenario.

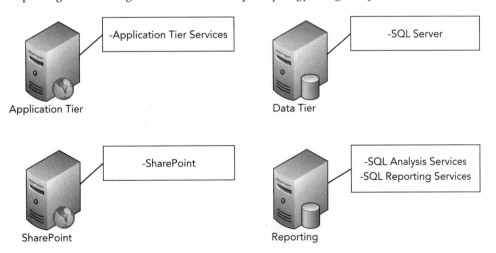

FIGURE 2-3: Existing server used with Team Foundation Server

> **NOTE** *Because SharePoint 2010 and later editions have higher system require-ments, such as for RAM, and can be intensive on server resources, we actually recommend that you have a separate server environment for SharePoint. This is especially the case if you are taking advantage of the rich dashboard features available when using the Enterprise edition of SharePoint.*
>
> *This configuration will ease the management and system resources requirement for your Team Foundation Server environment. It will also make sure that Team Foundation Server and SharePoint are not competing with one another for hard-ware resources on the same server.*

For high-availability scenarios, clustering of machines is available at each point in the archi-tecture. As previously discussed, the Team Foundation Server application tier machines can be located behind a network load-balancing device. The SQL Server instances referred to by the Team Foundation Server application and team project collections can also be clustered. Figure 2-4 shows an example of a larger topography that includes high-availability scaling.

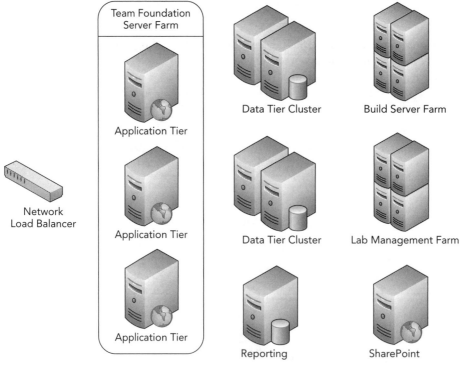

FIGURE 2-4: Larger topography that includes high-availability scaling

Hardware Requirements

Table 2-3 shows the hardware requirements for a single-server installation, where the application tier and data tier reside on the same physical machine. However, keep in mind that these numbers are *minimum* recommendations, and, obviously, the more hardware you can throw at a problem, the better, especially if you use the environment more heavily. You will want to continue to monitor the environment for performance and utilization to scale the resources as necessary.

TABLE 2-3: Hardware Requirements for Single-Server Installation

NUMBER OF USERS	CPU	HARD DISK	MEMORY
Fewer than 250 users	One single-core 2.13 GHz processor	125GB	2GB
250 to 500 users	One single-core 2.3 GHz dual-core processor	300GB	4GB

For a multiserver installation (where you have distinct physical servers for the application tier and the data tier), Table 2-4 lists the application tier hardware requirements, and Table 2-5 lists the data tier hardware requirements.

TABLE 2-4: Application Tier Hardware Requirements

NUMBER OF USERS	CPU	HARD DISK	MEMORY
500 to 2,200 users	One 2.13 GHz dual-core Intel Xeon processor	500GB	4GB
2,200 to 3,600 users	One 2.13 GHz quad-core Intel Xeon processor	500GB	8GB

TABLE 2-5: Data Tier Hardware Requirements

NUMBER OF USERS	CPU	HARD DISK	MEMORY
500 to 2,200 users	One 2.33 GHz quad-core Intel Xeon processor	2TB SAS Disk Array	8GB
2,200 to 3,600 users	Two 2.33 GHz quad-core Intel Xeon processors	3TB SAS Disk Array	16GB

Keep in mind that the application tier may be hosting SharePoint and/or SQL Server Reporting Services, in addition to Team Foundation Server. This might require you to bump up your hardware numbers in some form or fashion to account for the extra processing needed and the minimum requirements for those products.

Virtualization

Virtualization is a hot topic these days. Virtualization allows you to buy a large server and then virtually host several different servers on one physical machine. This allows an organization to make the most of a physical machine's resources. Some pieces of the Team Foundation Server environment can be safely hosted in a virtual environment, and some require careful consideration and performance tuning before being virtualized.

Ideally, the following pieces should be installed on physical servers or properly tuned virtual machines with peak performance specifications:

➤ SQL Server Database Engine

➤ SQL Server Reporting Services

➤ SQL Server Analysis Services

SQL Server is the foundation for holding all the information regarding Team Foundation Server. Should it become corrupted, the entire Team Foundation Server system will go down. To minimize the chances of database corruption, you should carefully consider the possible drawbacks before hosting SQL Server 2012 or higher in a virtualized environment. In some earlier editions of SQL Server, virtualization was not supported. However, this is no longer the case because there were quite a few improvements included in the latest versions.

> **NOTE** *Microsoft has a great list of frequently asked questions specifically about its support policy for running Microsoft SQL Server products in a hardware virtualization environment in this knowledgebase article:* http://aka.ms/SQLVirtualizationSupportPolicy. *We highly recommend that you follow the advice in this support article to ensure that your organization is in the best supported position available under a virtualized configuration.*

Specifically, for Team Foundation Server, you will want to monitor the disk I/O metrics to ensure that the virtualized database servers are able to keep up with the amount of I/O generated for database transactions that come from Team Foundation Server. No matter which virtualization technology you use, you will want to ensure that you set up the virtual environment for peak performance. The key is to continually monitor the performance indicators for the environment, and make appropriate modifications. Any degradation of performance should be reviewed, especially if you choose to virtualize your data tier server.

> **NOTE** *For some tips on properly setting up a virtual environment that will include SQL Server, see the recommendations in Chapter 22.*

The following can be safely installed in a virtualized environment with minimum to no impact on the Team Foundation Server system:

➤ Team Foundation Server application tier components

➤ SharePoint

➤ Team Foundation Build servers

➤ Team Foundation Proxy servers

➤ Test Controllers and Agents

➤ Release Management Server and Agents

> **WARNING** *Be careful when deciding to virtualize a server running Build Agents. A build will often require significant disk I/O and CPU resources, so virtualization may not be the best option. Build Controllers do not have the same requirements, so it is usually safe for them to run on virtualized environments.*

Planning for Software Prerequisites

In addition to the hardware requirements for Team Foundation Server, you will want to prepare for a new installation by ensuring that certain software prerequisites are met.

Operating Systems

Like Team Foundation Server 2012, Team Foundation Server 2013 supports only 64-bit Windows Server operating systems. However, Team Foundation Server can be installed on a 32-bit client operating system (for example, Windows 8). Table 2-6 lists the supported operating systems for the application tier server.

TABLE 2-6: Supported Operating Systems for Application Tier

OPERATING SYSTEM	ADDITIONAL NOTES
Windows Server 2008 R2 with Service Pack 1	64-bit only Standard, Enterprise, or Datacenter editions
Windows Small Business Server 2011 with Service Pack 1	64-bit only Standard, Enterprise, or Datacenter editions
Windows Server 2012	64-bit only Essentials, Standard, or Datacenter editions
Windows Server 2012 R2	64-bit only Essentials, Standard, or Datacenter editions
Windows 7 with Service Pack 1	Home Premium, Professional, Enterprise, or Ultimate editions
Windows 8	Basic, Pro, or Enterprise editions
Windows 8.1	Basic, Pro, or Enterprise editions

> **NOTE** *Team Foundation Server supports the capability to install on a server running a client operating system such as Windows 8.1. However, client operating systems will not support reporting features, integration with SharePoint products, or the ability to run a Team Foundation Server proxy.*

SQL Server

Team Foundation Server uses SQL Server to store its data, SQL Server Analysis Services to store an Online Analytical Processing (OLAP) cube for the data warehouse, and SQL Reporting Services as a presentation layer for rich reports. You can use the default instance or a named SQL instance for any of the components. Table 2-7 lists the supported versions of SQL Server.

TABLE 2-7: Supported SQL Server Versions

SQL SERVER VERSION	ADDITIONAL NOTES
SQL Server 2012 with Service Pack 1	Recommended Express, Standard, or Enterprise edition Express is used when installing Team Foundation Server using the "Basic" configuration wizard or when using Team Foundation Server Express Edition
SQL Server 2014	Express, Standard, or Enterprise edition

> **NOTE** *You can use an existing instance of SQL Server, as long as it meets certain requirements. See the latest version of the* Team Foundation Server Installation Guide *available on the Microsoft Downloads site at* http://aka.ms/TFS2013InstallGuide.

Included Edition

When purchasing Team Foundation Server 2013, you are able to install SQL Server 2012 Standard for limited use if you are installing on a single server. This "limited use" privilege permits you to use only that SQL instance for Team Foundation Server 2013 databases. This means that you would not be able to use the instance for any custom databases or other applications that you have installed within your organization.

You can use an additional production license of Team Foundation Server (for example, included with an MSDN Subscription) for installing the limited-use SQL Server license on a separate data tier server from the application tier server. You can read more about these licensing details in the latest version of the Visual Studio Licensing Whitepaper available at `http://aka.ms/VisualStudioLicensing`.

Enterprise Editions of SQL Server

If you are using an Enterprise edition of SQL Server that you have licensed separately, Team Foundation Server 2013 will take advantage of features made available only in the Enterprise edition. Following are some of the features that Team Foundation Server can take advantage of:

➤ **Online re-indexing**—This is particularly useful for the periodic maintenance jobs that Team Foundation Server runs to keep the SQL instance healthy, because it is capable of keeping the database online while it performs those steps. This can lead to better performance and reduced blocking calls.

➤ **Perspectives in Analysis Services**—The schema for the OLAP cube for the data warehouse will take advantage of a feature called *perspectives*. Perspectives in SQL Analysis Services allow a more focused view of the dimensions, measures, and data included in the OLAP cube.

➤ **Index compression**—Team Foundation Server will take advantage of index compression, which will help increase performance by reducing I/O and memory utilization. (This feature may require more CPU utilization, however, but shouldn't be a problem because I/O is typically the bottleneck for the data tier.)

➤ **Clustering data tiers for high availability and redundancy**—If you are looking to have a clustered data tier, then you will want to take advantage of the Enterprise edition because it allows you to have as many failover clusters as the underlying operating system supports.

➤ **Query optimizations**—Team Foundation Server can benefit from certain query optimizations available only in the Enterprise edition of SQL Server.

➤ **Data-driven subscriptions in Reporting Services**—This feature allows you to subscribe to a report and set up recurring e-mails, and so on, that use data to drive what parameters are set in each report that gets sent.

➤ **Scale-out deployment for Reporting Services**—This feature is particularly necessary if you decide to have multiple application tiers together as a Team Foundation Server farm, and want to have SQL Reporting Services installed on each of those front-end servers to be load balanced for high availability.

SharePoint Products

Team Foundation Server has the ability to integrate with a new or existing SharePoint environment. Starting with Team Foundation Server 2010, this integration is optional and not required for installation. You can choose to integrate with SharePoint at the time of installation or add it later.

Table 2-8 lists the supported version of SharePoint products that can be used for integration.

TABLE 2-8: Supported Versions of SharePoint Products

SHAREPOINT PRODUCT	ADDITIONAL NOTES
SharePoint Foundation 2010	
SharePoint Server 2010	Enterprise or Standard edition
SharePoint Foundation 2013	
SharePoint Server 2013	Recommended Enterprise or Standard edition

If you are using a full version of SharePoint Server such as SharePoint Server (SPS) 2010 or 2013, Team Foundation Server will take advantage of features available only in the full Enterprise edition (such as Excel Services). It does so by providing a set of "rich" dashboards that display charts contained in Microsoft Office Excel workbooks. The "rich" dashboards would not be available for your team portal sites when using the other versions of SharePoint products (SharePoint Foundation 2010 or 2013), but you would instead get a "lite" version of two dashboards based on SQL Server Reporting Services.

If you will be using a full version of SharePoint Server, you should consider installing the front-end components on different hardware than the hardware that will be used for running Team Foundation Server. This allows you to manage SharePoint independently of Team Foundation Server, which, in turn, allows you to lower your maintenance burden and prevent performance bottlenecks that may occur when both are running on the same server.

> **NOTE** *Chapter 15 provides a more in-depth look at integrating with SharePoint.*

Service Accounts

You will need several accounts. Table 2-9 lists the recommended service accounts that you will likely use when setting up your Team Foundation Server environment. The table assumes that you're using Team Foundation Server in an environment that uses Active Directory Domain Services.

TABLE 2-9: Recommended Service Accounts

SERVICE ACCOUNT	SAMPLE ACCOUNT NAME	ADDITIONAL NOTES
Team Foundation Server	yourdomain\TFSSERVICE	Should have the "Account is sensitive and cannot be delegated" option enabled. Do not use the same account you use to install Team Foundation Server.
Team Foundation Server Reporting	yourdomain\TFSREPORTS	Must be a user account (not Network Service). Should be given the "Allow log on locally" permission.

SERVICE ACCOUNT	SAMPLE ACCOUNT NAME	ADDITIONAL NOTES
Team Foundation Server Build	yourdomain\TFSBUILD	
Team Foundation Server Proxy	yourdomain\TFSPROXY	
Lab Management	yourdomain\TFSLAB	Must be a user account (not Network Service) and can be used with standard environments, even when not using virtual lab management features.

The following is a list of best practices for Team Foundation Server service accounts:

➤ Built-in service accounts such as Network Service are supported, except as noted in Table 2-9.

➤ The service account user should be an Active Directory account if the Team Foundation Server environment consists of more than one server.

➤ Service accounts should be given the "Log on as a service" permission, except the Team Foundation Server Reporting service account.

File Share Folders

As you are using certain features in Team Foundation Server, you will end up needing several shared folder locations. Table 2-10 lists the recommended folder share locations and their purposes. The suggested permissions for each of these shares is for full control for the TFSSERVICE and TFSBUILD service accounts, and read-only permissions for all team members, with the exception of libraries for Visual Studio Lab Management (which should include full control permissions for the TFSLAB service account).

TABLE 2-10: Suggested Folder Share Locations

DESCRIPTION	SUGGESTED NAME	PURPOSE
Build Drops	\\builds.tfs.contoso.local\Builds	Used by the automated build system to copy outputs of the build process. Should be contained on a file server separate from any build server hardware.
Symbol Server	\\symbols.tfs.contoso.local\Symbols	Used by the automated build system for publishing debugging symbols. Should be contained on a file server separate from any build server hardware.
Lab Management Library	\\library.lab.tfs.contoso.local\LabLibrary	Used by the lab management system for storing virtual machine and environment templates

SMTP Server

One of the nice features in Team Foundation Server is the ability to set up custom alerts with different events that occur on the system. This allows users to self-subscribe to receiving e-mails for a multitude of different scenarios that may occur—for example, when a work item is assigned to a user, a triggered build has failed, or a check-in occurs to a particular folder in version control.

To ensure that your team members will be able to take advantage of this functionality, you must have a Simple Mail Transfer Protocol (SMTP) server that will accept e-mail traffic from the Team Foundation Server application tier server(s). Beginning with Team Foundation Server 2012, support was introduced for advanced SMTP authentication settings such as a user name and password as well as support for Windows authentication. SMTP servers no longer need to be configured only to accept anonymous e-mail delivery from Team Foundation Server servers.

Firewall Concerns and Ports Used

To ensure the best connections between the servers in the Team Foundation Server environment and also client connectivity, you will want to ensure that certain ports are opened at each firewall that network traffic may flow through. Table 2-11 lists the default ports that Team Foundation Server uses for network traffic.

TABLE 2-11: Required Ports

PORT	DESCRIPTION
8080	Team Foundation Server Application Tier
8081	Team Foundation Server Proxy
9191	Team Foundation Server Build Service
80	SharePoint Default Website
17012	SharePoint Central Administration
1433	SQL Server
1434	SQL Browser Service
2382	SQL Server Analysis Services Redirector
2383	SQL Server Analysis Services
80	SQL Server Reporting Services

Source: *Team Foundation Server 2013 Installation Guide*

Friendly DNS Names

To ease future scenarios where you may want to move to new hardware, upgrade to new versions of Team Foundation Server, or scale out components, you may want to create friendly DNS entries that point to the individual components for Team Foundation Server. Additionally, it is helpful to have something "friendly" to provide to end users as a connection address instead of server names that can be cryptic.

It is particularly important for the new Web Access features and for the Source Server information permanently stored inside of debugging symbols that the endpoint used for Team Foundation Server components does not change over the lifetime of the environment, including upgrades. Friendly DNS names set your team up for the best continuity of use of each of those component services.

> **NOTE** *You should set up each of the individual friendly DNS names for all of the different components listed in Table 2-12, even if they are currently all on the same server. You never know when you will want to scale out the environment to additional or different hardware. Having these friendly DNS names configured and used by the Team Foundation Server environment will allow you the most in flexibility for the change of infrastructure scenarios that will come in the future.*

Table 2-12 lists the suggested friendly DNS entries that you should create for your Team Foundation Server environment (even if it is only a single server). Each of these entries can either be DNS A or CNAME records and assume an internal DNS suffix of domain.local.

TABLE 2-12: Friendly DNS Records

DNS RECORD ENTRY	POINTS TO
tfs.domain.local	Application Tier server or Network Load Balancer IP for Team Foundation Server Application Tier server farm. Used for Team Foundation Server Application Tier, Team Web Access, and SQL Reporting Services.
data.tfs.domain.local	Data Tier server or SQL Server Cluster IP. Used for location of the configuration database, team project collection databases, and the relational warehouse database.
warehouse.tfs.domain.local	SQL Server Analysis Services instance
india.proxy.tfs.domain.local	One friendly DNS entry for each remote location with a proxy server (optional)
sharepoint.tfs.domain.local	Separate friendly DNS entry for the SharePoint server if it is separated from the application tier server (optional)
lab.tfs.domain.local	System Center Virtual Machine Manager server used for Team Foundation Server Lab Management (optional)
builds.tfs.domain.local	The file share server(s) containing the build drops. This file share could also be set up for Distributed File System (DFS) or BranchCache with a single endpoint using this friendly DNS name.
symbols.tfs.domain.local	The file share server(s) containing the Symbol Server repository. This file share could also be set up for Distributed File System (DFS) or BranchCache with a single endpoint using this friendly DNS name.

> **NOTE** *For more information about how to configure all of the components of Team Foundation Server to use friendly DNS names instead of the default server names, as well as the scenarios where this is helpful, visit the blog post by Ed Blankenship at* `http://aka.ms/FriendlyDNSTFS`.

Legacy Visual Studio Versions

If team members are using older versions of Visual Studio, you will want to ensure they are able to connect to Team Foundation Server 2013. Microsoft provides excellent documentation describing compatibility between Team Foundation clients and Team Foundation Server 2013, including any software or patches required. You can find this documentation at `http://aka.ms/TFS2013Compatibility`.

The latest updates to the Visual Studio 2012 and 2013 versions of Team Explorer will work natively with Team Foundation Server 2013, but support for Git is only provided with the Visual Studio Tools for Git extension.

Earlier versions of Team Explorer can connect to Team Foundation Server 2013 after some additional installations. The Visual Studio 2010 version of Team Explorer has a *Forward Compatibility Update* available to allow users to connect to a Team Foundation Server 2013 environment. Existing essential functionality that was available in the IDE is maintained after installing the update. However, no new features available in the Visual Studio 2013 release are made available with the update. Those users can install Visual Studio 2013 or Team Explorer 2013 to use side by side with the older version of the IDE.

Even with the forward compatibility update installed, you will not be able to perform many of the administrative activities such as creating a team project in an older version of Visual Studio. For administration activities, be sure to use a Visual Studio version that matches the server version.

If you have team members who will be using older versions of Visual Studio (such as Visual Studio 2008, Visual Studio 2005, Visual Studio 2003, Visual Studio 6, and so on) or other development environments that support the Microsoft Source Code Control Interface (MSSCCI), then you can install the latest version of the Team Foundation Server 2013 MSSCCI Provider currently available on the Visual Studio Gallery. The MSSCCI Provider enables team members to perform essential version control operations in the legacy development environments. As with the Forward Compatibility Update, those team members should have Visual Studio 2013 or Team Explorer 2013 installed and running side by side to ensure they have access to the rest of the features of Team Foundation Server 2013.

> **NOTE** *Visual Studio 2012 introduced the ability for round-tripping support of Visual Studio solutions and projects between Visual Studio 2012 and Visual Studio 2010 SP1 without requiring an "upgrade" of the solution and projects. This allowed for some team members to begin using the new functionality of Visual Studio 2012 without requiring the entire team to upgrade at the same time as long as they are at least using Visual Studio 2010 with Service Pack 1.*
>
> *This support is continued in Visual Studio 2013 so other team members can work with the same solutions and projects in Visual Studio 2013, Visual Studio 2012, and even Visual Studio 2010 SP1.*
>
> *Not all Visual Studio project types will support this round-tripping functionality. Many of the common project types are supported. If you have a project that does not support this, you can move it to a separate Visual Studio solution designed to be opened only in old versions of the Visual Studio IDE. More information about which project types have round-tripping support with Visual Studio 2012 or 2010 SP1 and which ones don't can be found at* `http://aka.ms/VS2013Compatibility`.

SUMMARY

This chapter reviewed possible ways that you can approach gaining support for adopting Team Foundation Server and examined potential timelines for adoption. You learned how to identify the key players on your teams who will be instrumental in the success of the adoption.

There are many different ways for structuring your team project collections and team projects, and this chapter discussed the different possibilities and limitations that should help you formalize the most appropriate strategy for your teams.

You learned about the different hardware recommendations and software prerequisites that will be required for certain functionality. Additionally, being prepared also means ensuring that the environment and accounts are ready before installation, so we presented a list of suggested items to check off.

In Chapter 3, you learn how to actually install and set up your new Team Foundation Server environment. You also learn how to set up the prerequisites, and identify where each component of the Team Foundation Server environment should be installed. Finally, you learn about the process of configuring Team Foundation Server and creating the first team project.

3

Installation and Configuration

WHAT'S IN THIS CHAPTER?

➤ Preparing to install Team Foundation Server 2013

➤ Installing and configuring Team Foundation Server 2013

➤ Creating your first team project with Team Foundation Server 2013

Before the 2010 release, installing and configuring Team Foundation Server could have easily consumed an entire weekend or more. Installation errors were difficult to diagnose, configuration was done entirely via the command line, and configuration options were largely inflexible. Thankfully, the 2010 release of Team Foundation Server was a monumental leap forward when it came to installation, configuration, and administration.

There were significant improvements again in Team Foundation Server 2012, and the 2013 release further expedites the installation and configuration process.

Team Foundation Server 2013 provides a GUI-based configuration and administration console, a flexible architecture with options for choosing which components you want to use, robust validation logic before each configuration step, and many more fit-and-finish features.

In this chapter, you will learn how to install and configure Team Foundation Server 2013. Some advanced configuration areas will be reserved for later chapters, but after reading this chapter, you will be able to install and configure a simple Team Foundation Server deployment in a matter of minutes.

WHAT YOU'LL NEED

Before starting your installation, you should acquire the installation media for all of the components you will need. It is also a good idea to think about which updates you may need (such as service packs), and which clients and optional components you want to use with Team

Foundation Server 2013. You should also download and review the latest Team Foundation Server 2013 Installation Guide, as it is updated periodically.

Team Foundation Server 2013

There are several ways to obtain Team Foundation Server 2013. By far, the most common is via an MSDN subscription. When purchased with an MSDN subscription, all editions of Visual Studio 2013 include one server license and one client access license (CAL) for Team Foundation Server 2013. MSDN subscribers can log in to `http://msdn.microsoft.com/subscriptions` to download software. Team Foundation Server 2013 can be found as part of the Developer Tools, and then the Visual Studio 2013 category.

Another common way for organizations to obtain Team Foundation Server is via a volume licensing agreement. You may need to contact the volume licensing administrator at your organization to get access software from Microsoft's Volume Licensing Service Center (VLSC). Usually, only a handful of administrators at an organization have access to download software from the VLSC.

> **NOTE** *Most of the download packages available to MSDN subscribers and volume licensing customers are provided as* `.iso` *files. An* `.iso` *file is essentially a container of multiple files and directories packaged together as a single file. An* `.iso` *file can be mounted as a virtual CD/DVD drive, or it can be burned to physical CD/DVD media. Windows Server 2012 and Windows 8 and 8.1 include support for mounting* `.iso` *files, and no additional software is required to be installed. For more details on working with* `.iso` *files, see* `http://aka.ms/UsingMsdnDownloads`*.*

Team Foundation Server 2013 is also available via traditional retail channels. If you purchased Team Foundation Server 2013 via retail, you will receive physical DVD media in the software box.

Team Foundation Server 2013 is also available via a lightweight web installer. From the Microsoft website, you can download a small (< 1MB) bootstrap setup utility and run it. This utility will then download the required packages to a temporary directory and proceed with the installation. With a fast Internet connection, this can be the easiest way to install Team Foundation Server, as it doesn't require downloading and mounting `.iso` files.

Finally, Microsoft makes a 90-day, fully functional trial edition of Team Foundation Server 2013 available for download. Team Foundation Server 2013 trial edition can be downloaded at `http://aka.ms/TFS2013Downloads`, along with other trial editions of Visual Studio 2013 (such as Visual Studio Ultimate 2013).

> **USING A TRIAL EDITION**
>
> The trial edition of Team Foundation Server 2013 is a great way to evaluate the product before making a purchasing decision. But you should set a reminder for yourself at least 45 days before the end of the trial so that you can decide whether to make a purchasing decision, or if you decide not to purchase, whether any important data must be migrated off your Team Foundation Server trial deployment.
>
> Depending on the reseller you choose, and the purchasing process used by your organization, it can sometimes take a few weeks to fulfill your purchase. You don't want to find yourself locked out of your development project while you're waiting for an order to be processed.
>
> Upgrading from a trial edition to a paid edition is a simple process that just involves changing the product key. The steps are outlined at `http://aka.ms/Tfs2013ChangeKey`.

Team Foundation Server 2013 Installation Guide

Before starting your installation, you should download the latest version of the Team Foundation Server 2013 Installation Guide. This guidance is updated on a regular basis by Microsoft, and it contains detailed system requirements, checklists, step-by-step instructions, and other important information required to install and configure Team Foundation Server 2013. This chapter provides additional context and walkthroughs to supplement the Installation Guide, but it is not a replacement for the guide itself.

You can download the latest Team Foundation Server 2013 Installation Guide at `http://aka.ms/tfsInstallGuide`.

> **NOTE** *The Installation Guide is provided as a* `.chm` *file. Because of security restrictions on viewing* `.chm` *files obtained from the Internet, you may have difficulties opening the file. Before viewing this guide, you may have to save it locally, right-click the file, and select Properties. In the properties dialog box, select Unblock followed by OK. You can now double-click the file to open it.*

SQL Server 2012

In Chapter 2, you learned about how Team Foundation Server 2013 makes use of SQL Server 2012 to store your data. If you are using an existing deployment of SQL Server, you won't need to download installation media. However, if you are planning to use a separate SQL Server deployment for your Team Foundation Server 2013 instance, you may need to obtain the appropriate SQL Server media.

SQL Server Express 2012 can be used with Team Foundation Server 2013. But you will not be able to take advantage of reporting capabilities with Team Foundation Server 2013 unless you use SQL Server Standard edition (or higher). If you want to use the Express edition, this will be installed for you automatically by Team Foundation Server 2013 (if it isn't already installed).

If you plan to set up a separate instance of SQL Server 2012 Standard edition (or higher), you can obtain this installation media by using the same channels described earlier (MSDN, VLSC, retail, or trial). A limited-use license of SQL Server 2012 Standard edition is included with your license of Team Foundation Server 2013.

> **NOTE** *As discussed in Chapter 2, Team Foundation Server 2013 supports SQL Server 2012 with SP1 as well as SQL Server 2014. Support for SQL Server 2008 has been dropped with the Team Foundation Server 2013 release.*

> **NOTE** *See the Visual Studio 2013 and MSDN Licensing whitepaper at* http:// aka.ms/VS2013Licensing *to help you understand the licensing implications for each edition of SQL Server. For example, even though you can download SQL Server 2012 SP1 (any edition) or SQL Server 2012 SP1 Enterprise edition via your MSDN subscription, you must license this software separately. Using it with Team Foundation Server 2013 is not included in your MSDN subscriber product use rights.*

Operating System

In Chapter 2, you learned about the operating systems supported by Team Foundation Server 2013. Installing and configuring your operating system is beyond the scope of this chapter, but is an important step for you to undertake before you can set up Team Foundation Server 2013.

As you learned in Chapter 2, Team Foundation Server 2013 can be installed on a client operating system (Windows 7 with Service Pack 1, Windows 8, or Windows 8.1). Installing on a client operating system will provide you with most of the capabilities of Team Foundation Server, including source control, work-item tracking, test case management, build automation, and Lab Management. If you wish to use reporting and/or SharePoint integration, or your Team Foundation Server deployment will be used by more than a few users, you should install Team Foundation Server on a supported Windows server operating system.

SharePoint

In Chapter 2, you learned about how SharePoint can be used as a supplemental workspace for your development project. If you wish to use SharePoint Foundation 2013 with Team Foundation Server 2013, this can be automatically installed and configured during your Team Foundation Server 2013 configuration. If you want to use another edition of SharePoint (such as SharePoint Server 2013 or SharePoint Server 2010), you should install and configure this separately.

Client Software

You should also consider which client software you want to use with Team Foundation Server 2013. Chapter 4 covers several types of software clients, such as Visual Studio, Eclipse, Project, and Excel. At a minimum, to complete the exercises in this chapter, you should install Team Explorer 2013.

> **NOTE** *Team Explorer 2013 can be downloaded at* `http://aka.ms/TeamExplorer2013`*. Team Explorer is also included with Visual Studio Professional, Premium, and Ultimate editions, as well as with Microsoft Test Professional. So if you have any of these products installed, you won't need to download and install Team Explorer separately.*

Service Packs and Other Updates

Microsoft periodically releases service packs and other updates for the Visual Studio line of products, including Team Foundation Server. Before making Team Foundation Server available to your development team, you may want to think about which updates you need to apply after you have installed and configured the server. By installing updates before bringing the server online, you can minimize potential downtime in the future when the service has active users.

There are several types of updates provided by Microsoft. The most common include the following:

➤ **Service packs**—Service packs are by far the most well-tested and supported updates provided by Microsoft. It is highly recommended that you install service packs because they usually fix several bugs, improve stability and performance, and occasionally add or improve features.

➤ **Cumulative updates**—Shortly after the Team Foundation Server 2010 Service Pack 1 release, the product team moved to a model of producing cumulative update packages regularly. These cumulative updates are a rollup of all fixes that the team has addressed in response to customer issues. Cumulative updates receive an appropriate level of testing and we recommend that all Team Foundation Server customers apply them when they become available.

➤ **Hotfixes**—Hotfixes (also called QFEs, which means Quick Fix Engineering) are provided by Microsoft to address specific issues. Because hotfixes don't receive as much testing as a service pack or cumulative update does, they can sometimes introduce new issues. For this reason, you should consider installing a hotfix only if it addresses a specific issue you have observed in your environment.

> **NOTE** *Microsoft Support can help you determine if you need a specific hotfix. Hotfixes are usually described by a Microsoft Knowledgebase (KB) article. You can search the Microsoft Knowledgebase at* `http://support.microsoft.com/search/`. *Some hotfixes are available for download, and others require that you contact Microsoft Support to obtain access.*

➤ **General Distribution Release**—A General Distribution Release (GDR) falls somewhere between a hotfix and a service pack. GDRs are also well-tested and supported but generally address a narrower set of issues than a service pack does.

➤ **Feature packs**—Feature packs are updates that Microsoft provides, which add or enhance new features to existing products. Some feature packs are available only to customers with MSDN Ultimate subscriptions. This is a way for Microsoft to add extra value to the subscription-based licensing.

➤ **Team Foundation Server Power Tools**—While not technically an update, the Microsoft Visual Studio Team Foundation Server Power Tools provide a great set of enhancements and utilities for increasing your productivity. You can download the power tools at `http://aka.ms/TFS2013PowerTools`.

Once you have the installation media, and have configured your operating system and necessary prerequisites, you can begin to install Team Foundation Server 2013.

INSTALLING TEAM FOUNDATION SERVER

Setting up Team Foundation Server 2013 can be divided into two distinct phases: installation and configuration. During the *installation phase*, the components are copied onto your machine. During the *configuration phase*, you decide which optional components to enable, which accounts to use for permissions, which SQL Server instance to use, and other such settings.

> **NOTE** *A common practice within many organizations is to make use of a tool called Sysprep. This tool allows you to generalize an operating system and additional installed software, which makes it easier to deploy to multiple machines. However, not all software is compatible with the sysprepping process. One advantage of the dual-phase setup approach employed by Team Foundation Server is that you can now install it as part of a sysprepped image. Team Foundation Server configuration can then be deferred until after you have specialized your sysprepped image onto specific machines. Sysprepping Team Foundation Server 2013 after you have performed the configuration phase is not supported.*

To begin the installation phase, download and run the web installer or load your Team Foundation Server installation media. If you are using an `.iso` file, this may mean virtually mounting your `.iso` file as a DVD, as explained earlier, and then running `tfs_server.exe`.

On the first (and only) preinstallation screen you will be able to change the installation path and accept the license terms, as shown in Figure 3-1. Once you have accepted the license terms, select Install Now. The setup program will then proceed to copy and install all the required files to your machine. This is a much more streamlined installation process than previous versions.

FIGURE 3-1: Team Foundation Server setup screen

After the installation phase is complete, the Team Foundation Server Configuration Center will be automatically started. If you close this tool, you can always launch it again by navigating to the start screen and choosing Team Foundation Server Administration Console. Then, after the console appears, click the component you want to configure (such as Application Tier or Build Configuration), and click Configure Installed Features.

Next, you will learn about the variety of installation types available to you via the Team Foundation Server Configuration Center.

INSTALLATION TYPES

Team Foundation Server includes several wizards for configuring your server. This provides you with a guided (yet flexible) way of picking the best configuration experience for your desired usage of Team Foundation Server. The individual wizards can be accessed along the left-hand side of the Configuration tool, as shown in Figure 3-2.

The exact wizards available to you will depend on your operating system, and which components (if any) have already been configured (as indicated by a green check mark). Table 3-1 describes the individual wizards.

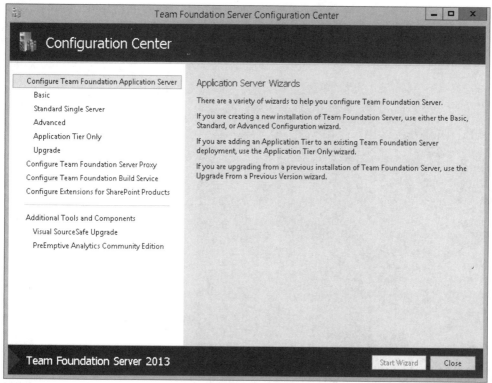

FIGURE 3-2: Team Foundation Server Configuration Center

TABLE 3-1: Available Wizards

WIZARD	DESCRIPTION
Basic	The Basic Wizard is the quickest and easiest way to get up and running with Team Foundation Server for small teams. The Basic Wizard enables you to use source control, work-item tracking, test case management, and Lab Management. However, Reporting Services and SharePoint integration will not be available using the Basic Wizard. These two components can be added later if you are installing Team Foundation Server on a Windows Server operating system. With the Basic Wizard, you can use an existing SQL Server instance, or let Team Foundation Server install and configure SQL Server 2012 SP1 Express edition for you.
Standard Single Server	The Standard Single Server Wizard assumes that you are installing Team Foundation Server on a single server. This wizard enables you to use source control, work-item tracking, test case management, Lab Management, reporting, and SharePoint integration. You should not use this wizard if you want to install using remote SharePoint or SQL Server deployments, or if you want to use a version of SharePoint other than SharePoint Foundation 2013.

Advanced	The Advanced Wizard provides maximum flexibility for your configuration. It also provides the same capabilities of Team Foundation Server as the Standard Single Server Wizard does. But the Advanced Wizard allows you to define remote systems for SharePoint, SQL Server, and SQL Server Reporting Services. This wizard also allows you to configure Kerberos authentication, to use a non-default instance of SQL Server, and to use editions of SharePoint other than SharePoint Foundation 2013. Finally, the Advanced Wizard gives you the option of disabling Reporting Services and/or SharePoint integration altogether, though you can always add these components later.
Application-Tier Only	The Application-Tier Only Wizard can be used to configure Team Foundation Server in a high-availability environment, as described in Chapter 22. You can employ multiple application tier nodes to provide load balancing and fault tolerance for your deployment. This wizard can also be used if you are moving your Team Foundation Server application tier from one server to another, or in a disaster-recovery scenario, as described in Chapter 23.
Upgrade	The Upgrade Wizard is used if you are upgrading from a previous version of Team Foundation Server. Upgrading is described in Chapter 27.
Configure Team Foundation Server Proxy	This wizard can be used to configure this machine as a Team Foundation Server proxy server. More information on configuring proxy servers can be found in Chapter 28.
Configure Team Foundation Build Service	This wizard can be used if you want to configure this machine as a build controller and/or one or more build agents. Team Foundation Build is detailed in Part IV.
Configure Extensions for SharePoint Products	This wizard should be used if you are planning on configuring Team Foundation Server to integrate with SharePoint running on a remote machine, or in a remote SharePoint farm. If you are using a farm, you will need to run this wizard on every machine in that farm.

The rest of this chapter uses the Basic Wizard as an example. If you are new to Team Foundation Server, you may want to consider using the Basic Wizard to set up your first Team Foundation Server deployment on a testing server. When you are ready to configure your actual Team Foundation Server deployment, you should spend some time reading the Team Foundation Server Installation Guide and Part V of this book to familiarize yourself with the various configuration types that are available, and map these to the needs of your development team.

For example, if you have a very large team, you may want to consider configuring Team Foundation Server in a dual-tier environment. If you have a geographically distributed team, you may want to set up Team Foundation Server proxy instances at remote sites. You may want to configure a dedicated build farm with multiple machines running build agents, and so on.

Next, you will begin a simple configuration using the Basic Wizard.

CONFIGURING TEAM FOUNDATION SERVER

From the Team Foundation Configuration tool, select the Basic Wizard and click Start Wizard. Click Next to advance past the Welcome page. You will be prompted to indicate which instance of SQL Server you want to use, as shown in Figure 3-3.

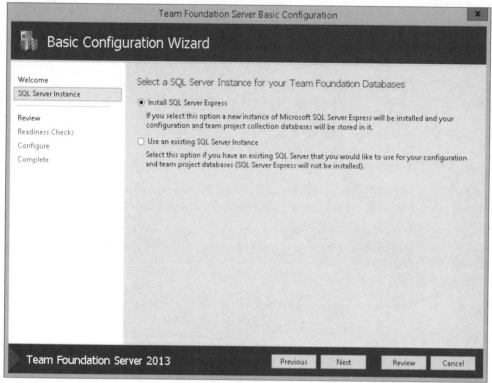

FIGURE 3-3: SQL Server instance selection page

You can choose an existing instance of SQL Server, or let the Basic Wizard install and configure SQL Server Express for you.

> **NOTE** *Letting Team Foundation Server install and configure SQL Server Express is a quick way to get up and running, and it should work well for a test server. But for a production server, you should consider taking the time to install and configure SQL Server 2012 SP1 Standard edition (or higher, if you have licensed it separately). This will make it easier to take advantage of capabilities like Reporting Services later on, and it will enable you to avoid the 10GB database size limitation imposed by SQL Server 2012 Express Edition. The Team Foundation Server Installation Guide includes step-by-step instructions for installing SQL Server Standard edition for use with Team Foundation Server.*

After selecting your SQL Server instance, click Next. You will be shown a list of the configuration settings you chose, such as those shown in Figure 3-4, and you will be given a chance to go back and make changes. The Basic Wizard has only a few pages, but other wizards have more.

FIGURE 3-4: Configuration settings review screen

When you are satisfied with your options, click Next. (Clicking Verify will also have the same effect.) The wizard will attempt to verify that the changes you are proposing will be successful if you proceed.

It is worth noting that no changes are being made to your server at this time. This process can be valuable in helping you discover that you may be missing a prerequisite, or it can warn you that certain configuration changes are going to be made for you.

When this step has finished, you will see a screen similar to Figure 3-5. If there are potential problems with your configuration, you will be shown any errors or warnings, usually with information on how to address them.

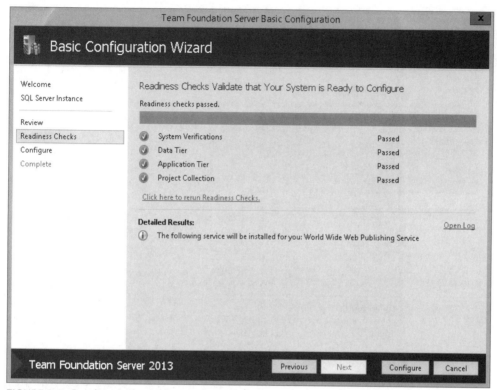

FIGURE 3-5: Readiness Checks page

Click Configure when you are ready to proceed with your configuration options. The wizard will attempt to configure Team Foundation Server using the options you selected. If you opted to install SQL Server Express as part of the configuration, this process may take several minutes. Otherwise, it should only take a few minutes.

When the configuration is finished, you should see a confirmation screen, as shown in Figure 3-6. Take note of any warnings or errors displayed on this page, as well as any informational notices (such as the message shown in Figure 3-6 indicating that an additional firewall port was opened during configuration). You can also access detailed log information by clicking the link at the bottom of this page of the wizard. Click Close when you are finished.

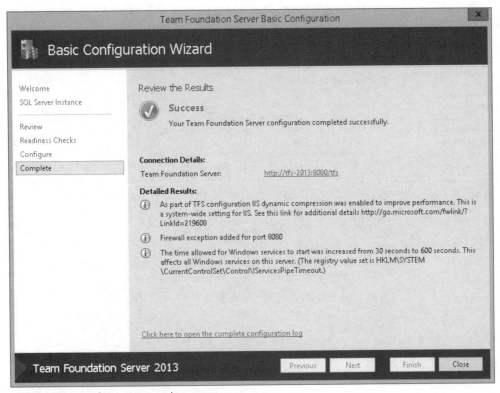

FIGURE 3-6: Configuration results page

At the conclusion of this step, you will have successfully configured an instance of Team Foundation Server 2013 on your machine. This instance is now running as a service, and you can begin to interact with it, or further configure it. You can even launch subsequent wizards from the Team Foundation Configuration Center, such as to configure a build controller and agent.

The Team Foundation Server Administration Console (shown in Figure 3-7) can now be used to monitor your server, to stop or start services, and to make additional configuration changes. Some common configuration changes include configuring a Simple Mail Transfer Protocol (SMTP) server (for e-mail alerts), enabling Kerberos authentication, assigning friendly names to the URLs used by clients to connect to Team Foundation Server, or adding a System Center Virtual Machine Manager (SCVMM) server to provide functionality for Lab Management.

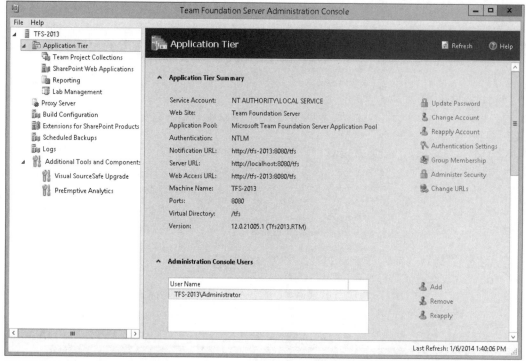

FIGURE 3-7: Team Foundation Server Administration Console

You may also want to add components that you skipped during the initial configuration, such as Reporting Services or SharePoint integration. The MSDN Library provides detailed instructions on how to perform all of these tasks, and more, at `http://aka.ms/TFS2013Manage`.

Now that you have your Team Foundation Server instance deployed, you can create your first team project.

CREATING YOUR FIRST TEAM PROJECT

A *team project* is the basic container of work used by Team Foundation Server. You will learn much more about team projects throughout the rest of this book. For now, you just need to know that you'll need to create a team project before you can store any source control, work items, or other artifacts in Team Foundation Server.

To create a team project with Team Foundation Server 2013, you must use Team Explorer 2013. Team Explorer 2013 is an add-on for Visual Studio 2013 that allows you to work with source control, work items, build definitions, and more, without ever leaving Visual Studio. Team Explorer also installs the necessary add-ins to work with Team Foundation Server 2013 from within Excel and Project. You will learn more about clients that can access Team Foundation Server 2013 in Chapter 4.

If you don't already have Team Explorer 2013 installed, you can either install it by itself (see the download link in the section, "What You'll Need," earlier in this chapter), or install Visual Studio Professional 2013 (or higher) and Team Explorer will be included automatically.

After Team Explorer 2013 is installed, launch Visual Studio 2013 from the Start screen.

> **NOTE** *Even if you installed Team Explorer 2013 standalone, instead of as part of Visual Studio Professional 2013 (or higher), you will still access Team Explorer 2013 from within the Visual Studio 2013 shell. This is why you access Team Explorer 2013 by opening Visual Studio 2013 from the Start screen.*

If the Team Explorer window is not already visible within Visual Studio, you can enable it by clicking View ⇨ Team Explorer. Team Explorer is shown in Figure 3-8. If this is the first time you have used this Team Foundation Server instance, you may be prompted to set up your Workspace mappings. You can do this now, or wait until you have a Team Project set up.

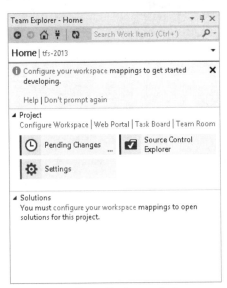

FIGURE 3-8: Team Explorer window

If you installed Team Explorer on the same machine as your Team Foundation Server 2013 deployment, your server name may already be populated for you (indicated by *localhost* or the computer name, as shown in Figure 3-8).

If you installed Team Explorer on a different machine, you should add your Team Foundation Server host manually by clicking the Select Team Projects link (near the top of the Team Explorer window). From the Connect to Team Foundation Server dialog box, click Servers to add a new server. Click Add and supply the address of your Team Foundation Server. You can find this in the

Team Foundation Server Administration Console under Application Tier ➪ Server URL (such as `http://tfs:8080/tfs`).

After you have added your server, click OK to close the first window, then click Close to close the next window, and then select the server you want to connect to in the drop-down box for "Select a Team Foundation Server." If you used the Basic configuration, you will have a single team Project Collection called `DefaultCollection`. Select this collection and click Connect.

> **NOTE** *A team Project Collection provides a way of grouping together one or more team projects. You learn more about team Project Collections later in this book.*

Click File ➪ New ➪ Team Project to launch the New Team Project Wizard shown in Figure 3-9. Provide a name for your team project and, optionally, a description. Click Next when finished.

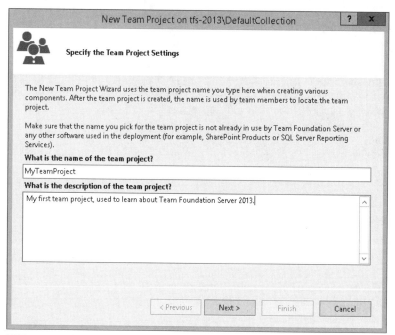

FIGURE 3-9: New Team Project Wizard

You will then be prompted to select the process template that you want to use for this new team project, and afterward, you will be asked how you want to configure source control for your project. For now, you can accept the default options and click Finish. The wizard will spend a few minutes creating your team project.

When you are finished, the Team Explorer window will display your team project, as shown in Figure 3-10. The appearance will differ depending on which source control option you chose in the previous wizard. You can now begin creating work items, source control, build definitions, and so on for this team project.

FIGURE 3-10: New team project

CONFIGURING FRIENDLY DNS NAMES

If you have followed the previous steps, then you now have a Team Foundation Server deployment that you can share with your team. You can start adding users to security groups (as explained in Chapter 24), and these users can begin connecting to your server. However, as mentioned in Chapter 2, there's one additional configuration step that you may want to take before advertising the address of your server, and that is to consider assigning friendly DNS names to the endpoints.

Refer to Chapter 2 for instructions on how to configure friendly DNS names for your Team Foundation Server endpoints. You can perform this step at any time in the future, but doing so now (before your server is being used) means your clients will only ever need to use these names.

SUMMARY

In this chapter, you learned how to install and configure a simple Team Foundation Server 2013 instance. Along the way, you learned about the incremental improvements Microsoft has made to installation and configuration in this release, such as a lightweight web installer. You also learned how to create a team project, which will become the basic container of work for your software development project.

In Chapter 4, you will learn more about the various client applications you can use to work with Team Foundation Server.

Connecting to Team Foundation Server

WHAT'S IN THIS CHAPTER?

➤ Understanding the basic Team Foundation Server architecture

➤ Understanding Team Foundation Server URLs

➤ Getting to know Team Foundation Server roles and security

➤ Connecting to Team Foundation Server from various development tools

➤ Understanding Team Explorer concepts, tools, and windows

At this point, you should now have a working Team Foundation Server Project Collection—either one that you have installed yourself using the instructions in Chapter 3 or one that has been provided for you. This chapter teaches you how to connect to an instance from the various products that can talk to Team Foundation Server; you also learn about some common troubleshooting techniques if you are unable to connect. But first, some more information on the Team Foundation Server architecture would be useful.

TEAM FOUNDATION SERVER ARCHITECTURE

Figure 4-1 shows the major logical servers available in a Team Foundation Server installation. The main Team Foundation Server application is hosted on the application tier. The initial contact from the client machine on your desktop is made to this application tier (AT) machine. From this, the client machine obtains all the other connection information to allow it to talk to the other components involved in a typical Team Foundation Server installation (the SharePoint portal, Analysis Services for reports, and so on).

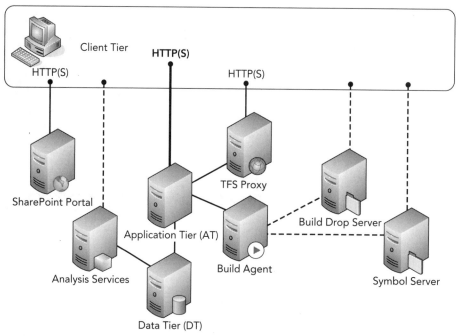

FIGURE 4-1: Logical architecture of a Team Foundation Server installation

> **NOTE** *For more detailed information on Team Foundation Server architecture and administration, see Chapter 21.*

Communication between the client and the application tier is performed using the Team Foundation Server Web Service Protocol. This is made up of a set of web services to which the client connects using the HTTP or HTTPS protocol, depending on how the application tier was configured. Authentication of the client connection is performed using Windows Integrated Authentication (also known as NTLM), Kerberos, or, if over an SSL/TLS encrypted connection, then Basic Authentication may be used.

For an on-premises Team Foundation Server, Windows Integrated Authentication is the typical form of authentication, unless the server has been explicitly configured otherwise. For Visual Studio Online, Internet identities (for example, Microsoft Account) and claims-based authentication are used. If using distributed version control, Basic Authentication will be used for Git operations.

On a Windows-based client machine, the client's default credentials for that server are used—usually the same credentials used to log in to the Windows machine in a domain environment. This provides for a seamless, single sign-on (SSO) capability.

You normally use the same credentials to talk to Team Foundation Server that you use to log in to your Windows workstation, and all the actions you perform against Team Foundation Server are audited against these credentials. On non-Windows machines, the credentials (domain, user name, and password) can be provided to allow authentication, or Kerberos can be configured if you require SSO infrastructure in your heterogeneous environments.

The majority of client/server communication in a Team Foundation Server instance is over HTTP or HTTPS. This is true for all the version control, work item tracking, SharePoint, and Reporting Services data. The exceptions to this are for connecting directly to the data warehouse running in Analysis Services from an analytics client (such as Microsoft Excel) or when communicating with the build drop location or Symbol server.

> **NOTE** *See Chapter 18 for more information on builds and Symbol servers.*

In addition to the application tier machine address, clients may also need to be configured with the address of a Team Foundation Server Proxy if used for remote development. A Team Foundation Server Proxy provides a way to cache requests for files from version control and test attachments. If two developers in a remote site request the same version of the same file, then the proxy server allows for the second developer to be served the file from the local proxy, rather than having to download the files over the wide area network (WAN) a second time.

> **NOTE** *For more information on the Team Foundation Server Proxy and working with geographically distributed teams, see Chapter 28.*

ADDRESSING TEAM FOUNDATION SERVER

A Team Foundation Server instance is referred to by the URL at which the actual application hosting Team Foundation Server is located. Figure 4-2 shows the basic makeup when connecting to Team Foundation Server.

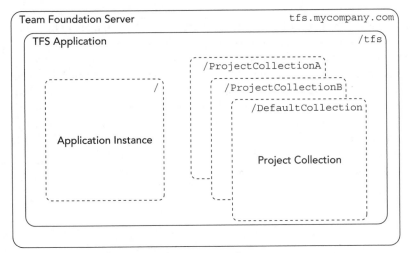

FIGURE 4-2: Team Foundation Server URL scheme

The URL is in the following format:

```
<protocol>://<serverName>:<port>/<virtualDirectory>/<collectionName>
```

The following is an explanation of the individual parts of the URL:

➤ `protocol`—This is the means used to connect to Team Foundation Server (HTTP or HTTPS).

➤ `serverName`—This is the Domain Name Server (DNS) name pointing to your Team Foundation Server application tier instance (or the network load balancer in front of it, if you are using a high-availability architecture). Note that the DNS name can be a friendly name that has been created in your organization to help locate the server. It doesn't have to be the actual machine name of your application tier. Also, if you ever plan on accessing the connection from outside of your company network (over the Internet), ensure that you use the fully qualified domain name such as `tfs.mycompany.com`.

➤ `port`—This is the port used to connect to the application tier. In a default installation, this is port 8080. The port can be omitted if it is the standard port for the protocol (that is, port 80 for HTTP or port 443 for HTTPS).

➤ `virtualDirectory`—This is the path in which the Team Foundation Server application was installed. By default, this is `tfs`. The `virtualDirectory` was added in Team Foundation Server 2010. In previous versions, the application was always installed at the root of the website that was hosting the application. However, in the 2010 release, this was moved down into the `tfs` folder to make it easier to host Team Foundation Server on the same default website as other applications on the server (such as SharePoint and the Reporting Services sites). This makes it significantly easier to have Team Foundation Server running on the standard port 80 or port 443, which, in turn, makes it much easier to make accessible over the Internet.

> **NOTE** *See Chapter 3 for more information on installation.*

➤ `collectionName`—This is the name of the project collection to which you are connecting. By default, Team Foundation Server has at least one project collection created—usually called `DefaultCollection`. However, as discussed in Chapter 3 and covered in depth in Chapter 21, multiple project collections can be created. In a graphical client such as Visual Studio or Eclipse, providing the URL of the Team Foundation Server instance is sufficient, and the user interface will then present the available project collections on that instance that are available for you to connect to. However, for many command-line tools, the full URL to your project collection is required. If the `collectionName` is missing, the server will assume that the collection marked as default is the desired one and will direct requests to it. If no collection is marked as default, then the URL will result in an error.

Following are some example URLs to connect to Team Foundation Server:

- ➤ `http://vsalm:8080/tfs`

- ➤ `http://vsalm:8080/tfs/DefaultCollection`

- ➤ `http://vsalm:8080/tfs/AdventureWorks`

- ➤ `https://tfs.codeplex.com/tfs/TFS01`

- ➤ `https://mycompany.visualstudio.com/`

- ➤ `https://tfs.mycompany.com/tfs`

Note that most of these URLs are not valid directly in a web browser. They are used as the root of the URL that the Team Foundation Server client uses to locate and communicate with the web services of that server instance. However, if you specify only the `virtualDirectory` part of the URL, or if the special name of `web` is used, this will redirect you to a web-based client for Team Foundation Server called Team Web Access (for example, `http://vsalm:8080/tfs/`, or `https://tfs.mycompany.com/tfs/`).

> **NOTE** *See the section "Accessing Team Foundation Server Through a Web Browser" later in this chapter for more information on Team Web Access.*

INTRODUCING TEAM FOUNDATION SERVER SECURITY AND ROLES

The significant functionality that Team Foundation Server has in relation to security, groups, and permissions can be very daunting at first. However, at its core, there are a few simple concepts to initially be aware of with Team Foundation Server security:

- ➤ Users
- ➤ Groups
- ➤ Permissions

> **NOTE** *For detailed information about Team Foundation Server security, see Chapter 24.*

Users

The on-premises version of Team Foundation Server uses Windows accounts for security. There is no separate concept of a Team Foundation Server user—just a Windows user who has permission to use Team Foundation Server resources. If Team Foundation Server is in an Active Directory environment (the preferred configuration), domain users can be granted permission to use Team Foundation Server. Local users may also be used (users defined locally to that machine in what is considered "Workgroup mode").

When you install Team Foundation Server, the user who installs and configures the product is required to have administrative permissions on the server. By default, that user is also granted the permissions of a Team Foundation Server administrator within the product.

The user details (user name, display name, e-mail address, and so on) are all taken from the Windows user details. Authentication of the users is performed using Windows authentication. This means that there is no separate infrastructure required to create or administer users specifically for Team Foundation Server. Existing user creation systems inside the company can be used, along with the handling of password policies, password resets, and so on.

Groups

Team Foundation Server has two types of groups that you must be concerned with:

➤   Windows security groups (domain, distribution, or local groups)

➤   Team Foundation Server groups

As you will learn in Chapter 24, the Windows security groups are basically a collection of users maintained by the Windows security systems. For example, to complete the installation of Team Foundation Server as described in Chapter 3, the user must be in the local Administrators group on the server.

Team Foundation Server has its own group structure maintained in the server. Within the system, there are three levels of groups:

➤   Server groups

➤   Team project collection groups

➤   Team project groups

Server groups impact the Team Foundation Server instance and are one of the few things in Team Foundation Server that cross the boundary between project collections. The default groups (detailed in Chapter 24) have hard-coded names that cannot be changed or removed from the server (for example, Team Foundation Administrators or Team Foundation Valid Users).

A user who is a member of the server group has permissions at the Team Foundation instance level. For example, users in the Team Foundation Administrators group can create new project collections. Users in the Team Foundation Valid Users group can connect to the Team Foundation Server instance and view which project collections are available (but they might not have permission to actually connect to a particular project collection). Modifications of the server groups must be performed using the Team Foundation Server Administration Console, as introduced in Chapter 3.

Team project collection groups are created as part of the collection creation process. The default groups and their members are detailed in Chapter 24. However, they control who is an administrator for the project collection, who can connect and use it, and so on.

Finally, *team project groups* control who can do what inside a particular team project. The main groups are as follows:

➤ **Project Administrators**—Members can perform all operations in the team project, including the assignment of security permissions to other users.

➤ **Contributors**—Members can add, modify, and delete items within the team project. You typically want your main development group for a team project to be a contributor.

➤ **Readers**—Members have read-only access to data in the team project.

➤ **Build Administrators**—Members have the ability to manage all aspects of test environments, configurations, and test runs.

A Team Foundation Server group membership is made up of Windows users and groups, or other Team Foundation Server groups. At each level, custom groups can be created and allocated certain permissions.

Permissions

Each user or group in Team Foundation Server can be allocated one or more of nearly 100 separate permissions available on the server controlling each aspect of the product. Each permission has an explicit Allow or Deny state.

Typically, when getting started with Team Foundation Server, you should stick with controlling access to the server by placing a user in one of the team project groups. Members of those groups then inherit a default set of permissions from, and get assigned into, other groups (such as the Team Foundation Valid Users group), allowing them to connect to the Team Foundation Server instance.

> **NOTE** *For more information about fine-grained control of users' permissions over the default Team Project Administrator, Contributor, or Reader, see Chapter 24.*

TEAM EXPLORER

Visual Studio Team Explorer is the client interface to Team Foundation Server. It provides the functionality necessary to be able to connect to and work with Team Foundation Server. All Visual Studio editions now include the Team Explorer client as part of the default installation. Team

Explorer Everywhere is also available to provide the client-side interface in the Eclipse IDE and cross-platform environments (on Mac, UNIX, or Linux machines).

Visual Studio Team Explorer is also available as a separate installation on the Team Foundation Server installation media, on the Team Explorer Everywhere media, or as a separate download. If installed on a machine without Visual Studio installed, it will install a cut-down version of Visual Studio (known as Visual Studio Shell), and, inside that, it will provide all the rich client-side functionality to work with Team Foundation Server.

Use of Team Explorer and Team Explorer Everywhere is covered by the Client Access License (CAL) required for a specific user to connect to Team Foundation Server, regardless of the number of machines from which the user connects.

Understanding Team Explorer in Visual Studio

By now, you should have provisioned a Team Foundation Server instance with a project collection and team project created by doing one of the following:

- ➤ Installing one yourself (following the instructions in Chapter 3)
- ➤ Downloading a trial virtual machine (VM) from Microsoft
- ➤ Signing up to Visual Studio Online
- ➤ Leasing a hosted Team Foundation Server solution from a hosting provider

You must now connect to your Team Foundation Server instance from the machine that you want to use for development.

Connecting to Team Foundation Server 2013 from Visual Studio 2013

The most common initial route is to attempt to connect to Team Foundation Server 2013 from Visual Studio 2013. Luckily, there are many ways to get connected.

You can click Team ➪ Connect to Team Foundation Server, or, from the Start page in Visual Studio, click the Open from Source Control link on the left-hand side. An alternative to Team Explorer is to click View ➪ Team Explorer, use Projects ➪ Connect to Team Projects in the header drop-down, and then click the Select Team Projects link.

Whatever way you use to connect, you are then presented with a rather dauntingly empty Connect to Team Project dialog box, as shown in Figure 4-3.

Typically, at this point, the drop-down to select a Team Foundation Server will also be empty. To add your server to the list, click the Servers button. This presents yet another empty dialog box—the Add/Remove Team Foundation Server dialog box. Click the Add button.

Finally, you can enter the details of the Team Foundation Server instance to which you wish to connect. Enter the name of your Team Foundation Server instance (vsalm or tfs.mycompany.com). At the bottom of the dialog box shown in Figure 4-4, you will be given a preview of the URL that will be used to connect to the Team Foundation Server.

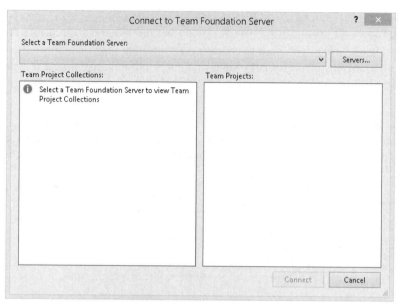

FIGURE 4-3: Connect to Team Project dialog box

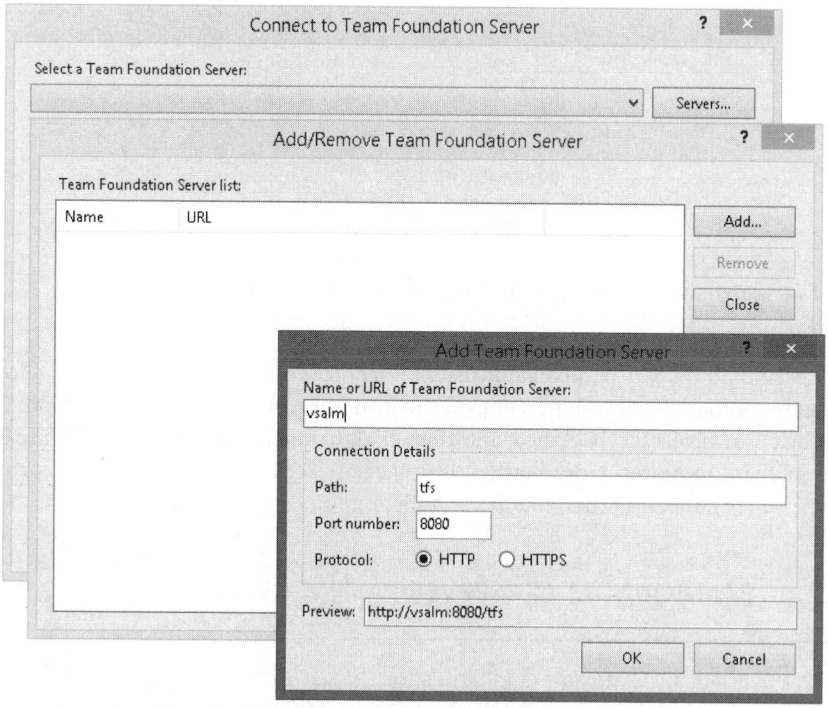

FIGURE 4-4: Add Team Foundation Server dialog box

For a default install of Team Foundation Server, this URL will be correct, as long as you have typed in the correct name for the server. However, if the URL is not correct (for example, you need to use HTTPS instead of HTTP, or perhaps you need to connect on a different port), you must alter the settings accordingly. Alternatively, if you have the URL that you should use to connect to your server, type it into the Name box at the top of the dialog box, and all the appropriate settings will be picked up.

Click OK to add the server to the list, and then click Close to get back to the Connect to Team Project dialog box. The dialog box should now be populated and a bit more welcoming. The example shown in Figure 4-5 is a more typical view of the dialog box once a few team projects and an additional team project collection have been created.

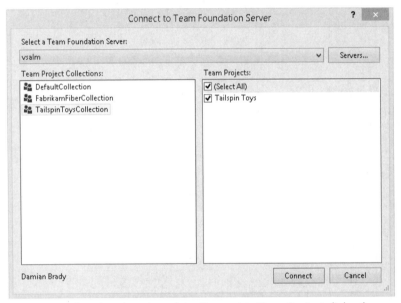

FIGURE 4-5: Populated version of the Connect to Team Project dialog box

Selecting a project collection on the left-hand side of the Connect to Team Project dialog box shown in Figure 4-5 gets Visual Studio to request the team projects available on that project collection. If you check the team project (or projects) check box and then click Connect, you control which team projects are displayed in Team Explorer. Note that while you are selecting the team projects at this point, it is actually the project collection that you are connecting to.

> ### STORING YOUR TEAM FOUNDATION SERVER PASSWORD ON WINDOWS
>
> On Windows-based systems, the default credentials for that site are used when connecting to Team Foundation Server. These are usually your Windows login credentials, which provide for a seamless SSO experience inside a domain.

However, sometimes you must log in to Team Foundation Server using a different set of credentials. This is especially true in the case where your Team Foundation Server is being hosted over the Internet in a different domain from the one you are logged in to. In situations in which the default credentials are not appropriate, Team Explorer will prompt you for your user name and password using the standard Windows authentication prompt.

You can also store these credentials so that they are always used for that server by Windows. On Windows 7 and later, click Start (or press the Windows key on your keyboard), and then type **Credential Manager**. Once there, add the Team Foundation Server instance that contains your project with the domain, user name, and password that you should use. You can also manage network passwords using the command-line tool CMDKEY.exe.

Team Explorer

Once connected, you should now see Team Explorer inside Visual Studio, as shown in Figure 4-6. If you do not see Team Explorer, go to View ➪ Team Explorer.

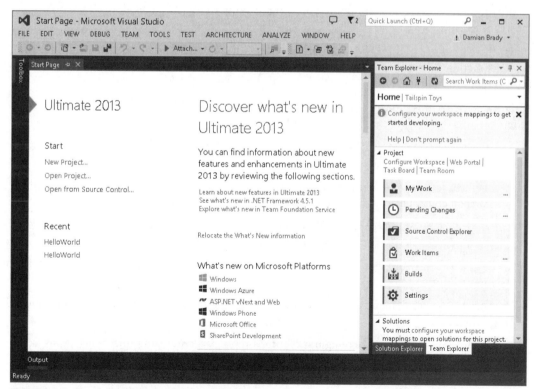

FIGURE 4-6: Team Explorer inside Visual Studio

The Team Explorer View has five buttons along the top:

➤ **Forward and Back**—Enables you to navigate between the different sections of Team Explorer

➤ **Home**—Returns Team Explorer to the home screen from which all other screens can be accessed

➤ **Connect**—Takes you to the Connect page in Team Explorer where you can choose which Team Project to work with

➤ **Refresh**—Re-requests the data in the Team Explorer view from Team Foundation Server. The data can take a while to populate

At the top of the Team Explorer View, you see the team project to which you are connected. You can be connected to only one team project and therefore one project collection at a time from Visual Studio, and you must use the Team ⇨ Connect to Team Foundation Server link or the Connect page in Team Explorer to swap connections.

Directly underneath the Team Project is an information section that will appear whenever an action is required. Under that are links and tiles that provide shortcuts to Team Web Access and pages within Team Explorer.

The links available to you will depend on the current state of your workspace. With Team Foundation Server 2013, at a minimum you will see a link to the Web Portal, the Task Board, and the Team Room.

Under these links are tiles for the major areas of Team Explorer. The first of these tiles is for the My Work section. This section is available only if you have Visual Studio Ultimate, Premium, or Test Professional edition installed.

After My Work are links to the different pages that represent the different parts of the system. The different pages or contexts available in Team Explorer are:

➤ My Work—Manage, suspend, and resume your work in progress and request a code review (see Chapter 6 for more information).

➤ Pending Changes—Work with pending changes, shelvesets, conflicts, and perform other version control tasks (see Chapters 6 and 7 for more information).

➤ Source Control Explorer—View and manage the source code tree for the project collection (see Chapter 11 for more information).

➤ Work Items—Add work items and view and manage work item queries (see Chapter 12 for more information).

➤ Builds—Create, modify, manage, and organize build processes (see Chapter 18 for more information).

➤ Settings—Manage the configuration of team projects and team project collections (see Chapter 21 for more information).

> **NOTE** *For a detailed explanation of compatibility between versions of the client and server, along with what was addressed in each version, see the article at* `http://tinyurl.com/Tfs2013Compat`.

Prior Visual Studio Versions

Before Visual Studio 2005, the source control programming interface popularized by Visual Studio was MSSCCI (Microsoft Source Code Control Interface, pronounced *"miss-key"*). The MSSCCI specification was originally designed for the Visual Studio integration with Visual SourceSafe (VSS) but was implemented by other development tool manufacturers, and implemented by other version control tool vendors.

When Team Foundation Server 2012 was released, the product team decided not to issue a compatibility patch for Visual Studio 2005. This incompatibility carries through to Team Foundation Server 2013. There is, however, an updated MSSCCI provider that works for this combination.

The Team Foundation Server team also makes an MSSCCI provider available on the Visual Studio Gallery at `http://aka.ms/TfsMSSCCI`. The MSSCCI provider requires that the corresponding version of Team Explorer be installed on the machine. A 64-bit version of the MSSCCI provider is also available.

Connecting to Team Foundation Server from Eclipse and Cross-Platform

As part of the Team Foundation Server 2013 release, Microsoft updated Team Explorer Everywhere. Team Explorer Everywhere contains two major components:

➤ Team Foundation Server plug-in for Eclipse

➤ Team Foundation Server cross-platform command-line client

While the full name of the product is actually Team Explorer Everywhere 2013 for Team Foundation Server 2013, it can work against the 2013, 2012, and 2010 versions of the server. Therefore, we recommend that you upgrade and install the latest version of Team Explorer Everywhere regardless of the Team Foundation Server version you currently have installed.

Unusually for a product in the Microsoft Visual Studio organization, Team Explorer Everywhere is written in Java and is supported across the major platforms, including Windows, Mac OS X, and forms of UNIX (such as Linux, HP-UX, Solaris, and AIX).

Team Foundation Server Plug-In for Eclipse

The plug-in for Eclipse provided as part of Team Explorer Everywhere installs as a standard Repository Provider plug-in inside development environments based on Eclipse 3.4 and above. This not only includes the latest versions of the standalone Eclipse IDE, but also tools such as Rational Application Developer, Adobe FlexBuilder, MyEclipse, and so on, as well as tooling to support embedded development. By providing the functionality as a standard plug-in to Eclipse written using 100 percent Java technologies like the rest of the Eclipse IDE, the plug-in is very easy to install and use for developers used to other version control providers in Eclipse.

As shown in Figure 4-7, Team Explorer Everywhere provides more than just version control capabilities to Eclipse. The entire Team Explorer 2013 experience as described earlier in this chapter is provided to Eclipse developers, meaning that all parts of a development organization can be peers when using Team Foundation Server to manage the development life cycle. Team Foundation Server treats source code or any other file as just a file. From a version control point of view, all code is created equal as far as Team Foundation Server is concerned.

FIGURE 4-7: Team Explorer Everywhere within Eclipse

The plug-in for Eclipse is installed from the Team Explorer Everywhere media, or via a download of the plug-in update site archive.

> **NOTE** *To install the Team Foundation Server plug-in for Eclipse, simply use the following update site in Eclipse (or install from the Eclipse Marketplace). This will ensure that you always have the latest released version of the plug-in installed:* `http://dl.microsoft.com/eclipse/tfs`.
>
> *If you would like to run the latest public pre-release version of the Eclipse plug-in, you can use the update site at* `http://dl.microsoft.com/eclipse/tfs/preview` *instead.*
>
> *For further information on getting started with version control using the Eclipse integration, see Chapter 6. Building Java applications using Team Foundation Server is also covered in Chapter 18.*

Cross-Platform Command-Line Client for Team Foundation Server

Team Explorer Everywhere also provides you with the ability to perform version control operations with many UNIX and Linux style operating systems using the cross-platform command-line client for Team Foundation Server (tf), as shown in Figure 4-8.

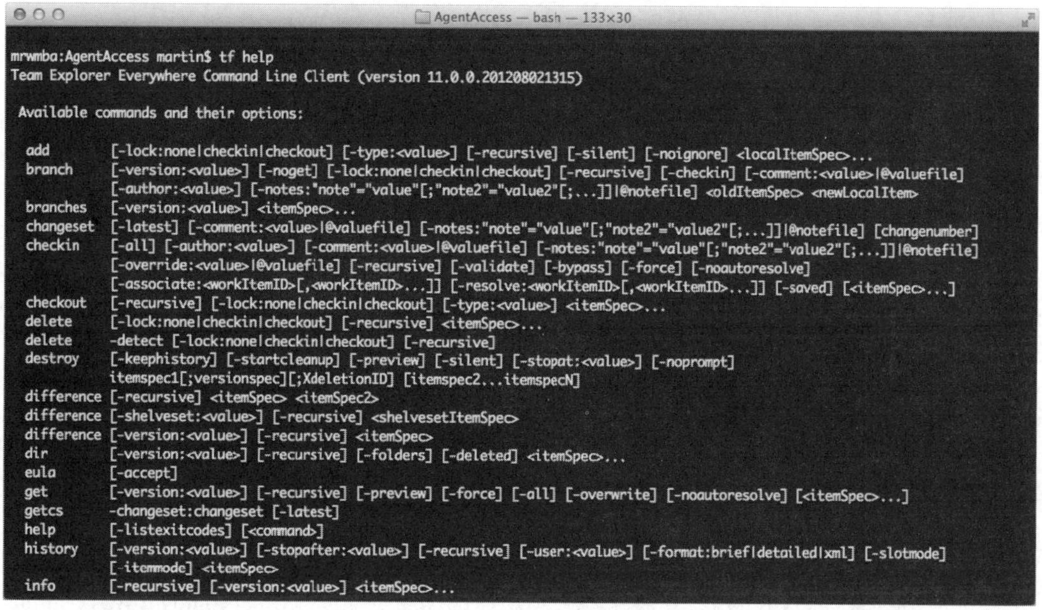

FIGURE 4-8: Cross-platform command-line client on Mac OS X

The command syntax is very similar to the version control command-line tool (tf.exe) installed on Windows as part of the Team Explorer installation. This allows for tools and scripts to be written against both flavors of the tool.

USE HYPHENS FOR MAXIMUM PORTABILITY

The Team Foundation Version Control command line accepts a number of parameters for each command. In most of the documentation and examples, parameters are prefixed by a forward slash character (/collection:TeamProjectCollectionUrl). However, in many UNIX shells, the forward slash character is an escape character. This means that, to actually pass a forward slash through to the tf command, you would need to escape it (usually with another forward slash).

continues

continued

To avoid this confusion, all versions of the command-line client are capable of accepting a hyphen or a forward slash to prefix a parameter. For example, `-collection:TeamProjectCollectionUrl` is a valid way to pass in the collection URL on both Windows and in all UNIX shells.

Therefore, if you are writing a script or a tool that makes use of the command line, use hyphens to ensure that the tool can run more easily on all platforms.

ALTERNATE WAYS TO CONNECT TO TEAM FOUNDATION SERVER

Besides installing Team Explorer or Team Explorer Everywhere, there are many other ways of connecting to Team Foundation Server. On the server itself, there is the Team Foundation Server Administration Console. But from the client, there are many different connectivity options, depending on what you want to do.

Accessing Team Foundation Server through a Web Browser

In Team Foundation Server 2013, an easy-to-use web-based client called Team Web Access (TWA) is installed by default on the application tier machines, and it is available under a special `web` directory under the `virtualPath` (`http://vsalm:8080/tfs/web`). This web-based client was completely rewritten in Team Foundation Server 2012. As shown in Figure 4-9, TWA is ideal for users who do not wish to install a dedicated Team Foundation Server client. It requires no additional software to be installed on the client machine, other than a modern web browser (the site works in Firefox, Safari, and Chrome, as well as Internet Explorer). It is also used in many places to provide a link that can be used to point to data in Team Foundation Server—for example, when passing around a link to a work item or shelveset.

At a high level, the following functionality is provided by TWA:

> Managing and prioritizing features, the Product Backlog, Sprint Backlog, and Task Boards

> Creating and editing work items and work item queries

> Managing areas, iterations, teams, groups, and security

> Managing e-mail alert subscriptions

> Read-only access to version control (including Source Control Explorer) as well as shelvesets, and the capability to compare and comment on versions of files in version control

> Queuing and managing build definitions

> Managing and running test cases and test suites

> Communicating via Team Rooms

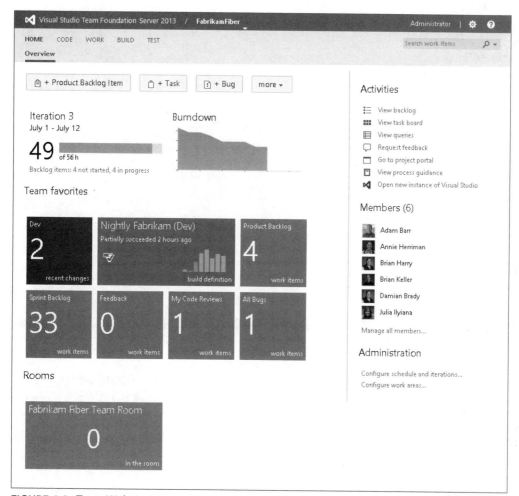

FIGURE 4-9: Team Web Access

When you initially browse to TWA, you are prompted to select which Team Project Collection, Team Project, and Team that you wish to connect to. In subsequent visits, you will see recent Team Projects and Teams listed for convenience.

Using Team Foundation Server in Microsoft Excel

As part of the Team Explorer installation process, team support is added to Microsoft Excel as a new tab on the Ribbon bar. This allows for the capability to add and edit work items directly from Excel spreadsheets, as shown in Figure 4-10.

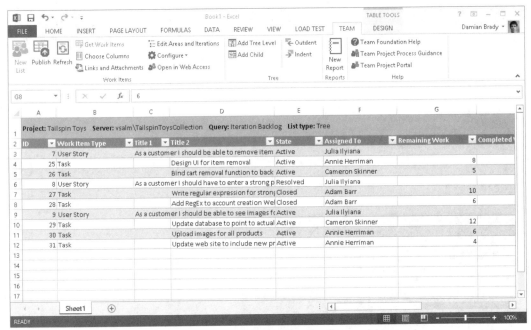

FIGURE 4-10: Adding and editing work items directly from Excel spreadsheets

To connect to Team Foundation Server from Excel, go to the Team Ribbon and click New List. Select the query that you would like to use as the basis of data to load into Excel. Or, if you would like to create a bunch of new work items, select Input List.

Usually, starting with a query is the easiest way, because you can still add and edit work items from it. You may add additional fields from the work item into the spreadsheet by clicking the Choose Columns button and adding additional columns into the list.

Note that if you select a hierarchical query—for example, a query that shows parent/child relationships such as an Iteration Backlog query in the standard `Iteration` folders created as part of an Agile process template—then you will have multiple Title columns for each level in the hierarchy, as shown in Figure 4-10. Adding a work item as a child of another is as simple as creating a new row and placing the title for that work item in the Title 2 column. If you need an additional column, or wish to quickly insert a new line to create the child node, click the Add Child button in the Team Ribbon.

To open an existing query as an Excel spreadsheet, you can right-click any work item query in Team Explorer and select Open in Microsoft Excel.

You can also easily generate several reports in an Excel workbook that analyze current status and historical trends based on the criteria specified in a flat (that is, not hierarchical) query. Right-click the query and select Create Report in Microsoft Excel. This will then connect Excel directly to Analysis Services to show the data directly from the Team Foundation Server data warehouse.

> **NOTE** *For more information on creating Team Foundation Server reports using Excel, see the MSDN documentation at* `http://tinyurl.com/Tfs2013ExcelReports`*.*

> **NOTE** *For more information on reporting, see Chapter 15.*

Using Team Foundation Server in Microsoft Project

In addition to providing Excel integration, the installation of Team Explorer also installs a Team Ribbon into Microsoft Project, as shown in Figure 4-11. This provides the capability to add and edit work items directly in Microsoft Project and to view data about the progress of the work items.

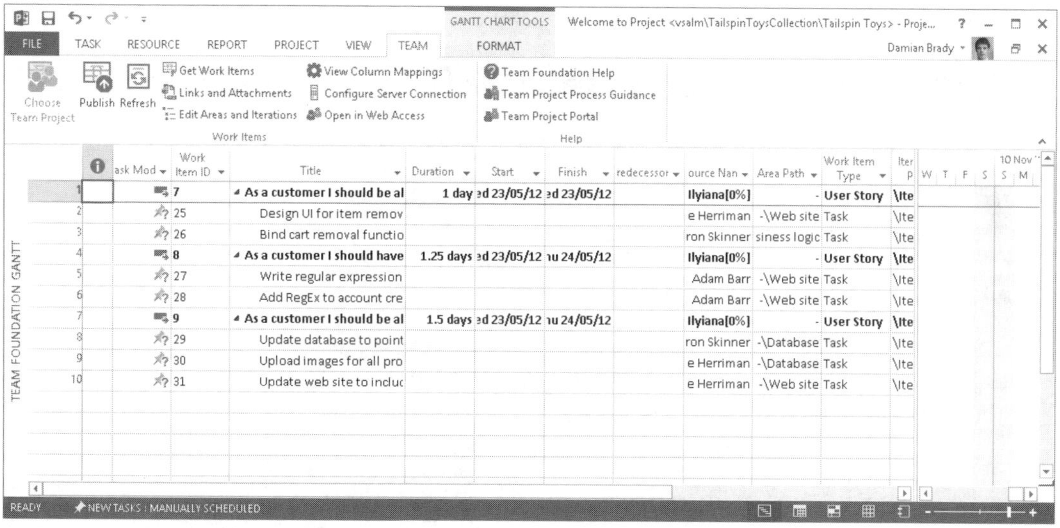

FIGURE 4-11: Team Ribbon in Microsoft Project

Because of the enhanced linking capabilities introduced in Team Foundation Server 2010, predecessors and successors can be created easily using Microsoft Project linked to work items, allowing you to control which work items depend on each other.

TEAM FOUNDATION EXTENSIONS FOR PROJECT SERVER

Introduced as a feature pack for Team Foundation Server 2010 Service Pack 1, the integration with Project Server now requires an installation of Extensions for Project Server. By enabling data flow between Team Foundation Server and Project Server, project managers can access up-to-date project status and resource availability across agile and formal software teams who work in Team Foundation Server. For more information, see the MSDN documentation at `http://tinyurl .com/Tfs2013ProjectServer`.

Windows Explorer Integration with Team Foundation Server

As part of the Team Foundation Server Power Tools (`http://aka.ms/TFS2013PowerTools`), Windows Shell Extensions can optionally be installed. Once it is installed, when you browse a folder that is mapped in a Team Foundation Server workspace, files and folders are decorated depending on the status (whether or not the files are checked out).

Right-clicking the file or folder provides access to some basic version control operations under the Team Foundation Server menu (see Figure 4-12) that can be very useful when working with Team Foundation Server outside of Visual Studio or Eclipse.

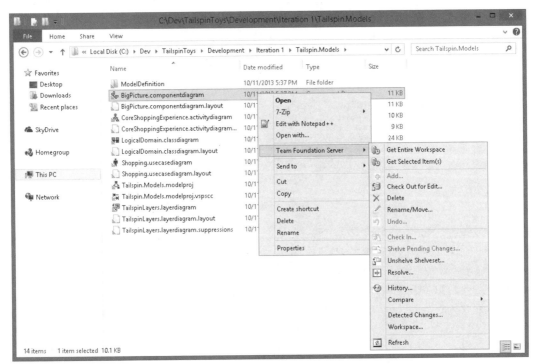

FIGURE 4-12: Windows shell extensions

Connecting Microsoft Test Manager to Team Foundation Server

Microsoft Test Manager is the dedicated interface for testers working with Team Foundation Server. It is installed as part of Visual Studio Test Professional, Visual Studio Ultimate, and Visual Studio Premium 2013.

The first time you start the application, you will be prompted to provide details about your Team Foundation Server instance. You are then able to select the Project Collection, Team Project, and Test Plan to which you wish to connect.

After the initial connection, your preference will be remembered, and you will automatically be connected to that Test Plan. To change Test Plan, or to connect to a different project or project collection, click the name of the Test Plan in the top right-hand corner of the screen, as shown in Figure 4-13.

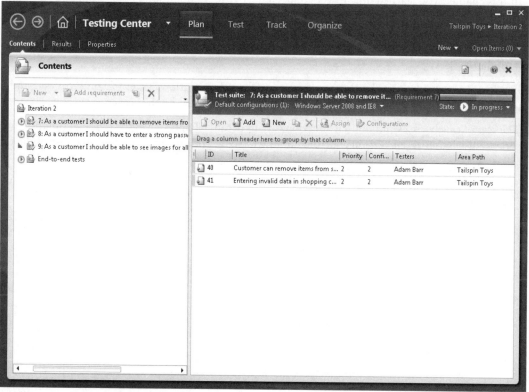

FIGURE 4-13: Microsoft Test Manager

Access to Team Foundation Server via Third-Party Integrations

Team Foundation Server supports a rich and vibrant third-party ecosystem through its powerful extensibility mechanisms, as outlined in Chapter 29. The same .NET object model installed as part of the Team Explorer integration is available for use by other third-party applications installed on your machine.

Integrations are available in other parts of Microsoft Office (such as Word and Outlook) from partners using these APIs. Also, many development tools and projects now integrate with Team Foundation Server using the extensibility hooks provided by Microsoft, or by wrapping calls to the version control command-line client.

SUMMARY

In this chapter, you learned how to get connected to Team Foundation Server from your desktop machine. You learned about the architecture of a typical Team Foundation Server installation and how the Team Foundation Server URL is used to provide the connection information to the server. The discussion also highlighted the basic access control and permissions system used by Team Foundation Server.

Finally, you learned about the client software for Team Foundation Server (Team Explorer) and how to begin using this interface to access the functionality provided by the server.

The rest of this book examines that functionality in detail. Chapter 5 begins that examination with a general discussion about version control and how to share your source code with the rest of the team.

PART II
Version Control

5

Overview of Version Control

WHAT'S IN THIS CHAPTER?

➤ Understanding the purpose, core concepts, and benefits of version control

➤ Understanding the differences between Team Foundation Version Control and Git-based repositories

➤ Analyzing the strengths and weaknesses of common version control products

Version control is the single most important tool you can use when developing software, regardless of the particular provider you use to give you version control functionality. Most software developers use version control tools in their day-to-day jobs, and yet, the fundamental concepts and reasoning behind version control are rarely discussed.

This chapter starts by explaining the fundamental concepts of version control and what functionality you typically find from a tool-independent viewpoint. Then we will discuss the similarities and differences between centralized and distributed version control systems. We then examine various important version control tools and analyze their strengths and weaknesses. The chapter concludes with a high-level look at the version control capabilities of Team Foundation Server, and looks at when Team Foundation Server is or is not the correct tool for your team.

WHAT IS VERSION CONTROL?

Version control is known by many names. "Source control" is frequently used, but the term "revision control" and even "software/source configuration management" (SCM) can be used to refer to the same broad set of functionality. Because a modern software project consists of much more than merely a set of source code, the term "version control" is used throughout this book, although the terms can be used interchangeably (and often are—even in the Team Foundation Server product).

Broadly speaking, *version control* provides the following capabilities:

➤ A place to store the source code, images, build scripts, and so on needed to build your software project

➤ The ability to track the history of changes to those files, and to view the state of the file at various points in the software life cycle

➤ Mechanisms and tooling to make it easy to work in parallel with a team of software developers on the same project

If you make a mistake when editing your code, a version control system lets you roll back time and get back to the state before you just accidentally deleted the past weeks' worth of work. A version control system allows you to know what code is running on someone's machine. Version control allows multiple teams of developers to work on the same files at the same time, and not get in each other's way.

Version control is so important that it is required for regulatory compliance in some industries, yet a remarkable number of organizations still do not use a version control system. Copying the folder containing your source code to another location is not a version control system—it is a backup. In the past, version control systems could be expensive, complex, and difficult to use. Today, version control is such a fundamental aspect of software development that, in its basic form, it is a commodity item and is increasingly easy to use. But even if you are a developer working on your own for a project, the safety net provided by a version control tool is worth the investment.

However, not all version control systems are the same. Even more confusing, some tools use the same words for very different activities. To thoroughly understand the nature of a version control system, you must be familiar with some core concepts.

Repository

In general, code is stored on a machine somewhere in a repository of some kind. The repository is usually represented as a tree of files, similar to the regular directory structures that everyone is familiar with in modern hierarchical file systems. However, the repository differs from a file system in one very important aspect: time. Whereas a file system is a collection of folders and files, a version control repository is a collection of folders and files and the changes made to those files over the repository's lifetime, thus allowing you to know the state of the files at any given point in time.

Additionally, a version control system must provide a number of features to make it useful. You need a way to share that version control repository with others on your team, make changes to the code, and share those changes with each other.

> **NOTE** *To keep things simple, this chapter's discussion refers to the repository as if there is a single master repository on a central server somewhere allowing your team to work. This is the traditional centralized version control system that many developers are familiar with today. However, not all version control systems work that way. In a distributed version control system (DVCS) such as Git, the machines work in a peer-to-peer manner. In other words, each machine has a copy of the full repository in its own right. This has some advantages and disadvantages that will be examined later in this chapter within the larger distributed version control discussion.*

Obviously, storing every version of every file can take up a lot of disk space. Version control systems frequently employ various tricks to ensure that the repository is efficient with storage. For example, Team Foundation Server will store the initial version of the file, and then store the changes between each version (known as deltas) for subsequent changes.

The "delta-fication" process in Team Foundation Version Control is actually much more complex than this. Optimizations are in place to ensure that this is done only for certain file types. It also ensures that recently accessed versions of files are cached in a ready-to-download state to avoid the computationally expensive task of rebuilding the file every time a developer requests a copy.

Working Copy

The files in the repository must be in a local area on the developer's machine. This allows the developer to work with the files, make changes to them, and debug them before he or she decides to check in or commit those changes to the repository. This local version is known as the workspace with Team Foundation Server, but in some version control systems, it can also be called a sandbox or working copy.

> **NOTE** *In Team Foundation Server, a workspace is actually more than just a working copy of the file system. Check out Chapter 6 for more information on workspaces.*

Using a local working copy of the repository, a developer can work in parallel with others on the team and know that the working copy of the code will not change until the developer performs a specific action. The developer will either make a change to the code or update the code from the repository by getting all the files that have changed since the last time he or she got a copy.

Working Folder Mappings

A working folder mapping is the link between the place in the repository where the files are stored and the place in your local file system where you have a working copy of that part of the repository. The terms working directory, workspace mapping, or *sandbox* can also be used to mean the working folder mapping.

> **NOTE** *Note that the terms "workspace," "working folder," and "sandbox" have been used in different version control systems to mean slightly different, but similar, things, which can be confusing when you are trying to understand a new version control system. This is one of the reasons it is important to understand the core concepts now so that this discussion can use a set of agreed-upon terms throughout the rest of the book. Each version control system you use is slightly different, and once you think about the problem in the way the tool allows you to work, it is often difficult to think about version control in other ways. This change in context is a problem that people encounter when moving from one version control system to another and, therefore, one that is addressed in Chapter 6 when discussing Team Foundation Server in more detail.*

Get/Clone/Pull

Once you have set up a working folder mapping, you must download the files from the repository to your local machine. In Team Foundation Version Control (TFVC) (as well as with some other version control tools) this process is known as *Get*. In Concurrent Version Systems (CVS) and Subversion (SVN), the same process is known as check-out—a word that means something slightly different in some version control systems like TFVC, as will be described shortly.

In a DVCS tool such as *Git*, you do not get individual files from the repository, but rather you clone the repository in its entirety. To initiate the creation of a local repository from a remote one, you would execute a *Clone* operation. This will retrieve an exact copy of the remote repository and place it on your local machine. While you are working on a local repository you might need changes from other team members. In this case you would execute a *Pull* request from your colleague's repository to update yours.

Add

What if you have no files in your repository? When you first start using a version control system, it is empty. In this case, you need to add some files. You select which files and folders to take from your local machine and add to the repository so that you can share them with the rest of your team. When you do this, you seldom want to add all of the local files.

For example, you might have some compiled binaries derived from your source or files that are generated by your tools in the source directory each time your code is built. You typically do not need or, indeed, want to share these files. Therefore, Team Foundation Server provides tooling to help you select which files from a folder you are actually interested in adding, and filters out those you want to exclude such as DLLs, compiled classes, and object files that are typically part of the build process and not the source code that you want to store.

Check-Out

If you want to work on a file, then some version control systems (such as Visual SourceSafe or Team Foundation Version Control when working in a mode known as a Server Workspace described later in this chapter) require you to inform the server that you are working on the file so that others on the team can know (and so that the server can check that you still have permission to edit the file). This operation is known as a check-out with Team Foundation Version Control.

In Visual SourceSafe (VSS), a single file can be edited by only one user at a time. Therefore, when a file is checked out, it is locked for editing for other users. In Team Foundation Server, the default behavior is that multiple people can edit the same file simultaneously (which is generally a best practice to allow a version control system to maximize productivity). However, you do have the option of locking the file as you check it out if you wish to prevent edits for some reason.

Note that the use of the term "check-out" is slightly different in this context as opposed to the use of the term in the context of CVS and SVN. In those systems, "check-out" means to download the files to your working copy locally. This is equivalent to a *Get* in Team Foundation Version Control.

A new mode of working was introduced in Team Foundation Server 2012 called a Local Workspace, and it's examined in Chapter 6. As with systems like SVN, with a Local Workspace in TFVC, you are not required to explicitly check out a file before working on it. Instead, you can edit any file that you can download. All files in your working copy are writable when you download them from version control and you just edit away. This has advantages because it means that there is much less friction when editing files locally, especially from tools outside of the main development environment. It also involves less frequent communication with the server, which makes working with the files offline much easier. However, you lose the ability to know exactly who on your team is currently working on which files.

Changeset/Commits

As you check out and edit files, you are building up a set of changes that will need to be applied to the repository when you wish to commit those changes. This set of changes to be done is called a changeset, commit, or changelist. The changeset consists of all the changes you have made to the files (for example, editing, adding, or renaming a file); in some version control systems, the changeset also contains metadata about the commit, such as which work items were associated with it or, in the case of Git, the original author of the changes that the committer is committing (which is important to track in many open source style workflows).

Check-in/Commit

At some point, you have a set of changes that you want to commit to the repository to share with your team, or draw a line in the sand as being at a point that you want to save your state with the repository. You want to commit your set of changes with the repository. This action is called a check-in in Team Foundation Server but can be called by other names (such as "commit") by other tools.

In more modern version control systems such as Team Foundation Server, Subversion (SVN), or Git, the check-in is performed on the repository as a single atomic transaction. That is, if, for some reason, your changes could not be applied to the repository (for example, if someone else has edited a particular file with a conflicting change while you were working on it or an upload of a file failed due to network issues), then none of the changes in your changeset are checked in until you resolve any issues preventing the check-in. In addition, if someone were to get a copy of the repository while you were doing your check-in, he or she would not get your changes. Only after your check-in has completed successfully are your changes visible to the rest of the team.

When you check in, you can also provide some additional data. In most version control tools, you can provide a comment describing the reason why you made the changes (and it is best practice to leave a meaningful comment). Team Foundation Server also provides the ability to provide additional metadata about each check-in, which will be described in more detail in Chapter 6.

Push

In Git there will be times when you need to send one or more commits from your local repository to a remote repository. This action is performed by executing a *Push* command to that repository. This is how a developer using a Git-based team project would send his or her work to the Team Foundation Server so that team members and the automated build process can use those files. Automated builds are described in Chapter 18.

History

As mentioned previously, a version control repository is like a file system that stores all the changes made to it. This extra dimension on the file system is known as the history. For a particular file or folder, the version control system can tell you everything that has happened to that file or folder over time. The history is one of the features that makes a version control system useful by allowing you to know what code you actually shipped to a customer who received a release at a given time. But it is also useful for many other things—for example, being able to go back in time and understand why the code is as it is now, to understand who has worked on a particular area in the past, or to figure out what has changed between two particular versions when suddenly something stops working that used to work well before.

The majority of version control systems provide the ability to label or tag files with a text description. This is a way of marking the repository to leave a meaningful name to a set of files in a particular version (for example, when you have done a build that you want to deploy). The label makes it easy to find that snapshot at a later time and to see what the repository contained at that instance.

Team Foundation Version Control provides for all of this history functionality; but, in addition, it makes it very easy to see what changes occurred to a file before it had been renamed. Similarly, changes that occurred before a file was branched or merged can be easily viewed from the file's history.

Branching and Merging

A branch is a copy of a set of files in a different part of the repository. This allows two or more teams of people to work on the same project at the same time, checking in changes as they go, but without interfering with the other teams. At some point in the future, you may want some or all of the code to join up again. This is when you need to merge the changes from one branch into the other branch. When merging changes from two files in separate branches, if the same bit of code has been edited differently in both places, then this is called a conflict, and the version control system will require someone to decide what the code should be in the merged version.

In most centralized version control systems, a branch is simply another folder at a different path that contains a copy of data from elsewhere in the repository. In Team Foundation Server, a branch folder is decorated differently, and branches are a first-class object with additional metadata and behavior to a regular folder, but they still live inside the repository. In Git, a branch lives outside the path of the repository and represents the versions of the files that particular repository has in that branch.

> **NOTE** *While Team Foundation Version Control logically shows branches in a different folder inside the repository, the files are not actually copied. A branch is just a pointer to where the files are stored in the repository. This saves space in the repository and allows branches to be lightweight and quick to create. When a file is first edited, the branch will contain the delta between that version of the file and the prior version on the parent branch.*

There are many ways to approach branching, and you should carefully consider what branching strategy you want to adopt. Chapter 10 provides more information on this.

If all you want to do is save your work in progress so that you can store a copy of it on the server, or possibly share it with others in your team without checking in the code, then you may also want to consider the shelving features of Team Foundation Version Control. Chapter 6 provides more information on shelving and unshelving.

CENTRALIZED VERSUS DECENTRALIZED VERSION CONTROL

In the world of version control systems, there are many options to choose from. To begin the selection process, it is important that you understand that version control systems fall into two basic categories, centralized and decentralized.

Centralized version Control

Centralized version control systems (CVCS) are structured so that there is a single, canonical copy of source code with which all team members interact. The most widely used of these systems are Visual SourceSafe (VSS), Subversion (SVN), and Team Foundation Version Control (TFVC). These systems are described further later in this chapter.

The typical usage scenario for a CVCS is that the developer performs a *Get* from the repository to create a local copy in his or her workspace. The developer then makes changes to the code base—adding, editing, deleting, and renaming files. All of these changes are isolated on the developer's local machine and are not visible to colleagues. When the developer is done, he or she *checks in* or *commits* the changes back to the central repository to allow other team members to retrieve those changes and integrate them with their ongoing development efforts.

This model provides a single "source of truth" for the code base as well as a single location to back up for disaster-recovery purposes. It also allows for the implementation of a central security model to restrict access to individual files, folders, or entire sub-trees.

Distributed Version Control Systems

Distributed version control systems (DVCS) have been around for more than a decade, but only in recent years have they gained widespread adoption with the creation of systems such as BitKeeper, Git, Mercurial, Veracity, and Bazaar. Git and Mercurial are probably the most well-known of these types of tools and have seen the widest adoption of DVCS to date. At the time of this writing, Git is emerging as the most important of this generation of version control systems due in no small part to the rapid rise of GitHub (`http://www.github.com`) as a central location for the sharing of open source projects. Git interoperability is a requirement of most modern DVCS systems, and Git's fast-import file format is now the de facto standard file format for the import and export of DVCS repositories.

Differences between Centralized and Distributed Version Control Systems

There are some common (but fundamental) differences between the way a DVCS tool operates versus the more traditional, centralized version control system tools discussed previously. The key difference is that the local developer machines have the capability of acting as a DVCS repository themselves and are peers to each other. Changes are not serialized as a set of versions in a centralized repository. Rather, they are stored as changes in the local repository, which can then be pushed or pulled into other users' repositories. While a centralized repository is not required, in many environments, it is common for a repository to act as the central hub that contains the master copy of the code on which the team performs automated builds and that is considered by the team to be the definitive version. Table 5-1 shows the strengths and weaknesses of a DVCS when compared to a CVCS.

TABLE 5-1: Strengths and Weaknesses of a DVCS

STRENGTHS	WEAKNESSES
It has full repository support when offline from others. It also has fast local repository access.	Using developer repositories can reduce the frequency with which changes are synced with the rest of the team, leading to a loss of visibility of the progress of the teams overall.
You can easily have multiple repositories and highly flexible topologies. You can use repositories in circumstances where branches might be used in a centralized server approach, which can, therefore, help with scalability. Because all the effort required to work with the repository is performed on the client, DVCS solutions typically have more modest hardware requirements on the server.	There is no centralized backup of progress for developers until changes are pushed to a central repository.

It encourages frequent check-ins to a local repository, thus providing the capability to track those changes and see the evolution of the code.

Current DVCS solutions lack some security, auditing, and reporting capabilities common to enterprise requirements, such as the ability to control access by path in version control. Access permissions are controlled at the repository level, not at the path level.

It is well-suited to many open source project workflows. It allows participation in the project without any centralized server granting permission. It works well for large projects with many partly independent developers responsible for certain areas.

Most centralized systems (such as SVN and Team Foundation Server) allow for optional locking of files to prevent later merge conflicts. The nature of DVCS tools makes this impossible.

Because of the way DVCS systems typically track changes, and because the nature of having distributed repositories means that merges happen more frequently, DVCS merges are usually less likely to produce conflicts, compared with similar changes merged from separate branches in a centralized version control system. However, merges can still obviously conflict, and the more the code has changed between merges, the more likely it is to require effort in performing the merge.

Because the entire repository is cloned to every machine, there can be an issue moving the large repositories across the network. This is often avoided by having multiple smaller repositories rather than just a single global repository.

As each working copy of the repository is a copy of the entire repository, including history, backups of that repository are implicit in each client. This increases the disaster recovery options without requiring any centralized overhead.

At the time of this writing, the integrated tooling or the tooling on Windows is not at the same level of maturation as the most popular centralized version control systems such as Team Foundation Version Control or Subversion.

DVCS systems provide a greater number of workflows when managing file versions. While this vast degree of freedom can be overwhelming to newcomers, once a basic workflow is established in the team it is quickly understandable.

COMMON VERSION CONTROL PRODUCTS

Many version control products have been created over time, and many are in use today. The most common tools used as of this writing are Visual SourceSafe (VSS), Subversion (SVN), Team Foundation Version Control (TFVC), and Git.

In Team Foundation Server 2013, Microsoft provided the ability to select a second version control repository engine in addition to TFVC during team project creation. You can now select either TFVC or Git as your version control engine. Distributed version control systems such as Git are becoming increasingly important players in the development ecosystem, especially in the open source community. This section also looks at distributed version control systems (DVCS).

Microsoft Visual SourceSafe

Visual SourceSafe (VSS) was originally created by One Tree Software and acquired by Microsoft in 1994. Microsoft Visual SourceSafe 2005 was the final release of the product, and it was scheduled for retirement from mainstream support in 2012. Despite its age, VSS, a pioneer in its day, is still a well-used version control product. It is very easy to install and set up, largely because it uses a file system–based repository and does not require a dedicated server. The early design did present some issues, however. Check-ins into the repository were not atomic and thus caused problems in team environments. Additionally, the file system–based approach could lead to instabilities in the repository, which gave VSS a reputation for sometimes corrupting the repository. Table 5-2 shows a contrast between the strengths and weaknesses of VSS.

TABLE 5-2: Strengths and Weaknesses of VSS

STRENGTHS	WEAKNESSES
VSS is easy to install and use.	This is an aging product; no longer actively developed.
VSS has broad support in developer tools.	It does not perform well over wide area networks (WANs).
VSS has wide adoption in the industry.	There are no atomic check-in transactions.
	It has very limited branch support (through sharing features).

Team Foundation Server is seen as Microsoft's replacement product for VSS. But Team Foundation Server also addresses far more scenarios (for example, work item tracking, reporting, team builds) for which VSS was never intended.

Apache Subversion

Subversion (SVN) is an open source version control project founded by CollabNet in 2000. SVN became a top-level project in the Apache Foundation in 2010. The system was originally designed to be a successor to the older open source CVS version control project. Since that time, it has surpassed the CVS market share and expanded beyond the original goal of replacing CVS. However, SVN is still heavily influenced by that design and should be familiar to CVS users.

While SVN has a large market share today, it is being challenged by distributed version control systems, most notably Git, in the open source space. But development of SVN is still continuing, and features continue to be added. Table 5-3 shows a contrast between the strengths and weaknesses of SVN.

TABLE 5-3: Strengths and Weaknesses of SVN

STRENGTHS	WEAKNESSES
SVN works under an open source licensing model (free to use).	Like CVS, SVN makes use of `.svn` directories inside the source folders to store the state of the local working copy and to allow synchronization with the server. However, it can have the effect of polluting the local source tree and can cause performance issues with very large projects or files.
SVN is in wide use by open source projects (but it is declining in favor of Git).	Renames are handled as a copy-and-delete operation in the repository, which can cause problems when merging branches.
The server works on a variety of operating systems.	Configuring authentication and performing certain administration functionality can be challenging in a Windows environment.
SVN provides broad support with developer tools on all platforms.	There is no shelving functionality.

Team Foundation Version Control

First publicly released in 2006, Microsoft Visual Studio Team Foundation Server is the reason you are reading this book, and so, by the end of this book, you will be very familiar with its functionality. Chapter 6 provides more information on the version control capabilities. However, it is worth highlighting the strengths and weaknesses of Team Foundation Version Control in this context, as shown in Table 5-4.

TABLE 5-4: Strengths and Weaknesses of Team Foundation Version Control

STRENGTHS	WEAKNESSES
It is more than just version control and provides tight integration with the work item tracking, build, and reporting capabilities of the product.	Offline support and support for occasionally connected developers is significantly improved on previous releases of Team Foundation Server, but centralized version control tools such as TFS and SVN will never be as strong at offline support as a Distributed Version Control tool such as Git.
It has first-class Visual Studio and Eclipse integration provided by the same vendor who provides the server.	A centralized server must be set up to allow check-in of code and collaboration of team members. However, you can have a centralized server set up quickly and easily for you at `http://www.visualstudio.com`.

continues

TABLE 5-4 *(continued)*

STRENGTHS	WEAKNESSES
It has many features appealing to enterprise-class customers, such as centralized security administration, integration with Active Directory for authentication, and single-sign-on (SSO), as well as SharePoint integration.	The server product runs only on Windows platforms, but a client is available cross-platform.
It is highly scalable.	
Shelveset support allows you to store changes on the server without committing to the main code repository.	
Check-in policies govern rules that the code should pass before you are able to commit it to the repository.	
Gated check-in support allows a build automation run to pass before the code is committed to the main repository.	
All data is stored in a SQL Server database for security and ease of backup.	

Git in TFS

The Git version control system is a free, open source DVCS that was designed and developed in 2005 by Linus Torvalds to support the development of the Linux kernel. Like all distributed version control systems, it allows for each developer to maintain a complete copy of the source repository on his or her local machine and makes it easy to share commits and entire branches between team members.

There is a large body of support for Git in modern development environments from native integration, such as in Apple's Xcode IDE, to support through plug-ins, like the EGit Eclipse plug-in, to hybrid integration such as Visual Studio 2013 provides, where you can either use command-line Git or Team Explorer integrated Git. For more information, see Chapter 7.

As stated earlier, Team Foundation Server 2013 now natively supports Git as a version control repository. This allows development teams to have the flexibility to work in a distributed fashion with each team member managing local commits while still allowing the TFS server to house the repository that is the "source of truth." This integration opens up the ability to link commits in Git to work items in TFS. It also allows Git branches to participate in automated builds. Let's look at the strengths and weaknesses of Git in TFS in Table 5-5.

TABLE 5-5: Strengths and Weaknesses of Git in TFS

STRENGTHS	WEAKNESSES
It is more than just version control and provides tight integration with the work item tracking, build, and reporting capabilities of the product.	The server product runs only on Windows platforms, but a client is available cross-platform.
Strong support for offline and occasionally connected development patterns with local repositories.	Does not have the ability to create shelvesets.
Makes merging of changes between branches and repositories much easier.	Gated check-in support is not available.
It has many features that appeal to enterprise-class customers, such as centralized security administration, integration with Active Directory for authentication, and single-sign-on (SSO), as well as SharePoint integration.	Does not have graphical support in Source Control Explorer, branch visualization, or changeset history tracking.
It is highly scalable.	"Source of truth" repository is defined only by convention.
All data is stored in a SQL Server database for security and ease of backup.	Security can only be set at the branch level on the server. No security control on local repositories.
Works with continuous integration automated builds.	

SUMMARY

This chapter introduced the basic concepts of version control and why it is needed. We then discussed the differences between centralized and distributed version control systems. You learned about some of the common version control tools in the market today and about their strengths and weaknesses.

Team Foundation Server is one of the leading tools in the market today. While it has some unique version control capabilities, and scales well from very small to very large teams, broadly speaking, when looking at the version control capabilities alone, it is comparable to most modern centralized version control systems in terms of feature sets, and with the addition of Git, it is a compelling alternative in the distributed version control area.

The key factor that makes many organizations choose to standardize on Team Foundation Server is the tight integration between work item tracking (which can include requirements, test cases, bugs, tasks, and so on), version control, build, and reporting features, all the way through the product. By closely binding your version control with your work item tracking, you get greater traceability. The intimate knowledge of the version control system by the build system gives rise to powerful build features, with no additional work by the administrators. The close link between builds and work items means that testers know which builds fix which bugs, what files in version control were affected, and which tests need to be re-run. It's the sum of the whole that really makes Team Foundation Server stand out from the competition.

As discussed, every version control system is different, and a developer's understanding of a version control system is key to effectively working with it. Chapter 6 delves deeper into the version control features offered by Team Foundation Server and how to work with them. The core concepts and tools will be discussed along with some help and advice in transitioning to Team Foundation Server from other version control systems.

Using Centralized Team Foundation Version Control

Version control is one of the primary reasons that people adopt Team Foundation Server. Most professional developers have had some prior experience with a version control system. The first thing you must come to terms with is that every version control system is different. While change can be unsettling at first, there are clear benefits in moving to Team Foundation Server's centralized version control system, called Team Foundation Version Control.

Team Foundation Version Control is a robust, powerful, and scalable version control infrastructure that you can rely on to support the needs of your software development efforts.

From teams of 1 to teams of 5,000 or more, Team Foundation Server is a mission-critical system supporting many organizations today. Team Foundation Version Control was built from scratch by Microsoft, and is not based on its previous version control offering, Visual SourceSafe (VSS).

Team Foundation Server stores all its version control data in a SQL Server database alongside the work item and build information. Team Foundation Server's version control systems are designed to work using Internet-based protocols. Centralized version control works great over high-latency network connections, such as those found in the typical enterprise wide area network (WAN), or over the public Internet. It provides highly flexible security and permission capabilities tied into an integrated authentication model.

This chapter first examines the fundamental concepts that you must understand to come to grips with the centralized version control model used by Team Foundation Server. Then we explain the common version control tool windows, along with how to access common version control operations and get started using Team Foundation Server Version Control on your first project.

In this chapter, you will look at the use of the version control command line and review special considerations to take into account when using Team Foundation Version Control cross platform. You will learn how to configure version control security and permissions in Team Foundation Server, and how to configure common settings for source control. Finally, you will see a short guide to Team Foundation Server for developers familiar with Microsoft VSS or Apache Subversion (SVN).

> **NOTE** *As noted in Chapter 5, version control goes by many names, including "source control," "revision control," and so on. This book mostly uses the term "version control" to indicate that Team Foundation Server can handle much more than source code, including everything that you use to create your product (such as build scripts, website images, and original artwork) that you wish to version alongside your source. However, the terms "version control" and "source control" can be used interchangeably. Even in Team Foundation Server, you will see references to both terms.*

But first, let's review getting started with Team Foundation Server Version Control. If you have used Team Foundation Server before or in previous versions, then feel free to skip that section and jump straight to "Learning What's New in Team Foundation Server 2013 Version Control."

GETTING STARTED WITH TEAM FOUNDATION SERVER VERSION CONTROL

Before diving into the details of Team Foundation Server version control, you will add a Visual Studio 2013 solution to version control. First, create a simple solution that you want to share with your team. Use a simple `HelloWorld` console application (although you could use any of your own applications). You must ensure that you are connected to Team Foundation Server. For more information on this, see Chapter 4, but, basically, in Visual Studio, go to Team ⇨ Connect to Team

Foundation Server, and then click Select Team Projects. Click the Servers link to configure server details, and then choose the project collection and team projects that you wish to connect to. Then click Connect.

Now add the solution to version control. Right-click the solution in Solution Explorer and select Add Solution to Source Control. You should see the screen shown in Figure 6-1.

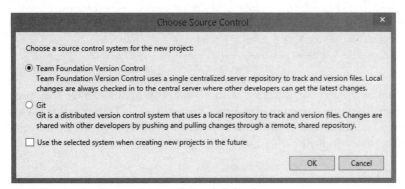

FIGURE 6-1: The Choose Source Control dialog box

Choose Team Foundation Version Control and click OK. You should be shown a new dialog box asking you to choose the Team Project to add your solution to, as shown in Figure 6-2.

FIGURE 6-2: Add to Source Control dialog box

> **NOTE** *If this is the first source code being added to your team project, then we recommend you reject the default of placing of your solution directly under the team project in version control. Instead, make a new folder called **Main** and place your solution in it—that is, $/MyTeamProject/Main/HelloWorld. This will put you in a good position should you want to adopt a branching strategy later on in your project development. Create the Main folder even if you have no idea what a branch is yet. Chapter 10 explains all about branching, and this folder will come in handy then.*

You are nearly there. To commit your changes so that other people on the team can see your project, you need to check in the files. To do this, open the Pending Changes page in Team Explorer (View ⇨ Other Windows ⇨ Pending Changes) and click the Check In button. You can provide a comment for your changes if you wish, as shown in Figure 6-3.

FIGURE 6-3: Pending Changes view

And there you have it. Your changes are now in Team Foundation Version Control. If you look in Solution Explorer, you will see a little padlock next to your files, as shown in Figure 6-4.

FIGURE 6-4: Version controlled files in Solution Explorer

If you right-click the files, you will see new menu options available, such as Get Latest, Check Out for Edit, and Compare, along with a Source Control submenu to allow you to View History, Undo Changes, and Shelve Changes. All of these commands and more will be explained later in this chapter, but first you will step back a little and review some concepts at the core of Team Foundation Server Version Control.

> **NOTE** *In Visual Studio, you can have a number of different version control providers. While Team Foundation Server is installed by default in Visual Studio 2013, if you have been using a different version control tool previously, you may not see the Team Foundation Server functionality. To switch to Team Foundation Server for version control, go to Tools ⇨ Options ⇨ Source Control, and ensure that your current source control plug-in is set as Visual Studio Team Foundation Server.*

LEARNING WHAT'S NEW IN TEAM FOUNDATION SERVER 2013 VERSION CONTROL

The Team Foundation Server 2013 product has seen a large number of changes including the introduction of Git repositories and general availability of a hosted Team Foundation Service. However, with respect to centralized version control, there have been relatively few changes since Team Foundation Server 2012. The biggest improvements related to Team Foundation Version Control for Team Foundation Server 2013 are in the UI.

The Team Explorer window in Visual Studio has undergone a lot of usability improvements and now represents a clean, easy-to-navigate way of working with Team Foundation Server. The layout of the Team Explorer windows has been completely reengineered to give you easy access to your projects. The Home page gives you one-click access to any Solutions you have in your Workspaces, and the Connect page lets you quickly navigate between Team Projects.

Similarly, there have been great improvements in the Code Explorer in Team Web Access. Web Access gives you very fine-grained visibility of changesets, with rich diff tools for file comparison right in the browser. Lightweight code commenting even gives you the ability to comment on changes directly in the browser.

A big drive in the previous Team Foundation Server 2012 release was to reduce friction in version control operations. This was done throughout the product from big new concepts, such as Local Workspaces, to moving UI that would have popped up in a modal window in the past into modeless experiences in the editor area or in the new Team Explorer.

In Team Foundation Server 2013, Microsoft has continued to make improvements around source control UI, while keeping the underlying Team Foundation Version Control functionality stable. If you are familiar with Team Foundation Server 2012, you will already be comfortable with the current version. If you're coming from an earlier version of Team Foundation Server or another version control system, you will find the Team Foundation Server Version Control Concepts section of this chapter very useful.

Team Foundation Version Control balances simplicity in day-to-day work with powerful functionality supporting the requirements of an enterprise version control system. But, to understand Team Foundation Server Version Control, you need to have a firm grasp of some fundamental concepts.

TEAM FOUNDATION SERVER VERSION CONTROL CONCEPTS

You can just dive in and start using Team Foundation Server Version Control with very little effort or training. However, at some point, you might bump into a couple of areas that prove confusing unless you understand the basics of how Team Foundation Server sees the world when it comes to centralized version control. The first fundamental concept you must understand is the notion of the *workspace*.

Workspace

One of the first problems with the term "workspace" is that it can be a somewhat overloaded term. For example, to Eclipse developers, the term "workspace" can mean the Eclipse workspace, which is entirely different from the Team Foundation notion of workspace, even though they both conceptually contain source code. To others familiar with version control systems, such as Polytron Version Control System (PVCS), or ClearCase, the term "workspace" also means something similar, but again quite different from Team Foundation Server. For SVN developers, the concept of a "workspace" is completely foreign, and they might assume that this is just the working copy (it is, but also more than just that).

A workspace can be thought of as the container that bridges the gap between your local computer and the Team Foundation Server repository. As shown in Figure 6-5, the workspace contains several important pieces of information.

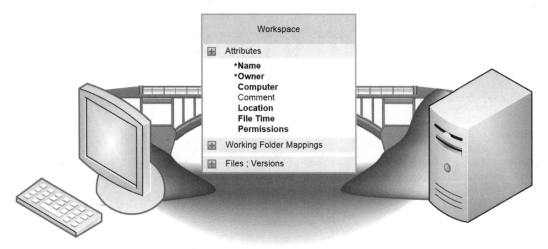

FIGURE 6-5: Workspace in Team Foundation Server

Workspaces are identified by a name and the hostname of the computer the workspace is for. The name can be up to 64 characters in length, and you can also provide a comment that may be a useful reminder if you have multiple workspaces on the same computer. The workspace also contains the working folder mappings that indicate which folders on your local machine map to which folders on the server.

CHANGING THE COMPUTER NAME OR OWNER FOR A WORKSPACE

The owner and computer name of the workspace are not editable in Visual Studio or Eclipse. However, you may occasionally need to edit these. To do this, use the `tf workspaces /updateComputerName:OldComputerName` or `tf workspaces / updateUserName:OldUserName` commands.

Note that the `updateCompterName` option does not move the workspace from one machine to another. You are telling Team Foundation Server that the hostname of the machine that this workspace is on has changed for some reason (that is, it was renamed or restored from a backup). Similarly, the `updateUserName` option doesn't change the owner of the workspace. It tells Team Foundation Server that your name has changed from, say, `DOMAIN\dbrady` to `DOMAIN\damianb`.

Under the hood, Team Foundation Server actually stored the Windows security identifier (SID) of the account. The update call simply tells the server to update its cache with the current user name for that same SID.

The version control system needs to store information in the workspace, such as which version of which files you have downloaded locally, which files you are in the process of editing, and so on. In Team Foundation Server 2013, the workspace state information can be stored in either of two locations, locally on disk or on the server. This leads to the terms *Local Workspaces* and *Server Workspaces*. In Team Foundation Server 2010 and below, the workspace state was always stored on the server (i.e., in what is now called a Server Workspace), but the default for new workspaces in Team Foundation Server 2012 and 2013 is a Local Workspace.

> **NOTE** *If you've upgraded an existing Team Project from Team Foundation Server 2010 or earlier, Server Workspaces will remain the default for that project.*

Local Workspaces

Local Workspaces were new to Team Foundation Server in the 2012 version and are available only from compatible clients, such as Visual Studio 2012 and 2013, or Team Explorer Everywhere, for Team Foundation Server 2012 or 2013. If you want to use a Local Workspace, you must be talking to a 2012 version of the server (or higher) and be using one of the newer clients. If you need to work on files from an older client, such as Visual Studio 2010 or Visual Studio 2008, at the same time as working on those files from a newer client, you will need to use a Server Workspace as described later in this section.

In a Local Workspace, state about that workspace is stored on the local disk. All the information is stored inside a folder called `$tf` (or `.tf` on UNIX-based file systems). The folder resides at the root of your workspace folder mappings. If there is no common root folder then it will reside at the root of the first active working folder mapping.

> **WARNING** *Because a Local Workspace stores information in a local data store that only Visual Studio 2012 and above knows how to read, Local Workspaces are invisible to Visual Studio 2010 and below.*
>
> *If you want to share a workspace between Visual Studio 2012 or 2013 and an earlier version of Visual Studio, you will have to convert your Local Workspace to a Server Workspace.*

In addition to storing the state information locally, Local Workspaces have a number of important differences to the way they work. The primary benefits of Local Workspaces are that you can edit files when offline from Team Foundation Server and that you can edit files outside of Visual Studio or Eclipse without performing an explicit check-out operation first.

To achieve this, when you perform actions, such as a check-in operation, or see what files you have pending changes for, the Team Foundation Server client will scan the contents of your Local Workspace and compare the contents of it with a copy of the last downloaded versions of those files (which are stored in a compressed form in the $tf folder). In this way, it can tell which files were edited, which files have been deleted locally, and which files have been added.

Edits are automatically added to your Pending Changes list; however, adds and deletes of files performed outside of Visual Studio or Eclipse are classified as Detected (or candidate) Changes. They are displayed to you, but not automatically added to your pending changes list in case you did not mean to add or delete that file from the version control repository. Handling Detected Changes is discussed later in this chapter.

If you perform rename or move operations outside of Visual Studio or Eclipse, then when the disk scanner runs it has no way to tell that these files are related and sees that as an Add and Delete of a file (add with the new name/path and delete with the old name/path). Therefore, in the Detected Changes experience, you are able to associate those two changes and promote them as a Rename.

Because no server communication is required before editing a file locally, you cannot prevent a user from editing the file when placing a lock on it. Locks are still available with a Local Workspace, but they function like a Check In lock in Server Workspaces—that is, a lock prevents someone from checking in their changes to that file.

The other downside of Local Workspaces is that as they store a local copy of files to enable you to compare and undo while off-line and because a scan of the disk is required to tell you which files you have edited, there is a tradeoff between the number of files in your Local Workspace and performance. Depending on the speed of your local hard drive, you may notice performance degradation in certain version control operations when working on workspaces containing more than 100,000 files; however, those scenarios are rare and the performance degradation is linear depending on the number of files you have locally.

Because Local Workspaces make it so easy to edit and work with files under version control, they became the default mode of working for all new workspaces created by Visual Studio 2012 and above, and Team Explorer Everywhere for Team Foundation Server 2012 and above. You can easily convert from Local to Server and vice-versa from the Edit Workspace dialog box in Visual Studio 2013 by going to File ➪ Source Control ➪ Advanced ➪ Workspaces ➪ Edit ➪ Advanced.

Server Workspaces

Server Workspaces are the mode of operation familiar to users of older versions of Team Foundation Server and the only option available when using older versions of Visual Studio, such as Visual Studio 2010 or Visual Studio 2008. If you had an existing workspace and upgraded the server to Team Foundation Server 2012 or 2013 from an earlier release, then that workspace would initially also be a server workspace.

With a Server Workspace, the information about the state of your workspace is stored on the server. The server remembers which versions of which files you have downloaded to your local computer, and also stores those files that you are in the process of changing, and any files that you have decided to lock so that others cannot edit those files at the same time as you do.

Using the workspace to remember the files and versions downloaded is one of the ways that Team Foundation Server can optimize performance for large workspaces. When you ask the server to Get Latest, it already knows what versions you have of all the files, so it can send you only the ones that have been modified. Additionally, because a Server Workspace stores the files you are currently working on, Team Foundation Server has the capability of highlighting this fact to others in your team who are also using Server Workspaces so that they know that someone else is currently editing a file that they were about to modify.

But, those benefits come at a tradeoff in terms of usability for developers. One of the most common aspects of Server Workspaces that people often find confusing (and frustrating for some developers using older versions of Team Foundation Server) is the fact that you must always tell the server when you do something to a file or folder in your workspace (such as editing the file, renaming it, or adding a file into a folder).

This mode of operation works well if you are always in Visual Studio or Eclipse and are always connected to your Team Foundation Server, as the IDE integrations automatically perform all the necessary version control operations on behalf of the user. But, it can lead to confusion when a developer drops out of the IDE and tries to work with the files.

For example, developers might open an image file in an external editor and get frustrated when they are unable to save the file because it is read-only, making them switch over to Visual Studio to explicitly check out the file.

Another common complaint with Server Workspaces is that developers might have deleted a file locally in Explorer, realized their mistake and then gone to Visual Studio to do a Get Latest to retrieve the latest version of that file only to be told by Visual Studio that "All files are up-to-date" and the deleted file has not been restored. This makes sense when you understand Server Workspaces, as you never told Team Foundation Server that you were deleting the file so it still assumes you have it. The file is easily recoverable by going to Get Specific Version and performing a Force Get; however, that requires a deeper understanding of Server Workspaces and the intricacies of Team Foundation Server workings than many developers wish to have when all they want to do is edit their files and check in their changes.

For this reason, Local Workspaces is the default when creating a new workspace in Visual Studio 2012 or 2013 against Team Foundation Server 2012 or 2013. However, Server Workspaces still exist for backward compatibility and for those users who prefer the functionality they offer or require the scalability in terms of the number of files in the workspace that a Server Workspace can provide.

Working Folder Mappings

As mentioned previously, part of the information contained in the workspace is the working folder mappings. At the simplest level, a *working folder mapping* says which folders on your local machine map to which folders in the repository. For example, if you were to map `C:\Local\MyTeamProject` to `$/MyTeamProject` and then download the files to your local machine by performing a Get Latest, you would have a copy of the latest versions of all the files from the server in your local directory.

> **NOTE** *.NET (and, therefore, Team Foundation Server) imposes a 260-character limit for the full file path, which stems from a limitation of certain APIs in Windows around file handling. Conventions for source code can result in long folder and file names. This is especially true for Java projects, but can be true with many large Visual Studio solutions. Therefore, a useful tip is to store source code in a folder off the root of a hard drive (such as C:\source) on Windows, or at a suitable mount point in UNIX file systems. This way, you will have more characters available for the files in your local path.*

With Team Foundation Server, working folder mappings are stored in your Team Foundation Server workspace. They are not shared between other people using the repository (unlike PVCS, for example). Viewing the current set of working folder mappings is very easy, as explained in the following:

➤ With Visual Studio, go to File ➪ Source Control ➪ Advanced ➪ Workspaces. Select your workspace and click Edit.

➤ With Eclipse, right-click on the project in Package Explorer and go to Team ➪ Manage Workspaces. Select your workspace and click Edit.

> **NOTE** *Alternatively, you can use the* `tf workfold` *command or the Team Foundation Sidekicks tool, available at* `http://www.attrice.info/cm/tfs/`.

Figure 6-6 shows the working folder mappings from Visual Studio. The example shows a fairly complex working folder mapping layout—it is much more usual to see an example with only one or two active working folder mappings. The figure demonstrates some additional working folder mapping features available in Team Foundation Server. Figure 6-6 also shows all the Advanced options of the workspace, which are usually hidden until the user presses the Advanced button. Take a closer look at the working folder mappings.

Active Working Folder Mappings

The first working folder mapping is straightforward. This maps the contents of `$/MyTeamProject/Main` to `C:\Dev\MyTeamProject\Main` recursively. If you create this working folder mapping and then perform a Get from `$/MyTeamProject/Main/HelloWorld`, the contents of that folder would be downloaded to `C:\Dev\MyTeamProject\Main\HelloWorld`.

Cloaked Working Folder Mappings

The second mapping in Figure 6-6 is not an Active mapping, but is cloaked. A *cloaked working folder mapping* tells the server that you do not wish to download the contents that are cloaked. In other words, you do not want them to appear in your local file system, nor do you want to get any files in that folder if the contents of that folder are changed on the server.

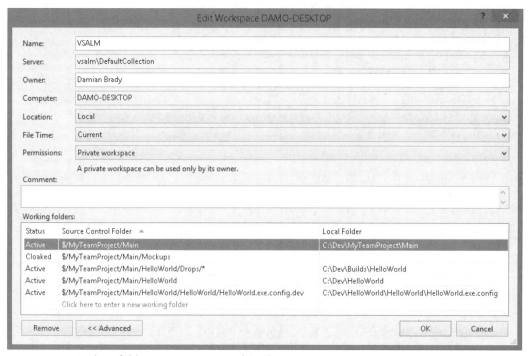

FIGURE 6-6: Working folder mappings in Visual Studio

In Figure 6-6, you see a cloaked working folder mapping that is a child of the previous Active recursive mapping for `$/MyTeamProject/Main`. This means that the large graphic files contained in the `$/MyTeamProject/Main/Mockups` folder are not downloaded to the local machine, saving bandwidth and disk space.

> ### COPYING COMPLEX WORKING FOLDER MAPPING CONFIGURATIONS
>
> A typical working folder mapping configuration can be quite simple. However, some version control trees require a more complex folder mapping to be used, which you may want to share with the team or copy to another workspace on a different machine. To copy the working folder mappings from another workspace, you have several options.
>
> From the Edit Workspace dialog box shown in Figure 6-6, you can copy and paste working folder mappings between different instances of the dialog box. You can even copy the mappings, paste them into a text editor, such as Notepad, to perform a mass edit of them, and then copy/paste those back into the working folder mappings section.
>
> From the command line, you can create a new workspace using the following command:
>
> ```
> tf workspace /new /template:workspacename[;workspaceowner]
> ```

In this way, you can specify an existing workspace to use as a template for your new workspace, taking the working folder mappings from that existing workspace. The `workspaceowner` is optional. If you do not provide it, the server will look for a workspace with that name belonging to your user. However, you can use the `workspaceowner` field to copy a working folder mapping set used by a colleague.

Recursive Working Folder Mappings

By default, a standard working folder mapping, as detailed previously, is applied recursively. When you map a folder to a location in the version control repository, a mapping is implicitly created for all subfolders. However, you can override the implicit mapping, as was done in the fourth line in Figure 6-6.

If you do not want a working folder mapping to be recursive, then you can use an asterisk as a wildcard to say that you wish to map only the server folder and its immediate files to your Local Workspace, as shown in the third line of Figure 6-6.

Mapping Individual Files

Despite the name, working folder mappings do not only apply to folders. They can actually apply to any path in version control, including individual files. For example, in Figure 6-6, the file called `HelloWorld.exe.config.dev` is being called `HelloWorld.exe.config` in the Local Workspace.

WORKSPACE PERMISSIONS

With Team Foundation Server 2005 and 2008, the owner of the workspace was set at the time the workspace was created, and could only be used by the owner of the workspace. With Team Foundation Server 2010, these restrictions were removed. Changing the owner is simply a case of editing the owner field in the Edit Workspace dialog box (see Figure 6-6). To control who can use the workspace, the owner can select from one of three *permission profiles* for his or her workspace: Private workspace, Public workspace (limited), or Public workspace.

Under the hood, a workspace actually has four permissions:

➤ `Read`—The `Read` permission exists but was not enforced in the shipping product. In theory, it would control who would have the ability to see that the workspace exists, what mappings it had, and what pending changes exist in the workspace. However, when Team Foundation Server 2010 was released, any valid users were able to view these properties just as they could do in the 2008 and 2005 releases.

➤ `Use`—The `Use` permission is more interesting. It dictates who is allowed to change the state of the workspace—to get files, check out files, and so on.

continues

continued

➤ CheckIn—The CheckIn permission is separated out so that, in certain cases, other people can use the workspace, but only the owner can check in those changes.

➤ Administer—The Administer permission controls who can change the mappings, name, owner, comment, computer, and so on, as well as who can delete the workspace and change the workspace permissions.

With Visual Studio, these permissions are set by choosing one of the three permission profiles mentioned previously. A *private workspace* is the default, and the behavior is similar to that familiar to users of Team Foundation Server before the 2010 release. Only the owner can use the workspace. The permissions for that workspace are owner: Read, Use, CheckIn, and Administer.

A *public workspace* (*limited*) means that any valid user may use the workspace, but only the owner is allowed to perform check-ins or change the properties of the workspace. In this case, the permissions for the valid users would be valid-user: Read, Use. If the owner sets a workspace to be a public workspace, then all valid users essentially have the same rights as the owner (that is, valid-user: Read, Use, CheckIn, and Administer). It also means that any valid user would also be allowed to change the owner of the workspace, and then set the workspace permissions back to Private, so this should be used with caution.

Public workspaces can be useful when different developers are sharing the same machine to make changes in parallel. With a public workspace, you can maintain a proper audit history to see which users actually checked in the changes from that particular machine. The limited public workspaces can also be used when you have requested that colleagues help you make some changes on a machine in your workspace, but you want them to do it under their own logon credentials and have a guarantee that they will not be able to check in those changes for you.

The Edit Workspace dialog box only allows you to pick from one of the three permission profiles. If you have more complex workspace permission requirements (such as sharing a workspace between a few specified users, rather than with all valid users), you can actually have full control using the .NET object model.

Get

Thus far in this chapter, you have seen the term "Get Latest" a few times already without explicitly knowing what it means. To download the files from a Team Foundation Version Control repository to your local file system, you perform what Team Foundation calls a *Get*. Note that this is a different term from the one used by SVN or CVS to perform this action (referred to in those systems as *check-out*). The term "check-out" means something else in Team Foundation Server, which you will learn about shortly.

When you get files from version control you can do one of two things:

➤ **Get Latest**—This downloads the latest versions of all the files as of the time you asked to start getting them.

➤ **Get Specific Version**—You can find Get Specific Version under the Advanced menu in source control. This downloads a version that you have specified by date, label, changeset number, or simply the latest version. This specification of the version is called a *versionspec* in Team Foundation Server.

FILE MODIFICATION TIMES

By default, with Team Foundation Server the modification time of the files in your workspace on your local machine is left as the current local time on your machine when you happened to perform the Get from version control that resulted in downloading a new version of the file. In Team Foundation Server 2012 and 2013, you can change this behavior by editing the File Time property in the workspace, as shown in Figure 6-6. If you change the File Time to be Checkin, then the next time you perform a Get, the modification of the file will be the time that version of the file was checked into Team Foundation Server (adjusted to local time on the computer). This can be useful if you have processes that you run locally that use the file's modification time to help it understand if it needs to include the file or not (for example, when running robocopy to deploy only change files to an ASP.NET site or running make or other timestamp-dependent build processes).

In Team Foundation Server, you get files only when you specifically tell the server that you want to. This means that you can ensure that you know the state of your files; but, again, this can be a little different from what VSS users expect who are used to getting the latest file as they perform a check-out.

VERSIONSPECS

In the Get dialog box shown in the following figure, there is a section for Version. Here, you specify what Team Foundation Server understands as a version specification, or *versionspec*. A versionspec specifies the version that you want to work with, and can be specified using one of the following types: changeset, label, date, workspace, or latest.

continues

continued

You learn more about changesets later in this chapter, but in brief, changesets are the fundamental unit of versioning in Team Foundation Server. Changesets have a numeric ID associated with them. A changeset versionspec is denoted by `C123456` to Team Foundation Server, where `123456` is the ID of the changeset.

A *label versionspec* says you want a version that belongs to a particularly named label. It is denoted by myLabel where *myLabel* is the label name.

Date versionspecs are denoted with a `D`, and then, in the command line, you can pass any date format supported by the .NET Framework on any of the date formats for the local computer (for example, `D2008-04-22T22:15`).

A *workspace versionspec* means the version most recently downloaded into the workspace. This is denoted by a `W`, meaning the current workspace (or `WworkspaceName;workspaceOwner`) when specifying a workspace written as a string.

Finally, the *latest* version is a versionspec in its own right denoted by `L` when written as a string. When you use the `Get Latest` command in Visual Studio or Eclipse, you are actually telling the client to perform a *Get* of versionspec `L`.

Certain commands (for example, when viewing the history of a file) can accept ranges of versionspecs denoted by the tilde character (~). Different types of version-specs can be mixed in those instances. For example, `D2004-04-11T18:37~L` would say you wanted a range of versions beginning with April 11, 2004 at 6:37 p.m. up until the latest version.

Check-Out

With a Server Workspace in Team Foundation Server, the initial files destined for your workspace would be marked read-only in your local file system. Before you start editing the files, you must *check out* the files from Team Foundation Server to let the server (and others on your team) know that you are editing the files. This happens automatically for you if you are editing files from within Visual Studio as soon as you start typing in the files. But you must do it explicitly if you want to edit the files outside Visual Studio when using a Server Workspace.

If you are using a Local Workspace (which is the default), there is no need to explicitly check out a file. If a file has been modified on your local file system, compared with the version you last did a Get for, then the file is marked as having a pending edit, and it can still be said by some that it is "checked out."

When you have finished with the file and want to commit it back to the repository, you perform a *check-in*.

As mentioned previously, the term "check out" is used by many version control systems, but means different things, depending on the system. In VSS, "check out" means "give me the latest version of the file and lock it so that no one else can edit it." In SVN (and also CVS), "check out" means "get the latest version."

Locks

By default, with both Local and Server Workspaces, Team Foundation Server does not automatically lock a file on check-out. That is, more than one person can edit a file at the same time. The first person to check in a file does so as normal. Subsequent people will be prompted to merge their changes with the other modifications that have been made since getting the previous version of the file if it was no longer the latest. This behavior is extremely useful in ensuring that teams can develop on the same code base in parallel (especially with files such as a Visual Studio `.vbproj` or `.csproj` that must be edited every time someone on the team adds or renames a file in the project).

However, there are times when you wish to temporarily prevent someone from making changes to a particular file or folder in source control. For this reason, Team Foundation Server provides two types of locks that you can place on a file in your workspace: a *check-out lock* or a *check-in lock*.

Check-Out Lock

Available only when working with a Server Workspace, a check-out lock will be familiar to users of older version control systems such as VSS or PVCS. It prevents other users from checking out the locked file while you hold the check-out lock. A check-out lock may not be placed on a file if other users already have that file checked out in their workspaces.

As an example, you might use a check-out lock when you are making some major or complex revisions to a file and you want to ensure that no one else makes any changes to that file until you are done because you do not want the additional complexity of having to merge their changes into yours before you check in.

One disadvantage of a check-out lock occurs when someone is using a Local Workspace. They do not have to explicitly check out the file to modify it, which means that a check-out lock will not be applied. Similarly, if a lock has been applied by someone else, the current user will not be prevented from editing the file. For those people using Server Workspaces, they cannot easily make that file editable in their Local Workspace, or work on it while you have the lock held. Therefore, you are reducing the ability of your team to work in parallel on the same codebase.

Check-In Lock

Check-in locks are available for both Local and Server Workspaces. With a check-in lock, other users can still edit the file on which you have placed the lock, but they will be unable to check it in until you have released the lock. Check-in locks can be placed on files that others have checked out, but, by placing the check-in lock on the file, you are guaranteeing that you will have the right of first check-in.

Using Locks Effectively

With any locks, you must ensure that your team communication is effective to explain why you need to lock the file. Locking should be used only where necessary because it reduces the ability of your team to work in parallel, and so can reduce productivity if overused.

In Source Control Explorer, you can see locks that other users might have on a file. If there are multiple changes, you might need to right-click the item, select Advanced ➪ Properties, and then look at the Status tab. However, it does not tell you what type of lock they have. To determine this information, you can use the `tf status /format:detailed` command.

Note that locking should be used only to temporarily lock a particular file or folder. The lock is held as part of the locking user's workspace. If you wish to restrict the ability of developers to edit a file or folder for a longer term (for example, if you want to restrict access to a branch in your codebase that represents the state of the code in production), then you should consider using version control permissions as detailed later in this chapter.

You can unlock a file at any time using the unlock command, but locks are also automatically released when you check in any changes related to that item in version control.

Check-In of Pending Changes

As you make changes to the files in your workspace, you are building up a list of *pending changes*. Any changes you make (edits, adds, deletes, undeletes, renames, moves, branches, merges, and so on) are stored as pending changes in your workspace.

In Team Foundation Server, when you wish to commit your list of changes to the server, you perform a *check-in*, as shown in Figure 6-7.

FIGURE 6-7: Pending Changes in Team Explorer

UNLOCKING FILES OF OTHER USERS

Occasionally, you will need to remove the lock placed on a file by another user in your system—for example, when that person has left the company, or is unavailable for a long period of time. To perform this operation, you need the `UnlockOther` permission in version control, which is granted to team project administrators by default.

If you have permission, you can easily unlock individual files using the command-line `tf lock /lock:none` command, from the Team Foundation Server Sidekicks tool, or from the Team Members Team Foundation Server Power Tool in Visual Studio.

If you need to remove locks because the users have left the company and they will no longer be working on the codebase, then the easiest way is to delete their workspaces. This will not only remove the locks contained in the workspaces, but also free up the resources associated with keeping track of that user's workspace. To do this, use the command-line `tf workspace /owner:FormerUserName` to find the workspaces belonging to that user and then the `tf workspace /delete WorkspaceName;FormerUserName` command, or the Team Foundation Sidekicks utility available from `http://www.attrice.info/cm/tfs/`.

A check-in is performed as a single atomic transaction. During the check-in operation, the server first checks to see if you are able to perform the check-in for these files (that is, you have the "Check in" permission for the files set to Allow), that there are no check-in locks on the files, and that you are attempting to check in a change of the latest version of the file. If, for some reason, the check-in cannot occur (for example, because someone else has edited a file while you had it checked out and has committed the changes), then the entire check-in operation will fail. You will be informed of the reason, along with instructions on how to take corrective action. This is a different behavior from systems such as VSS that do not have the notion of an atomic check-in.

Assuming you are able to check in the files, the modified files are uploaded to the server and committed to the version control repository, along with any comment that you may have provided with the change. Once a set of changes has been committed, it is known as a *changeset*. (Changesets are examined in more detail shortly.)

Related Work Items

While performing a check-in, it is best practice to also associate the change with a *work item* (such as a bug, task, feature, requirement, user story, and so on). In this way, you can easily get end-to-end traceability of requirements on through to changes of code, and into builds, which is a key feature of Team Foundation Server.

COMMENTING ON YOUR CHECK-INS

As is common with version control systems, when performing a check-in to Team Foundation Server, you can provide a comment to summarize your change. It is a best practice to add a comment, and with Team Foundation Server, you can actually enforce this by using a check-in policy. In previous versions of Team Foundation Server, the Changeset Comments Policy was available as part of the Team Foundation Server Power Tools, but in Visual Studio 2012 and 2013 and Team Explorer Everywhere for Team Foundation Server 2012 and 2013, it now ships as standard. Adding comments means that when you look at the history later, it is easy to quickly see why changes were made.

When providing comments, you should concentrate on *why* you were making the change, not *what*. For example "edited HelloWorld.cs" or "Fixed bug 1234" are not particularly useful comments because you could easily get that information from looking at the details of the changeset. Instead, the comment "Refactored code into more discrete methods to make it easier to test and maintain" would be much more useful.

> **NOTE** *For more information on work items, see Part III (Chapters 12 through 16) of this book.*

Included and Excluded Changes

When checking in files, the changes that you wish to be included in the check-in operation are listed in the Included Changes section of the Pending Changes page. You can exclude changes by dragging them from the Included Changes section over to the Excluded Changes section or by right-clicking on the files and selecting Exclude. When you exclude a file from being checked in, this is remembered in future Visual Studio sessions. This might be useful, for example, if you have edited a web .config file to switch on some debugging to help you with a bug that you are trying to fix, but you do not want to accidentally check that file in.

With excluded changes, you can drag-and-drop them back into the Included Changes section or right-click on them and select Include if you want to check them into a future changeset. Alternatively, you can right-click Perform an Undo to restore the file back to the version it was before you started editing it.

Detected Changes

In the Excluded Changes section in Figure 6-7, you can also see an area for Detected Changes. This is important, as it shows changes that the Local Workspace disk scanner has detected that have occurred outside Visual Studio, for which you might wish to pend changes. Clicking on the Detected Changes link will show the Promote Candidate Changes dialog box (see Figure 6-8).

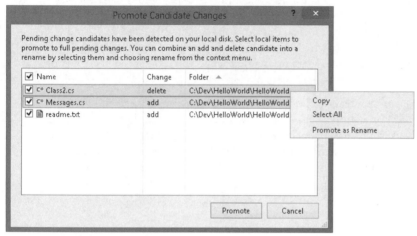

FIGURE 6-8: Promote Candidate Changes dialog box

In the example shown in Figure 6-8, three changes have been detected that occurred outside of Visual Studio. The file readme.txt was added into a folder covered by the working folder mappings and Class2.cs was renamed to Messages.cs. As discussed earlier in this chapter, if renames are performed inside Visual Studio or Eclipse, then the appropriate rename pending change will be created and stored in the history for that file. However, if the files were renamed outside of Visual Studio or Eclipse, then this will show up as an add and a delete of the file. To tell Team Foundation Server that this is a rename and therefore maintain the full history, you can select both changes, right-click, and select Promote as Rename, as shown in Figure 6-8.

Ignoring Files

If the Local Workspace disk scanner has detected files that you never wish to be part of version control, you can specify that they be ignored by right-clicking on the file and selecting the appropriate option, as shown in Figure 6-9.

This will create a file called .tfIgnore containing the details of the filename (or pattern) that should be ignored. Once checked in, other team members will inherit these ignore settings, which allows you to ensure that they do not accidentally add the files that you have said should be ignored by Team Foundation Server.

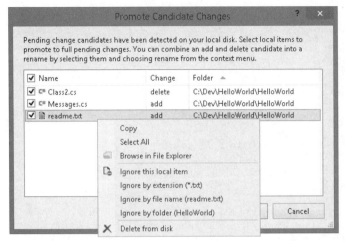

FIGURE 6-9: Ignoring changes from the Promote Candidate Changes dialog box

.TFIGNORE FILE SYNTAX

The syntax of the .tfIgnore file allows for more complex ignore patterns than are possible to configure using the menu options in the Promote Candidate Changes dialog box. The .tfIgnore file is a text file and the settings in it apply recursively to all folders below it in the workspace unless the pattern is prefixed by the \ character. Wildcards such as * and ? are allowed, and you can begin the ignore pattern with a path to make it more specific (but wildcard patterns are not permitted in the path portion, just in the filename portion of the pattern). A hash (#) character at the start of the line allows you to create a comment for documentation purposes. An exclamation point (!) means that you would like to specifically include files of that pattern when they might otherwise be ignored because of the project collection global exclusion patterns or by a .tfIgnore file higher up in the folder hierarchy. Finally, to make it easier to apply a .tfIgnore pattern cross-platform, a path separator character can be either a forward slash (/) or a backward slash (\) character and they are interpreted as path separators on Windows and UNIX file systems alike.

Because of the similarity of the .tfIgnore file syntax to similar files for other version control systems, such as .cvsIgnore, .svnIgnore, or .gitIgnore, it is often possible to convert ignore file patterns designed for one system to the other just by copying the file and renaming it.

continues

continued

The following is an example of a `.tfIgnore` file:

```
# An example .tfIgnore file

# Excludes all files ending in .txt in Alpha\Beta
# and all its subfolders.
Alpha\Beta\*.txt

# Excludes all files ending in .cpp in this folder only.
\*.cpp
# Excludes all files ending in .cpp in this folder
# and all subfolders.
*.cpp
# If "Contoso" is a folder, then Contoso and all its children are
# excluded. If it is a file, then only the "Contoso" in this
# folder is excluded.
\Contoso
# Include .dll's in the \lib folder inside this project
!\lib\*.dll
```

Check-In Notes

While checking in files, it is often useful to capture metadata about the change from the person committing the check-in. For example, who performed a security review of the changes or a reference to a third-party ticketing system? In other version control systems, this is often implemented by the developers adopting a convention when providing check-in comments. However, Team Foundation Server provides a mechanism for capturing structured data about a check-in—the *check-in notes*.

In the Pending Changes page of Team Explorer, you have direct access to the check-in notes to capture data about the check-in, as shown in Figure 6-7. Check-in notes are all text-based responses and other than a simple check to enforce that a value has been entered, no other validation is available. A check-in note could be many lines (in fact, up to 2GB of data). However, typically it is just a single name or value.

To configure the check-in notes for a team project in Visual Studio, go to Team ➪ Team Project Settings ➪ Source Control. Click the Check-in Notes tab, as shown in Figure 6-10.

From the Check-in Notes tab, you can add, edit, remove, and reorder check-in note titles, as well as make any check-in note field mandatory. If a check-in note is required, then, when a user attempts to perform a check-in without providing a value for that field, the user will be prompted for a value before being allowed to check in.

Check-in Policies

A check-in policy is a piece of code that runs in the client performing the check-in, which validates if the check-in is allowed to occur. For Visual Studio, this code is written in .NET. In Eclipse or the cross-platform command-line client, the check-in policy is written in Java. Figure 6-11 shows the check-in policies available in a standard installation of Visual Studio 2013.

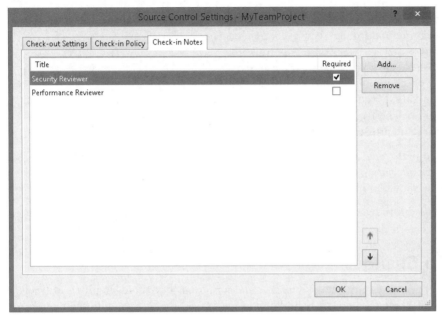

FIGURE 6-10: Check-in Notes tab

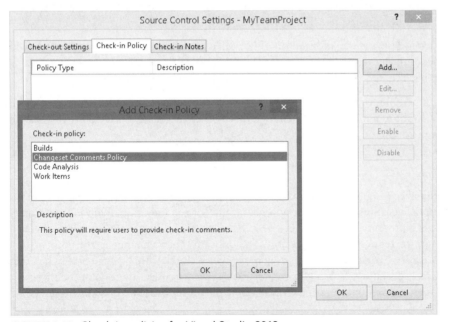

FIGURE 6-11: Check-in policies for Visual Studio 2013

Additional check-in policies are available as part of the Team Foundation Server 2013 Power Tools. Also note that the check-in policies enforced by Team Explorer Everywhere in Eclipse and the cross-platform command-line client must be configured from a Team Explorer Everywhere client by a user with appropriate permission. This is because those clients use a separate (Java-based) implementation for check-in policies. Once configured by the administrator in Visual Studio and in Eclipse, the check-in policies will be in effect for all users checking in affected files to that team project.

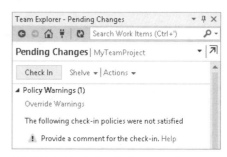

FIGURE 6-12: Policy Failure warning

If a user attempts to perform a check-in that fails validation of the check-in policy, the user will be warned about the policy failure, as shown in Figure 6-12.

If necessary, it is possible to override the policy by clicking the Override Warnings link and entering a comment.

Undo Pending Changes

Even the best developers sometimes make mistakes and wish that they could simply revert their changes instead of checking them in. In Team Foundation Server, this is accomplished by performing an Undo Pending Changes. This will allow you to select which changes you wish to undo, and those files will be rolled back to the previous version that you downloaded into your workspace (not the latest version on the server, because that could be different).

If the change you are undoing is the addition of a file (called an *add*), the pending add is removed from your list of pending changes. However, the file is not automatically deleted from the disk, allowing you to go back to add that file if you have mistakenly undone the change.

Note that undoing a pending change reverts the state of the file back to the point at which you last checked it in. If you want to actually undo a change that you have already checked in, you should look at the `rollback` command covered later in this chapter.

Changeset

When you perform a check-in, all the information about that single atomic check-in operation is stored as a *changeset*. The changeset is the fundamental unit of versioning in Team Foundation Version Control. It is represented by a number—the changeset ID, which is a unique incrementing number across the entire Team Project Collection. The only way that a change to the contents of a version control repository can occur is by creating a changeset. In fact, this is true even when creating the version control repository. When you create a team project collection, one of the things that the setup process does is check in the root of the version control repository $/ as changeset 1.

REMOVING SOURCE CONTROL FILES FROM YOUR LOCAL FILE SYSTEM

You can see that changeset numbers are the unique unit of versioning in Team Foundation Server by noting how to remove a file from your local file system when using a Server Workspace without deleting it from version control.

Occasionally, you will have a file in your workspace that you do not want locally for some reason, but you want to leave it in version control. The obvious course of action is just to go out to the file system and delete it from the disk. This works fine with the new Local Workspaces in Team Foundation Server 2013, but with a Server Workspace it would cause problems. In that case, it is because you have not told Team Foundation Server that you have deleted it locally, so if you perform a Get Latest on the folder, because the server thinks you already have that file version in your Server Workspace, it doesn't send the file to you again until someone makes a change to that file.

However, if you perform a Get Specific Version on the file or folder and set the changeset to 1, the file will be deleted locally and will show in Source Control Explorer as Not Downloaded. Performing a Get Latest on the file will download it again.

Why does this work? Because changeset 1 is the changeset that was created when the team project collection was created, and the root of the version control repository ($/) was checked in. By saying that you want to get the version of the file at changeset 1, you are telling the server you want to get that file as it was at a point in time, which is represented by changeset 1. The file didn't exist at changeset 1, and so it is deleted from your local file system.

You'll be glad to know that if you are using Local Workspaces, which are the default in Team Foundation Server 2013, then you don't have to deal with any of these peculiarities; just delete the file locally and do a Get when you want it back. However, understanding the behavior helps understand changesets in Team Foundation Server regardless of which workspace type you use.

The changeset contains all the information about the change—what adds, edits, renames, deletes, branches, merges, and so on, occurred at that instant—along with the additional information of what work items were associated with the change, any check-in notes, and check-in policy compliance. The date of the changeset, and who checked it in, are also tracked by the server for auditing purposes. Note that this is different from VSS, where the date on the client machines actually could affect the date of that file in the version control repository.

Changeset IDs increment across the whole Project Collection. For example, a check-in to $/TeamProjectA/FileX.txt could be changeset 25, and the next check-in might affect

`$/TeamProjectB/FileY.txt`, making that changeset 26. Therefore, if you view the history of a single file, you will see the IDs of the changesets in which changes occurred to that file. Files are not individually versioned as they are in VSS, but their version is the ID of the changeset in which they were altered, as shown in Figure 6-13.

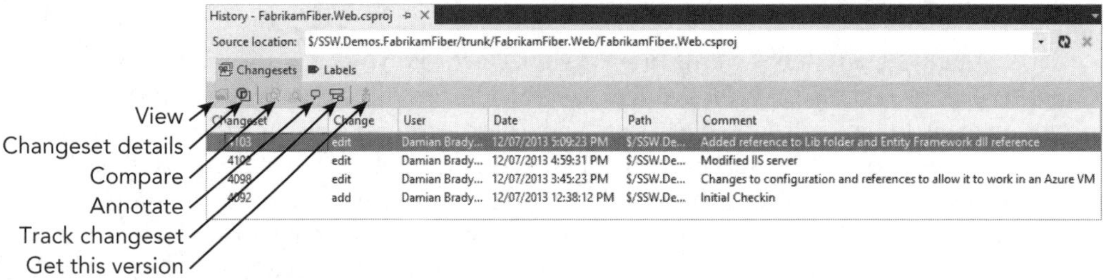

FIGURE 6-13: History view in Visual Studio 2013

The changes that occurred in a changeset are immutable—you cannot go back in time and rewrite history. However, the owner of a changeset (or an administrator) is able to edit the changeset comment and check-in notes after the event. In addition, a work item may be linked to a particular changeset at any point after the changeset is created, and that work item would show up in the associated work items channel when viewing the changeset details.

> ### ROLLING BACK A CHANGESET
>
> Occasionally, a change will be committed to the repository that needs to be reverted. In Team Foundation Server 2010, rolling back a change was only available from the command line. However, since Team Foundation Server 2012 you have been able to roll back a change from the history view by right-clicking, or from the changeset details page in Team Explorer.

Shelvesets

Sometimes, when you work on a set of files, it is useful to store the changes on the server without committing those changes to the main code line that the rest of the team is working on. Perhaps because you want to save progress on a particularly large change, you might want to share a set of changes with a colleague on a different machine. Team Foundation Server provides a simple mechanism to help in those instances—the *shelveset*.

A set of pending changes can be saved to the server in a shelveset—a process called *shelving*. A shelveset is uniquely identified by the owner and a name given to the shelveset.

Shelvesets share much in common with changesets. They can contain the same metadata (work item associations, check-in notes, comments, and so on). However, they are not versioned in the same way. If the same person saves a set of changes to a shelveset with the same name, the contents of that shelveset will be overridden with the contents of the new shelveset. In addition, shelvesets can be deleted. Unlike when a file is deleted in version control, if you delete a shelveset, the contents of that shelveset are gone. A shelveset cannot be undeleted. Therefore, a shelveset is a temporary store of data on the server, but one whose lifetime is controlled by the owner of the shelveset.

To get the contents of a shelveset into a workspace, you first find the shelveset and then you *unshelve* it. To find a shelveset belonging to you or another user, go to the Pending Changes page in Team Explorer and select Find Shelvesets from the Actions menu. You can unshelve into different workspaces, on different computers. You can e-mail the name of a shelveset to a team member, and that person can find it by your user name, look at the details, compare the files in it with other versions, and even unshelve the contents into their workspace, provided they have suitable working folder mappings for the shelved files.

For many instances, judicious use of shelvesets can be a quick and easy way of passing around and storing version control data with your team, and can reduce the need for temporary private branches of code. However, shelvesets do take up some resources on the server, so you should delete old shelvesets when no longer needed.

Shelvesets are used by the My Work feature covered later in this chapter and the gated build and buddy build features discussed in Chapter 18.

Branches

Generally speaking, a *branch* in Team Foundation Server can be thought of as a folder that contains a copy of the source tree from another area in the tree taken at a point in time. A branch is useful when parallel areas of development are required.

> **NOTE** *For more information about branching concepts, see Chapter 5.*
> *For more detail and best practices on how to branch and merge with Team*
> *Foundation Server, see Chapter 10, and for some examples of using branching in*
> *common version control scenarios see Chapter 11.*

In Team Foundation Server 2005 and 2008, a branch was exactly that—a folder. However, in Team Foundation Server 2010, branches were promoted to be a first-class citizen. As shown in Figure 6-14, a branch has a unique icon in source control to distinguish it from regular folders. It also can contain additional metadata (such as the owner), and description, as well as the relationships between it and other branches.

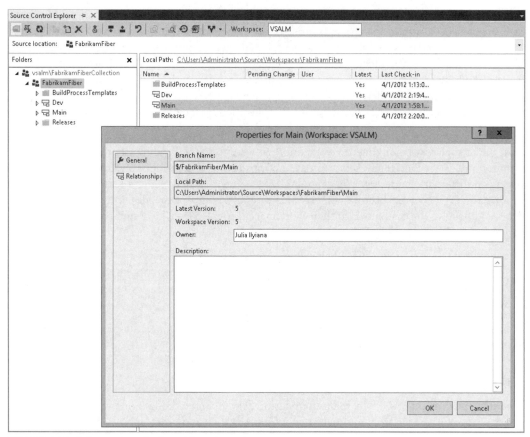

FIGURE 6-14: Information displayed for a branch

You can convert an existing folder to a full branch object very easily by right-clicking the folder in Source Control Explorer and selecting Branching and Merging ➪ Convert to Branch. If you created a `Main` folder when adding your solution to version control at the beginning of this chapter, then convert this to a full branch now.

USING SOURCE CONTROL EXPLORER

The *Source Control Explorer* (see Figure 6-15) provides a view of your current Team Foundation Version Control workspace. You can show the Source Control Explorer by clicking the link in the Team Explorer home page or in Visual Studio by going to View ➪ Other Windows ➪ Source Control Explorer.

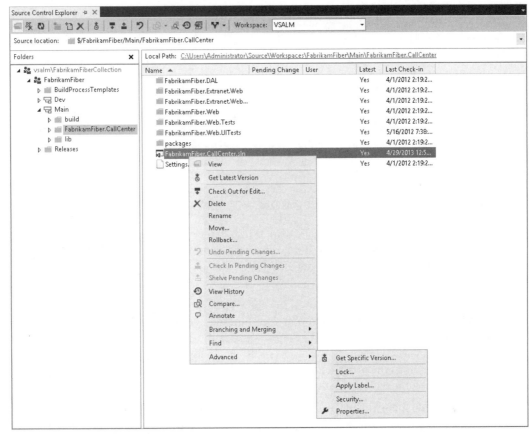

FIGURE 6-15: Source Control Explorer

Apart from the files and folders, the Source Control Explorer contains several useful areas. In Visual Studio 2013, the toolbar for the source control editor is inside the control—not part of the main Visual Studio toolbars. In addition to shortcuts to a variety of actions, the toolbar also contains the Workspace selection drop-down menu, which shows you which workspace you are currently viewing in Source Control Explorer, and allows you to quickly switch between workspaces or manage workspaces.

BE CAREFUL WHEN SWITCHING WORKSPACES

In Visual Studio 2013, a lot has been done to reduce friction and also to allow you to be very productive with version control without having to understand the concept of workspaces. Therefore, you often have just a single workspace when starting out with Team Foundation Server. However, if you do create additional workspaces, be cautious that switching the workspace you are looking at in Source Control Explorer does not affect the workspace viewed in the Pending Changes page (which is switchable separately in the Pending Changes page when you have multiple workspaces available).

The Source Location shows the server path that you are currently navigating. You can type in or paste a server path if you know exactly where you want to browse. When you press Enter, you will navigate to that area. If you click the drop-down arrow, you can navigate up the folder hierarchy from your current location. The Local Path shows which folder maps to the server path being viewed. If a mapping is present, Local Path is clickable, and doing so will open a Windows Explorer window showing that local path.

From Source Control Explorer, you can view, add, delete, and undelete files, as well as check in, check out, branch, merge, view history, view properties, and perform all other version control operations. Think of Source Control Explorer as your master control area for Team Foundation Version Control.

MANAGING SOLUTION SOURCE CONTROL BINDINGS

The mapping between a solution in Visual Studio and the version control settings is stored in the `.sln` file. If you wish to customize the bindings, or remove them entirely, then go to File ⇨ Source Control ⇨ Change Source Control while editing a file in the solution.

If you used the VSS upgrade wizard to import a VSS repository into Team Foundation Server, you should find that your bindings for the solution have been automatically converted for you. If not, you can use the `tfpt bind` command in the Team Foundation Server Power Tools to do this in an automated way. Or you can fix the bindings the first time you open the solution by removing the old bindings and adding the new ones in the Source Control dialog box.

However, if you manually moved your source over from the latest version from VSS or any other version control system, you might have to modify the bindings the first time you open the solution. Equally, if you have been provided with a copy of some source code that was previously checked into a Team Foundation Server repository that you do not have access to, then you can use this dialog box to remove the bindings.

Chapter 9 provides more information on migrating from legacy version control systems.

Viewing History

To view the history of a file or folder, in Source Control Explorer, right-click the file or folder, and select View History from the context menu. This opens a new document tab in Visual Studio.

The new History window is now a tabbed document window in Visual Studio. This allows you to open multiple History windows for research, something that was not possible in Visual Studio 2010 or below. The History window also provides a view of both the changesets associated with the file or folder, as well as any labels.

You have several options when you click the Changeset tab. You can select a changeset and click the View button to view the file version for that particular changeset. You can click the Changeset Details button to view the details for a particular changeset, including all the files that make up the changeset and any associated work items. You can compare two different versions of a file or folder to see the differences. Clicking the Annotate button allows you to see, line by line, who made what changes to a particular file.

You can select a changeset and click the Get This Version button. This will replace the current version of this file in your workspace with the selected version, enabling you to easily return to an earlier version of a file. Finally, you can right-click a file version and click Rollback Entire Changeset. The effect of this is to revert all the changes that were made in that changeset. Note that this applies not just to this file, but to all files in the selected changeset.

The History window also allows you to track the changes across multiple branches, merges, and renames.

> **NOTE** *Chapter 10 provides more information on branching and merging.*

Labeling Files

A *label* is a marker that can be attached to files and folders. This marker allows all the files and folders labeled together to be retrieved as one collective unit. Labeling was available in previous versions of Visual Studio, but it had some issues. Labeling an item could sometimes be a tedious and complex process, and labeling a large number of files could be very slow.

To create a new label, in Source Control Explorer, right-click the file or folder you want to label, and from the Advanced context menu, select Apply Label. This opens the New Label window, as shown in Figure 6-16.

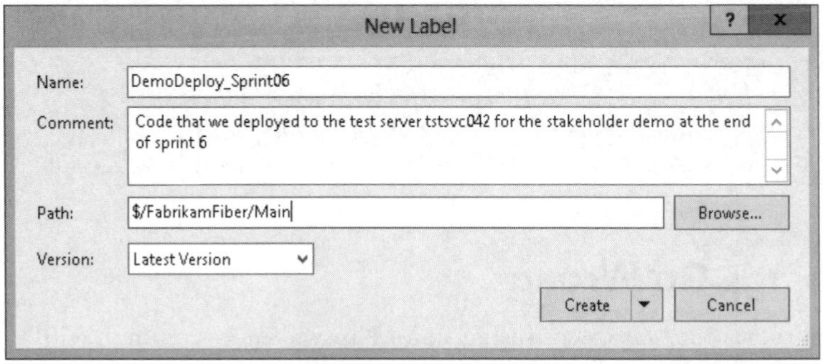

FIGURE 6-16: New Label window

In this window, you can enter the label name and a comment. You can also select the version that you want to label. You can choose to label by Changeset, Date, Label, Latest Version, or Workspace Version. Click the Create button to create the label.

Notice that the Create button is a drop-down arrow. Clicking the arrow provides you with two options. You can create the label as is, or you can create the label and then edit it. If you select Create and Edit, the label will be created, and you will be presented with a new tab, as shown in Figure 6-17.

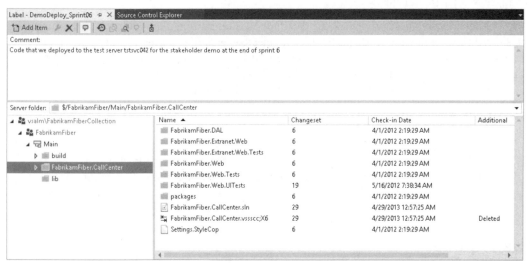

FIGURE 6-17: Using Create and Edit to create a label

This tab allows you to make multiple changes to the label. You can add new files to the label. You can change the version of an individual file that the label is currently applied to. And you can remove files from the label. All of this is made easily accessible by using a tree-view control.

> **NOTE** *In Team Foundation Server, labels can be edited at any point after they are created by any user who has the "Administer shelved changes" permission set to Allow. This is very different from VSS, where labels are fixed once created, and more like the tagging behavior in SVN. Because of this reason, labels in Team Foundation Server should not be used for strict auditing purposes.*

Recovering When Things Go Wrong

Occasionally, you can get your workspace into a confusing state. This was more common with Server Workspaces when you were initially learning Team Foundation Server and were doing a lot of changes outside of the IDE. However, even with Local Workspaces things can sometimes get confusing when you get started.

Once you understand Team Foundation Version Control, you will find that this never happens to you. However, until you understand how the server thinks about version control, the following tips can help you get your workspace back into a state that is more understandable. If you find that you have a development workflow that requires you to take any of the following steps as part of a normal day, then you are doing something wrong, and you should look again at how you are using Team Foundation Version Control.

Get Specific, Force Overwrite, Force Get

The Get Specific Version dialog box has options to "Overwrite writable files that are not checked out" and "Overwrite all files even if the local version matches the specified version." These two options can help you if you are using a Server Workspace, but have been editing files outside of Visual Studio or Eclipse and you want to replace them with the server version.

The default behavior when doing a Get is to warn you when you attempt to download a new version of a file that is writable locally, and not to download it. This is to prevent overwriting of changes that you may have made locally and wanted to keep.

If you force a Get, you will download all files again, even if the server thinks you already have a copy in your workspace. This allows you to recover from the situation where you have deleted a file locally in a Server Workspace but have not told Team Foundation Server, and so it will normally not send the file to you when you perform a Get because it thinks you have it. The Force options are almost never required when using a Local Workspace.

Detect Local Changes in Eclipse

You can detect local changes in the Team Foundation Server plug-in for Eclipse, available as part of Team Explorer Everywhere. You can do this by selecting Detect Local Changes from the Actions menu in Team Explorer, or by right-clicking a project in Package Explorer. If you have a Local Workspace, a full disk scan will be performed to detect changes. Even when used with a Server Workspace, your Local Workspace will be compared with the server version, and the plug-in will attempt to check out files that you have changed.

Re-Create the Workspace

If all else fails, then the nuclear option is to go to the Manage Workspaces dialog box (File ➪ Source Control ➪ Workspaces in Visual Studio), delete your workspace, and create it again. Move any files that were in your local working folders to a temporary directory, and start all over again.

This is the Team Foundation Server equivalent of rebooting your version control state. When you delete a workspace, all information about what files you have downloaded, what locks you might have invoked, and what files you had checked out is removed. Therefore, this option should not be taken lightly but is guaranteed to get you back into a known good state.

KEEPING ON TASK WITH MY WORK

If you have Visual Studio Ultimate 2012 or 2013, or Visual Studio Premium 2012 or 2013 installed, then you will see the My Work section in Team Explorer. This feature was added to Visual Studio 2012 and was designed to help you switch context between activities, thus allowing you to suspend and resume tasks and bring along all the information and tool windows you need to work on those tasks.

A common problem with development is how long it takes you to get "into the zone" when solving a problem or developing a feature. For example, imagine that you are working on a new complex task; you have it partially implemented, but the code is nowhere near finished yet. You have a set of files open in Visual Studio, a bunch of tool windows just in the position you are working, and a set of breakpoints and watches that you have set up to help you solve the exact problem you are working on. But then an urgent bug fix is found that needs your immediate attention, or maybe colleagues are requesting that you do a code review so that they can get their work checked in and move onto the next task. Getting back to where you were before the interruption can take a long time, not just getting your brain back into gear, but also all the mechanics of getting the files open again, and the windows and breakpoints set up how you wanted them.

The My Work page in Visual Studio aims to help you get back into the zone as quickly as possible and stay in the zone as much as possible by centralizing all your activities together. This makes it easier for you to switch contexts when the inevitable interruptions occur and also makes it even easier to keep your team up to date with what you are working on.

As previously stated, the My Work page is available only if you have Visual Studio Ultimate 2012 or 2013, or Visual Studio Premium 2012 or 2013 installed on your machine. If you have one of those versions installed then you will see My Work is the first tile of your Team Explorer home page. Clicking the link will take you to the My Work page shown in Figure 6-18.

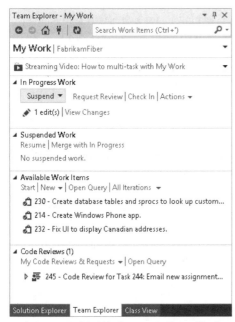

FIGURE 6-18: My Work page in Team Explorer

Note that the My Work page automatically picks up what your team context is from Team Explorer and shows you work items assigned to you in the Available Work Items section. If you compare the available work items in Figure 6-18 with the agile planning task board view on the web, as shown in Figure 6-19, you can see the same three tasks assigned to Damian Brady.

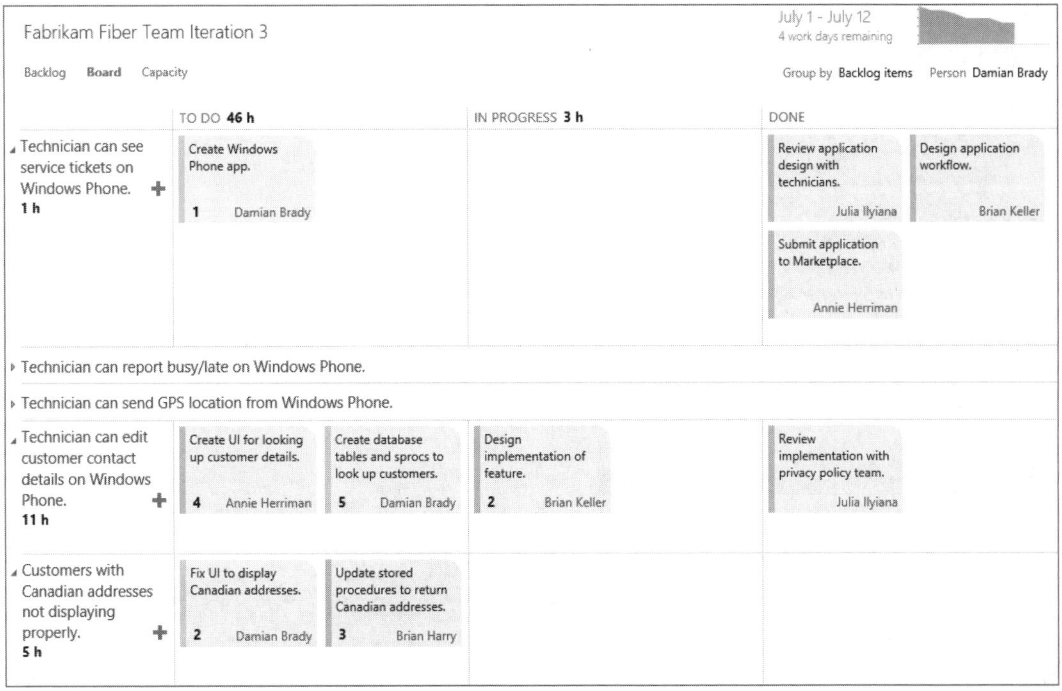

FIGURE 6-19: Agile task board displaying work to do

NOTE *The Agile planning tools are covered in detail in Chapter 14.*

In this example, start work on Task 214, which is to create a Windows Phone application. To track what you are working on (and also to let the team know that you are working on it), you drag the task from Available Work Items up to In Progress Work. You could also right-click the task in the Available Work section and select Add to In Progress. The My Work page will now look as shown in Figure 6-20.

When you move the work item from Available to In Progress, Visual Studio updates the status of the work item accordingly. This makes it easy for you to remember what you are currently working on, but also allows your team members to see what is happening when they check in with the task board, as shown in Figure 6-21, where the highlighted task has moved over to the In Progress column.

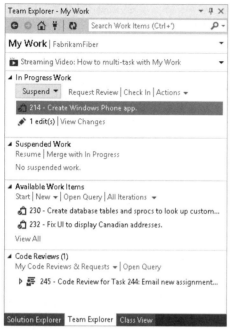

FIGURE 6-20: My Work updated

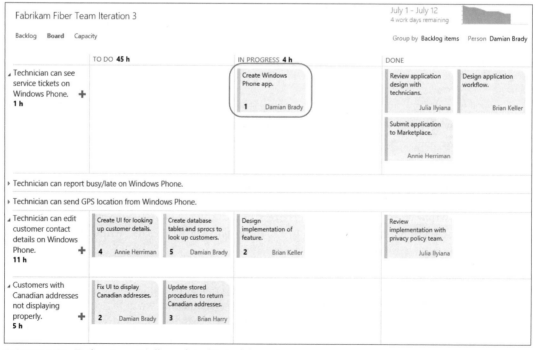

FIGURE 6-21: Task automatically updated in task board

LIMITED SYNCHRONIZATION OF IN PROGRESS WORK

Moving work items between states on the boards in Team Web Access is distinct from moving them between sections in My Work. In Visual Studio, you are identifying the items you are working on right now, while the State of a work item represents its state in the sprint as a whole. A work item may be In Progress without anyone actively working on it.

Moving from Available to In Progress in My Work will change the status of your work item to In Progress; however, moving it back to Available or suspending work will not reset the value to To Do. Similarly, moving a work item to In Progress on the board will not move it to In Progress in Visual Studio.

This limited synchronization makes sense if you consider that a single developer may have a number of workspaces or Visual Studio instances running in different locations, each of which is being used for working on different tasks. Indeed, a team member may not be using Visual Studio at all in the case of designers or database specialists.

As you start to make changes for your task, the state of your version control changes are shown in the My Work page along with a `View Changes` link to take you to the pending changes page to see more information, as shown in Figure 6-22.

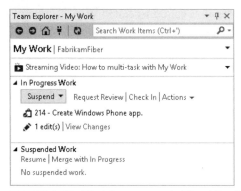

FIGURE 6-22: Work in progress in Visual Studio

Then a coworker drops by your desk and asks you to take a quick look at the code review that she just sent, as she needs to get the fix checked as soon as possible. You want to *suspend* your current work so that you can go do the code review and then come back to your task later. Simply press the Suspend button in the My Work page.

When you press the Suspend button, it will create a new shelveset for you containing your changes in version control. The shelveset will, by default, have the title of the first work item you added to your In Progress Work section, but you can edit the name before pressing the Suspend button again, as shown in Figure 6-23.

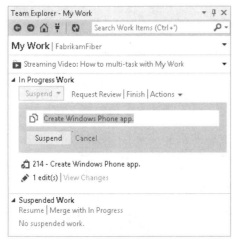

FIGURE 6-23: Suspending work

In addition to creating the shelveset, Visual Studio also stored the windows that you had open, the position of your tool windows and breakpoints, and so on as properties on that shelveset.

Next, you will do the code review as requested and send over your comments. A step-by-step guide to the code review process in Visual Studio appears later in the chapter.

Once you have finished reviewing your coworker's code, you are ready to pick up where you were. Returning to the My Work page in Team Explorer, you see that your Suspended Work section contains what you were last working on, as shown in Figure 6-24, which is very handy in case you had forgotten. Select the suspended work and press Resume.

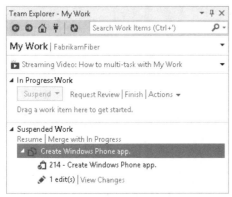

FIGURE 6-24: Resuming suspended work

This quickly unshelves the changes, restores the files that you had open, opens tool windows, and restores your breakpoints.

Note that if you forget to resume your work immediately, but instead do what many people do and just come back to your desk and start working on something else, you can select the suspended work and merge it with the current work in progress (thanks to the changes in Team Foundation Server 2012 to support merge on unshelve and all the automerge improvements).

When the task is complete, you can press the Check In link directly in the My Work page. That will take you to the Pending Changes page to review your changes, enter a comment, and check in. Note that if you are associating a work item on check-in as Resolving the work item, then when you perform the check-in, the work item will automatically be moved onto its next state, which in your case is Done.

The work item is then updated in the team task board, and a link is created between the changeset created and the work item you associated the change with. All this happened simply and easily by using the My Work page.

> **NOTE** *The My Work page is so useful that you might find yourself going there a lot. A quick keyboard shortcut to get to the My Work page from anywhere in Visual Studio is Ctrl+0, then M. For a complete list of keyboard shortcuts in Team Explorer see* `http://aka.ms/TEKeys2013`*.*

MANAGING CODE REVIEWS

Code reviews are formal or informal reviews of code by a lead or peer developer before a developer checks in his or her source code changes. Following are some examples of what code reviewers look for when they review the code:

➤ Best practices

➤ Potential bugs

➤ Performance

➤ Security threats

➤ Following internal coding standards

➤ Previous code review suggested changes

Visual Studio Premium 2013 and Visual Studio Ultimate 2013 contain a code review feature that, in conjunction with Team Foundation Server 2013, allows a rich code review experience.

> **NOTE** *While the Premium 2013 and Ultimate 2013 editions of Visual Studio contain a rich code review experience, code reviews can still be carried out by developers not using one of those Visual Studio SKUs by using Team Foundation Server shelvesets to pass around the files to be reviewed and by making use of Check-In notes to record the code reviewer for a particular changeset.*

> **NOTE** *Team Foundation Server 2013 introduces a feature called* lightweight code comments *for commenting on changes from within the browser. In Team Web Access, team members can add notes to an entire changeset or shelveset, a single file, or even to individual lines within a file. Users can reply to comments, creating a hierarchy of messages like a message board.*

Requesting a Code Review

You can request a code review of your current pending changes from the Home page of Team Explorer from the My Work page, as shown in Figure 6-25, or from the Actions menu in the Pending Changes page of Team Explorer. Alternatively, if you would like to request a code review of changes already committed to the repository, then you can right-click a changeset in the History view and request a review from there, as shown in Figure 6-26.

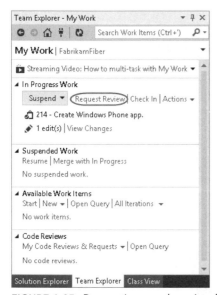

FIGURE 6-25: Requesting a code review from the My Work page

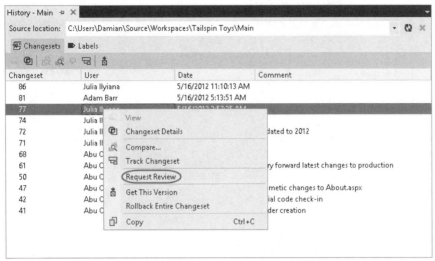

FIGURE 6-26: Requesting a code review of a changeset from the History view

Regardless of how you request the code review, you will be taken to the New Code Review page of Team Explorer, as shown in Figure 6-27. Here, you enter the name of the people you want to perform your review (you must provide at least one name, but you may request several reviewers). You also provide a title for the code review (which is taken from the Changeset comment or any currently associated work items by default). Then you can specify an area path for your code reviews—by default, these are scoped to the Team Project, but if you have areas defined for the different elements of your project, then you might want to have reviews categorized by these areas. Finally, you can add a description about what it is in particular you want the reviewers to focus on and press Submit Request. Behind the scenes, a new Code Review Request work item is created to help track the status of your review with a Code Review Response work item to track the responses. If this is a review of pending changes (as opposed to a review of a checked-in changeset), then a new shelveset will be created in Team Foundation Server containing your selected changes.

Performing a Code Review

Your team members will see your Code Review requests appear in their own My Work view, as shown in Figure 6-28, from where they can open them. Selecting the link below the Code Reviews section heading in the My Work page allows you to filter the reviews to show code reviews that you have initiated, your reviews and requests for reviews sent to you, incoming code review requests, and recently finished or recently closed reviews.

> **NOTE** *You may want to configure an e-mail alert so that team members are notified on new Code Review requests by e-mail as soon as they are created or when someone leaves comments for them on a requested review. That way, if users are not in Visual Studio or not using the My Work page, they will know about a Code Review request. You can edit alerts by going to Team ⇨ Project Alerts in Visual Studio or by viewing the page directly in Web Access.*

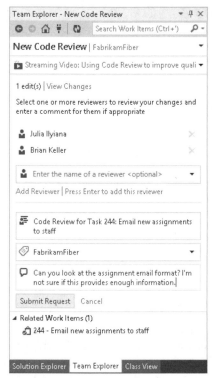

FIGURE 6-27: Creating a New Code Review request

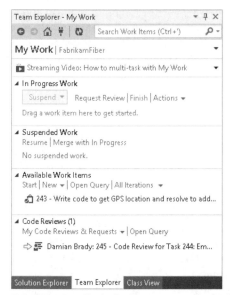

FIGURE 6-28: Code Review requests in the My Work Page

Incoming requests are indicated by the arrow next to them, as shown in Figure 6-28. You can open a Code Review request by double-clicking it, which will show you the Code Review page in Team Explorer, as shown in Figure 6-29. You can see the details of the code review, the reviewers, related work items, files, and any comments left by other reviewers.

The first thing you should do is use the links at the top of the code review, as shown in Figure 6-29, to indicate whether you Accept or Decline the Code Review request. This step is completely optional but is useful to let others on your team know that you are signing up to do the code review. If you decline the request, then you should provide a comment as to why you don't need to review it. You may also want to add additional reviewers if you think that someone else on the team should give a second opinion on the changes.

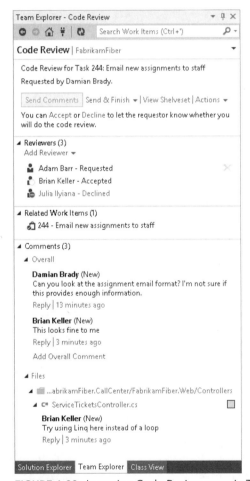

FIGURE 6-29: Incoming Code Review page in Team Explorer

Once you have accepted the code review, you can inspect each file in the review. Clicking a file will open it in the diff view. From here you can select an area of code, right-click, and leave a comment on particular line ranges. You can right-click a particular file in the Code Review page and select Add File Comment to leave an overall comment for the entire file. You can also use the check boxes against the files in the Code Review page to indicate that you have reviewed that file, also shown in Figure 6-30.

FIGURE 6-30: Conducting a code review in Visual Studio

Finally, you can leave an overall comment on the review and then click the Send and Finish link shown in Figure 6-30 to indicate whether the code review is good (i.e., can be checked in) or needs work before being checked in (and possibly another code review).

Completing the Code Review

As you receive code review comments, you will see them arrive in the My Work page in Team Explorer. You may also want to sign up for e-mail alerts so that you are notified when you get code review comments back. From the Code Review page in Team Explorer, shown in Figure 6-31, you can view the shelveset that contains the code review changes and easily unshelve the changes back into your workspace. Doing so allows you to make any changes as appropriate based on the comments from your team before checking the code in. For each comment provided, you may reply to that user if you need to have further discussion on a point. You can also use the check marks on the right side of the page to keep track of when you have completed all the changes you want to make to files based on the feedback.

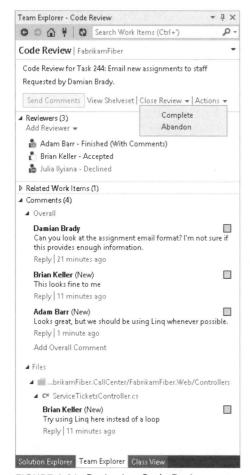

FIGURE 6-31: Reviewing Code Review responses

Finally, assuming the code review is now complete, you can close the review as Complete or Abandoned. Use Abandoned if the comments that came back indicated that you needed to rethink your changes and will be sending those for another code review, or mark as Complete if you have responded to all the comments and taken action as appropriate.

TEAM FOUNDATION SERVER VERSION CONTROL IN ECLIPSE

So far, this chapter has mostly focused on the experience when performing version control operations inside Visual Studio 2013. However, Team Foundation Server is available inside a number of environments, not just older versions of Visual Studio (such as Visual Studio 2012, Visual Studio 2010, and Visual Studio 2008, which have Team Foundation Server integration), but also even older versions or IDEs that support the Microsoft Source Code Control Interface (MSSCCI) API for version control.

Team Explorer Everywhere is available to help you connect to Team Foundation Server from within Eclipse or from UNIX-based operating systems such as Mac OS X, Linux, Solaris, AIX, or HP-UX. With the 2012 release of Team Foundation Server, Microsoft made Team Explorer Everywhere available free of charge to anyone with the appropriate license to connect to a Team Foundation Server (i.e., anyone who has a Team Foundation Server Client Access License). Previously, Team Explorer Everywhere was available as a separate commercial tool from Microsoft and before that from a partner company called Teamprise. But, because of the popularity of Team Foundation Server for use in enterprises for their Eclipse and cross-platform development, as well as their .NET development, the decision was made to increase the investment in those integrations and make it part of the core Team Foundation Server offering.

Team Explorer Everywhere is an implementation of the Team Foundation Server protocol written entirely in Java, using the same web services that the .NET implementation uses. Therefore, the Team Explorer Everywhere clients run anywhere that Eclipse and Java run, not just on Windows, but on Mac, Linux, and many common UNIX platforms. Microsoft is fully committed to keeping Team Explorer Everywhere and Eclipse up to date so that developers in Eclipse can be full contributors to a software development team using Team Foundation Server.

While many of the experiences in working with Team Foundation Server in Eclipse are similar to working inside Visual Studio 2013, as shown in Figure 6-32 (especially the Source Control Editor, work item tracking, and build automation functionality), there are a few differences because of the way that version control tools typically integrate with an Eclipse environment.

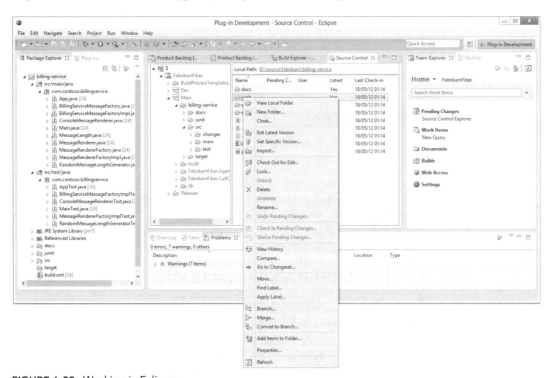

FIGURE 6-32: Working in Eclipse

ECLIPSE WORKSPACES VERSUS TEAM FOUNDATION SERVER WORKSPACES

Unfortunately, the word "workspace" in the Eclipse and Team Foundation Server worlds means different, yet slightly overlapping, things. A Team Foundation Server workspace was defined earlier in this chapter. The Eclipse workspace contains a set of Eclipse projects, along with the set of user preferences for that instance and other configuration data.

However, the set of projects in an Eclipse workspace maps well into the concept of working folder mappings in a Team Foundation Server workspace. To reduce the complexity of dealing with multiple concepts called "workspace," the Team Foundation Server plug-in for Eclipse allows for only one active Team Foundation Server workspace per Eclipse workspace. In Team Explorer Everywhere for Team Foundation Server 2013, you can easily switch which Team Foundation Server workspace is the active one from the Pending Changes page in Team Explorer.

Installing the Team Foundation Server Plug-In for Eclipse

To install the Team Foundation Server plug-in from the media, go to Help ➪ Install New Software in Eclipse. This displays the Available Software wizard. Click the Add button to add an Eclipse update repository, and then enter the location as `http://dl.microsoft.com/eclipse/tfs`. Then click OK.

Select the check box for the Team Foundation Server plug-in for Eclipse. Optionally, you can uncheck the setting for "Contact all update sites during install to find required software." This works because a typical Eclipse-based product contains the requirements for Team Explorer Everywhere, and not checking external update sites will reduce the installation time.

ALTERNATIVE INSTALLATION METHODS

The recommended way to install Team Explorer Everywhere in Eclipse is via the Eclipse marketplace or the Eclipse update site given previously. However, you can also download Team Explorer Everywhere from the Microsoft Download Center or from MSDN.

Go through the rest of the wizard and accept the license terms. Once you click Finish, the Team Foundation Server plug-in should be installed, and you will be prompted to restart Eclipse (which you should do).

This will add the Team Explorer view to Eclipse, and a Team Foundation Exploring perspective that you can use to connect and work with Team Foundation Server resources.

Sharing Eclipse Projects in Team Foundation Server

Now that you have the Team Foundation Server integration installed, the next thing you want to do is add your Eclipse project into Team Foundation Server so that it is shared with the rest of the team. This is done in a similar way to the "Add solution to source control" functionality in Visual Studio.

However, in Eclipse, version control providers make this functionality available by right-clicking the project in Eclipse and selecting Team ⇨ Share Project. This displays a list of version control repository types. As shown in Figure 6-33, Team Foundation Server will now be available in that list.

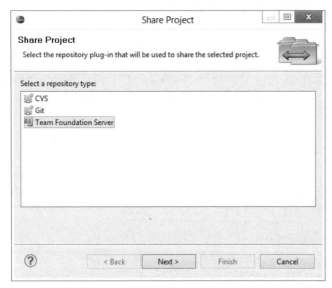

FIGURE 6-33: Team Foundation Server displayed as a repository type

Select Team Foundation Server. On the next screen, you will be prompted to select your Team Foundation Server. If you have not set up an existing Team Foundation Server connection, then you will be prompted for the name or fully qualified URL for your Team Foundation Server instance.

Note that if your Team Foundation Server instance is not installed at `http://server_name:8080/tfs`, you will want to ensure that you share your Team Foundation Server address with the development team using the fully qualified URL (that is, `https://fabrikam.tfspreview.com`) instead of the hostname to ensure that the right connection settings are used.

Once you have selected the server, you will be asked to pick the project collection and team project in which you wish to share your Eclipse project, as shown in Figure 6-34.

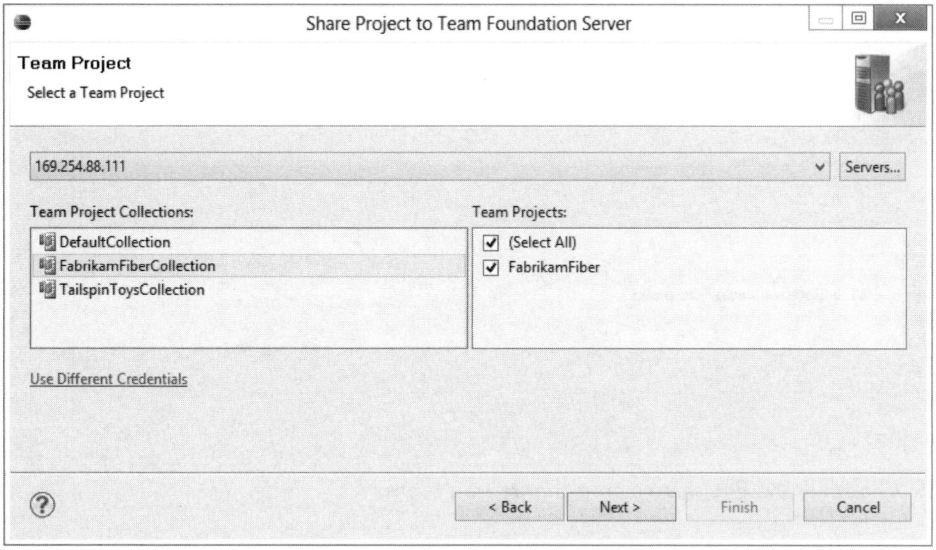

FIGURE 6-34: Sharing a project with Team Foundation Server

Then, on the following page in the wizard, you will be prompted to select which Team Foundation Server workspace to use to share your project. Note that you may wish to use multiple Team Foundation Server workspaces on the machine to keep your Eclipse workspaces separate, or your Eclipse and Visual Studio workspaces separate. However, a single workspace can safely be shared by both Visual Studio and Eclipse on the same machine, should you have both applications installed.

If you have never connected to the Team Foundation Server project collection from this machine before, a new private workspace will have been created for you by default. Select the workspace you require (or add a new one and then select it) and click Next.

You will then be presented with the page shown in Figure 6-35, which asks you where to place your project in the version control repository. Put your project into a folder called `Main` if you think you might want to use the branching features of Team Foundation Server in the future.

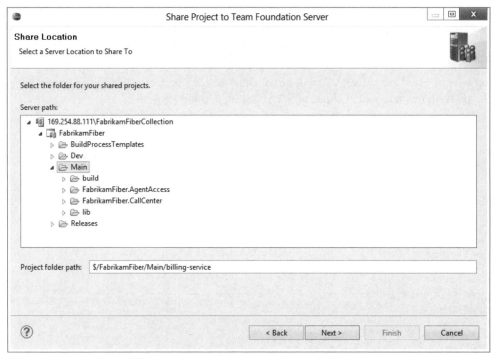

FIGURE 6-35: Choosing where to share a project in version control

The final page in the Share Project Wizard will confirm the details of the sharing, allowing you to review the details before you click Finish. Note that the plug-in will automatically create any required working folder mappings.

Once shared, the project resource in Package Explorer will be decorated, indicating that they are under Team Foundation Server version control; however, they are not available on the server for others to use until you have checked in the files that you are sharing.

You can check in your files from the Pending Changes page in Team Explorer or by right-clicking your project and selecting Team, Check-in. The Pending Changes page in Team Explorer should have been opened for you as soon as you finished sharing the project; however, if you ever lose the Team Explorer window from your perspective, go to Windows ➪ Show View ➪ Other ➪ Team Foundation Server ➪ Team Explorer. You can position the Team Explorer window where it most makes sense to your workflow.

Once you have navigated to the Pending Changes page, check your project into Team Foundation Server by clicking the Check In button, as shown in Figure 6-36.

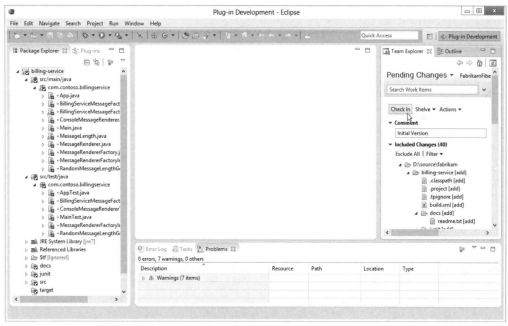

FIGURE 6-36: Check In button in Pending Changes page

Once you have checked in your files, you can work with the rest of your team using Team Foundation Server just as the .NET developers would in Visual Studio. In Eclipse, the version control functionality is available by right-clicking a file and selecting Team from the context menu.

Importing Projects from Team Foundation Server

If someone else on your team has already added the Eclipse project to Team Foundation Server, you will want to download the project locally to work on it. In Eclipse, this is accomplished by importing the project into your Eclipse workspace. You can run the Import Wizard by connecting to Team Foundation Server through the Team Foundation Server Exploring Perspective, performing a Get on the files using Source Control Explorer, and then right-clicking the project folder and selecting Import from the context menu.

A simpler way to run the Import Wizard is to go to File ⇨ Import in Eclipse. Under the Team node, you will find Team Foundation Server if you have the plug-in correctly installed. Connect to the Team Foundation Server project collection and select your workspace in the same way as detailed previously when you looked at the Share Wizard. Then you need to select which project to import, as shown in Figure 6-37.

FIGURE 6-37: Selecting projects to import

You should select the folder that directly contains the Eclipse project (i.e., the one containing the `.project` file). Note that if you have multiple projects to import, you can Shift-click to select a range, or Ctrl-click the individual projects (Command-click on the Mac). With Team Explorer Everywhere, it is recommended that you share your Eclipse `.project` files with Team Foundation Server. However, if you do not, you will want to check the "Show the New Project Wizard for folders that are not Eclipse projects" option on this dialog box so that you can define your project settings.

Finally, you will be given a confirmation page explaining which projects you will be importing before you click Finish to download the files to your local machine.

Now that you have a project in the workspace, right-clicking a file managed by Team Foundation Server and selecting the Team menu will show the available version control functions.

Differences between the Eclipse and Visual Studio Clients

Microsoft is fully committed to supporting the needs of Eclipse developers using Team Foundation Server, but there are some differences between the functionality available in one client over the other. For example, Eclipse developers are often familiar with the notion of *synchronize* (a perspective allowing you to easily see the differences between your Local Workspace and the server repository), and so the Team Foundation Server plug-in for Eclipse provides this capability. The closest alternative in Visual Studio would be a folder compare.

However, the Eclipse integration is designed to provide support for development activities in Eclipse, and so some Team Foundation Server administration activities (such as creating new team projects) are not supported outside of Visual Studio.

Team Foundation Server Version Control from the Command Line

You can manipulate the version control repository from the command line by using the `tf` command (which is short for "Team Foundation"). In fact, the command-line tool offers much more flexibility and functionality.

> **NOTE** *In Visual Studio 2013 in Windows 8 and above, the command-line tools are not added to your start page by default. This means using the global search in Windows will not find them unless you add them to your start page manually.*

On Windows platforms, the command line ships as part of Visual Studio Team Explorer, which is installed as part of Visual Studio 2013. From a VS2013 command prompt, you can use the `tf help` command to see the available functionality. On non-Windows platforms, the command-line client is available as part of Team Explorer Everywhere. Unzip the command-line client and put the `tf` command in your path. You can then use the `tf help` command to get a list of the commands available.

> **NOTE** *The majority of the documentation for the command-line client describes arguments prefixed by a forward-slash character (/). However, certain UNIX shells use the / character as an escape character, meaning that if you wanted to use it on the command line, you would have to escape it (that is, use //). Therefore, both the Windows and cross-platform versions of the `tf` command support the hyphen character (-) as a prefix to arguments. For example, the following commands are identical on Windows:*
>
> ```
> tf checkin /comment:"This is a test"
> tf checkin -comment:"This is a test"
> ```

The cross-platform and Windows clients are broadly compatible with mostly the same commands and arguments supported across versions, allowing for reuse of scripts and integrations using the command-line interface. However, they do come from two different implementations of the command-line interface. The Windows version is written in .NET, and the cross-platform implementation is in Java. Therefore, there are some small differences. However, the majority of functionality is the same with both clients.

Getting Help

As mentioned previously, you can use the `tf help` command to see a list of commands available. To see the syntax for a single command, type `tf help` *command*, where *command* is the name of the command you want to see more about.

> **NOTE** *Consult the MSDN documentation online at* `http://aka.ms/TFS2013cmd` *for more information regarding use of the* `tf` *command line.*

Using the Command Line

Following is an example that shows a very basic way of working with the command line to demonstrate how it works. Assuming you have never connected to Team Foundation Server before, the first thing you must do is create a workspace on your local computer.

```
tf workspace -new -collection:http://servername:8080/tfs/
    defaultCollection -login:user@DOMAIN,Passw0rd MyWorkspace
```

In this example, `MyWorkspace` is the name of your workspace and `http://servername:8080/tfs/defaultCollection` is the URL to your team project collection. You are passing in your credentials with the command. Note that if you do not provide any credentials when you are working on Windows, or you are using Kerberos on non-Windows platforms, you will connect with the credentials of the currently authenticated user. If you are trying to connect to a hosted TFS instance on `visualstudio.com` from a non-Windows system, then you will need to have enabled basic authentication in your user profile and use those credentials. Once you have created the workspace, the credentials used are cached in the current user's profile, unless told otherwise.

Next, you create a working folder mapping:

```
tf workfold -map -workspace:MyWorkspace $/TeamProject/Main/Path.
```

Here you are creating a working folder mapping in `MyWorkspace` between the server path `$/TeamProject/Main/Path` and the current directory (`.`).

Now, you download the code:

```
tf  get
```

Then you can edit the files (using the text editor of your choice—in this case, `vi`, but you might choose Notepad on Windows). Note that as you are using Local Workspaces by default in Team Foundation Server 2013, you do not need to explicitly check out the file first.

```
vi myfile.txt
```

Then you want to check the status of your pending changes to make sure the list of edits that you want to make is correct.

```
tf status
```

The status command will perform a full disk scan and automatically pend any edits that you have made. If you created or deleted any files, these will be shown as candidates, but you have to explicitly add or delete them using the `tf add` or `tf delete` commands if you want to check those changes in. Next, you check in the pending changes in `MyWorkspace`:

```
tf checkin -comment:"Making changes from the command line"
```

Your changes have now been checked in and a changeset has been created. You can look at those changes from any of the other version control clients by performing a Get to download the changes you just committed using the command line.

TEAM FOUNDATION VERSION CONTROL POWER TOOLS AND THIRD-PARTY UTILITIES

The functionality provided by Team Foundation Server is so rich, and the extensibility through the Team Foundation Server .NET or Java-based API's so straightforward, that a number of Power Tools and third-party utilities have been created to expose that functionality in easier-to-use ways. While there are too many to mention them all here, the following sections detail some of the more invaluable ones that should be in every Team Foundation Server power user's arsenal.

Microsoft Visual Studio Team Foundation Server Power Tools

The Team Foundation Server Power Tools are created by the Team Foundation Server team itself at Microsoft, and provide a number of great features that might not have been ready to put into the final release at the time it was published, or were not considered necessary for the majority of users. Many of the features originally delivered in Power Tools (such as Annotate, folder diff, rollback, and so on) appeared first in the Power Tools before arriving in the full product in a later release.

> **NOTE** *The Power Tools are available free from* http://aka.ms/TFS2013PowerTools

The main Power Tools install some extensions into Visual Studio, as well as a new command-line client on Windows called `tfpt`. The Power Tools include the following, which are of particular interest in the version control area:

- ➤ **Windows shell extensions**—This is a TortoiseSVN-like extension to both Windows Explorer and the common file dialog boxes, which allow many basic source control operations from Windows without having to run Visual Studio or the command-line tool.

- ➤ **Command-line (tfpt) tool**—`tfpt help` shows a list of the commands available, including `tf online`, which will compare your local working folder with what the server thinks you have in your workspace. It will also help you manage adds, edits, deletes, and so on for files that you might have changed outside of Visual Studio or while offline and using a Server

Workspace. Another useful command is `tfpt scorch`, which will ensure that your local working folders match exactly what the server thinks you should have—any additional files are deleted, while any modified files are re-downloaded and replaced.

Team Foundation Server MSSCCI Provider

The MSSCCI provider enables integration of Team Foundation Server version control with products that support the older MSSCCI API originally created for VSS but adopted by many IDE developers. The MSSCCI provider is developed by the team at Microsoft responsible for Team Foundation Server.

> **NOTE** *The MSSCCI provider is available as a free download from* `http://aka`
> `.ms/MSSCCI2013`

Because this provider was created long after the original developers probably created the tool using the API, and because it is for a version control system very different from the ones that the developers of the IDE would have tested against, your mileage may vary. Many people use this in lots of different development environments. However, the download page for the MSSCCI provider states that it is tested against the following products:

➤ Visual Studio 2005

➤ Visual Studio .NET 2003

➤ Visual C++ 6 SP6

➤ Visual Basic 6 SP6

➤ Visual FoxPro 9 SP2

➤ Microsoft Access 2007

➤ SQL Server Management Studio

➤ Enterprise Architect 7.5

➤ PowerBuilder 11.5

➤ Microsoft eMbedded VC++ 4.0

VERSION CONTROL SECURITY AND PERMISSIONS

Team Foundation Server is highly configurable, and contains a very fine-grained and flexible security model. This is especially true for version control.

Before you start using the version control features widely in your team, you should determine which individuals will take on the responsibility of being an administrator. The majority of the developers on the team would typically be classified as contributors. The way you organize your roles should be determined by a matter of convenience and organizational requirements.

> **NOTE** *For more information on security and privileges, see Chapter 24.*

Version control has a very flexible permissioning model that can control exactly what is permissible at the folder and even file level. You can view the security settings for a file or folder by right-clicking it in Source Control Explorer from Visual Studio, and selecting Advanced ⇨ Security.

Figure 6-38 shows the Security dialog box and the inherited security settings. To alter the settings for the folder or branch, select the setting to toggle between explicit allow or deny, or to allow if the inherited permission would allow that action. To disable inherited permissions for that item, turn the Inheritance off, as shown in Figure 6-38.

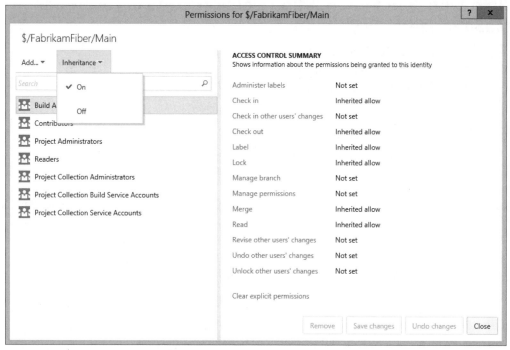

FIGURE 6-38: Settings in Security tab

SWITCHING VERSION CONTROL TO TEAM FOUNDATION SERVER

Chapter 9 details your options for moving the code from your old version control system into Team Foundation Server. However, in addition to bringing your code over, you must also ensure that your developers are comfortable with Team Foundation Server's version control capabilities. Regardless of the version control system you used in the past, Team Foundation Server is going to behave differently from what you are used to.

The first thing to understand is that Team Foundation Server is much more than just version control. The true value of Team Foundation Server comes from the tight integration between version control, work item tracking, build, and test data, all stored in the same SQL Server database, allowing you to track the progress of your entire Application Development Lifecycle.

In terms of the version control capabilities, however, there are differences that usually trip up unsuspecting developers who have previously used the most common version control systems outside of Team Foundation Server (in particular, VSS and SVN).

Working with Team Foundation Version Control for Visual SourceSafe Users

Team Foundation Version Control was designed to feel familiar to VSS users. Similar terms and concepts, such as Get, check-out, check-in, and so on, are used to describe similar actions. However, despite these similarities there are some fundamental differences between VSS and Team Foundation Server.

Speed, Reliability, and Scalability

One of the first things you will notice about Team Foundation Server is that operations such as check out, get latest, or even just navigating down into folders are significantly faster than in other version control systems, especially if you have been using VSS over a WAN. Team Foundation Server was designed for modern, Internet-style protocols and stores all of its data in a SQL Server database. By contrast, a VSS repository is a collection of files stored in a network folder accessed by using standard Windows file-sharing protocols, which do not scale well over high-latency networks.

Because Team Foundation Server uses a real SQL Server database for storage, the reliability of that store is very high. With VSS, there is no atomic check-in process, and the transfer of data to the repository is non-transactional. Therefore, if there was a loss of connectivity between the VSS client and the network share during a version control operation, the integrity of the affected files (and, thus, the repository as a whole) could be affected. This data integrity issue does not affect Team Foundation Server because of the difference in architectures.

VSS was recommended for teams of 20 or fewer developers, whereas Team Foundation Server can scale to thousands of active users. By using flexible architectures, Team Foundation Server can scale well when server resources become the limiting factor, or when you want to ensure server up-time.

> **NOTE** *Chapter 22 provides more information about scalability and high availability with Team Foundation Server.*

Versions

As discussed earlier in this chapter, Team Foundation Version Control determines file versions based on the changeset in which they were modified. Therefore, file versions do not increment individually. The first time VSS users look at the history of a file and see a nonsequential series of numbers in the history is often the first time that they realize they are talking to a fundamentally different version control tool. With Team Foundation Server, the date and time of the change is recorded by the server, not the client, so issues around dates and times caused by an incorrect clock on a VSS client disappear.

Pinning and Sharing

Team Foundation Server does not have an exact equivalent to the pinning and sharing features of VSS. Frequently, these were used as basic branch support, whereas Team Foundation Version Control now has full branch and merge capabilities, encouraging more robust software engineering practices.

> **NOTE** *Chapter 10 provides information on branching and merging.*

Labels and History

In VSS, labels could be thought of as a point in time in the repository, and labels appear in the History view. All changes before that point in time were included in the label. The closest equivalent to this in Team Foundation Version Control is the changeset, which is the fundamental unit of versioning in the repository. If you record the changeset at which a build is performed, you know exactly which versions of files it contains.

In Team Foundation Version Control, labels are more flexible. Now you can pick and choose which version of a file is included in that label—and you can edit that later on. You can think of a label in Team Foundation Version Control as tagging which file versions make up that label. Because labels are so different in Team Foundation Version Control, they do not show up as points in time in the standard view of a file's history, but are instead shown on a separate tab in the History view.

Team Foundation Server stores and displays history differently than VSS. In VSS, when you create a new file inside a folder, it creates a new version of the parents in addition to the new child. The same is true for renames, deletes, and updates.

In Team Foundation Version Control, this is just recorded on the child item, and no new version is created for the parents. The most noticeable effect of this is that the "Last Check-in" time of a parent folder does not change when a change is made inside the folder or to one of its children. To determine when the last changes were made to a folder in Team Foundation Version Control, you right-click the folder and select View History, which is a significantly faster operation than its VSS counterpart.

Keyword Expansion

VSS has a feature called *keyword expansion* where source code could include certain keywords such as `$Author: $`, `$Revision: $`, or `$Date: $`, and the appropriate data would be inserted into the tag on every check-in to version control. This was especially useful when no integration into VSS was available inside the IDE, and so finding out any of this information was often a fairly slow task in the separate VSS client application, or when viewing a printout of code.

However, keyword expansion did present many issues when comparing the differences between file versions, or when performing merges. Team Foundation Version Control takes a fundamentally different approach, and does not alter the contents of your files as you check them in. Therefore, keyword expansion is no longer supported. VSS users are often surprised by this, but the powerful IDE integration combined with the speed and performance of Team Foundation Server means that this is rarely an issue once you get over the fact that it is not there.

Concurrent Editing of Files

Team Foundation Version Control is capable of supporting multiple developers editing the same file at the same time, and has powerful merge functionality to facilitate and resolve conflicts that might occur as a result. The feature is usually enabled in most team project process templates, and is a boon to developer productivity.

In VSS, check-outs and check-ins occur only when making an edit to a file. In Team Foundation Version Control, a check-out is required for all modifications, including renames, moves, and deletes. The check-in operation will also commit all those changes in a single atomic transaction, including any adds, edits, moves, renames, and deletes. Because of this, it is much easier to maintain a repository that is always consistent.

New Features in Team Foundation Server

VSS developers should familiarize themselves with the many new features offered by Team Foundation Server, as described in this chapter and the rest of this book. Shelving is one such feature that is often overlooked by new developers because equivalent functionality is not available in VSS.

Using Team Foundation Version Control for Subversion Users

With previous versions of Team Foundation Server, moving from Subversion was often the most painful transition for developers because of the difference between that version control model and the one employed by Server Workspaces. However, a Subversion user is going to have a much easier time using and understanding the Local Workspace model that is the new default for Team Foundation Version Control. For that reason, if you are migrating users over from Subversion, it is recommended that you have them in an environment where Local Workspaces are available.

Again, the key difference to understand is that Team Foundation Server is much more than just a version control tool, and comes with very tight integration to work item tracking, build, and test management. It also comes with a slightly different terminology.

Differences in Terminology

SVN (and CVS) users are used to a different set of terms than those used by Team Foundation Version Control, as outlined in Table 6-1.

TABLE 6-1: Terminology Differences Between SVN and Team Foundation Version Control

SVN	TEAM FOUNDATION VERSION CONTROL
Check-out	Get Latest (and also Map Working Folder)
Update	Get Latest (or Get Specific Version)
Commit	Check-in
Revision	Changeset (see also versionspec)
Add	Add
Delete	Delete
Copy	Branch
Move	Move, rename
Revert	Rollback
Status	Status, pending changes list
Diff	Compare
Blame	Annotate
Log	History

Shell Extension Functionality

A popular method of accessing SVN from Windows platforms is via the TortoiseSVN Windows Shell Extensions. Equivalent shell extension functionality is available as part of the Team Foundation Server 2013 Power Tools, which, as mentioned earlier, is a separate free download from Microsoft.

Differences in History

Team Foundation Version Control tracks renames as a specific change type, meaning that renames can easily be tracked in history, rather than appearing as a delete and add. Viewing the history for a specific file allows you to view the history before a rename occurred, and also changes that occurred in a previous branch before the file was merged into the current location. In Visual Studio, a full graphical visibility of merge history is available alongside the branch hierarchy, allowing you to easily see in which branches a particular change has been merged.

Administration and Setup

Setup of Subversion is initially driven by a typical installer on Windows, or a package management system on most UNIX-style operating systems. However, the initial configuration of the server for use by the team requires extensive use of the command line and editing of configuration files. Security configuration is more complex, and configuring Subversion to delegate to Windows user accounts for authentication requires work. The Subversion server does run on many platforms, but as a result, can feel a little alien to an administrator used to Windows-based systems.

Setup and administration of Team Foundation Server is performed via a set of wizards and graphical tools on Windows. Initial setup of a basic Team Foundation Server installation providing version control, build, and work item tracking functionality is very straightforward, and will install any prerequisites (such as IIS or SQL Server Express) if not present or no existing full SQL Server installation is available. Team Foundation Server can be installed on client versions of Windows, such as Windows Vista, Windows 7, or Windows 8, but for a large team, we recommend that it be installed on a full server version of Windows. Team Foundation Server can even be installed on editions of Windows Server that include a domain controller such as Windows Server 2012 Essentials.

> **NOTE** *Chapter 9 provides more detail about the tools and techniques available to help migrate your source code from another version control system into Team Foundation Server.*

SUMMARY

This chapter introduced you to all the core concepts in Team Foundation Server's centralized version control (Team Foundation Version Control), and provided some insights on how to get started and use the tooling in day-to-day development. You also learned about where to find settings and configuration for the server, and how to manage security permissions. You learned about the common difficulties people have when switching version control from VSS or SVN.

> **NOTE** *Chapter 10 provides a more detailed explanation and guidance relating to branching and merging. Chapter 11 provides more detailed walkthroughs of using version control in specific scenarios.*

Chapter 7 will introduce you to the new distributed version control system supported by Team Foundation Server.

7

Distributed Version Control with Git and Team Foundation Server

WHAT'S IN THIS CHAPTER?

➤ Introducing Distributed Version Control concepts

➤ Learning about Visual Studio integration with Git

➤ Learning about using Git command-line tools with Team Foundation Server

Version control is one of the primary functions of Team Foundation Server and, as a result, has seen major changes in each release. These changes have improved upon the core version control functionality: providing features, enabling new workflows, and extending the scale of TFS to still greater levels. In each of these changes, up until TFS 2013, the core concept of Team Foundation Version Control as a centralized version control system has remained intact. TFS 2013 breaks from tradition and provides the entirely new concept of a distributed version control tool: Git.

Version control systems can be split into three types. With a check-out/edit/check-in system, such as TFS server workspaces, you are required to explicitly check out a file before you can make changes locally and check the changes back in to the server. TFS enforces this workflow by marking your local files as read-only until the file is checked out. In some configurations, checking out a file implies taking a lock as well, which prevents other developers from checking out the file and eliminates concurrent development and the corresponding potential for merge conflicts.

With an edit/merge/commit system, such as TFS Local Workspaces, you do not have to explicitly check a file out or negotiate with the server before you make changes. Instead, your files are writable on disk and you can simply open the file with your text editor to make changes. Because there is no automatic file locking, other developers can also make changes to the same files you are editing. When that happens, you will have to get their changes and merge them with yours before you can check in your changes.

With a distributed version control system such as Git, the client/server model is discarded in favor of a decentralized model. Instead of checking in directly to a server, you commit the changes to a local repository on your computer before pushing these changes to the server to share them with your team. Having a repository locally enables even more concurrent development for a team of developers and provides more flexibility for branching and merging.

In this chapter, you will look at the concepts of distributed version control, especially how Git manages changes in local repositories and how those changes are synchronized with a server repository. You will learn about new branching and merging workflows, including the "topic branch" workflow. Finally, you will discover how to work with Git repositories from Visual Studio as well as the command line.

> **NOTE** *For an introduction to using Git in TFS from Xcode, watch Martin Woodward's introduction video at* `http://channel9.msdn.com/Events/Visual-Studio/Launch-2013/AT110`.

DISTRIBUTED VERSION CONTROL CONCEPTS

Distributed version control systems were first adopted broadly by open source communities to address the difficulties they had working with a central version control server. Unlike a typical office environment where developers are connected over a fast network connection to the server, open source developers tend to be spread out across the globe and it's unlikely that every contributor has a fast connection to the server. In fact, some contributors may not have reliable network access at all.

To address this problem, distributed version control systems provide a full copy of the repository to every contributor when they "clone" the repository from the server. This clone isn't merely a copy of every file being placed in the working directory, though developers do have that. This repository is a full-fidelity copy, including every file as it existed at each version throughout the lifetime of the project. This allows you to view history, examine previous versions of files, perform diffs and roll back changes without having to connect to a server. You can even commit changes to the local repository.

Unlike a centralized version control system, where checking in changes places them in the server repository for other users to access immediately, committing changes in a distributed system is a process split up into two steps. When you *commit*, your changes are recorded in your local repository. When you *push* these changes, they are made available to other developers.

Git

The Git version control system was created by Linus Torvalds when he grew dissatisfied with the existing version control systems used to manage the development of the Linux kernel. He developed Git as a distributed system to allow the many developers working on the kernel to coordinate their changes effectively.

Git, when capitalized, refers to the version control system itself, including the format of the repository and the protocols that tools use to communicate with each other. The reference implementation of this system is a set of tools called git, without capitalization, or sometimes "git core."

This distinction is important because while git is the reference implementation of the system, it is not the only implementation. Linkable libraries exist for many programming languages including C, C#, Java, and even JavaScript, which allows authors of development tools to easily include Git repository management in their products. This wide support is owed to the simplicity and flexibility of the Git repository format.

> **NOTE** *Microsoft Visual Studio and Team Foundation Server use the libgit2 and LibGit2Sharp libraries for repository management, which provide a powerful Git library and a helpful .NET object model. These are open source libraries maintained by Microsoft, GitHub, and others in the community. For more information, see* `http://libgit2.github.com`.

Repository

In order to enable this offline, concurrent development strategy, the repository format of a distributed version control system differs from the repository format of a centralized version control system. In a centralized tool, such as Team Foundation Version Control, each new changeset builds on the last. Although two developers can make changes concurrently, their check-ins are serialized.

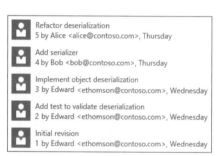

FIGURE 7-1: Concurrent changes checked in to Team Foundation Version Control

Figure 7-1 illustrates the results of concurrent changes by Alice and Bob. Both developers retrieved changeset 3 and started making changes. Bob checked his changes in first, as changeset 4. When Alice went to check her changes in, she was forced to get Bob's changes, merge them with her own, and then continue checking in to produce changeset 5.

If Alice and Bob were using a distributed version control tool, however, they would both be able to commit changes to their local repositories independently. Figure 7-2 shows the starting point for these changes: Again, each developer will begin working at the same time, making their changes against changeset 3.

FIGURE 7-2: Starting history for both developers

Again, Bob will make a change and commit it, producing changeset 4 (see Figure 7-3).

Alice will also make a change, but unlike in the centralized version control system, she does not need to merge her changes with Bob's in order to commit. In fact, she cannot merge her changes with Bob's because he has only committed his changes, he has not yet published them. Instead, she commits changeset 5, which contains only her changes, as illustrated by Figure 7-4.

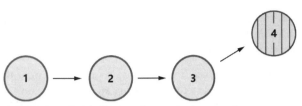

FIGURE 7-3: Bob's history after a single commit

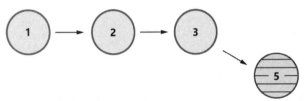

FIGURE 7-4: Alice's history after a single commit

Once Bob does publish his change, Alice will be able to take it and "pull" it into her repository. Once she does, she can merge her commit with Bob's to produce a new commit that reflects both changes. Instead of merging before the commit, she merges their changes after the commit, and history appears as Figure 7-5.

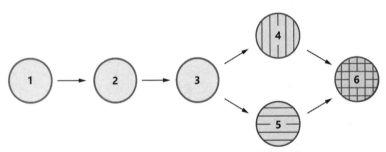

FIGURE 7-5: Alice's history after merging commit 5 from Bob

> **NOTE** *These examples use simple integers to represent the commits in order to simplify the presentation. Later you will learn how Git creates commit IDs that are unique to the repository.*

Because each Git repository contains the full history, including all the files, care should be taken to organize them into small, manageable units. A TFVC repository is meant to scale to large collections of applications, often from many teams. A Git repository should instead contain a single application at most. Many applications may need to be split along logical component boundaries to ensure that the repositories and working directory remain small.

Graph

Unlike Team Foundation Version Control, which requires changes to occur in a linear fashion, you can see that distributed version control systems allow changes to be made in two repositories at the same time. The repository history diverges as each developer makes a commit in their local repository before merging back together when the changes are integrated. This divergence takes place at the repository level itself: Instead of treating history as a linear flow, Git models history internally as a graph.

Some tools will display this internal representation in a graphical view, like the tool shown in Figure 7-6.

Most tools, however, do not display the actual history graph because it can become very complex with many contributors. These tools will instead simplify the history to provide a list of commits in reverse chronological order, like the one in Figure 7-7 from Visual Studio.

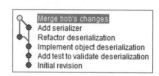

FIGURE 7-6: Viewing history as a graph

Commit

A commit is a snapshot of the repository at a point in time, similar to a changeset in Team Foundation Version Control. Unlike TFVC, however, you cannot simply use monotonically increasing integers to represent the commit ID because there is no central server to assign these numbers. Two repositories could not simply use the "next" integer for a commit ID, or else two different repositories would create a commit ID 4 as the new commit based on commit ID 3. Having two commits with ID 4 in the universe of repositories would be confusing and make merging repositories very difficult.

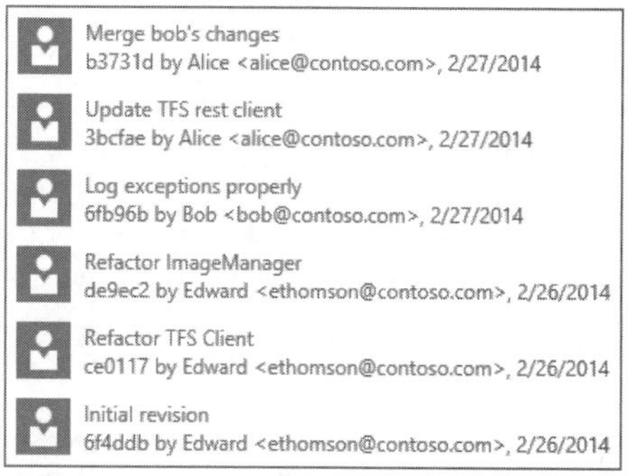

Instead, Git generates commit IDs based on the contents of the commit itself, applying the SHA1 hash algorithm to the data to produce a unique identifier. This 160-bit hash value is represented as a string of 40 hexadecimal characters. For example:

```
661ebb2c07ca7630240cd0c1a7487461d90d3825
```

This is certainly a more difficult ID to work with than, say, the number 4. Fortunately, you do not usually need to talk about a commit with its full ID; instead, you can talk about the "abbreviated commit" with its first few characters. Often, seven characters is enough to refer to a unique ID in the repository, so most tools would allow you to refer to this commit as:

```
661ebb2
```

FIGURE 7-7: Viewing history with reverse chronological sorting

Branches

You've seen that the Git history model allows for parallel lines of development to occur between different repositories. This concept is very similar to the process of working in different development branches. In fact, branches in Git are implemented on top of the history model as simple pointers to commits in the graph. As a result, branches in Git differ from branches in Team Foundation Version Control: Instead of a branch being applied to folders inside the repository, a branch applies to the entire repository.

If, in the previous example, Alice and Bob had each created a new branch for their changes and named it after themselves, Alice's repository would show both her branch and Bob's, as in Figure 7-8.

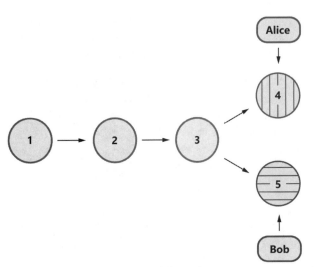

FIGURE 7-8: Alice's history with branches

When Alice went to merge Bob's branch into hers, her branch would then advance to point to the new commit which reflects the merge of their changes (see Figure 7-9).

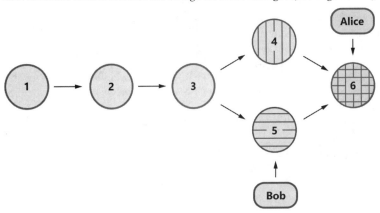

FIGURE 7-9: Alice's history after merging Bob's branch

Topic Branches

Because Git represents branches as a simple pointer to a commit, you can create branches quickly and with little overhead. This is in contrast to a centralized version control system where creating branches often requires an administrator to set up the branch, and users need to manage their working folder mappings to include it. The complexity of creating branches often discourages you from doing so, except for features that are so large that the work needs to be split up over multiple changesets and are destabilizing enough that it would disrupt other developers.

A distributed version control system, on the other hand, encourages you to create "topic branches" for any work you perform, whether it's a complex feature that will take weeks to complete or a simple one-line bugfix. By creating a branch, you can keep your work isolated from the main line, or "master," branch, and merge it when you are ready. In longer-lived topic branches, you should take regular merges from the master branch in order to keep up to date and make your merge back to master simpler.

When everybody works in a topic branch system, you see short-lived branches diverging from the master branch before being merged back in, as illustrated in Figure 7-10.

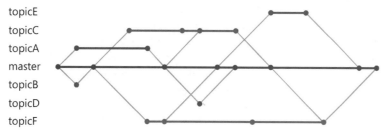

FIGURE 7-10: Typical branch graph in a topic branch

Although this branching structure may look confusing, you generally only need to worry about the master branch and the topic branch that you're directly working on. When you look only at the relationship between the topicF branch and the master branch, as in Figure 7-11, you see a simpler view that shows how the topic branch was created from master, how commits were made in both branches, and how the merges occurred between them.

FIGURE 7-11: The topicF branch and master

HEAD

Git has a special branch called "HEAD," which does not usually point to a commit as a regular branch would, but instead points to another branch. Git uses this to track the branch that you are currently working on. If we extend Alice's repository to show HEAD, we would see it pointing to the "Alice" branch, as in Figure 7-12.

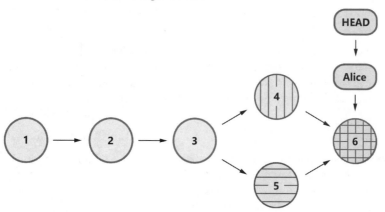

FIGURE 7-12: Alice's history depicting HEAD

Because the current branch is maintained as a simple pointer, Git makes it very easy to switch branches: The HEAD pointer is simply updated to the new branch and the working directory is updated with the changes. You will see this workflow in the section "Branching and Merging" later in this chapter.

> **NOTE** *It is possible for HEAD to point to a commit instead of a branch. When this occurs, you are not working on a branch and are instead said to have a "detached HEAD."*

Working Directory

The working directory, as you might expect, is similar to a working folder in Team Foundation Version Control and contains the files as they exist in the current branch. You can add, edit, and delete files in the working directory as you would expect, and commit them when you are finished.

Unlike working folders in Team Foundation Server, however, a working directory applies to the entire repository. This allows you to easily switch from one branch to another within the same working directory. Checking out a new branch is as simple as updating the files on disk that have changed and does not require any changes to working folder mappings.

Because there are no working folder mappings, however, you cannot use them to limit the size and scope of what you have on your local disk. Instead, you are encouraged to create a repository for a single, small component and use multiple repositories if you need multiple components. This will benefit your working directory as well as the size of your repository's history.

Index

Git introduces a new concept called the index, which contains the changes that will be included in the next commit. The index is sometimes also called the "stage," and you are said to stage your changes when you add them to the index. The index is similar to the pending changes list but with an important distinction: When you stage a file, it is the contents at the time you stage it that will be included in the next commit. If you modify that file further without staging it again, the new changes will not be committed.

This distinction allows you fine-grained control over your commits, though it can be confusing when you transition to Git from another version control system. Because of this added level of complexity, Visual Studio's Git integration does not display the index and instead shows the Included Changes list and Excluded Changes list similar to Team Foundation Version Control.

You will need to use the index when you work with the git command line. You will see how to add and remove files from the index in the section "Using Git Command-Line Tools" later in this chapter.

Although this is not a comprehensive guide to Git or distributed version control, understanding these concepts should provide you with the knowledge to begin using the Git version control system. In the next sections, you will discover how to use Visual Studio to manage your Git repository and how to work with Git from the command line.

MICROSOFT VISUAL STUDIO INTEGRATION

Beginning with Visual Studio 2013, Visual Studio adds Git repository management capabilities and brings the most commonly used functions directly into Team Explorer. This provides a similar interface to version control operations, whether you're using Git or Team Foundation Version Control, so existing TFS users should be able to get started with Git quickly.

In this section, you learn how to get started with a Git repository in Visual Studio and how to make changes to files in the working directory and commit them. You learn how to create and manage branches and how to merge changes from one branch into another. Finally, you learn how to publish your changes to other developers, and fetch and merge their changes into your repository.

Getting Started with a Repository

As you learned earlier in this chapter, when you work with a Git repository, you make changes in your working directory and then commit those changes to the Git repository that exists locally. Often, this local repository is a copy of an existing repository from a version control server, but if you are just getting started with a new project, you will also want to start with a new repository. Visual Studio provides the ability to get started either way, by cloning an existing repository or initializing a new one.

Cloning a Git Repository Hosted in Team Foundation Server

Like other features of Team Foundation Server, Git repository management is located in Team Explorer. To clone a Git repository, navigate to the Team Explorer ⇨ Connect page, and then click Select Team Projects.

If you have not connected to your Team Foundation Server before, click Servers to set your server up. Once connected, a list of the Team Projects on your server will be displayed (see Figure 7-13). Select the Team Project that contains your Git repository and click Connect. The remote Git repository will then be added to the Connect page.

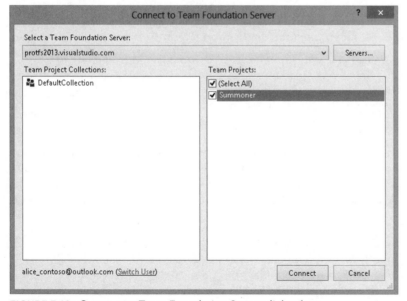

FIGURE 7-13: Connect to Team Foundation Server dialog box

Once the Team Project has been added to the Connect page, you can right-click the project and select Clone. You will be prompted to enter the local path to clone to, as shown in Figure 7-14. Once you enter the working directory path and click Clone, the repository will be downloaded from the server and checked out into the working directory you specified.

Cloning a Git Repository Hosted Outside TFS

Although Team Foundation Server 2013 provides easy-to-use Git repository hosting, there are many options for hosting your repositories. Some hosting providers, like CodePlex, provide free hosting for open source projects in publicly readable Git repositories, while others, like Visual Studio Online, provide hosting only for private repositories. Some providers, like GitHub, provide hosting for both public and private repositories.

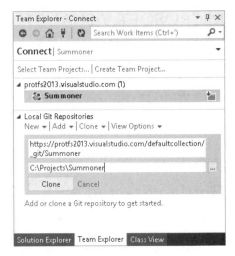

FIGURE 7-14: Clone a Team Project

> **NOTE** *Because distributed version control systems work on a peer-to-peer basis, the only thing that makes a repository authoritative is convention. When you and your peers agree to publish your changes to a repository, you have decided to make that repository the "server repository." As a result, it's very easy to set up a simple Git repository server on your local network just by exposing a file share.*
>
> *Unfortunately, when you set up your own server repository, you often miss out on the features that are included when you use a hosting platform, such as integrated work item tracking and continuous integration. It is often more convenient to use a product or a hosting provider that can offer these amenities to you.*
>
> *Hosting your repositories in Team Foundation Server provides many unique capabilities like push auditing, unified management, and Active Directory integration. You can learn more about these features at* `http://www.edwardthomson.com/blog/hosting-git-repositories-in-tfs`*.*

To clone a remote Git repository hosted in a different provider, navigate to Team Explorer ➪ Connect page. In the Local Git Repositories section, click Clone and in the text box, enter your Git server URL. In the second text box, you should enter the local path for your working directory. When you click the Clone button, the repository will be downloaded and checked out to the working directory you specified.

> **WARNING** *In Visual Studio 2013, Git repositories cannot be accessed using the SSH protocol. Visual Studio does support both file shares and HTTP or HTTPS repositories. If you were instructed to clone using SSH, contact your server administrator for instructions on using HTTPS instead.*

Most of the features you will learn about in subsequent sections are available to you regardless of the Git server you use, but some features are available only when your repositories are hosted in TFS. The features that are only available with TFS servers will be noted explicitly.

Initializing a New Repository

Because Git repositories are frequently transferred from a local computer to the server, and from one developer to another, they are necessarily very lightweight. As a result, creating a new repository is a quick and simple operation.

To create a Git repository for an existing Visual Studio Solution, navigate to Solution Explorer. Right-click on the solution and select Add to source control. In the Choose Source Control dialog box, shown in Figure 7-15, select Git.

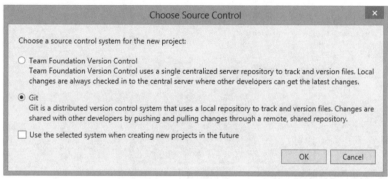

FIGURE 7-15: Choose Source Control dialog box

FIGURE 7-16: A newly created Git repository

You can also create a repository in a new, empty directory that is not associated with a solution by navigating to the Team Explorer ⇨ Connect to Team Projects page. In the Local Git repositories section, click New and enter the path where you want to create a working directory. When you click Create, your working directory and Git repository will be created, and the new repository will appear in the list of Local Git Repositories (see Figure 7-16).

You can begin making changes to the files in your repository and commit them immediately. You will learn how to share this Git repository with other developers in the section "Synchronizing with the Server."

Opening a Repository

All the repositories that you've worked with previously appear in the Team Explorer Connect page under the Local Git Repositories section. Repositories appear here when you clone or initialize them with Visual Studio, when you select Open from the Team Explorer Connect page, and when you open a Visual Studio solution that is inside a Git working directory.

CREATING A GIT REPOSITORY WHEN CREATING A NEW PROJECT

You can create a Git repository at the same time you create a new solution by clicking Add to source control in the New Project Wizard (see the following figure). The Select Version Control dialog box will open as soon as your solution is created.

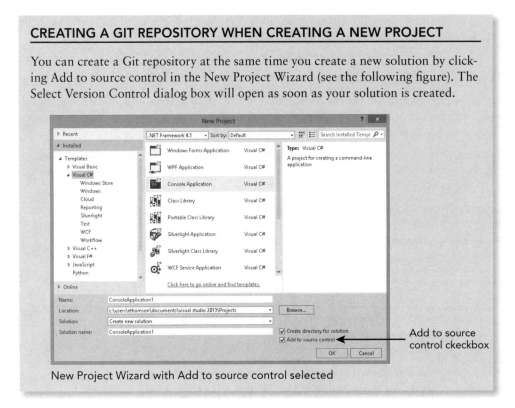

New Project Wizard with Add to source control selected

To start working with a Git repository, simply find it in the list and double-click it. The Team Explorer Home page will then open with this repository selected. If your repository contained a Visual Studio Solution, that solution will appear in the Solutions section of the Home page (see Figure 7-17). Double-clicking the Solution will open it. As you make changes to the files in your working directory, you will see these changes reflected throughout Visual Studio: in editor windows, in Solution Explorer, and in Team Explorer.

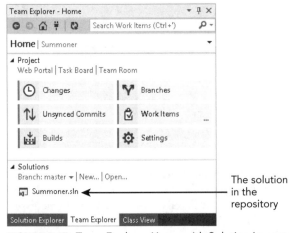

FIGURE 7-17: Team Explorer Home with Solution imported

Making Changes in a Working Directory

In order to commit changes to a repository, you start by editing the files directly in the working directory. Once you are happy with the working directory changes, you can commit them to the repository and, ultimately, publish these changes with your peers.

Included and Excluded Changes

Git does not require you to perform any special operations before you begin making changes to a file such as checking it out or locking it. You only need to open that file, make your changes and save the file. Git will scan your repository's working directory to determine what files have changed.

When you first change a file, it will appear in the Team Explorer Changes page in the Included Changes section (see Figure 7-18). Files listed in this section will be included in the next commit you perform. If you want to make changes to a file but *not* include it in the next commit, you can right-click on a file in the Included Changes list and select Exclude. This will move the file to the Excluded Changes list, which is useful if you are making simple, temporary changes that you will undo in the future or if you want to split the changes you are making over several commits. When you are ready to include the file, you can right-click on it and select Include to move it back to the Included Changes list.

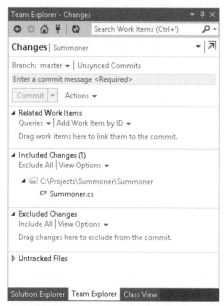

FIGURE 7-18: An edited file in the Included Changes list

> **NOTE** *Conveniently, you can make changes outside of Visual Studio, with any text editor you like, and those files will be reflected in the Changes list. Visual Studio listens for file system events that occur within your Git working directory and updates the Changes list accordingly.*

New files that are added to the working directory are not immediately managed by Git; instead of appearing in the Included Changes list, added files appear in the Untracked Files list. This is to prevent new files from being inadvertently added to the repository without your knowledge.

When a new file appears in the Untracked Files list, you can add it to the repository by right-clicking on it and selecting Add. The file will be moved to the Included Changes list and will be included in your commit.

Ignoring Files

Generally, you want to promote items in the Untracked Files list to be Included Changes. If you have files in your Untracked Files list that you do not want tracked by your version control tools, such as local configuration files, you probably want these to be ignored completely by Git so that they do not clutter your view of the repository.

Git uses a file called `.gitignore` to manage the list of ignored files. When Git detects a new file in your working directory, it compares the name against the contents of the `.gitignore` file. If the filename matches a line in the ignore file (wildcards are allowed), it will not be reported as a new file.

To ignore an untracked file in Visual Studio, simply right-click on its name in the Untracked Files list and select Ignore This Local Item. Its filename will be added to the `.gitignore` file and you will not be notified of its presence again.

There are often many files in your working directory that you want to ignore, such as build output, temporary files written by text editors, and the Visual Studio user preferences file. When you initialize a new repository with Visual Studio, a default `.gitignore` will be set up in your repository for you so that you do not have to configure their ignore settings in every repository you create.

If you created your repository outside of Visual Studio, you should download this default `.gitignore` from `https://github.com/github/gitignore/blob/master/VisualStudio.gitignore` and add it to your repository.

Undoing Changes

Sometimes you make a change in your working directory that you do not want to commit: Whether you've made a temporary change to help test other changes, or if you've decided to abandon the changes you were making, it's very easy to undo them and replace them with the version from HEAD.

To examine the changes that you've made to a file, find the file in the Team Explorer Changes page, right-click on it and select Compare With Unmodified. This will open the file in the Diff Editor, which shows the file as it exists in HEAD on the left and the working directory version of the file on the right, as shown in Figure 7-19.

From within the Diff Editor, you can directly edit the contents of the working directory copy on the right-hand side. This lets you back out small changes to areas of the file, bringing the contents from the origin version, one line or one region at a time.

If you want to undo all the changes you've made to a file, you can right-click on the file in the Team Explorer Changes page and select Undo. Any changes you've made locally will be lost and the file contents will be replaced with the version of the file in HEAD.

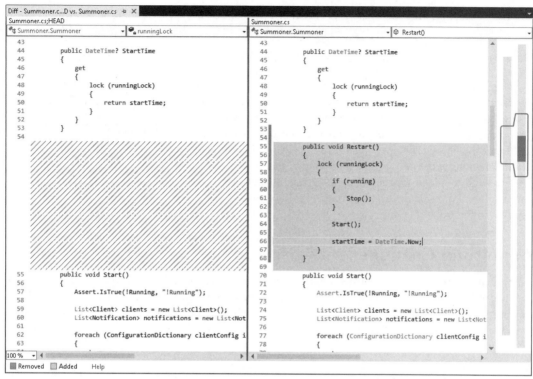

FIGURE 7-19: Changes to be committed, in the diff viewer

Renames

In the previous section, "Distributed Version Control Concepts," you learned that Git commits are stored as snapshots of the repository at the time of the commit. Commits are not stored as a list of "deltas" or changes from the previous commit, they simply reflect the entire state of the repository. This means that there's no way to represent that a file in your Included Changes is a rename.

Despite that, you can select a file in Solution Explorer and change its name and this rename is reflected in the Included Changes list, as you can see in Figure 7-20.

FIGURE 7-20: Team Explorer showing a rename in the Included Changes list

Instead of instructing the version control system to perform a rename, as in Team Foundation Version Control, Git simply detects that the rename occurred when it examines the working directory for changes. Any files that are newly added in the working directory are compared to the previous version of any files that were deleted. If an added file is similar to a deleted file, Git does not display this change as an add and a delete; it shows it as a rename.

Git can even take this a step further and detect similar files in complex renaming situations such as a "circular rename":

1. Rename `File1.cs` to a temporary filename like `temp`.

2. Rename `File2.cs` to `File1.cs`.

3. Rename `temp` to `File2.cs`.

In this situation, you haven't added or deleted files, so comparing the working directory to the contents of HEAD would suggest only that `File1.cs` and `File2.cs` have changed. Git will analyze these changes, however, comparing the modified versions in the working directory to the previous versions to determine whether the files were "rewritten." If a file is very dissimilar to its previous version, it will be treated as if the file was deleted and re-added for the purposes of rename detection. This allows Git to detect even complex rename cases, as shown in Figure 7-21.

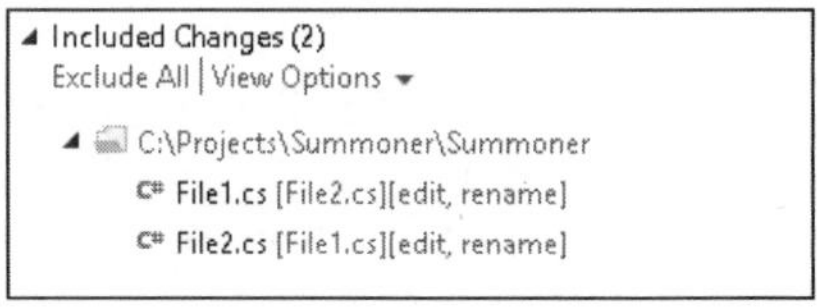

FIGURE 7-21: Circular renames in Git

Committing Changes

An advantage of working in a distributed version control system, and committing directly to a local repository, is that you can commit your changes without publishing them to other developers. For example, if you are fixing several bugs, you can fix each bug in a discrete commit, which allows your version control history to accurately reflect your changes, and allows reviewers to examine each change independently.

Reviewing Your Changes

Although committing locally allows you to create several independent commits before publishing them to your peers, each of these commits should still be of high quality and able to stand on its own. To help maintain quality, you should review your changes before you commit them.

Open the Team Explorer Changes page to see what changes are about to be committed. Examine the items in the Included Changes list to make sure that it is the complete list of changes that you want included. Make sure that the files in the Excluded Changes list and the Untracked Changes list should not be included in the commit. To get more detailed information about the changes, right click on a file and select Compare with Unmodified to open the file in the Diff Editor.

Associating Work Items

Team Foundation Server embraces the notion of integration between version control and work item tracking and that performing work on source control should be linked to a development task or a bug. As a result, Visual Studio provides work item tracking integration with Git commits, just like with TFVC.

> **NOTE** *Integrated work item tracking is only available when your Git repository is hosted in Team Foundation Server.*

You can associate work items with your commit from within the Team Explorer Changes page, in the Related Work Items Section located directly above the Included Changes list. Click the Queries button to display your work item queries, and then select the work item query to run. In the Query Results Editor, navigate to the work item you want to associate your commit with, and double click it to add it to the list of associated work items. Alternately, if you know the ID of the work item that you want to associate, you can simply click Add Work Item by ID and enter the ID in the text field.

When you commit this change, the work item link is stored with the commit in your local repository. When you push the commit to the server, the work item will be updated to reflect your changes and will be linked with the commit.

Committing

When you have reviewed your changes and associated work items, you are ready to provide a commit message that describes your changes and save the commit. By convention, the first line of the commit message is a brief summary of the changes in the commit. If you want to provide additional information, leave a blank line before writing a detailed description. When you are done, simply click the Commit button to update your repository.

Branching and Merging

Branching is a critical component of software development that allows you to create parallel lines of development for your software. You can have a stable development branch that reflects the current version that contains bug fixes only, while another branch reflects the next version and contains unstable or less mature new feature work.

Creating a Branch

To create a new branch, start by navigating to Team Explorer ➪ Branches. The Branches page shows all the branches that exist in your local repository, with the current branch displayed in bold. Click the New Branch option to expose the branch creation options, shown in Figure 7-22, and enter the name of your new branch in the branch name text box.

Your new branch will be created from the current branch by default. In a topic branch workflow, you should select the master branch to create your branch from. Select the Checkout branch option in order to switch to your new branch immediately so that as soon as you click Create, you will be working on that new branch. If you have changes in the working directory when you create the branch then they will remain as changes to be committed in the new branch.

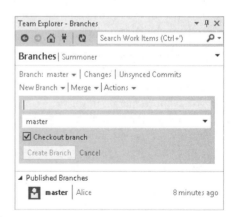

FIGURE 7-22: Branch creation options

Switching Branches

Because Git branches at the repository level, switching branches is trivial because there are no working folder mappings to change. When you switch branches in Git, the working directory contents

are simply updated with the contents of the branch you're switching to. To switch branches, navigate to the Team Explorer Branches page, right-click the branch and select Switch.

You can switch branches even if you have changes in your working directory, provided none of those files are also changed in the target branch. Your local changes remain in the Team Explorer Changes page, and will be applied to the new branch during your next commit.

If you have made changes to files that have also changed in the branch, you will receive an error message, like the one you see in Figure 7-23. You will need to either commit or undo your changes to switch branches.

FIGURE 7-23: Conflicting changes prevent switching branches

Merging Branches

Branches provide a helpful way to isolate parallel lines of development, but this isolation isn't helpful unless you can easily take the changes from one branch and apply them to another. For example, you

may have a stable branch that contains the current version of your software and only receives bug fixes. After you have fixed a bug in the stable branch, you want to take that change and merge it into your development branch so the bug is fixed there, too. Similarly, if you are working with a topic branch strategy, you want to merge your topic branch into the master branch once the topic is finished and ready to be included broadly.

To perform a merge, open the Team Explorer Branches page and click the Merge button. In the source branch combo, select the branch that contains the changes that you want to merge; in the target branch combo, select the branch that should receive those changes. In a topic branch strategy, you would select your topic branch as the source and your master branch as the target, as shown in Figure 7-24.

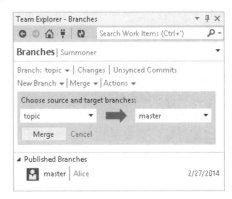

FIGURE 7-24: Merging changes from "topic" to "master"

When you click Merge, your working directory will switch to the target branch and any changes from the source branch will be merged. If a file has only changed in the source branch, and not the target, that file will simply be brought over into the target. If a file has changed in both branches, Git will try to automerge those changes by taking the modified regions in the source file and the modified regions in the target file to produce a new file that contains both changes (see Table 7-1).

TABLE 7-1: The Results of an Automerge

COMMON ANCESTOR	SOURCE BRANCH	TARGET BRANCH	AUTOMERGE RESULT
Line one	Changed in source	Line one	Changed in source
Line two	Line two	Line two	Line two
Line three	Line three	Line three	Line three
Line four	Line four	Line four	Line four
Line five	Line five	Changed in target	Changed in target

If both branches contain changes to the same file, with changes in the same regions, the file cannot be automerged. This file will be marked as a conflict and you will have to resolve the conflict manually and commit the merge when you are done.

MERGING BRANCHES IN GIT VERSUS TFVC

Although merging branches is generally similar between Git and TFVC, Git does have two advantages that make merging more convenient.

➤ Git allows you to merge any two branches, unlike Team Foundation Version Control, which maintains a branch hierarchy and requires that merges move up and down that hierarchy. The following figure shows a branch hierarchy in TFVC: In this hierarchy, you cannot merge changes directly from the Working branch to the Grandparent branch without first merging those changes to the Parent branch. Git has no such restriction.

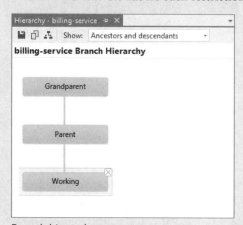

Branch hierarchy

➤ Because Git encourages workflows that branch and merge regularly, merges tend to occur more frequently. As a result, merges are smaller and have fewer conflicts.

Resolving Conflicts

When merging two branches produces conflicts, the Team Explorer Changes page will provide a message at the top of the page notifying you that your merge did not complete and you must resolve the conflicts to continue. Clicking the Resolve the conflicts link (see Figure 7-25) takes you to the Resolve Conflicts page.

FIGURE 7-25: Conflict notification in the Team Explorer Changes page

Clicking the Resolve the conflicts link (shown in Figure 7-25) takes you to the Resolve Conflicts page. The Resolve Conflicts page lists each conflict that exists in the working directory, and you must resolve each of them to complete the merge. Select a conflict to show the conflict resolution options (see Figure 7-26).

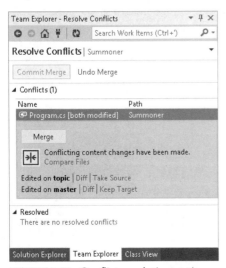

FIGURE 7-26: Conflict resolution options

To see the changes that led to the conflict, you can click the Compare Files button. This will open the Diff Editor with the file in the source branch on the left and the target branch on the right, allowing you to see the regions that conflicted directly. To look at only the changes that occurred in one of the branches, click the Diff button next to the source or target branch.

If you want to take the changes from the source branch, overwriting the changes that occurred in the target branch, you can click Take Source. Similarly, if you want to keep the changes from the target branch, overwriting the changes that occurred in the source branch, you can click Keep Target.

More often, however, you want to merge the changes in the branches manually. Click the Merge button to open the file in the Merge Editor, shown in Figure 7-27. The Merge Editor shows you the file as it exists in the source branch on the left and the file as it exists in the target branch on the right. The file below these branched versions contains the result of the merge. You must edit the file in the bottom row to include the source and target changes, as appropriate. Once you have finished, save the file to accept your changes and resolve the conflict.

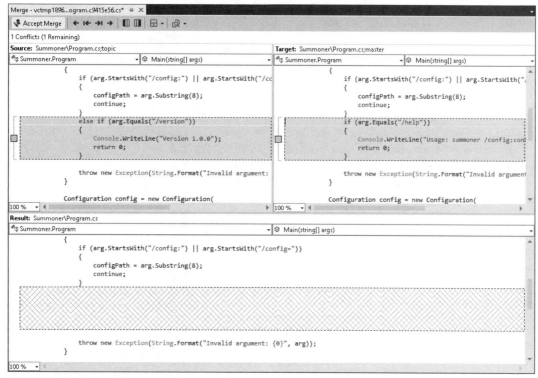

FIGURE 7-27: Merge Editor resolving a conflict

Once all conflicts have been resolved, the Conflicts list empties and indicates that there are no conflicts remaining. Any time you have a merge with conflicts you should perform a build and test pass locally before committing your changes. Once you have validated the merge results, click the Commit Merge button.

> **NOTE** *The Diff Editor included in Visual Studio provides powerful three-way merging functionality for resolving conflicts, but like text editors, merge tools can be a personal preference. Visual Studio reads the Git* `merge.tool` *configuration settings, so if you prefer to use your own merge tool, you can configure it according to the* `git-mergetool` *documentation, available at* `https://www.kernel.org/pub/software/scm/git/docs/git-mergetool.html`.

Synchronizing Changes with the Server

Downloading changes from other developers and publishing your changes are crucial parts of working with other developers on a project. In a typical collaborative workflow you will pull changes from the server into your repository and merge them with any changes you made before pushing your changes to the server.

Pulling Changes from the Server

Pulling changes from the server downloads any commits that your peers have made and merges those changes into your local repository.

An advantage of the topic branch workflow is that you are not working directly in the master branch, so you can pull the changes from the server's master branch into your own without worrying about merge conflicts. This will keep your master branch in sync with the remote but not force you to merge the changes with your topic branch until it is convenient.

To pull changes from the server, first switch to the master branch. Then navigate to Team Explorer ➪ Unsynced Commits. At the top of the Unsynced Commits page is the Incoming Commits list, which shows all the changes that are new on the server and will be merged into your local repository, as shown in Figure 7-28.

When you have reviewed the incoming changes, click Pull to merge them into your master branch. In a topic branch

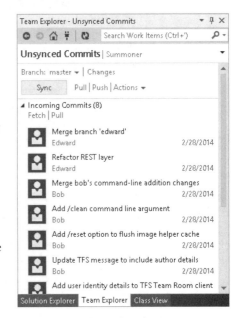

FIGURE 7-28: Incoming changes

workflow, this will generally complete without conflicts, so you can switch back to the topic branch that you're working on and merge the changes from your master branch when it's convenient.

Examining Changes

To see the changes that were pulled into your branch, go to the Team Explorer Branches page, right-click on the master branch and select View History. This will open the History Editor, displaying the commits in reverse chronological order, as shown in Figure 7-29.

To see more detailed information about one of the changes, double-click on it to open the commit details in Team Explorer. This will show you the complete commit details as well as the list of files that were modified in this commit (see Figure 7-30). You can double-click on any file to open the file in the Diff Editor, with the previous version on the left and the contents of that commit on the right.

If, however, you know the file that changed but not the commit that contained the change, you can view the changes that were made in a particular file. If you have the file open in an Editor window, right-click in the window and select Source Control ➪ History. Otherwise, you can navigate to the file in Solution Explorer, right-click on the file and select View History. This gives a list of every commit that has changed the current file, but not what was changed.

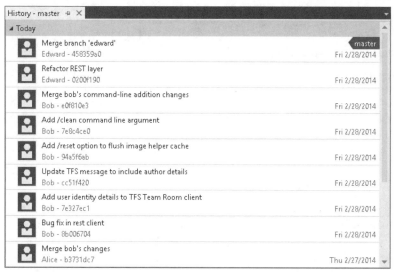

FIGURE 7-29: History view

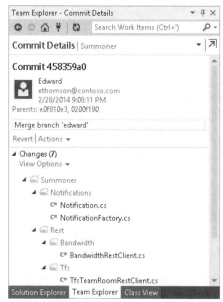

FIGURE 7-30: Commit details

For a more in-depth view of the changes, you can view the "annotated history" of a file by right-clicking on the file and selecting Source Control ➪ Annotate. This will add a new column on the right side of the Editor window, which shows the last commit that changed each line (see Figure 7-31). The annotated history view is useful in determining what commit introduced a bug or a change in behavior, and it can be helpful in quickly identifying the author who made the change along with providing more information. Unsurprisingly, annotated history is also frequently called the "blame" history.

```
Program.cs;68d7e9ea (Annotated)    ⏸ ✕   Program.cs        History - master
6f4ddb10  Edward  2/26/2014                configPath = arg.Substring(8);
                                           continue;
                                       }
94a5f6ab  Bob    2/28/2014           if (arg.StartsWith("/reset"))
                                       {
                                           ImageHelper.Instance.Reset();
                                       }
7e8c4ce0  Bob    2/28/2014           if (arg.StartsWith("/clean"))
                                       {
                                           ImageHelper.Instance.Clean();
                                       }
525e6ef2  Alice  2/28/2014           if (arg.Equals("/help"))
                                       {
                                           Console.WriteLine("Usage: summoner /config:co
                                           return 0;
                                       }
68d7e9ea  Alice  3/3/2014            if (arg.Equals("/version"))
b7b26672  Alice  2/28/2014             {
                                           Console.WriteLine("Version 1.0.0");
                                           return 0;
                                       }
6f4ddb10  Edward  2/26/2014
                                     throw new Exception(String.Format("Invalid argumer
100 %  ▾  ◀
```

FIGURE 7-31: Annotated history

Pushing

Pushing your changes to the server uploads the commits that you've made in your local branch and then sets the server's branch to point to the same commit that your local branch points to. The server will not merge any changes for you; instead, you must merge any changes on the server with your local branch before you push it. The server enforces that you have performed the merge to ensure that you do not accidentally overwrite any changes on the server.

Visual Studio allows you to pull any changes on the server, merge them with your local branch, and then push the results back up to the server in a single step called "synchronizing." Synchronizing is most useful when you have finished making changes in your topic branch and are ready to merge it into the master branch and push it to the server. First, switch to the master branch and perform the merge from your topic branch to master. Then, navigate to Team Explorer ➪ Unsynced Commits and press the Sync button. Your master branch will be synchronized with the server and the changes from your topic branch will now be merged.

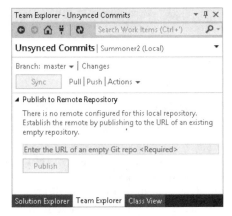

FIGURE 7-32: Publishing a new repository to the server

For a new repository that you want to publish to a server for the first time, you will not be able to synchronize. Instead, when you navigate to Team Explorer ➪ Unsynced Commits, you will be prompted for the remote server URL. Enter the Git repository URL that was provided when you created the repository and click Publish, as shown in Figure 7-32.

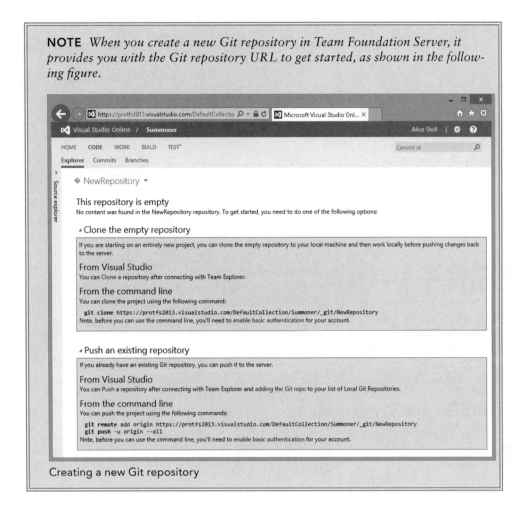

NOTE *When you create a new Git repository in Team Foundation Server, it provides you with the Git repository URL to get started, as shown in the following figure.*

Creating a new Git repository

USING GIT COMMAND-LINE TOOLS

You saw in the previous section that Visual Studio provides straightforward access to working with Git repositories but, like TFVC, not all version control operations are available in Visual Studio. If you want to perform more advanced Git repository operations, or if you just prefer a text-based interface to a graphical user interface, you will want to use the command-line tools.

The command-line tools, Git for Windows, are a version of the git core utilities developed to manage the Linux kernel repository. The original git core tools remain primarily targeted at running in Unix environments and as a result are written in a mixture of languages including Bourne shell scripts, Perl, and Python, and expect to be able to invoke standard Unix utilities that are not typically available on a Windows system.

The Git for Windows project takes the git core tools, packages them with a minimal set of the Unix utilities, and provides a helpful installer to handle setting up this environment for you. Git for

Windows also includes an alternate command-line environment, Git Bash, which provides a Unix-like command-line experience. You are not required to use Git Bash, however; you can perform these operations directly from a command prompt or from PowerShell.

> **WARNING** *You may see Git for Windows referred to as "msysgit," although this is not generally correct. Git for Windows is the name of the project that provides the git core tools for Windows users in an easy-to-use installer. msysgit is actually the environment used to develop and build Git for Windows itself.*

In this section, you learn how to install Git for Windows and how to use some of the most commonly used commands. You will also discover the posh-git interface for PowerShell, which can be helpful when working from the command line.

> **NOTE** *This section is not a comprehensive tutorial of the git core tools; it is meant to provide an introduction to how they work and how to use them alongside Visual Studio. Even if you prefer to use the interface in Visual Studio, understanding how the command-line tools work is helpful to understanding how the Git version control system works. For more information on using the git command-line tools, refer to* Pro Git *by Scott Chacon, available at* http://git-scm.com/book.

Installing Git for Windows

Visit http://msysgit.github.io/ to download the latest version of Git for Windows in a helpful self-extracting installer. The installer will offer you many options that allow you to make expert-level configuration settings. You can simply accept the defaults because they are generally safe, but two options deserve explanation.

> **NOTE** *Martin Woodward provides a detailed explanation in his article "Setting Up the Perfect Git Command Line Environment on Windows" at* http://www.woodwardweb.com/git/setting_up_the.html.

Setting Your PATH Environment Variable

By default, Git for Windows will modify your PATH environment variable to include the git command-line tool so that you can use it from either a command prompt or PowerShell. If you choose to not modify the PATH, you will have to use the Git Bash environment to use git. If you choose to include the entire set of Git for Windows tools in the PATH, you will have Unix tools available at the command line, some of which override Windows tools of the same name. These options are only suggested if you are very familiar with Unix.

Setting Your Line Ending Conversion

Git supports line ending conversion to support development in heterogeneous environments. Typically, Windows uses two characters to represent the end of a line, using a carriage return

(ASCII 13) and a line feed (ASCII 10) character, while Unix uses a single newline character (ASCII 10). Most modern applications can read and write files in either format but some legacy applications expect a particular format.

This line ending conversion is optional, but recommended. You should select the "Checkout Windows-style, commit Unix-style" option, even if you are only working on Windows and never collaborating with developers on Unix platforms. Some Git tools perform line-ending conversion by default and do not honor this configuration setting; they will expect the repository to contain Unix-style line endings always.

If you were to configure Git to always write Windows-style line endings, but use one of these deficient tools that did not honor this configuration, it would lead to inconsistent settings in both your repository and your working directory.

Working with Git for Windows

One the installation has finished, you can start working with the git command-line tools as soon as you open a new command shell or a new instance of PowerShell. You will see the examples illustrated with command shell, but you should use whichever you prefer. If you are a PowerShell user, make sure to see the section "Using Posh-Git" later in this chapter.

Cloning Git Repositories Hosted in Team Foundation Server

If you have cloned a repository using Visual Studio and you want to work with the git core tools, you do not need to clone a repository again. You can simply open the working directory in a command prompt and run the git commands in your working directory. If you would prefer to clone using the command line instead, you must first discover the URL of the server repository by opening Team Web Access.

In a web browser, navigate to the Team Project that contains the Git repository you want to clone; then navigate to the Code page, and select the Git repository to clone. Click the Clone button, shown in Figure 7-33, to open a text field that contains the URL of the server repository.

Once you have copied the URL of the server repository, you can simply run the `git clone` command.

```
git clone http://servername:8080/tfs/DefaultCollection/_git/Project C:\Project
```

In this example, the server repository located at `http://servername:8080/tfs/DefaultCollection/_git/Project` will be cloned to a new local working directory, `C:\Project`.

> **NOTE** *When you are prompted for your user name and password, you can simply press Enter twice to provide your Active Directory credentials to your Team Foundation Server. If you are using TFS hosted in Visual Studio Online, you should instead enter your Alternate Credentials, as described at* `http://aka.ms/VSOAlternateCredentials`.

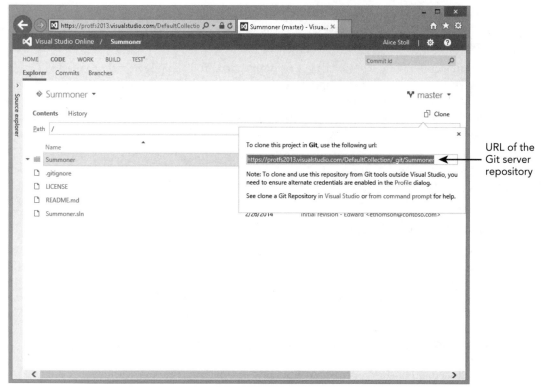

FIGURE 7-33: The server repository URL in Team Web Access

Making Changes in the Repository

As you learned previously, Git does not require you to notify the version control system before you start making changes in the working directory. However, the git core tools do not have the Include Changes and Excluded Changes list, as you saw in Visual Studio, so you will need to update the Git index to reflect your changes after you have made them.

Making Changes and Staging Them for Commit

As you make changes in the working directory, you can use the `git status` command to look at the working directory and report the changes you've made. New files in the working directory will be reported as "untracked" and modified and deleted files will be reported as "unstaged changes." None of these changes have been added to the index and these changes will not be included in the upcoming commit. Figure 7-34 shows the status of a Git repository with unstaged changes.

If you want to prepare these changes to be committed, you need to "stage" them. To stage new files or modified files, add them to the index with the `git add` command. To stage deletions of removed files, use the `git rm` command. Figure 7-35 shows the status of a git repository with a mix of staged and unstaged adds, modifications, and deletes. The staged changes will be included in the next commit; the unstaged changes will remain unstaged.

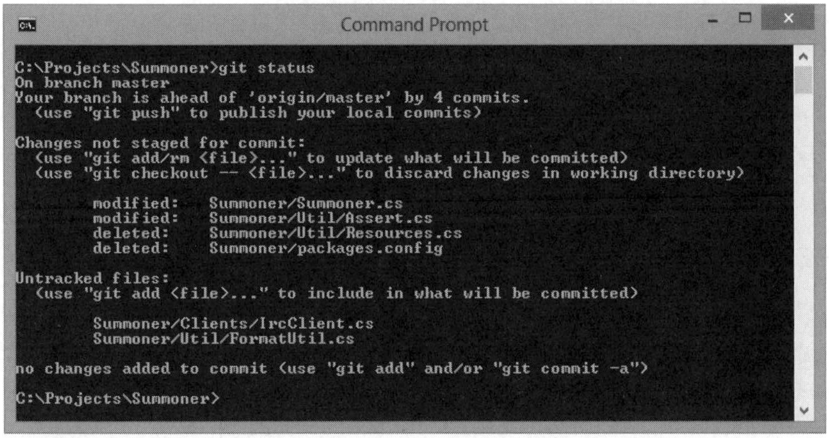

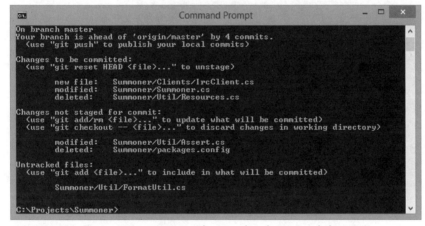

FIGURE 7-34: Git repository status with unstaged changes

FIGURE 7-35: Git repository status with staged and unstaged changes

> **NOTE** *You can use the shorthand command* `git mv`, *which renames the source file to the target file on disk, removes the source filename from the index, and adds the target filename to the index.*
>
> *As you learned earlier, you do not have to use* `git mv` *because Git repositories detect renamed files using heuristics instead of storing rename information in the repository. There is no difference between using* `git mv` *and simply renaming the file yourself, staging the deletion of the source file with* `git rm` *and staging the addition of the target with* `git add`.

Reviewing Your Changes and Committing Them

When you have finished making changes and are ready to commit them, you should first review them for accuracy.

Check the status of your repository to ensure that you have staged all the changes you want included; review the list of unstaged changes carefully, making sure that there are no files that should be included in the upcoming commit. Because you can stage incremental file changes to the index, occasionally you may stage changes to a file and then edit that file further, which will cause you to have both staged and unstaged changes to the same file. In this case, you should review the changes on a line-by-line basis.

To see this deeper comparison of the changes that you have staged, you can compare the staged changes against the HEAD commit.

```
git diff --staged
```

This will show you each line that you have changed and staged for commit, easily decorated to identify the changes. Added lines will be prefixed with a "+" while removed lines will be prefixed with a "-". Unchanged lines have no prefix, and are provided for context (see Figure 7-36).

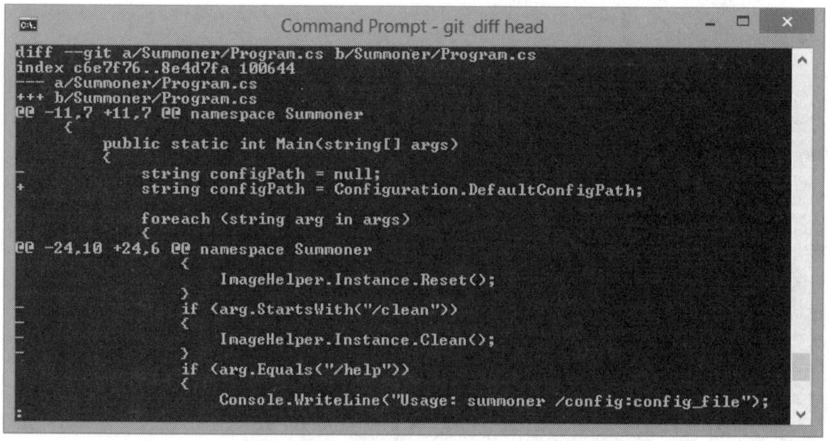

FIGURE 7-36: Output of git diff showing changes in a single file

When you have reviewed your changes and are ready to commit them, simply run the following:

```
git commit
```

You will be prompted to enter a commit message that describes the changes that you're making. Again, the first line should be a brief summary of the change, followed optionally by a blank line and additional details. When you have finished, save the file and exit your text editor, and your changes will be committed.

Viewing History

You learned earlier that Git stores its history in a graph, but in the examples you've seen, history has been portrayed as a flattened list of commits, sorted reverse chronologically. To see the actual graph, with history diverging and merging, you can use the `git log` command as shown in Figure 7-37. Specify the `--graph` option to display the graph format, the `--decorate` option to show labels on the commits that indicate the location of the branches, and the `--oneline` option to show a compact display, with one commit per line.

```
Command Prompt - git  log --graph --branches --decorate --oneline
*7e9e (HEAD, new_topic, master) Merge branch 'version_arg'
|
| * b7b2667 (version_arg, topic) Add /version argument
| *   700f07c Merge branch 'help_arg'
| |\
| * | 525e6ef (help_arg) Add /help command line argument
| |/
| *   458359a (origin/master) Merge branch 'edward'
| |\
| * | 0200f19 Refactor REST layer
| |/ /
| *   e0f810e Merge bob's command-line addition changes
| |\ \
| * | | 7e8c4ce Add /clean command line argument
| * | | 94a5f6a Add /reset option to flush image helper cache
| |/ /
| * | cc51f42 Update TFS message to include author details
| * | 7e327ec Add user identity details to TFS Team Room client
| * | 8b00670 Bug fix in rest client
| |/
| *   b3731dc (origin/alice) Merge bob's changes
| |\
| | * 6fb96bc (origin/bob) Log exceptions properly
| * | 3bcfae7 Update TFS rest client
```

FIGURE 7-37: Git log with graph visualization

Branching and Merging

Creating a branch with the git command-line tools is simple and quick, just like creating a branch in Visual Studio. To create a new topic branch based on the master branch, you use the `git branch` command:

```
git branch new_topic master
```

Once created, you can switch to the topic branch:

```
git checkout new_topic
```

Note that you can also perform this branch creation and branch switching from within Visual Studio. In fact, Visual Studio will watch the git repository and update Team Explorer as you create branches and switch to them. You can see Team Explorer updated to reflect the new branch in Figure 7-38.

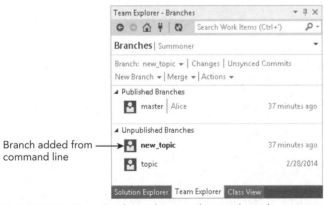

Branch added from command line

FIGURE 7-38: Team Explorer showing the new branch

After you have made changes and committed them in your topic branch and you are ready to merge the topic branch into master, you need only to switch to the master branch and merge the topic branch in.

```
git checkout master
git merge topic
```

If the merge is successful, it will complete immediately and produce a new commit. However, if any merge conflicts occurred, you will be notified that you must resolve them before continuing.

You can edit each file manually and stage the resolved file, or you can resolve the conflicts in Visual Studio, using the helpful Diff Editor that you've already seen. Visual Studio will even detect the conflicts as soon as the merge produces them, and allow you to resolve them from the Team Explorer Resolve Conflicts page.

Once you have staged a resolution for all your conflicts, you can `git commit` the results to complete the merge. You can then synchronize your changes with the server to publish your topic branch to your peers.

Synchronizing with the Server

When working with Visual Studio, you pull changes from the server, merge them with your own, and then push your changes to the server. This is the same workflow you should follow when working from the command line.

Pulling Changes from the Server

In order to retrieve changes from the server, merging the changes in the server's master branch into your master branch, first switch to the master branch using `git checkout master`, and then use the `git pull` command.

```
git pull origin
```

In this example, the argument "origin" refers to the name of the Git server. Because git provides peer-to-peer access to other repositories, you can actually configure many remote repositories that you share changes with. By convention, "origin" is the remote repository that you first cloned from.

As in Visual Studio, the `pull` command both fetches the new commits on the server and merges them into your repository. The `git pull` command is actually a combination of the `fetch` and `merge` command. If you are on the master branch, locally, this is the equivalent of:

```
git fetch origin
git merge origin/master
```

> **WARNING** *A variation on the git pull workflow is to "rebase" your changes on top of the upstream changes. This can be accomplished by:*
>
> ```
> git pull origin --rebase
> ```
>
> *which is the equivalent of:*
>
> ```
> git fetch origin
> git rebase origin/master
> ```
>
> *Instead of performing a merge commit, this takes your local changes that have not been pushed upstream and re-applies them on top of the upstream changes. As a result, the repository history does not appear to diverge and merge; it appears like a straight line. This may be visually appealing, but it obscures the actual direction that development took and if a bad merge occurs, it can hide the source. As a result, you should generally merge the server's changes unless your development team has a convention to the contrary.*

Pushing Your Changes

To publish your changes to the server, you use the `git push` command to upload a branch to the server.

```
git push origin master
```

In this example, as with the `pull` command, the argument "origin" refers to the name of the Git server. The argument "master" refers to the name of the branch you wish to push; the changes in your master branch will be pushed to the server's master branch.

If there are other changes on the server that you do not yet have in your repository, your push will fail. You will be prompted to merge those changes into your repository and push again. To retrieve the server's changes and merge them into your repository, use the `git pull` command. After resolving any conflicts, you can push your newly merged changes to the server.

Using Posh-Git

Posh-Git is a set of PowerShell scripts that provide user interface enhancements when you're using the git command-line client. Posh-Git provides two simple, but powerful, features: an extension to your shell's prompt that provides a brief report of your repository's status, and command-line completion for git commands and branches.

Installing posh-git is simple: Download the latest version from `http://dahlbyk.github.io/posh-git/`, extract the Zip file, and run the included `install.ps1` script from a PowerShell prompt. The installer updates your startup profile so that posh-git will be loaded by default every time you start PowerShell; to rerun your startup profile to take advantage of posh-git immediately, follow the instructions provided in the installer.

Now, you can simply change directories into your git repository. As soon as you enter the working directory, your prompt will change to include additional information about your repository status. In a working directory with no changes, you will simply see the prompt include the name of the currently checked out branch.

```
C:\Projects\Summoner [topic]>
```

Switching branches by using the `git branch` command updates the prompt immediately to reflect this change. The color of the branch name indicates its relation to your server repository, as shown in Table 7-2.

TABLE 7-2: Posh-Git Remote Branch Indicators

COLOR	STATUS
Blue	Your branch is "up to date" with the server's branch; your local branch points to the same commit as the server's branch.
Green	Your branch contains new commits that you can push to the server.
Red	The server's branch contains new commits that you can pull.
Yellow	Both your branch and the server's branch contain new commits since the last time you synced. You should pull commits from the server and then you can push your commits.

If you have any staged or unstaged changes in your working directory, a summary of the status will be displayed in your prompt after the branch name. For example, if you add a file to the working directory and stage a change to an existing file, the prompt will indicate those changes.

```
C:\Projects\Summoner [topic +0 ~1 -0 | +1 ~0 -0 !]>
```

The first group of status indicators shows the staged changes in the working directory; the second group of indicators shows the unstaged changes in the working directory. Table 7-3 explains the status indicators in detail.

TABLE 7-3: Posh-Git Working Directory Status Indicators

SECTION 1: STAGED CHANGE INDICATORS	
+	Number of new files in the working directory that are staged for addition
~	Number of modified files in the working directory that have staged changes
-	Number of deleted files in the working directory that are staged for removal
SECTION 2: UNSTAGED CHANGE INDICATORS	
+	Number of untracked files in the working directory that are new and not staged
~	Number of modified files in the working directory that are not staged
-	Number of deleted files in the working directory that are not staged
!	Number of unresolved conflicts

Having these indicators in your prompt is an exceptionally helpful way to have a constant, unobtrusive view of your repository status.

Posh-Git also provides command-line completion for git commands. This lets you type **git ch** and press Tab, and posh-git will complete this to `git checkout`. You can type **git stat** and press Tab, and posh-git will complete this to `git status`. Similarly, posh-git provides command-line completion for git branches. You can type **git checkout ma** and posh-git will complete this to `git checkout master` (provided you don't have any other branches that start with "ma").

If you're a PowerShell user, posh-git will quickly become an indispensable part of your Git workflow. If you're not a PowerShell user, the simple utility of posh-git may make you reconsider.

SUMMARY

In this chapter, you learned about Git, the concepts of distributed version control systems and how they differ from centralized version control. You learned how Git integrates into Visual Studio and how to take advantage of common version control operations with Git, including making changes and committing them, pushing your changes to other users, pulling changes from the server, and branching and merging with the topic branch workflow strategy. You have also learned some basics about how to work with Git repositories from the command line.

In Chapter 8, you will learn how you can work with Team Foundation Server Version Control from heterogeneous environments.

Version Control in Heterogeneous Teams

WHAT'S IN THIS CHAPTER?

➤   Understanding heterogeneous teams

➤   Working with Xcode

➤   Working with Eclipse

➤   Working from the command line

WHAT ARE HETEROGENEOUS TEAMS?

Heterogeneous teams are ones that comprise team members who focus on different technologies, languages, and tools. A typical example of a heterogeneous team is a team that maintains an application with a web front-end written in ASP.Net MVC, an iPad app, a Windows Phone app, and an Android app sitting on a business logic layer composed of RESTful APIs written in C# that calls out to Java web services. The system may also create batches of data as CSV files that get pushed over FTP to a folder where a COBOL application on the mainframe picks them up at a specified time each night for further processing.

Inside this team, you have Microsoft .NET developers, Java developers, COBOL developers, Objective-C developers, and C++ developers all needing to work together to create a seamless application suite. Typically, each group would have its preferred version control tool that would integrate with its toolset.

WORKING TOGETHER SEAMLESSLY

Managing changes in separate version control repositories based on the technology in use means that creating builds and gathering check-in data, as well as coordinating changes, become much more complex. Team Foundation Server offers these kinds of teams the ability to coordinate their version control tooling by offering two types of version control repositories that will work across all of these platforms.

Team Foundation Version Control allows teams that want to use a centralized version control system to have an integrated experience regardless of platform. When working on a Windows operating system, the team members can use Team Explorer. Team members that use the Eclipse IDE can install the Team Explorer Everywhere plug-in to gain many of the benefits derived from Team Explorer.

Team members working on iOS, Linux, or Solaris can still install Eclipse with Team Explorer Everywhere to access Team Foundation Version Control. If the team member is working on a machine without a graphical user interface, Team Explorer Everywhere ships with a command-line client that will let you perform all of the version control functions from a command line.

Team Projects based on a Git repository allow any team member across any platform and using any IDE to utilize Team Foundation Server as their remote version control repository. Many IDEs are able to integrate with Git out of the box, such as Apple's Xcode, and there are a number of Git implementations that allow use across Windows and non-Windows platforms alike.

XCODE DEVELOPMENT

Developers of iOS applications usually use Apple's Xcode development environment to support their application development efforts. The Xcode IDE has built-in support for Subversion and Git version control repositories. Because Team Foundation Server has the option to create a team project with a Git version control repository, Xcode developers can easily connect to a Git-based team project using the built-in functionality.

Using a Git-Based Team Project

To connect your Xcode IDE to the Git repository in your team project, you will first need to clone the team project's repository. Start by opening up Web Access and navigating to your team project. Click on the Code link to bring up the source control page. If you have an empty repository, you will see a page similar to Figure 8-1.

At the bottom of this page, you will see a section titled "Push an Existing Repository." There are two git commands in this section. The git remote command has a URL argument. You will need this URL to connect from Xcode.

If you already have code in the repository, you will need to look to the right side of the page. There you will see a Clone link. Click this link to display the URL needed to pass to Git to clone your repository, as shown in Figure 8-2.

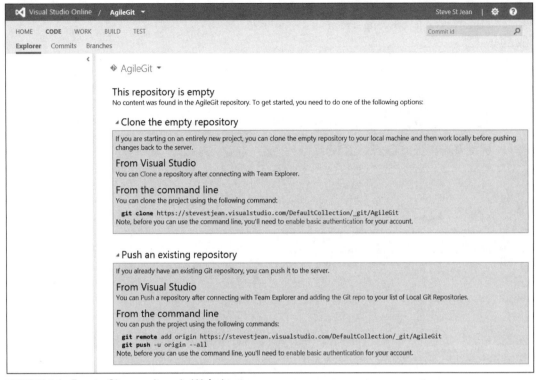

FIGURE 8-1: Empty Git repository in Web Access

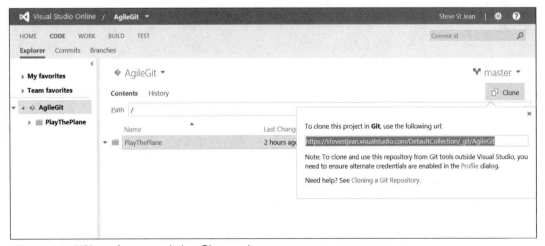

FIGURE 8-2: URL to clone an existing Git repository

Once you have that URL, you open your Xcode IDE and click on the *Check out an existing project* link on the Welcome to Xcode screen as shown in Figure 8-3.

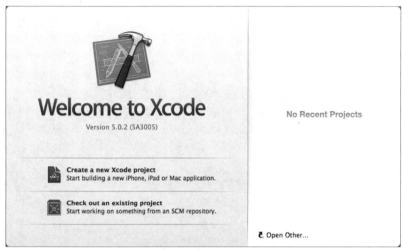

FIGURE 8-3: Welcome to Xcode dialog box

In the Check Out dialog box, enter the URL you copied from Web Access into the Repository Location text box, as shown in Figure 8-4.

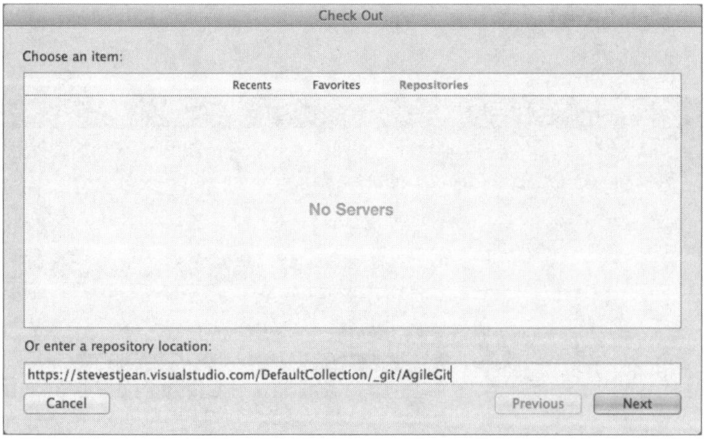

FIGURE 8-4: Set remote repository location

Xcode may prompt you for your credentials, as shown in Figure 8-5. Enter your user name and password and click the Next button.

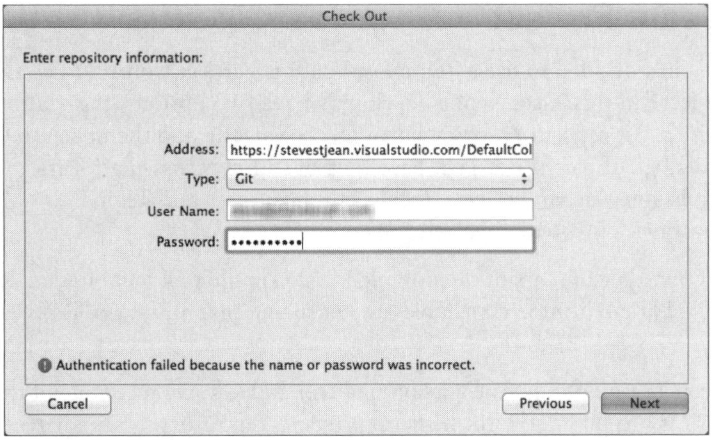

FIGURE 8-5: Enter repository credentials

ALTERNATE CREDENTIALS FOR VISUAL STUDIO ONLINE

If you are attempting to connect to a Git repository hosted on Visual Studio Online, you will need to configure Alternate Credentials on your account. Some applications that work outside the browser use Basic Authentication credentials and other applications have problems with user names that are e-mail addresses. To support these tools, Visual Studio Online lets you configure alternate credentials. For more information, see http://aka.ms/VSOAlternateCredentials.

Once Xcode has found the repository and verified your credentials it will ask you to select a directory in which to check out the project. Select a folder and click the Check Out button, as shown in Figure 8-6. When this step completes, Xcode will open with your project loaded.

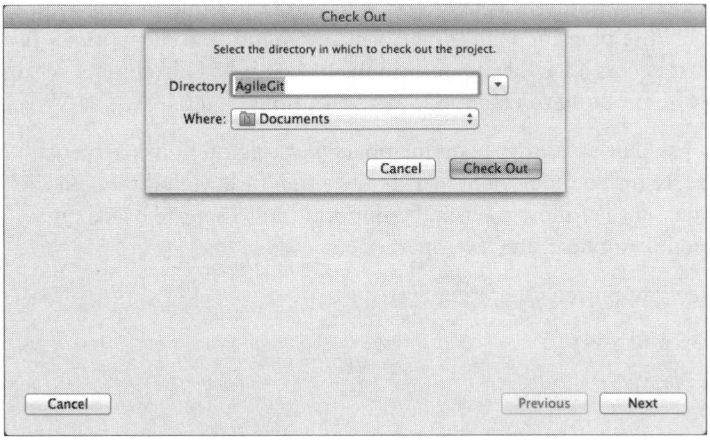

FIGURE 8-6: Enter repository credentials

Using a TFVC-Based Team Project

What happens if the organization has decided to use a Team Foundation Version Control (TFVC)–based repository for its team project? In this case, Xcode developers have two options, they can create their own team project with a Git repository, or they can use Git locally and then push to the TFVC repository using a tool called git-tf. Git-tf is a Java-based, open source, cross-platform, command-line tool that serves to bridge the gap between local Git repositories and Team Foundation Version Control repositories in a team project.

Installation is as simple as extracting the contents of the downloadable zip file to a local folder, adding the extracted folder to your PATH environment variable, and ensuring that `java.exe` is also in your PATH.

Because of the differences between Team Foundation Version Control and Git, we recommend that the team select a single Git repository to interact with the team project's repository. So in my team, I would use `git tf clone` to clone the TFVC repository from Team Foundation Server. I would then Push to a shared Git repository. The rest of my team would use `git clone` to clone the shared Git repository, and we would develop our application there. When we are done, I would Pull from the shared Git repository and then commit all of the work to TFVC using `git tf checkin`. Nobody else in my team needs to interact with the TFVC repository.

> **NOTE** *For more information and typical workflows on the git-tf tool, see* `http://gittf.codeplex.com`.

ECLIPSE DEVELOPMENT

Back in 2009, Microsoft acquired a company that created a Team Foundation Server extension for the Eclipse IDE called Teamprise. That product was later renamed to Team Explorer Everywhere (TEE) and currently includes an Eclipse plug-in, a cross-platform command-line client, and a Java SDK for building custom tools that access TFS. The team responsible for it has also built a set of Team Build extensions that allow Team Build to compile Java applications that use Ant or Maven.

Team Explorer Everywhere's Eclipse plug-in allows team members working on non-Microsoft technologies to interact with their Team Foundation Server. It is written in Java and runs on the operating systems and Java versions in the following lists. It supports IDEs that are based on Eclipse 3.5 to 4.3, including Rational Application Developer.

➤ Team Explorer Everywhere Supported Operating Systems

  ➤ Windows 8.1 (x86 and x64)

  ➤ Windows 8 (x86, x64)

- ➤ Windows 7 (x86, x64)
- ➤ Windows Vista (x86, x64)
- ➤ Windows XP (x86)
- ➤ Linux with GLIBC 2.3 to 2.11 (x86, x86_64, PowerPC)
- ➤ Mac OS X 10.8+ (Intel only)
- ➤ Solaris 8 to 11 (SPARC,x64)
- ➤ AIX 5.2 to 7.1(32- and 64-bit)
- ➤ HP-UX 11i v1 to v3 (PA-RISC, Itanium)
- ➤ Team Explorer Everywhere Supported Java Versions
  - ➤ Oracle Java 1.5+ or IBM Java 1.5+ on Microsoft Windows
  - ➤ Apple Java 1.5+ on Mac OS X
  - ➤ Oracle Java 1.5+ on Linux or Solaris
  - ➤ IBM Java 1.5+ on Linux or AIX
  - ➤ HP Java 1.5+ on HP-UX

Team Explorer Everywhere has a look and feel that is very similar to the look and feel of Team Explorer for Visual Studio. Because of this design similarity, almost all of the workflows are similar between the two Team Foundation Server clients. As such, most of the help and tutorial documentation that applies to Team Explorer applies to Team Explorer Everywhere.

One of the new features of Team Explorer Everywhere 2013 is that it exposes functionality from both TFVC- and Git-based team projects right in the plug-in in a manner similar to Team Explorer.

Installing Team Explorer Everywhere

The easiest way to install Team Explorer Everywhere on a computer with Internet access is to use the Microsoft update site. Simply open Eclipse, navigate to the Help menu, and click Install New Software. When the Install dialog box appears, click the Add button, as shown in Figure 8-7.

The Add Repository dialog box will appear. In the Name field, enter something memorable like "Team Explorer Everywhere" and set the location of the update site to `http://dl.microsoft.com/eclipse/tfs`, as shown in Figure 8-8.

Click the OK button, which will bring up the list of features in the Install dialog box. Here, select the TFS Plug-in for Eclipse check box, as shown in Figure 8-9.

Choose the Next button to download the metadata for Team Explorer Everywhere. When it finishes downloading, the Install Details dialog box will be displayed, as shown in Figure 8-10. Review the add-ins to be installed and click the Next button.

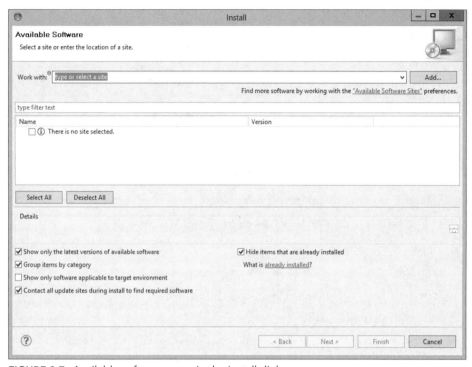

FIGURE 8-7: Available software page in the Install dialog

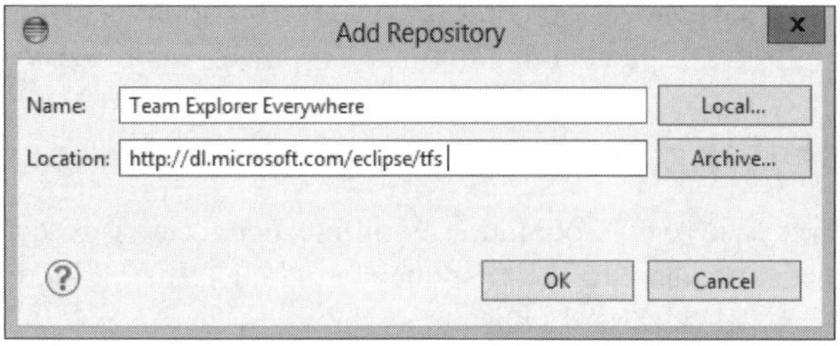

FIGURE 8-8: Add Repository dialog box

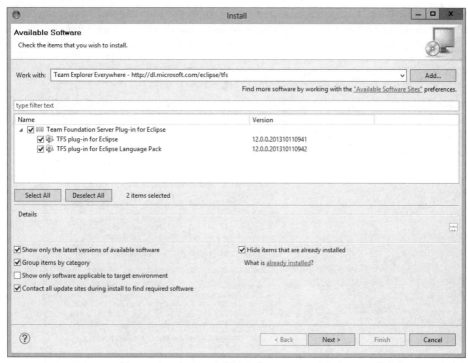

FIGURE 8-9: Feature selection in the Available Software page in the Install dialog

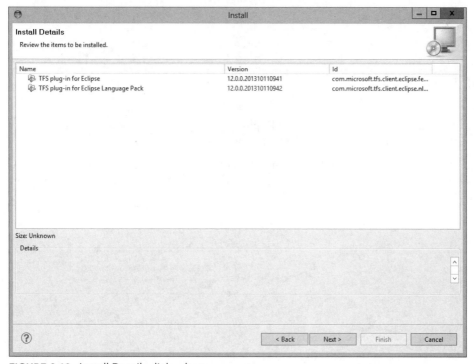

FIGURE 8-10: Install Details dialog box

In the Review Licenses dialog box, select "I accept the terms of the license agreements" and click the Finish button, as shown in Figure 8-11. Eclipse will now download and install Team Explorer Everywhere. When the installation is complete, you will need to restart Eclipse.

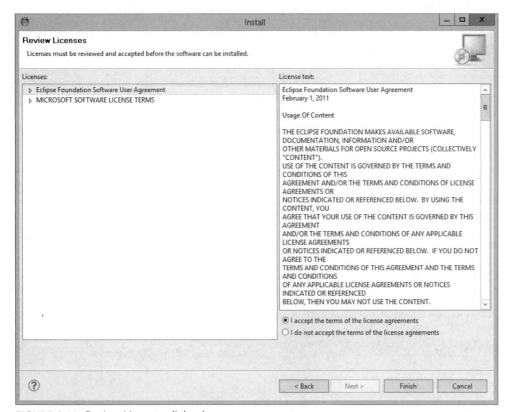

FIGURE 8-11: Review Licenses dialog box

Once Eclipse is restarted, you can access Team Explorer Everywhere's windows by selecting Window ⇨ Open Perspective ⇨ Other, as shown in Figure 8-12.

In the Open Perspective dialog box, select Team Foundation Server Exploring and click OK, as shown in Figure 8-13. The Eclipse workbench now has a section holding Team Explorer, as shown in Figure 8-14.

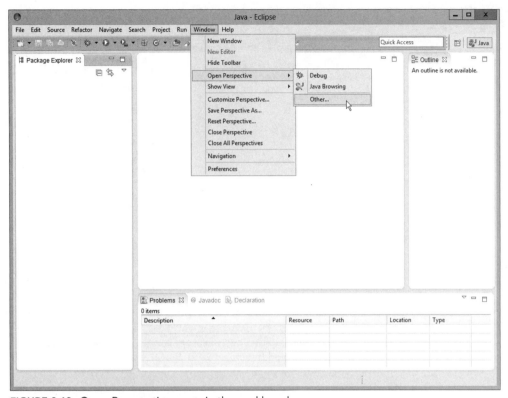

FIGURE 8-12: Open Perspective menu in the workbench

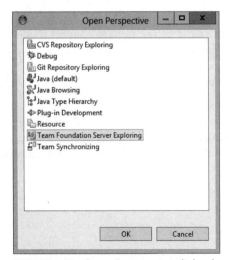

FIGURE 8-13: Open Perspective dialog box

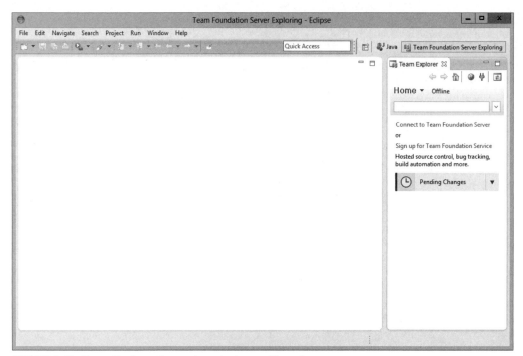

FIGURE 8-14: Team Explorer Everywhere in the workbench

Connecting Team Explorer Everywhere to Team Foundation Server

Now that you have Team Explorer Everywhere installed into Eclipse, you need to connect it up to your Team Foundation Server. Start by clicking on the Connect to Team Foundation Server link in Team Explorer, as shown in Figure 8-14. In the License Agreement page of the Add Existing Team Project dialog box, click the "I have read and accept the terms in the License Agreement" and click the Next button, as shown in Figure 8-15.

In the Team Project page, click the Servers button, as shown in Figure 8-16. In the Add/Remove Team Foundation Server dialog box, click the Add button. In the Add Team Foundation Server dialog box, enter the name of your Team Foundation Server in the Name or URL of Team Foundation Server text box, as shown in Figure 8-17, and click OK.

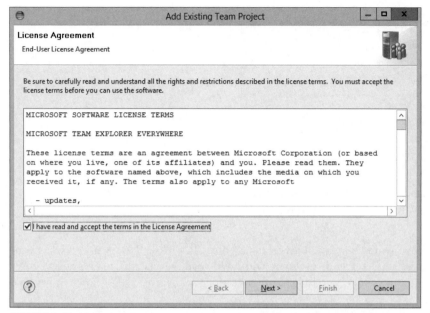

FIGURE 8-15: License Agreement page

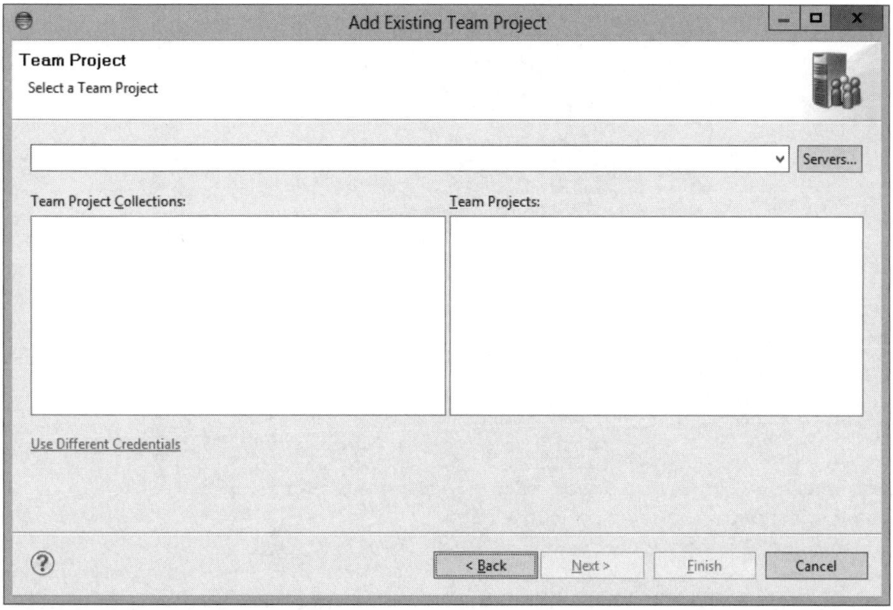

FIGURE 8-16: Team Project page

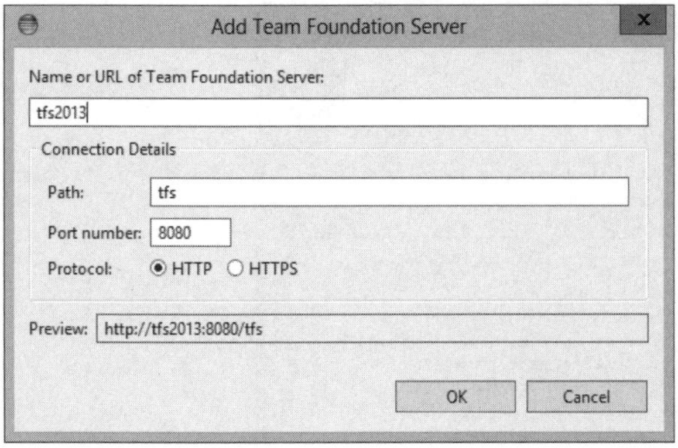

FIGURE 8-17: Add Team Foundation Server dialog box

Back in the Add/Remove Team Foundation Server dialog box, click Close. Now you can select your Team Foundation Server in the server drop-down, which will load the available team project collections. Select your team project collection to load the collection's team projects, as shown in Figure 8-18.

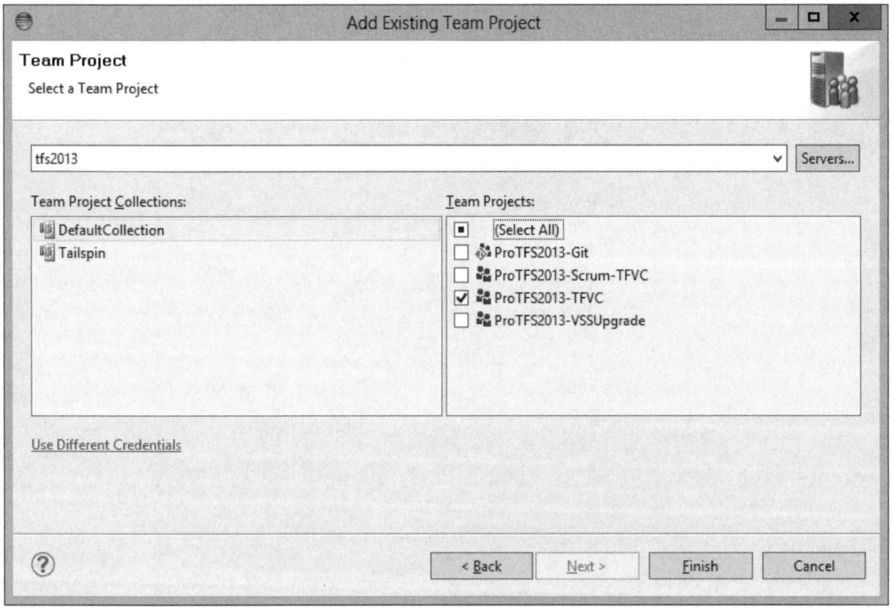

FIGURE 8-18: Team Project page with team project selected

To complete the process, click Finish. This will finalize the connection between Team Explorer Everywhere and Team Foundation Server. Your IDE is now ready to work with Team Foundation Server, as shown in Figure 8-19.

FIGURE 8-19: Team Explorer Everywhere connected to TFS

Using Team Foundation Version Control

Once Team Explorer Everywhere is installed and connected to your TFVC-based team project, you can click the Source Control Explorer link in TEE to open the Source Control Explorer window, as shown in Figure 8-20.

Store an Existing Eclipse Project in TFVC

One of the first things you have to do is take the source code for your project and place it into your team project. To do this you will have to have your project open in Eclipse and TEE connected to TFS.

Start by right-clicking on your project in Package Explorer and selecting Team ➪ Share Project from the context menu, as shown in Figure 8-21.

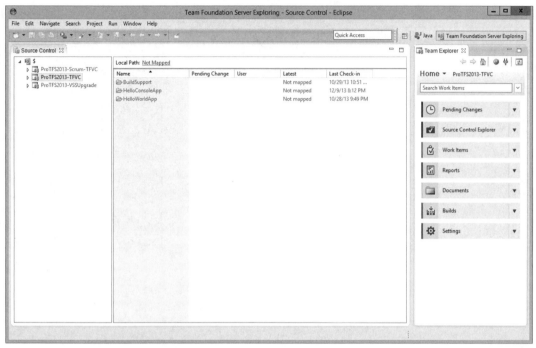

FIGURE 8-20: Source Control Exploresr in Eclipse

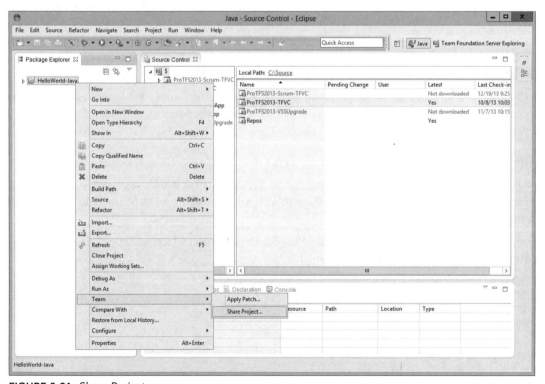

FIGURE 8-21: Share Project menu

This will bring up the Share Project Wizard. Select Team Foundation Server from the repository plug-in list, as shown in Figure 8-22, and then click Next.

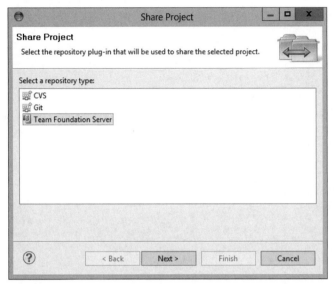

FIGURE 8-22: Selecting the repository plug-in

When the Server Location step appears, navigate to your team project. Note that the Eclipse project name is appended to the selected folder in the Project folder path text box, as shown in Figure 8-23. Once you have your path selected, click Next.

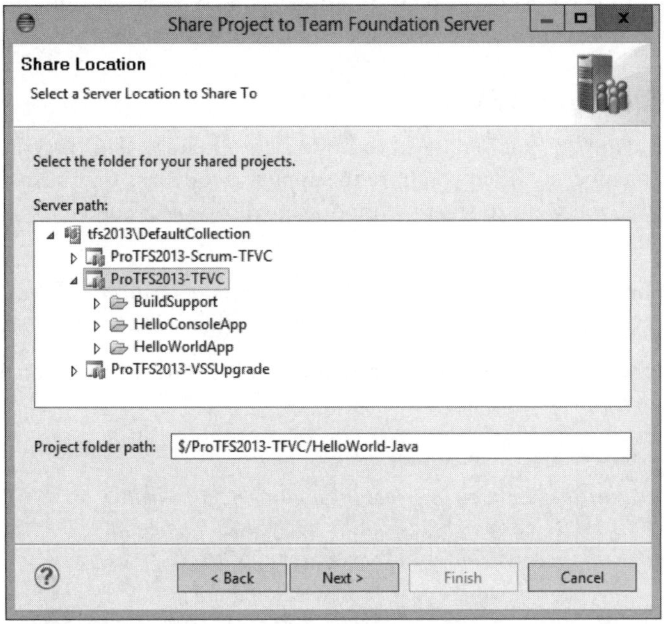

FIGURE 8-23: Selecting a server location

Review your configuration and then click Finish, as shown in Figure 8-24. This will create a set of pending changes (adds) in version control, as shown in Figure 8-25.

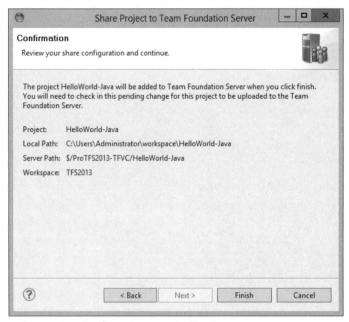

FIGURE 8-24: Confirmation pane in Share

In the Pending Changes pane, enter a comment and then click the Check in button as shown in Figure 8-25 to commit your changes to the repository. Congratulations, you have successfully shared your Eclipse project in Team Foundation Server.

Import an Existing Eclipse Project from TFVC

Now that you have your source code available, you will need to bring it into Eclipse. This is typically done when you get a new team member or when you have to support a codebase that hasn't been touched for a while. In either case, you want to start by importing your project code into Eclipse.

Start by selecting File ➪ Import... to open the Import Wizard's Selection pane. Expand the Team node and select Team Foundation Server as an Import Source, as shown in Figure 8-26. Click Next.

In the Projects Selection pane, select the folder containing your application's `.project` file and click Next, as shown in Figure 8-27.

> **NOTE** *If you want to import multiple Eclipse projects, you can select multiple folders in the tree view using Ctrl+left-click on each folder, or you can select a range of folders by left-clicking on the first folder and then using Shift+left-click on the last folder.*

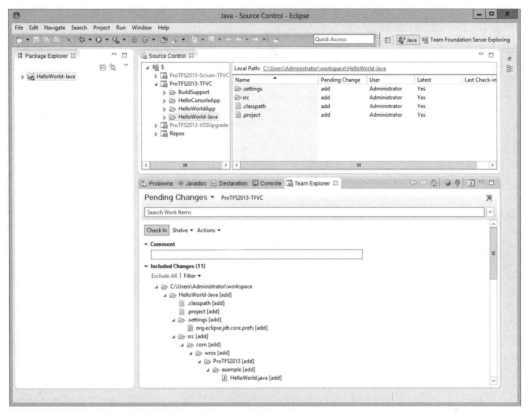

FIGURE 8-25: Pending Adds in Source Control Explorer

FIGURE 8-26: The Select pane in the Import Wizard

FIGURE 8-27: Projects Selection in the Import Wizard

When the Confirmation pane is displayed, review the list of Eclipse projects that have been selected for import. When you are satisfied with the list, click Finish, as shown in Figure 8-28.

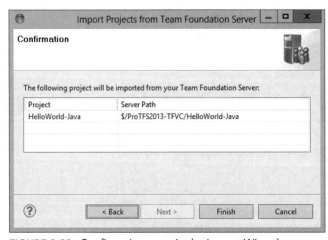

FIGURE 8-28: Confirmation pane in the Import Wizard

Team Explorer Everywhere will download the project's source code into your Eclipse workspace and load the Eclipse Project into Package Explorer, as shown in Figure 8-29. You are now ready to work with your application code.

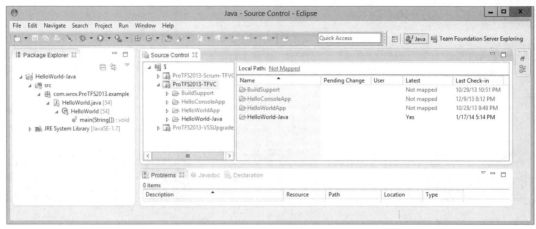

FIGURE 8-29: Eclipse project open in Package Explorer

Add, Delete, Edit, Rename, Check-Out, and Check-In Files

Team Explorer Everywhere provides much of the same functionality to Eclipse developers as Team Explorer provides to Visual Studio developers. The features, commands, and even the look and feel are almost identical. Because of this, the information contained in Chapter 6 relating to check-out, check-in, adding, deleting, and renaming files in version control is also applicable to Eclipse developers.

> **NOTE** *Because of the similarity between Team Explorer Everywhere and Team Explorer, much of the documentation available to Team Explorer users is also applicable to Team Explorer Everywhere users. For more information on using Team Explorer Everywhere, see Adopting Team Explorer Everywhere on MSDN at* http://aka.ms/AdoptingTEE.

Using Git

Eclipse developers working with a Git-based team project can use the EGit plug-in to access their team project repository just like any other Git repository. EGit is maintained on the Eclipse website and can be found in the Eclipse Marketplace or at http://www.eclipse.org/egit. When working with Git-based team projects stored on Visual Studio Online, you need to enable Alternate Credentials on your account so that basic authentication can be used to connect to the Service. For information on enabling Alternate Credentials in Visual Studio Online see http://aka.ms/VSOAlternateCredentials.

WORKING WITH THE CROSS-PLATFORM COMMAND-LINE CLIENT

Team members whose development machines are running an operating system that doesn't provide a GUI in which to run Eclipse and Team Explorer Everywhere can still participate in your team project. For those team members, Microsoft provides the Team Explorer Everywhere Command-Line Client (CLC), which can be used to access the team project's version control repository from a command shell.

Install and Connect

The first step is to download the Command-Line Client files from Microsoft. The Command-Line Client is part of Team Explorer Everywhere and can be downloaded from the Team Explorer Everywhere download page at `http://aka.ms/DownloadTEE`. When you click the Download button you will be given the option to select the files to be downloaded. Select the `TEE-CLC-12.0.0.zip` file's check box and click Next, as shown in Figure 8-30.

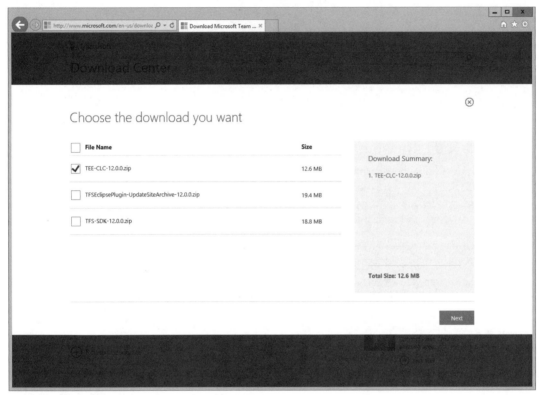

FIGURE 8-30: Team Explorer Everywhere download page

Once the zip file is downloaded, copy the archive over to the target machine and extract the files from the archive. Now you will need to change the system/shell's PATH environment variable to include the folder where the archive was unzipped. You will also need to add the Java Runtime Environment or Java Development Kit location to the PATH or set the JAVA_HOME environment variable to point to your Java installation.

Once that is complete, open a command prompt and type **tf** and hit Enter. You should see output from the Command-Line Client, as shown in Figure 8-31.

> **NOTE** *For additional information about any of the tf commands, type **tf help** followed by the name of the command you want information about. So to see how the* merge *command works, type **tf help merge**.*

FIGURE 8-31: Command-Line Client help

AUTHENTICATION

Every interaction with Team Foundation Server is constrained by your rights within TFS. When you perform a version control operation, TFS needs to be able to authenticate you prior to performing the operation.

When using the `tf` command-line tool you must provide your credentials by adding the `-login:<username>,<password>` option to the `tf` command. For example, if you want to perform a check-in, you would use `tf checkin -login:tfs2013\steve,myPassword`. The user name can be specified in `domain\username` or `username@domain` format.

If you want to let Team Explorer Everywhere cache your credentials, you can set the `TF_AUTO_SAVE_CREDENTIALS` environment variable to any value. When this value is set, the next usage of the `-login` option will save the credentials to the credential cache. From that point on, those credentials will be used for each invocation of the `tf` command.

For more information see `http://aka.ms/CLCAuth`.

Creating a Workspace Mapping

Before you can perform any version control operations, you need to review and accept the Microsoft Software License Terms. To view the License, type **tf eula** and press Enter. When the License is displayed, it will prompt you for acceptance. Type **y** or **yes** and press Enter. If you want to accept the License without these steps, you can type **tf eula /accept**.

Now that the legal stuff is out of the way, you will need to create a workspace on your machine that connects it to Team Foundation Version Control in your team project. In the first command in Figure 8-32, we are creating a workspace called MyApp inside the http://tfs2013:8080/tfs/ DefaultCollection team project collection.

FIGURE 8-32: Mapping a server folder to a local folder

Next you need to create a folder mapping from a location in version control to your local machine. You'll start by creating a local folder called **MyApp** in C:\, and then you'll use the tf workfold command to map the folder in version control to your local folder, as shown in Figure 8-32.

Performing a Get from Team Foundation Server

To perform version control activities, you need to change you working folder to the local directory that Team Foundation Server knows about so you type **cd c:\MyApp** and press Enter. Once there, you can use the tf get command to retrieve the latest version of all of the files in your project from source control, as shown in Figure 8-33.

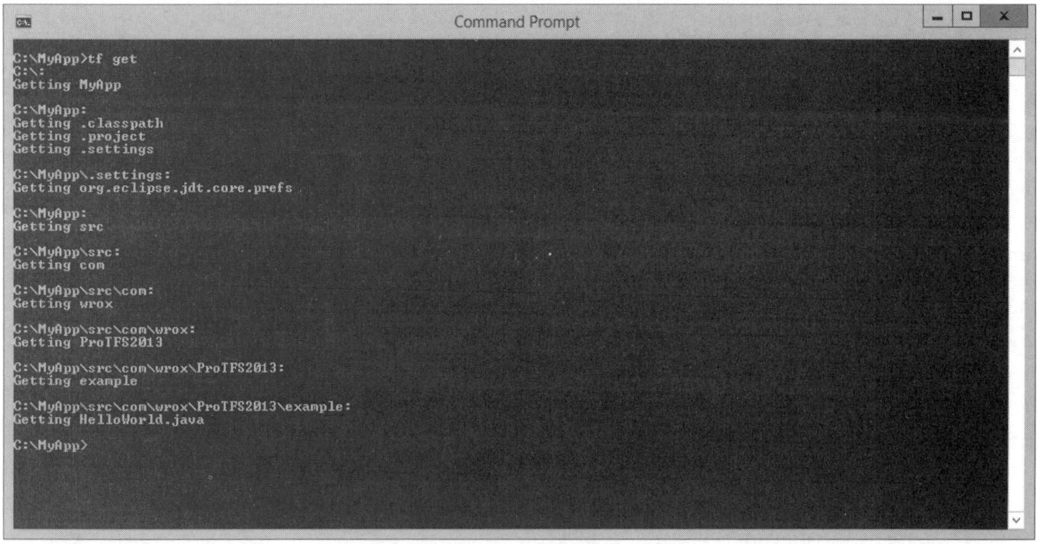

FIGURE 8-33: Retrieving the latest version from version control

Editing Files and Committing Changes

Now with that done, you can make changes to your files. When you're ready to check in your changes, you can issue a `tf status` command to see what is changed in my workspace. Figure 8-34 shows that you have made an edit to the `HelloWorld.java` file. To commit that change to version control you'll use the `tf checkin` command with the `/comment` parameter to add a comment to your check-in, as shown in Figure 8-34.

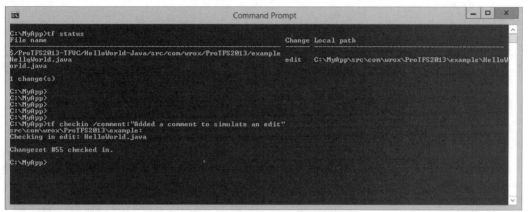

FIGURE 8-34: Reviewing and committing changes

To show that these changes were actually committed to Team Foundation Server, you can open Eclipse, go to your project folder in Source Control Explorer, and get the history of changes to that folder. As you can see in Figure 8-35, Changeset 55 contains the comment that you added when you checked in your edits.

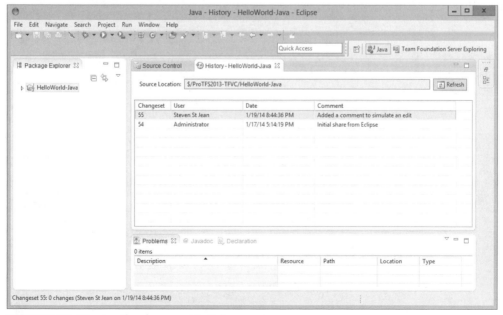

FIGURE 8-35: Viewing the changeset in Eclipse

> **NOTE** *For more information on using the Team Explorer Everywhere Command-Line Client, see* `http://aka.ms/CLCBeginnersGuide`. *For help with the available commands, see the Team Explorer Everywhere Command-Line Reference on MSDN at* `http://aka.ms/CLCCommands`.

SUMMARY

In this chapter, you learned what constitutes a heterogeneous team and how Team Foundation Server supports those teams across disparate operating system and development platforms. You were shown how Xcode developers can use Team Foundation Version Control and Git-based team projects to safeguard their source code.

Additionally, you were introduced to Team Explorer Everywhere both as a plug-in to the Eclipse IDE as well as in a command-line client for use in situations where development occurs in a non-GUI-based environment.

In Chapter 9, you learn how you can migrate your source code from legacy version control systems into Team Foundation Server.

Migration from Legacy Version Control Systems

WHAT'S IN THIS CHAPTER?

➤ Understanding the difference between upgrade and migration

➤ Comparing tip versus history migration techniques

➤ Migrating from Visual SourceSafe using the wizard

➤ Understanding Team Foundation Server Integration Platform

➤ Getting to know third-party tools for other legacy systems

Most teams adopting Team Foundation Server don't have the good fortune of starting from the very beginning with their applications. More than likely, there is an existing repository of source code that teams will want to move in some capacity into Team Foundation Server so they can continue software development from there.

That team may be using the latest version of Microsoft Visual SourceSafe (VSS) only to find themselves in an unsupported scenario since July 2012, which was when Microsoft discontinued mainstream support for Visual SourceSafe 2005. The team's goal may be to move to a new version control system, such as Team Foundation Server or Visual Studio Online, so that they can receive support if they are in a situation where they might need it in the future. They may also be using one of the other available version control systems—either commercial or open source.

One thing is certain: The process of moving to a new version control system gives you the rare opportunity to reorganize and clean up parts of the source code organization that has needed attention. This chapter explores the different options available for migrating existing source code into Team Foundation Server.

MIGRATION VERSUS UPGRADE

Team Foundation Server administrators may say that they want to *migrate* from a previous version of Team Foundation Server to Team Foundation Server 2013. More than likely, they mean that they want to *upgrade* to the newer version. If the Team Foundation Server administrator chooses the incorrect approach, the team will experience a loss of data and more work through the transition to Team Foundation Server 2013.

Upgrade

The term *upgrade* refers to the process of using the Team Foundation Server Upgrade configuration wizard to move data from a previous version of Team Foundation Server to the latest version. This scenario is different from setting up a new Team Foundation Server 2013 server and then attempting to "move" source code and work items into that new server. Upgrades are always fully supported and are tested in many configurations before being released. In an upgrade, data on the server is transformed at the database level, and all data and metadata are preserved.

By using the appropriate configuration wizard, the process is capable of using a full-fidelity upgrade to keep all of the data and history with the least amount of effort for the administrator and the team members using the server.

There are also different types of upgrades, such as the following:

➤ **In-place upgrade**—Defined as an upgrade that, when complete, will use the same set of hardware running the current Team Foundation Server version.

➤ **Migration-based upgrade**—Defined as an upgrade involving a second, duplicate set of hardware that will host the new version of Team Foundation Server when the process is complete. Note that, despite having a similar name, a migration-based upgrade is *not* a migration.

> **REFERENCE** *Chapter 27 examines topics related to the process of upgrading Team Foundation Server from previous versions.*

Migration

A *migration* refers to the process of replaying actions from one system into another system. One of the key differences, as compared to an upgrade, is that a migration is a *lower fidelity data transfer*. In Team Foundation Server, only version control and work item tracking data can be migrated between servers. Build data, reports, and numerous other pieces of metadata cannot be migrated. In general, available migration tools have significantly less testing than the upgrade process, and most available tools have limited support (because they are released out-of-band for the normal release).

In the case of a migration, the data transformations are done using only the public APIs, which are limited to providing only certain pieces of information while moving data. The result of these limitations is that some data is lost or distorted in the process of migration. Examples of this are artifact IDs (changeset numbers, work item IDs), date timestamps, area paths, and iteration paths.

> **NOTE** *Matthew Mitrik, a program manager on the Team Foundation Server Version Control team, has written several blog posts about this particular concept and discusses each of the different scenarios. For more information, visit* `http://aka.ms/TfsUpgradeOrMigration`.

MIGRATING HISTORY OR LATEST VERSION

One of the first determinations your team must make is whether you want to migrate all of the source code history from your legacy version control system or just take the latest version (which is sometimes referred to as the *tip* version) at a particular milestone. Most teams will immediately answer, "We want the history. We cannot move without all of the history." However, that may not always be the wisest choice for your team.

The clear advantage of migrating history is the ability to immediately benefit from all of the history your team has been putting into the version control system over time. Source code history can be extremely valuable when you need to determine how long a change has been included in the product, how it was first introduced, or who introduced it.

Another advantage of moving the history to Team Foundation Server is the ability to take the legacy servers that housed the existing source code out of commission. Not having to support two separate systems can definitely be a strong benefit for some teams in terms of maintenance, cost savings, and licensing cost savings.

However, there are possible downsides to migrating the source code history into a new system such as Team Foundation Server. Following are some of those downsides:

➤ **Testing**—Migrations should be treated like any type of software development project. Time and effort should be dedicated to testing the migration numerous times in a test environment to ensure that the migration occurs exactly as planned and the end-result is what you expect.

➤ **Third-party purchase**—It is possible that the team may want to leverage a third-party migration tool that is commercially available. This involves purchasing a license and a potential support contract for help from the vendor when using the migration tool.

➤ **Custom software development**—It is also possible that a custom tool or Team Foundation Server Integration Platform adapter will need to be developed and tested. This is particularly the case whenever a tool is not available commercially.

➤ **Playback execution time**—In addition to planning, development, and testing time as part of a migration effort, you must also consider the amount of time it will take to actually play back all of the history into Team Foundation Server. Essentially, each action that has ever occurred in the legacy version control system must be committed in sequence into Team Foundation Server.

Ultimately, the return on investment for moving the source code history should be determined and weighed against the downside. If the team does end up moving over only the tip version, it can always leave around the legacy version control system in a read-only state to allow team members to research history in the archive if needed.

> **NOTE** *For more information about this particular topic, the hosts of the Developer Smackdown podcast and their guest, Ed Blankenship, discuss Team Foundation Server Migrations. This episode is available as an mp3 download at* `http://aka.ms/EdPodcastMigration.`

MIGRATING FROM VISUAL SOURCESAFE

If a team is currently using Microsoft Visual SourceSafe (VSS), then it is in luck. Team Foundation Server 2013 includes a streamlined VSS Upgrade Wizard that will take a VSS repository and migrate it into a team project in Team Foundation Server or Visual Studio Online.

WHERE DID VSSCONVERTER.EXE GO?

In Team Foundation Server 2012, the `VSSConverter.exe` tool was updated and renamed to `VssUpgrade.exe`. Unlike the VSS Upgrade Wizard, which is designed to streamline the most common upgrade scenario, this tool allows a much finer grain of control.

This tool includes several features that the wizard does not currently support, including the following:

➤   Move entire repository or only specified folders.

➤   Map locations from the legacy repository to new locations in the Team Foundation Server version control repository.

➤   Analyze the VSS repository for corruption and other migration issues before migration begins.

➤   Map VSS users to Active Directory (AD) domain user accounts.

➤   Update source control bindings during migration from VSS bindings to the appropriate Team Foundation Server bindings in the Visual Studio solution and projects.

The link in the Visual SourceSafe Upgrade section of the Team Foundation Server 2013 Administration Console links to the Visual SourceSafe Upgrade Tool page that is compatible with Team Foundation Server 2010, 2012, and 2013. As of this writing, the page does not explicitly state compatibility with Team Foundation Server 2013.

For more information on the VssUpgrade.exe utility which also supports Team Foundation Server 2013, see `http://aka.ms/Tfs2012VSSUpgrade.`

> **NOTE** *Microsoft Visual SourceSafe 2005 Standard Edition mainstream support ended July 10, 2012. When Microsoft ends mainstream support for a product, it ceases to release non-security hotfixes, provide telephone support, and supply other mainstream support options. Certain extended support options may be available to some companies for some of the benefits, but such companies must have acted within 90 days from the end of mainstream support to take advantage of them. The most up-to-date information about the support life cycle for Visual SourceSafe 2005 is available at* `http://aka.ms/SupportVSS`*. A company can also contact its Microsoft representative to inquire further about support options after mainstream support ended.*

The VSS Upgrade Wizard plays back each of the check-ins into Team Foundation Server during the migration. It does so by creating changesets of files that were checked in at relatively the same time by the same user and with the same comment. Also, the changes must not conflict with one another to be included in the same changeset. For example, if a user added a specific file and then deleted it in the relatively same time period, then those two actions will not be committed in the same changeset during migration.

One of the outcomes that will be noticed is that the date and timestamp for the new changesets will be set to the time that the migration action actually occurred, instead of the original time. The original check-in date and timestamp will be stored in the changeset's comment for reference purposes. Additionally, the original user will not be stored in the comment if that user is not mapped appropriately. If the user is mapped appropriately, the user name will be in the changeset's user name field.

This section examines the different options that teams have available if they want to migrate the full history from VSS into the Team Foundation Server version control repository.

Preparing to Use the VSS Upgrade Wizard

The very first step before attempting to begin a migration effort is to ensure that the VSS repository has been fully backed up. This provides the ability to restore it to its original state if there are any errors that occur during the migration. Be sure to always run the migration utility against a copy of the database, instead of against the actual database.

One key step is to ensure that, if the VSS database version is older than the latest version (Visual SourceSafe 2005) then the database should be upgraded before the migration occurs. The DDUPD utility can be used for upgrading to the latest version after installing Visual SourceSafe 2005.

A second important step before starting the wizard is to run the Visual SourceSafe ANALYZE utility on your VSS repository. This will check the integrity and fix any structural errors.

> **NOTE** *More information on the VSS ANALYZE utility can be found at* `http://aka.ms/VssAnalyze`*.*

Your development team may choose to not migrate all of the history stored in the VSS repository and instead choose to migrate only a subset of that history. Your team might decide that it only needs the last year's history to reduce the amount of migration execution time needed. If that is the case, the administrator should use the archive functionality available in VSS to archive all content before the selected date.

> **WARNING** *Using the archive functionality in VSS will permanently remove the source code and history specified. Be sure to back up the VSS database before taking this step if you need to keep that data.*

For those instances where migration execution time needs to be minimized as much as possible, ensure that all of the servers and computers needed in the migration exist on the same local network or even on the same network switch. The servers and computers that will be used in the migration effort are the migration computer that will be executing the VSS Upgrade Wizard, the server hosting the file share that contains the VSS database, and the Team Foundation Server.

Finally, prepare the team for the migration by informing it of the timeframe when the migration will occur. For example, some teams will start a migration at the close of business on Friday so that the migration can be executed during the weekend, and the new location will be available by the beginning of the business day on Monday. Ideally, the team will have checked in all files, removed any check-outs, and not used the VSS database while the migration is occurring. To ensure that only the upgrade wizard has access to the repository, permissions can be removed from the file share for all users except the account that will be executing the migration.

Using the Visual SourceSafe Upgrade Wizard

Once you are ready to migrate, the first step is to download and install the latest copy of the wizard. To do that, open the Team Foundation Server Administration Console and navigate to Additional Tools and Components, and then navigate to the Visual SourceSafe Upgrade. On the right, you should see a link to download and install the latest version, as shown in Figure 9-1.

Once you have downloaded the wizard, run `tfs_VssUpgrade.exe` to start the installer. The installation wizard screen will appear and ask you for an installation path and to accept the license terms and conditions, as shown in Figure 9-2. Click Install to continue.

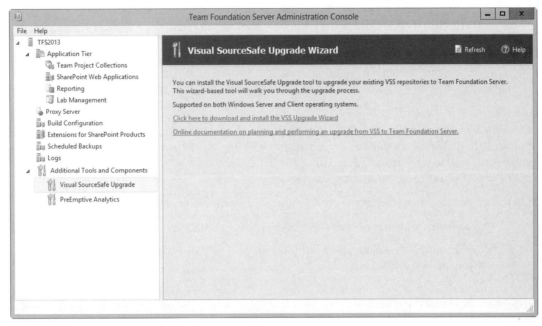

FIGURE 9-1: Visual SourceSafe Upgrade in the Administration Console

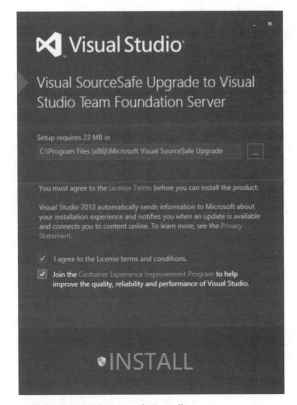

FIGURE 9-2: VSS Upgrade Installer

> **NOTE** *To streamline the process further, the installer contains a copy of the Visual SourceSafe object model. This means that there is no need to have Visual SourceSafe or other prerequisites already installed on the machine from which you are performing the migration.*

Once the wizard is installed, it can be launched from the Start menu under Microsoft Visual Studio 2012 ➪ Team Foundation Server Tools ➪ VSS Upgrade Wizard, or by running `VssToTfs.exe` from the installation path. (The default path is `C:\Program Files (x86)\Microsoft Visual SourceSafe Upgrade\VssToTfs.exe`.)

On the wizard welcome screen, you need to provide the following information:

➤ **Visual SourceSafe Repository**—The folder that contains the `srcsafe.ini` file

➤ **Visual SourceSafe Admin password (optional)**—The password for the administrator account of your repository

Once you have specified a valid repository, you can click the List Available Projects link to attempt to load the repository and enumerate the projects, as shown in Figure 9-3. When you are ready, click Next.

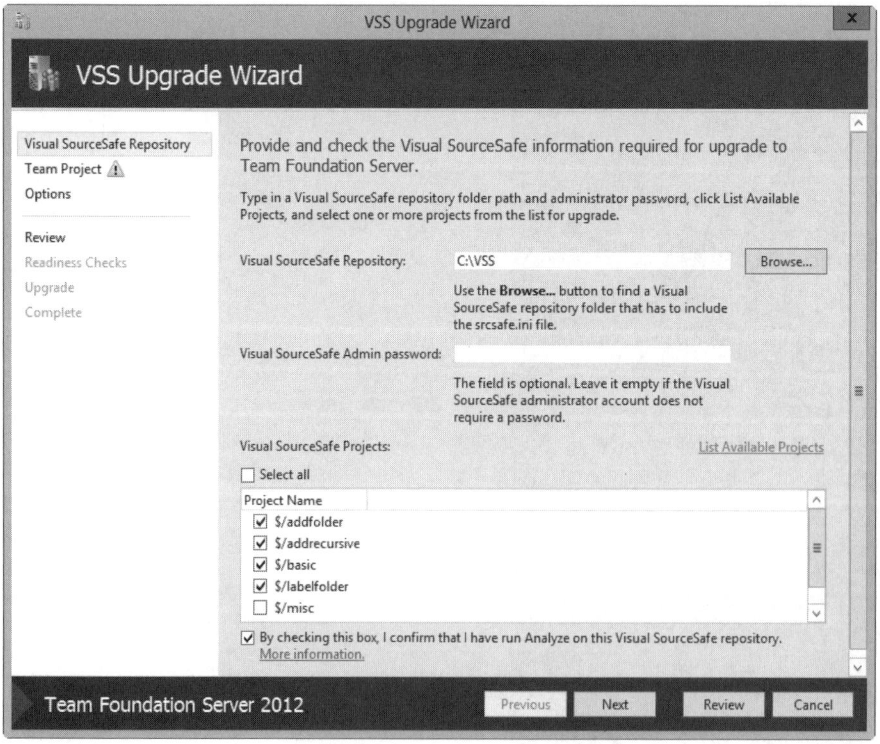

FIGURE 9-3: VSS Upgrade Wizard options screen

The following screen (see Figure 9-4) asks you for a destination team project. The destination team project can be a local Team Foundation Server instance or Visual Studio Online. It is required that this team project does not contain any existing source code folders. Click the Browse button to select an appropriate destination. Click Next to proceed to the upgrade options screen.

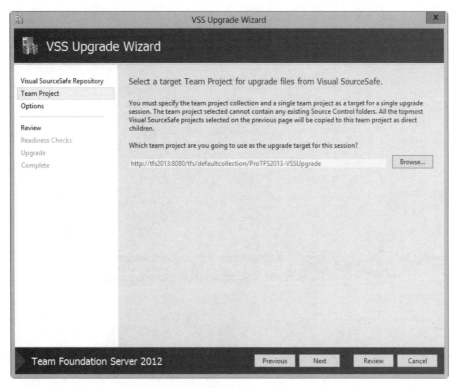

FIGURE 9-4: Target team project screen

The upgrade options screen (see Figure 9-5) allows you to choose the fidelity of the upgrade. There are two options:

➤ **Full history**—Migrate all changes back to the very first commit.

➤ **Tip**—Migrate only the latest version of each file.

The VSS Upgrade Wizard also requires a SQL Server instance for temporary storage during the upgrade process. It is best if this SQL Server instance is local or close to the upgrade wizard machine. This minimizes the latency and ensures that the migration can proceed as fast as possible.

Once you have selected an upgrade option and a valid SQL Instance, select Next. After performing a series of readiness checks, click Next to start the upgrade process. The time the wizard takes to run will depend upon the options that you chose and how many changes there are. The wizard shows the progress and the current actions being performed, as shown in Figure 9-6.

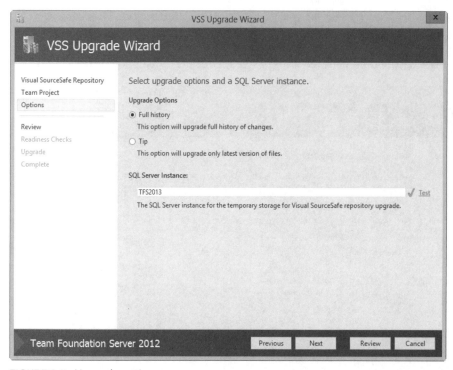

FIGURE 9-5: Upgrade options screen

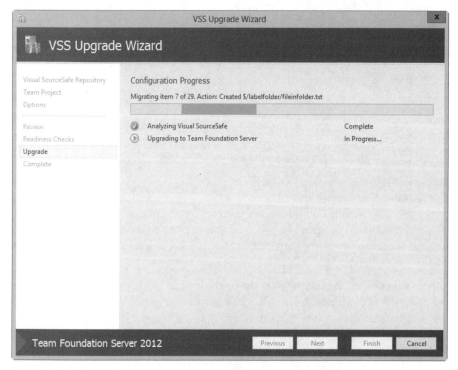

FIGURE 9-6: Upgrade progress screen

Once the upgrade process is complete, you will be able to view an Upgrade Report. This report details the migration settings—the number of changes, files, and folders migrated. The report will also display any warnings or problems that were encountered. You can see an example of the report in Figure 9-7.

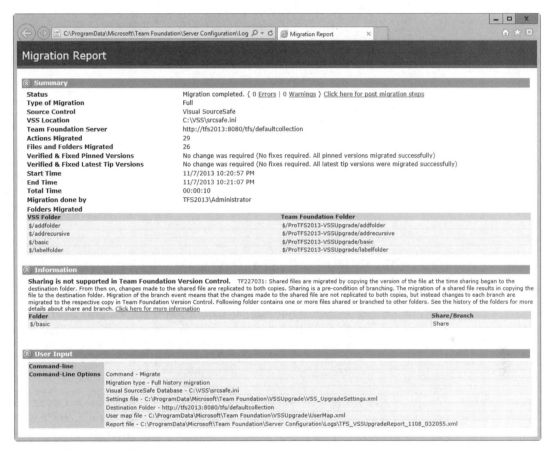

FIGURE 9-7: Upgrade Report

One of the limitations of the upgrade wizard is that the date-timestamp for the changesets in Team Foundation Server will be the time the migration occurred, rather than the original check-in time. However, as you can see in Figure 9-8, the original VSS commit time is preserved in the comments of the changeset.

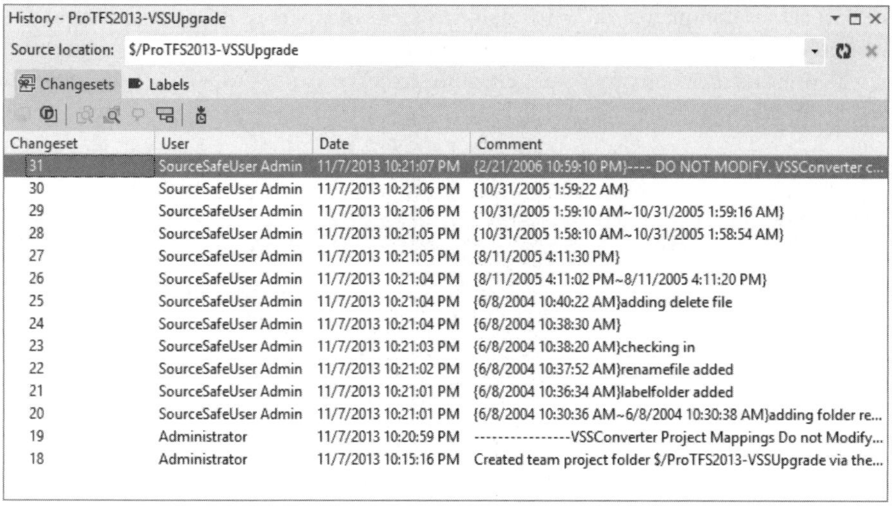

FIGURE 9-8: View history dialog box showing the original VSS timestamps

TEAM FOUNDATION SERVER INTEGRATION PLATFORM

The Team Foundation Server product team at Microsoft has dedicated resources for creating a platform called the Team Foundation Server Integration Platform, which enables customers to build migration and synchronization tools. It is essentially an entire framework that includes a user interface (UI) for configuring the migration/synchronization run, a service for executing the actions, and even a conflict resolution experience for situations when the tool is unable to handle migration/synchronization actions.

Microsoft has provided the free utility and source code on a dedicated CodePlex project site at http://tfsintegration.codeplex.com/. Occasional updates are uploaded to the CodePlex project site, and the Visual Studio ALM Rangers have created quite a bit of documentation that is available to get you started. Figure 9-9 shows a screenshot of the Team Foundation Server Integration Platform configuration utility.

> **NOTE** *As of this writing, the Team Foundation Server Integration Platform has not been recompiled against the 2013 object model. However, the 2012 Integration Platform is fully compatible with Team Foundation Server 2013. To use it you must install either Team Explorer 2012 or the Team Foundation Server 2012 Object Model Installer on the machine hosting the Integration Platform. The Object Model Installer can be found at* http://aka.ms/ TFS2012OMInstaller.

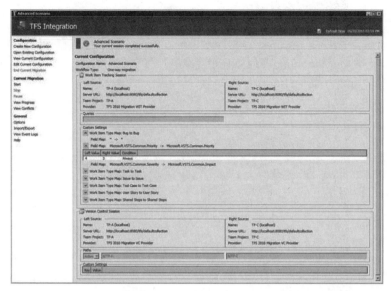

FIGURE 9-9: Team Foundation Server Integration Platform configuration utility

The Team Foundation Server Integration Platform can assist with migrating both version control artifacts and work items from legacy systems to Team Foundation Server using an adapter system. The Team Foundation Server adapters have been created, and all that you need to do is create a version control or work-item tracking adapter for the legacy system.

Examples for creating custom adapters, as well as other adapters, are available out of the box. Following are some of the adapters that were available as of this writing:

➤ Team Foundation Server 2008, 2010, and 2012 Version Control

➤ Team Foundation Server 2008, 2010, and 2012 Work Item Tracking

➤ Rational ClearCase

➤ Rational ClearQuest

➤ SharePoint List

➤ SharePoint Document Library

➤ File System

If the system you want to migrate from is a custom in-house system, you can create a custom adapter using the API available in the Team Foundation Server Integration Platform. There are samples of both types of adapters available in the source code for the Team Foundation Server Integration Platform to get you started.

> **NOTE** *As mentioned earlier in the chapter, some items are not migrated when using the tool, and this should be taken into consideration when deciding on whether the tools meet your requirements. The following artifacts are not migrated by the built-in adapters:*
>
> ➤ Permissions
>
> ➤ Labels
>
> ➤ Shelvesets
>
> ➤ Work item queries
>
> ➤ File encodings
>
> ➤ Pending changes
>
> ➤ Check-in notes
>
> ➤ Workspaces
>
> ➤ Subscriptions
>
> ➤ Test cases
>
> ➤ Check-in policies
>
> ➤ Reports
>
> ➤ Team portal
>
> ➤ Process templates
>
> ➤ Builds
>
> ➤ Warehouse data

POPULAR THIRD-PARTY MIGRATION TOOLS

Several third-party tools are available commercially that can be used by teams that don't have a tool available for them or don't feel like building a custom adapter for the Team Foundation Server Integration Platform. Let's take a look at a couple of them.

Subversion, CVS, and StarTeam

The team at Timely Migration has built a tool that is very successful at migrating source code history from a Subversion (SVN) repository to Team Foundation Server. It handles many common situations, such as migrating full or selected history, discovering branches and creating them in Team Foundation Server, and converting tags into Team Foundation Server version control labels.

In addition to SVN, the Timely Migration tool supports migrating from a CVS or StarTeam repository with similar features as the SVN migration tool.

> **NOTE** *For more information about the Timely Migration tool, visit the website at* http://aka.ms/TimelyMigration. *There is a charge for the tool, as well as any support hours needed during the test and actual migration execution runs. You can download a trial version of the tool, which is a fully featured evaluation edition that allows you to test migrations before purchasing the product. However, it obscures the contents of each file when it is checked in to Team Foundation Server.*

ClearCase

Thankfully, the Team Foundation Server Integration Platform includes an adapter that will allow teams to migrate from an IBM Rational ClearCase source control repository to Team Foundation Server. You can choose to migrate either full history or selected history with the available adapters.

More information about the Team Foundation Server Integration Platform was presented earlier in this chapter.

> **NOTE** *You can also use Team Foundation Server Integration Tools, which has a compiled copy of the platform and is the minimally necessary tool for migrating from ClearQuest. The Integration Tools release can be located in the Visual Studio Gallery at* http://aka.ms/TFSIP.

SUMMARY

Migrating source code from a legacy system can be a tough endeavor for administrators and teams. This chapter reviewed the different techniques and tools necessary for migrating from a legacy system, whether that be using the new Visual SourceSafe Upgrade Wizard, the Team Foundation Server Integration Platform on CodePlex, or one of the popular third-party commercial tools. You also learned about some suggestions for ensuring a smooth migration no matter which legacy source control system your team has been using.

In Chapter 10, you will learn about the branching and merging features available in Team Foundation Server Version Control. You will learn about the new branching and track changes visualization tools, as well as some common best practices for branching and merging strategies.

10

Branching and Merging

WHAT'S IN THIS CHAPTER?

➤ Understanding branching terminology and concepts

➤ Getting to know common branching strategies

➤ Using the branching and merging tools with TFVC

➤ Using the branching and merging tools with Git

Branching and merging in version control can open up a whole world of possibilities for improving development productivity through parallelization. Yet, for many developers, branching and merging are slightly scary and full of uncertainty. Because of a lack of good tooling in the past, many developers still shy away from branching and merging, despite Team Foundation Server having good support for both. At the other extreme, some people who see all the great branching and merging functionality available can go a little crazy with their newly found power. Overuse of branching and merging can impact developer productivity and reduce the maintainability of their repository as a result.

With the addition of Git as a supported version control repository in Team Foundation Server 2013, you now have two different methods of branching and merging available to your teams.

No matter which side of the spectrum you find yourself on, this chapter explains the fundamental principles behind the important branching and merging strategies, and it provides some key guiding principles to help you apply them to your organization's needs. This chapter highlights the branching and merging tooling available with Team Foundation Server 2013, and then concludes by walking you through the application of this tooling with some examples.

DIFFERENCES BETWEEN TFVC AND GIT WHEN BRANCHING AND MERGING

As you saw in Chapter 5, Team Foundation Server supports a centralized version control system, Team Foundation Version Control (TFVC), and a distributed version control system, Git. Some of the main differences between these two technologies lies in how they approach the idea of a "source of truth" for your versioned items.

In centralized version control repositories, the source of truth is the repository located within the server. The local client can have one or more copies of the source code on disk in the form of multiple workspaces, but local clients don't have the ability to keep historical versions nor do they actually have access to those historical versions if they are disconnected from the server. This means that all branching and merging support comes from the server and not the local client.

In distributed version control systems there is no single "source of truth." Every team member has a full copy of the entire history of the source tree plus any branches they are working on. In addition, they have the same branching and merging facilities as the server does. As such, each client has the ability to perform branching and merging locally as well as on the Team Foundation Server copy of the repository. This feature is extremely flexible and powerful, which can also make it difficult to be successful if you aren't familiar with how branching and merging work.

One of the biggest differences you will initially encounter is how your source repository is visualized within Team Foundation Server. Team Foundation Version Control–based repositories are visualized and manipulated through Source Control Explorer and Team Explorer. This allows for visual manipulation of the repository and visualization of the branch relationships and changeset history, which you will see later in this chapter.

While you can use Team Explorer to manage commits, branching, and merging in your Git-based work, you do not have the same tooling to visualize branch relationships, changesets, and merge history.

Because these models are different, we will make note of which repository type is applicable to each topic when there is a difference.

BRANCHING DEMYSTIFIED

Lots of terms and concepts are peculiar to the world of branching and merging. The following sections provide some definitions and context for those basic terms and concepts.

Branch

As stated in Chapter 5, a *branch* is a copy of a set of files in a different part of the repository that allows two or more teams of people to work on the same part of a project in parallel. When you create a branch in Team Foundation Version Control in Team Foundation Server 2013, it doesn't actually create new copies of all those files on the server. It just creates a record pointing to them—one reason why creating a new branch containing thousands or even millions of files can be done quickly.

When using Git for version control, you will be able to create branches locally. When you feel the code is ready, you can share them with other team members and the Git repository hosted within your Team Project in Team Foundation Server.

Merge

A *merge* takes the code in two branches and combines them into one codebase. For example, if you had two teams of developers working on two branches, and you wanted to bring the changes together, you would merge them. If the changes consisted simply of edits to different files in the branches, the merge would be simple—but it can get more complicated, depending on what was edited in both branches.

For example, if the same line of the same file was edited in both branches, the person performing the merge must make a decision as to which change should win. In some circumstances, this will result in a *hybrid merge*, where the combination of the *intent* behind the two changes requires a different result than the text in those versions being combined. When you branch using centralized version control, Team Foundation Version Control keeps track of the relationship between branches, as shown in Figure 10-1.

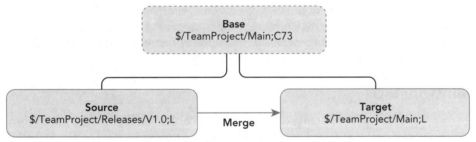

FIGURE 10-1: The relationship between the source and target branches

The branch containing your changes that you want to merge is called the *source* branch. The branch you want to merge the changes into is the *target* branch. The common ancestor between them is the *base version*. When you merge, you can select a range of changes in the source branch to merge into the target branch.

When you branch using distributed version control, Git keeps track of the relationship between the branches. Because each developer has a full copy of the Git repository, Git can search for a common ancestor when performing a Merge. This makes merging between local branches and remote copies of the repository very easy.

Conflict

If the same file has been edited in both the source and target branches, Team Foundation Server may flag this as a *conflict*. In Team Foundation Server 2012 RTM, the merge experience for centralized version control was simplified, but if the same file had been edited in both branches, it was flagged as a conflict, even if the changes are to completely different sections of the file. With the 2012.1 Update, the merge tools now check to see if the changes to the same file are actually overlapping and will only generate a conflict in this case.

For certain changes (such as a file that was edited in two different places), Team Foundation Server can make a good guess about what should happen (you want to see a file containing the changes from both places). This is called an *automerge*. In Team Foundation Server 2012, the number and type of conflicts that can be automerged were increased from earlier releases. And, unlike earlier releases, Team Foundation Server will automerge the file for you if it is safe to do so but allow you to review those changes to ensure that the desired merge behavior has been performed. For example, if two different bugs were fixed, you probably want both changes. However, if the two changes were just fixing the same bug in two different ways, perhaps a different solution is in order. In most cases, where the development team has good communication, the changes are a result of different changes being made to the file. Automerge usually does a great job of merging them together, making it easy for the developer to validate the changes.

There can also be many cases where the actual outcome is unclear, so automerging is not available. For example, if you deleted the file in one branch and edited it in another, do you want to keep the file with the changes or have it removed? The person performing the merge is responsible for deciding the correct *conflict resolution* based on an understanding of the code and communicating with the team members who made the conflicting changes to understand their intent.

As with life in general, conflict is never good in version control. Making the decision about the correct conflict resolution in version control can be a complex and time-consuming process. Therefore, it is best to adopt a branching strategy that minimizes the likelihood of conflicts occurring. However, conflicts will occur, and Team Foundation Server provides the tooling to deal with them, so conflicts should not be feared.

Branch Relationships

When you branch a folder in Team Foundation Version Control, the relationships between those branches form a standard hierarchical relationship. The source of the branch is the parent, and the target of the branch is the child, as shown in Figure 10-2. Children who have the same parent are called *sibling* branches.

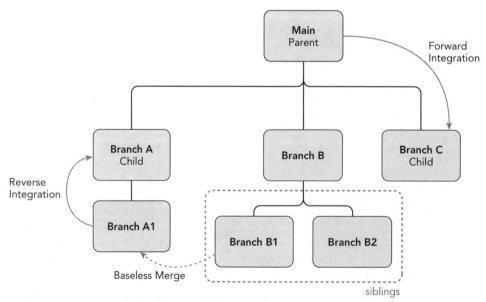

FIGURE 10-2: Hierarchical relationship in branches

In Git, all branches in a repository are related at some point in their past, so the hierarchy of branches is not relevant.

Baseless Merge

A *baseless merge* occurs when two arbitrary branches in centralized version control merge without reference to a base version. This is sometimes necessary if the source code was originally imported in a flat structure without the branch relationship being in place, or if you want to merge between a branch and another branch not a direct parent or child (for example, `Branch A1` and `Branch B1` in Figure 10-2).

Because no base version is being used to compare against, the probability of the server detecting conflicts occurring between the two branches is much higher. For example, if a file were renamed in one branch and edited in the other, it will show up as a file delete conflicting with the file edit, and then a file add that gives no hint as to which file it was related to, or that there was an edit intended for this file in the other branch. For this reason, baseless merges are discouraged with Team Foundation Server 2013 and a warning will appear whenever a baseless merge operation is selected in Visual Studio. Standard merging (one with a base version) through the Visual Studio or Eclipse clients are the encouraged method—and only one branch up or down (a parent to a child or vice versa) is allowed. Therefore, your branching model should attempt to constrain most merges between parent and child branches to minimize the amount of baseless merging required.

In Git, all branches in a repository have a common ancestor somewhere in their history. Git is very good at finding these common ancestors. This means that every merge is considered a standard merge and there is no concept of a baseless merge in Git.

Forward/Reverse Integration

Forward integration (FI) occurs when you merge code from a parent branch to the child branch. *Reverse integration* (RI) occurs when you merge code from a child branch to the parent branch. The terms FI and RI are specific to centralized version control repositories. They are often thrown around quite freely during a branching debate, so it is important to understand what they mean. If you are doing feature development in branches, it is common to use FI at various points during the feature development cycle, and then to use RI at the end. See the section "Feature Branching" later in this chapter for more information.

Push/Pull

In a decentralized version control repository the language used is relative to the branch you are working with. There is no parent or child, so the notion of Forward or Reverse is irrelevant. Instead, when you request changes from another branch, you are performing a *Pull* operation. When we send changes to another branch, you are performing a *Push*.

COMMON BRANCHING STRATEGIES

Depending on the organization of your team, and the software that you need to develop, you can adopt numerous branching strategies, all with various pros and cons. However, just as every strategy in chess is made up of simple moves, every branching strategy uses one or more combinations of some basic techniques. This section details some of the basic techniques, how they are used, and why.

When developing your own branching strategy, you should take into account the needs of your organization. In all likelihood, you may adopt a strategy that combines one or many of the basic techniques described here.

When looking at any strategy for branching and merging, you should keep in mind the following important rules:

➤ Prefer simplicity over control.

➤ Branch only when you really need to. (You can branch after the fact if you need to.)

➤ If you ever want to merge two branches together, keep the time between the branch and the merge to a minimum.

➤ Ensure that your branch hierarchy matches the path you intend your merges to follow.

> **NOTE** *For additional guidance on branching and merging with Team Foundation Server, see the "Visual Studio Team Foundation Server Branching and Merging Guide" project on CodePlex at* `http://vsarbranchingguide`
> `.codeplex.com/`. *This guidance is created by a community of Visual Studio ALM Rangers, and it combines the knowledge of Microsoft engineers and consultants with Microsoft Most Valued Professionals (MVPs) and other technical specialists in the community. The guidance also includes hands-on labs, along with a set of diagrams. Although the guidance caters to very complex branching and merging requirements, it can also be a useful starting point when creating your own branching plan.*

No Branching

It may be counterintuitive, but the simplest branching technique is to not branch at all. This should always be your default position. Do not branch unless you need to. Remember, you are using a version control tool that tracks changes over time. You can branch at any point in the future from any point in the past. This gives you the luxury of not having to create a branch on the server "just in case." You create branches only when you need them. This strategy does not preclude your team from creating local branches for their work if you are using a Git-based team project. In that case, your team members will simply push their changes to the server from their local branches when they feel their work is ready.

In Team Foundation Version Control, all branching is performed on the server, so there are things you can do to prepare yourself to make branching easier in the future if you decide you need a branch.

Figure 10-3 illustrates the most important thing that you should do if you think you might possibly need to branch in the future. When you first create your Team Foundation Version Control–based team project in Team Foundation Server, create a folder called `Main` and check it in. Then, right-click the folder in Source Control Explorer and select Branching and Merging ⇨ Convert to

Branch to get to the screen shown in Figure 10-4. This gives you an easy point to branch from in the future, and it also makes you think about the areas of your source code that live in the same branch together, which will help you in the future if you ever do decide to branch.

FIGURE 10-3: A branch called Main

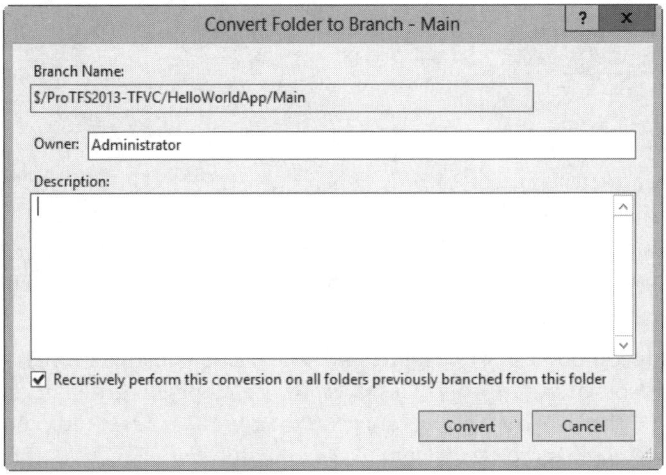

```
Convert Folder to Branch - Main                          [ ? ] [ X ]

Branch Name:
$/ProTFS2013-TFVC/HelloWorldApp/Main

Owner:  Administrator

Description:
|




☑ Recursively perform this conversion on all folders previously branched from this folder

                                        [ Convert ]   [ Cancel ]
```

FIGURE 10-4: Convert Folder to Branch screen

With no branching, you have only one branch of code to work in for all teams. This technique works great when you have small teams working on the same codebase, developing features for the same version of the application and supporting only one version of the application at a time. At some point, no matter how complex your branching strategy evolves to support your business needs, you need at least one stable area that is your main (or mainline) code. This is a stable version of the code that will be used for the build that you will create, test, and deploy.

However, during stabilization and test periods, while you are getting ready to release, it may be necessary for the team to not check in any new code into the codebase (undergo a *code freeze*). With smaller teams working on a single version, this does not impact productivity because the people who would be checking in code are busy testing to ensure that the application works, as well as getting ready for deployment.

With this technique, there is no way to start work on something new before the final build of the current version has been performed. The code freeze period, therefore, can be very disruptive because there is no way to start work on the next version until the current one has shipped. It's these times when other strategies become useful for teams of any size, even a team of one.

Branch per Release

For teams that employ branching, the most common branching technique is *branch per release*. With this technique, the branches contain the code for a particular release version, as shown in Figure 10-5.

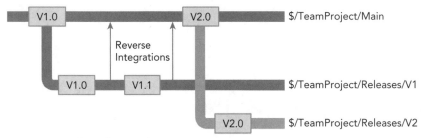

FIGURE 10-5: Branch per release

Development starts in the Main branch. After a period of time, when the software is considered ready, a branch is made to the V1 branch, and the final builds are performed from it. It is then released into production (with the code in the final production build getting a label to indicate which versions of which files were in that version). Meanwhile, development of new features for version 2 (V2) continues on the Main branch.

Say some bugs are discovered in production that must be addressed, and a small change is necessary to reflect how the business needs something to work. However, the development group does not want to include all the work for V2 that has been going on in the Main branch. Therefore, these changes are made in the V1 branch, and builds are taken from it. Any bug fixes or changes that must also be included in the next version (to ensure the bug is still fixed in that next release) are merged back (reverse-integrated) into the Main branch. If a bug fix was already in the Main branch, but needed to go into V1, it might simply be merged (forward-integrated) into it. At a certain point, the build is determined to be good, and a new V1.1 build is performed from the V1 branch and deployed to production.

During this time, development on the next version can continue uninterrupted without the risk of features being added into the code accidentally and making their way into the V1.X set of releases. When it is decided that V2.0 is ready to go out the door, the mainline of code is branched again to create the V2 branch, and then the V2.0 build is created from the new branch. Work can continue on the next release in the Main branch, but it is now easy to support and release new builds to customers running on any version that you want to keep supporting.

Branch per release is very easy to understand and allows many versions to be supported at a time. It can be extended to multiple supported releases very easily, and it makes it trivial to view and compare the code that was included in a particular version of the application. Branch per release is well-suited to organizations that must support multiple versions of the code in parallel—such as a typical software vendor.

However, for a particular release, there is still no more parallelism of development than in a standard "no branching" strategy. Also, if the organization must support only two or three versions at a time (the latest version, the previous version, and, perhaps, the version currently being tested by the business), this model can lead to a number of stale branches. While having lots of old, stale branches doesn't impact the performance of Team Foundation Server, or even cause any significant additional storage requirements, it can clutter the repository and make it difficult to find the versions you are interested in—especially if the organization frequently releases new versions. If this is the case, you may want to move old branches into an Archive folder, and have only the active branches (the versions that the development team are currently supporting) in the Releases folder.

Code Promotion Branching

An alternative to branch per release is *code-promotion branching* (or *promotion-level branching*). This technique involves splitting the branches into different promotion levels, as shown in Figure 10-6.

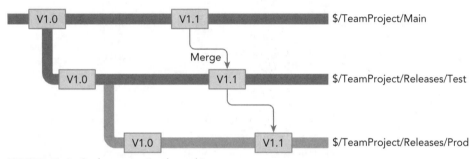

FIGURE 10-6: Code promotion branching

As before, development starts with just the Main branch. When the development team is ready to test the application with the business, it pushes the code to the Test branch (also often called the QA branch). While the code is being tested, work on the next development version is carried out in the Main branch. If any fixes are required during testing, they can be developed on the Test branch and merged back into the Main branch for inclusion in the next release. Once the code is ready to release, it is branched again from Test to Prod. When the next release cycle comes along, the same is done again. Changes are merged from Main to Test, and then Test to Prod.

Code-promotion branching works well in environments that have a single version running in production but have long test-validation cycles that do not involve all of the development team. This allows development to continue on the next version in Main while test and stabilization of the build occurs in the Test branch. It also makes it trivial for the development team to look at the code currently on each system. Finally, the branch structure makes it easy to create an automated build and deployment system using Team Foundation Build that can automatically update the QA/Test environment as code is pushed to the QA branch.

> **NOTE** *For more information on the build capabilities of Team Foundation Server 2013, see Part IV of this book.*

Feature Branching

The previous branching strategies all involve a single team working on the system in its entirety as it works toward a release. All features for that release are developed in parallel, and the build can be deployed only when all features in flight have been completed and tested. However, in large systems, or systems that require very frequent deployment (such as a large commercial website), *feature branching* (or *branch per feature*), as shown in Figure 10-7, can be useful.

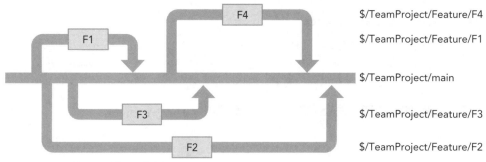

$/TeamProject/Feature/F4

$/TeamProject/Feature/F1

$/TeamProject/main

$/TeamProject/Feature/F3

$/TeamProject/Feature/F2

FIGURE 10-7: Feature branching

Feature branching is used when a project requires multiple teams to be working on the same codebase in parallel. In Figure 10-7, you see four feature teams working in separate branches (F1, F2, F3, and F4). Note that in a real branching structure, the feature branches themselves would likely have meaningful names such as FlightSelling, InsuranceExcess, or whatever shorthand is used by the project to refer to the feature under development. The Main branch is considered "gold code," which means that no active development goes on directly in this branch. However, a feature must be reverse-integrated into this branch for it to appear in the final release build and for other teams to pick it up.

Initially, F1 is started with a branch from Main. But, while it is being developed, a second and third team start F2 and F3, respectively. At the end of development of the feature, F1 is merged back into the Main branch, and the F1 branch is deleted. Then that team starts on feature F4. The next feature to finish is F3, followed by F2. At each point, once the feature is merged into the Main branch, a new version of the software is released to the public website. But only one version is ever supported at any time.

Feature branching allows for a large amount of parallel development. However, this comes at the cost of delaying the pain of integrating each team's changes until the feature is complete, and you are merging the feature branch back into Main branch. For example, in Figure 10-7, when merging the F2 branch, all changes and inevitable conflicts introduced by features F1, F2, F3, and F4 must be analyzed and resolved.

The longer a period of time that code is separated into branches, the more independent changes occur and, therefore, the greater the likelihood of merge conflicts. To minimize conflicts, and to reduce the amount of *integration debt* building up, you should do the following:

➤ **Keep the life of a feature short.** Features should be as short as possible and should be merged back into the Main branch as soon as possible.

➤ **Take integrations from the** Main **branch regularly.** In the example shown in Figure 10-7, when F1 is merged back into Main, the feature teams still working on their features should merge those changes into their feature branches at the earliest possible convenient point.

➤ **Organize features into discrete areas in the codebase.** Having the code related to a particular feature in one area will reduce the amount of common code being edited in multiple branches and, therefore, reduce the risk of making conflicting changes during feature development. Often, the number of teams that can be working in parallel is defined by the number of discrete areas of code in the repository.

When using feature branching, the whole team doesn't necessarily have to be involved. For example, one or two developers might split off from the rest of the team to go work on a well-isolated feature when there is a risk of the merge not being possible (they are working on a proof of concept), or when it is decided that the current release should not wait for that particular feature to be implemented.

IMPLEMENTING BRANCHING STRATEGIES IN CENTRALIZED VERSION CONTROL

So far, this chapter has covered a lot of the theory behind branching. This section puts that theory into action as it walks you through implementing a branching strategy using the branch tools available with Team Foundation Server 2013 and a Team Foundation Version Control–based Team Project.

The Scenario

For this example, you'll look at a fictional organization called Tailspin Toys that has installed Team Foundation Server and is using the version control functionality. Say that you are a member of the internal IT team, which supports an order-fulfillment intranet site critical to the operation of the business. The team has only one version of the site in production at any one time. However, because of the criticality of the software, the IT team has lengthy test cycles involving a series of experts from the business to ensure that the software is working as required.

The IT team has a single team project called IT and a single ASP.NET web application checked into the team project root folder at $/IT/Orders. They also have an automated build set up in Team Foundation Server.

The team has some issues when it comes to managing sources. The development process is plagued by problems and inefficiencies. There are significant periods when developers are forbidden from checking in to the repository while getting ready for a release. The delays cause the developers to end up creating large shelvesets filled with changes that become unmanageable.

Occasionally, urgent bugs are required to be fixed in the production codebase. This is done by the developer getting the label that represents the production codebase, adding the fix, building it on a local machine, and manually pushing the modified files out to production. Ensuring that the correct files are pushed to production and the source code fix is added back into version control is a manual process that has caused some problems. There have been instances where fixes to production were missing when the next version rolled out and had to be repeated again.

But, luckily, there are some people in the development organization who recognize the problems and want to come up with a branching plan to alleviate some of them. You have been selected to roll out this plan.

The Plan

After some careful consideration, the team decides that a code-promotion strategy fits their organization quite well. Figure 10-8 shows the plan that the organization has decided to adopt.

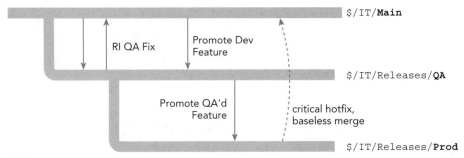

FIGURE 10-8: Example branch strategy

The code will consist of the following three branches, as suggested by the code-promotion branching strategy:

➤ Main—The main development effort is conducted here. This is the branch from which the regular continuous integration build is performed, and where new features are developed.

➤ QA—The code will live here while it is being tested by the business. Because these test periods can be lengthy, new code development will carry on in the Main branch. Any fixes or modifications to the version under test will be performed directly on the QA branch and reverse-integrated back into Main. An automated build will be created that will run early in the morning during the week. The results of that build will be pushed to the QA web server daily for testing by the business the following day.

➤ Prod—This represents the code currently running in production. Code normally goes from Main to QA into Prod. A build is also created for this branch so that urgent hotfixes can be checked in and repeatedly built. Urgent hotfixes like this are very much the exception, though. If an urgent hotfix is performed, a baseless merge is performed to push that fix back into Main. Note that the results of the Prod build are first deployed to a test environment to ensure that they work as expected before manually running a script that pushes the code to production.

Implementation

Figure 10-9 shows the current codebase.

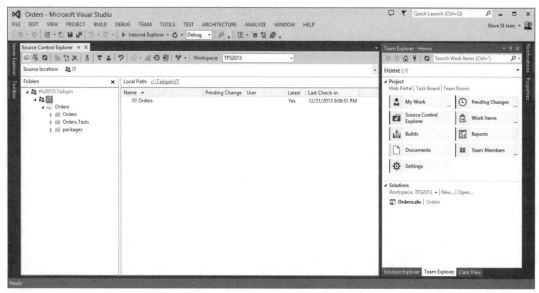

FIGURE 10-9: Current codebase in Source Control Explorer

The first thing you want to do is to move the code currently at the root of the team project in version control into a `Main` branch. This will be the most disruptive of the changes because it will require the build to be reconfigured, and team members to re-sync their workspaces. So, you decide to do this late one night, a few weeks before the IT team is due to push a release to the test team.

To move the code into a branch, you right-click the `Orders` folder containing the solution and select Move. Then you manually enter a path of **`$/IT/Main/Orders`** in the Move dialog box shown in Figure 10-10. Note that the `Main` folder does not have to exist at this point. Moving the files to that location will cause Team Foundation Server to create the parent folder.

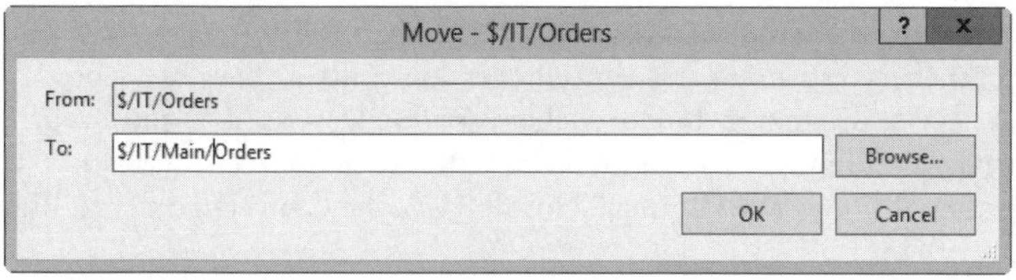

Move - $/IT/Orders	?	X
From: $/IT/Orders		
To: $/IT/Main/Orders	Browse...	
	OK	Cancel

FIGURE 10-10: Entering a path in the Move dialog box

As soon as this is done and checked in, you edit the build definition's workspace so that it looks at only the `Orders` Source Control Explorer folder under the `Main` folder, as shown in Figure 10-11.

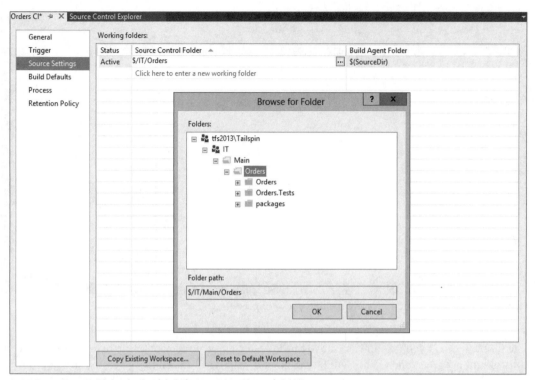

FIGURE 10-11: Editing the build definition's working folders

You also modify the Process for the build to remove the solution file from the old location, and add it in again at the new location, as shown in Figure 10-12. You then manually queue a new build to ensure that everything is working well. Everything works, so you send an e-mail notifying the team of the change to version control, and you go home for the evening.

Now, as an aside, note that the source is in the correct path, but the `Main` folder is not yet a branch. In Team Foundation Server, branches are a first-class entity in version control. They are represented by a different icon and have additional metadata such as Owner, Description, and Branch Relationships. To convert a folder to a branch, you right-click the folder in Source Control Explorer and select Branching and Merging ⇨ Convert to Branch. This displays the Convert Folder to Branch dialog box, as shown in Figure 10-13.

Note that to convert a folder to a branch, you must have the Manage Branch permission in Team Foundation Server. Also, once you have converted a folder to a branch, no folders above or below it may be a branch.

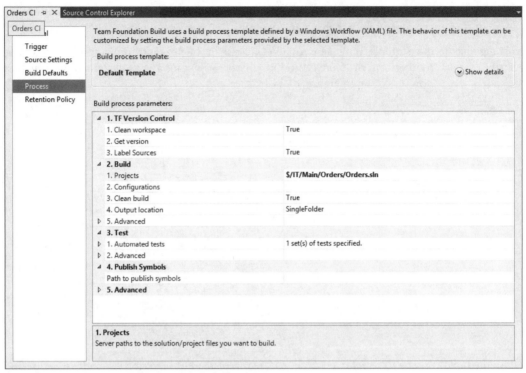

FIGURE 10-12: Modifying the Process for the build

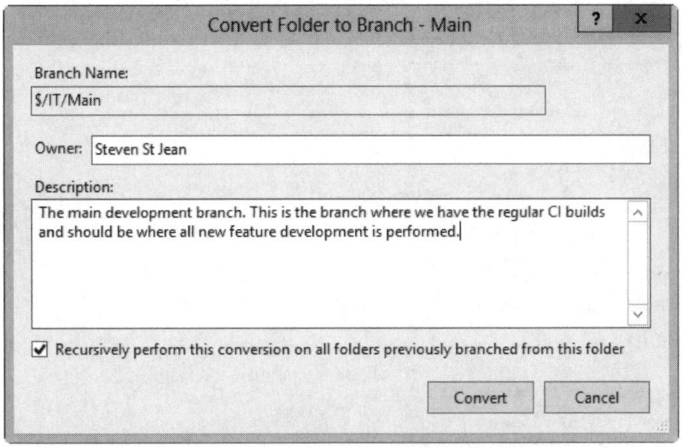

FIGURE 10-13: Convert Folder to Branch dialog box

If people had already created new branches from the Main folder, you would want to ensure that the check box shown in Figure 10-13 is selected because this will also convert those folders to branches. But this does not apply in our Tailspin Toys example.

In the future, if you ever need to convert a branch back to a regular folder, go to Visual Studio and select File ⇨ Source Control ⇨ Branching and Merging ⇨ Convert to Folder.

Now get back to the example implementation. You come in the next morning and start to get the branches set up. You perform the Convert to Branch operation on `Main` as described previously, and the source tree is now as shown in Figure 10-14.

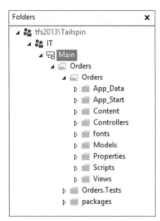

FIGURE 10-14: Main as a branch folder

When the build is ready to be released to the QA team, instead of invoking the code freeze period that used to be enforced, you take the latest version of code and branch it to create the `QA` branch. You do this by right-clicking the `Main` branch and selecting Branching and Merging ⇨ Branch, which displays the Branch dialog box for a branch (see Figure 10-15).

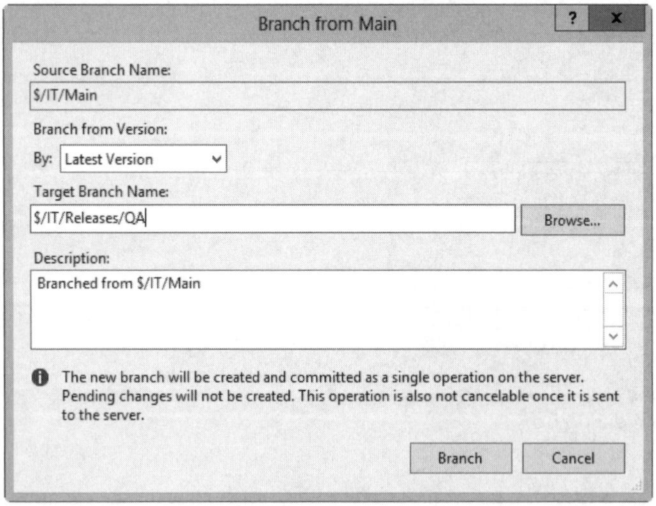

FIGURE 10-15: Branch dialog box for the Main Branch

In this dialog box, you enter the full path that you would like to create, which, in this example, is $/IT/Releases/QA. If the Releases folder does not already exist, it will be created automatically as part of this operation. As shown in Figure 10-15, there is a warning that this will be committed to the repository as part of a single transaction.

This behavior is slightly different from that experienced when branching a folder or file. When you branch a folder or file in the Visual Studio or Eclipse clients, it is assumed that you are making a copy of the file in your local workspace as well. Figure 10-16 shows an example of the Branch dialog box when a file is selected.

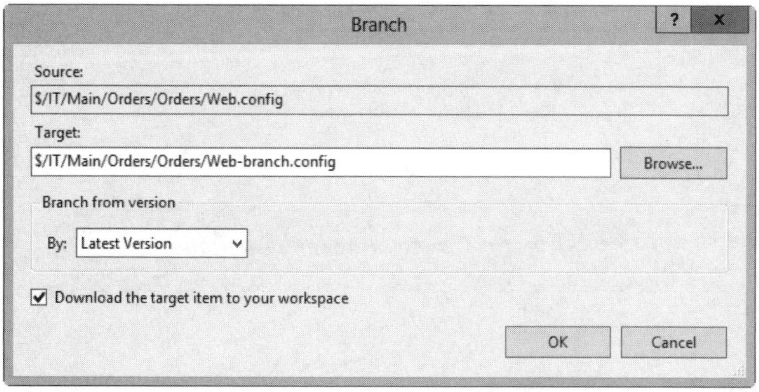

FIGURE 10-16: Branch dialog box when a file is selected

If you had selected a folder outside an existing branch, you would also get the option to convert the folders to a full branch in Team Foundation Server—but you do not have to. This is a subtle point. While branches are first-class objects in Team Foundation Server, you can branch any folder or file to another place in the repository. This is a great way to copy areas of the repository to a different part of the repository, but make the history of changes that occurred in the old location easily accessible in the new one. In Team Foundation Server, a rename is actually implemented under the covers as a simultaneous branch and a delete of the source location.

In the instance of branching a file or folder, this is done as a two-phase operation. The branch changes are made in your workspace, and then you check these in.

However, in the majority of instances, you want to branch an entire path in version control. Usually, you will not be making changes to the files or performing validation before check-in.

So, performing these in a single atomic transaction is a much more efficient use of server resources. (This is functionally equivalent to the tf branch command line with the /checkin option supplied.) Therefore, you perform the branch as indicated in Figure 10-15 and the source tree is now as shown in Figure 10-17.

A new build definition (called Orders QA) is created for the QA branch, with a scheduled trigger of 6 a.m., Monday to Friday. That way, a fresh build is ready and waiting for the test team each morning if changes have been made to the QA branch during the day.

FIGURE 10-17: QA branch created

> **NOTE** *Chapter 18 provides more information on creating build definitions.*

Dealing with Changesets

During initial testing, you notice a small bug with the stylesheet on Internet Explorer 6 on Windows XP. None of the development team was old-fashioned enough to be running this configuration, but it is still commonly found in the company, so the team decides to create a fix for it.

The modification is made to the Site.css file in the QA branch and checked in as changeset 6. The next scheduled build (Orders QA_20131231.1) picks up this change and adds it to the code running in the test environment. Once the fix has been verified, it must be merged into the Main branch.

For merges like this, it is best if the merge is performed as soon as possible, and by the developer that made the change. That way, it is fresh in his or her mind and isn't forgotten, or the fix misunderstood. The testing team has set a policy that the related bug cannot move to the Closed state until an urgent fix has been merged into the Main branch—which is a sensible policy.

To merge that code, the developer right-clicks the source branch (in this case, the QA branch) and selects Branching and Merging ⇨ Merge. This displays the Merge Wizard dialog box, as shown in Figure 10-18.

The developer opts to merge selected changesets to ensure that only the change the developer is aware of is picked up. The developer checks that the target branch has been identified as Main, and then clicks Next. This displays the changesets selection page.

On this page, you can select a single changeset or a continuous range of changesets that you want to merge. In the case of the example testing team, it has just the one changeset it is interested in (6), so the developer selects that and clicks Next, as shown in Figure 10-19. This provides a final confirmation page and, when the developer clicks Finish, the merge is performed. The pending changes page now looks like Figure 10-20.

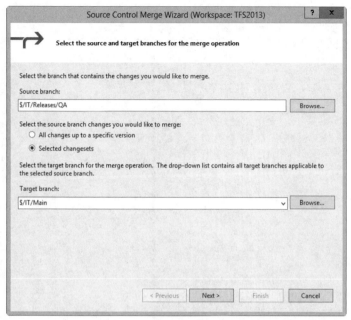

FIGURE 10-18: Source Control Merge Wizard

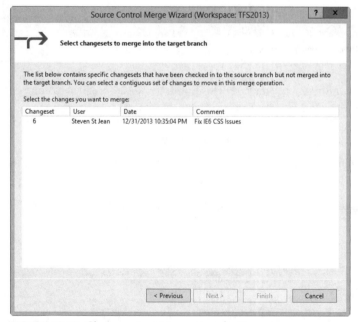

FIGURE 10-19: Changeset merge range selection page

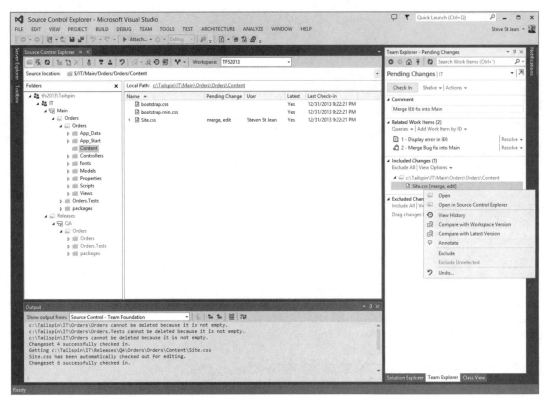

FIGURE 10-20: Displaying the results of a merge

The stylesheet file currently has a pending merge on it. At this point, it is good practice to compare the current version of the file with the latest version to ensure that the change you are making is still the correct one, as shown in Figure 10-20. In this case, it is, so the developer associates the changeset with the original bug, checks in the merge, and then marks the bug as Done.

At this point, if you right-click the file in Source Control Explorer and select View History, you will see the History for the file, as shown in Figure 10-21 (once the tree nodes have been expanded).

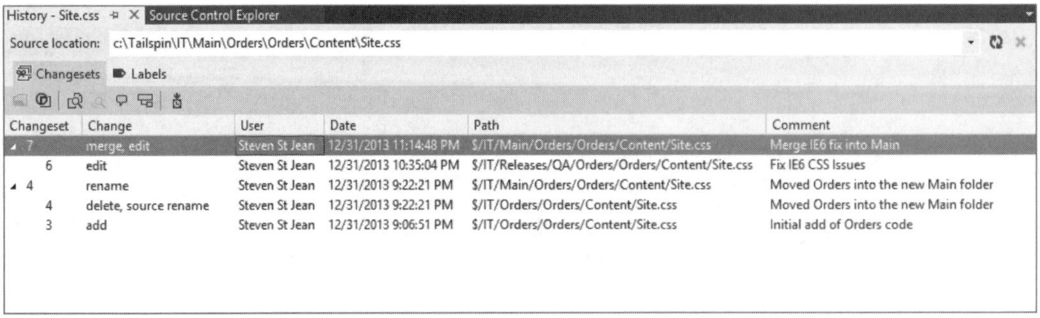

Changeset	Change	User	Date	Path	Comment
▲ 7	merge, edit	Steven St Jean	12/31/2013 11:14:48 PM	$/IT/Main/Orders/Orders/Content/Site.css	Merge IE6 fix into Main
6	edit	Steven St Jean	12/31/2013 10:35:04 PM	$/IT/Releases/QA/Orders/Orders/Content/Site.css	Fix IE6 CSS Issues
▲ 4	rename	Steven St Jean	12/31/2013 9:22:21 PM	$/IT/Main/Orders/Orders/Content/Site.css	Moved Orders into the new Main folder
4	delete, source rename	Steven St Jean	12/31/2013 9:22:21 PM	$/IT/Orders/Orders/Content/Site.css	Moved Orders into the new Main folder
3	add	Steven St Jean	12/31/2013 9:06:51 PM	$/IT/Orders/Orders/Content/Site.css	Initial add of Orders code

FIGURE 10-21: History for the file

In Figure 10-21, you can see the merge of the changes back into Main at changeset 7. By expanding the node, you can see the changes made to that file in the source branch (in this case, the edit of the file in the QA branch in changeset 6). Then, further back in history, you can see the rename (move) of the file when the code was moved under the Main folder. Finally, if you expand that rename node, you can see all the history of the file before it was in the current branch structure.

Another way to visualize this change and see that it made it into the correct branches is to right-click changeset 7 in the History view and select Track Changeset. This displays the Select Branches dialog box (see Figure 10-22), which allows you to select which branches you would like to view.

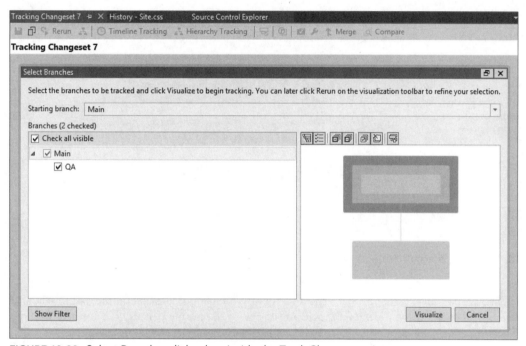

FIGURE 10-22: Select Branches dialog box inside the Track Changeset view

For the example scenario, the developer selected the Check All Visible check box and clicked the Visualize button. Initially, this sequence will show a hierarchical view of branches, which are colored according to which branches the changes in changeset 7 made it into. If you were to look at Figure 10-23 in color, you would see that everything showed up green to indicate that everything was good.

An alternative visualization is available by clicking the Timeline Tracking button, as highlighted in Figure 10-23. This displays the changes in a familiar timeline style view, as shown in Figure 10-24. Again, if this were in color, you would see that all the branches are green, which means that the code made it to where it should be.

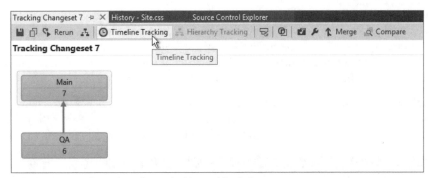

FIGURE 10-23: Branches shown in hierarchical view

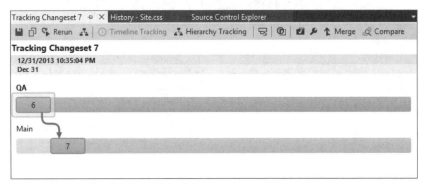

FIGURE 10-24: Timeline Tracking view

Back at Tailspin Toys, the IT product has undergone a bunch more testing on the QA branch, and development continues in the Main branch. At the end of the testing period, it is decided that the application is working properly, so the build created with the stylesheet fix in changeset 7 (build Orders QA_20131231.1) is deployed to production.

However, all is not well. Once deployed to production, the Chief Information Officer (CIO) of the company notices an incorrect footer file at the bottom of the main page. The page still contains text that reads, "My ASP.NET MVC Application." While this doesn't affect functionality in any way, the CIO would like the issue fixed ASAP because she is about to demo the application to the board of directors.

It's a small, low-risk fix. In days gone by, this would be exactly the sort of thing for which a member of the IT team would jump into the production environment and just fix it. However, it's exactly the sort of change that can be forgotten about back in the development branch. So, to ensure that the change is not overlooked, the team decides to do it in version control using the new branch plan.

First, they must create the Prod branch. There are two ways to do this. One is to create the branch from the label applied as part of the build process. Another is to branch by the changeset that included the required fix. Now take a brief look at both methods and see which is more appropriate for this example scenario.

Branch from Label

As previously discussed, it is possible to create branches after the fact by right-clicking in Source Control Explorer and selecting Branching and Merging ➪ Branch as well as from the `tf branch` command line.

In the Branch from QA dialog box, select Label from the Branch Version drop down, as shown in Figure 10-25, and then click the ellipsis (. . .) button to find the label created by the build process. (By default, each build labels the files included in that build with the build number.) Enter the target branch name of `$/IT/Releases/Prod` and click Branch.

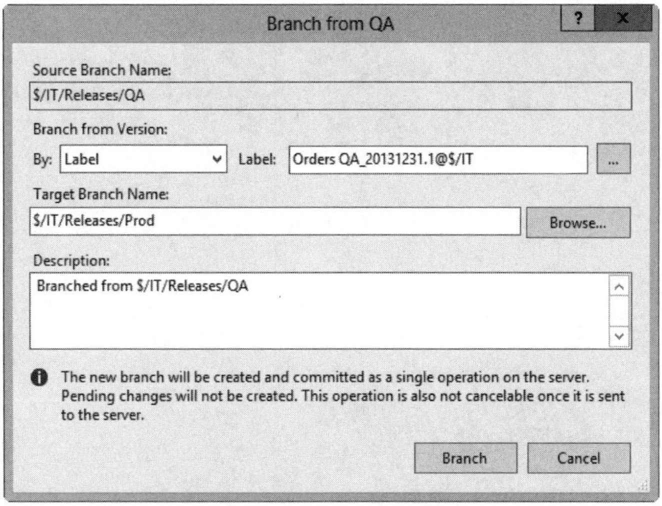

FIGURE 10-25: Branch by Label in Visual Studio

To do the same thing from the command line, the developer opens up a Developer Command Prompt for VS 2013 and enters the following command:

```
tf branch $/IT/Releases/QA $/IT/Releases/Prod /version:L"
  Orders QA_20121231.21@$/IT" /checkin
```

Whichever way you perform a branch by label, the advantage is that it will branch only the files included in the specified label, and that label was created automatically by the build process to include only the files in the workspace definition of the build at the time the build was performed.

The major downside is that, as stated in Chapter 6, labels in Team Foundation Server are editable. Someone with appropriate permissions could have edited the label and removed or included certain key files after the label was created by the build process. This is unlikely in the example Tailspin environment, but it is possible.

Branch from Changeset

From the build report shown in Figure 10-26, you can see the build associated with changeset 6 was successful. As discussed in Chapter 6, the changeset represents a unique (immutable) point in time in the version control repository. Therefore, if you were to branch from changeset 6, this would include the files at the exact state that they were in when the build was performed.

FIGURE 10-26: Build report

The team decides to branch by changeset 6 so as to include all changes up until changeset 6 in the QA branch when creating the Prod branch. To do this, the developer right-clicks the QA branch in Source Control Explorer and selects Branching and Merging ➪ Branch. The developer then changes the "Branch from Version" to changeset 6, and sets the Target Branch Name to be $/IT/Releases/Prod.

Once the branch is created, the version control repository then looks like Figure 10-27.

If you were to right-click the Main branch and select Branching and Merging ➪ View Hierarchy, you could see a visualization of the current branch structure, as shown in Figure 10-28. If you hover the mouse over each branch, you see a tooltip with the additional metadata about that branch, including any description that you entered.

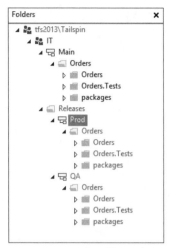

FIGURE 10-27: Prod branch created

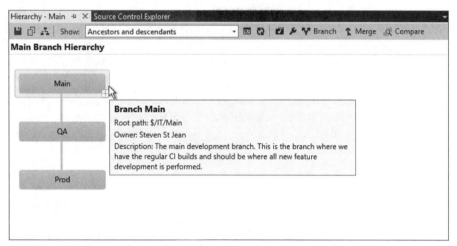

FIGURE 10-28: Current branch hierarchy

At this point, the developer can now create a fix in the Prod branch. The developer edits the offending cshtml file and checks it in as changeset 11. The developer then creates a build and deploys this to production. Now you must ensure that the fix is in the appropriate branches so that it also gets included in the future releases.

To do this, you right-click the Prod branch, and select View History. Then, you right-click the changeset and select Track Changeset. As before, you select the Check All Visible check box and click Visualize. The change will show in green in the Prod branch only, as represented by the bottom box in Figure 10-29.

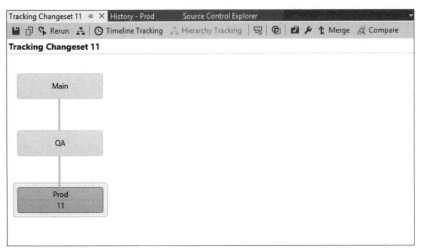

FIGURE 10-29: Change being visualized for the changeset

To merge this change into Main, the developer now has two choices: a ladder merge or a baseless merge. If you find that during your branch process you frequently must perform baseless merges or merges through other branches (ladder merges), this is a good indication that the model is no longer optimized for the typical circumstances encountered in your environment, and you may want to revise it.

However, in the Tailspin scenario, making ad hoc changes to production is very much an exception case. So, the IT team wants to optimize the branch plan for the usual case of a change starting in Main, getting promoted on to QA, and then to Prod. So the developer must use a ladder merge or a baseless merge to go from Prod to Main.

Ladder Merge

As shown in Figure 10-29, the team has a change in Prod. To get that fix into Main using standard merges, the developer must first merge it into the QA branch and then, from there, into Main. This is because in Team Foundation Server, a standard merge can flow from parent to child, or vice versa.

To merge the changes, from the Tracking Changeset view shown in Figure 10-29, the developer uses the mouse to drag and drop the Prod branch up to the QA branch. This will display the standard Merge Wizard shown earlier in Figure 10-18. The developer clicks the Selected changesets radio button and clicks Next to display the changeset selection page shown earlier in Figure 10-19.

On this page, the developer would select the desired changeset and click Finish. The developer then checks in the merged file, and clicks the Rerun button in the Tracking Changeset view to show the change in the QA branch. Finally, the developer drags and drops the QA branch to the Main branch and repeats the process through the Merge Wizard.

In this particular example, because of when the change occurred in production, it actually would have been possible to get the change into Main in this way. However, if the change had been required when there was a different (newer) version of the software in the QA branch, you may have not wanted to merge the changes in this way. Instead, you could have opted to do a baseless merge directly into Main, and then the change would make it back up to the QA branch with the next release to the test team.

Now take a look at how to plug in that option for the Tailspin Toys example scenario.

Baseless Merge

To discourage baseless merges, the simple drag-and-drop approach is not available inside Visual Studio 2013. Instead, the developer must right-click the Prod branch and select Merge. The Source Control Merge Wizard (refer to Figure 10-18) is displayed with the available parent or child target paths shown in the drop down. In your example, $/IT/Releases/QA would be the only option shown. But to perform a baseless merge, press the Browse button and then select the Main branch. The merge dialog box then shows a warning (as shown in Figure 10-30) that a baseless merge is going to be performed.

> **NOTE** *The same action could be performed from the command line using a command such as the following:*
>
> ```
> tf merge /baseless /recursive /version:11
>     $/IT/Releases/Prod $/IT/Main
> ```

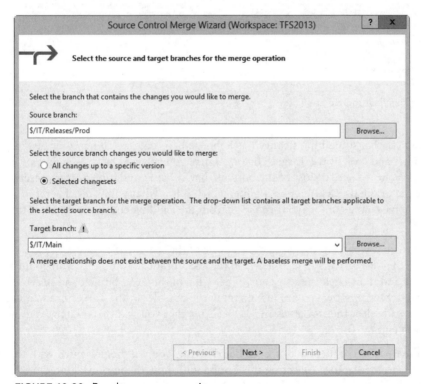

FIGURE 10-30: Baseless merge warning

In your example, as in the case with many active development environments, development has been ongoing by the rest of the team and additional check-ins have occurred in the Main branch. Therefore, it is highly likely that a conflict will occur. As discussed previously, Team Foundation Server 2013 will automatically attempt to merge those conflicts for you, if possible. For example, if a developer was editing on part of the file in the Main branch, and the change occurred to an unrelated part of the file in the Prod branch, these changes would be merged automatically even though this is a baseless merge. Sadly, in your example scenario, someone has renamed the _Layout.cshtml file in the Main branch to _MainLayout.cshtml. If you had performed the ladder merge, as described in the previous section, Team Foundation Server would have been able to use the common base version to detect the rename operation and merge the changes into the file with the new filename. However, as this is a baseless merge (with no common base version for comparison), Team Foundation Server can use only the current state of the two branches when making its calculations. It therefore has no way to determine that the rename on _Layout.cshtml occurred after a point in time in which the branch that ended getting branched to Prod was performed. Therefore, Team Foundation Server thinks that you want to add _Layout.cshtml back into Main, but it knows that a file used to exist by this name and is clever enough to check with you first to see if that is what you really wanted to do by showing you the conflict dialog box, as shown in Figure 10-31.

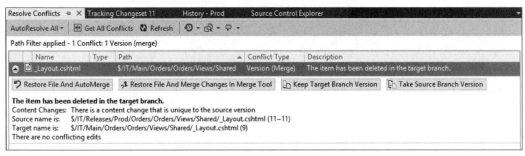

FIGURE 10-31: Resolving baseless merge conflicts

In this instance, you can see that something strange has happened. To dig into things a bit further, you right-click the conflict and look at the Target History. There you can see that _Layout.cshtml was renamed to _MainLayout.cshtml. Most of the options that Team Foundation Server presents requires you to restore the original _Layout.cshtml file, which is not what you want. Therefore, you undo the pending merge change on _Layout.cshtml from the Pending changes page in Team Explorer and try again.

This time, you now know that you want to merge the changes of the specific file _Layout.cshtml in the Prod branch with the file _MainLayout.cshtml in the Main branch. To do this, you go into Source Control Explorer and right-click the _Layout.cshtml file in the Prod branch and select Branching and Merging ➪ Merge. Now you are just merging the one file. In the Target Branch, you press the Browse button and select the _MainLayout.cshtml file that you want your changes to be merged into, as shown in Figure 10-32.

This will again show the Resolve conflicts dialog box, but this time you will be presented with the option to Merge Changes in Merge Tool. Selecting this option will show the improved integrated merge tool in Visual Studio 2013, as shown in Figure 10-33.

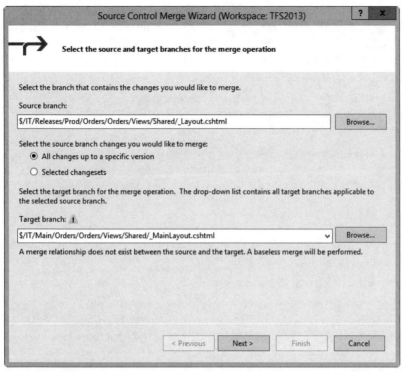

FIGURE 10-32: A baseless merge of a single file

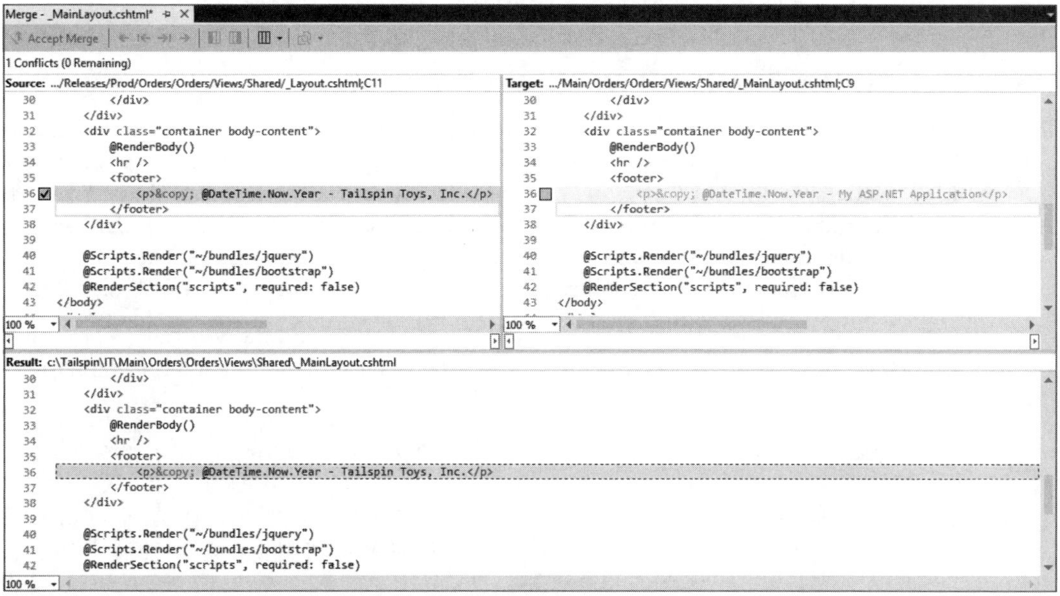

FIGURE 10-33: Resolving conflicts inside Visual Studio 2013

The change from the source version on the left-hand side is selected and any additional changes necessary to correctly merge the file are performed on the contents in the Results pane at the bottom on the merge tool. The developer then presses the Accept Merge button to inform Team Foundation Server that the conflict on that file has been resolved.

> **NOTE** *If desired, external diff and merge utilities can be configured in Visual Studio under Tools ⇨ Options ⇨ Source Control ⇨ Visual Studio Team Foundation Server ⇨ Configure User Tools.*
>
> *To find out more about configuring external diff and merge utilities for use with Visual Studio, see* `http://aka.ms/ExternalDiffMerge`*. James Manning has a blog post detailing the configuration parameters necessary for many of the common tools at* `http://aka.ms/ExternalDiffMergeEx`*.*

The developer can now check in the merge by using the command line or Visual Studio. Following is the command to execute a check-in from the command line:

```
tf checkin /recursive /noprompt $/IT/Main
```

> **NOTE** *For more information on using the* `tf merge` *command to perform merge operations (including additional examples), see the MSDN documentation at* `http://aka.ms/tfmerge`*. For more information about past merges from the command line for a known source and destination branch, see the Help documentation for the* `tf merges` *command on MSDN (*`http://aka.ms/tfmerges`*) or type* **`tf help merges`** *at a Developer Command Prompt.*

Tracking Change through Branches

As you have seen thus far, the branch visualization tooling in Visual Studio 2013 provides some powerful capabilities for viewing your branch hierarchy and tracking the progress of changes through it. Using the View Hierarchy functionality, you can immediately see the relationships of the branches in your source tree, and navigate to their locations in the repository. By selecting Track Changeset for a changeset in the History view, you see into which branches that change has been made, and you can even merge the change into other branches by dragging and dropping between branches.

The Tracking Changeset visualization has some additional features not always displayed in simple examples, such as those presented here. Figure 10-34 shows an example from a more complex branch hierarchy.

In the example shown in Figure 10-34, the original change occurred in the `FeatureB` branch as changeset 86. This was reverse-integrated into the `FeatureInt` branch as a standard merge in changeset 87. That change was then merged into `Main`. But not all files were copied over as part of the merge, as the cross-hatching and the asterisk next to changeset 88 indicates. This should instantly be an area to investigate which files were checked in and why. Double-clicking the branch will show the changeset details to begin the investigation.

Then, rather than a standard merge back down from Main into the V2.0 branch, you can see that three baseless merges have occurred to get all the changes into that branch (changesets 89, 90, and 91). Finally, a single baseless merge took all the code into the V3.0 branch. Figure 10-34 shows that the changes have yet to make it into the FeatureA branch or into the V1.0 and V1.1 branches. Clicking the Timeline Tracking button displays the timeline view for changeset 86, as shown Figure 10-35.

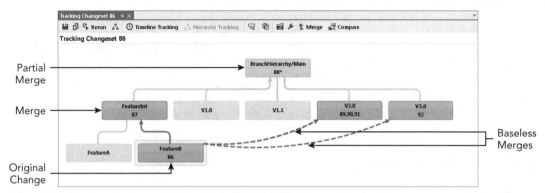

FIGURE 10-34: Complex branch hierarchy in Tracking Changeset visualization

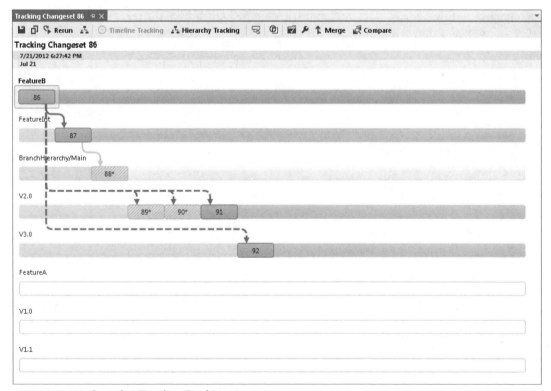

FIGURE 10-35: Complex Timeline Tracking view

This view does not show the relationships between branches (the hierarchy) but instead shows the merges as they happened. The sequence of events around the partial merges into Main and V2.0, and the subsequent full merge into V2.0, are therefore much more clearly represented. Hovering over each branch provides additional metadata, including its owner and description.

IMPLEMENTING BRANCHING STRATEGIES IN GIT

When discussing the implementation of branching strategies in a Git-based world, you have to separate the discussion into server-side local branching activities. Many of the strategies and implementations already discussed were based on the fact that the Team Foundation Version Control–based repositories perform all of their branching on the server. Local copies of those branches are implemented as separate folders within your Workspace or even as separate Workspaces on your machine. With Git, you have the full power of branching and merging both locally and between the local and remote repositories.

No Branching Strategy

As described earlier, this strategy is the simplest to use. It is simply a single branch residing within the team project. Team members can branch and merge locally for any purpose, but they all must Push and Pull from the single Master branch on the Team Foundation Server.

To implement this strategy, start by cloning the Master branch from the team project into your local Git repository, as shown in Figure 10-36.

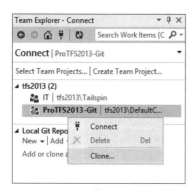

FIGURE 10-36: Clone a team project repository.

Now you have a local master that is considered a published branch, as shown in Figure 10-37.

This branch is your link back to the team project and the starting point for all of your local branches. Now you can click on the New Branch link, which opens up a section where you can name your branch. You're expanding the HelloWorld app's pool of languages so call the branch **ExpandLangs**, as shown in Figure 10-38.

Notice also that you have your local master branch as the source and the Checkout branch check box is selected. Click on the Create Branch button and your branch is created, checked out, and you are switched to it as denoted by the bold type in Figure 10-39. Notice that the `ExpandLangs` branch is Unpublished. This means that it doesn't have a counterpart on the remote repository.

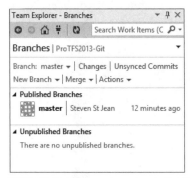

FIGURE 10-37: Local master is Published

FIGURE 10-38: Create a branch

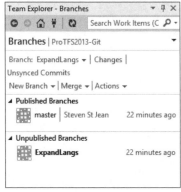

FIGURE 10-39: New branch

Now you can implement our feature and make as many commits as you like to the branch. When your work is complete on the branch, you can go back to the Branches page in Team Explorer, right-click on the `ExpandLangs` branch, and select View History, which will show that you have changes that aren't in your local master, as shown in Figure 10-40.

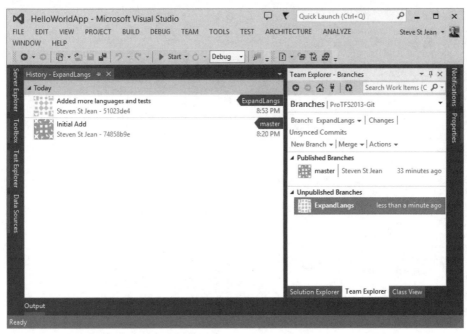

FIGURE 10-40: ExpandLangs branch history

To merge those changes back to `Master`, you click the Merge link in the Branches page, which expands the Merge section. Here, you select `ExpandLangs` as your source and `Master` as your target and click the Merge button, as shown in Figure 10-41.

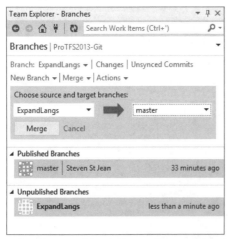

FIGURE 10-41: Merge ExpandLangs to local Master

Now you have your local Master branch updated. You can now Push your local changes up to the team project's repository by switching to the Master branch and then navigating to the Unsynced Changes page, selecting your Commit, and clicking the Push link, as shown in Figure 10-42.

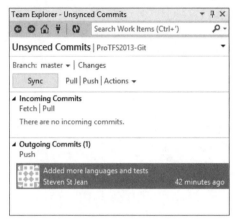

FIGURE 10-42: Push changes from a local branch to remote repository

Feature Branching Strategy

Feature branching in Git has been the subject of many discussions since its release. The main thing to understand is that the reason for feature branching is the same regardless of the version control tool used; only the implementation will differ.

In Git, you already use a local feature branch to implement your code locally. But what happens if you are working with a couple of colleagues on that feature? You will either all have to have your own local branch of Main and share code between each of your local repositories or you need some central place to share code.

For this to work, you can create a branch locally and then publish that branch back to the team project so your colleagues can Pull the branch locally and work on it.

Let's assume that you need a feature branch to add an About page to your application. You're working with two other developers so you need a common feature branch. You've already got a local copy of Master, as shown in Figure 10-37. You can create a local branch from Master called **AboutPage**, as shown in Figure 10-43.

Then you right-click on the AboutPage branch and select Publish Branch, as shown in Figure 10-44. This will make the branch available to your colleagues in your team project repository, as shown in Figure 10-45.

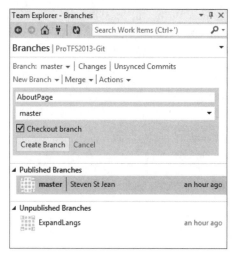

FIGURE 10-43: Create an AboutPage branch from Master.

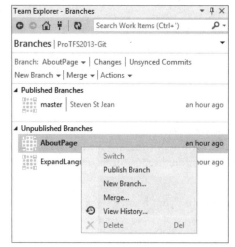

FIGURE 10-44: Publish branch

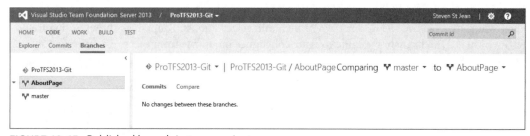

FIGURE 10-45: Published branch in team project

Now you can each make changes locally and then commit them to your local `AboutPage` branch. When you're ready, you can go to the Unsynced Commits page, select your commits, and click the Push link to push them to the `AboutPage` branch in the team project, similar to Figure 10-42. Looking back at the repository in **Web Access**, you can now see in Figure 10-46 that the difference between the `AboutPage` branch and `Master` is your commit.

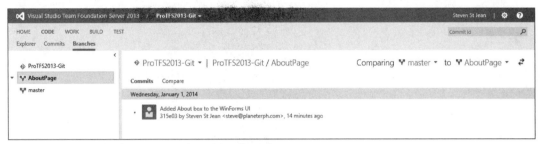

FIGURE 10-46: Pushed commit in AboutPage branch

Now your colleague Tatiana needs to create a local branch from the `AboutPage` branch in the team project. She will go to her Branches page in Team Explorer and click the New Branch link. In the New Branch section, she will change the source drop-down from `master` to `origin/AboutPage`, as shown in Figure 10-47. This will default the name of the local branch to `AboutPage`, which is fine. She then clicks the Create Branch button to create the branch.

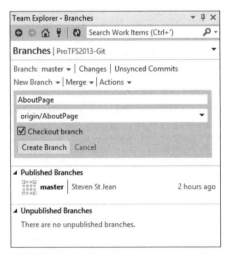

FIGURE 10-47: Creating a local AboutPage branch

She now opens the branch and makes changes to the application in one or more local commits. When she is done, she pushes her changes to the team `AboutPage` branch in the team project as you did earlier.

When you go to your Unsynced Changes page, you can click the Fetch button in the Incoming Commits section to show her commits. You can then Pull those commits into your local branch by clicking the Pull link, as shown in Figure 10-48.

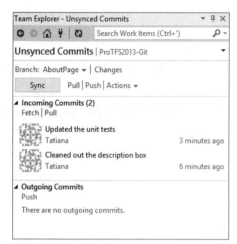

FIGURE 10-48: Pulling a team member's Commits

Your entire team can keep doing these steps until the entire feature is complete. You can then merge the AboutPage branch with Master to deliver your work to the next release.

SUMMARY

As you can tell from this chapter, the branch and merge capabilities of Team Foundation Server not only allow for some complex software configuration management scenarios, but also provide the tooling to help understand what is happening with changes in your version control repository.

While conflicts are always going to happen with any parallel development process, Visual Studio 2013 and Team Foundation Server 2013 have tooling to help resolve and manage merge conflicts to make branching and merging easier.

With the arrival of Git as a first-class version control repository choice within Team Foundation Server, you now have the ability to perform branching and merging locally, as well as on the server.

The chapter looked at the terminology used in branching, discussed some common branching techniques, and then provided a detailed walkthrough of implementing a basic branching strategy in an organization using the tools provided for Team Foundation Server 2013. Finally, this chapter examined the changeset tracking functionality available in Team Foundation Version Control to determine to which branches a particular change has propagated.

Chapter 11 builds on the knowledge gained so far in this book, and provides some best-practice guidance over a few scenarios common across development teams (such as how to organize the structure of the repository, manage third-party dependencies, and manage the dependencies for internally developed libraries, such as common framework code). Chapter 11 also looks at the practicalities of using Team Foundation Server to manage Team Foundation Server artifacts, such as process templates, custom build assemblies, custom tools, and so on.

11

Common Version Control Scenarios

WHAT'S IN THIS CHAPTER?

➤ Organizing folders within the branch structure

➤ Managing and storing third-party dependencies

➤ Managing source code and binaries for internal shared libraries

➤ Storing customization artifacts to manage Team Foundation Server in the version control repository

A few scenarios are common across development teams when managing source code for their applications and managing Team Foundation Server. Organizing and architecting the structure of the version control system can have a direct effect on improving the way applications are managed and built. This chapter explores some of those scenarios and discusses possible solutions to tackle each of them. When illustrating these scenarios, we will be using a Team Foundation Version Control–based team project, although you could use a Git-based team project just as easily.

SETTING UP THE FOLDER STRUCTURE FOR YOUR BRANCHES

One common issue that development teams have centers on the organization of their source control repositories. Over time, these repositories can become unruly and downright difficult to locate. The common question around the office can sometimes be, "Where is that located in source control?"

By providing some organization to the version control repository in Team Foundation Server, you can provide your team with better discoverability of source code assets. You can also introduce best engineering practices that will make it easier to compile your applications locally and on automated build servers.

Figure 11-1 shows a sample folder structure within a branch. Notice how the folders are inside the folder indicated as a branch in Team Foundation Server version control. Essentially, the idea is to store within the same branch all of the artifacts necessary for building, testing, architecting, and so on, the product or product family. This allows you to create as many branches as the team needs to contain everything necessary for the development effort.

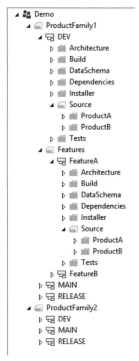

FIGURE 11-1: Sample folder structure within a branch

Later on, when you are creating a build definition that will build the entire product family, it will be useful to scope the build to the branch so that it has access to all of the artifacts that would be necessary to compile, test, and package the product family. Each of these folders and its purposes will be examined in this chapter.

Application Source Code

The primary version control folder needed for most teams is one that contains the source code for a family of products. This folder is named Source in the branch shown in Figure 11-1. Each product can be contained in a separate subfolder, and any shared libraries that are used only by the products in the product family can have subfolders under the Source folder as needed.

Additionally, teams may choose to store the source code for the automated unit tests in this folder because the unit test projects are traditionally included in the same Visual Studio solution as the product's Visual Studio projects. The development team is usually the team that manages artifacts in this version control folder, and the creation and management of unit tests is typically owned by developers.

Automated Tests Source Code

The testing or quality assurance team may end up generating source code for automated tests such as Coded UI, web performance, and load, as well as for other types of tests. They need a location in which to store the source code that implemented those automated tests, so the version control folder named `Tests` in the branch shown in Figure 11-1 serves that purpose.

By including the source code in the same branch as the rest of the product family, it can easily be managed across the branching structure, and it can be included to be compiled or even run in automated builds that use the branch as its source. Including the Visual Studio projects for your automated tests in the same build as your application is also a requirement for queuing automated test runs from Microsoft Test Manager to run inside of an environment.

Architecture Assets

Software architects can create valuable architecture diagrams that might also be helpful to team members implementing and testing the product family. Visual Studio 2013 Ultimate provides some powerful architecture tools, including a Visual Studio project type for modeling projects that enable the capability to store UML and other architecture diagrams in a meaningful way. The architecture assets also need a version control folder in the branch, which is shown in Figure 11-1 with the name of `Architecture`.

Alternatively, the architecture modeling projects and diagrams can be stored in the `Source` folder mentioned earlier in order to be included in the same Visual Studio solutions. The idea is to ensure that they are included in the same branch alongside the rest of the assets for the product family.

Again, by including them in the same branch, the architecture components and artifacts could be used in an automated build process. Specifically, you could perform architectural validation during compilation using the layer diagrams stored in the Visual Studio architecture modeling projects.

Database Schema

Database developers also produce artifacts to manage the schema and data in the databases used in the product family. Their artifacts can be stored in the same branch folder as well. To offer change management for the database schema, Visual Studio 2013 also includes a project type for database schema management that integrates with version control repositories. This functionality was available in Visual Studio 2012 by installing the SQL Server Data Tools add-in but is now available in all versions of Visual Studio 2013. Thus, to edit a stored procedure, you would use the same version control techniques as editing a source code file for an application.

The folder named `DataSchema` in Figure 11-1 is used to store database schema artifacts in the branch. The automated build process can even use the database schema "source code" contained in this version control folder to compile the schema into a deployable unit for creating a new database from the schema or update an existing database automatically to the latest schema version.

Installer Assets

If your development team needs to produce installers for the product to ship to customers, or to internal business users, or even to ease deployment of server or web applications, then a version control folder should be created inside the branch to store the installer artifacts. This particular folder is represented in the example branch in Figure 11-1 as the folder named `Installer`. This allows for the automated build process to have easy access within the same branch to the source code necessary to compile the merge modules and/or installers.

Build and Deployment Assets

Finally, there might be artifacts that the development team may want to store that are necessary during the build process or for deployment reasons. A version control folder dedicated to these artifacts is helpful. The version control folder for these artifacts is shown in Figure 11-1 with the name of `Build`.

You don't necessarily need to store the build workflow process template (`.XAML`) file itself in this folder. However, it is certainly an option if your team decides to store build process templates inside the branch. If you store the build process template file inside the branch, then each of those branched build process template files must be registered for use in the build system before they can be used by a build definition.

> **NOTE** *Chapter 19 provides more information about managing and registering build process templates.*

THIRD-PARTY SOURCE CODE AND DEPENDENCIES

Traditionally, teams should not store binaries in version control. This best practice has evolved because team members would check in the `bin` and `obj` folders created after compiling a solution or project in Visual Studio. Those folders, and particularly the binaries that get created, should generally not be stored in version control even with Local Workspaces. Problems may arise when storing those folders in a server workspace because Team Foundation Server marks files coming from version control as read-only, which prevents Visual Studio or MSBuild from being able to overwrite those files.

The idea around this is that you should store in the version control branch only those source code files necessary to create the binaries and let the automated build system compile the source code into the necessary binaries. The build drop folders can then be stored on a file share that is backed up regularly and retained appropriately. Even though the Visual Studio Online (VSO) has introduced the concept of storing the build drop folders inside Team Foundation Server, it does not store them inside or check in to the branch but rather has a separate location inside the server for the outputs of compilation. This is only done in this manner because VSO doesn't have a way to talk to your drop folder within your firewall.

> **NOTE** *The practice of not storing the binaries in the version control repository can also be generally applied for other types of compiled "outputs," depending on the circumstance. For example, storing the compiled help file (that is, a .CHM file) in the version control repository would generally not be recommended because it can be compiled during an automated build process. Instead, the source files used for creating the compiled help file would be stored in version control.*

However, the guideline of not storing binaries in the version control branch does not apply when it comes to managing third-party dependencies.

One folder you might have noticed in the branching structure shown in Figure 11-1 that has not been discussed yet is the Dependencies folder. This folder is exactly the version control branch location that can be used to manage the third-party dependencies. Let's take a look at two methods for managing a Dependencies folder and discuss the strengths and weaknesses of both approaches.

Folder inside the Branch

The first approach is based on the premise that everything necessary for the product family is stored inside the branch folder. This means that a Dependencies folder could be created inside the branch folder, as shown in Figure 11-1, and used to manage the third-party dependencies.

Subfolders can be created to manage the different types of third-party dependencies that might be needed by the products in the product family. For example, a UIControls subfolder can be created to store third-party custom UI controls, or an EnterpriseLibrary subfolder can be created to store the assemblies that come from the Microsoft Enterprise Library. You might even create further subfolders to isolate the different major versions that might become available for the dependency. Separating and organizing the dependencies into subfolders will help ease the management and discoverability of the dependencies over time.

The first benefit that comes from storing the Dependencies version control folder inside the branch is that it allows the development team to manage changes to dependencies just like any other change to the products. For example, the new version of a dependency could be updated in the DEV branch for developing and testing, but the RELEASE and MAIN branches continue to use the older version until the update is merged and promoted to those branches. This approach allows for effective source configuration management of the dependencies of your application because the teams can choose when to "take" changes to the dependencies by performing the updates themselves.

Another benefit is that it allows for relative references to be used in the HintPath property for file references in Visual Studio project files. Visual Studio and MSBuild can use the HintPath property to resolve the references in a project at compile time. Using relative paths in the file reference (instead of an absolute path that may include the branch name) ensures that the reference can be properly resolved by Visual Studio, or automated build servers, no matter what the physical structure ends up being for storing branches in version control.

Listing 11-1 shows how the relative path would be used if the Visual Studio project file for ProductA used a dependency in the Dependencies folder, as shown in Figure 11-1.

LISTING 11-1: HintPath property in Visual Studio project file branch dependency folder

```xml
<?xml version="1.0" encoding="utf-8"?>
<Project ToolsVersion="4.0" DefaultTargets="Build" xmlns=
    "http://schemas.microsoft.com/developer/msbuild/2003">
<!-- Section Removed for Brevity -->
  <ItemGroup>
    <Reference Include="EnterpriseLibrary">
      <HintPath>..\..\Dependencies\EnterpriseLibrary.dll</HintPath>
    </Reference>
    <Reference Include="System" />
    <Reference Include="System.Data" />
    <Reference Include="System.Deployment" />
    <Reference Include="System.Drawing" />
    <Reference Include="System.Windows.Forms" />
    <Reference Include="System.Xml" />
    <Reference Include="System.Core" />
    <Reference Include="System.Xml.Linq" />
    <Reference Include="System.Data.DataSetExtensions" />
  </ItemGroup>
  <ItemGroup>
<!-- Section Removed for Brevity -->
</Project>
```

A drawback to this approach is that each product family's set of branches contained in version control has a copy of dependencies that might be used by multiple product families. This can potentially cause more data storage to be used in the Team Foundation Server database. It also means that, if an update must be committed for all product families, the update must be made in each product family's branching structure independently.

However, the benefits outweigh the potential drawback in this particular case. This also ensures that teams have a better understanding of the dependencies used by the products in their product family. Teams can also actively manage the time when new dependencies are integrated into their product family's branch and actually take the update themselves on their own schedule to prevent disruption.

This approach can be considered the preferred method for managing dependencies because it falls in line with the concept of storing everything needed for an application inside the branch's root folder. It also provides for the minimal amount of drawbacks, which are negligible in the larger view of software development.

Folder at Team Project Level

Another alternative for storing dependencies inside version control is to use a common `Dependencies` version control folder across several product families. This folder is scoped at the team project level, as shown in Figure 11-2.

The main benefits of this approach are that the storage space is not an issue, and teams have the capability to make a change to a dependency that would be picked up by all product families. Even when using this approach, the same type of subfolder organization that was described for the "folder inside branch" option can be used and is encouraged for the same beneficial reasons described for that option.

Because this common version control folder is used to centrally manage all dependencies, the work of the responsible teams can be affected, and products in the different product families can also be affected if a dependency being used causes changes that break the applications. This causes the teams to immediately fix their applications to address the breaking change in

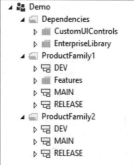

FIGURE 11-2: Alternative approach with a common Dependencies version control folder

each of the branches for their product families. Teams must also address the breaking change in a branch that contains production source code (such as a RELEASE branch) before they can produce a meaningful build that works with the updated dependency. This approach does not allow the development teams to "take" changes as needed, and to fit them into their normal development cycles. Another immediate drawback that will surface is that the relative references in the Visual Studio project files may not resolve correctly, depending on the physical placement of the branches in the version control repository.

This approach can also be susceptible to breaking the file references when renaming or reorganizing version control folders in the future. For example, if a Visual Studio project file in the DEV\Source\ ProductA version control folder included a file reference to the Enterprise Library assembly in the common `Dependencies` version control folder, the `HintPath` would be listed as a relative path in the project file, as shown in Listing 11-2.

LISTING 11-2: HintPath property in Visual Studio project file with common folder dependency

```xml
<?xml version="1.0" encoding="utf-8"?>
<Project ToolsVersion="4.0" DefaultTargets="Build" xmlns=
    "http://schemas.microsoft.com/developer/msbuild/2003">
<!-- Section Removed for Brevity -->
  <ItemGroup>
    <Reference Include="EnterpriseLibrary">
      <HintPath>..\..\..\..\Dependencies\EnterpriseLibrary\
        EnterpriseLibrary.dll</HintPath>
    </Reference>
    <Reference Include="System" />
    <Reference Include="System.Data" />
    <Reference Include="System.Deployment" />
```

continues

LISTING 11-2: *(continued)*

```
        <Reference Include="System.Drawing" />
        <Reference Include="System.Windows.Forms" />
        <Reference Include="System.Xml" />
        <Reference Include="System.Core" />
        <Reference Include="System.Xml.Linq" />
        <Reference Include="System.Data.DataSetExtensions" />
      </ItemGroup>
      <ItemGroup>
    <!-- Section Removed for Brevity -->
    </Project>
```

However, if `Features` branches were created, as shown in Figure 11-3, then the `HintPath` property would no longer be valid because it would need an extra "`..\`" to represent the extra path level that the `Features` branches are now sitting under.

FIGURE 11-3: Features branches

Finally, if you use this approach, ensure that the common `Dependencies` version control folder is included in the workspace definition for any build definitions, in addition to the branch that contains the source code needed by the automated build, as shown in Figure 11-4.

FIGURE 11-4: Including the Dependencies folder in the workspace definition

INTERNAL SHARED LIBRARIES

Companies may have multiple development teams that all work separately on the product families that each of the teams owns. At some point, those development teams may come to the realization that they want to have common types and source code to be shared among the products. There are certainly benefits to having one code base for the common library. For example, bug fixes, new functionality, and performance improvements can be introduced to multiple product families easily, and this allows for common usage patterns across the teams.

The key to a successful shared library strategy is to treat the package of common libraries as a completely separate "product family" internally. This means that it would ideally have its own release cycle (even if it is on the same cadence as another product family) and its own product backlog, and it would be owned by a specific team (whether a dedicated team or a team that also works on another product family).

The shared library product family is essentially treated as though it is a third-party dependency by the teams that want to use the shared library. It's just a third-party dependency built internally. A significant example of this is how the .NET Framework (common library) is developed alongside Visual Studio and Team Foundation Server in the Developer Division at Microsoft, both of which have dependencies on the .NET Framework.

For the following discussion, refer to the sample product families and common libraries shown in Figure 11-5. You will notice that both product families have a dependency on the shared libraries.

Choosing a Location in Version Control

The first decision that must be made is the location in version control in which to store the source code for the shared libraries. Two common choices come up with Team Foundation Server:

➤ Dedicating a branching structure in the same team project

➤ Dedicating a branching structure in a different team project

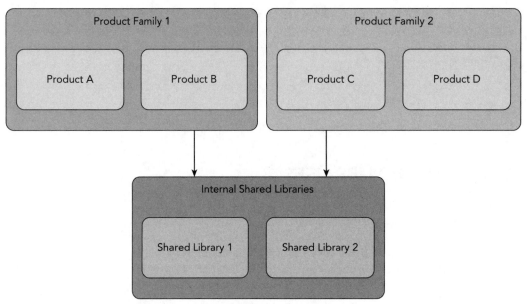

FIGURE 11-5: Product families with a dependency on shared libraries

Dedicating a Branching Structure in the Same Team Project

If the shared libraries are considered to be grouped together with multiple product families in one team project, you might want to contain the source code for those shared libraries in the same team project. This is especially the case if the release cycle for the shared libraries is on a similar cadence as the other product families in the same team project. The release cycle of the shared libraries must be set to "release" and stabilized before the release of the other product families. This is to ensure that any bug fixes are included, new features are implemented, and the shared libraries are tested sufficiently before any of the product family teams need to release their products.

Figure 11-6 shows an additional branching structure for the common libraries alongside the other related product families in the same team project. The team that owns the development of the shared libraries now has its own mechanism for managing change in version control.

A different area path node structure and team can even be created to isolate the work item artifacts related to the shared libraries. This allows managers and executives to still pull reports and work item queries across the entire team project, which provides a high-level view of the progress across multiple product families and the shared libraries. Figure 11-7 shows how those area paths might be defined in the same team project.

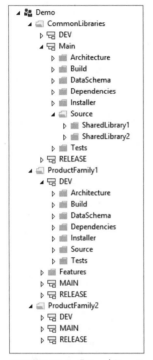

FIGURE 11-6: Branching structure for the common libraries alongside the other related product families in the same team project

If this approach is taken, you can also ensure that you have separate build definitions to create the binaries that the other product family teams will end up using as dependencies in their products. Figure 11-8 shows how the build definitions for common libraries might show up alongside the build definitions of other product families in the same team project.

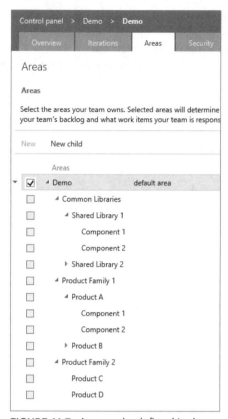

FIGURE 11-7: Area paths defined in the same team project

Dedicating a Branching Structure in a Different Team Project

Let's say that the development teams for multiple product families have a dependency on the common libraries, and those product families exist across multiple team projects. In this case, you can either choose one of the existing team projects or, if needed, create a new team project for managing the source code and release for the common libraries. The concept is essentially the same except that the new branching structure, build definitions, and area paths would exist in that new team project.

Storing Library Assemblies as Dependencies

Once you have defined the location for the branching structure for the common libraries, and you have created build definitions that run successfully to produce the binaries, the product family teams are ready to take a dependency on those shared libraries in their Visual Studio projects.

The process is very similar to how the team would manage this dependency as any other third-party dependency. Team members would choose when to take a new version of the dependency based on their release schedule and how they want to support their products against the new version of the shared libraries. They then find a build with high quality and navigate to its drop folder to grab the binaries and check them into the respective `Dependencies` folder, as described earlier in this chapter.

FIGURE 11-8: Build definitions for common libraries

It is important to ensure that the product family teams choose a build coming from a build definition that includes source indexing and publishing of its symbols to a Symbol Server. This approach is used as opposed to grabbing the binaries compiled on a developer's machine from Visual Studio. This allows the developers to still debug and step through source code, even without having the Visual Studio projects in the same solution.

ENABLING DEBUGGING FOR SHARED LIBRARIES USING SYMBOL AND SOURCE SERVER

One common reason that developers would like to include the Visual Studio projects for the shared libraries in the same solution as their products is to make it easier to step through the source code of the shared libraries at debug time. By taking advantage of Source and Symbol Server support in Team Foundation Server Build and Visual Studio, those developers can achieve that goal, even when using a file reference for the dependency.

To support this, the development team will need to check in a binary that has been produced from a build definition configured for Source Server indexing, and then publish the symbols to Symbol Server. The development team will also need at least read-only access to the branches that contain the source code for the shared libraries—regardless of whether those folders exist in the same team project or a different team project.

continues

continued

This is one of many scenarios that can be solved by using Source Server and Symbol Server. Chapter 18 provides more information about enabling Source and Symbol Server support in automated builds. You can also find additional information about the Symbol Server and Source Server features available in Team Foundation Server by visiting this blog post by Ed Blankenship: `http://bit.ly/SymbolServerTFS`.

Branching into Product Family Branches

You may also choose to have a separate branching structure in the same or different team project, and then branch the source code folders from the shared library branch into the other product family branches. This allows developers to have copies of the shared library projects inside the same solution, and then use project references to those shared library projects.

To enable this, you must create a branch by selecting Branching and Merging ⇨ Branch from the context menu of the shared library folder, as shown in Figure 11-9.

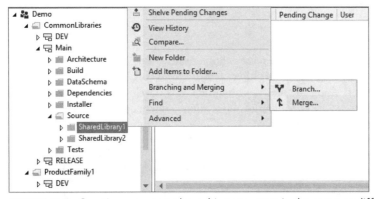

FIGURE 11-9: Creating a separate branching structure in the same or different team project

Once you select the Branch command, the Branch options dialog box shown in Figure 11-10 is displayed. Notice how this branch dialog box is different than the branch dialog box displayed when creating a branch from an actual branch folder. This difference exists because you are attempting to create a branch inside of an already existing branch root folder. Because the SharedLibrary1 folder is not considered a branch, it will just be created with a version control branching relationship as a folder at the target location.

One drawback for this approach is that you will not be able to take advantage of branch or track changes visualizations. It is solely a branching relationship in version control that exists to allow for merging changes into the branching structures of multiple product families.

The team should be careful about how the shared libraries are then deployed because each would be compiling the shared library separately in the respective build definitions. The team could get in a situation where it is deploying two assemblies with the same name, version number, and so on but with different content in it.

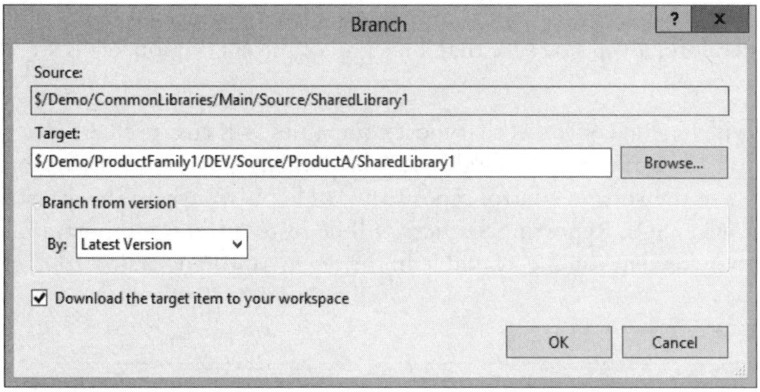

FIGURE 11-10: Branch options dialog box

This also demonstrates another drawback. The shared libraries can start to quickly diverge on different paths if not managed appropriately. For example, one development team may introduce a new exception-handling routine, and another team could introduce a different exception-handling routine at the same time. Later, those two teams could merge their changes back to the original parent branch for the shared library and end up with two exception-handling routines.

MANAGING ARTIFACTS USING TEAM FOUNDATION SERVER

Team Foundation Server administrators often find that they need a place to organize and store artifacts needed for managing Team Foundation Server. Interestingly, this is where the version control repository can help out those administrators. A dedicated team project can be created to store, in one convenient location, all of the artifacts that would be necessary to manage Team Foundation Server.

This team project (named, for example, TFS) can be stored in the default team project collection, and its access can be limited to the administrators of the system. For example, you can provide access for this team project only to members of the Team Foundation Server Administrators security group.

From time to time, other developers may help out with some of the custom tools that can be created to extend Team Foundation Server, or build engineers may need access to use or contribute to the master build process templates. In those situations, you can create specific team project security groups to allow privileges on an ad hoc basis without giving full access to the entire team project's repository.

The following sections explore the different types of artifacts that you might organize in this team project. Each suggestion is certainly optional and depends on your particular scenario. The premise is that you want to effectively organize the artifacts necessary to manage Team Foundation Server.

SQL Reporting Services Encryption Key Backup

In disaster-recovery scenarios, one of the commonly misplaced artifacts is a backup of the SQL Reporting Services encryption key. Without this key artifact, you could experience problems with a full restore after a disaster. Therefore, always be sure that a backup of the encryption key is stored in the TFS team project.

The thinking behind storing it in version control is that most companies will ensure that they have a backup of the key Team Foundation Server databases. The databases can be easily restored from those backups, and access to the version control repository can happen early in the disaster-recovery process. At the point when SQL Reporting Services will be restored, the administrator will have access to the encryption key backup file available in the newly restored version control repository.

> **WARNING** *To protect the contents of the encryption key, you need a password when creating the encryption key backup file. Therefore, be sure to make a note of the password in the appropriate location, according to your company's internal security guidelines.*
>
> *It may be acceptable for some employees at some companies to store a text file alongside the encryption key backup file and check in that text file to the same location in the version control repository. If that option is not an acceptable practice in your organization, then ensure that the administrators will have ready access to retrieving the password during a disaster-recovery scenario.*

Figure 11-11 shows the encryption key backup file available in the root of the team project's version control repository folder.

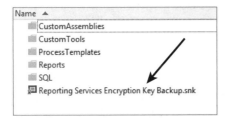

FIGURE 11-11: Location of encryption key backup file

> **NOTE** *Chapter 23 provides more information about disaster-recovery procedures for Team Foundation Server. Also, more information about the procedure for generating an encryption key backup file for SQL Reporting Services is available at* http://aka.ms/BackupReportingServicesKey.

Process Templates

A primary reason why administrators want to manage artifacts is to be able to manage the change of process templates used in the team projects on the Team Foundation Server. Work item type definitions are the primary source of changes to the process templates in most organizations.

You should create a folder structure that is set aside especially to manage the changes to the process templates. This allows for each change to go through a check-out/check-in procedure and be audited to include the date and time the change was made, the user who made the change, and the details about the change (for example, changeset comments and associated work items). This process is very similar to how source code changes would be made to an application being built by a development team.

You can leverage each of the version control features available in Team Foundation Server. For example, you can create two branches to maintain the changes to the process templates. One branch would be for the version of the process templates used on the *testing* Team Foundation Server environment, and one branch would be used to store the version of the process templates used in the *production* Team Foundation Server environment. This allows administrators to make changes that can be tested out first in a separate environment, and then merge those changes to the production branch when the quality of those changes has been determined.

Additionally, the TFS team project can even contain continuous integration build definitions for automatically deploying the changes to the process template's work item type definitions to the appropriate environment whenever the change is checked in to the appropriate branch. One build definition could be created for each branch to deploy to that specific environment (for example, deploy to the production environment when changes are made to the Production branch).

> **NOTE** *Chapter 13 provides more information about process templates, making changes to work item type definitions, and automatic deployment of those changes using a Team Foundation Server build.*

Figure 11-12 shows the branches created for managing process templates in the TFS team project's version control repository.

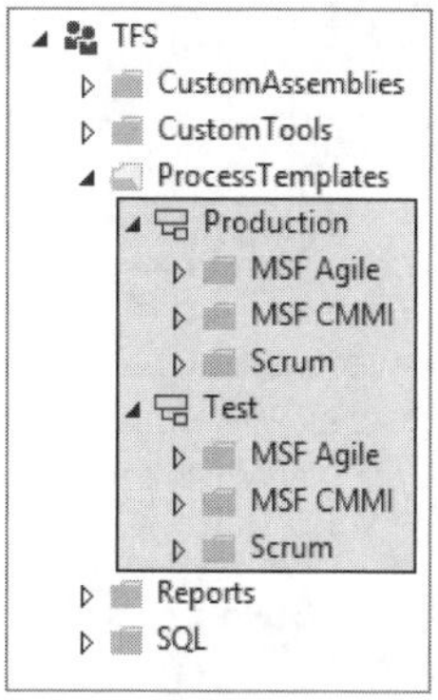

Custom Build Assemblies

In Team Foundation Server, build servers (specifically build controllers and agents) can monitor a version control folder for custom assemblies that should be used during the build process and deploy them automatically. This feature is particularly useful for companies that have large numbers of servers in their build farm and want an effective deployment tool and change control method for the custom assemblies. It is also useful for teams who want to leverage the hosted elastic build servers feature of Visual Studio Online.

FIGURE 11-12: Branches created for managing process templates

These custom assemblies can contain custom build workflow activities or even custom MSBuild tasks used by Visual Studio projects. By creating a version control folder in the TFS team project, the custom assemblies can be managed from a central location alongside other artifacts used to manage Team Foundation Server.

Interestingly, this version control folder is not used exclusively by the build servers but can also be used by end-user machines connecting to Team Foundation Server. There could be custom types or custom UI editors used by custom build process parameters that would need to be resolved whenever an end user queues a build manually. The Visual Studio clients will monitor the specified location and load the assemblies appropriately to resolve those custom types. For this reason, be sure to provide all users of Team Foundation Server read-only access to this version control folder.

> **NOTE** *Chapter 19 provides more information about creating custom build activities and deploying those activities to the servers in the build farm.*

Each build controller should be configured to point to this version control folder for deploying custom build assemblies. Figure 11-13 shows the Build Controller Properties dialog box and the field to set for monitoring the version control folder. The figure also demonstrates how the properties correspond to the version control folder created in the TFS team project.

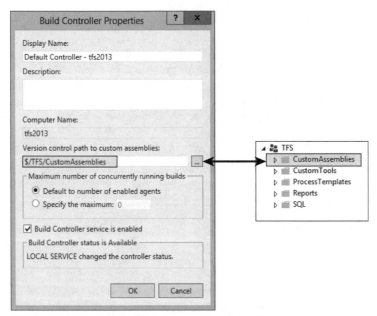

FIGURE 11-13: Build Controller Properties dialog box

Master Build Process Templates

Another version control folder that can be created in the TFS team project's version control repository is a folder used to store all of the master build process template .XAML files. After build engineers have architected a build process template that will work for several build definitions, it is nice to have such templates stored and managed from a central location.

Build definitions in the same team project collection can be configured to use the master build process templates, even if those build definitions are defined in a different team project.

> **NOTE** *Chapter 19 provides more information about architecting and customizing build process templates.*

Source Code for Custom Tools

Custom tools and extensions can be created to further enhance the features available in Team Foundation Server using the Team Foundation Server Software Development Kit (SDK). The TFS team project's version control repository is the perfect location for managing the source code to use for building those custom tools.

Build definitions can be created for the suite of custom tools that compile and package those tools using the source code stored in the TFS team project's version control repository. The work item tracking artifacts in the TFS team project can even be used to manage the releases for the custom internal tools built for Team Foundation Server.

Following are examples of the types of tools that could be created and stored in this version control repository:

➤ Custom check-in policies

➤ Custom build workflow activities and build tasks

➤ Custom work item controls

➤ Web Service event handlers for Team Foundation Server events

➤ Custom testing data collectors (or diagnostic data adapters)

➤ Migration utilities and Integration Platform adapters

➤ Custom Code Analysis rules

➤ Global Code Analysis spelling dictionary

➤ Custom IntelliTrace event collectors

Figure 11-14 shows an example of the version control folders that can be created to store the source code for custom tools that extend Team Foundation Server and Visual Studio.

FIGURE 11-14: Version control folders used to store the source code for custom tools

SUMMARY

The version control repository can quickly become unruly if left up to a team. By introducing some organization (and, specifically, some targeted methods), not only will the discoverability of the source code be improved but the method in which the application is developed is also improved. This is especially the case when third-party dependencies and internal shared libraries are needed by the application.

Additionally, storing artifacts used to manage Team Foundation Server in version control folders will allow administrators to easily access all of those artifacts in one location. You will also be able to locate key artifacts needed in disaster-recovery scenarios, as well as have a common place to manage source code for extensions to Team Foundation Server and Visual Studio.

Part II of this book has explored the features available in the version control repository in Team Foundation Server. Part III introduces the features available in the work item tracking system of Team Foundation Server. You will learn about project management, work item tracking, and reporting capabilities of Team Foundation Server. Chapter 12 introduces you to the concepts of the work item tracking system and provides the fundamentals for managing projects and work using Team Foundation Server.

PART III
Project Management

12

Introducing Work Item Tracking

WHAT'S IN THIS CHAPTER?

➤ Getting to know the additions and enhancements to project management capabilities in Team Foundation Server 2013

➤ Understanding work items and process templates

➤ Managing and querying work items

In Part II, you learned about the support that Team Foundation Server 2013 has for source control. In Part III, you will learn about how Team Foundation Server 2013 helps with project management.

Project management can involve many aspects of developing software, such as tracking remaining work and open bugs, determining how much work you can commit to with your available resources, and even helping to enforce a standard process of interaction between your team members. You will see that Team Foundation Server 2013 provides capabilities to help you achieve all of these things and more.

In this chapter, you will start by learning about the enhancements to project management available in this release. This chapter also provides an overview of work item tracking, including some ways to manage and query work items from Visual Studio, Excel, Project, and other clients. You will also learn about the importance of process templates, including an overview of the process templates provided by Microsoft for use with Team Foundation Server 2013.

Subsequent chapters in Part III of this book will also familiarize you with process template customization (Chapter 13), describe the use of the new Agile Planning tools (Chapter 14), provide an in-depth look at using reporting and SharePoint dashboards to get real-time insights into how your software development project is going (Chapter 15), and discuss the implementation of integration between Team Foundation Server and Microsoft Project Server (Chapter 16).

PROJECT MANAGEMENT ENHANCEMENTS IN TEAM FOUNDATION SERVER 2013

In Team Foundation Server 2012, Microsoft made significant strides to align Team Foundation Server with Agile methods. In Team Foundation Server 2013, the focus has broadened to support Agile project management at a larger scale. This section highlights some of the most significant improvements and additions you will find in this release, as well as those introduced in Team Foundation Server 2012. This will allow those readers coming from Team Foundation Server 2010 or 2008 to get up to speed on the significant differences that the 2012 and 2013 releases bring. If you are brand new to Team Foundation Server, concepts such as work items will be explained in greater detail later in this chapter.

Rich Work Item Relationships

According to Microsoft, the top-requested project management feature by users of the first two releases of Team Foundation Server (2005 and 2008) was representing rich relationships between work items. In these releases of Team Foundation Server, it was only possible to relate work items with one another via a simple linking mechanism. But these links didn't provide any explicit meaning, directionality, or cardinality.

For example, a common project management use case for many software development projects is to be able to model parent/child relationships between work items, such as for capturing a feature catalog or for detailing the tasks required to implement a particular requirement. You could link these work items together using early releases of Team Foundation Server, but the links didn't carry enough meaning to convey proper parent/child relationships. Without directionality, it's not easy to discern which work item is the parent and which work item is the child in this representation. Furthermore, without cardinality, there isn't a mechanism for restricting that each child work item could only have (at most) one parent work item.

Beginning with Team Foundation Server 2010, Microsoft introduced rich relational linking between work items. You can model rich relationships between work items using a variety of link types. These link types can also include directionality and cardinality. Team Foundation Server 2013 ships with many link types, but the following are the most common:

➤ **Parent/child**—This is a useful link type for representing hierarchies such as feature catalogs, or for detailing task work items (children) that will be used to implement a requirement or user story (parent). Any work item can have zero or more child work items, and zero or one parent work item.

➤ **Tests/tested by**—This link type is primarily intended to model the relationships between test-case work items and the requirements or user stories that they test. This makes it easier to determine the quality of a given requirement or user story by examining the recent results for its related test cases. A work item can test zero or more work items.

➤ **Successor/predecessor**—The successor/predecessor link type is used to indicate work items that have a dependency relationship with one another. For example, designing the user interface for a web page is generally a predecessor to writing the code and markup that will provide the implementation of that web page. A work item can have zero or more successor and/or predecessor links to other work items.

➤ **Related**—The related link type is the same as the legacy linking system found in Team Foundation Server 2005 and 2008. These link types are not directional and provide no additional context about the type of relationship. If you had linked work items in a project that was upgraded to Team Foundation Server 2013, those relationships will be represented by the related link type.

You will discover that rich work item relationships provide the basis for other features and enhancements across the project management capabilities of Team Foundation Server 2013, such as enhanced querying and reporting. It is also possible to define your own link types if you wish, although for most teams, the provided link types will be sufficient. More information on creating custom link types can be found at `http://aka.ms/WICustomLinks2013`.

> **NOTE** *Team Foundation Server 2013 does not have a mechanism for ensuring that your links are semantically correct. For example, it's possible to create circular chains of successor/predecessor links or tests/tested-by relationships between two work items that don't involve a test case. If you notice that you have invalid link types in your project, you can easily delete them at any time.*

Test Case Management

Test cases are represented as work items in Team Foundation Server 2013. This makes it possible to create rich relationships between the code you are implementing and the results of your quality assurance (QA) efforts.

For example, test case work items can be linked (via tests/tested-by link types) to requirement work items. As tests are run, results can be reported on by querying a given requirement work item, navigating to the related test cases, and viewing the results of recent test runs. Many of the new default reports make use of this information to expose new perspectives on software quality.

> **NOTE** *You learn more about the role that testing plays in Team Foundation Server 2013 in Chapter 26.*

Agile Portfolio Management

In Team Foundation Server 2013, Microsoft added an additional category of work items to assist in managing a project at a portfolio level. A management team can define high-level goals and can assign work to those goals in a hierarchical manner. Individual teams can work with their own backlogs, while managers can see the progress of multiple projects across the entire scope of work for one or more projects.

By default, the out-of-the-box templates for Team Foundation Server 2013 contain one additional layer to the hierarchy, called the Feature category. However, Team Foundation Server now gives you the ability to create up to five levels of portfolio backlog. For example, you may have an Initiative work item that contains Goals, which are further broken down into Features. This hierarchy is fully supported in the Team Web Access user interface.

> **NOTE** *To add additional work item categories, you will need to modify the process template for your project. For more information on customizing process templates, see Chapter 13.*

Enhanced Reporting

One of the primary reasons Microsoft designed Team Foundation Server as an integrated solution (including source control, project management, build automation, and so on) is to enable multidimensional views into software development projects. Effectively managing a software project is not unlike managing other complex projects. Making smart decisions requires you to have a rich set of information resources available, usually in real time, which can help to inform resource allocations, prioritizations, cuts, schedule changes, and other important evaluations.

The rich work item relationships that exist within Team Foundation Server 2013 enable Microsoft to significantly enhance the types of reports available. As just one example, parent/child relationships between user stories and tasks can produce a report showing the amount of work required in order to finish implementing any given user story. By further analyzing the tests/tested by links, you can get a view into software quality for those same user stories based on the results of your test cases. There are countless other examples.

Starting in the 2010 release, Microsoft made it much easier to customize existing reports, or create new ones. The ad hoc reporting capabilities allow you to create reports from just a work item query.

Basic reporting has now been included in Team Web Access with the addition of work item charts and Team Favorite tiles. These simple reporting elements can give insights into the state of your project at a glance.

> **NOTE** *You learn more about reporting with Team Foundation Server 2013 in Chapter 15.*

SharePoint Server Dashboards

Most software development projects involve many stakeholders. In addition to the core programming team, a team may include project managers, business analysts, testers, architects, and so on. There may also be external stakeholders—such as end users or executive management—who have a vested interest in monitoring the progress of your project. Most of these people don't use Visual Studio; so how do you effectively communicate project status to everyone?

Microsoft has integrated Team Foundation Server with SharePoint for this reason. Whenever you create a team project with Team Foundation Server 2013, you can optionally create a new SharePoint site (or use an existing one). This site can be used as a dashboard to provide everybody on your extended team with a view into your project. Your SharePoint site provides a web-based view of reports from your team project, along with a document repository where you can store artifacts such as specifications and storyboards.

> **NOTE** *At the time of writing, you cannot create a SharePoint site for Team Projects created in Visual Studio Online.*

> **NOTE** *In Chapter 15, you will learn about how these SharePoint dashboards can be used and customized for your team.*

Agile Planning Tools in Team Web Access

When planning for Team Foundation Server 2013, Microsoft noted that there was a significant shift among development organizations toward the group of Agile development methods. To help support teams moving toward these methods, this release of Team Foundation Server includes some "must-have" features to help you plan your backlog, track velocity, understand your capacity, plan each iteration (or sprint), view a burndown of hours for each iteration, and view how work is flowing through your project. These tools will be immediately familiar to teams that practice Scrum.

While creating these tools, the Microsoft team wanted to ensure that usage was not limited to the practitioners of Scrum or Agile development methods, but rather was available and usable by any development team using Team Foundation Server. To support this, every process template that ships with Team Foundation Server 2013 supports the agile planning and tracking tools. You can also modify a custom or third-party process template to support these new features. You will learn more about process template customization in Chapter 13.

Significant improvements have been made in the Team Web Access interface in the 2013 release. These include color-coding of work item types, drag-and-drop management of work items, and customization of columns on the agile boards. Many more small UI changes have been included in the various minor releases.

> **NOTE** *In Chapter 14, you learn more about managing teams and using the Agile Planning tools.*

WORK ITEMS

If you're new to Team Foundation Server, you may be wondering what exactly a work item is after reading the preceding section. A *work item* is the basic building block of the project management capabilities in Team Foundation Server. Microsoft defines a work item as ". . . a database record that Team Foundation uses to track the assignment and progress of work."

Work Item Types

There are many kinds of work items, known as *work item types*. An instance of a work item type is a work item, in much the same way that, in object-oriented programming (OOP), an instance of a class is an object. A work item can represent explicit work that needs to be completed (or has been completed), such as with a *Task* work item type. Work items can capture details of the software you are building, such as with *Requirement* or *User Story* work item types. Work items can be used to capture problems, such as the *Bug* work item type (which indicates a problem with your software) or the *Issue* work item type (which might describe a problem with tooling, processes, or people that may be slowing down your project, or even preventing work from happening). In Team Foundation Server 2013, *Feature* work items have been added for managing a portfolio of work. Team Foundation Server 2013 includes other default work item types as well, and you can even create your own.

> **NOTE** *You learn more about work item type customization in Chapter 13.*

Work items include a handful of key elements, as shown in Table 12-1.

TABLE 12-1: Work Item Elements

ELEMENT	DESCRIPTION
Field	*Fields* contain the information that can be captured as part of a work item. Some fields are shared by all work item types (called *system fields*). Examples of system fields include *Title* (a one-line description of your work item), *ID* (a number that is globally unique across your team project collection), and *Assigned to* (which can be a user, such as a developer, who is working on a fix for a bug work item). Other fields might be specific to a given work item type, such as the *Steps to reproduce* field, which is found in the Bug work item type and describes how a bug was discovered.
Rule	*Rules* can dictate which values are allowed for given fields. For example, you might decide that the Priority field for bugs should be assigned a value of 0, 1, or 2 and cannot be left blank.
Form	A *form* describes the way work items are displayed by work item clients such as Visual Studio. (You will learn more about some of the ways to view and interact with work items later in this chapter.)

State	*States* indicate where in your project workflow a work item is. For example, a Bug work item type in the MSF for Agile Software Development process template starts out in an *Active* state when it is first created. Once a developer declares that the code has been written or modified to fix a bug, the developer changes the state of the Bug work item to *Resolved*. If a tester can verify that the bug can no longer be reproduced, the tester changes the bug work item state to *Closed*. But if a tester can still reproduce the bug, it will need to be reactivated (that is, the tester will change the state of the bug back to Active). This signals to the developers that they still have work to do.
Transition	*Transitions* are similar to rules, but they define how a work item moves from one state to another. In the previous example, a bug work item must begin in an Active state, and can then move into a Resolved or Closed state. But, from a Resolved state, it is also possible to move back to an Active state. This is all defined by the transition model as part of the work item type. Additionally, transitions can dictate that certain fields should be required in order to move from one state to another. For example, to move a bug from an Active to a Resolved state, a developer must assign a *Reason* (such as Fixed, As Designed, Cannot Reproduce, and so on).
Link	Work items can include *links* to other work items, using any of the link types you read about in the preceding section.
History	Work items also contain a full *history* that includes information about all changes to fields and transitions.

Figure 12-1 shows an example of a bug work item form that has been resolved by the developer. This screenshot is taken from a bug that was created with the MSF for Agile Software Development process template. You will learn more about process templates later in this chapter.

Figure 12-2 is a state diagram showing the transitions for the default Bug work item type included with the MSF for Agile Software Development process template. State diagrams for each work item type are included with the documentation for the process templates provided by Microsoft. They are useful for understanding how a work item behaves.

Areas and Iterations

Most of the system fields available for work items (such as Title and ID) are fairly self-explanatory. But there are two important fields—Area and Iteration—that warrant further discussion.

The Area field is a versatile one that can be used to create logical categories for your work items. In Team Foundation Server 2013, when you define a Team, a corresponding Area is created by default. This helps organize work items according to the team responsible for delivering them. There are a number of other ways you can use areas, and another common approach is to define an area for each logical part of your application.

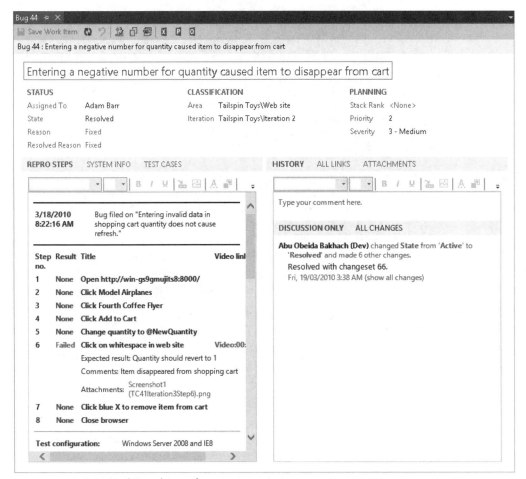

FIGURE 12-1: Bug (Agile) work item form

For example, in Figure 12-1, this bug is assigned to the `Tailspin Toys\Web site` area to indicate that it is part of the web application being developed by the `Fabrikam Fiber Web Team` for the `Tailspin Toys` team project. The complete string that is used for this designation is referred to as an *area path*. Other area paths might include `Tailspin Toys\Database` or `Tailspin Toys\Mobile Application`, or can be several levels deep, such as `Tailspin Toys\Web site\Shopping cart\Update controller`.

The Iterations field is useful for project planning, and it can indicate a timeframe for when you plan to address a work item. In Figure 12-1, this work item is assigned to `Tailspin Toys\Iteration 2`, where `Tailspin Toys` is the name of the team project and `Iteration 2` is the specific iteration this work item is assigned to.

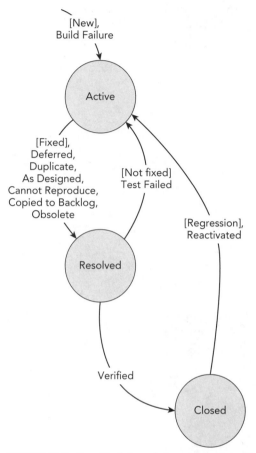

FIGURE 12-2: Bug (Agile) work item type state diagram

You can name your iterations whatever you'd like; some teams choose sequential iterations (such as Iteration 1, Iteration 2, and so on), while others choose to map them to milestone releases (such as Beta 1, Beta 2, and so on). You can also create trees of iterations and employ a blend of naming strategies, such as `Tailspin Toys\Version 2.0\Beta 1\Iteration 2`. In addition, Iterations allow you to set start and end dates, as shown in Figure 12-3. This metadata is used in the Agile Planning tools discussed later in this chapter.

You are not required to use iterations and areas to categorize your work items, but they can be very useful for querying, managing, and reporting on your work items as your team project grows. When used effectively, areas and iterations can allow you to employ a single team project for dozens or even hundreds of applications across many years of iterative releases.

A team project administrator can manage the list of valid areas and iterations from within Visual Studio by selecting Team ⇨ Team Project Settings ⇨ Work Item Areas and iterations by clicking Team ⇨ Team Project Settings ⇨ Work Item Iterations. This launches the Team Project's Control Panel in the Web Access portal. Figures 12-3 and Figure 12-4 show the screens for editing iterations and areas, respectively.

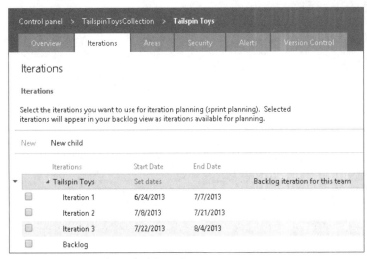

FIGURE 12-3: Iteration administration

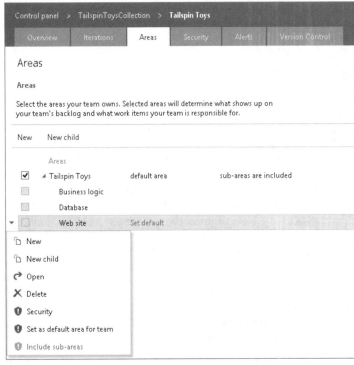

FIGURE 12-4: Area administration

A nice feature of area and iteration administration is that you can use the Security option in the context menu, as shown in Figure 12-4, to define granular permissions for indicating who is allowed to modify or even read work items in each part of your team project. For example, maybe you work for a government security contractor and there are bugs of a sensitive nature that should only be viewed by team members with a certain security clearance. Or maybe you are building a prototype of the next version of your application and want to restrict access to minimize the potential for leaks that your competitors could get access to. These sorts of restrictions are possible by using iteration and area security settings.

At any time, you can return to the Area and Iteration settings to add, rename, move, or delete areas and iterations. If you rename or move areas or iterations for which there are existing work items, those work items will automatically be reassigned by Team Foundation Server using the new name or location you choose. If you delete an area or iteration for which there are existing work items, you will be prompted for the value that Team Foundation Server should use to replace the iteration or area value in affected work items.

You will discover that work items are used throughout Team Foundation Server. They form the basis of many of the reports you will read about in Chapter 15. They can be linked to changesets (which you read about in Part II) to provide more information about what changes were made to a set of files and why. They can be used by project managers and team leaders for project planning, and they are used to help control which work team members should be focused on, and how they should interact with other team members.

Work items, work item types, and all of the activities involving work items (editing, querying, reporting, and so on) are usually referred to collectively as the *work item tracking* capability of Team Foundation Server. Now that you understand the basics of work items, you are ready to learn about process templates, which include the definitions for work item types.

PROCESS TEMPLATES

A *process template* defines the default characteristics of any new team project. Process templates are a powerful concept in Team Foundation Server. A process template includes the default work item types, reports, documents, process guidance, and other associated artifacts that provide you with everything you need to get started with your software project.

Choosing the right process template is an important step in creating a new team project. You should carefully choose the best process template for your team's preferred work style and the type of project you are working on. This section will help you understand the types of process templates available. While you are reading this section, you should be thinking about the following types of questions:

➤ How does your team work today?

➤ Is there anything about how your team works today that you'd like to change?

➤ Do you need a formal process, or do you work better as a more agile team?

➤ Are there areas of your process where you prefer to be more agile, but other areas where you need to be more formal? (For example, maybe you want to manage your team's iterations in an agile manner, but decisions about requirements require formal negotiations with your customer.)

➤ Do you have resources to invest in and maintain your own custom process template, or would one provided by Microsoft or a reputable third party be a better solution?

➤ What other stakeholders should be involved in the decision-making process for answering these questions?

If answering these questions proves difficult for you or your team, you may want to start with a small pilot project first and see how your team performs when using one of the existing process templates. You can then use the findings from that pilot to determine which process template to start with, and what changes (if any) need to be made to that process template before using it for subsequent projects. Process template customization is covered in Chapter 13.

Embracing the *right* process template can have a transformational effect on an organization by providing everyone on the team with a predictable and repeatable process for capturing and communicating information, making decisions, and ensuring that you are delivering on customer expectations. This, in turn, can drive up software quality and development velocity, which ultimately delivers more value to your customers.

MSF for Agile Software Development

The MSF for Agile Software Development 2013 process template included with Team Foundation Server 2013 is designed for teams who are practicing agile methodologies, such as Scrum or Extreme Programming (XP). These methodologies have their roots in the now-famous Agile Manifesto (www.agilemanifesto.org/).

> **NOTE** *MSF version 1 was introduced by Microsoft in 1993, and version 4 was first codified as a set of process templates with the release of Team Foundation Server 2005. MSF provides guidelines, role definitions, and other materials to help organizations deliver IT solutions, including software development projects. Many of the guiding principles of MSF align closely with those of the Agile Manifesto.*

A key tenet of agile methodologies is that requirements will evolve over time, both as business needs change and as customers begin to use interim releases of your software. For this reason, the MSF for Agile Software Development process template assumes that teams will be frequently refining requirements and reprioritizing work by maintaining a common backlog of requirements (which are captured as user stories in this template). Periods of work are time-boxed into short lengths of time (iterations). Prior to each iteration, the development team works with the customer to prioritize the backlog, and the top user stories on the backlog are then addressed in that iteration.

Another important aspect of agile methodologies is, as the Agile Manifesto describes it, valuing "individuals and interactions over processes and tools." This doesn't mean that processes and tools shouldn't be used at all, but instead that they sometimes can get in the way of empowering people to communicate and work together in order to make smart decisions.

This is also reflected in the MSF for Agile Software Development process template, which defines a relatively small number of states, fields, transitions, and work item types as compared with other process templates such as the MSF for Capability Maturity Model Integration (CMMI) Process Improvement process template. By keeping the process simple, the goal is to prevent any unnecessary burdens from getting in the way of people making the right decisions.

The following are the work item types available in the MSF for Agile Software Development process template:

➤ Bug

➤ Issue

➤ Task

➤ Test Case

➤ User Story

➤ Feature

> **NOTE** *There are a few additional work item types present in all of the Microsoft-supplied process templates (and available to be added to custom and third-party process templates), which cannot be created directly, but are instead created during special situations. Code Review Request and Code Review Response work items are used to provide the code review functionality, which you read about in Chapter 6. Feedback Request and Feedback Response work item types are created during the process of requesting feedback and provid- ing feedback from stakeholders, which are covered in* Professional Application Lifecycle Management with Visual Studio 2013 *(*http://www.wiley.com/ WileyCDA/WileyTitle/productCd-1118836588.html*). Finally, the Shared Steps work item is essentially a special instance of a Test Case. You learn more about shared steps and test cases in Chapter 26. Most team members won't interact with shared steps directly, so they are excluded from the preceding list.*

The MSF for Agile Software Development process template works well with the Agile Planning tools and Task Boards in Team Foundation Server 2013.

> **NOTE** *You can explore the MSF for Agile Software Development 2013 process template in depth, including more detail on each of the included work item types, at* http://aka.ms/MSFAgile2013.

MSF for CMMI Process Improvement

The *MSF for CMMI Process Improvement 2013* process template is designed for teams who want to, or may have to, take a more formal approach toward developing software. This process template is based on the Capability Maturity Model Integration (CMMI) for Development, which was developed by the Software Engineering Institute, a part of Carnegie Mellon University. CMMI defines not only a framework for developing software, but it also prescribes ways for an organization to constantly improve its processes in an objective and repeatable way. An organization can even become certified by an outside appraiser who can verify whether or not it is performing at one of five CMMI maturity levels.

CMMI is a popular model for developing software by such organizations as systems integrators (SIs) and software factories. There is very little subjectivity in the model, so it allows an organization to represent its services using a standard that is well understood globally and can be appraised and certified by a neutral third-party organization. CMMI is also used for developing many mission-critical systems by organizations such as NASA or defense contractors. In fact, the Software Engineering Institute at Carnegie Mellon was originally funded by the United States Department of Defense to help them find better ways of managing their projects.

As you might expect, the MSF for CMMI Process Improvement process template is more complex than its Agile counterpart. The CMMI template includes the following work item types:

➤ Bug

➤ Change Request

➤ Issue

➤ Requirement

➤ Feature

➤ Review

➤ Risk

➤ Task

➤ Test Case

> **NOTE** *The Feedback, Code review, and Shared Steps work item types are also omitted from this list for the same reason as mentioned previously in the discussion of the MSF for Agile Software Development process template.*

In addition to including three additional work item types, the work item types themselves are also more complex in the CMMI process template than in the Agile process template. Compare the screenshot of a bug work item form from the Agile process template, shown earlier in Figure 12-1, with a bug work item form from the CMMI process template, shown in Figure 12-5. Take note of the additional fields, such as Root Cause, Triage, and Blocked, which were not in the bug work item from the Agile process template. There are also additional tabs across the lower half of the bug work item from the CMMI process template.

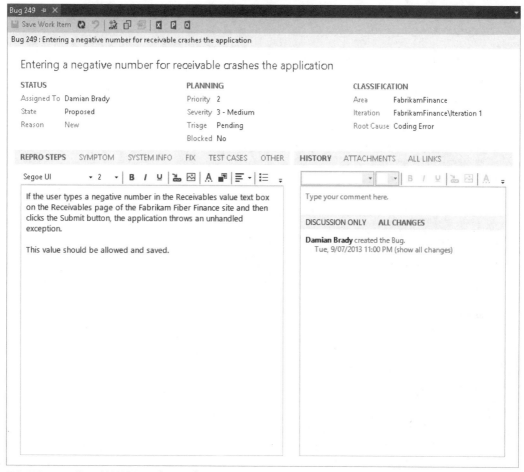

FIGURE 12-5: Bug (CMMI) work item form

The states and transitions of work item types from the CMMI process template are also more complex than in the Agile process template. Now compare the state diagram of the bug work item type from the Agile process template, shown in Figure 12-2, with the state diagram of the bug work item type from the CMMI process template, shown in Figure 12-6.

The key difference you should notice between these two state diagrams is that the CMMI process template introduces an additional state—Proposed. This explicit decision stage is required in the CMMI process template before a developer is ever assigned to work on a bug. This should cause the team to ask such questions as, "Is this really a bug, or does this represent a request to change the way certain functionality was designed? Will fixing this bug have unintended side effects on other parts of the software? If you choose to work on this bug, how should it be prioritized against your other work?"

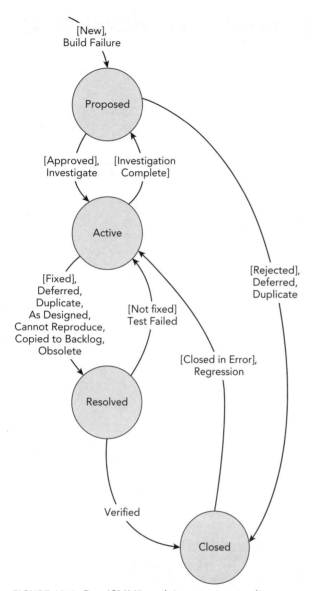

FIGURE 12-6: Bug (CMMI) work item type state diagram

This shouldn't imply that those aren't important questions to be asking even if you are using the Agile process template, and a seasoned team practicing an agile methodology will likely already be mentally following this checklist as they triage bugs. But the CMMI process template makes this step explicit, which helps to ensure that this step takes place for every bug, regardless of the experience level of the development team.

Another way of thinking of CMMI is to realize that by following the model, NASA isn't guaranteed that it will never again develop a rocket that fails because of a software defect. But if NASA is following CMMI correctly, then it can guarantee that an agreed-upon process was used to make decisions leading up to that defect. And conversely, in the event of a defect, it can audit the process that was used, examine the assumptions that went into the decision-making process, and learn from those mistakes in the interest of refining its process and helping to ensure that the same mistake never happens again.

It is also important to point out that using the MSF for CMMI Process Improvement process template alone will not ensure that an organization can successfully pass a CMMI certification audit. This is akin to the fact that simply having a smoke alarm and a fire extinguisher on hand won't keep a family safe if they don't know how to properly use and maintain this equipment.

But Team Foundation Server 2013, along with the MSF for CMMI Process Improvement process template, can be very useful for helping an organization that wants to adopt CMMI as its model of development. Team Foundation Server features such as end-to-end traceability, multidimensional reporting, rich linking (between work items, and with other artifacts such as builds and changesets), and preservation of history are all incredibly useful capabilities that can help an organization to prepare for and pass a CMMI audit.

> **NOTE** *You can explore the MSF for CMMI Process Improvement 2013 process template in depth, including more detail on each of the included work item types, at* `http://aka.ms/MSFCMMI2013`.

CMMI DEVELOPMENT METHODOLOGY

There is a common misconception that CMMI dictates a waterfall, or "Big Design Up Front," development methodology. While there is certainly a strong correlation between teams practicing waterfall methodologies and those following a CMMI model, CMMI actually does not define a development methodology. You can choose to use an agile development methodology along with the MSF for CMMI Process Improvement process template if you want to, although you might have a hard time selling agile diehards from your team on the value of the additional rigor imposed by its processes.

As a compromise solution, another approach is to pick and choose the aspects of the CMMI process template that are most interesting to you, and incorporate those into the Agile process template as a custom process template. For example, maybe you like the explicit decision point created by having your bugs begin in a Proposed state before being activated, but you don't see a need for the additional work item types in the CMMI template. In this example, you could start with the Agile process template and import the Bug work item type from the CMMI process template.

Visual Studio Scrum

While there are many development methodologies that make up the agile movement, Scrum has established itself as the most popular for the time being. Scrum defines clear roles, responsibilities, and activities that team members practicing Scrum must follow.

A team practicing Scrum uses a standard vocabulary to define what they are doing. Teams hold *daily scrum meetings* (meetings where team members talk about what they did yesterday, what they will do today, and anything that might be blocking them—called an *impediment*). Instead of a project manager, a team practicing Scrum is usually led by a *Scrum Master.* There are other terms as well, which you can learn about in any of the dozens of books about Scrum, or from the hundreds of Scrum user groups or trainers around the world.

The Visual Studio Scrum 2013 process template was introduced specifically to help teams who want to practice Scrum and use Team Foundation Server 2013. The first version was made available a few months after Team Foundation Server 2010 first shipped. The current version now ships in the box with Team Foundation Server 2013; in fact, it was also made the default process template for team project creation.

So, you might now be wondering, if the MSF for Agile Software Development process template is designed to support any of the agile development methodologies—including Scrum—what is the purpose of the Visual Studio Scrum process template? The Visual Studio Scrum process template was created to provide teams practicing Scrum with the *specific* artifacts and terminology used universally by teams who have adopted Scrum.

Instead of User Stories or Requirements, Visual Studio Scrum uses *Product Backlog Item* work item types. Instead of Issues or Risks, Visual Studio Scrum uses *Impediment* work item types. *Sprints* are represented by the Iteration Path, and the dates you use to define your Sprints are used when rendering your *burndown* and *velocity* reports. The Agile Planning Tools discussed in Chapter 14 were created specifically with the Scrum template in mind. In short, if you practice Scrum or are considering practicing Scrum, the Visual Studio Scrum process template is designed to help you do so while making the most of Team Foundation Server 2013.

> **NOTE** *You can explore the Visual Studio Scrum 2013 process template in depth, including more detail on each of the included work item types, at* `http://aka .ms/Scrum2013`.

COMPROMISING WITH SCRUM

If you want to practice Scrum, the Visual Studio Scrum process template provides a great option for doing so. But you shouldn't feel locked into this process template if there are other process templates you like better, such as the MSF for Agile Software Development process template.

For example, you may prefer some of the additional reports that are included with the Agile process template. You can still use the Agile process template and practice Scrum, but you will just need to make some mental translations between the terminology you use as a Scrum team and the way the Agile process template expects you to enter information (such as referring to Product Backlog Items as User Stories).

Third-Party Process Templates

Several third parties provide process templates for use with Team Foundation Server 2012 and 2013.

There are several great third-party process templates available, but you should carefully consider the support and road map implications of adopting a third-party process template. For example, when the next version of Team Foundation Server is released, will the process template be upgraded to take advantage of new or improved features? And if so, what is the upgrade path for migrating existing projects to the new version of the process template?

If you aren't prepared to take over the maintenance of the process template in the event that the third party chooses to stop investing in it, then you might want to consider one of the aforementioned process templates that are built and supported by Microsoft.

Custom Process Templates

Finally, you might decide that none of the process templates provided by Microsoft or third parties fit the needs of your team or your development project. While you could certainly create your own process template from scratch, a far more common approach is to start with an existing process template and customize it to suit your needs. You can learn about customizing process templates in Chapter 13.

Now that you understand your options for choosing a process template, the next section will introduce you to some of the different ways you can manage your work items.

MANAGING WORK ITEMS

There are many ways of accessing your work items within Team Foundation Server 2013. Because work items will be used by many stakeholders across your team (including programmers, testers, project managers, and so on), and most of these roles don't use Visual Studio as their primary tool, you will discover that Microsoft provides many client options for accessing work items.

In this section you will be introduced to using Visual Studio, Excel, Project, and Team Web Access to access your work items. This chapter won't cover every aspect of accessing work items from each of these clients, but it will give you a better idea of the ways each client can be used, as well as the relative benefits of each, and provide you with pointers to detailed documentation for each client.

The list of clients in this section isn't exhaustive. There are also dozens of third-party clients, a few of which are examined in this section. Testers might use Microsoft Test Manager (discussed in Chapter 26). Eclipse users can utilize Team Explorer Everywhere. You can even write your own clients using the Team Foundation Server object model if you want to.

Using Visual Studio

In Chapter 4, you learned about using Team Explorer to work with Team Foundation Server 2013. Team Explorer not only provides access for Visual Studio users wanting to connect to Team Foundation Server, but it also installs the add-ins required to work with Excel and Project. So, even if you don't plan on using Visual Studio, if you want to use Excel or Project with Team Foundation Server, you should install Team Explorer.

> **NOTE** *The examples in this chapter assume that you are using Team Explorer 2013. While it is possible to use older versions of Team Explorer to connect to Team Foundation Server 2013, you will not be able to access some of the new features in the product. In particular, because earlier editions of Team Explorer (2005 and 2008) aren't aware of the rich relational-linking capabilities of Team Foundation Server 2013, you won't be able to manage these link types or use the newer querying capabilities to navigate your work items.*
>
> *You can still use older versions of Visual Studio along with Team Explorer 2013. Team Explorer 2013 will be installed "side by side" with your legacy version of Visual Studio, and you can access it by opening the Visual Studio 2013 shell. You can continue to use your legacy Visual Studio client to check in code changes, and then switch to Team Explorer 2013 to update your work items.*

Creating Work Items

Work items are easy to create using Visual Studio. Open the Team Explorer window of Visual Studio 2013 and click on the `Work Items` entry. Now, click on the `New Work Item` menu. The drop-down menu will reveal the work item types that are available in your team project. Click the work item type that you want to create an instance of. An empty work item form will appear, similar to that shown in Figure 12-1.

The new work item form will vary in appearance based on the work item type you chose to create. For the most part, filling out the work item form is self-explanatory, but there are a few things to notice when creating and editing work items.

The first is that your work item won't have an ID until it has been successfully saved for the first time. Remember that the ID is a number that is globally unique across your team project collection, numbered sequentially, starting with 1. This means that the first work item you save within a new team project won't have an ID of 1 if there are existing team projects in your team project collection that also contain work items.

For now, your work item probably says something like "New Bug 1" at the top of the form. The number 1 isn't your work item's ID; it's just a temporary number used by Visual Studio to track unsaved work items in this session. In fact, until it is saved, Team Foundation Server won't know about your work item.

Before you can successfully save this work item, you will need to assign a Title to it at a minimum. There may be other required fields as well, depending on the work item type you selected. An error message at the top of the form will indicate any remaining fields that you must complete. Some required fields may appear on other tabs.

Another thing you'll notice about work items is that you can't skip states. A work item must be saved in one state prior to moving to the next state. For example, if you refer back to Figure 12-2, you will notice that a bug from the MSF for Agile Software Development process template generally moves from Active to Resolved to Closed.

You can't immediately create a new bug and save it in the Resolved state, however, even if you already fixed the bug that you found, and you're just creating the bug work item as a record of what you did. You must first save it in an Active state, change the state to Resolved, and then save it again.

This may seem cumbersome at first, but the reason you can't immediately change the state of a new work item is that the work item type may define rules that must be satisfied as a work item transition from one state to another. Additionally, the meaning of some fields changes during a work item's life cycle, so each time you save in a new state, the available choices for a field may change. For example, when you create a new bug using the Agile process template, the Reason field helps to indicate how a bug was discovered. When you are transitioning the same bug from Active to Resolved, the Reason state indicates why you are doing so (the bug was fixed, or couldn't be reproduced, or was a duplicate, and so on).

The interface for creating and editing work items with Visual Studio is very straightforward. What can be difficult to master is an understanding of all of the fields found throughout the work item types, their transitions, when to use them, and so on.

For the process templates provided by Microsoft, the documentation is very thorough and is recommended reading to help you decide how to best adopt these process templates within your team. But wholesale adoption of these templates isn't for every team. You should feel empowered as a team to decide which fields are more or less important than others. You may even decide to add to or simplify the work item types to better meet your needs. Process template customization is covered in Chapter 13.

DELETING WORK ITEMS

A common complaint by people who are new to using work items with Team Foundation Server is that work items can't (easily) be deleted. This was a design decision by Microsoft. Organizations do not want bugs, requirements, or other important work items in a project to be accidentally (or maliciously) deleted, so there isn't an option within Visual Studio or the other clients you'll read about in this chapter for deleting work items.

continues

continued

Team Foundation Server 2013 makes deletion possible from a command prompt. Open a Visual Studio command prompt and type `witadmin destroywi /?` for the command-line syntax help. This action is not reversible, so take care when using it. As a general rule, destructive operations are only available from the command line and require Administrative permissions.

Microsoft's recommended approach is to transition work items as appropriate instead of deleting them. For example, if you examine the state diagram in Figure 12-2, you will see that valid reasons for resolving a Bug work item include indicating that the bug can't be reproduced, it's obsolete (maybe it refers to a feature or functionality that has been removed or changed), or it's a duplicate of a bug that already exists.

While it might be tempting to just want to delete these work items instead of resolving them using one of these reasons, the resolution data might prove useful later for a QA lead to discover that a tester isn't doing his or her job effectively when filing these erroneous bugs. It's easy to generate a report later on showing, for example, all of the bugs created by a tester that were later discovered to be duplicates of existing bugs. But if those same work items are deleted, they won't show up in such a report.

CHANGING A WORK ITEM TYPE

In Team Foundation Server, the fields for each work item type can be vastly different. For this reason, it is not possible to simply change the type of a work item. This is a common complaint by people familiar with alternative process management tools such as Atlassian's Jira.

Even though changing a work item type is not supported in Team Foundation Server, both the Team Web Access and Visual Studio interfaces provide convenient ways to create a copy of a work item. The copied work item can be a different type, and all data in corresponding fields will migrate across. This includes all links to work items.

For more information on copying work items, see the blog post at `http://aka.ms/ChangeWIType`.

Work Item Queries

Now that you know how to create work items, the next task you should learn about is how to find them. You can type the ID of the work item directly in the Search box in Team Explorer, but this assumes that you know the ID of all of your work items. Chances are you'll want to use queries most of the time.

The process template you are using probably includes some useful built-in queries already. Open the `Work Items` page of Team Explorer to reveal the `My Queries` and `Shared Queries` folders under the `Queries` node. The contents of the `Shared Queries` folder are visible to everybody on the team, whereas `My Queries` provides a personal location to save queries, which may only be useful to you. By keeping specialized queries in `My Queries`, you can avoid creating too much clutter for your fellow team members.

> **NOTE** *You should consider using permissions to lock down queries within the Shared Queries node. This will prevent someone from accidentally overwriting a shared query with their own, which might cause unexpected results for others. You can set security on a query or query folder within Team Queries by right-clicking it and selecting Security.*

If you have an existing query, you can simply double-click it to run it. Your results will vary based on the type of query you run and the number of matching work items in your team project, but it will look something like the query results shown in Figure 12-7.

	ID	Work Ite...	Title	State	Assigned ...	Remainin...	Complete...	Story
	7	User Story	As a customer I should be able to remove items from my shopping cart.	Active	Julia Ilyiana			2
	25	Task	Design UI for item removal	Active	Annie Herr...	8		
	26	Task	Bind cart removal function to back end	Active	Cameron S...	5		
	8	User Story	◢ As a customer I should have to enter a strong password when creating a new ac...	Resolved	Julia Ilyiana			3
	27	Task	Write regular expression for strong password	Closed	Adam Barr	10		
	28	Task	Add RegEx to account creation Web page	Closed	Adam Barr	6		
	9	User Story	◢ As a customer I should be able to see images for all items.	Active	Julia Ilyiana			9
	29	Task	Update database to point to actual images	Active	Cameron S...	12		
	30	Task	Upload images for all products	Active	Annie Herr...	6		
	31	Task	Update web site to include new product images.	Active	Annie Herr...	4		

FIGURE 12-7: Results of a tree query

The query results shown in Figure 12-7 are from a Tree of Work Items query. This query type returns a list of work items matching your query and groups them according to their parent/child relationships. In this example, there are top-level User Story work items that are linked to child task work items.

Another type of query is Work Items and Direct Links. This type of query is similar to the Tree of Work Items query, except that you are not limited to parent/child links. For example, you can specify that you want to see all user stories and their test cases as represented by a tested-by link type. You can even construct a query that shows all of your user stories that *do not* have linked test cases; this is useful for spotting potential holes in your test plan.

Finally, the Flat List query type does not show any link types and is the basic type of query found in all versions of Team Foundation Server.

From within the query results window, you can open a work item simply by double-clicking it. You also have several options available to you from the toolbar located at the top of the query results window. You can place your mouse over these toolbar icons to learn more about them. The available options will vary slightly between query types, but all of them allow you to create new work items (linked to any work items you have highlighted); to link the work item you have highlighted to another existing work item; to open your query results in Microsoft Project, Outlook, or Excel (more on this later); to edit the query you are working with; and to change which columns are displayed in your query results (and in which order).

The query editor shown in Figure 12-8 is the result of having opened the query from Figure 12-7 and clicking Edit Query.

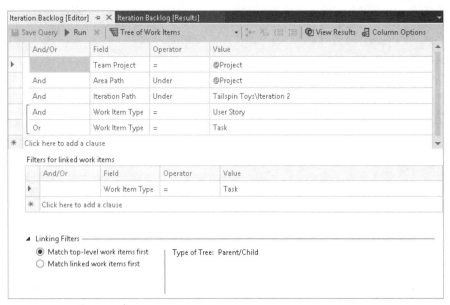

FIGURE 12-8: Query editor

Even if you've never used queries with Team Foundation Server before, this query should be fairly straightforward to reverse-engineer to learn what it does.

The first row (`Team Project = @Project`) means that your query results should be scoped to the team project where the query is saved. If you delete this row, your results may return work items from the entire team project collection. `@Project` is a *query variable*. Query variables are converted into their respective values when the query is executed. So, for this project, `@Project` will resolve to "Tailspin Toys." By using query variables, you can write more flexible queries. The two other query variables available to you are `@Me` (which is converted into the user name of the currently logged-in user) and `@Today` (which is converted into today's date).

The next row of the query (`AND Area Path Under @Project`) indicates that work items from any area path of this project can be included because the area path specified is the top-level area path (for this project, that means that `@Project` will resolve to the `\Tailspin Toys\` area path). You could change this clause to something like AND Area Path Under Tailspin Toys\ Web site if you wanted to restrict results to work items related to your website. Because you are using the Under operator, if you had further sub-paths (such as Tailspin Toys\Web site\ Shopping cart), these would be included as well. If you wanted to restrict the results so that the area path matched exactly what was specified in the rightmost column, you could change the operator to the equals sign (=).

The third clause (AND Iteration Path Under Tailspin Toys\Iteration 2) is similar to the second clause. This means that work items must be assigned to an iteration of Iteration 2 (or anything under this path).

Clauses four and five are grouped together (as shown by the vertical bracket on the far-left side of the query). This means that they should be interpreted together, in much the same way that math operations within parentheses or brackets are interpreted together. These clauses, when interpreted together, mean *Return work items with a work item type of User Story OR a work item type of Task.*

Finally, because the query type for this query is a "Tree of Work Items," there is a second grid (labeled "Filters for linked work items"), which allows you to specify any constraints on the child work items that are returned. In this example, only task work items will be returned as children.

> **NOTE** *Work item queries can be very powerful, and the options for creating queries are endless. A full guide for understanding how to use queries can be found at* http://aka.ms/TFSQueries2013.

Using Microsoft Excel

Microsoft Excel is another popular client for editing work items. If you have installed Team Explorer 2013 on a machine with Microsoft Excel (2007, 2010, or 2013), you will have a Team tab available from the Office Ribbon, which allows you to interface with Team Foundation Server 2013.

There are two ways of opening work items in Excel. One option is to open query results from within Team Explorer and then, from the query results toolbar, click Open in Microsoft Office ⇨ Open Query in Microsoft Excel. The other approach is to start in Excel, open the Team tab from the Office Ribbon, and then click New List. You will be prompted to select your Team Foundation Server and team project, along with the query for the work items you want to manage. Or, instead of a query, you can start with an empty list. This allows you to enter new work items, or to select individual work items to add to your list by clicking Get Work Items.

Managing work items in Excel is a fairly rich experience. You can create new work items, make edits to existing work items, and even manage Trees of Work Items. Figure 12-9 shows the results of the same query you saw earlier. Note that parent/child relationships are represented here as well. Parent work items have their titles listed in the Title 1 column, and their children have their titles listed in the Title 2 column. If you added a third level to the tree, grandchild work items would be listed in a column named Title 3, and so on.

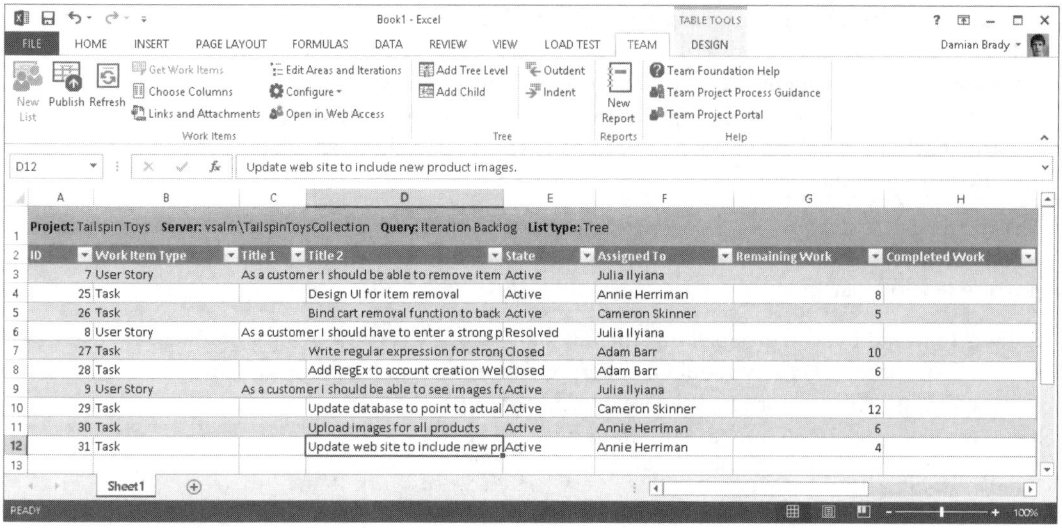

FIGURE 12-9: Work items in Excel

You can make any changes you want to within your Excel grid. You can add new work items for a Tree of Work Items query by clicking an existing work item and clicking Add Child from the Team tab of the Ribbon. To create a new work item, you can simply place your cursor on a new row at the bottom of your grid, and start typing.

Note, however, that none of your work will be persisted to Team Foundation Server until you click Publish from the Team tab of the Ribbon. Even if you save the Excel workbook file, your work items won't be synchronized to Team Foundation Server until you publish them. Similarly, you won't see any changes that have occurred in Team Foundation Server until you click the Refresh button in the Team tab.

> **NOTE** *In order to access the Publish button from the Team tab, your cursor will need to be within a cell that is a part of your work item grid. Otherwise, the Publish button will be disabled.*

You will receive an error message if the values you entered for work items in Excel do not conform to the validation rules or state transition workflow for the work item type. At this point, you can even view the offending work items using the same form view you are familiar with from Visual Studio.

> **NOTE** *Excel is a useful tool for making bulk edits of work items, for quickly importing several work items between team projects, or for people who just prefer working with Excel over Visual Studio. You can read more about using Excel as a work item client at* http://aka.ms/TFSExcel2013.

Using Microsoft Project

Microsoft Project is one of the most popular project management tools in the world and supports integration with Team Foundation Server. If you have installed Team Explorer 2013 on a machine with Microsoft Project Professional (2007, 2010, or 2013) or Standard, you will have a Team menu that allows you to interface with Team Foundation Server 2013.

As with Excel, you can either start with a query in Team Explorer (and choose Open in Microsoft Office ⇨ Open Query in Microsoft Project), or you can open Project and use the Team menu to access a query of work items from Team Foundation Server. Figure 12-10 shows work items being managed by Microsoft Project.

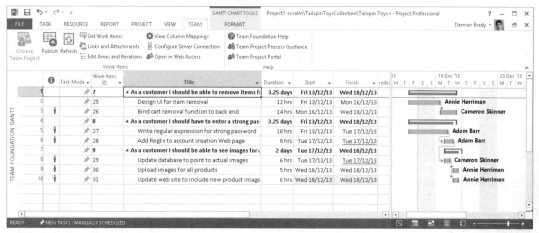

FIGURE 12-10: Work items in Project

Project will also display work items according to their parent/child relationships. A major benefit of using Project to view your work items is that it's easy to visualize dependency relationships (successor/predecessor) using the built-in Gantt chart visualization that Project is popular for. In Figure 12-10, it's easy to see that some work items have dependencies on others, which can be helpful for teams deciding how to prioritize their work.

Like Excel, changes to work items that you make within Project are not synchronized to Team Foundation Server until you click Publish from the Team menu.

> **NOTE** *You can learn more about using Project for managing work items at* `http://aka.ms/TFSProject2013`.

Using Team Web Access

Team Web Access provides yet another way of managing your work items. You learned about how to connect to Team Web Access in Chapter 4. Team Web Access provides a rich, web-based way of accessing Team Foundation Server. An obvious benefit of Team Web Access is that users do not need to have any software other than a web browser. Figure 12-11 shows Team Web Access being used to manage work items.

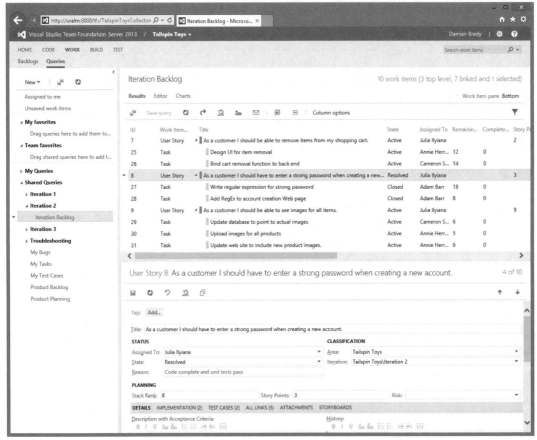

FIGURE 12-11: Team Web Access

Team Web Access provides a surprising number of features for a web-based client. You can edit queries, manipulate work items, manage tasks with the task board, manage security, and manage team members.

Team Web Access makes an ideal work item client for users who don't have Team Explorer installed. Some organizations even encourage end users to file bugs and enhancement requests about their software using Team Web Access.

> **NOTE** *You can read more about using Team Web Access as a work item client at* http://aka.ms/TFSWebAccess2013.

> **NOTE** *If you are interested in using Team Web Access as a way for end users to file and track bugs and enhancement requests, you should consider the Limited Access or Work Item Only View version of Team Web Access. When users connect to Team Foundation Server using the Limited Access View, they do not need to have a client access license (CAL) for Team Foundation Server. For more details on enabling Limited Access View for your end users, see* `http://aka.ms/TFSWIOV`.

Using Third-Party Tools

In addition to the tools mentioned previously, several third-party tools are available that integrate with Team Foundation Server 2013 and make use of work items. The following sections examine just a small sampling of the many tools that integrate with Team Foundation Server 2013.

AIT Tools Suite

The folks at AIT GmbH & Co. in Germany have created a number of free add-ons to the Team Foundation Server system. They include tools to check dependencies between branches of code, generate documentation and change logs during your build, and allow you to use Microsoft Word to edit work items.

AIT WordToTFS is an add-in to Microsoft Word that allows the user the ability to create, modify, and delete work items. You can import work items directly into a Word document or refresh existing work items from the data stored in Team Foundation Server. Once you have finished making changes to the work items, you can publish those changes back to Team Foundation Server so that the rest of your team can see them.

You can download the AIT Tools Suite programs for free at `http://tinyurl.com/AITToolsSuite`.

TeamCompanion

TeamCompanion (by Ekobit) is an add-in to Microsoft Outlook that provides most of the same functionality as Team Explorer but from within a tool that you probably always have open. This is an excellent UI for those team members who live in Outlook, such as project managers. From TeamCompanion, you can create new work items from received e-mails, send work items as an e-mail, and send the results of a query as the body of an e-mail.

TeamCompanion can also schedule queries to run at intervals and let you know something in the query results has changed in a manner similar to Outlook's ability to show you that you have new e-mails. You can also view reports, manage alert subscriptions, or use the powerful work item search capabilities.

A free trial version of TeamCompanion can be downloaded from `http://teamcompanion.com`.

PROJECT SERVER INTEGRATION

Earlier in this chapter, you learned about how Microsoft Project can be used to create project plans with your work items in Team Foundation Server 2013. But organizations that utilize Project Server may also be interested in the capability of Team Foundation Server 2013 to integrate with their Project Server 2007, 2010, or 2013 deployments.

This integration allows planning and status information from your development team, using Team Foundation Server, to flow through to your project management office, using Project Server. This enables the software development team to use a single tool—Team Foundation Server—for managing their work while allowing Project Server users to easily report on and participate in project management activities from those same projects. Project Server Integration is discussed in detail in Chapter 16.

SUMMARY

In this chapter, you learned about the project management capabilities of Team Foundation Server 2013, with a focus on work item tracking. You first learned about some of the major features related to project management that have been improved or introduced in this release. You were introduced to work items, including the key components that make up work item types. You discovered the importance of process templates, which include predefined work item types, and you read overviews of several of the most popular process templates available for use with Team Foundation Server 2013. Finally, you were introduced to a variety of ways that you can manage your work items with Team Foundation Server 2013, including from within Visual Studio, Excel, Project, and through integration with Project Server.

In Chapter 13, you will learn about how work items and process templates are defined, and how you can customize them to best suit the needs of your team.

13
Customizing Process Templates

WHAT'S IN THIS CHAPTER?

➤ Understanding the artifacts contained in a process template

➤ Using the Process Template Editor

➤ Learning about custom work item controls

➤ Deploying custom work item controls to client machines

WROX.COM CODE DOWNLOADS FOR THIS CHAPTER

The wrox.com code downloads for this chapter are found at http://www.wrox.com/go/proftfs2013 on the Download Code tab. The code is in the Chapter 13 download and individually named according to the names throughout the chapter.

Although Team Foundation Server contains several great out-of-the-box process templates, and several quality third-party process templates exist in the supporting ecosystem, you may find the need to customize the process template in a multitude of different ways. Tools are available for editing the artifacts necessary for customizing a team project's process template.

This chapter introduces you to these tools and the different types of customizations available. You will also learn how to easily deploy changes to work item type definitions through the use of the automated build system in Team Foundation Server.

It is important to note that customizable process templates are currently enabled only for the on-premises Team Foundation Server product and not for the hosted Visual Studio Online offering at the time of this writing. It may be something that is enabled in the future but until then, customers using the Visual Studio Online are not able to customize their process templates.

ANATOMY OF A PROCESS TEMPLATE

Process templates are built around the concept that a process should enable you, rather than hinder you. If you implement too little of a process, you must expend significant effort to stay on track. The inroads you make on a project will fully depend on the organizational skills of your team. The infrastructure will not support or enforce your process. Too much process inhibits productivity and velocity.

Process templates in Team Foundation Server provide a way to introduce the process to the entire team without getting in the way. When you create a new team project, process templates are used to set up the work items, work item queries, agile tools settings and preferences, shared document libraries, dashboards, reports, and more. A process template is a collection of files, including XML files, documents, and reports.

Before you start exploring the contents of a process template, you might want to download an existing one by going to the Process Template Manager. From the Team Explorer home hub, you can choose the Settings link to take you to the Settings page where you will see a Process Template Manager link in the Team Project Collection page section, as shown in Figure 13-1.

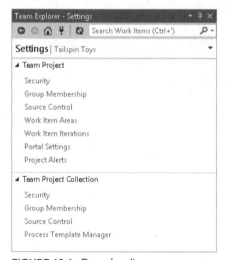

FIGURE 13-1: Downloading a process template

Next, you select a process template, click the Download button, and then choose the location where you want to save the process template files. Figure 13-2 shows the Process Template Manager dialog box.

Plug-In Files

Plug-in files are artifacts essential to the New Team Project Wizard. Each plug-in file defines the tasks that will end up running during the wizard. The displayed screens used for gathering information during the wizard are also defined in the plug-in files.

Each plug-in reads the list of tasks and dependencies and creates an automation sequence that will run during the team project creation wizard experience.

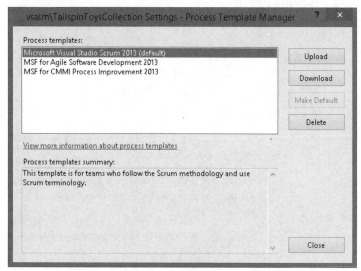

FIGURE 13-2: Process Template Manager dialog box

Table 13-1 lists each of the plug-in folders, plug-in files, and a description of what each file contains. Figure 13-3 also shows the directory layout inside a process template where each of the configuration files is stored.

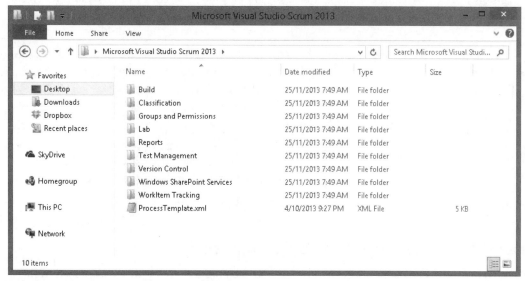

FIGURE 13-3: Directories in a process template

TABLE 13-1: Process Template Plug-In Files

FOLDER	PLUG-IN FILE	DESCRIPTION
Build	Build.xml	Defines the tasks to configure the initial security permissions assigned to identities for Team Foundation Server Build, and it uploads the build process template files.
Classification	Classification.xml	Defines the initial iterations and areas of a team project
Groups and Permissions	GroupsandPermissions .xml	Defines the initial security groups of a team project and their permissions
Lab	Lab.xml	Defines the tasks to configure the initial security permissions assigned to identities for Visual Studio Lab Management
Reports	ReportsTasks.xml	Defines the initial reports for a team project and sets up the report site.
Test Management	TestManagement.xml	Defines the test management files to upload, which will create the initial test variables, configurations, settings, and resolution states of a team project. These settings are used by Microsoft Test Manager.
Version Control	VersionControl.xml	Defines the initial security permissions for version control, check-in notes for a team project, and whether exclusive check-out is required
Windows SharePoint Services	WssTasks.xml	Defines the project portal for the team based on a template for a SharePoint site; also defines template files and process guidance
WorkItem Tracking	WorkItems.xml	Defines the initial work item types, queries, and work item instances of a team project. This plug-in also defines the settings to use for the agile-based planning tools in Team Web Access.

Source: MSDN Library (http://aka.ms/ProcessTemplatePlugIns)

Default Security Groups and Permissions

Each team project can contain security groups, and each has a set of permissions scoped to the team project level. The process template can create default team project security groups that can be used for setting permissions in each of the other plug-ins for the team project, as well as which permissions should be initially granted or denied for those security groups. For example, the Microsoft Visual Studio Scrum 2013 process template defines the following default team project security groups:

➤ Readers

➤ Contributors

➤ Build Administrators

> **NOTE** *Additionally, the Team Project Creation Wizard will create a security group called* Project Administrators *that will be granted all permissions. You do not have to define the group in the process template to be created.*

Figure 13-4 shows an example of what the Visual Studio Scrum 2013 process template defines for the default security groups.

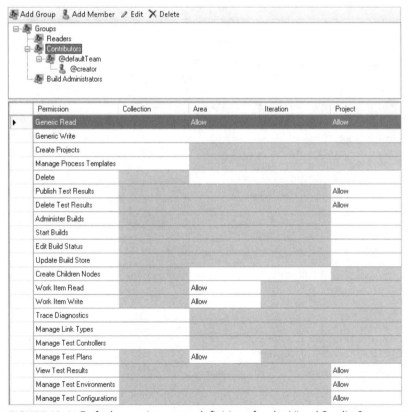

FIGURE 13-4: Default security group definitions for the Visual Studio Scrum process template

> **NOTE** *Chapter 24 provides more information about managing security privileges and permissions.*

Initial Area and Iteration Nodes

If there will be standard area path and iteration path nodes that should be available for each new team project, you can define those initial nodes in the process template. Figure 13-5 shows the default iteration nodes created when using the Visual Studio Scrum process template.

Work Item Type Definitions

Work item type definitions are the files that contain information about which states, transitions, fields, and form layouts exist on a particular work item type. Work item type definition files are by far the most commonly customized artifacts in a process template. The process template's main work items file lists each of the work item type definitions that should be included, as well as the location of the individual work item type definition files, as shown in Figure 13-6.

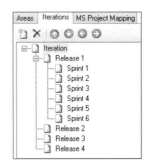

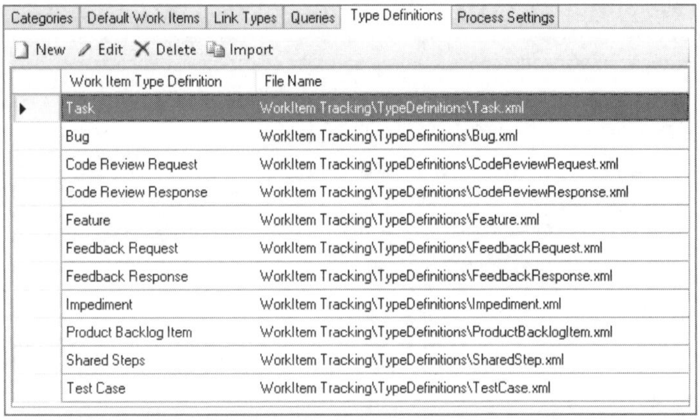

FIGURE 13-5: Default iteration nodes

Work Item Type Definition	File Name
Task	WorkItem Tracking\TypeDefinitions\Task.xml
Bug	WorkItem Tracking\TypeDefinitions\Bug.xml
Code Review Request	WorkItem Tracking\TypeDefinitions\CodeReviewRequest.xml
Code Review Response	WorkItem Tracking\TypeDefinitions\CodeReviewResponse.xml
Feature	WorkItem Tracking\TypeDefinitions\Feature.xml
Feedback Request	WorkItem Tracking\TypeDefinitions\FeedbackRequest.xml
Feedback Response	WorkItem Tracking\TypeDefinitions\FeedbackResponse.xml
Impediment	WorkItem Tracking\TypeDefinitions\Impediment.xml
Product Backlog Item	WorkItem Tracking\TypeDefinitions\ProductBacklogItem.xml
Shared Steps	WorkItem Tracking\TypeDefinitions\SharedStep.xml
Test Case	WorkItem Tracking\TypeDefinitions\TestCase.xml

FIGURE 13-6: Work item type definitions to be included and the location of files

> **NOTE** *Chapter 12 provides more information about the default work item types available in the standard process templates.*

Work Item Fields

One of the defining parts of the work item type definition is the list of fields contained for that work item type. Each field can have the attributes shown in Table 13-2 that define it.

TABLE 13-2: Field Attributes

FIELD	DESCRIPTION
Name	This is the friendly name used for the work item query. Each field in a team project collection must contain a unique name.
Field Type	This attribute defines the type of data that will be stored in the field. Among all of the types available, the following types are commonly used: String, Integer, Double, DateTime, PlainText, and Html. The correct type should be chosen, because it cannot be changed after the field is created in the team project collection.
Reference Name	This attribute defines a longer name for use in organizing multiple fields. Each field in a work item type definition must contain a unique reference name. You will probably want to distinguish your company's custom fields by prefacing the reference name with your company name (for example, Contoso .MyNewCustomField).
Help Text	This describes the field's purpose to the end user. The help text is displayed whenever hovering over a field's label on the work item forms.
Reportable	This attribute indicates how the field will be handled when the data warehouse jobs process it. The possible values for this attribute are None, Dimension, Detail, and Measure. For example, the number of hours remaining for a task would be defined as a measure, but the task's priority and to whom it is assigned would be defined as dimensions. Fields marked as a Detail do not show up in the Analysis Services warehouse cube, but they do show up in the relational data warehouse.
Formula	If the value for the Reportable attribute is Measure, the Formula attribute identifies how the warehouse will aggregate the values for the field. In most cases, you should use Sum.
Reportable Reference Name	By default, the name used for the data warehouse is the *reference name*. However, if fields in multiple team project collections must have a different reference name, but still be reported as the same field, this attribute can be defined. The reportable reference name should be unique for each team project collection.
Reportable Name	In addition to the reportable reference name, a friendly reportable name is offered as well. It is similar to the name of the field and is used in the warehouse.
Sync Name Changes	If you have a field meant to store a value for a user account/person and this attribute is set to true, Team Foundation Server will update the contents of the field as changes are made to the display names in Active Directory, User Profiles, and so on.

> **WARNING** *You must be careful not to create too many fields, but, rather, reuse them across work item types, team projects, and team project collections as necessary. By reusing the same reference names (or reportable names if different) for fields, you also benefit from being able to report the same data across team projects and team project collections, even if they are using different process template types. You can even create work item queries that use the same field across multiple team projects for showing up as a column in the query results.*
>
> *The maximum number of fields for all work item types in a team project collection is approximately 1,000. Additionally, approximately 1,000 reportable fields can be defined across all team project collections for one Team Foundation Server instance. These maximums happen to correspond to the number of columns that can be created in a SQL Server table, less some overhead used by Team Foundation Server.*

Work item fields can also contain rules applied to the field at run time. Multiple rules can be specified to be applied for a single field. Table 13-3 shows some examples of common field rules that can be used.

TABLE 13-3: Field Rule Examples

RULE	DESCRIPTION
DEFAULT	This rule allows for a value to be specified as the default value for a field. This can be the current date/time, user information, another field's value, or a specified literal value.
ALLOWEDVALUES	This rule indicates a list of values allowed for this field. This can be a list of literal values or an entry for a global list. For example, you might want to constrain the values of a Priority field to the integers 1 through 4.
REQUIRED	This rule indicates that the field is required to contain a value.
VALIDUSER	This rule indicates that the value of the field must contain the name of a valid user who has permissions to access Team Foundation Server.
SERVERDEFAULT	This rule is particularly useful in states and transitions whenever the current user, or the current date and time, should be stored in a particular field.
COPY	This rule can be used to copy a value from another field, date/time from the clock, current user information, or from a specified literal value.
READONLY	This indicates that that field cannot be edited.
ALLOWEXISTINGVALUE	This rule allows for an existing value to still be valid even if it is removed as an allowed value in the future. This applies as long as the field does not change values.

Several rules have optional `for` and `not` attributes that can be specified to indicate whether that rule applies to a security group (`for` attribute) or does not apply to the security group (`not` attribute). For example, a `REQUIRED` rule can be added to a field for the `Contributors` security group by specifying the group in the `for` attribute, but the `Project Administrators` security group can be excluded by specifying the group in the `not` attribute.

> **NOTE** *More information about the available work item rules can be found in the MSDN documentation article titled "Working with Field Rules" at* `http://aka.ms/WITFieldRules`*.*

Work Item States and Transitions

Work items can be classified in different states, and a workflow between those states can be defined using transitions. Each transition can contain a *reason* for the transition. For example, a bug can be in the state of Active, and then transitioned to the Resolved state with a reason of Fixed, Duplicate, As Designed, Cannot Reproduce, Deferred, and so on. The combination of state and reason can be used for reporting and for work item queries to further distinguish between work items in the same state.

Each work item can have only one initial transition that can contain multiple reasons. Figure 13-7 shows the states and transitions for the Bug work item type in the MSF for Agile Software Development 2013 process template. Figure 13-7 also shows the available reasons for the transition between the Active and Resolved states.

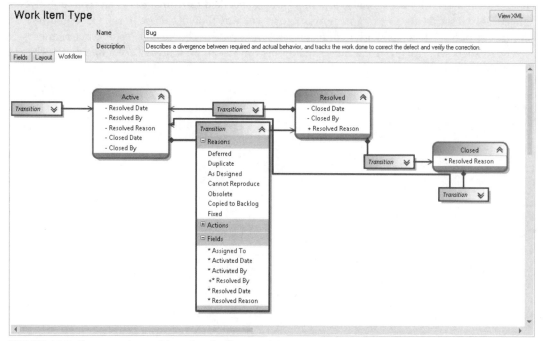

FIGURE 13-7: States and transitions for the Bug work item type

Rules for States and Transitions

Previously in this chapter, you learned that rules can be applied to fields globally for the work item type. Rules can also be applied at the state level or at a particular transition or reason. A combination of all the rules is applied based on the rules defined at the field, state, transition, and reason scopes. Figure 13-8 shows the different field rules specified for the `Microsoft.VSTS.Common` `.ResolvedBy` field on the transition between the Active and Resolved states.

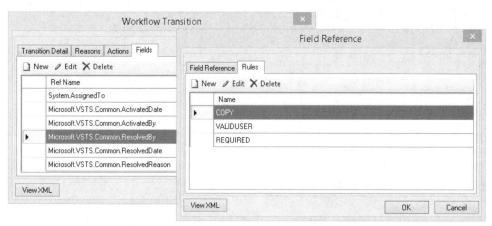

FIGURE 13-8: Different field rules

You can also restrict certain transitions using the same `for` and `not` attributes used for certain field rules. Figure 13-9 shows those attributes being specified for transition between the Active and Resolved states. As an example in this figure, you are allowing those in the Contributors security group to move the work item from the Active state to the Resolved state, but members of the Readers security group can never make this transition, even if they are a member of the Contributors security group.

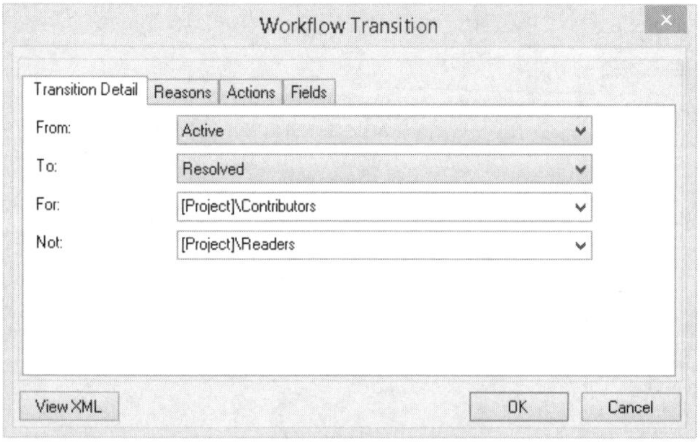

FIGURE 13-9: Attributes being specified for transition

Work Item Form Layouts

Once all of the fields and the workflow of states and transitions have been defined, you can specify what the work item form will look like when it is opened in any of the Team Foundation Server client tools. The layout is specified by using a set of items. Figure 13-10 shows a partial example of a layout for the Bug work item type in the MSF for Agile Software Development process template.

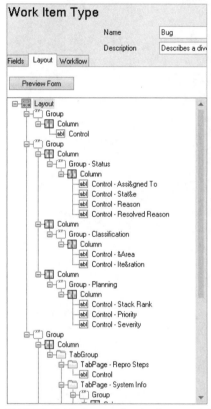

FIGURE 13-10: Layout for the Bug work item type

Following are the items that can be used on the form:

➤ **Group**—This container can include one or more columns, and optionally it can specify a display name for the container.

➤ **Column**—A column is contained within a group, and it can be either a fixed width, or have a percentage-based width relative to the other columns in the same group.

➤ **Control**—This item can be added to other container units, and it allows the presentation of a work item control that can edit a field or display other information.

➤ **Tab Group**—This container begins a new grouping of tab pages.

➤ **Tab Page**—This container stores all of the items that would exist inside a particular named tab.

CONSIDERATIONS FOR DIFFERENT CLIENT LAYOUTS

Work item type definitions can actually specify multiple layout sections that target specific clients. For example, you might specify a particular layout when a work item is opened in Visual Studio Team Web Access, versus one displayed for the Visual Studio Team Explorer client. Following are the available work item form layout values:

➤ **WinForms**—This layout target is used in the Visual Studio Team Explorer client, and additionally in Microsoft Test Manager.

➤ **Web**—This layout target is used by Visual Studio Team Web Access.

➤ **JavaSWT**—This layout target is used by Visual Studio Team Explorer Everywhere, which displays within Eclipse-based products.

➤ **Unspecified**—If no other display targets are specified, clients can ultimately fall back to using the Unspecified layout.

The current version of the Process Template editor available in the Team Foundation Server 2013 Power Tools does not support editing multiple work item form layouts. If you choose to use multiple work item form layouts, you must use the XML editing approach described later in this chapter.

Standard Work Item Controls

Several standard work item controls are available for displaying and editing fields in the form layout. Table 13-4 describes each of the available standard work item controls.

TABLE 13-4: Standard Work Item Form Controls

CONTROL	DESCRIPTION
Field	Used for standard field editing and can accommodate many of the different field types without any special editing features
Date Time	Has special editing features available for date/time fields. For example, this control can be used to provide a standard calendar control that the user can use to edit a field.
HTML Field	Allows an end user to edit with rich text for HTML fields. A new rich editing toolbar is displayed immediately above the control to allow the end user to easily reach the commonly used rich editing options available for an HTML field.
Links	Does not specify a particular field to edit, but instead allows a user to edit the different links of multiple link types currently set on a work item. The control additionally has filter options to filter certain types of work item link types, work item types, and external link types from showing in an instance of the links control.

Attachments	Provides the end user with the ability to manage the file attachments on a work item. However, it does not modify a particular work item field.
Work Item Classification	Used only for editing the Area Path and Iteration Path fields and displays the available nodes in a tree control
Work Item Log	Shows a view of the historical revisions for a work item, including the comments for each of the revisions. Additionally, end users can specify a rich-text comment to be stored with a particular revision of the work item as soon as the end user saves the work item changes.
Label	Allows for a label to be specified on the work item form. The label can specify a plain-text value and include a link to a static URL or a dynamic-based link that uses several supported macros, such as @ReportServicesSiteUrl, @ReportManagerUrl, @PortalPage, @ProcessGuidance, and @Me.
Webpage	Can display literal HTML data, or point to a static or dynamic-based URL that can also use any of the support macros mentioned on the label control. Additionally, the UrlPath attribute can contain string parameters (similar to when using format strings in the .NET method String.Format()) and specify another field's value for use as the parameter to the dynamic URL.
Associated Automation	Used on the Test Case work item type to display and/or edit the associated automation for the Test Case work item
Test Steps	Used on the Test Case work item type to show and/or edit the test steps for the Test Case work item

Source: MSDN Library (http://aka.ms/WorkItemFormControls)

Work Item Categories

Team Foundation Server 2010 introduced a new work item tracking feature called *work item categories*. This feature allows for work item types with different names in different team projects to be used in external tools, in reporting, and in work item queries. For example, one team project may have a work item type with the name of "Bug" where another has a work item type called "Defect" that need to appear together in metrics on reports that pull data from both team projects.

Microsoft Test Manager is one example of an external tool that uses the work item categories to create and select work items based on their categories. Multiple work item types can be included in a work item category, and one is identified as the default work item type for the individual category.

Figure 13-11 shows the default work item categories specified in the Visual Studio Scrum 2013 process template.

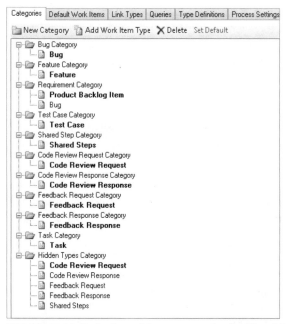

FIGURE 13-11: Default work item categories for Visual Studio Scrum 2013 process template

The Hidden Types Category is unique in that it specifies the set of work item types that you do not want users to create manually. By default, the feedback and code review work item types are included in this category because of tools specially made for those user experiences. Each of the different user interfaces then no longer exposes the work item types included in this category in the lists of available work item types to use for creating a new work item.

Team Foundation Server 2013 introduced a new Features Category in its process templates. Work items belonging to this category represent high-level goals in the project portfolio. They will be shown at a high level in the Web Access UI and can be useful for managing groups of backlog items.

Work Item Link Types

Team Foundation Server 2010 introduced the concept of *rich link types*, which can be used throughout Team Foundation Server for reporting and querying work items. These rich link types truly allow full traceability between work items stored in Team Foundation Server. Each link type can have a specific topology and also have a different name that describes each end of the link.

Table 13-5 shows the available standard defined link types.

TABLE 13-5: Standard Defined Link Types

FORWARD NAME	REVERSE NAME	LINK TYPE REFERENCE NAME	TOPOLOGY
Successor	Predecessor	System.LinkTypes.Dependency	Dependency
Child	Parent	System.LinkTypes.Hierarchy	Tree
Related	Related	System.LinkTypes.Related	Network
Tested By	Tests	Microsoft.VSTS.Common.TestedBy	Dependency
Test Case	Shared Steps	Microsoft.VSTS.TestCase .SharedStepReferencedBy	Dependency

Source: MSDN Library (http://aka.ms/WITLinkTypes)

You can also create custom link types for your own purposes in customized process templates. Following are the different types of link topologies available in Team Foundation Server:

➤ **Network**—Link types of this topology have essentially no rules and no directionality. You can have circular relationships, and the link looks the same from both ends. Figure 13-12 shows the network topology.

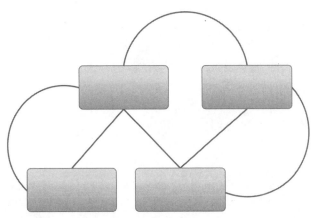

FIGURE 13-12: Network topology

➤ **Directed Network**—Link types of this topology are network links, except that there is directionality. You can specify a name that appears at each link end. In other words, the link looks different depending on which side you view it. Figure 13-13 shows the directed network topology.

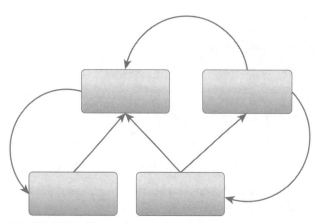

FIGURE 13-13: Directed network topology

➤ **Dependency**—Link types of this topology are like directed network links in that they have directionality, but they also have an additional constraint to prevent circular relationships. Figure 13-14 shows the dependency topology.

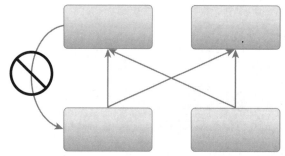

FIGURE 13-14: Dependency topology

➤ **Tree**—Link types of this topology are essentially trees that enforce a one-to-many relationship and do not allow circular relationships. Figure 13-15 shows the tree topology.

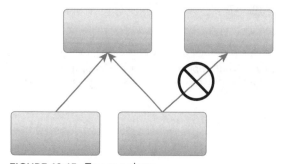

FIGURE 13-15: Tree topology

Global Lists

Global lists are available at the team project collection level to allow for managing common lists used in the work item tracking system. For example, a company might have a list of departments that it would like to use in multiple work item types across several team projects. The company can specify an ALLOWEDVALUES field rule that includes only the values listed in the global list created for the departments. Anytime the list must be updated, the global list can be edited, and this does not involve deploying new work item type definitions to each of the team projects.

Global Workflows and Fields

Team Foundation Server 2010 Service Pack 1 introduced a new concept to manage global fields and workflows. Global fields and workflows were primarily added to support the Project Server Integration feature released to synchronize changes between Team Foundation Server and Project Server.

You can also take advantage of this new concept natively in Team Foundation Server 2013. Essentially, by defining a global workflow for a team project collection or specific team project, you are defining which fields should exist on all work item types across all of the team projects, or for the specified team project. Additionally, you can define global lists in the global workflow definition.

> **NOTE** *You can find more information about global workflows in the MSDN documentation article at* http://aka.ms/WITGlobalWorkflows.

Initial Work Items

The process template can also contain a list of work items that will be initialized during the team project creation process. This is useful if each new team project should contain a certain set of startup work items to kickstart the team project. By default, the standard out-of-the-box process templates no longer define any default work items.

Work Item Queries and Folders

Certain work item queries and their organizational folder structure should be defined for a new team project in the process template. The standard work item queries should be included. Additionally, the default security and privileges for the work item query folders can be specified.

Figure 13-16 shows the default work item queries and query folders specified in the MSF for Agile Software Development process template.

Microsoft Project Column Mappings

The Microsoft Project column mappings file correlates work item fields to fields defined in a Microsoft Project file. Figure 13-17 shows the default Project column mappings defined in the MSF for Agile Software Development process template. This is not the same as the mappings used for fields in a Project Server integration implementation. These mappings are used only if you want to open work items or a work item query directly in the Microsoft Project client when it is not connected to a Project Server.

FIGURE 13-16: Default work item queries and query folders

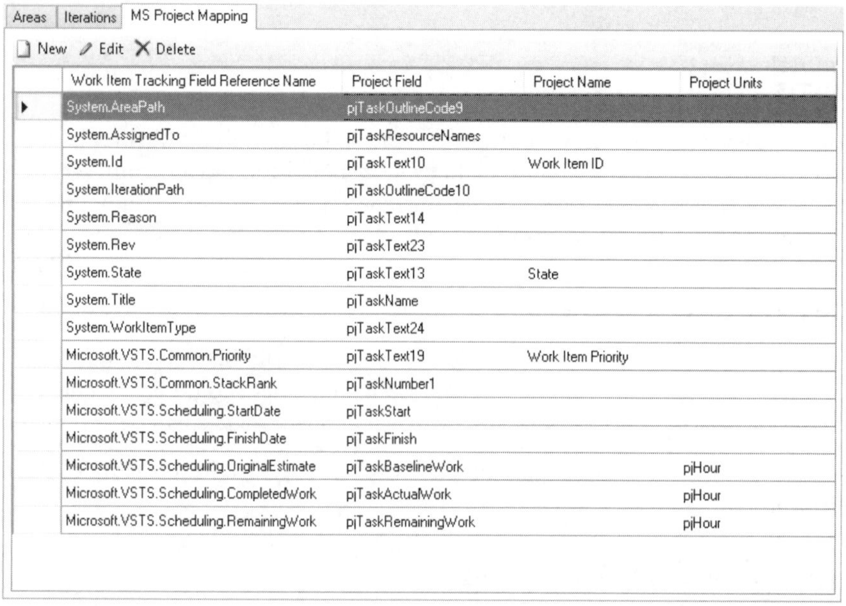

Work Item Tracking Field Reference Name	Project Field	Project Name	Project Units
System.AreaPath	pjTaskOutlineCode9		
System.AssignedTo	pjTaskResourceNames		
System.Id	pjTaskText10	Work Item ID	
System.IterationPath	pjTaskOutlineCode10		
System.Reason	pjTaskText14		
System.Rev	pjTaskText23		
System.State	pjTaskText13	State	
System.Title	pjTaskName		
System.WorkItemType	pjTaskText24		
Microsoft.VSTS.Common.Priority	pjTaskText19	Work Item Priority	
Microsoft.VSTS.Common.StackRank	pjTaskNumber1		
Microsoft.VSTS.Scheduling.StartDate	pjTaskStart		
Microsoft.VSTS.Scheduling.FinishDate	pjTaskFinish		
Microsoft.VSTS.Scheduling.OriginalEstimate	pjTaskBaselineWork		pjHour
Microsoft.VSTS.Scheduling.CompletedWork	pjTaskActualWork		pjHour
Microsoft.VSTS.Scheduling.RemainingWork	pjTaskRemainingWork		pjHour

FIGURE 13-17: Default Project file column mappings

Each mapping can additionally specify an `IfSummaryRefreshOnly` optional attribute, which indicates that if a Project task is a summary task it will never publish its value back to Team Foundation Server, but it will allow new values in Team Foundation Server to overwrite the value in the Project file. This is particularly useful for calculated fields in Project that should not be pushed back into Team Foundation Server.

> **NOTE** *More information about customizing the Microsoft Project field mappings files can be found in the MSDN Library at* `http://aka.ms/ WITProjectClientMappings`.

Version Control Permissions and Settings

The process template can also include the settings and permissions on the version control repository of the team project created during the team project creation wizard. For example, the "Enable multiple check-out" setting, "Enable get latest version on check-out" setting, and required "Check-in notes" can be provided. Permissions for each group can also be specified.

Figure 13-18 shows the default permissions available to the `Contributors` security group in the MSF for Agile Software Development process template.

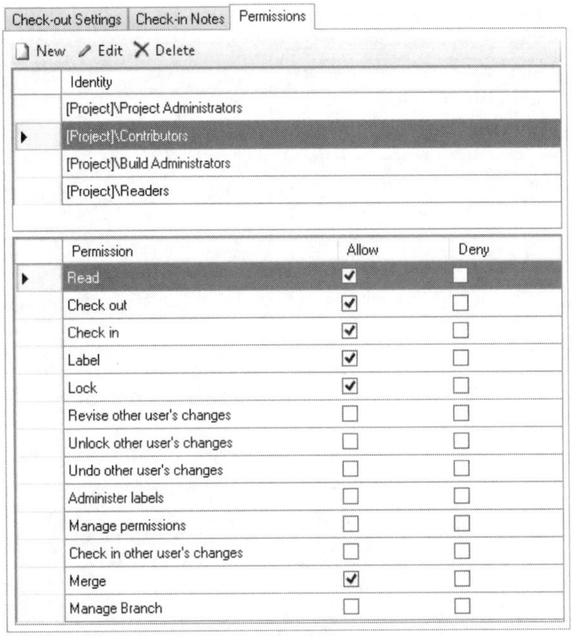

FIGURE 13-18: Default permissions

SharePoint Project Team Portal Document Library Settings

If a SharePoint team project portal is created during the team project creation wizard, then the initial content for the document libraries in that new SharePoint site can be specified in the process template. Additionally, the process guidance documents for the process template are specified.

Figure 13-19 shows the default document libraries, folder structure, and some of the documents available after a team project is created using the MSF for Agile Software Development process template.

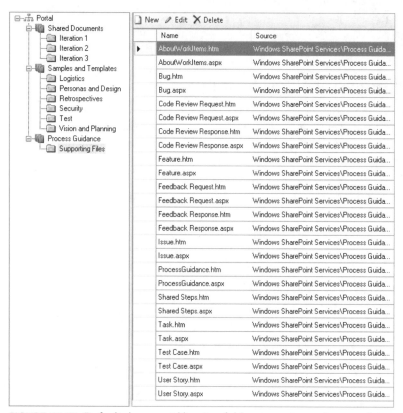

FIGURE 13-19: Default document libraries, folder structure, and some of the available documents

> **WARNING** *You cannot customize the Microsoft Excel reports and SharePoint dashboards by customizing the process template files. These artifacts are created for a team project depending on the selection you make in the New Team Project Wizard.*

SQL Reporting Services Report Definitions

The initial folder structure and reports in the related Reports site can also be specified in the process template. Figure 13-20 shows the list of each of the folders and SQL Reporting Services report definition files that will be uploaded to the Reports Manager site during the team project creation wizard for the MSF for Agile Software Development process template.

Server Path	File Name
Bugs\Bug Status	Reports\Bug Status.rdl
Bugs\Bug Trends	Reports\Bug Trends.rdl
Bugs\Reactivations	Reports\Reactivations.rdl
Builds\Build Quality Indicators	Reports\Build Quality Indicators.rdl
Builds\Build Success Over Time	Reports\Build Success over Time.rdl
Builds\Build Summary	Reports\Build Summary.rdl
Project Management\Burndown and Burn Rate	Reports\Burndown and Burn Rate.rdl
Dashboards\Burndown	Reports\Burndown - Dashboard.rdl
Project Management\Remaining Work	Reports\Remaining Work.rdl
Project Management\Status on All Iterations	Reports\Status on All Iterations.rdl
Project Management\Stories Overview	Reports\Stories Overview.rdl
Project Management\Stories Progress	Reports\Stories Progress.rdl
Project Management\Unplanned Work	Reports\Unplanned Work.rdl
Tests\Test Case Readiness	Reports\Test Case Readiness.rdl
Tests\Test Plan Progress	Reports\Test Plan Progress.rdl
Dashboards\Burn Rate	Reports\Burn Rate - Dashboard.rdl

FIGURE 13-20: Folders and SQL Reporting Services report definition files

USING THE PROCESS TEMPLATE EDITOR

Instead of editing each XML file by hand, you can use the Process Template Editor included with the latest version of the Team Foundation Server Power Tools. The Process Template Editor comprises a set of tools integrated into Visual Studio Team Explorer that allow you to edit work item type definitions and process template definition files, export/import work item type definitions, and create/modify global lists, and it includes a work item field explorer to view details about the fields included in a team project collection.

Installing the Process Template Editor

The Team Foundation Server Power Tools installer is available from the Visual Studio Gallery and is updated regularly.

The quickest way to find the latest download for the Power Tools installer is to go to your preferred search engine and use the search term "Team Foundation Server Power Tools." Currently, a list of all the Power Tools for the entire Visual Studio product line is listed at http://aka.ms/TFPowerTools.

Before you begin installing the Power Tools, be sure to have all instances of Visual Studio completely closed because the installer will be setting up and configuring several Visual Studio add-ins.

> **NOTE** *Always be sure that you are using the latest version of the Team Foundation Server Power Tools. The Team Foundation Server product team at Microsoft continually improves the Power Tools with bug fixes and new features. Traditionally, a new version of the Power Tools has been released every three to six months.*

Working with a Process Template

Instead of editing work item type definitions directly on the server (which is an option), it is a best practice to download the process template, store it in version control, and then edit it offline. When the changes you have made are ready and tested in a test environment, you can then deploy those updates to your production Team Foundation Server team project collection(s).

> **NOTE** *Chapter 11 provides more information about storing process templates and managing other Team Foundation Server artifacts in the version control repository.*

Whenever you have the process template stored in an offline location, you can open the `ProcessTemplate.xml` file contained in the root folder for a process template, and the Process Template Editor window will display in Visual Studio. Figure 13-21 shows the root Process Template Editor window when opening the Visual Studio Scrum process template.

From the root window, you can edit all of the individual parts of the process template easily. For example, you can edit the work item type definitions by navigating to the Process Template ⇨ Work Item Tracking ⇨ Type Definitions node. Then select a work item type and click the Edit button. Many of these different parts were shown in earlier figures for this chapter in each heading that discussed the process template artifact types.

> **NOTE** *If you are interested in learning more about using the Process Template Editor, you can read through the help documentation included in the Team Foundation Server Power Tools installer. For 64-bit operating systems, the default location for the help documentation is* `C:\Program Files (x86)\Microsoft Team Foundation Server 2013 Power Tools\Help\ProcessEditor.mht`.

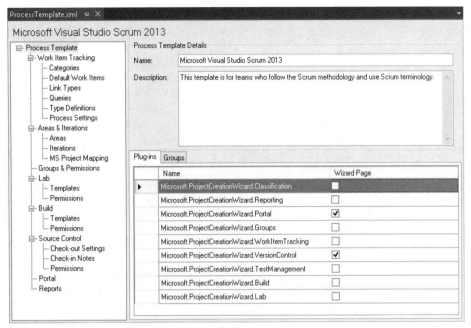

FIGURE 13-21: Process Template Editor window

Using an XML Editor and WITAdmin

An alternate approach for managing process template and work item type definitions is to edit the XML files with your preferred XML file editor, and then use the command-line tools to export and import the work item type definitions. The XML schema is completely documented in the MSDN Library and is available in the following locations:

➤   **Process Template Schema Reference**—http://aka.ms/ProcessTemplateSchema

➤   **Work Item Type Definition Schema Reference**—http://aka.ms/WITSchema

The command-line tool named witadmin.exe is actually a tool installed whenever you install Visual Studio Team Explorer (or another Visual Studio 2013 product). From a Developer Command Prompt (and with the appropriate server permissions), you can perform several administrative functions to manage the work item tracking system.

Table 13-6 shows a few of the available commands, but you can always discover the full list by executing witadmin.exe /? at a Visual Studio command prompt window.

TABLE 13-6: Sample Commands for witadmin.exe

COMMAND	DESCRIPTION
Listfields	Particularly useful when you need a list of all of the fields in a team project collection and their details. Each of the entries will even list all of the work item types and team projects that the field is being used by. When used with the `/unused` switch, you can also get a list of fields that exist in the team project collection that are completely unused.
Changefield	Allows you to update certain attributes for an existing field after it has been created. For example, you can update any of the name attributes, but you will notice that not all attributes can be changed. An example of this is the work item type field. You are mostly not able to change the work item type unless it is between `HTML` and `PlainText`.
Deletefield	Will completely remove a field once it is unused by any work item type in any team project in the team project collection. It will also remove the field from the warehouse during the next warehouse processing cycle if this was the last team project collection using the specified field to be deleted.
Listwitd	Helpful for listing the work item types available in a team project
Renamewitd	Allows you to rename an existing work item type even if there are already work items of that type created in a team project. For example, you may decide to rename the Requirement work item type to User Story or Feature at some point in the future.
destroywi, destroywitd	Allows you to completely destroy a particular work item or a work item type, and all its existing work items, in a team project. The data is not destroyed in the warehouse and will remain until a full rebuild occurs.
exportwitd, importwitd	Allows for exporting and importing work item type definitions from a team project. If a work item type currently exists, it will be replaced with the new work item type definition. Existing work items will use the new definition after it is imported.
Listlinktypes	Lists the available set of link types in a team project collection
exportlinktype, importlinktype	Allows for exporting and importing new link types for the team project collection. If the link type already exists, it will be updated.
exportcategories, importcategories	Allows for exporting and importing new work item category definitions for a specific team project. If the work item category already exists, it will be updated.
exportgloballist, importgloballist, destroygloballist	Allows for exporting, importing, and destroying global list definitions for a team project collection, respectively. If a global list has the same name, it will be replaced with the newly imported global list definition.

exportprocessconfig, importprocessconfig	Allows you to customize several process configuration elements to meet your Agile planning and Scrum processes. Many of these elements control the interactive tools and visual displays provided in Team Web Access. This can also be useful when using the MSF CMMI and third-party process templates to configure the agile planning tools appropriately.
exportglobalworkflow, importglobalworkflow	Allows you to export or import the global workflow definitions, which allows you to share definitions of fields and list items among multiple types of work items, as previously discussed in this chapter

DEPLOYING UPDATES TO PROCESS TEMPLATES

Now that you have a grasp of how to fully customize your process template, you can use that new process template in several ways. You can deploy your process template in one of two scenarios:

➤ Updating individual components of an existing team project

➤ Using it in the team project creation wizard for new team projects

Uploading Process Templates in Team Foundation Server

To allow project collection administrators to create a new team project using the customized process template, you must add the process template to the available process templates for the team project collection. You can manage the available process templates by using the Process Template Manager window described earlier in this chapter (and shown in Figures 13-1 and 13-2).

You will notice that an Upload button is available. During the upload process, the process template will be validated for compliance, and any errors encountered during validation will be displayed in a message box. If the upload button is not enabled, you are likely connected to a hosted Visual Studio Online instance. Because Visual Studio Online does not currently support customized process templates, the Upload button will be disabled.

Editing Work Items on an Existing Team Project

The most common way to deploy updates for a process template for an existing team project is updating the work item type definitions. You can use the `witadmin.exe importwitd` command-line tool option for importing a new definition for an existing work item type definition in a team project.

Concerns

Updating work item type definitions for existing team projects can be particularly risky. You should always ensure that you are testing your work item type definition updates in a test environment that includes waiting for a successful warehouse processing cycle to occur without any errors from the updates.

Some work item type definition changes have minimal impact, where others might take a little more effort to be fully implemented. For example, adding a new reportable field to an existing work item type definition does not impact the health of the Team Foundation Server, unless it conflicts with a field in another team project collection that has the same name, but different attributes. You will begin seeing a problem whenever the next warehouse processing cycle begins, because the conflicting field definitions will block further warehouse processing.

An additional scenario that has a higher impact would be changing the state name for an existing work item type definition. You must handle all existing work items in the old state name. Also, there may be existing work item queries that have used the particular state name and standard reports that rely on the old state name, all of which must get updated.

> **NOTE** *One method you might use for changing a state name on existing work items is to create a temporary transition from the old state name to the new state name. You can then update the work item type definition with the temporary transition. Then, move all of the work items in the old state to the new state using that temporary transition. Remove the temporary transition, and then upload the final work item type definition without the old state and the temporary transition to update the team project.*

When adding field rules you will want to think about the impact of those changes on the existing work items in a team project. For example, if you were to add a new REQUIRED field rule, or change the values in the ALLOWEDVALUES rule list, you could potentially use a combination of ALLOWEXISTINGVALUE and DEFAULT field rules to ensure that the existing work items are still considered valid work items. You can then update all of the existing work items using a tool such as Microsoft Excel to bulk-edit the field value in all of the existing work items.

Using an Automated Build to Deploy Work Item Type Definition Changes

When you are editing source code for an application, it is helpful to have regular automated builds to compile and deploy the application for testing. Similarly, when making changes to work item type definitions in version control, it is helpful to have an automatic deployment process. You can use a customized build process template that will automatically deploy multiple work item type definitions to multiple team projects. You can create an automatic deployment build for both Production and Test branches that contain the process templates that would deploy to their respective Team Foundation Server environments.

An automated deployment process for work item type definitions should ideally have the following features:

➤ Specify multiple team projects to update.

➤ Specify multiple work item types to update.

➤ Back up each of the existing work item type definitions currently in use.

➤ Copy the latest version of the work item type definition and backups to a build drop folder.

➤ Indicate errors during the deployment process in the build log.

Additionally, the following standard build features would be included because it is an automated Team Foundation Server build:

➤ Build versioning

➤ Labeling the source code for the process template

➤ Getting the latest version of the process template

➤ Associating changesets and work items

➤ Gated check-in, continuous integration, scheduled, and so on

> **NOTE** *There is a work item type definition deployment build process template available with instructions for use on Ed Blankenship's blog at* `http://aka.ms/DeployTFSProcessChanges`. *This build template was originally created for Team Foundation Server 2010, but has been updated to support Team Foundation Server 2012. At the time of this writing this has not been tested for Team Foundation Server 2013, but it would serve as a great starting point.*
>
> *See Chapter 18 for more information about automated builds and build process templates.*

CUSTOMIZING AGILE TOOLS

The Agile planning and developer productivity tools that you will learn more about in Chapter 14 provide several customization options for your process templates. This is nice because you can essentially get the tools to work with even customized process templates not based on any Agile methodology.

Here you will review a few of the top customization topics for the new common process configuration and agile process configuration files available in a process template. To read more about these files, visit this MSDN article: `http://aka.ms/CustomAgileProcessConfig`.

Metastates and Backlogs

Team Foundation Server 2012 introduced a concept called *metastates*. Metastates are important because these tools need a way of defining what to show in certain situations. For example, the My Work page in Team Explorer has a section that displays available work items that a team member can use to start working on something. However, it only really wants to display "open" work items to team members so they are not inundated with a long list of work items. The problem though is how to limit the work item states that are considered "open." This is where metastates come in.

In Team Foundation Server 2013, configuration of the metastates and agile project management tools has been combined into a single `ProcessConfiguration.xml` file. This file contains the defined metastates used for each work item category as well as (if appropriate for that group) the columns that will be displayed, and fields included in the quick addition panel of Team Web Access. The following is an excerpt from the definition of the requirement category:

```
<RequirementBacklog category="Microsoft.RequirementCategory"
    pluralName="Backlog items" singularName="Backlog item">
  <States>
    <State value="New" type="Proposed" />
    <State value="Approved" type="Proposed" />
    <State value="Committed" type="InProgress" />
    <State value="Done" type="Complete" />
  </States>
  ...
</RequirementBacklog>
```

You will notice that each of the states defined in the work item type definitions maps to known metastates. There are three categories of metastates in Team Foundation Server. Table 13-7 defines the available metastates for each of these categories.

TABLE 13-7: Allowed Metastates and Descriptions

STATE	WORK ITEM TYPES	DESCRIPTION
Proposed	All	Indicates work items that are new, not yet committed, or not yet being worked on. Work items in this state appear on the product backlog page. Sample states that could fall into this metastate: New, Proposed, Approved, and To Do.
InProgress	All	Indicates work items that have been committed or are actively being worked on. Work items in this state are removed from the product backlog page because they have been committed to an iteration or sprint. Sample states that could fall into this metastate: Active, Committed, In Progress, and Resolved.
Complete	All	Indicates work items that have been implemented. The effort represented by backlog items in this metastate is included in calculating the team's velocity. Sample states that could fall into this metastate: Closed and Done.
Resolved	Bugs	Indicates bugs that have been resolved but not yet verified

Requested	Feedback	Indicates feedback items that have been requested but have not yet been received or responded to
Received	Feedback	Indicates feedback items that have been received by the recipient but have not yet been completed
Reviewed	Feedback	Indicates feedback items that have been received and completed by the recipient
Declined	Feedback	Indicates feedback items that have been received by the recipient, but were declined and not completed

Effort, Remaining Work, and Stack Rank

Two of the most important fields used in the Agile planning tools involve the estimated effort for a product backlog item and the remaining work on tasks. The following is an excerpt from the `ProcessConfiguration.xml` file that demonstrates the defaults used in the MSF for Agile Software Development 2013 process template. Notice that you can even specify the units used for the values in the remaining work field for the Task work item type. If you want to use something other than hours, such as story points, this would be where you would edit this setting:

```xml
<TypeFields>
  <TypeField refname="System.AreaPath" type="Team" />
  <TypeField refname="Microsoft.VSTS.Scheduling.RemainingWork"
    type="RemainingWork" format="{0} h" />
  <TypeField refname="Microsoft.VSTS.Common.StackRank" type="Order" />
  <TypeField refname="Microsoft.VSTS.Scheduling.StoryPoints" type="Effort" />
  <TypeField refname="Microsoft.VSTS.Common.Activity" type="Activity" />
  <TypeField refname="Microsoft.VSTS.Feedback.ApplicationStartInformation"
    type="ApplicationStartInformation" />
  <TypeField refname="Microsoft.VSTS.Feedback.ApplicationLaunchInstructions"
    type="ApplicationLaunchInstructions" />
  <TypeField refname="Microsoft.VSTS.Feedback.ApplicationType"
    type="ApplicationType">
    <TypeFieldValues>
      <TypeFieldValue value="Web application" type="WebApp" />
      <TypeFieldValue value="Remote machine" type="RemoteMachine" />
      <TypeFieldValue value="Client application" type="ClientApp" />
    </TypeFieldValues>
  </TypeField>
</TypeFields>
```

Additionally, the product backlog prioritization tools will update the "stack rank" of the items automatically as they are reprioritized. The tool uses the field defined for `Order` and automatically fills in values so that the backlog items are able to be sorted from lowest to highest order.

Defining the Team

By default, teams in Team Foundation Server projects are defined based on the Area Path nodes that the team owns. However, if you don't use Area Path to define your teams, you could use an alternate field. For example, you might have a custom field on all of your work items with the name of Department that defines which work items belong to which team. You can specify that by setting the *Team* field to use in the process configuration file:

```
<TypeFields>
  <TypeField refname="System.AreaPath" type="Team" />
</TypeFields>
```

Other Process Configuration Customizations

Other common types of process configurations are available in the `ProcessConfiguration.xml` file. The following list includes a few examples of additional customizations:

➤ Add or remove fields from the "quick add" pane in the product backlog view. For example, in addition to setting a title you might also want to specify an effort estimate with each new item.

➤ Add or remove columns from the backlog and iteration views.

➤ Change the list of activities that task work items and team members can be assigned to.

➤ Change the working days to be used when calculating the iteration's capacity and rendering the live burndown chart. By default, Saturday and Sunday are considered nonworking days, but you can remove or include additional weekdays as nonworking days.

➤ Configure the types of work items to be used as parents and children in the different tooling options.

➤ Customize the options available and the work item fields used for the stakeholder feedback tools.

➤ Change the accent color assigned to a work item of a particular type.

COMMON WORK ITEM TYPE CUSTOMIZATIONS

Certain customizations are commonly made to the existing process template. The following discussions provide an overview of some of those common customizations.

Adding New States

Teams often might not feel that the states provided in the standard process templates fit well with their team's process. They might decide that a new state should be created in the workflow.

If you can avoid adding too many states, you can make it easier for end users to understand and use these new states during normal day-to-day interaction with work items. This will also reduce the amount of effort required to customize reports to take advantage of each of those states. Instead, you can use the combination of states and reasons to help you distinguish between work items in a specific state when querying or reporting on work items.

Adding a state can be done pretty easily. For example, if you wanted to add a Proposed state to a work item type definition, you might add a snippet similar to the following in the work item type's XML file:

```
<WORKFLOW>
  <STATES>
    <STATE value="Proposed">
    </STATE>
    <STATE value="Active">
      <FIELDS>
        <FIELD refname="Microsoft.VSTS.Common.ClosedDate">
          <EMPTY />
        </FIELD>
        <FIELD refname="Microsoft.VSTS.Common.ClosedBy">
  . . .
```

You might also want to move around some of the field rules (for example, empty out the Closed Date and Closed By fields), as well as change some of the existing transitions to take advantage of the new state.

> **NOTE** *A full how-to article about adding a new state to a work item type defini-tion is available in the MSDN Library at* `http://aka.ms/WITCustomizeStates`.

However, adding a state does mean that certain reports will be affected. For example, some of the following reports in the MSF for Agile Software Development process template may be impacted:

➤ **Bug Status Report**—This report has a stacked area chart that lists bugs by state and has a particular color assigned to each state. Additionally, it shows the number of bugs in the Resolved and Active state assigned to each team member.

➤ **Stories Overview Report**—This report shows how many bugs are open for each user story and displays them in a segmented bar chart by state.

➤ **Status on All Iterations**—This report shows how many bugs exist in each iteration path and displays them in a segmented bar chart by state.

Displaying Custom Link Types

The `Links` control allows for rich interaction with the link types available in Team Foundation Server, including any custom link types you create for your process template. You can take advan-tage of the `Links` control to create an additional instantiation of a `Links` control on your work item form that filters by work item type, work item link type, and/or external links.

In the MSF for Agile Software Development process template, you will notice a tab named Implementation on a User Story and Task that displays any parent and children tasks and user stories. It also allows for easily creating new links scoped to the particular link type.

One example customization you might make would be to specify a new tab for tracking dependencies between work items. For example, you might add the following XML entry into the form layout for the work item type definition. Notice that the `System.LinkTypes.Dependency` link type is used for filtering for this particular links control instantiation:

```xml
<Tab Label="Dependencies">
  <Control Type="LinksControl" Name="Dependencies">
    <LinksControlOptions>
      <LinkColumns>
        <LinkColumn RefName="System.Id" />
        <LinkColumn RefName="System.WorkItemType" />
        <LinkColumn RefName="System.Title" />
        <LinkColumn RefName="System.AssignedTo" />
        <LinkColumn RefName="System.State" />
        <LinkColumn RefName="Microsoft.VSTS.Scheduling.OriginalEstimate" />
        <LinkColumn RefName="Microsoft.VSTS.Scheduling.RemainingWork" />
        <LinkColumn RefName="Microsoft.VSTS.Scheduling.CompletedWork" />
        <LinkColumn RefName="Microsoft.VSTS.Scheduling.StartDate" />
        <LinkColumn RefName="Microsoft.VSTS.Scheduling.FinishDate" />
        <LinkColumn LinkAttribute="System.Links.Comment" />
      </LinkColumns>
      <WorkItemLinkFilters FilterType="include">
        <Filter LinkType="System.LinkTypes.Dependency" />
      </WorkItemLinkFilters>
      <ExternalLinkFilters FilterType="excludeAll" />
      <WorkItemTypeFilters FilterType="includeAll" />
    </LinksControlOptions>
  </Control>
</Tab>
```

Synchronizing Name Changes

For work item fields that contain names of people, handling name changes can be particularly tricky. The names used for fields such as the Assigned To field are actually the display names for each Active Directory account, and are synchronized from Active Directory if you are using an on-premises edition of Team Foundation Server. If you are using a hosted Visual Studio Online instance, this will be the display name that users have entered in their personal profile details for their account.

You can specify an attribute on work item fields named `syncnamechanges` and set its value to `True` to indicate that the particular field should be automatically updated across all existing work items any time the display name changes. This should help the management of work items tremendously, and ensure that work items are not orphaned to users who have experienced name changes.

The following XML excerpt for a field definition demonstrates the use of this attribute:

```xml
<FIELD name="Assigned To" refname="System.AssignedTo" type="String"
       reportable="dimension" syncnamechanges="true">
  <HELPTEXT>The person currently working on this bug</HELPTEXT>
```

```
    <ALLOWEXISTINGVALUE />
    <VALIDUSER />
</FIELD>>
```

You can also use the `witadmin.exe changefield` command-line tool option to update an existing field's `syncnamechanges` value.

> **NOTE** *Team Foundation Server can actually detect if multiple accounts use the same display name in Active Directory. The display name used in work item fields in this case would be a disambiguated name that is a combination of the Active Directory display name, and the full user name, in the format of* DOMAIN\ user.

INTRODUCING CUSTOM WORK ITEM CONTROLS

The standard work item controls provide plenty of functionality for editing the work item fields that can be created in Team Foundation Server. However, there may be additional functionality that you would like to add to the work item forms or custom editors for the work item fields. You can do this by creating custom work item controls and deploying them to all of the end users' machines to use while editing work items.

Custom work item controls do not have to edit a work item field at all. Several of the standard work item controls (such as the `Webpage` control) do not contain any fields and only display information. An example of this would be a custom work item control to pull information from an external system related to the opened work item.

Work Item Clients

A different implementation of the custom work item control must be created based on the client that will be displaying the work item control. The following clients are currently available for displaying custom work item controls:

➤ **Visual Studio Team Explorer**—Windows Forms control

➤ **Microsoft Test Manager**—Windows Forms control

➤ **Visual Studio Web Access**—jQuery-based control

➤ **Visual Studio Team Explorer Everywhere**—Java SWT control

Team Web Access Custom Work Item Controls

Because Team Web Access was completely rewritten in Team Foundation Server 2012, the model for creating a custom work item control completely changed and is now fully supported. You will end up creating a jQuery-based control and then deploy it using the Web Access extensions administration experience. This allows you to not worry about deploying anything to the server.

For more information, check out these two blog posts by Serkan Inci for creating and deploying a new Team Web Access custom work item control:

➤ http://aka.ms/TWACustomControls

➤ http://aka.ms/TWADeployCustomControls

Preferred and Fallback Control

If a particular client does not have an implementation of the custom control, or cannot locate the custom control, you can specify a control in the work item form's layout section of the work item type definition to be used. You can then specify the preferred control to use if it is deployed.

The following work item form layout excerpt demonstrates the use of the preferred control attribute:

```
<Control Type="FieldControl" PreferredType="MyCustomControl"
    FieldName="System.AssignedTo" Label="Assigned To" LabelPosition="Left" />
```

Work Item Control Interfaces

To create a custom work item control for Windows Forms, you must essentially create a new Windows Forms control that implements specific interfaces in the Team Foundation Server SDK. The following sections describe some of the most common interfaces that can be implemented for work item controls.

IWorkItemControl

The IWorkItemControl interface is actually the primary interface to be implemented and is required for custom work item controls. It contains the base functionality for a custom work item control, and its members are used by the work item form in Visual Studio Team Explorer.

Listing 13-1 shows the full signature for the IWorkItemControl interface.

LISTING 13-1: IWorkItemControl interface definition

```
// C:\Program Files (x86)\Microsoft Visual Studio 12.0
    \Common7\IDE\PrivateAssemblies
    \Microsoft.TeamFoundation.WorkItemTracking.Controls.dll

using System;
using System.Collections.Specialized;

namespace Microsoft.TeamFoundation.WorkItemTracking.Controls
{
    public interface IWorkItemControl
    {
        StringDictionary Properties { get; set; }
        bool ReadOnly { get; set; }
        object WorkItemDatasource { get; set; }
        string WorkItemFieldName { get; set; }
```

```
        event EventHandler AfterUpdateDatasource;
        event EventHandler BeforeUpdateDatasource;

        void Clear();
        void FlushToDatasource();
        void InvalidateDatasource();
        void SetSite(IServiceProvider serviceProvider);
    }
}
```

Table 13-8 shows common members used to provide the base functionality for the work item control.

TABLE 13-8: Common Members Used to Provide Base Functionality

MEMBER	DESCRIPTION
WorkItemDatasource	Contains a reference to the actual WorkItem object (and must be cast properly to the Microsoft.TeamFoundation.WorkItemTracking .Client.WorkItem type). It can end up being null during initialization, so be sure to handle the situation gracefully.
WorkItemFieldName	Contains the name of the field used by the work item control for editing. This is something defined in the work item type definition's form layout section in the control definition. Not all controls need to edit work item fields, so the value for this property could be empty.
Properties	Provides all of the properties defined in the work item type definition's control item. In Team Foundation Server 2013, you can even use a CustomControlOptions type, which contains custom properties to be used by the control.
ReadOnly	Specifies whether the control should render itself as read-only to the end user
BeforeUpdateDatasource/ AfterUpdateDatasource	These events should be implemented and raised before and after data is flushed to the data source (the work item).
Clear	May be called by the work item system. It indicates to the control that the control should be cleared.
FlushToDatasource	Called by the work item system to indicate that the value stored by the control should be saved to the work item object immediately. This often occurs when the end user chooses to save the work item.

continues

TABLE 13-8 *(continued)*

MEMBER	DESCRIPTION
InvalidDatasource	Called by the work item system to indicate to the control that it should redraw itself. Typically, the control will refresh its display by reading the data from the work item object.
SetSite	Provides a pointer to the IServiceProvider object that allows you to take advantage of Visual Studio services such as the DocumentService or the IWorkItemControlHost service. You do not have to store this service provider reference if you will not be using any of the services provided by Visual Studio.

IWorkItemToolTip

The label for the custom control can display a tooltip with information about the work item field or the custom control. You can decide what and how to display the tooltip implemented by the IWorkItemToolTip interface. Listing 13-2 shows the full interface signature for the IWorkItemToolTip interface.

LISTING 13-2: IWorkItemToolTip interface definition

```
// C:\Program Files (x86)\Microsoft Visual Studio 12.0
    \Common7\IDE\PrivateAssemblies
    \Microsoft.TeamFoundation.WorkItemTracking.Controls.dll

using System.Windows.Forms;

namespace Microsoft.TeamFoundation.WorkItemTracking.Controls
{
    public interface IWorkItemToolTip
    {
        Label Label { get; set; }
        ToolTip ToolTip { get; set; }
    }
}
```

Once each member is set, you can then make a call to ToolTip.SetToolTip(string) to provide a meaningful tooltip when the end user hovers over the label.

IWorkItemUserAction

The IWorkItemUserAction interface is implemented when the control requires some type of user action (such as the control or work item field being in a bad state and you want to prevent the user from saving the work item). Listing 13-3 provides the full interface definition for the IWorkItemUserAction interface.

LISTING 13-3: IWorkItemUserAction interface definition

```
// C:\Program Files (x86)\Microsoft Visual Studio 12.0
     \Common7\IDE\PrivateAssemblies
     \Microsoft.TeamFoundation.WorkItemTracking.Controls.dll

using System;
using System.Drawing;

namespace Microsoft.TeamFoundation.WorkItemTracking.Controls
{
    public interface IWorkItemUserAction
    {
        Color HighlightBackColor { get; set; }
        Color HighlightForeColor { get; set; }
        string RequiredText { get; set; }
        bool UserActionRequired { get; }

        event EventHandler UserActionRequiredChanged;
    }
}
```

Following are some of the interface members:

➤ `RequiredText`—This property stores the friendly error message displayed to the end user about what action needs to be taken. It is commonly displayed in an information bar in Visual Studio at the top of the work item form.

➤ `HighlightBackColor`/`HighlightForeColor`—These properties store the background and foreground colors that should be used in your custom control to stay consistent with the theme of the work item form.

➤ `UserActionRequired`—This property indicates to the work item form whether the control needs input from the user.

➤ `UserActionRequiredChanged`—This event should be raised any time the `UserActionRequired` property is changed by the control.

IWorkItemClipboard

The `IWorkItemClipboard` interface provides functionality to your control for integrating with the clipboard functionality in Visual Studio. Listing 13-4 provides the full interface definition for the `IWorkItemClipboard` interface.

LISTING 13-4: IWorkItemClipboard interface definition

```
// C:\Program Files (x86)\Microsoft Visual Studio 12.0
     \Common7\IDE\PrivateAssemblies
     \Microsoft.TeamFoundation.WorkItemTracking.Controls.dll

using System;

namespace Microsoft.TeamFoundation.WorkItemTracking.Controls
```

continues

LISTING 13-4 *(continued)*

```
{
    public interface IWorkItemClipboard
    {
        bool CanCopy { get; }
        bool CanCut { get; }
        bool CanPaste { get; }

        event EventHandler ClipboardStatusChanged;

        void Copy();
        void Cut();
        void Paste();
    }
}
```

Each of the methods should be implemented and should handle the appropriate user-initiated command. If any of the Boolean properties (such as CanCopy) are changed, the ClipboardStatusChanged event should be raised to indicate to the work item form that the clipboard status for the control has been updated.

> **NOTE** *A group of developers has teamed together and released a set of commonly requested custom work item controls (including their source code) on a CodePlex project available at* `http://witcustomcontrols.codeplex.com/.`

Deploying Custom Controls

Once you have implemented the appropriate interfaces on your work item control, you must compile the .NET project and deploy both the compiled assembly that contains the custom work item control and a work item custom control deployment manifest file. Each of the artifacts should be deployed to one of the following locations for Visual Studio 2013 and Microsoft Test Manager 2013 clients. The clients will search for custom work item controls in the following order:

➤ **Value Name Entries in Registry**—If you want to store the artifacts in a custom folder, you can add a custom value list to the following registry key to point to that custom folder. Note that this registry key does not exist unless it is manually created by you or a custom installer.

```
[HKEY_LOCAL_MACHINE\SOFTWARE\Microsoft\VisualStudio\12.0
    \WorkItemTracking\WorkItemTracking\CustomControls\LookInFolders]
    "C:\\CustomControls\\MyCustomLocation"=""
```

➤ **Common Application Data 2013–Specific Location**—For example, `C:\ProgramData\Microsoft\Team Foundation\Work Item Tracking\Custom Controls\12.0\`

➤ **Local Application Data 2013–Specific Location**—For example, `C:\Users\UserName\AppData\Local\Microsoft\Team Foundation\Work Item Tracking\Custom Controls\12.0\`

➤ **Visual Studio Private Assemblies Location**—For example, `C:\Program Files (x86)\Microsoft Visual Studio 12.0\Common7\IDE\PrivateAssemblies\`. Storing custom work item controls in this folder is not recommended.

➤ **Common Application Data Location**—For example, `C:\ProgramData\Microsoft\Team Foundation\Work Item Tracking\Custom Controls\`

➤ **Local Application Data Location**—For example, `C:\Users\UserName\AppData\Local\Microsoft\Team Foundation\Work Item Tracking\Custom Controls\`

One of the first three approaches is recommended when deploying your custom work item controls to a team member's machines.

Work Item Custom Control Deployment Manifest

The work item custom control deployment manifest file has a `.wicc` extension. It contains the full class name for the custom work item control, as well as the name of the assembly that contains the custom work item control. That is the filename for the file where `.wicc` is the file's extension, as in `MyCustomControl.wicc`. The contents of the custom control deployment manifest would contain something similar to Listing 13-5.

LISTING 13-5: Work item custom control deployment file

```xml
<?xml version="1.0"?>
<CustomControl xmlns:xsi="http://www.w3.org/2001
    /XMLSchema-instance" xmlns:xsd="http://www.w3.org/2001/XMLSchema">
  <Assembly>Wrox.CustomWorkItemControl.dll</Assembly>
  <FullClassName>Wrox.CustomWorkItemControl.MyCustomControl</FullClassName>
</CustomControl>
```

Using the Custom Control in the Work Item Type Definition

Once the work item custom control artifacts have been deployed to each of the client machines, you can then configure the control definition in the work item type definition's form layout section by setting the `Type` attribute as shown here. The value for this attribute is the filename of the custom work item control deployment manifest, without the `.wicc` extension.

```xml
<Control Type="MyCustomControl" FieldName="System.AssignedTo"
    Label="Assigned To:" LabelPosition="Left" />
```

Remember that you can now use the *preferred* and *fallback* controls mechanism discussed earlier in the chapter to make a better experience for your team members.

SUMMARY

Process templates are the most customized part of Team Foundation Server. They allow teams to easily modify their process and have the tool help them with day-to-day activities for managing their process. In this chapter, you learned about the different artifacts that make up a process template, how to deploy changes to the work item type definitions, and how to edit work item type definitions to include common customizations.

You also learned about custom work item controls and the specific Team Foundation Server SDK interfaces that should be implemented when creating the custom work item control. Deployment of those work item controls to each of the client machines was also covered.

In Chapter 14, you will learn how to manage your teams using the new Agile-based planning tools in Team Web Access.

14

Managing Teams and Agile Planning Tools

WHAT'S IN THIS CHAPTER?

➤ Defining and managing your portfolio and product backlog

➤ Planning an iteration while balancing resource capacity

➤ Tracking your work using task boards

➤ Understanding options for customizing the agile planning and tracking tools

➤ Communicating with your team using Team Rooms

➤ Discovering how the development team can request feedback from stakeholders on specific features or requirements

➤ Learning how project stakeholders can use the Microsoft Feedback Client to provide rich feedback about your software

The Agile Manifesto defines several guiding principles that have implications on the ways in which teams manage projects. Instead of attempting to define an entire project schedule up front, as with a waterfall methodology, an agile team allows the plan to evolve over time. Work is broken down into multiple successive *iterations*, each of which might last between one and four weeks.

Teams practicing an agile development methodology tend to embark upon a journey of mutual discovery with their customers to determine new work dynamically, based on changing business priorities or on feedback from work done in previous iterations. The customer, or at least a proxy for the customer, is considered a virtual member of the team and participates in defining and prioritizing (and often re-prioritizing) work over time.

The pursuit to embrace agile development, with dynamic schedules and evolving requirements, has meant that many of the tools and techniques used for traditional project management are no longer sufficient. Agile practitioners have needed to look for different ways of capturing work, balancing resource capacity, tracking status, and so on.

Scrum, which is by far the most popular agile development methodology in use today, defines such tools, terminology, and methodology. Future work is captured and prioritized on a product backlog, which can then be committed into specific iterations, called sprints. Each sprint has its own sprint backlog in which work is further decomposed into smaller units of work. This work is tracked to completion on a *task board*, which usually takes the form of sticky notes on a whiteboard.

Team Foundation Server 2013 has embraced these concepts by providing a set of web-based tooling for managing your product backlog, decomposing your work into iterations, and tracking your work using a digital task board. Anyone familiar with or practicing Scrum should feel immediately at home with this set of tooling, although it cannot be understated that this same set of tooling can be adopted by any team who wants to use it, even if they aren't practicing Scrum per se. One of the design principles of Team Foundation Server has always been that teams can use any process they want to, and Team Foundation Server provides the right level of flexibility and customization to support such a process.

In this chapter, you learn about the web-based tooling available within Team Foundation Server 2013 to support agile project management and tracking. This book is not a true primer on how to run a project using a Scrum (or any other) development methodology, but there are several great books to choose from that cover this topic.

Later in this chapter, you will also explore the new tools available for teams that allow them to communicate with each other and be notified of useful events in real time. You will also learn how team members can request feedback from stakeholders. Stakeholders are then able to respond to that request using a new Feedback Client that they can then submit, which will then be available for the requesting team to manage and process.

DEFINING A TEAM

Team Foundation Server 2013 defines the notion of a team, which you can use to organize people who are working together. This should not be confused with the concept of a team project within Team Foundation Server, which is a large container of work, consisting of source control and work items that all share a common process template. A team project usually contains multiple teams, and each team can have its own product backlog, iterations, and task board. A single person might also participate in more than one team. For instance, a graphic designer might be a shared resource responsible for contributing artwork to different teams.

> **NOTE** *For more information about making decisions about the scope and size of your team projects, see Chapter 2 about planning your Team Foundation Server deployment.*

To create a team, follow these steps:

1. Open a browser and visit the Team Web Access home page for your team project. You can access this by clicking the Web Access link in Team Explorer. The address takes the format of `http://<server>:<port>/tfs/<collection-name>/<team-project-name>`.

2. Now open the administrative context by clicking the gear icon in the upper-right corner. If you do not have administrative privileges for your team project, you need to contact your team project administrator to perform these steps. On this screen you should see a list of any teams already configured for your team project.

3. Click New Team to display the Create New Team dialog box, as shown in Figure 14-1. You can provide a name and description for your team and specify what default permissions new team members should inherit. From the Settings tab, you can declare any users who should be team administrators.

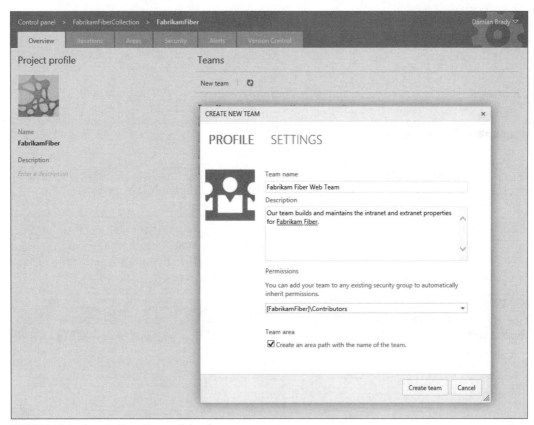

FIGURE 14-1: Create New Team dialog box

The Create New Team dialog box also lets you create an area path for this team. You were introduced to the concept of areas in Chapter 12. Areas provide a way for you to categorize your work within a team project. You can choose to create areas for each of your teams, so that (for example) bugs that are filed against the \Fabrikam Fiber Web Site area path are automatically routed to the Fabrikam Fiber Web Team.

4. Click Create Team when you are finished to create your team and return to the list of teams on your team project. Click your team in this list to display the team administrative dialog box shown in Figure 14-2. From here you can easily add new team members or team administrators. You can also change the name of your team or the description, or choose an image to represent your team.

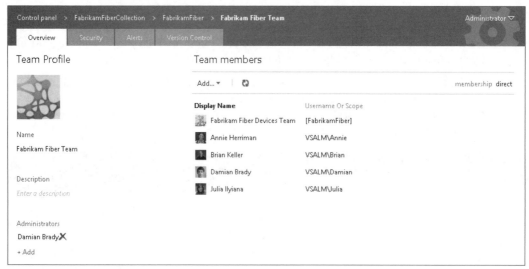

FIGURE 14-2: The team administrative dialog box

You are able to add whole Team Foundation Server groups to teams as well as individuals. If you have added groups, you can toggle between seeing individual members and their teams by clicking on the membership filter at the top right of the list.

5. Click the Iterations tab to select the iterations your team is participating in, as shown in Figure 14-3. In Chapter 12, you also learned how to manage iterations and assign start and end dates to them. On this screen, you are indicating which iterations your team is using to structure its work. You should ensure that the iteration dates do not overlap.

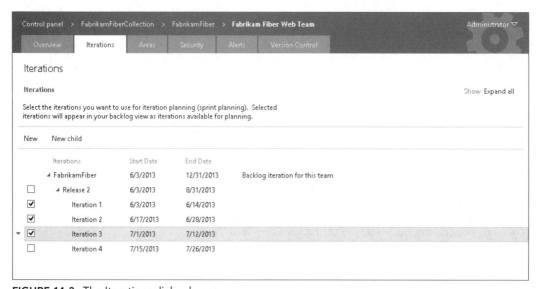

FIGURE 14-3: The Iterations dialog box

Your iterations need to be hierarchical, consisting of at least one parent and one child. This is required so that your backlog iteration (representing unscheduled work) can exist at the root or parent node, and specific iterations (representing scheduled work) are represented by child nodes. In Figure 14-3, `Release 2` is the parent node representing the backlog iteration. You can select a new backlog iteration by highlighting that iteration, clicking the small drop-down arrow to the left of the iteration name, and then selecting Set as Team's Backlog Iteration. But you need to first ensure that your desired backlog iteration has at least one child iteration.

> **NOTE** *It may be necessary to create different iteration structures for each team within your team project. For example, if your Web Team is using the term "Sprint 3" to define an iteration that begins on March 1, but your Database Team thinks of Sprint 3 as beginning on April 15, each team should have its own iteration structure. You can use any naming convention you want for this, such as* `WebTeam\Sprint3` *and* `DataTeam\Sprint3`*. This way, each node can have its own start and end date independently.*
>
> *If your organization's goal is to report across multiple teams, it is recommended that you not take this approach and attempt to align the team's iteration schedules appropriately. You can even have some teams on differing lengths as long as the time spans are equally divided. For example, one team may work on four-week iterations and another may work on two-week iterations. That can be accommodated by placing two child iteration nodes for each four-week iteration node. One team would select the four-week iteration node and the other would select the two children that represent the two-week iterations.*

Similarly, click Areas to configure which area paths your team is using to manage its work, as shown in Figure 14-4. You can select multiple areas, or the root area path, although if you have many people using your team project you might want to use areas to more carefully segregate work—for example, based on application, project, team, and so on.

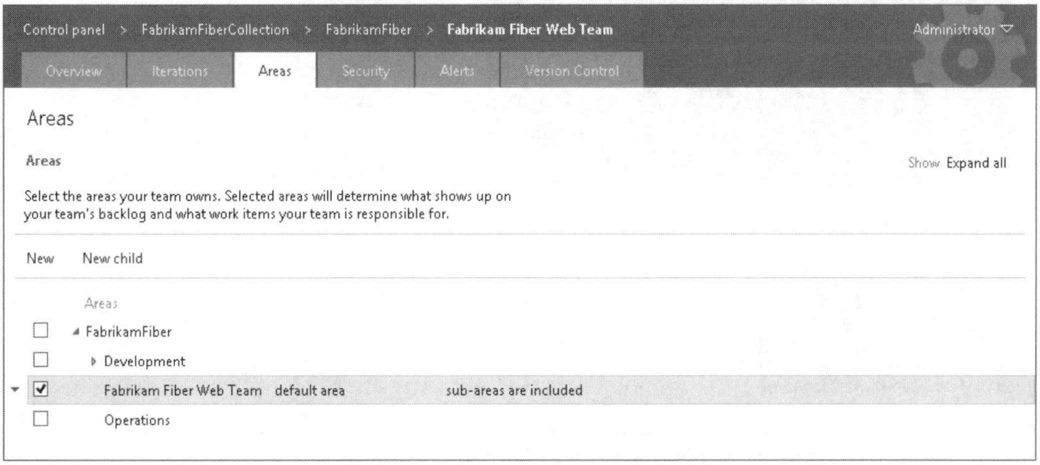

FIGURE 14-4: The Areas dialog box

You can use the Security tab to configure permissions for your team, and you can use the Alerts tab to configure e-mail notifications for your team. For example, you might want to automatically send an e-mail to any team member if a work item assigned to that person changes. Or you can e-mail the entire team if a daily build fails.

Finally, you can click the Version Control tab to change permissions specific to source code files and folders if you are using Team Foundation Version Control, or repositories and branches if you are using Git.

6.   Close the administrative context when you are finished, and return to Team Web Access. You can now access the team home page for any team you are a member of by clicking the drop-down to the right of "Visual Studio Team Foundation Server 2013" in the header of the Team Web Access view and selecting the appropriate team. For example, Figure 14-5 shows the home page for the Fabrikam Fiber Web Team.

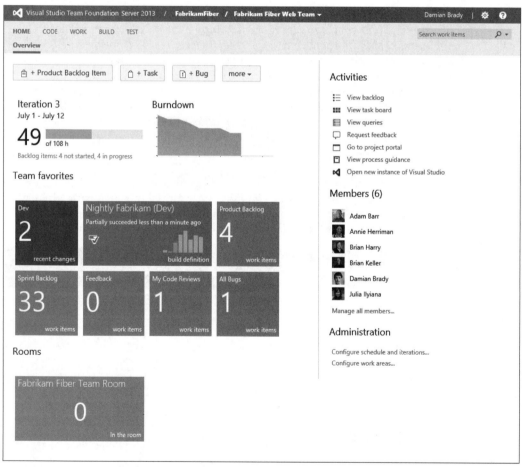

FIGURE 14-5: Home page for the Fabrikam Fiber Web Team

If you just created a brand-new team, your home page won't yet look as rich as the one shown in Figure 14-5. The top half of this view shows information relevant to your current iteration. The status bar on the left shows the amount of work remaining as compared to the capacity of your team (in this example, 49 hours of work have been completed and the team has a total capacity of achieving 108 hours of work). The burndown graph is a trend that shows how remaining work has decreased (or increased) over time during your current iteration. You learn more about iteration capacity and burndown visualizations later in this chapter.

The bottom half of this view shows any Team Favorites you have configured. These can represent work item queries—such as open bugs or in-progress tasks. They can also display graphs of recent builds or even recent changesets that have been checked into a particular branch. To add Team Favorites to this view, you should first open a relevant work item query, branch, or build within Team Web Access. You can then click the small drop-down arrow located to the left of the object and select Add to team favorites, as shown in Figure 14-6. This adds a new tile to your team's home page, which can make it easy for the entire team to see the metrics you believe are most important to track. You can then drag and drop each of the tiles to reorganize the final view.

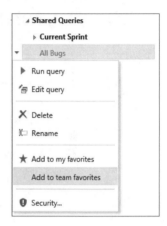

FIGURE 14-6: Add to team favorites option

Next you will see how to define and manage your team's product backlog.

MAINTAINING PRODUCT BACKLOGS

A product backlog is essentially just a list of work that your team has identified but hasn't yet scheduled for implementation. The product backlog is a useful tool for collaborating with customers or other project stakeholders. As new work is requested by your stakeholders, you can track it in a central location on the product backlog. You can also estimate and prioritize this work, usually with input from your customer or stakeholders to help determine which items are most important to deliver first.

The 2013 release of Team Foundation Server introduces the concept of Agile Portfolio Management. While in previous versions, the product backlog was defined without a hierarchy, now you can define your work at multiple granularities. This allows you to define high-level goals or features that contain multiple product backlog items.

All of the standard process templates that come with Team Foundation Server have been updated to provide support for this new hierarchy. Each template includes a new *Feature* work item type for this purpose.

Managing the Backlog

From your team's home page, click View Backlog to display your product backlog, such as the one shown in Figure 14-7. In Team Foundation Server 2013, a small colored bar has been added next to work items to indicate the work item type. In Figure 14-7, you can see one red Bug in our backlog surrounded by blue Product Backlog Items. The "quick add" panel at the top of this page, shown as a light gray box, enables you to quickly enter new work as it is identified. You can select the type of work to add (such as Product Backlog Item or Bug), provide a title, and press Enter (or click Add) to quickly add this work to your backlog. When you do this, you automatically create a new work item within Team Foundation Server.

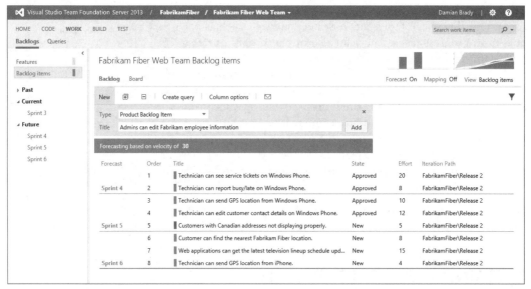

FIGURE 14-7: Product Backlog hub

If you highlight a row within your backlog, any new work you add from the Quick Add panel is inserted above this highlighted row. The exception to this rule is when you have highlighted the last row in your backlog; new work is added at the end of your backlog.

> **NOTE** *The screenshots in this chapter reflect a team project created with the Visual Studio Scrum 2013 process template included with Team Foundation Server 2013. The terminology varies slightly if you are using either the MSF for Agile Software Development 2013 or MSF for CMMI Process Improvement 2013 process templates, but you can still take advantage of the same tooling. You can even customize this tooling for use with your own custom or third-party process templates. Customization options are discussed later in this chapter.*

You can easily reprioritize work by dragging and dropping it on the backlog. Changes you make here are saved to Team Foundation Server in the background. You can also double-click an item in this view to open the work item editor to provide additional detail or make changes.

NOTE *If you have used previous versions of Team Foundation Server then you are used to changing priority by hand-editing a field within each work item. But notice that the Priority field is no longer visible within Team Web Access or Visual Studio when viewing work items. Backlog Priority is now a hidden field by default. The recommended way of setting this value is to use the Team Web Access view to drag items up and down the backlog. Behind the scenes, Team Web Access uses large integers and an algorithm to assign Backlog Priority values. The use of large integer values here makes it possible to insert a work item between two items on a backlog without needing to make updates to each of the surrounding items.*

Team Foundation Server 2013 introduces a few new options at the top of your backlog. You can click Create query to create a work item query representing the current view. You can change the columns that are shown by clicking Column options, and you can even e-mail your backlog by clicking the envelope icon.

Teams practicing Scrum will be familiar with a concept known as *velocity*. Velocity is a metric used to calculate the amount of work that a team is able to deliver for a given iteration. It is usually measured in story points on Scrum teams. Other teams may prefer to do their estimations in hours, or days, or ideal days, and so on. Regardless of the estimation technique used by your team, you can use the product backlog view to get a sense for when you will be able to deliver items on your backlog. The only requirement is that you should be consistent with your estimation techniques. For example, when some people on the team are estimating in days and other people are estimating in story points, it's difficult to create consistent plans.

Toggle forecast lines on or off by clicking the On/Off link in the upper right of this page labeled "Forecast." Forecast lines display, as shown in Figure 14-7, to indicate when work is estimated to be delivered based on your current team's velocity. This approach requires that you have estimated your backlog items by providing a value for effort. Do this by double-clicking each item in your backlog to provide this additional level of detail.

NOTE *Most teams practicing Scrum also transition the state of an item on the backlog from New to Approved at the time that the team provides an Effort estimate. You are not required to follow this protocol, but it can be helpful for differentiating between truly new work (which might only be in the "idea" stage) and work that your team has taken time to estimate.*

The Forecasting Based on Velocity Of text box enables you to experiment with different values to see the effect that given values for velocity might have on delivering work. For example, you might be able to ask for additional funding from your customer to hire new team members and speed up the rate at which items are delivered. Or you might know that there are several upcoming holidays that will affect your team's ability to deliver. You can also click the velocity column graph in the upper-right corner of this screen to see your historical velocity for the preceding (and current) iterations.

The forecast lines are purely estimates. In order to actually schedule work for a given iteration, you can drag and drop it onto either the current or future iterations listed on the left-hand side of this view. When you drag and drop work onto an iteration, the value in the Iteration Path column is updated to reflect the assigned iteration, and the Iteration field is updated within the work item in Team Foundation Server.

Teams practicing Kanban will be familiar with the Cumulative Flow diagram visible on the upper right of the product backlog page that was introduced in the 2012 Update 1 release. This diagram shows you how your backlog items are moving through their state transitions over time. It shows up to 30 weeks of data and is an easy way to visualize how your team is working, highlighting any bottlenecks.

> **NOTE** *Even though you have assigned work to a particular iteration, it continues to show up in your product backlog until you have transitioned the work item to a state that shows it is in progress. For the Scrum process template, work is considered to be in progress when it reaches the Committed state. By convention, most teams typically wait until they have broken work down into child tasks before they transition it to a Committed state. Next, you find out how to break work down.*

Agile Portfolio Management

If you are familiar with Team Foundation Server 2012, you'll notice a few new additions to the backlog page in the 2013 release to support the new portfolio management functions.

Click the On/Off link next to the Mapping label below the graphs to toggle mapping of backlog items to features. A Features panel will open on the right of the screen, enabling you to drag backlog items into features to group them.

You will also notice a link next to a View label in this section. Clicking the link expands a drop-down with various views of your backlog. The text in the drop-down options and the views they trigger varies between process templates, but there is some consistency. The first option will show you a flat view of your backlog items. The subsequent views will show you hierarchical views. For example, if you are using the Visual Studio Scrum 2013 process template, you will be able to see the Backlog items to Features hierarchy, or the Backlog items to Tasks hierarchy.

> **NOTE** *When you're on the Backlog items page, Team Web Access will only give the option of forecast lines if you're viewing a flat list of items. To see forecast lines, you must choose the basic view.*

Team Web Access introduces an entirely new Features page accessible via the link on the left of the page. The Features page is very similar to the backlog page but it allows you to manage the work items above your backlog items in the hierarchy. You can switch between various views in a similar way to the Backlog items page. In the case of the Visual Studio Scrum 2013 template, you can see a flat list of Features, Features to Backlog items, or even Features to Tasks, which shows you two levels of hierarchy.

> **NOTE** *In Team Foundation Server 2013, the backlog board has been moved. In the previous release, the board was another option under the top-level Work hub. The backlog board can be considered another view of the Backlog items page so it exists as a link at the top of the page. This is consistent with the board for an Iteration, and the board for Features.*

PLANNING ITERATIONS

After you have identified the work that you want to deliver for a given iteration, you can click an iteration from the list on the left-hand side of the product backlog view to open the iteration planning view shown in Figure 14-8. This figure shows an iteration that is mid-sprint, meaning that the team has already completed some work and is preparing to finish this iteration.

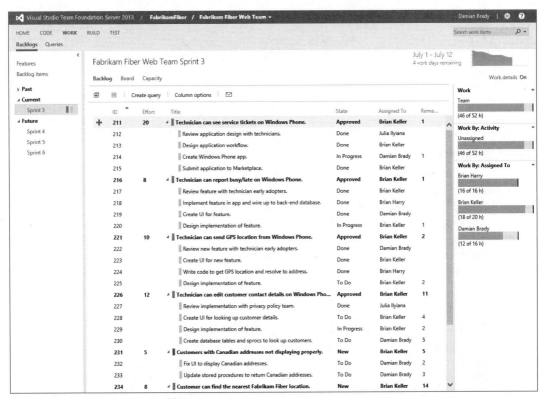

FIGURE 14-8: The Iteration Backlog view

When you first add items to an iteration (such as a Product Backlog Item or a Bug) you are only declaring your intention to deliver this functionality. The next phase of planning this work is to actually break it down into the individual tasks that people on your team need to complete in order to perform the work. When you hover over a Product Backlog Item, you can click the plus (+) sign that appears to display the dialog box shown in Figure 14-9, which enables you to add a new task work item as a child to the parent you clicked on.

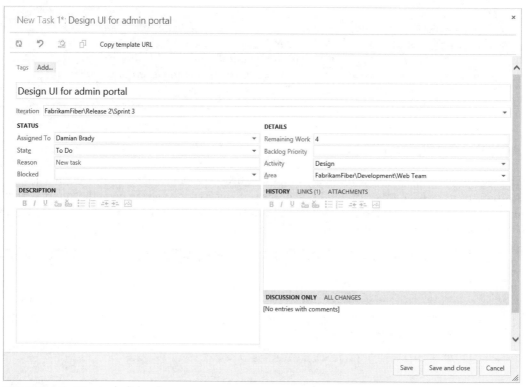

FIGURE 14-9: New task dialog box

You should provide a title for this task and, if possible, an estimate for the amount of remaining work. By default, remaining work is assumed to be provided in hours, but you can also customize this (see the section "Customization Options" later in this chapter). You can assign this to a team member who will complete this work, but you are not required to do so. Save this work item and proceed to break down the rest of your work into child tasks. If you haven't already done so, set the state of parent work items to Committed as each item is broken down.

> **NOTE** *A common question that many people have is about the relationship between effort, provided earlier when defining an item for the backlog, and remaining work, provided for tasks. Effort is typically a rough estimate used to provide a quick indication about the size of work in relation to other items on the backlog. Remaining work values in your iteration should be much more precise, and represent the additional level of planning and estimation analysis that has been given to considering how a given feature or user story will be implemented. As a team gains experience, it becomes better at providing more realistic estimates while the product backlog is being defined.*

As you begin to create tasks with values for remaining work, you will notice that the capacity graphs on the right-hand side of this screen begin to render. These graphs are broken into three areas:

➤ **Work**—shows the total amount of work remaining for this iteration, calculated as the sum of the remaining work across all task work items.

➤ **Work By: Activity**—enables you to categorize the amount of remaining work into categories. When creating tasks, you can use the activity field to categorize tasks, such as Development, or Testing, and so on. If you don't provide a value for activity, work simply shows up as Unassigned.

➤ **Work By: Assigned To**—shows the amount of remaining work that is assigned to each person on your team.

Click the Capacity tab to assign the capacity for each of the members of your team, as shown in Figure 14-10. The Capacity Per Day column enables you to specify the average number of hours per day that a given resource is working on tasks. The Activity column enables you to specify the discipline of a team member, which is necessary if you want to view capacity by activity type. Finally, you can use Days Off to define days that a team member is sick or on holiday, and you can use Team Days Off to define days that the whole team will be unavailable, such as during a holiday or company retreat.

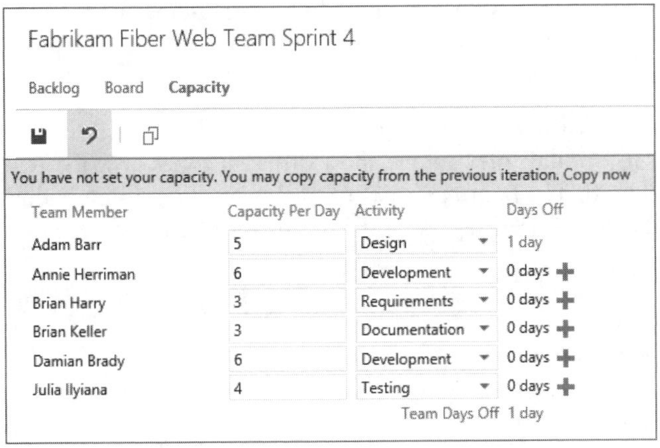

Fabrikam Fiber Web Team Sprint 4			
Backlog Board **Capacity**			
💾 ↻ ⊡			
You have not set your capacity. You may copy capacity from the previous iteration. Copy now			
Team Member	Capacity Per Day	Activity	Days Off
Adam Barr	5	Design ▾	1 day
Annie Herriman	6	Development ▾	0 days ➕
Brian Harry	3	Requirements ▾	0 days ➕
Brian Keller	3	Documentation ▾	0 days ➕
Damian Brady	6	Development ▾	0 days ➕
Julia Ilyiana	4	Testing ▾	0 days ➕
		Team Days Off	1 day

FIGURE 14-10: Capacity planning for iteration

The values you enter for this table are specific to this team and this iteration. So a shared resource who works on multiple teams might have different values for Capacity Per Day or Days Off depending on the team. Also a resource who works five hours per day on one iteration might work only two hours per day during a subsequent iteration. If you like the capacity settings for the team from the previous iteration or just like a quick start, you can even copy those values by clicking Copy Now to copy capacity from the previous iteration tool, as shown in Figure 14-10.

After you assign capacity values for your team, the capacity indicators on the right change to either green, if a resource is at or under capacity, or red, if there is too much work given the planned capacity. The iteration plan is designed to be viewed on a regular basis so that you can make adjustments to the plan as needed. For example, if a team member is sick, you might need to reschedule work that was originally planned for this iteration. You can drag and drop parent items from this list onto other iterations on the left-hand side of the page.

TRACKING WORK

When you are satisfied with the iteration plan, it's time to start writing code, authoring documentation, designing user interfaces, and doing all the other work that's required to develop great software. During the course of this activity, it can be helpful to have a single location to easily determine the status of the work that everybody is doing.

Scrum teams typically use a task board for this purpose. In its simplest form, a task board takes the form of a whiteboard with sticky notes on it that you move from the left side of the board (work that is not yet started) to the middle (work that is in progress) to the right (completed work). Similarly, Kanban teams often use these boards to help visualize the flow of backlog items through various phases.

Physical boards work very well for teams that are co-located, especially if they share a team room, because anybody can quickly look up at the whiteboard to determine the state of the team's work. Of course, this approach has its challenges for teams who work in different geographic locations, have individual offices, or even spread across multiple floors or buildings.

Team Foundation Server 2013 provides digital versions of these boards that overcome the limitations imposed by traditional physical boards. There are Kanban boards available for managing Features and Product Backlog Items, and task boards for managing individual Iterations.

Using the Kanban Board

To view a Kanban board, choose either the Features or Backlog items view, and then click Board at the top of the page. The boards are very similar; they simply show different types of work items. Figure 14-11 shows a Backlog Kanban board. The board consists of tiles that represent individual Product Backlog Items or Features, and columns that represent the progress of each item.

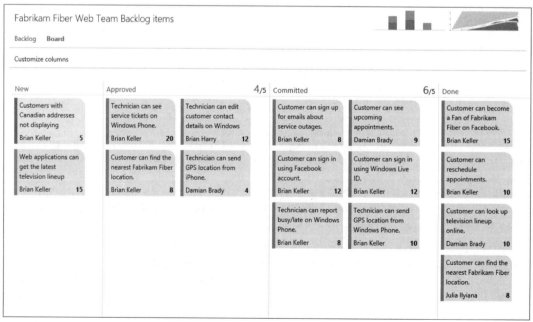

FIGURE 14-11: Kanban board

To change the state of a backlog item or feature, you can drag and drop the tiles to move them between columns, provided the process template transitions allow you to do so.

> **WARNING** *Moving a Feature or Backlog item from one column to another does not affect the children of that work item. To mark a backlog item or feature as completely "done," you need to ensure all child work items have an appropriate completed status.*

A key concept in Kanban is limiting work in progress. This means that a team should not have too many items in one column, as this represents a potential bottleneck. With the exception of the first and last columns (which represent brand new and completed work items, respectively) you will see two numbers in the column header. These represent the number of backlog items currently in the column, and the "work in progress limit" assigned to that column. You will see how to customize the work in progress limit soon. In Figure 14-11, you can see the team has committed to more items than the work in progress limit for the Committed state. Team Foundation Server will not prevent you from committing to more items, but it will alert you by coloring the header red.

By default, the columns map one-to-one with the available states for the work items. You can click the Customize columns link to add additional columns with the Customize Columns dialog box shown in Figure 14-12.

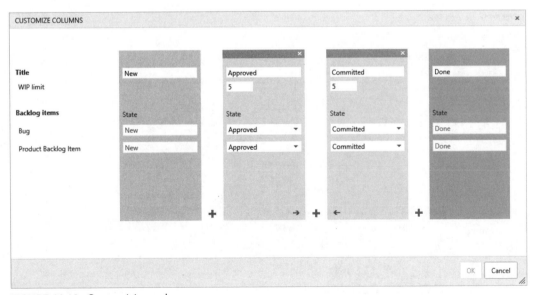

FIGURE 14-12: Customizing columns

The Customize Columns dialog box allows you to add and remove columns using the plus (+) signs between columns and the crosses at the top right of each column respectively. You also can change the display name of a column, change its work-in-progress limit, and change the work item state that that column maps to.

This feature allows you to manage your portfolio or backlog in more detail than your process template may allow. Teams can take advantage of this feature to temporarily introduce columns for situations such as external audits, deployment or test processes, or even code reviews.

> **NOTE** *Changes you make using the Customize Columns dialog box are local to that Web Access board and do not change the available states for the process template. New columns represent pseudo-states that will not be available for selection when changing the state of a work item, and name changes will only be shown on the board.*
>
> *Be careful when adding and removing pseudo-states as they will show in the Cumulative Flow graph if at least one work item has moved into that pseudo-state at any point in time. If you are frequently adding and removing pseudo-states, your Cumulative Flow graph can become very messy.*

Using the Task Board

Agile task boards will be familiar to anyone coming from Team Foundation Server 2012, but there have been some useful changes in this release. To view an individual iteration's Task board, select an Iteration and then click Board at the top of the page to see a task board like the one in Figure 14-13.

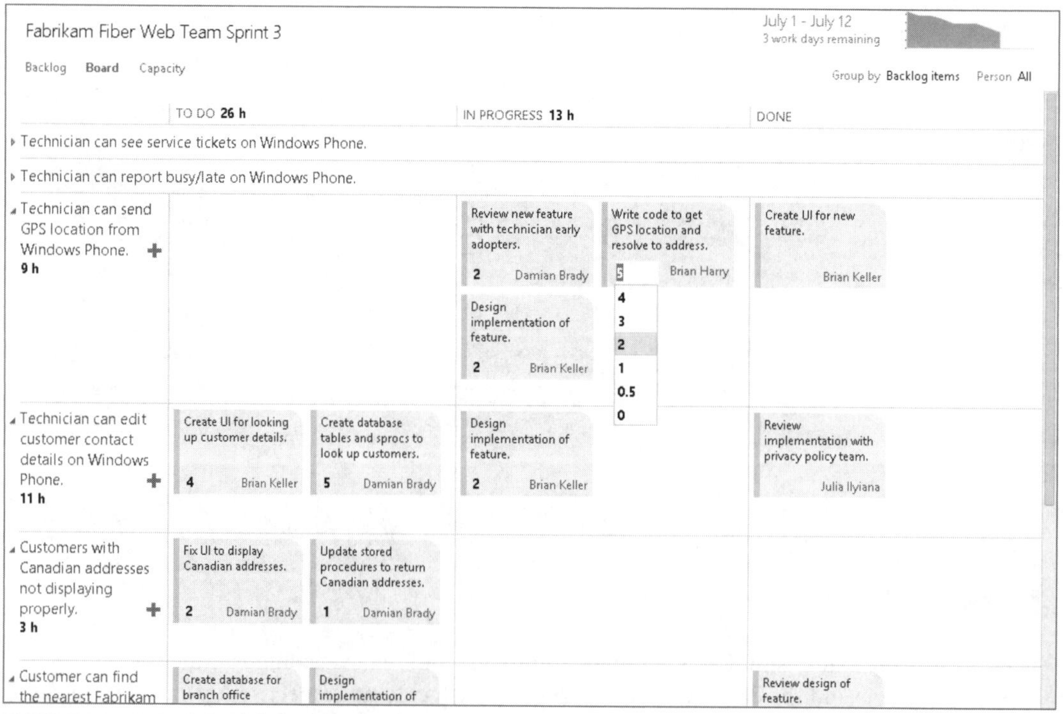

FIGURE 14-13: Agile task board

Each row on this task board represents a parent backlog item from your current iteration. The tiles on this task board represent the individual child tasks that you created. Each task begins in the To Do column. When a team member is ready to begin a task, he or she can drag and drop it onto the In Progress column. As the team member makes progress against a given task, he or she can click the number on the task to update the remaining work. If he or she has finished a task, he or she drags it into the Done column to automatically set the amount of remaining work to zero. Clicking the name of the team member for a given task opens a drop-down menu that enables you to quickly reassign work. Similarly, clicking the number of hours remaining opens a drop-down menu allowing you to change the remaining hours.

Click a task to open it in a full editor, such as the one previously shown in Figure 14-9. This is often helpful if you want to add more detail to a task or comment on its progress.

> **NOTE** *The task board understands the rules and limitations of the underlying process template your team project is based upon. For example, consider a scenario where you have prematurely moved a task from In Progress to Done—perhaps by mistake, or perhaps you realized there is additional work that needs to be finished. If you try to move work from the Done column back to the In Progress column, you receive an error message indicating that work that is In Progress cannot have a value of 0 for remaining work. To fix this, click the task to open the full editor and assign a new value for remaining work.*

The entire interface is touch-friendly. If you have a touch-screen monitor, such as in a shared team room, you can configure it to display your task board and make it easy for team members to update the status of their work whenever they walk by it. And because everything is stored in Team Foundation Server, remote workers can access the same view in any modern web browser and device to see what their colleagues are working on and provide their own status updates.

If you find yourself constrained for space in this view, you can collapse finished backlog items by clicking the arrow to the left of the parent work item title. You can also use your browser's zoom functionality (usually Ctrl plus a hyphen or a ++ sign) to fit more work on a single screen.

You can change the view to focus on individual team members by clicking the Person: All link and selecting the name of any team member. This highlights the work assigned to that team member, making it easier to differentiate from the rest of the team's work.

You can also click the Group By: Backlog items link to change the view such that tasks are organized by the team member they are assigned to, instead of by their parent work item. This is a helpful view for team meetings, where team members might be expected to tell their peers what they worked on yesterday and what they are planning to work on today. This view is also helpful for seeing whether there are any team members with too much work remaining and whether other team members might have the capacity for picking up some of that work.

As work is finished, the team can transition parent backlog items to a state of Done. Open a parent backlog item by clicking the title of the item on the left-hand side of the screen. This state transition is not done automatically when all of the tasks are finished because there may be additional checkpoints or quality gates in place before work is considered to be truly finished. For example, you might want to request feedback from your project's stakeholders to ensure that everybody is satisfied with the work as it has been implemented. You will explore requesting feedback from stakeholders later in this chapter.

The burndown chart in the upper-right corner of this screen displays a trend of the remaining work over time for your iteration. This chart is updated in real time as your team completes work (or identifies new work) during the course of an iteration. You can display the burndown chart in full screen by clicking it, as shown in Figure 14-14.

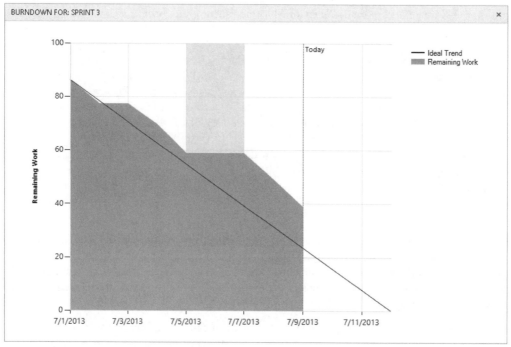

FIGURE 14-14: Burndown chart

CUSTOMIZATION OPTIONS

As mentioned previously, the examples in this chapter follow the default experience you get by using the Visual Studio Scrum 2013 process template for a team project. If you are practicing Scrum today, then you are likely already familiar with the types of tools available in this chapter. But even if you aren't practicing Scrum or using the Scrum process template, you can still benefit from these tools.

Depending on the process template you choose, the default terminology and views might vary. For example, a team using the MSF for CMMI process template tracks Requirements instead of Product

Backlog Items as the primary backlog work item type to be planned. An MSF for CMMI Software Improvement 2013 task board contains four columns (Proposed, Active, Resolved, and Closed) instead of the three shown earlier for a Scrum project (To Do, In Progress, and Done).

If you are using a team project that was created using one of the process templates provided by Microsoft with Team Foundation Server 2013 (Scrum 2013, MSF for Agile 2013, or MSF for CMMI Process Improvement 2013) then this tooling is preconfigured automatically to work with your team projects. If you are upgrading an existing team project from an earlier release of Team Foundation Server, then you need to perform some additional steps in order to begin using the agile planning and tracking tools mentioned in this chapter. These steps are outlined at http://aka.ms/ TeamProjectUpgrade2013.

> **NOTE** *Upgrading from previous versions of Team Foundation Server is covered in more detail in Chapter 27.*

There are also several ways you can customize these tools to change their appearance and behavior. For example:

➤ Add or remove fields from the "quick add" pane in the product backlog view. For example, in addition to setting a title, you might also want to specify an effort estimate with each new item.

➤ Change the available states for work items in the feature, backlog, and iteration boards.

➤ Change the list of activities that task work items and team members can be assigned to.

➤ Change the working days to be used when calculating capacity and rendering the burndown graph. By default, Saturday and Sunday are considered nonworking days, but you can modify these.

➤ Configure the types of work items to be used as parents and children throughout the tooling.

➤ Change the color used for different work item types in the backlogs and boards.

The types of customizations and other process template customizations are covered in more detail in Chapter 13.

TEAM ROOMS

Team rooms are a new feature in Team Foundation Server 2013. A team room provides an online area that encourages and captures communication between team members, regardless of their physical location. Team rooms are created for each team defined in a project, but you can create additional rooms for any purpose.

On your team's home page, you will see a tile showing the number of people currently in your team room. To open a team room, click the room tile. Figure 14-15 shows an example team room interaction.

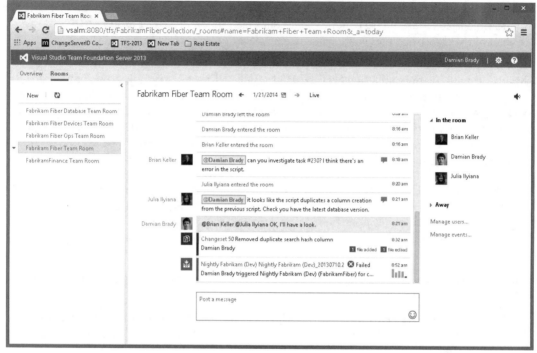

FIGURE 14-15: Team room

The main area of the page shows the conversation between team members as well as any Team Foundation Server events that team members have chosen to be notified about. You can change the date you are looking at using the calendar links at the top of the page. Contributing is as easy as typing in the "Post a message" text area and pressing Enter. Messages are primarily text, but can be enriched in a number of ways.

Clicking on the smiley face icon gives you access to various *emoticons*. These will also replace known character combinations in your message. For example, :(will be replaced by a face with a frown.

You can mention a specific team member using the @ character, and when you type @, a drop-down will appear to help you choose valid members. As a team member, you will be notified if you're mentioned in a message, and your name will appear with an orange background and border, as in Figure 14-15.

Finally, you can link directly to any work item using the # character. In Figure 14-15, you can see a link to work item #230. This is a rich link that can be clicked on to view and edit the work item details.

> **NOTE** *Team rooms are only officially available in Team Web Access, but a Visual Studio extension has been created by MVPs Utkarsh Shigihalli and Tarun Arora. You can download the extension at* `http://aka.ms/VS2013TeamRooms`.

On the left of the page, you will see all the rooms you have permission to enter. You can click on any of these to enter the room and start chatting with the other members of your team.

On the right side of the page, you can see everyone who is currently in the room. You can also click the small arrow next to Away to see people who have access to the room but are not currently present. Finally, you can manage the users who have access to the room and the Team Foundation Server events that will be surfaced in the main chat area.

To invite other Team Foundation Server members to a team room, click on the Manage users link. This dialog box allows you to add individual users or entire teams to the team room.

Team rooms can also surface Team Foundation Server events such as the check-in and build failure visible in Figure 14-15. To manage the events that are shown, click the Manage events link. You will see a dialog box with four categories of events, as in Figure 14-16.

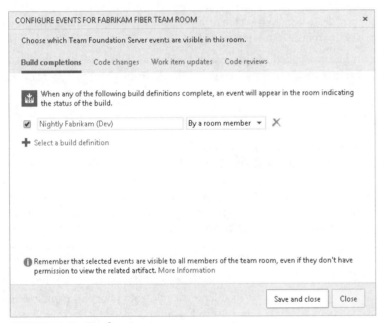

FIGURE 14-16: Configuring team room events

This dialog box enables you to subscribe to multiple events for build completions, code changes, work item updates, and code reviews. You can further filter these to only members of the room, and in the case of work item updates and code reviews, restrict them to a specific area path.

STAKEHOLDER FEEDBACK

You have learned about the importance of engaging with your software development project's stakeholders to ensure that you have a clear understanding of what your stakeholders want you to build before you start implementing it. However, regardless of how much time you spend up front during this requirement's elicitation phase, the first iteration of software you create is rarely going to meet all of their expectations.

There are a variety of reasons for this: Technical challenges might get in the way of the originally planned implementation; business requirements may evolve from the time when you first captured them to the time that you implement the first working code; the opinions of users can be fickle, even influenced by seeing the software in action for the first time; you may not have truly understood what your stakeholders were asking for when you were capturing their requirements; or, you may not have had time to implement all the requirements in the initial release.

These possibilities will be anticipated by any agile software development team that embraces the fact that software development is something of an art form, requiring iterative cycles of requirement gathering, implementation, and feedback, which in turn informs an additional round of requirements and changes that must be implemented. However, the challenge for any team is in finding a way to effectively capture feedback from its stakeholders in a manner that can be analyzed, synthesized, and acted upon. This problem is made harder when stakeholders are time-shifted or geography-shifted away from the software development team. Even if the development team shares a common location with its stakeholders, finding a systematic way of gathering feedback from all of its stakeholders on a recurring basis can be a burdensome task.

In Visual Studio 2013, Microsoft has integrated the process of collecting stakeholder feedback directly into its application life-cycle management tooling capabilities. In this chapter, you find out how to use this tool to solicit and capture feedback from your stakeholders in a rich, actionable way.

Requesting Feedback

The first step toward getting great feedback from your stakeholders about your software is to properly frame the question of what you are asking for feedback on. The question of whether or not your software provides the right level of functionality is a very different question from whether or not your software is designed properly. Functionally, a tractor can get you from your house to your office in the morning, but it is probably not what you feel comfortable being seen in as you pull into the parking lot at work. But early on in a software development iteration, the team may be focused squarely on strictly implementing the required functionality with the understanding that it can make it look nice later on. Unless you properly scope your request to the stakeholders when you ask for feedback, you may get a lot of feedback on things that you haven't yet started to address in the software.

With Team Foundation Server 2013, you can request specific feedback from your stakeholders by visiting the Team Web Access home page for your project or team. In the list of Other Links, click Request feedback. You are presented with the dialog box shown in Figure 14-17, which allows you to specify what you are requesting feedback on and from whom.

> **NOTE** *If you don't see Request Feedback under the list of activities, this indicates that your Team Foundation Server instance has not been configured to use an SMTP e-mail server. Your Team Foundation Server administrator will be able to configure this using the Team Foundation Administration Console on the application tier server.*
>
> *You will also need to ensure that your user account has appropriate licensing access level to request feedback. Only users with Visual Studio Test Professional 2013, Visual Studio Premium 2013, or Visual Studio Ultimate 2013 are permitted to request feedback using this capability. This can be configured using the Administration features of Team Web Access, as described in more detail in Chapter 24.*

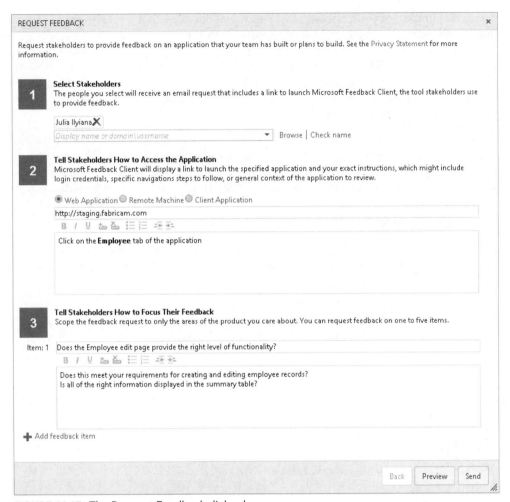

FIGURE 14-17: The Request Feedback dialog box

Follow these steps in the dialog box to request feedback from your stakeholders:

1. Specify the names of the users you want to request feedback from. These users need to be recognized as users who have access to your team project.

2. Specify how users should access the functionality you are asking them to test. For a web application, users might need to access a staging server (potentially in a Lab Management environment) that contains a recently deployed build. For other applications users might need to remote into another machine or install an interim build. Use this space to give the users any specific instructions they need in order to get started with your software.

3. Specify up to five aspects of your software that you want feedback on.

When specifying what you want to collect feedback on, be as specific as possible. You can also use the area below each feedback title to provide additional instructions that might help your stakeholders access certain features or scope their feedback to what you care most about. When applicable, you might want to also specify the things that you do *not* want feedback on. For example, if you know that the staging server you are using is very slow and doesn't reflect the performance of your production environment, then you might want to mention this to the users so they don't waste time giving you a lot of feedback on the performance of the application. If the user interface hasn't yet received attention from a designer (affectionately known as "programmer art"), be sure to specify this as well, so users don't spend time critiquing anything other than the application's functionality. The 2013 release of Team Foundation Server added rich text capabilities to the feedback fields to allow you to highlight important points.

After you have told your users how to access your software and what you are looking for feedback on, click Preview to see the e-mail that your stakeholders will receive. Click Send to deliver an e-mail to the stakeholders you specified earlier and also create Feedback Request work items (up to five, one for each item you added in Step 3) for you to track this request in Team Foundation Server.

Providing Feedback

After you have requested feedback from your stakeholders, they will receive an e-mail like the one shown in Figure 14-18. Before stakeholders can provide feedback, they need to first install the Microsoft Feedback Client by clicking the Install the Feedback Tool link in the e-mail.

FIGURE 14-18: Request feedback e-mail

> **NOTE** *The Feedback Client is freely downloadable from Microsoft and does not require a Team Foundation Server client access license. Users will, however, need to have appropriate permissions to your Team Foundation Server instance. At a minimum, users will need to be a member of the Limited access level group. See* http://aka.ms/TFS2013FeedbackPermission *for details.*

After the feedback tool is installed and stakeholders are ready to give feedback, they can click the Start Your Feedback Session link in the e-mail to open the Feedback Client shown on the left side of Figure 14-19. The menu at the top enables the stakeholders to dock the Feedback Client on either side of the monitor or to float the window to another monitor. The instructions provided on this first page are from the feedback request that you created earlier. After the stakeholders have installed or otherwise launched the application for which they are providing feedback, they can click the Next button to start giving feedback.

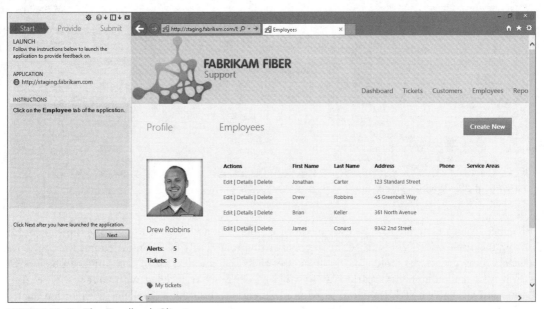

FIGURE 14-19: The Feedback Client

Figure 14-20 shows a stakeholder in the middle of providing feedback on this web application. The top half of the Feedback Client scopes the specific questions the stakeholder has been asked to address. In this case, you asked if the right information is displayed in the summary table. The stakeholder responded by asking if an Employee ID column can be added to this table. The stakeholder then used the Screenshot button to capture a snippet of the table and double-clicked that snippet so that he could annotate it with a red rectangle showing where the Employee ID column should go.

> **NOTE** *By default, Microsoft Paint is used to edit a screen clipping any time the user double-clicks within the Feedback Client. You can configure the Feedback Client to use your own favorite image-editing tool by clicking on the gear icon at the top of the window. For example, if you want to make annotations with a tool like SnagIt, you can configure it as your tool of choice. For more information, take a look at* `http://bit.ly/VSFeedbackwithSnagIt`.

FIGURE 14-20: Providing feedback

The Feedback Client can also be used to capture video and audio recordings while the stakeholder is using the application. This can be the next best thing to actually being in the room, watching over the shoulder of the stakeholder as he or she uses the application. A video recording can be a powerful way of truly understanding the way in which a user tends to interact with your software. Audio annotations enable a stakeholder to provide commentary about his experience without having to take the time to type notes. Video and audio contextualize the feedback you get from your stakeholders so that you can better understand how to respond to it.

After a stakeholder is finished providing feedback on a particular feedback item, he or she can provide a star rating before clicking Next. If there were other feedback items specified in this request, the stakeholder would now be prompted with each one sequentially. At the end of the feedback session, the stakeholder has an opportunity to review the feedback he or she has captured before submitting it to Team Foundation Server. This creates new Feedback Response work items (one for each Feedback Request, which was created earlier), which include all of the artifacts captured by the Feedback Client (video recordings, text and audio annotations, screen clippings).

The software development team can view the feedback responses using the built-in Feedback work item query (see Figure 14-21). If a piece of feedback results in a new bug or new requirement, the team can use the New Linked Work Item button to create a new work item linked to this specific Feedback Response work item. By linking the feedback directly from the stakeholders into the new work item, you can provide additional context and traceability for the developer who is assigned to implement the fix or new requirement specified in that work item.

As feedback is reviewed and any necessary actions have been taken (such as fixing bugs or implementing requirements), you can transition the State field of each Feedback Response to Closed.

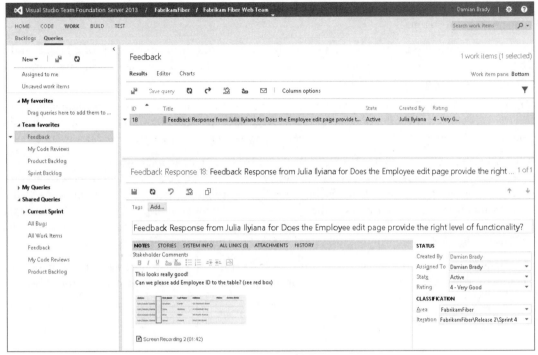

FIGURE 14-21: The Feedback Requests work item query results

Voluntary Feedback

Stakeholders can also provide unsolicited or voluntary feedback at any time by launching the Feedback Client directly instead of from a feedback request e-mail. They are first prompted to connect to the appropriate Team Foundation Server instance and team project where they want to provide feedback. After doing so, they can file feedback using video, audio, text, and screen clippings as they did previously. The one thing to be careful of here is that Feedback Response work items created when using a voluntary feedback method do not show up in the default Feedback Requests work item query. Instead, you should write a custom query to search for all work items of the type called Feedback Response. Feedback that is generated by the Feedback Client in an unsolicited manner will, by default, have a title that starts with Voluntary.

SUMMARY

In this chapter, you discovered the new tools available with Team Foundation Server 2013 for planning and tracking work in an agile manner. You found out how to use the product backlog view for defining and managing items that your team may schedule and implement in the future, as well as the new feature hierarchy available in Team Foundation Server 2013. You then saw how to break down work for an iteration into tasks and examine the remaining work for these tasks against the capacity of your team.

You also learned about using the digital boards to track work during the course of a project and an iteration so that everybody on the team can easily understand what their colleagues are working on and how much work is left to deliver.

You learned about the new team rooms that facilitate communication between team members and notify them of Team Foundation Server events, regardless of where they are. You saw how to subscribe to relevant events so the team can see what is happening with your server at any time.

You learned how you can request scoped feedback from your stakeholders to get actionable data that can help you refine your application development. You learned about the new Feedback Client that can capture rich information—including video recordings, text and audio annotations, and screen clippings—from your users as they give feedback about your applications. Finally you learned how you can use this feedback to create actionable bugs or new requirements that your team can use to ensure that you are continuing to build the right software to please your stakeholders.

In Chapter 15, you will have the opportunity to learn about the rich reporting features of Team Foundation Server 2013 as well as collaboration integration with team portals hosted in Microsoft Office SharePoint Server.

15
Reporting and SharePoint Dashboards

WHAT'S IN THIS CHAPTER?

➤ Learning about the changes and new features

➤ Understanding the Team Foundation Server data warehouse

➤ Understanding the tools available to create and manage reports

➤ Using the new Work Item Charting in Web Access

➤ Creating and customizing reports using Excel

➤ Extending and customizing the data warehouse and dashboards

One of the key value propositions for Team Foundation Server has always been the reporting features that it provides. When you have your source control, work-item tracking, and build and test case management systems all integrated in a system like Team Foundation Server, the reporting can provide powerful insight into the status of your projects. The data collected and the reports provided by Team Foundation Server gives your projects a level of transparency that allows you to react and adjust to changing conditions.

In this chapter, you will first learn about the Work Item Charting tools that are new in Team Foundation Server 2013 Web Access. Then you will see changes that were first introduced in Team Foundation Server 2010 and the minor changes since. These changes are designed to support multiple team project collections on a single server and, thus, improve reporting capabilities. You will then learn about the three data stores in the Team Foundation Server data warehouse. This chapter also provides an overview of how to set up and configure the integration with SharePoint, and how to take advantage of the excellent reporting features. Finally, you will learn how to customize project portals and warehouse adapters.

WHAT'S NEW IN TEAM FOUNDATION SERVER 2013?

Team Foundation Server 2010 included a significant investment in the reporting infrastructure and capabilities. This prior investment means that very little has changed in the reporting features of the product in the 2012 and 2013 releases. However, Microsoft has begun a significant push to give you the ability to report against more current data by introducing Work Item Charting, which allows you to visualize the results of your work item queries. They are continually improving the feature set of Team Foundation Server through roughly quarterly updates. Work Item Charting will continue to be improved in these updates.

For customers who are upgrading from Team Foundation Server 2010, this news will bring some comfort. There were almost zero schema changes to the relational warehouse database and the Analysis Services cube, which means all your custom reports and dashboards should continue to work without modification. Contrast this to upgrading from the 2008 version to the 2010 version where the entire structure changed and almost all reports needed to be rewritten from scratch.

Following are the biggest changes for reporting and SharePoint integration since Team Foundation Server 2008:

➤ Work Item Charting has been added to Web Access.

➤ Cross-collection reporting is now supported.

➤ A relational warehouse schema is now supported.

➤ The Analysis Services cube schema is more usable.

➤ An optional, but richer, SharePoint integration is now supported.

➤ Excel-based reporting features have been added.

Work Item Charting in Web Access

Work Item Charting is a new feature in Team Foundation Server 2013 that allows you to visualize the results of work item queries in a myriad of formats including pie, bar, column, and stacked bar charts, as well as showing the data in a Pivot table format. Figure 15-1 shows the results of the My Work Items query in each of these formats on a single dashboard.

The Work Item Charting capabilities are included in the on-premises version of Team Foundation Server as well as Visual Studio Online. To create a chart, open the Team Foundation Server Web Access portal and navigate to your team's home page. Click on the View queries link in the Activities section. As you can see in Figure 15-2, there is an All Bugs query that returns all of the Bug work items for the Mobile System team.

Looking just below the All Bugs query results title, you can see three links, the standard Results and Editor links and the new Charts link. Clicking the Charts link brings up the Charts page for the All Bugs query, as shown in Figure 15-3. Each query now has its own page for charts of the results of that query. Each page can hold multiple charts and is visible to the entire team.

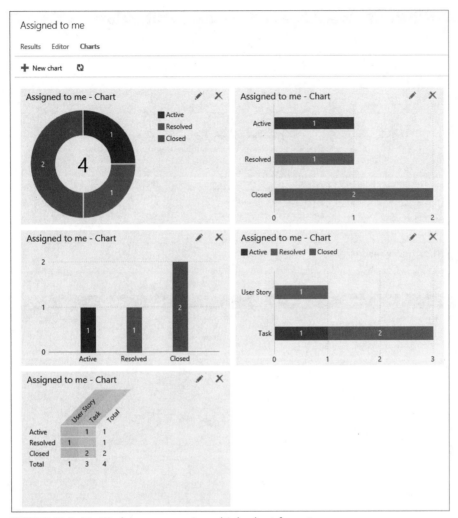

FIGURE 15-1: My Work Items query in multiple chart formats

To create a new chart for this query, simply click the New chart link in the toolbar. This will bring up the Configure Chart dialog box, as shown in Figure 15-4. We have filled in the values in Figure 15-4 to create a pie chart that shows the query results by Assigned To field value. We have renamed the chart to All Bugs By Assignment. Notice that the Configure Chart dialog box shows an example of the chart that changes as we change the criteria.

When the chart has been configured, you can click OK and the chart will be saved to the Charts page for the All Bugs query, as shown in Figure 15-5. It will now update as the underlying query results change.

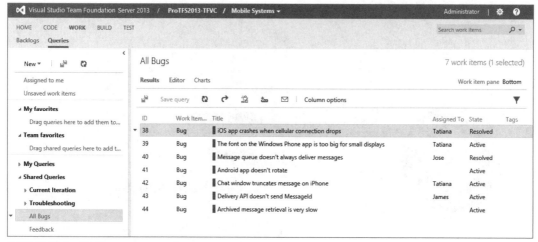

FIGURE 15-2: All Bugs query results

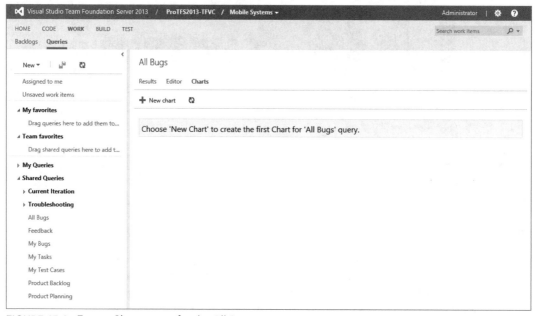

FIGURE 15-3: Empty Charts page for the All Bugs query

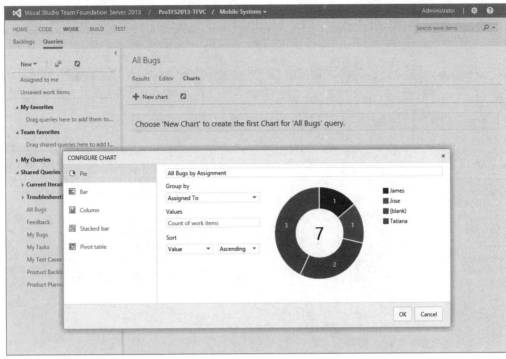

FIGURE 15-4: Configure Chart dialog box

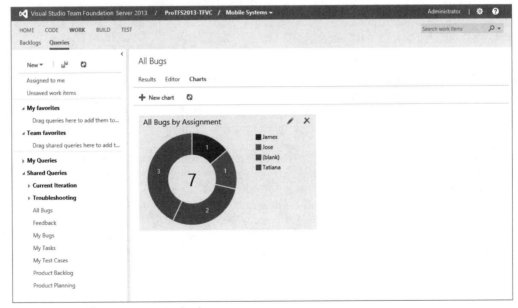

FIGURE 15-5: All Bugs query single chart

The Charts page can hold multiple views of your data. We have created two additional charts for the All Bugs query, as shown in Figure 15-6. If you need to change the criteria for a chart, you can simply click the pencil icon on that chart to open the Configure Chart dialog box.

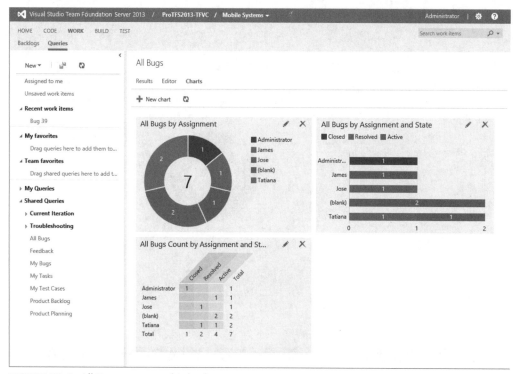

FIGURE 15-6: All Bugs query multiple charts

Different queries will provide different fields to Group By. For example, my All Bugs Query's pie chart could only Group Work Item Type, Assigned To, and State, whereas the Assigned To Me query has the ability to be grouped by Work Item Type, State, Area Path, and Iteration Path. The fields available are dependent on the types of work items returned in the query results.

> **NOTE** *This section has shown the charting functionality in Team Foundation Server 2013 RTM. As of this writing, Visual Studio Online has already provided the ability to Pin charts to the team home page. This feature will be provided to on-premises Team Foundation Server installation in one of the Team Foundation Server 2013 Updates.*

Cross-Collection Reporting Support

Team Foundation Server 2008 allowed a single relational warehouse and cube per server. Ironically, organizations that were large enough to need multiple Team Foundation Servers were the same organizations that most needed aggregated reporting across their entire organizations.

Team Foundation Server 2010 allowed organizations like this to consolidate their multiple, separate servers into a single logical server. Now that they have a single logical server, they also have a single data warehouse across which they can do reporting.

Team project names are unique within a team project collection. Because of this, the data warehouse schema was modified to support a hierarchy of collections and projects.

None of the reports included with the out-of-box process templates are configured for cross-project or cross-collection reporting. However, it is possible to modify the Team Project filter on the reports to select multiple projects.

Changes to the Relational Warehouse

Before Team Foundation Server 2010, customer feedback reflected that the latency for reporting from the cube was too high. Customers wanted their work-item updates to be available in reports almost immediately.

A common example was a daily stand-up meeting, whereby the team would be looking at the Remaining Work report and question why the report showed that an individual or team hadn't made any progress. Often, it turned out that they had, in fact, updated their work items, but those updates hadn't been processed in the cube before the report was rendered.

> **NOTE** *One of the useful features that arrived in Team Foundation Server 2012 was the task boards. At the top of each task board page is a miniature burndown chart, updated automatically every time you update any work item in the current iteration. This is also true for the velocity graph at the top of the product backlog screen and the capacity graph at the right of the sprint backlog screen.*
>
> *Because this graph is not using the data warehouse functionality, it is always up to date and does not incur any delays in updating. This makes it an ideal candidate for pasting into, say, a project status e-mail.*
>
> *For more information, see Chapter 14.*

Until the 2010 release, reporting against the relational warehouse was not supported. Since the 2010 release, that is no longer the case. There are now several views on top of the warehouse to support reporting. These views make it easier to query for data and keep compatibility with future versions. Additionally, the naming conventions have been standardized to help differentiate fact tables and dimension tables. For example, `dbo.Work Item` is now called `dbo.DimWorkItem`, which identifies it as a dimension table.

> **NOTE** *A more detailed discussion about fact tables and dimensions is provided later in this chapter.*

Along with supporting queries against the relational warehouse, the work-item tracking warehouse adapters were updated for improved performance. The new adapters are now capable of moving data from the operational store to the relational warehouse much faster than in previous releases. The goal for the adapters was to keep the latency for work-item tracking less than five minutes during normal operations.

In the 2012 release, the only schema changes to the relational warehouse were:

➤   The addition of the Start Date and End Date to the iterations

➤   The removal of some of the fields that were used internally in the 2010 release for configuration of the warehouse

Changes to the Analysis Services Cube

Although the cube in Team Foundation Server 2005 and 2008 provided useful data and was reasonably well-used by customers, there was room for improvement. Along with supporting the architecture improvements, the changes in Team Foundation Server 2010 improved usability, query performance, and processing performance.

The main changes to the cube schema starting with Team Foundation Server 2010 include the following:

➤   The `Current Work Item` and `Work Item History` measure groups were combined into the `Work Item` measure group. Now you just include the `Date` measure to show historical trends.

➤   Area and iteration dimensions have been folded into the `Work Item` dimension as true hierarchies.

➤   Some dimension names have been updated to make them more meaningful and provide context, especially when looking at the entire list. For example, `Platform` is now `Build Platform`.

➤   Dimensions starting with `Related` have been moved to the `Linked Work Item` dimension.

A more detailed discussion of measures is presented later in this chapter.

The main additions to the cube schema starting with Team Foundation Server 2010 include the following:

➤   Work-item hierarchy and linking are now supported in the cube through the `Linked Work Item` and `Work Item Tree` dimensions.

➤   Work-item types can now be grouped into categories. For example, the Bug category can group Bug and Defect work-item types together. This is useful if you have different terminology across your team projects and need a meaningful report across all of them.

➤ Area Path and Iteration Path are now available as attributes on the Work Item dimension. This allows you to show a flat string (rather than a hierarchy) on your reports.

➤ As shown in Figure 15-7, display folders have been added to the Work Item dimension to make it easier to group fields, rather than display one long list.

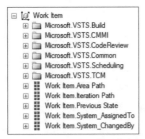

FIGURE 15-7: Display folders on the Work Item dimension

> **NOTE** *For more information on the data warehouse changes and the reasons behind them, refer to John Socha-Leialoha's three-part blog post titled "Upgrading Team Foundation Server 2008 Reports to 2010" (Part I at* http://aka.ms/UpgradeTfsReports1; *Part II at* http://aka.ms/UpgradeTfsReports2; *and Part III at* http://aka.ms/UpgradeTfsReports3). *Also see the official MSDN documentation, "Changes and Additions to the Schema for the Analysis Services Cube," at* http://aka.ms/TfsCubeChanges.

Optional and Richer SharePoint Integration

Integration with SharePoint is an important feature for Team Foundation Server. However, the installation and configuration of the integration was a significant source of problems. Along with the other architectural changes designed to support different server topologies, SharePoint integration is optional.

If you want to use the SharePoint integration features, you can configure SharePoint at install time or at a later time. The configuration options are designed to be flexible.

Team Foundation Server 2013 integration is available with both SharePoint 2010 and SharePoint 2013.

> **WARNING** *The reporting and SharePoint integration features are not available when Team Foundation Server is configured in the Basic configuration, when Team Foundation Server Express is used, or when installed on a client operating system (such as Windows 8). If you have any of these configurations and would like to enable the reporting features, you must use a Standard or Advanced configuration on a server operating system.*

TEAM FOUNDATION SERVER DATA WAREHOUSE

The Team Foundation Server reporting and data warehouse features comprise three data stores, as shown in Table 15-1.

TABLE 15-1: Team Foundation Server Reporting Data Stores

DATA STORE	DATABASE NAMES	CHARACTERISTICS
Operational	Tfs_Configuration, Tfs_Collection	Normalized, optimized for retrieving the most recent data, and transactional
Relational warehouse database	Tfs_Warehouse	Has a star schema, and includes all historical data designed to be used for analysis
Analysis Services cube	Tfs_Analysis	Data is preaggregated, preindexed, and includes advanced analysis features.

Along with these three data stores is a set of scheduled jobs that move data between the stores:

➤ Warehouse adapter jobs (sometimes called *sync jobs*) periodically copy changes from the operational store to the relational database.

➤ Analysis processing jobs instruct the cube to begin either an incremental or full process.

Figure 15-8 shows a high-level representation of this data movement and processing.

FIGURE 15-8: High-level architecture of the Team Foundation Server data warehouse

Operational Stores

The operational stores in Team Foundation Server are nothing more than the databases that support the normal day-to-day operations of the server. In previous versions of Team Foundation Server, there were different databases for the different feature areas (for example, the `TfsWorkItemTracking` and `TfsVersionControl` databases). In Team Foundation Server 2010, the contents of these databases were merged into a single `Tfs_Collection` database for each team project collection.

The schema of these databases is optimized for Team Foundation Server commands, rather than reporting. The data in these databases is changing all the time and does not lend itself to historical reporting and analysis.

The operational stores should not be accessed directly. The only supported interface for accessing them is through the Team Foundation Server object model.

Relational Warehouse Database and Warehouse Adapters

Each component in Team Foundation Server has different requirements for storing data in the relational warehouse database. The warehouse adapters for each operational store are responsible for transferring data to the data warehouse for their store.

Although the warehouse adapters are set to run on a schedule, they are also triggered and run on-demand when data changes. This keeps the latency in the relational warehouse low.

The warehouse adapters are also responsible for making schema changes in the relational warehouse and cube. For example, when you add a new field to a work-item type and mark it as reportable, the warehouse adapter will perform a schema change and add a new column to the relational warehouse, as well as make changes to the cube definition.

The dynamic nature of these data adapters allows the structure and mechanics of the data warehouse to be hidden from project administrators. This is one of the unique benefits of reporting in Team Foundation Server. You can define your work item types in a single place using relatively straightforward schema and tools. You then automatically get access to rich reporting features based on these customizations. You never have to deal with database schema changes or updating cube structures.

The downside of this, however, is that if you want to make customizations to either the relational warehouse or cube, you must deploy them as a custom warehouse adapter. If you don't, your customizations will be lost when the warehouse is rebuilt.

The relational warehouse database stores data in a set of tables organized in a star schema. The central table of the star schema is called the *fact table*, and the related tables represent *dimensions*. For example, the dbo.FactCurrentWorkItem table has one row for every work item stored in the work-item tracking operational store. A dimension table stores the set of values that exist for a given dimension. For example, a Person dimension is referenced by the Work Items fact table for the Assigned To and Closed By properties. You'll learn more about fact tables and dimensions later in this chapter.

Querying the Relational Warehouse Database

In Team Foundation Server 2010, writing reports against the relational warehouse database using Transact-SQL (TSQL) queries became officially supported. As a rule of thumb, you'll generally want to use the cube for historical reports, or reports that require a lot of slicing and dicing using parameters or aggregate data. The cube is preaggregated and indexed, and is ideal for this sort of reporting.

The relational warehouse, on the other hand, allows you to create reports that pull loosely related data together in ways not possible with the cube.

Following are the nine views against which you can query and write reports with some level of assurance that they will work when the server is upgraded to a future version of Team Foundation Server:

➤   CurrentWorkItemView

➤   WorkItemHistoryView

➤   BuildChangesetView

➤   BuildCoverageView

➤   BuildDetailsView

➤   BuildProjectView

➤   CodeChurnView

➤   RunCoverageView

➤   TestResultView

The other views that begin with v and end with Overlay are used for processing the cube, and, as such, aren't meant for use in your own reports.

The relational warehouse is an ideal store to use if you require reports with a lower latency than the cube can provide.

> **NOTE** *As with previous versions of Team Foundation Server, fields that have the* Html *data type are not stored in the relational warehouse. Therefore, they are not available in the cube. For reporting against those fields, you must use the Work Item Tracking object model to query and retrieve them.*

Querying the Current Work-Item View

Using the CurrentWorkItemView, you can query the relational warehouse and retrieve a list of work items without using the Work Item Tracking object model. For example, following is a work item query (WIQ) that returns all non-closed bugs assigned to John Smith in the Contoso project:

```
SELECT
[System.Id],
[Microsoft.VSTS.Common.StackRank],
[Microsoft.VSTS.Common.Priority],
[Microsoft.VSTS.Common.Severity],
[System.State], [System.Title]
FROM WorkItems
WHERE [System.TeamProject] = 'Contoso'
AND   [System.AssignedTo] = 'John Smith'
AND   [System.WorkItemType] = 'Bug'
AND   [System.State] <> 'Closed'
ORDER BY
[System.State],
[Microsoft.VSTS.Common.StackRank],
[Microsoft.VSTS.Common.Priority],
[Microsoft.VSTS.Common.Severity],
[System.Id]
```

And here's an equivalent query that retrieves the same data from the relational warehouse:

```
SELECT
[System_Id],
[Microsoft_VSTS_Common_StackRank],
[Microsoft_VSTS_Common_Priority],
```

```
[Microsoft_VSTS_Common_Severity],
[System_State],
[System_Title]
FROM CurrentWorkItemView
WHERE
[ProjectPath] = '\ContosoCollection\Contoso'
AND [System_AssignedTo] = 'John Smith'
AND [System_WorkItemType] = 'Bug'
AND [System_State] <> 'Closed'
ORDER BY
[System_State],
[Microsoft_VSTS_Common_StackRank],
[Microsoft_VSTS_Common_Priority],
[Microsoft_VSTS_Common_Severity],
[System_Id]
```

DYNAMICALLY RETRIEVING THE WEB ACCESS ADDRESS

One of the things that people want to do is provide a hyperlink from a work item in a report to the Web Access view of that work item. This is useful, because it allows others to interact with the work item without needing Visual Studio installed.

To be able to create the hyperlink, you need to know the address of the server. Additionally, instead of surfacing the URL as a report parameter, or hardcoding it, it is ideal to somehow retrieve it from the database. But how, you might ask?

From within a SQL query of the relational data warehouse, this can appear to be difficult at first. However, with the `ToolArtifactDisplayUrl` field in the `DimToolArtifactDisplayUrl` table, you can easily find it.

The following SQL query essentially takes the first artifact display URL and retrieves the first half of the string before `/CollectionName/WorkItemTracking/WorkItem.aspx?artifactMoniker=`. This means that it will continue to work regardless of whether the server is configured with a virtual directory (`/tfs/`) or not, as well as HTTPS, custom port numbers, and so on.

```
SELECT TOP 1
  SUBSTRING(
    ToolArtifactDisplayUrl,
    0,
    PATINDEX(
      '%/' + ProjectNodeName + '%',
      ToolArtifactDisplayUrl
    )
  + 1
) + 'web/' as WebAccesBaseUrl
FROM    DimToolArtifactDisplayUrl
INNER JOIN DimTeamProject tp
ON
tp.ParentNodeSK = DimToolArtifactDisplayUrl.TeamProjectCollectionSK
WHERE   ToolType = 'WorkItemTracking/Workitem'
AND ProjectNodeTypeName = 'Team Project Collection'
```

Querying the Work-Item History View

You can construct an "as of" query that returns only the last records for each work item that was modified before a certain date. For example, the following "as of" query returns the remaining work as of the end of December 2011:

```
SELECT System_Id, Microsoft_VSTS_Scheduling_RemainingWork
FROM WorkItemHistoryView WHERE System_ChangedDate < '1/1/2012'
AND System_RevisedDate >= '1/1/2012'
AND RecordCount > 0
AND ProjectPath = '\ContosoCollection\Contoso'
```

Other Considerations for Querying the Relational Warehouse

The relational warehouse is not suitable for all queries and, therefore, some will be faster using the Work Item Tracking object model that uses the operational store. Team Foundation Server 2010 introduced multiple project collections, and these collections share the same relational warehouse and cube.

The following are important considerations to keep in mind when writing queries against the views:

➤ Use `ProjectPath` or `ProjectNodeGUID` as the filter. A team project's name is not necessarily unique across multiple collections on the same logical server, whereas the project's path is fully qualified with the collection name and a project's GUID is also unique.

➤ Use unique keys for joins. For example, a work item ID is no longer guaranteed to be unique within the warehouse, because the same work item ID could exist in different team project collections.

➤ Be aware of compensating records. Whenever a work item is updated, a pair of records is added to the warehouse. The first record negates the previous record. This makes querying the relational warehouse faster for some types of queries.

> **NOTE** *For more information on compensating records, see "Compensating Records" on MSDN at* http://aka.ms/TfsCompensatingRecords, *and "Work Item Tracking Compensating Records" at* http://aka.ms/TfsCompensatingBlog.

Analysis Services Cube

The fact tables in the relational warehouse are suitable for reporting on current information. However, reporting on historical trends of data over time requires duplicating the data for every time interval that you want to report on.

Each time the cube is processed, the relational warehouse data is aggregated, summarized, and stored. The cube is a single central store to report against without having to aggregate across the different operational stores.

The cube contains *dimensions*, *facts*, *attributes*, and *measures*. Table 15-2 and Figure 15-9 show the definitions and the relationships of these items, respectively.

TABLE 15-2: Cube Terminology

TERM	DESCRIPTION
Dimension	Dimensions enable the data to be sliced in many ways. Data values are associated with a set of dimensions, allowing you to show aggregate results sliced using a specific set of dimension values.
Fact	Facts are data that can be associated with multiple dimensions. This data may also be aggregated. Fact tables hold these values.
Attribute	Under each dimension, you'll find a set of attributes, and possibly hierarchies (areas and iterations are hierarchies). Each attribute is connected to a column in the corresponding dimension table in the relational warehouse.
Measure	Measures are values that correspond to columns in the corresponding fact table.

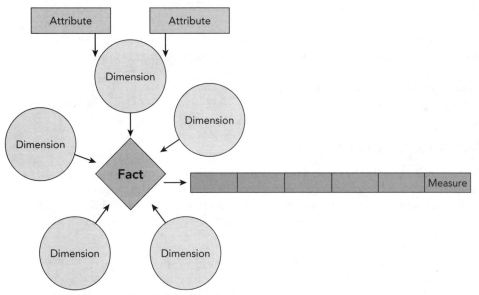

FIGURE 15-9: Relationships of objects in the cube

> **NOTE** *For more information, see "Perspectives and Measure Groups Provided in the Analysis Services Cube" on MSDN at* http://aka.ms/Tfs2013Cube.

Cube Perspectives

In the cube, *perspectives* are groups of related dimensions and measure groups. A perspective is a subset of the features and objects of a cube. They are useful because you don't have to scroll through the whole *Team System* cube to get to where you need to be.

Perspectives are available only when you are using the Enterprise edition of SQL Server Analysis Services. A license for only the Standard edition is included with Team Foundation Server, so you'll need to license the other edition separately if you want to use cube perspectives.

Cube Processing

The Analysis Services cube is processed periodically on a schedule. The processing is triggered by two built-in Team Foundation Server jobs that correspond to the two different processing types:

➤ **Full Process**—Re-creates the cube from its definition, and processes every object in the cube. The default processing interval is every day at 2 a.m. for a full process.

➤ **Incremental Process**—Processes only objects that have changes since the last full or incremental process. The default processing interval is every two hours for an incremental process.

If the previous cube process failed, or the cube schema has changed, the next process is upgraded from an incremental process to a full process.

> **NOTE** *If you would like to change the processing interval, see the article "Change a Process Control Setting for the Data Warehouse or Analysis Services Cube" on MSDN at* `http://aka.ms/Tfs2013CubeConfig`.

Data Warehouse Permissions

Users within Team Foundation Server are not automatically granted access to the relational warehouse or cube. They must be explicitly granted access. The reason for this is that there are no fine-grained permissions provided or security trimming performed in the warehouse. When users have permission to view the warehouse, they have full access to the warehouse data for all team projects in all team project collections.

In some organizations, it is perfectly acceptable to allow any individual with work-item access in a particular project to have access to the whole data warehouse. However, in other more regulated industries and organizations, these permissions are reserved for a smaller subset of users.

To grant access, the `TfsWarehouseDataReader` role exists in both the `Tfs_Warehouse` relational database and the `Tfs_Analysis` cube. Users and groups can be added to these roles to allow them access to the resources.

> **NOTE** *For more information, see the article "Grant Access to the Databases of the Data Warehouse for Visual Studio ALM" at* `http://aka.ms/Tfs2013CubeAccess`.

SHAREPOINT INTEGRATION

Once you have the standard reporting features working correctly, you can optionally configure integration with SharePoint. SharePoint integration is comprised of the following parts:

➤ Team Foundation Server Extensions for SharePoint

➤ Excel Services and dashboard compatibility

SharePoint Extensions

In order for a team project to have SharePoint integration, Team Foundation Server must have an association with a SharePoint web application. In order for this association to be configured, the SharePoint server must have the Team Foundation Server Extensions for SharePoint Products installed and configured.

There is no requirement that SharePoint be installed on the same server as Team Foundation Server, or even managed by the same people. Many organizations already have an existing SharePoint farm, and Team Foundation Server can integrate with the farm, as long as the Extensions are installed and configured.

The Extensions include site templates, web parts, and SharePoint timer jobs that maintain the associations between team projects and project portals, among other things.

> **NOTE** *For more information, see "Extensions for SharePoint Products" at* `http://aka.ms/TFS2013SPExt`.

Excel Services and Dashboard Compatibility

Excel Services is a feature of the Enterprise edition of SharePoint. It allows an Excel workbook to be rendered on the SharePoint server and presented to the user as a web page. This is incredibly useful because of the following:

➤ For report producers, pivot tables and pivot charts can easily be created in Excel.

➤ For report consumers, no extra software is required. The reports are simply web pages.

> **NOTE** *For detailed instructions on manually integrating Team Foundation Server and SharePoint, you should consult some articles on MSDN. See "How to: Set up remote SharePoint Products Team Foundation Server" at* `http://aka.ms/TFS2013SetupSP`, *and "Configure Team Foundation Server Extensions for SharePoint Products" at* `http://aka.ms/TFS2013SPExt`.

Adding a Project Portal and Reports to an Existing Team Project

For a number of reasons, you might not have a project portal or reports associated with your team project, such as in the following scenarios:

➤ The server or team project collection may not have had reporting or SharePoint integration configured when the team project was created.

➤ The process template used to create the team project may not have included the reporting or SharePoint tasks.

➤ Creating a SharePoint site might have been skipped during the project creation wizard.

➤ The connection between the team project and project portal may have been removed, or been invalid, before an upgrade.

During a TFS 2005/2008 to 2013 upgrade, the TFS installation was first upgraded to TFS 2010 before upgrading to TFS 2013. If the 2005 or 2008 server was imported to 2010 rather than upgraded, the project portal and reporting settings would have been lost.

Fortunately, with the help of the Team Foundation Server Power Tools, it's easy enough to add either a project portal or the default reports from a process template after the fact. From a Visual Studio command prompt, you can use the following commands:

➤ `tfpt addprojectportal`—Create a project portal for an existing team project that doesn't currently have one.

➤ `tfpt addprojectreports`—Create (or overwrite) the reports for an existing team project.

Additionally, you can use Visual Studio and navigate to the Team menu bar, `Team Project Settings`, and then `Portal Settings` to modify the association of a team project with a SharePoint site at any time, as shown in Figure 15-10.

CREATING REPORTS

Reporting is a powerful feature in Team Foundation Server. It breaks down the usual barrier within teams that is often caused by a lack of information. Team Foundation Server provides a powerful set of reports in the box, and provides the capability to add additional reports based on your needs.

Tools

Because reporting in Team Foundation Server is based upon SQL Server, any tool that can produce reports from SQL Server can be used. Following are the main tools that Team Foundation Server is designed to work with:

➤ Excel for pivot tables, pivot charts, and dashboards

➤ SQL Server Report Builder

➤ SQL Server Business Intelligence Development Studio (BIDS)

➤ SQL Server Data Tools

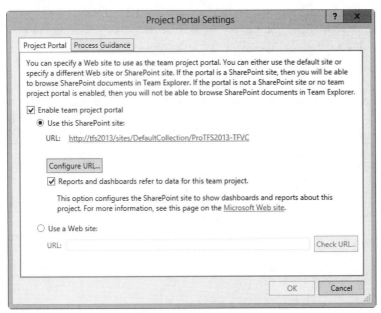

FIGURE 15-10: Portal Settings dialog box

Each of these tools has different capabilities, as well as an associated learning curve. Figure 15-11 shows this comparison.

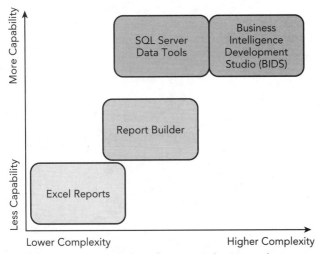

FIGURE 15-11: Comparison of report authoring tools

Excel Reporting from a Work-Item Query

Creating reports with Excel has the lowest barrier to entry. It's powerful enough for most purposes, and leverages a tool that most people are already familiar with. Perhaps the most impressive new reporting feature, originally introduced in Team Foundation Server 2010, is the capability to create reports from work item queries.

Although many people working with previous versions of the product used Excel to create reports based on the cube, it was still not approachable for many. You first had to be given access to the cube, be told the server name, and then wade through all the dimensions to find the ones you wanted in your report.

Starting with Team Foundation Server 2010, you can go from a Work Item Query to a pivot chart report in as little as two steps. No special knowledge is required. To do this, open Team Explorer, select the `Work Items` link, and start by expanding either the `Shared Queries` or `My Queries` folder. Then, right-click one of the queries and select Create Report in Microsoft Excel, as shown in Figure 15-12.

FIGURE 15-12: Selecting the Create Report in Microsoft Excel option

The first thing that happens is that Excel translates the Work Item Query into a query for the Analysis Services cube. After that, it presents a New Work Item Report dialog box, as shown in Figure 15-13. From this dialog box, you select which fields that you would like to pivot by, as well as the type of reports to generate.

> **WARNING** *Sometimes translating the Work Item Query can take longer than expected. The more columns that you have in your query, the longer the translation will take. It's a good idea to have only the columns that you want to pivot on in your query before you try generating a report.*

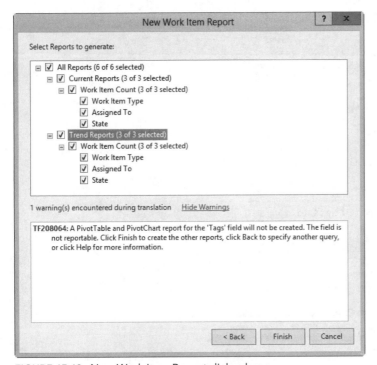

FIGURE 15-13: New Work Item Report dialog box

There are two different types of reports:

➤ **Current reports**—These reports show the current state of the work items, represented as pie charts, as shown in Figure 15-14.

➤ **Trend reports**—These reports show the historical trend of the work items, represented as area charts, as shown in Figure 15-15.

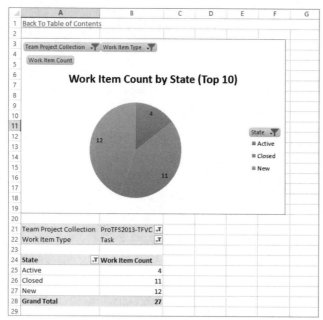

FIGURE 15-14: Current Report pivoted by State

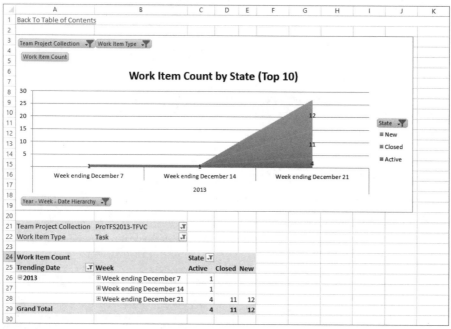

FIGURE 15-15: Trend Report pivoted by State

Once the reports are generated, you have a workbook prepopulated with the Analysis Services database connection. You can further filter and customize the automatically generated reports, or create entirely new reports.

> **NOTE** *For more information, see "Creating Reports in Microsoft Excel by Using Work Item Queries" at* http://aka.ms/Tfs2013ExcelReports.

SQL Server Reporting Services Reports

SQL Server Reporting Services provides a powerful reporting platform. Along with allowing you to run rich reports, Reporting Services also provides the following features:

➤ **Subscriptions**—Reports can be executed on a regular schedule, and the results can be e-mailed to the team (for example, a weekly progress report).

➤ **Data-driven subscriptions**—Reports can be executed and the parameters or delivery schedule can be dynamically changed based upon the results of a database query. For example, you could send a daily e-mail to team members who have high-priority bugs open.

➤ **Caching and snapshots**—If a report is particularly complex, or is refreshed regularly, you can configure caching and snapshots to improve performance.

➤ **Linked reports**—By using linked reports, you can create multiple reports with different parameters off a single base report (for example, a remaining work report with different area and iteration parameters for different teams within a project).

These Reporting Services reports are also the most accessible. For example, they are available from the following:

➤ Directly from the Report Manager website

➤ Integrated in Visual Studio Team Explorer

➤ As web parts on the SharePoint project portal

Permissions

Before you can access SQL Server Report Builder from the Report Manager website, you must be granted the appropriate permission. In addition to this permission, if you want to publish your report for others to use, you will need that permission as well. The `Team Foundation Content Manager` role is created as part of the Team Foundation Server configuration and includes both of these permissions.

> **NOTE** *For more information, see "SQL Server Reporting Services Roles" at* http://aka.ms/Tfs2013SSRSRoles.

SQL Server Report Builder

Report Builder provides a Microsoft Office–like report authoring environment. Using the tool, you can create and edit reports directly from the Reporting Services server.

You can download and install SQL Server 2012 Report Builder from `http://aka.ms/sql2012rb`. Once it is installed, you can access Report Builder from the Start menu under the `Microsoft SQL Server 2012 Report Builder 3.0` folder.

To build a simple report, open Report Builder and select the Chart wizard icon on the design surface. When the New Chart Wizard appears, click the Create a dataset radio button and then click Next. Then, on the Data Source Connections screen, select Browse. When the Select Data Source screen appears, select the `Tfs2010OlapReportDS` shared data source from your Reporting Services Server, as shown in Figure 15-16. Continue through the wizard. When prompted for Data Source credentials, select Use the current Windows user.

FIGURE 15-16: Select Data Source screen

On the Design a query screen shown in Figure 15-17, drag the `Work Item.Area Path` dimension attribute and the `Work Item Count` measure onto the query pane and click Next.

On the Choose a chart type screen, select a Column or Bar chart and click Next. On the Arrange chart fields screen shown in Figure 15-18, drag `Area_Path` from the available fields list to the Categories list. Then drag `Work_Item_Count` to the Values list and click Next.

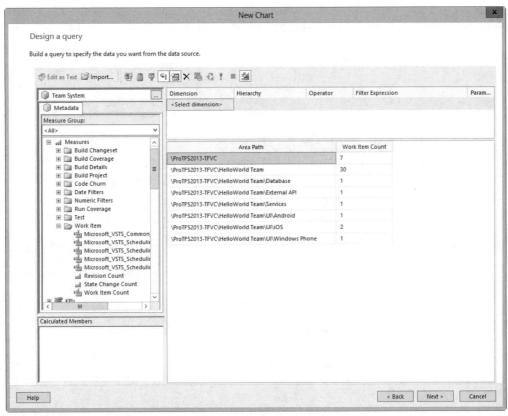

FIGURE 15-17: Design a query screen

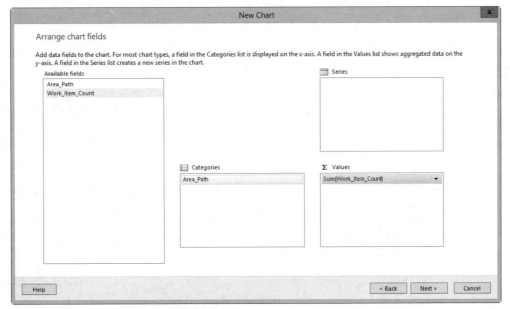

FIGURE 15-18: The Arrange chart fields screen

Select a chart style and, when the wizard completes, select Run from the Ribbon (or press F5). The report should be rendered, and you should see something similar to Figure 15-19.

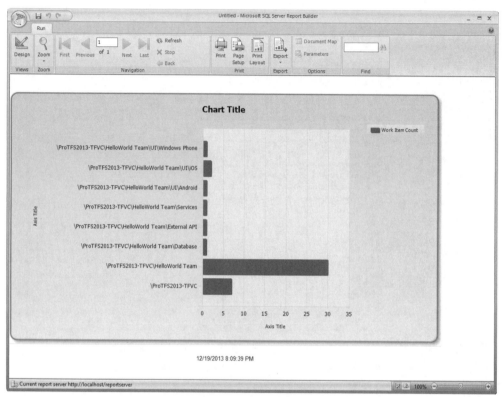

FIGURE 15-19: Example report created with Report Builder

When you are finished with your report, you can save it to your Reporting Services server and share it with other team members.

> **NOTE** *For more information, see "Getting Started with Report Builder" at* `http://aka.ms/RBGettingStarted`.

> **NOTE** *Both SQL Server 2008 R2 and SQL Server 2012 include Report Builder 3.0. This version includes new wizards and many other improvements over the previous versions that make it a compelling choice for report authors.*

SQL Server Business Intelligence Development Studio and SQL Server Data Tools

SQL Server provides an integrated environment for developing cubes, data sources, and reports. This tool has a different name depending on the version of SQL Server you have installed. In SQL Server 2008 and 2008 R2, this tool is called Business Intelligence Development Studio (BIDS). In SQL Server 2012, this tool is called SQL Server Data Tools (SSDT). To install BIDS, run the Setup program for SQL Server 2008 or 2008 R2 and select the Client Components check box when you specify the components to install. In SQL Server 2012, you will select SQL Server Data Tools instead. Because BIDS and SSDT are add-ins to Visual Studio, they will install the Visual Studio shell if you don't already have it installed. BIDS and SSDT are usually installed with an older-than-current Visual Studio Shell, so BIDS 2008 R2 runs inside Visual Studio Shell 2008, and SSDT 2012 runs inside the Visual Studio 2010 shell. These tools can be installed side by side on a computer with newer versions of Visual Studio.

If you need to create complex and rich reports like the ones that are included with the product, you should refer to the white paper by John Socha-Leialoha. The paper is called "Creating Reports for Team Foundation Server 2010," and it's available at `http://aka.ms/Tfs2010Reports`.

SETTING DEFAULT REPORT PARAMETERS WITH LINKED REPORTS

The reports that are included in the Scrum, Agile, CMMI process templates are very powerful while, at the same time, very generic. (These process templates are examined in more detail in Chapter 12.)

For them to be generic, a lot of their behavior is driven through parameters. For example, there are parameters for areas, iterations, and work-item types. Without any customization, each time users open the report, they must select the correct parameters before the report is meaningful to them.

If you have multiple teams using a team project, and they are using different area paths to keep their work items separate, the default parameter settings of the reports can be frustrating. Even if you're the only team working in a team project, you might want quick access to reports with preconfigured iteration parameters.

With the use of linked reports, you can predefine a set of parameters for a report and have it appear as a new report without creating an actual copy of the original report.

For more information, see the following blog posts:

➤ "Customizing Report Parameters—Cube Reports" at `http://aka.ms/TfsReportParams1`

➤ "Customizing Report Parameters—SQL Reports" at `http://aka.ms/TfsReportParams2`

SharePoint Dashboards

SharePoint dashboards are a feature made possible through the integration between Team Foundation Server 2013 and SharePoint 2010 or 2013. Each dashboard is made up of three different types of web parts:

➤ **Team Foundation Server web parts**—These access the operational store, and show the current data in the system. They are interactive and can be used to update work items.

➤ **Page Viewer web parts**—These display SQL Server Reporting Services reports. They pass through parameters and cache results.

➤ **Excel Services web parts**—These render charts from Excel workbooks stored in a SharePoint document library. They use the Single Sign-On (SSO) or Secure Store Service (SSS) to authenticate to the cube server.

When Team Foundation Server is integrated with the Enterprise edition of SharePoint (which includes Excel Services), the dashboards will display Excel Services web parts. For servers that don't have Excel Services available, the dashboards will use Page Viewer web parts and display Reporting Services reports.

Both the Agile and the CMMI process templates come with the following dashboards. However, only the first two dashboards are available on a server without Excel Services:

➤ **My Dashboard**—Quickly access work items assigned to you.

➤ **Project Dashboard**—Review progress with the team. Shows the Task Burn Down and Burn Rate reports.

➤ **Progress Dashboard**—Track progress toward completing an iteration.

➤ **Bugs Dashboard**—Monitor bug activity.

➤ **Build Dashboard**—Monitor code coverage, code churn, and build activity.

➤ **Quality Dashboard**—Troubleshoot software quality issues with the team.

➤ **Test Dashboard**—Monitor test progress and find gaps in test coverage.

> **NOTE** *For more information, including detailed descriptions and samples of each of the dashboards, see "Dashboards (Agile)" at* `http://aka.ms/Tfs2013AgileDash` *and "Dashboards (CMMI)" at* `http://aka.ms/Tfs2013CMMIDash`.

Accessing Dashboards

The easiest way to access dashboards for a team project is to select the Documents link in Team Explorer, and then select the Show Project Portal link, as shown in Figure 15-20. This will then open the default web browser and navigate to the SharePoint site associated with that team project.

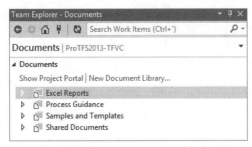

FIGURE 15-20: Show Project Portal link in Team Explorer

If there is no project portal associated with the team project, then the documents link will not be available on the home screen.

Customizing a Dashboard

The default dashboards have no filters applied and, therefore, the first customization you'll want to make is to scope them to the area and iteration that your team is currently using.

To create a customized dashboard for your team, follow these steps:

1. Browse to an existing dashboard on your project portal site.

2. Select the Copy Dashboard button in the site toolbar, as shown in Figure 15-21.

FIGURE 15-21: Toolbar showing Copy Dashboard button

3. On the Copy Dashboard Page screen shown in Figure 15-22, enter a Dashboard File Name and Title for the new dashboard. Then, click the Copy Dashboard button.

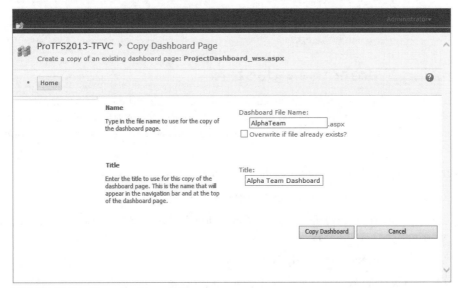

FIGURE 15-22: Copy Dashboard Page screen

Now you can modify the web parts on the dashboard to show details specific to your team.

ADVANCED CUSTOMIZATION

A few advanced customization topics to briefly look at include:

➤   Customizing project portals

➤   Customizing warehouse adapters

➤   `TfsRedirect.aspx`

Customizing Project Portals

Project portals are designed to be customized to the team or the organization's needs. Beyond the simple customization available within SharePoint, you can modify the process template to change project portals created in the future. Following are a few scenarios that you might want to do this for:

➤   Your organization has an existing SharePoint site template, and you want to modify it to include the Team Foundation Server dashboards.

➤   You want to modify the existing Team Foundation Server site templates to include your customizations for future project portals.

➤   You want to change the visual appearance of the portal site.

> **NOTE** *For more information, refer to the white paper, "Customizing Team Foundation Server Project Portals," by Phil Hodgson at* `http://aka.ms/ TfsProjPortals`*.*

Customizing Warehouse Adapters

As discussed earlier, if you want to make customizations to either the relational warehouse or cube that are beyond simple field changes, you must deploy them as a custom warehouse adapter. If you don't deploy the changes as an adapter, your customizations will be lost when the warehouse is rebuilt.

A custom adapter must know how to do the following:

➤   Create the schema in the relational warehouse.

➤   Retrieve and transform data from the operational store, and load it into the relational warehouse.

➤   Create the schema in the analysis database.

➤   Create a warehouse adapter sync job and schedule it.

> **NOTE** *For more information, refer to the Team Foundation Server 2010 sample warehouse adapter from Nick Ericson in the MSDN Code Gallery at* `http://aka.ms/Tfs2010SampleAdapter`. *Even though it is for Team Foundation Server 2010, it will work with Team Foundation Server 2013 once you update the project references.*

TfsRedirect.aspx

If you look at the Link property for the Page Viewer web parts on the dashboards, you'll see that they're set to a value like the following:

```
/sites/DefaultCollection/FabrikamFiber/_layouts/TfsRedirect.aspx?tf:type=Report&tf:
    ReportName=Dashboards/Burndown&tf:ShowToolbar=0&Width=381pt&Height=180pt
```

`TfsRedirect.aspx` is a special piece of glue that helps SharePoint, Reporting Services, and Team Foundation Server work together. For example, several items on a project portal that point to other related resources are:

➤ Team Web Access

➤ Process Guidance

➤ Reports on the dashboard pages

Because these settings are stored only in Team Foundation Server and can be changed at any time, SharePoint uses the `TfsRedirect.aspx` page to retrieve them.

By specifying the `tf:Test` parameter, you can see the underlying settings, which may be useful in debugging project portal configuration problems. For any existing project portal, simply append the following to the site URL:

```
/_layouts/TfsRedirect.aspx?tf:type=ReportList&tf:Test=1&tf:clearcache=1
```

> **NOTE** *For more information, see "Using TfsRedirect to Display Reports in TFS 2010 Dashboards" at* `http://aka.ms/TfsRedirect`.

SUMMARY

In this chapter, you learned about the compelling new Work Item Charting features that were introduced in Team Foundation Server 2013. You also learned about the reporting features introduced in Team Foundation Server 2010, as well as the changes incorporated into the 2012 release. In addition, you learned about the various data stores in the system and how data flows between them.

This chapter covered the two main reporting technologies (Reporting Services and Excel Services), along with the tools to create and customize the reports. This chapter also described how to quickly and easily create a report from a simple Work Item Query. Finally, this chapter looked briefly at some advanced customization topics.

Chapter 16 takes a look at how you can integrate Team Foundation Server with Microsoft Project Server and receive up-to-date project status and resource availability reports across multiple teams.

16

Project Server Integration

WHAT'S IN THIS CHAPTER?

➤ Getting to know the benefits of Project Server for Software Development Teams

➤ Understanding scenarios where integration may be helpful

➤ Introduction to the key steps necessary to integrate Team Foundation Server and Project Server

➤ Review the necessary software to be installed on a project manager's machine

In some organizations, working with traditional project managers or project management offices (PMOs) is a fact of life for development and software engineering teams. Many of those software engineering teams wonder how they can better interact with project managers or PMOs without having to enter project tracking data twice or even worry about another system.

Project Server, and Project Client, which connects to it, have become popular tools of choice for those in the PMO community just as Team Foundation Server has been leveraged by software development teams. This chapter discusses the key parts of both products and how to begin integrating them for a better overall project planning and tracking experience.

OVERVIEW

Software development tasks may also be part of a larger project that contains activities and tasks outside software engineering work. Those tasks outside the software engineering process could have dependencies on software engineering milestones and deadlines. For example, after a software project is "done," it still needs to be deployed to an IT environment, users need to be trained, marketing updated, and so on. Teams could certainly track those non-software development tasks in Team Foundation Server, but it may not always be the appropriate solution depending on the project. This is a place where the integration between Project Server and Team Foundation Server really shines and gives you the best holistic approach for everyone involved.

There certainly are useful and innovative project management features in Team Foundation Server, including many of the purpose-built Agile planning tools for managing software releases. There are also really great tools and features built into Project Server that do not necessarily make sense to be implemented in Team Foundation Server. Finally, there is a middle ground of features common to both platforms. Integration provides the ability to utilize those features that are great in each toolset.

The integration between Team Foundation Server and Project Server was initially shipped in Service Pack 1 for Team Foundation Server 2010. It's now included natively in Team Foundation Server since the 2012 release and supports integration with Project Server 2010 with Service Pack 1, or Project Server 2013.

If you want to try this integration, a demo environment is available to download at `http://aka.ms/ProjectServerTFSIntegrationVM2012`, which includes a set of step-by-step walkthroughs of how to use the tools. It was originally built for integration in Team Foundation Server 2012, but it is very easy to take that environment and upgrade it to use Team Foundation Server 2013 and Visual Studio 2013. Those simple upgrade steps are available in a blog post at `http://aka.ms/UpgradeProjectServerTFS2013VM`.

Project Server Essentials

Project Server is particularly great at solving a few scenarios that some development and testing teams are facing. Not all teams and organizations need these types of scenarios addressed, but those that do might find some comfort with leveraging them in Project Server. The following list describes some scenarios that have come from organizations that have software development teams contributing to their projects:

➤ **Budgeting and cost of projects**—Project Server is able to apply costs to resources used, which can include people and other material resources. It can then use those costs at a project level to track an overall budget, especially across an organization's portfolio of projects in progress.

➤ **Visibility into tracking shared resources**—Because an organization may have multiple projects in progress, some team members might need to contribute to multiple projects. Project Server is able to help "book" shared team members and has tools to track when a particular team member will be over-used across multiple projects.

➤ **Portfolio analysis**—Project Server provides an organization with deep insight into its overall portfolio of projects. This also includes the ability to customize the project request life cycle from the early inception phases to include project costing estimates all the way to the completion of selected projects. Project Server's portfolio analysis features also allow organizations to help address a situation in which you have a certain budget available for projects in a given year, but you're wondering which projects to select for approval to deliver the highest value to the organization for the budget we have available?

➤ **Cross-project dependencies and deliverables**—Project Server is able to track the effects of your current project when another project's deliverables are starting to fall behind.

➤ **Schedules** — Project Server is very much date-aware so that project managers are able to schedule tasks and get estimates of project completion dates and task critical paths to meet deadlines.

➤ **Timesheets and administrative time**—Teams that need to perform time tracking can do so with Project Server.

➤ **Vacation, holidays, and time off**—By tracking when team members will not be available because of company holidays, vacation, and other types of time off, Project Server is able to help project managers with tracking overall project schedules and team members' availability based on that information.

➤ **Non-people project resources**—Certain projects may have non–people-related resources, such as manufacturing equipment, event locations, and so on, that need to be tracked within a project's schedule and budget. Project Server can track those along with people-related tasks and resources.

If any of these benefits sound particularly interesting to your organization then you may want to look into integrating Project Server with your Team Foundation Server instance. The integration of the two becomes an extremely powerful platform for tracking your projects and software releases.

Bidirectional Synchronization

One of the nice parts about the Team Foundation Server and Project Server integration is that it is a two-way synchronization once it is set up. This means that project managers can make changes and publish them to Project Server, which then gets pushed over to Team Foundation Server. Then developers/testers can make changes in Team Foundation Server that are sent over as project change requests to Project Server, which a project manager can approve and include in his or her projects.

Both clients have additional information displayed to the team member so that they can view details about the integration. For example, team members using Visual Studio and Team Foundation Server will notice a new tab on the work item form named *Project Server*, which contains fields related to the integration, as shown in Figure 16-1. Additionally, the history of the work item will begin to show all of the different synchronization events that occur for that work item.

Similarly, when the integration is set up and an enterprise project is mapped in Project Server, a project manager will be able to open his or her enterprise project in Microsoft Project and notice a few fields related to Team Foundation Server. Figure 16-2 shows a project plan including fields that identify whether the plan should be published to the Team Foundation Server Team Project and as what work item type. There is a new view added to the project plan called "Team Foundation Gantt (Project Server)," which is where the additional fields are added.

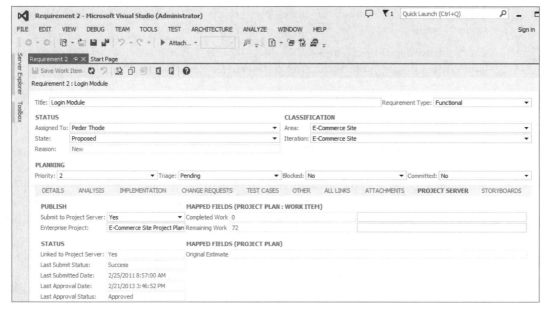

FIGURE 16-1: Project Server tab on the work item form

FIGURE 16-2: Microsoft Project Plan with Team Foundation Server-specific columns

Work Item Synchronization Life Cycle

A Team Foundation Server administrator should understand the life cycle of a Team Foundation Server work item, as it is synchronized with a task in an enterprise project stored in Project Server. Let's begin the discussion with a simple example showing the steps a project manager would take to add a task to the project plan in Project Server and wanting to submit it to Team Foundation Server.

1. The project manager opens his or her enterprise project from Project Server in Microsoft Project.

2. The project manager then adds a new task (or chooses an existing task) and changes the field value of "Publish to Team Project" to Yes and provides a value for the Work Item Type field, such as Requirement, User Story, Product Backlog Item, or Task depending on the process template being used.

3. The project manager then saves and publishes the enterprise project plan back to Project Server. Project Server then takes the line marked to publish and creates a work item in Team Foundation Server. At that point, any changes will be synchronized across.

4. For example, now that the work item is created in Team Foundation Server, the development manager can make changes such as creating children implementation tasks and updated assignments and effort fields. Those changes will then get submitted to the Project Server to be approved.

5. However, the update changes have not been made to the enterprise project plan just yet. Enterprise projects in Project Server have a concept of Status Update Approvals before they are committed to the project plan. The project manager visits the Approval Center in Project Server to approve each of the status updates that have come from Team Foundation Server.

6. The project manager will open the enterprise project again, which includes the new status updates, and then save and publish the enterprise project back to Project Server, which then completes the synchronization life cycle.

The last two steps may not seem obvious if you have not interacted with Project Server before. By default, all status updates not made by the project manager need to be approved. As mentioned previously, this is done by the project manager in the Approval Center, as shown in Figure 16-3.

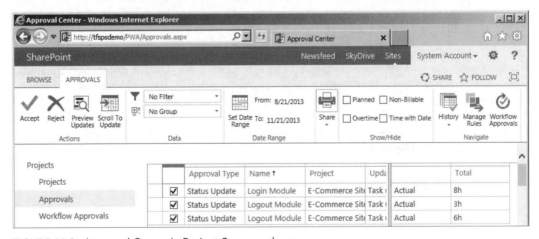

FIGURE 16-3: Approval Center in Project Server web app

The second item that may not be obvious is the publishing step. After any changes by the project manager, those changes need to be published back to Project Server before they are completely committed. This step allows project managers to make interim draft changes to their project plan without making it "final."

These two steps may seem to be burdensome to some project managers, so they can set up an auto-approval rule to remove one of the steps. Beginning in Project Server 2010 Service Pack 1, project managers can also add an auto-publish rule as well, which will remove the second step. However, some project managers prefer the granularity of this approach. These two concepts are important for administrators of the integration to understand because this will likely come into play when team members are concerned that something has completely synchronized from Team Foundation Server.

The steps of the second life cycle covered here occur when the items start with the development team and are synchronized over to Project Server. There are a few differences from the life cycle mentioned previously:

1. A development manager creates a new product backlog item and children tasks for the individual work that will be done to implement that product backlog item. The development manager then opens the Project Server tab on the product backlog item's work item form and sets the value of the Submit to Project Server field to Yes, and then chooses the name of the enterprise project in the Enterprise Project field. The development manager will then save the work item and notice in the history field submitted to Project Server for approval.

2. The new item has not appeared on the project plan yet. The project manager needs to open up the Approval Center in Project Server and approve the status updates.

3. The project manager then opens up the enterprise project plan from Project Server and saves and publishes the project plan to incorporate the newly synchronized item. At this point, the work item in Team Foundation Server will show as fully approved and synchronized. The project manager will also notice that the single summary item will have a roll-up from all of the child tasks, including the assigned-to list and how many hours are remaining/completed for each of those team members.

You will notice in step 1 that the development manager chose to submit only the parent product backlog item and not the product backlog item and the child tasks. The development manager could have taken the latter approach, but by sending over only the parent, the synchronization process will roll-up the resource information automatically, and updates from the children are automatically synchronized to the parent level as a summary to Project Server. That way, teams can work with their project managers and choose to send over only summary level information updates or send over even the details of the implementation tasks.

Default Field Mappings

By default, a limited number of fields are synchronized between Project Server and work items in Team Foundation Server. Some fields depend on the work item type and which process templates are used for team projects in Team Foundation Server. Table 16-1 discusses a sampling of the default field mappings that you will find.

TABLE 16-1: Default Field Mappings

TEAM FOUNDATION SERVER FIELD	PROJECT SERVER FIELD	PROJECT SERVER STATUS QUEUE FIELD
Title	Task Name	Title
Assigned To	Resources	Resources
Completed Work	Task Actual Work	Resource Actual Work
Remaining Work	Task Remaining Work	Resource Remaining Work
Original Estimate	Baseline Work	
Start Date	Task Start	Resource Start
Finish Date	Task Finish	Resource Finish

You might notice from the table that two fields are stored for certain fields in Project Server. This is because of the "approvals" workflow for a particular item in an enterprise project. The value may be different from what is contained in the fully published enterprise project and what is currently in the status approval queue.

You can also customize these field mappings, including adding additional fields to synchronize. Also, additional steps are required if you are using the Scrum process template for your team project in Team Foundation Server. More information about how to customize the field mappings and what additional steps are necessary if you are using the Scrum process template can be found in the MSDN article at `http://aka.ms/CustomizeTFSPSFields`.

Mirror Fields

Because of the "approval" cycle in Project Server, there are times when the value of the work item field may differ from what is currently in Project Server. This can be more prominent when a project manager declines a status update approval. These types of situations can be monitored and are the reason that work item types in Team Foundation Server have additional work item fields called *mirror fields*.

Mirror fields are used to store the intermediate value before status updates are approved. Mirror fields are essentially a "second set of books." For example, the mirror field for the Remaining Work field is named Project Remaining Work. Whenever the values of those two fields are not the same then it is an intermediate state where a status update has not been approved yet or has been declined.

MONITORING WORK ITEM SUBMISSIONS TO PROJECT SERVER

As an administrator, you will likely want to monitor the flow of status updates between Team Foundation Server and Project Server. You can create a work item query to find problems in the synchronized-by filtering on `Project Server Last Submit Status = Failure`. This will return a list of work items that have an issue in the synchronization that you can then troubleshoot.

For more information about this process, you can read about additional troubleshooting steps at `http://aka.ms/MonitorTFSPSIntegration`.

Team Foundation Server Global Workflows

A new concept was introduced for work item type definitions and process templates called global workflows, which simplify the Project Server and Team Foundation Server integration. Global workflows are not dedicated to this integration only, but can be used in other scenarios as well.

Global workflows define a certain set of fields and rules that should exist on every work item type, even if not defined in the work item type definition. Global workflows can be scoped to either a team project or a team project collection. They can also define global lists that should exist and be used by fields defined in the global workflow fields.

Global workflows are used for several Project Server integration-specific fields that are needed and simplify the process of easily defining those fields. Those administrators able to customize work item type definitions need not worry about specifying the fields defined in the global workflow, which simplifies maintenance of those definitions. If you are customizing what fields are mapped to Project Server, you may also want to make appropriate customizations to the global workflow for your team project collection as well.

You can find out more about Global Workflows by reading the MSDN article at `http://aka.ms/ TFSGlobalWorkflow`.

Relationship between Team Projects and Enterprise Projects

Each team project in Team Foundation Server can have multiple Project Server enterprise projects mapped to it. However, it is important to know that an enterprise project in Project Server can be mapped only to a single team project in Team Foundation Server. This relationship should be considered as your company forms its team project structuring strategy, as discussed in Chapter 2.

INITIAL CONFIGURATION

Configuring integration between Team Foundation Server and Project Server has some fairly simple initial steps that you must perform only one time. One step needs to be performed any time a new enterprise project is created that will contain tasks synchronized with Team Foundation Server. This section covers the essentials for setting up the integration.

Necessary Permissions

As an administrator, you want to make sure that the proper permissions are provided to the service accounts used to run both Team Foundation Server and Project Server. This is one area that you will want to make sure is completely implemented. It is commonly overlooked and will cause problems if not set up correctly. The following list provides a summary of the necessary permissions:

➤ For Project Server 2010 and Project Server 2013, you must grant the Team Foundation Server service account Full Control permissions for the Project Server Service Application so it can be accessed properly.

➤ You must also grant the Team Foundation Server service account the permissions required to access each mapped instance of Project Web Access (PWA). These differ by Project Server version, so see the reference link in the paragraph following this list for the specific details.

> ➤ Team members assigned tasks in enterprise projects in Project Server synchronized to Team Foundation Server should be recognized as Contributors to the team project.

> ➤ Team members assigned to work items in Team Foundation Server synchronized to Project Server should exist in the Enterprise Resource Pool in Project Server and should be granted permissions to log in to Project Web Access.

Be sure to double-check the last two bulleted items. They both seem to be an area that many teams forget to ensure. You can find out more information about the necessary permissions for the integration and how to provide those permissions by reading the MSDN article at `http://aka.ms/ TFSPSPermissions`.

Command-Line Tool for Configuration

The command-line tool used to administer the integration between Team Foundation Server and Project Server is named `TfsAdmin.exe`. It is available whenever you install any version of Visual Studio 2013 because all versions include the Team Explorer components. You will find the tool by opening a command prompt window and navigating to the following directory for 32-bit operating systems:

```
cd %ProgramFiles%\Microsoft Visual Studio 12.0\Common7\IDE
```

and the following directory for 64-bit operating systems:

```
cd %ProgramFiles(x86)%\Microsoft Visual Studio 12.0\Common7\IDE
```

Project Server Installation Components

Additionally, you will need to install the Team Foundation Server Extensions for Project Server on each web-tier and application-tier server that hosts a Project Server 2010 or Project Server 2013 installation that will synchronize with Team Foundation Server.

The Team Foundation Server Extensions for Project Server are available as part of the Team Foundation Server 2013 ISO image, as shown in Figure 16-4.

FIGURE 16-4: Team Foundation Server ISO/DVD image with Project Server Extensions folder

One-Time Integration Steps

As mentioned earlier, some one-time steps are necessary to map the Project Server and Team Foundation Server instances so that they know about each other for synchronization. The following is a quick overview of each of these steps; more information can be found in the MSDN article at http://aka.ms/TFSPSConfiguration.

1. Register the Project Web Access (PWA) instances that will contain enterprise projects for synchronization with Team Foundation Server. You perform the first step by running this command line, using the appropriate values for your setup:

```
TfsAdmin ProjectServer /RegisterPWA
                       /pwa:http://project.contoso.local/pwa
                       /tfs:http://tfs.contoso.local:8080/tfs
```

2. You will want to map the Project Web Access (PWA) instance to the team project collections it will synchronize with. You can perform this step by running the following command line and replacing the appropriate values for your setup:

```
TfsAdmin ProjectServer /MapPWAToCollection
                       /pwa:http://project.contoso.local/pwa
                       /tfs:http://tfs.contoso.local:8080/tfs/DefaultCollection
```

3. You will then define the field mappings for each of the team project collections that will participate in the synchronization. You can use either the default field mappings or a customized set of field mappings as described earlier in this chapter:

```
TfsAdmin ProjectServer /UploadFieldMappings
         /collection:http://tfs.contoso.local:8080/tfs/DefaultCollection
         /useDefaultFieldMappings
```

Once these three steps are finished, the synchronization will be ready, and you should not need to run these commands again in the future. You have one more step for each enterprise plan, which is covered in the next section.

Mapping Enterprise Projects to Team Projects

Now that the initial integration has been configured for Team Foundation Server and Project Server, there is one final action for each enterprise project that you want to participate in the synchronization. You need to do this step each time project managers create new enterprise projects, so you need to communicate to your project managers that they must let a Team Foundation Server administrator know when they have created new enterprise projects.

This step needs to be done only once for each enterprise project. The enterprise project needs to be mapped to a team project, and you should specify the types of work items that should participate for synchronization with the particular mapping:

```
TfsAdmin ProjectServer /MapPlanToTeamProject
         /collection:http://tfs.contoso.local:8080/tfs/DefaultCollection
         /enterpriseproject:"E-Commerce Site Project Plan"
         /teamproject:"Engineering"
         /workitemtypes:"User Story,Task"
```

The final option for work item types will change depending on the process template used by your team project. The previous example's command-line entry used the MSF Agile process template. If you are using the Scrum process template, you may want to specify for Product Backlog Items and Tasks to be used. For the MSF CMMI process template, you might specify Requirements and Tasks.

You might also notice that the list of work item types includes a comma to separate each of the work item types but does not include a space character between each list entry. Spaces are not accepted, so be sure to watch for the proper syntax when you run this command-line entry in the future.

Necessary Software for Project Managers

The next thing to remember is that project managers using Project Server will need to have the appropriate software installed on their machines if they want to open enterprise projects that are published. The minimal install necessary for a project manager's machine is as follows:

➤ Microsoft Office Project Professional 2007, Microsoft Project Professional 2010, or Microsoft Project Professional 2013

➤ Team Explorer for Visual Studio 2013 (`http://aka.ms/TeamExplorer2013`)

> **TEAM FOUNDATION SERVER CAL REQUIREMENT FOR PROJECT MANAGERS**
>
> Even though Team Explorer needs to be installed to get the proper add-ins available in Microsoft Project, a Team Foundation Server Client Access License (CAL) is *not* needed for project managers if they will be connecting only to Project Server. If they need to look at details and interact in other ways with Team Foundation Server that require a CAL, then you will still need a CAL for the project manager. You can find out more information about this requirement in the MSDN article at `http://aka.ms/TFSPSConfiguration`.

SUMMARY

As you can see, the Project Server and Team Foundation Server integration can be extremely beneficial for certain teams and organizations to bring their project managers and software engineering teams better in line with one another.

In this chapter, you learned about the integration between Project Server and Team Foundation Server. You reviewed the scenarios about when Project Server makes sense and where it excels, as well as the types of situations in which the integration might be beneficial.

You also reviewed the features and benefits of the integration and the steps necessary to set up the integration. Finally, you reviewed what was necessary for project managers to have installed on their machines.

You begin the next part of the book in Chapter 17, which discusses the automated build system of Team Foundation Server.

PART IV
Team Foundation Build

17

Overview of Build Automation

WHAT'S IN THIS CHAPTER?

➤ Getting to know build automation

➤ Scripting a build

➤ Using build automation servers

➤ Adopting build automation

After version control, automating the build is the second most important thing you can do to improve the quality of your software. This chapter defines build automation and examines why it benefits the overall software engineering process. This is followed by a look at the high-level capabilities and limitations of Team Foundation Server, and a comparison with other common build systems in use today. Finally, some general advice is provided to assist in adopting build automation in your environment today.

Subsequent chapters of this book dive deeper into Team Foundation Server's build capabilities, discuss how to customize the build process, and demonstrate this by working through a series of common build customizations used in real-world scenarios.

WHAT'S NEW IN BUILD AUTOMATION

Team Foundation Server 2013 and Visual Studio Online have shipped with some improvements to the automated build system that make it easier to get an automated build running and to quickly extend the build functionality. These improvements include the ability to host your build servers in Windows Azure, store build outputs in the Team Foundation Server or Visual Studio Online server, and extend your build to perform custom actions using PowerShell scripts. Each of these will be discussed further in this and in the following chapters of Part IV.

Hosted Build Service

Within the Visual Studio Online service ecosystem is a capability known as the *Hosted Build Service*. This service provides a relatively unlimited pool of build machines that are managed by Microsoft and hosted in Windows Azure. The services provided mimic the Team Foundation Build architecture described in Chapter 18 but without the cost of hardware acquisition, setup, and maintenance.

Visual Studio Online provides a hosted build controller that will provision a temporary build agent to service your build request. The output of the build will be placed in the new server build drop location in your Visual Studio Online account or in a version control folder that you specify.

The build agents provided in the service have a plethora of preinstalled software packages that your build can utilize. Anything else it needs will have to be pulled from your version control repository during the build.

> **NOTE** *To get a list of the software packages provided on the hosted build agent you can view the official list of software at* `http://aka.ms/SoftwareOnHostedBuild`. *You can see a live list of the available software packages by browsing to* `http://listofsoftwareontfshostedbuildserver.azurewebsites.net/`.

If you find that you need software that is not provided by Microsoft, you still have the option to register additional build controllers and agents that run on premises. These machines are registered with your Visual Studio Online account, but their configuration is fully controlled by you.

Server-Based Build Drops

In all versions of Team Foundation Server, you have the option to either have the build process copy all of the outputs of compilation to a folder on a file server known as the build drop or to not copy any files off the build agent machine. In Visual Studio Online and Team Foundation Server 2013, you now have the option to have the outputs of compilation stored in a special location on the server. The reason for this addition is that when the Hosted Build Service in Visual Studio Online was implemented, it didn't have any way to access your local file share. Storing the outputs of compilation on the server solved this problem.

Some of the nice side-effects of this change is that now your build drops can be managed by Team Foundation Server so you don't have to go to IT to get access to a file share for your build outputs. The server drops are also backed up with all of the other Team Foundation Server data.

> **REFERENCE** *Server drops are discussed further in Chapter 18.*

LET'S BUILD SOMETHING

Imagine building a house. You visit the site every day and see nothing but a muddy field. The construction team tells you, "Yup, we're making excellent progress. The doors are all done and look great. Walls are 80 percent there. Plumbing is ready to go, and the kitchen is ready to drop in." Every day that you visit, you see that same muddy field. The construction teams tell you how well progress is going. Sometimes they regale you with stories about how they decided the doors were not going to be up to the job, so they threw them on a bonfire and built new ones from scratch that can open both ways, and even have little flaps ready should you ever decide to get a cat.

But you never see any progress—just a muddy field with lots of busy people running around looking stressed.

Then, the day before you are due to move in, everything arrives on site at the same time. Things are stuck together in a hurry—but it takes longer than everyone seemed to think it would. The day draws on, night begins to fall, and everyone gets tired, but they heroically continue trying to get the thing to fit together.

In the morning, you take a look at your house. It's a house for sure. A couple of the rooms are not quite finished yet, because they didn't fit when they arrived onsite. A few of the screws are missing, none of the paint is the color you would have chosen, and many things aren't exactly how you'd envisioned them when you drew up the plans six months ago. More embarrassingly for you, now when you see the house you think of several places where it would have been great to have an extra power outlet, and you realize you will probably never get to use the expensive hot tub that you asked for. You can't help wondering why they spent all that time putting cat flaps in your doors when you are allergic to cats, and yet they didn't get the toilet plumbed in the main bathroom.

Now, try to imagine how your customers feel when dealing with something as ephemeral as software. How do you show progress to a customer? How do you know how complete you are? How do you know if everything works? How do you know if you are done with a particular feature or if a feature is done enough to move onto the next one?

The only way to know all this is to assemble your software together and try it out as a whole, to run your application, or to visit your website. Sure, some areas are missing or not quite functional yet. But once you are able to see your application running, you know how close you are to finishing, and it is also very easy for your customer to know how things are going. Once the customer sees it for real, he or she might say that a particular feature you thought was only partially implemented is actually enough to do what he or she wanted. The customer can suggest some course corrections early on, which will make everyone happier with the end result. But you didn't have to change too much to get there.

The problem is that assembling your application can take time. But by making an investment in automating this experience as you go through the software development process, you not only ensure that you can accurately measure and demonstrate progress, but you also remove a huge source of error when it comes to that last-minute push to completion.

If you are serious about the quality of the software you deliver then you need to be serious about build automation.

WHAT IS BUILD AUTOMATION?

Build automation is the process of streamlining your build process so that it is possible to assemble your application into a usable product with a simple, single action. This entails not just the part of code a particular developer is working on but other typical activities such as the following:

- ➤ Compiling source code into binaries
- ➤ Packaging binaries into installable modules such as MSI files, XAP files, JAR files, DMG images, and so on
- ➤ Running tests
- ➤ Creating documentation
- ➤ Deploying results ready for use

Only after the parts of your application come together can you tell if your application works and does what it is supposed to. Assembling the parts of an application is often a complex, time-consuming, and error-prone process. There are so many parts to building the application that, without an automated build, the activity usually falls on one or two individuals on the team who know the secret. Without an automated build, even they sometimes get it wrong, with show-stopping consequences that are often discovered very late, making any mistakes expensive to fix.

Imagine having to recall an entire manufacturing run of a DVD because you missed an important file. Worse still, imagine accidentally including the source code for your application in a web distri-bution or leaving embarrassing test data in the application when it was deployed to production. All these things made headlines when they happened to organizations building software yet they could have easily been avoided.

Integration of software components is the difficult part. Developers work on their features in isolation, making various assumptions about how other parts of the system function. Only after the parts are assembled do the assumptions get tested. If you integrate early and often, these integra-tions get tested as soon as possible in the development process—thus reducing the cost of fixing the inevitable issues.

It should be trivial for everyone involved in the project to run a copy of the latest build. Only then can you tell if your software works and does what it is supposed to. Only then can you tell if you are going to have your product ready on time. A regular, automated build is the heartbeat of your team.

In Visual Studio, a developer can usually run his or her application by pressing the famous F5 key to run the code in debug mode. This assembles the code together on the local workstation and executes it, which makes it trivial for the developer to test his or her part of the code base. But what it doesn't do is ensure that the code works with all the latest changes committed by other members of the team. In addition, pressing the F5 key simply compiles the code for you to run and test manually.

As part of an automated build, not only can you test that the code correctly compiles, but you can also ensure that it always runs a full suite of automated tests. This instantly gives you a high degree of confidence that no changes that have been introduced have broken something elsewhere.

Pressing the F5 key is easy for a developer. You want your automated build to make it just as easy to run your application—if not easier. This is where a build automation server plays a part.

The build automation server is a machine that looks for changes in version control and automatically rebuilds the project. This can be on demand, on a regular schedule (such as nightly or daily builds), or can be performed every time a developer checks in a file—a process that is often referred to as *continuous integration*. By giving you rapid feedback when there is a problem with something that has been checked in, the software development team has the opportunity to fix it right away when it is fresh in the mind of the person just checking in code. Fixing the issue early minimizes the cost of the repair as well as the impact the problem code would have on the development efforts of your team members.

However, before you can set up a continuous integration build on a build server, you must script your build so that it can be run with a single command.

MARTIN FOWLER ON CONTINUOUS INTEGRATION

The term *continuous integration* (CI) emerged from Agile software development methodologies such as Extreme Programming (XP) at the turn of the millennium. Martin Fowler's paper on continuous integration from 2000 is still worth reading today at `http://www.martinfowler.com/articles/continuousIntegration.html`.

Note that, as originally described, the term refers to increasing the speed and quality of software delivery by decreasing the integration times, and not simply the practice of performing a build for every check-in. Many of the practices expounded by Fowler's paper are supported by tooling in Team Foundation Server—not simply this one small feature of the build services. However, the term *continuous integration* has come to be synonymous with building after a check-in has occurred and is, therefore, used by Team Foundation Server as the name for this type of trigger, as discussed in Chapter 18.

Scripting a Build

The most basic form of build automation is to write a script that performs all the operations necessary for a clean build. This could be a shell script, batch file, PowerShell script, and so on. However, because of the common tasks that you perform during a build (such as dependency tracking, compiling files, batching files together, and so on), a number of specialized build scripting languages have been developed over the years.

Make

The granddaddy of specialized build scripting languages is *Make*. Originally created at Bell Labs by Dr. Stuart Feldman in 1977, Make is still commonly used on UNIX-based platforms to create programs from source code by reading the build configuration as stored in a text-based file called *makefile*. Typically, to build an executable, you had to enter a number of commands to compile and link the source code, also ensuring that dependent code had been correctly compiled and linked. Make was designed specifically to help C programmers manage this build process in an efficient manner.

A makefile defines a series of targets, with each command indented by a tab inside the target:

```
#Comment
target: dependencies
<TAB>command
```

For example, a simple Hello World application could have the following makefile:

```
# Define C Compiler and compiler flags
CC=gcc
CFLAGS=-g

# The default target, called if make is executed with no target.
all: helloworld

helloworld: helloworld.o
    $(CC) $(CFLAGS) -o $@ $<    # Note: Lines starts with a TAB

helloworld.o: helloworld.c
    $(CC) $(CFLAGS) -c -o &@ $<

clean:
    rm -rf *o helloworld
```

Note that one of the main features of Make is that it simplifies dependency management. That is to say that to make the executable helloworld, it checks if the target helloworld.o exists and that its dependencies are met. helloworld.o is dependent on the C source file helloworld.c. Only if helloworld.c has changed since the last execution of Make will helloworld.o be created and, therefore, helloworld.

The previous script is the same as typing the following commands in sequence at the command line:

```
gcc -g -c -o helloworld.o helloworld.c
gcc -g -o helloworld helloworld.o
```

In a simple makefile like the one shown previously, everything is very readable. With more complex makefiles that do packaging and deployment activities, it can take a while to figure out which commands are executed in which order. Make uses a declarative language that can be difficult to read for developers used to coding in more imperative languages (like most modern program languages are). For many developers, it feels like you must read a makefile slightly backward—that is, you must look at the target, and then follow all its dependencies, and then their dependencies, to track back what will actually occur first in the sequence.

Since its inception, Make has gone through a number of rewrites and has a number of derivatives that have used the same file format and basic principles, as well as providing some of their own features. There are implementations of Make for most platforms, including NMAKE from Microsoft for the Windows platform.

Apache Ant

Ant is a build automation tool similar to Make, but it was designed from the ground up to be a platform-independent tool. James Duncan Davidson originally developed Ant at Sun Microsystems. It was first released in 2000. According to Davidson, the name "Ant" is an acronym for "Another Neat Tool." It is a Java-based tool and uses an XML file, typically stored in a file called build.xml. With its Java heritage and platform independence, Ant is typically used to build Java projects.

Ant shares a fair number of similarities with Make. The build file is composed of a project that contains a number of targets. Each target defines a number of tasks that are executed and a set of dependencies. Ant is declarative and does automatic dependency management. For example, a simple Hello World application in Java could have the following build.xml to compile it using Ant:

```xml
<?xml version="1.0" encoding="utf-8"?>
<project name="helloworld" basedir="." default="package">

    <target name="compile">
        <mkdir dir="${basedir}/bin" />
        <javac srcdir="${basedir}/src"
                destdir="${basedir}/bin"
                debug="on"
                includeAntRuntime="false"/>
    </target>

    <target name="jar">
        <jar destfile="${basedir}/helloworld.jar"
            basedir="${basedir}/bin" />
    </target>

    <target name="clean">
        <delete file="helloworld.jar" />
        <delete dir="${basedir}/bin" />
    </target>

    <target name="package" depends="compile,jar">
        <!-- Comments are in standard XML format -->
    </target>

</project>
```

The tasks in Ant are implemented as a piece of compiled Java code implementing a particular interface. In addition to the large number of standard tasks that ship as part of Ant, a number of tasks are available in the open source community. Manufacturers of Java-related tooling will often provide Ant tasks to make it easier to work with their tools from Ant.

Ant scripts can get quite complex, and because the XML used in an Ant script is quite verbose, scripts can quickly get very large and complicated. Therefore, for complex build systems, the main `build.xml` file can be broken down into more modular files.

Ant is so common among the Java community that most of the modern IDEs ship with a version of Ant to allow automated builds to be easily executed from inside the development environment as well as with tooling to help author Ant scripts.

Apache Maven

Maven is an open source project management and build automation tool written in Java. It is primarily used for Java projects. The central concept in Maven is the Project Object Model (`pom .xml`) file that describes the project being built. While Maven is similar in functionality to Make and derivations such as Ant, it has some novel concepts that define a distinct new category of build tools, making Maven worth discussing in this book.

Make and Ant allow a completely free-form script to be coded, and for you to have your source files located in any manner. Maven takes the not-unreasonable assumption that you are performing a build and uses conventions for where files should be located for the build process. It applies the Convention over Configuration software design paradigm to builds. The main advantage of this paradigm is that it helps you find your way around a Maven project because they all must follow certain patterns to get built (at the disadvantage of losing some flexibility).

The other main difference between Maven and the Make-inspired build tools is that it takes dependency management to the next level. While Make and Ant handle dependencies inside the project being built, Maven can manage the dependencies on external libraries (which are especially common in many Java projects). If your code takes a dependency on a certain version of a library, then Maven will download this from a project repository and store it locally, making it available for build. This helps the portability of builds because it means that all you need to get started is Java and Maven installed. Executing the build should take care of downloading everything else you need to run the build.

> **NOTE** *For more information about Maven, visit* `http://maven.apache.org/`.

NAnt

NAnt (`http://nant.sourceforge.net/`) was inspired by Apache Ant, but it was written in .NET and designed to build .NET projects. Like Ant, it is also an open source project and was originally released in 2001. Interestingly, according to the NAnt FAQ, the name NAnt comes from the fact that the tool is "Not Ant," which, to extract Ant from its original acronym, would mean that NAnt was "Not Another Neat Tool." But, in fact, NAnt was a very neat way of performing build automation, and it was especially useful in early .NET 1.0 and 1.1 projects.

Syntactically very similar to Ant, NAnt files are stored with a `.build` suffix such as `nant.build`. Each file is composed of a project that contains a number of targets. Each target defines a number of tasks that are executed and a set of dependencies. There are tasks provided to perform common .NET activities such as `<csc />` to execute the C# command-line compiler tool.

The main problem with NAnt files is that they are not understood by Visual Studio, and so changes made to the Visual Studio solution files (`.sln`) and project files must also be made in the NAnt file; otherwise, the dependencies would not be known to the automated build script. To execute a build using the `.sln` file or the `.vbproj`/`.csproj` files, you must install Visual Studio on the build server and use the `devenv` task to drive Visual Studio from the command line, which most people avoid.

MSBuild

MSBuild is the build system that has been used by Visual Studio since Visual Studio 2005. However, the MSBuild platform is installed as part of the .NET Framework, and it is possible to build projects using `MSBuild.exe` from the command line without using the Visual Studio IDE.

Visual Studio keeps the MSBuild file up-to-date for the project. In fact, the `.csproj` and `.vbproj` files that are well known to developers in Visual Studio are simply MSBuild scripts.

MSBuild was heavily influenced by XML-based build automation systems such as Ant or NAnt, and also by its predecessor NMAKE (and therefore Make). MSBuild files typically end with a `*proj` extension (for example, `TFSBuild.proj`, `MyVBProject.vbproj`, or `MyCSharpProject.csproj`). The MSBuild file follows what should by now be a familiar pattern. It consists of a project, and inside the project, a number of properties and targets are defined. Each target contains a number of tasks.

Following is an example of a simple MSBuild script that you could execute from a Visual Studio command prompt with the command `msbuild helloworld.proj`:

```
<?xml version="1.0" encoding="utf-8"?>
<Project xmlns="http://schemas.microsoft.com/developer/msbuild/2003"
         DefaultTargets="SayHello" >

  <PropertyGroup>
    <!-- Define name to say hello to -->
    <Name>World</Name>
  </PropertyGroup>

  <Target Name="SayHello">
    <Message Text="Hello $(Name)!" />
  </Target>

</Project>
```

However, MSBuild has some notable exceptions. In addition to simple properties in a `PropertyGroup`, as shown previously (which can be thought of as key-value pairs), there is also a notion of an `Item`. `Items` are a list of many values that can be thought of as similar to an array or enumeration in programming terms. An `Item` also has metadata associated with it. When you create an `Item`, it is actually a .NET object (implementing the `ITaskItem` interface). There is a predefined set of metadata available on every `Item`, but you can also add your own properties as child nodes of the `Item` in the `ItemGroup`.

Another way that the use of MSBuild differs from tools such as Ant or NAnt is that Visual Studio and Team Foundation Server ship with a number of templates for the build process. These are stored in an MSBuild script with a `.targets` extension. They are usually stored in `%ProgramFiles%/MSBuild`, `%ProgramFiles(x86)%/MSBuild` or in the .NET Framework folder on the individual machine. The actual build script created by Visual Studio usually just imports the relevant `.targets` file and provides a number of properties to customize the behavior of the build process defined in the `.targets` file. In this way, MSBuild shares some slight similarities to Maven in that a typical build pattern is presented, which the project customizes to fit.

In an MSBuild script, reading the file from top to bottom, the last place to define a property or target wins (unlike in Ant, where the first place defined is the winner). This behavior means that anything you write after you import the `.targets` file in your MSBuild script will override behavior in the imported build template.

The standard templates provided by Microsoft include many `.targets` files that are already called in the standard template prefixed with `Before` or `After`, which are designed as hook points for your own custom logic to run before or after these steps. A classic example would be `BeforeBuild` and `AfterBuild`. It is considered good practice to override only targets designed to be overridden like this, or to override properties designed to control the build process. The imported `.targets` files are typically well-commented and can be read if you would like to learn more about what they do.

The following is a basic `.vbproj` file as generated by Visual Studio 2013 for a simple `Hello World` style application. Hopefully, you will now recognize and understand many of the elements of the file. Notice that is doesn't contain any actual `Targets`—these are all in the imported `Microsoft.VisualBasic.targets` file, including the actual callout to the Visual Basic compiler. The `.vbproj` file just contains properties and `ItemGroups`, which configure how that `.target` file behaves:

```xml
<?xml version="1.0" encoding="utf-8"?>
<Project ToolsVersion="12.0" DefaultTargets="Build"
        xmlns="http://schemas.microsoft.com/developer/msbuild/2003">
  <Import Project="$(MSBuildExtensionsPath)\$(MSBuildToolsVersion)
                   \Microsoft.Common.props"
          Condition="Exists('$(MSBuildExtensionsPath)\$(MSBuildToolsVersion)
                   \Microsoft.Common.props')" />
  <PropertyGroup>
    <Configuration Condition=" '$(Configuration)' == '' ">Debug</Configuration>
    <Platform Condition=" '$(Platform)' == '' ">AnyCPU</Platform>
    <ProjectGuid>{1B7AC2CB-6612-475A-837D-A7CAB495109E}</ProjectGuid>
    <OutputType>Library</OutputType>
    <RootNamespace>HelloWorld</RootNamespace>
    <AssemblyName>HelloWorld</AssemblyName>
    <FileAlignment>512</FileAlignment>
    <MyType>Windows</MyType>
    <TargetFrameworkVersion>v4.5</TargetFrameworkVersion>
  </PropertyGroup>
```

```xml
<PropertyGroup Condition=" '$(Configuration)|$(Platform)' == 'Debug|AnyCPU' ">
  <DebugSymbols>true</DebugSymbols>
  <DebugType>full</DebugType>
  <DefineDebug>true</DefineDebug>
  <DefineTrace>true</DefineTrace>
  <OutputPath>bin\Debug\</OutputPath>
  <DocumentationFile>HelloWorld.xml</DocumentationFile>
  <NoWarn>42016,41999,42017,42018,42019,42032,42036,42020,42021,42022</NoWarn>
</PropertyGroup>
<PropertyGroup Condition=" '$(Configuration)|$(Platform)' == 'Release|AnyCPU' ">
  <DebugType>pdbonly</DebugType>
  <DefineDebug>false</DefineDebug>
  <DefineTrace>true</DefineTrace>
  <Optimize>true</Optimize>
  <OutputPath>bin\Release\</OutputPath>
  <DocumentationFile>HelloWorld.xml</DocumentationFile>
  <NoWarn>42016,41999,42017,42018,42019,42032,42036,42020,42021,42022</NoWarn>
</PropertyGroup>
<PropertyGroup>
  <OptionExplicit>On</OptionExplicit>
</PropertyGroup>
<PropertyGroup>
  <OptionCompare>Binary</OptionCompare>
</PropertyGroup>
<PropertyGroup>
  <OptionStrict>Off</OptionStrict>
</PropertyGroup>
<PropertyGroup>
  <OptionInfer>On</OptionInfer>
</PropertyGroup>
<ItemGroup>
  <Reference Include="System" />
  <Reference Include="System.Data" />
  <Reference Include="System.Xml" />
  <Reference Include="System.Core" />
  <Reference Include="System.Xml.Linq" />
  <Reference Include="System.Data.DataSetExtensions" />
</ItemGroup>
<ItemGroup>
  <Import Include="Microsoft.VisualBasic" />
  <Import Include="System" />
  <Import Include="System.Collections" />
  <Import Include="System.Collections.Generic" />
  <Import Include="System.Data" />
  <Import Include="System.Diagnostics" />
  <Import Include="System.Linq" />
  <Import Include="System.Xml.Linq" />
  <Import Include="System.Threading.Tasks" />
</ItemGroup>
<ItemGroup>
  <Compile Include="Class1.vb" />
  <Compile Include="My Project\AssemblyInfo.vb" />
  <Compile Include="My Project\Application.Designer.vb">
    <AutoGen>True</AutoGen>
    <DependentUpon>Application.myapp</DependentUpon>
```

```
    </Compile>
    <Compile Include="My Project\Resources.Designer.vb">
      <AutoGen>True</AutoGen>
      <DesignTime>True</DesignTime>
      <DependentUpon>Resources.resx</DependentUpon>
    </Compile>
    <Compile Include="My Project\Settings.Designer.vb">
      <AutoGen>True</AutoGen>
      <DependentUpon>Settings.settings</DependentUpon>
      <DesignTimeSharedInput>True</DesignTimeSharedInput>
    </Compile>
  </ItemGroup>
  <ItemGroup>
    <EmbeddedResource Include="My Project\Resources.resx">
      <Generator>VbMyResourcesResXFileCodeGenerator</Generator>
      <LastGenOutput>Resources.Designer.vb</LastGenOutput>
      <CustomToolNamespace>My.Resources</CustomToolNamespace>
      <SubType>Designer</SubType>
    </EmbeddedResource>
  </ItemGroup>
  <ItemGroup>
    <None Include="My Project\Application.myapp">
      <Generator>MyApplicationCodeGenerator</Generator>
      <LastGenOutput>Application.Designer.vb</LastGenOutput>
    </None>
    <None Include="My Project\Settings.settings">
      <Generator>SettingsSingleFileGenerator</Generator>
      <CustomToolNamespace>My</CustomToolNamespace>
      <LastGenOutput>Settings.Designer.vb</LastGenOutput>
    </None>
  </ItemGroup>
  <Import Project="$(MSBuildToolsPath)\Microsoft.VisualBasic.targets" />
  <!-- To modify your build process, add your task inside one of the
       targets below and uncomment it.
       Other similar extension points exist, see Microsoft.Common.targets.
  <Target Name="BeforeBuild">
  </Target>
  <Target Name="AfterBuild">
  </Target>
  -->
</Project>
```

Windows Workflow Foundation

Although this chapter has familiarized you with specialized build scripting languages, so far no mention has been made of other programming and scripting methods that could also be used to create a build (such as PowerShell, batch files, or even UNIX shell scripts). But one such general-purpose framework is worth mentioning here because of its use by the build automation functionality in Team Foundation Server—*Windows Workflow Foundation* (WF).

WF is a programming framework from Microsoft used for defining and executing workflows. The WF version used by Team Foundation Server is version 4.5 and is part of the .NET Framework 4.5. WF can be coded using the XML-based XAML markup or in any .NET language directly against the Windows Workflow Foundation APIs, which ship with the .NET Framework.

Unlike the specialized build languages, WF contains no functionality built in for dependency management—or even methods for mass manipulation of files. Therefore, its use by Team Foundation Server for build automation might seem a little odd at first. However, WF provides a couple of capabilities that traditional build scripting languages do not.

The build scripting languages do not typically store states between instances, but workflow is all about state. WF maintains state, gets input and sends output to the world outside of the workflow engine, provides the control flow, and executes the code that makes up the work.

In addition, most build scripting languages control the execution on a single machine. The state persistence nature of WF brings with it the ability to take components of the build and deploy them across multiple machines. This means that you can split some of the workload of your build across several machines and bring the results back together before proceeding with the rest of the build process. For example, you could perform compilation on one machine, while generating documentation from the source on another, and bring them both together when you package your build. This capability provides another weapon in your arsenal when trying to reduce the overall time for a build to complete, and thus tightening the feedback loop for your builds.

For activities that require more traditional build capabilities (such as amassing a bunch of files together and compiling them), the WF templates used by Team Foundation Server rely on the traditional build scripting languages—typically MSBuild.

Chapters 18 and 19 explain more about WF and how it is used by Team Foundation Build. The rest of this chapter looks in more detail at the concept of a build automation server.

USING BUILD AUTOMATION SERVERS

Once you have a single command that can run your build, the next step is to run it periodically. This ensures that the product in version control is not only always in a runnable state, but also removes yet another manual step in the chain and fully automates the build process. Having the build runnable on a server ensures that the build is repeatable on a machine other than the one used by the developer to code the project. Just this simple act of separation helps to ensure that all dependencies are known about and taken into account by the build, which is what helps build repeatability.

In the earliest days of build automation, the build was performed periodically (typically weekly, nightly, or daily) using a simple cron job or scheduled task.

Building on every single check-in to the version control system requires a machine with dedicated build server logic. It was exactly this logic that was built for a project being implemented by a company called ThoughtWorks (an IT consultancy focused on Agile software development practices).

The Continuous Integration (CI) build server logic was then later extracted into a standalone project, which became CruiseControl.

CruiseControl

CruiseControl (`http://cruisecontrol.sourceforge.net/`) is an open source build server implemented in Java. Therefore, it runs on many platforms, including Windows and Linux. At the heart of CruiseControl is the build loop that periodically checks the configured version control system for changes to the code and, if a change is detected, will trigger a new build. Once the build is complete, a notification can be sent regarding the state of the build.

Configuration of CruiseControl is performed using a single `config.xml` file. Because of its long life as a vibrant and active open source project, many extensions have been contributed to CruiseControl over time. Many different version control systems (including Team Foundation Server) can be queried by CruiseControl using these extensions. An equal number of notification extensions exist including e-mail, a web-based console, instant messenger, or even a system tray application in Windows. Output from the build (including results of unit tests, code coverage reports, API documentation, and so on) is available via the web interface.

While any build process can, in theory, be executed by CruiseControl, it is typically used to automate Ant builds. Therefore, it is typically used to build Java projects.

As discussed, Team Foundation Server is supported by CruiseControl as a version control repository. However, data about the build and build notifications are kept within the CruiseControl system.

CruiseControl.NET

CruiseControl.NET (`http://www.cruisecontrolnet.org/`) is an open source build server, but, as the name suggests, it is implemented using .NET. It was loosely based on the original Java version of CruiseControl, and it was also originally developed by the same ThoughtWorks consultancy.

Configuration of CruiseControl.NET is typically performed by editing an XML file called `ccnet.config`. It is also capable of working with a number of version control systems, including Team Foundation Server, and because of its focus on .NET developers, it is capable of building .NET projects by using NAnt or MSBuild scripts and notifying the developers of the results.

Hudson/Jenkins

Hudson is another open source build server implemented in Java. Hudson was the original name for the server but after a bit of an acrimonious falling out between the main community maintainer of the project and the holders of the Hudson trademark, a community fork of the project was created called *Jenkins*. In recent years, they have become a popular alternative to CruiseControl, not least because of an easy-to-use web-based interface for configuring new builds, rather than relying on manual editing of XML files.

While Hudson/Jenkins is capable of building a number of projects (including Ant and even MSBuild), it has some special features for handling Maven builds and tracking dependencies between the builds for Maven projects, which is what makes it worth calling out in particular in this book.

Hudson is capable of working with many version control tools, including Team Foundation Server. However, like all external build systems, data about these builds is kept inside the Hudson system, though it does have some useful build reporting capabilities.

Team Foundation Server

Build automation is so vital to improving the quality of software development that, since its original release in 2005, Team Foundation Server has included build automation capabilities. Internally, the feature was known by the name "Big Build," but people refer to the build automation component of Team Foundation Server as Team Build or Team Foundation Build.

MSBuild first shipped with Visual Studio in 2005, and the original incarnation of Team Foundation Build in 2005 was based heavily around MSBuild. A build was defined by an MSBuild script called `TFSBuild.proj` located in a folder under `$/TeamProject/TeamBuildTypes/BuildTypeName` in Team Foundation Server version control.

When a build was triggered, the `TFSBuild.proj` file was downloaded to the build server and executed. Results of the build were published back to the server, and, importantly, metrics about it were fed into the powerful Team Foundation Server data warehouse. Additionally, the build results were automatically linked with entries in the Team Foundation Server work item tracking engine.

However, in the original 2005 release, the capabilities of Team Foundation Build were very limited. There was no built-in process for triggering builds—they had to be triggered manually, or users had to configure their own jobs to trigger builds periodically or listen for check-ins and trigger continuous integration builds.

Thankfully, the 2008 release of Team Foundation Server saw huge improvements in the build capabilities. In fact, Team Foundation Build was probably the single biggest reason to upgrade from Team Foundation Server 2005. In 2008, you had the ability to trigger builds by one of several trigger types, including scheduled builds and continuous integration style builds.

The 2010 release saw even more improvements to Team Foundation Server's build capabilities. The biggest of these was the move from a totally MSBuild-based solution to one using WF as the build orchestration engine. This had several important advantages, including the ability to easily surface common build configuration properties into the user interface in Visual Studio, as well as the ability to distribute a build across multiple servers (or Build Agents).

While you get very rich integration in Team Foundation Server within the version control, build, and work item tracking functionality, it is important to note that the build automation capabilities of Team Foundation Server can be used only with Team Foundation Server version control or Git. While this should not be an issue for readers of this book, it is an important element to factor in when planning your migration to Team Foundation Server. Only after your source code is in Team Foundation Server does it make sense to switch on its build automation capabilities.

ADOPTING BUILD AUTOMATION

Hopefully, by now, you are suitably convinced that build automation is something that you want to do. But how should you go about adopting build automation as a practice?

The first step is to ensure that you have a single command that you can run to fully build and package your product ready for deployment. If you use Visual Studio then this is very easy because most Visual Studio project types are easily built using MSBuild. However, if you have components developed in Java or other software languages then you will need to do some work to put together your build script using the most appropriate scripting language (such as Ant or Maven).

Next, you should ensure that everyone knows how to build the project and that all the developers can run this from their machines.

Once the build is easy to run, the next step is to periodically run the build to ensure that you always have a clean code base. If you have sufficient resources, and your build is fast enough, then strive for a continuous integration style of build and ensure that you have a fast (and hopefully fun) method of notification to tell the developers when the build has been broken. A simple e-mail notification will suffice and should be used at a minimum, but you can be more creative if you would like.

> ### BRIAN THE BUILD BUNNY
>
> Some ways of making the team pay attention to the state of the build are more imaginative than others. A popular way of encouraging the team to pay attention to the current state of the build is to make creative and eye-catching build status notification mechanisms. While wall displays and lava lamps are a good way of communicating this information to the team, Martin has even gone so far as to connect a talking, moving robot rabbit into Team Foundation Server. For more information on this project (including a prize-winning YouTube video and full source code), see http://aka.ms/BrianTheBuildBunny.
>
> Sadly, the company that created Brian the Build Bunny is no longer in business.

Just this simple step of running the build regularly will significantly affect the productivity of your team. No longer will developers need to roll back changes they have downloaded because they do not compile in their environment. At this point in your adoption of build automation, the trick is to keep things fun, but to gradually introduce a little peer pressure to ensure that the build status is usually good. If a build fails for some reason, that build failure should be the team's immediate priority. What change to the system made the build fail? Who just broke the build? Fix the build and then resume normal work.

If you are developing a website, then make your build automatically deploy to a server so that people can easily play with the latest version of the code. If you are building a client-side application, try to package it so that it can easily be executed by anyone involved in the project. MSI files or ClickOnce installers are good ways of doing this on Windows, but DMG images for the Mac, RPM/DEB files on Linux, or Eclipse Update sites for Eclipse developers are all great ways of making it easy to run the latest build.

Once the team has become familiar with the notion of builds happening automatically, and gotten into the habit of ensuring that the build is "good" at all times, you can gradually raise the bar on determining what makes a good build.

To begin with, simply being able to compile the build and package it for deployment is good enough. Next, you want to introduce things such as automated unit tests (again, slowly at first) so that not only does the build compile, but it also actually works as originally intended. You can also introduce other code-quality indicators at this point, such as ensuring that code meets team-wide coding standards. Over time, you can introduce targets—such as 20 percent of code being covered by the unit tests—and then gradually increase this percentage. In Team Foundation Server, you can also increase quality by making the build run before the code being checked in is committed to the version control system. This feature is known as Gated Check-in and is discussed in Chapter 18. Using the Lab Management features described in Chapter 26, you can even deploy your complex n-tier application out to a series of servers in your lab, and then execute full integration tests in that environment, to validate your build. For the developer, this is still incredibly easy; all she has to do is check in her code.

The trick is to be constantly improving the quality of your builds but still ensuring that checking in and getting a clean build is fast and easy. By keeping the feedback loop between a check-in and a working, deployable product to test as short as possible, you will maximize the productivity of your team, while also being able to easily demonstrate progress to the people sponsoring the development activity in the first place.

SUMMARY

This chapter provided a glimpse of what's new in build automation in Team Foundation Server 2013. It explained what build automation is and the benefits it brings. You learned about some of the various ways to script an automated build and how to run that build periodically using a build automation server. Finally, the chapter provided tips on how to adopt build automation, in general, inside the organization.

Once you have migrated your source code into Team Foundation Server, getting builds configured is an important next step. As discussed in this chapter, if you are already using an existing build automation server, then most of these are already able to use Team Foundation Server as a version control repository from which to draw when automating the build. However, there are several advantages to using Team Foundation Server's built-in build automation capabilities—primarily the integration you get between the version control and work item tracking systems, but also the excellent reporting capabilities provided by Team Foundation Server. The regular builds act as a heartbeat to which you can track the health of your project once all the data from version control, work item tracking, and build automation is combined in the reports provided by Team Foundation Server.

Things have been somewhat generalized in this chapter because build automation is important regardless of the technology or platform you choose to use. However, Team Foundation Server has some innovative features around build automation.

Chapter 18 describes in detail how to create automated builds inside Team Foundation Server. It describes all the features that Team Foundation Server provides, and it highlights new features in the 2013 release. You will learn about the architecture of the Team Foundation Build system and how to work with builds. Finally, the build process will be examined in detail, describing what it does and how it works.

18

Using Team Foundation Build

WHAT'S IN THIS CHAPTER?

➤ Getting to know the build automation features provided by Team Foundation Server

➤ Understanding the Team Foundation build architecture

➤ Installing a build controller and build agent

➤ Working with builds

➤ Understanding the build process

➤ Editing build process parameters

➤ Building both .NET and Java projects with Team Foundation Server

This chapter introduces the build automation capabilities of Team Foundation Server, the core concepts, and how to install the build server functionality. You will learn how to create your own builds based on the standard build process templates, along with how to use and manage them.

> **NOTE** *For information on customizing the standard build process, see Chapter 19.*

INTRODUCTION TO TEAM FOUNDATION BUILD

The build automation capabilities of Team Foundation Server have probably undergone the most significant change since the initial release of Team Foundation Server 2005. Originally, the build functionality extended MSBuild to allow for a basic level of build automation integrated with Team Foundation Version Control and work item tracking.

In the 2008 release, the build system came of age in its own right as a fully enterprise-ready build automation system. That release introduced new first-class concepts into Team Foundation Server, such as the build definition and build agent, and it also had flexible build triggering functionalities provided out of the box. However, the build process was still tightly tied to MSBuild.

The 2010 release introduced even more features into the build automation area. The biggest change was the introduction of Windows Workflow Foundation as the main build orchestration mechanism. The actual compilation of solutions is still handled by the specialized build language (such as MSBuild for .NET solutions, but also Ant or Maven for Java-based projects). However, the rest of the process is governed by a build process template written using Windows Workflow Foundation.

> **NOTE** *For more information on these build languages, see Chapter 17.*

Other notable features new in the 2010 release include gated check-in support, private builds, build notifications, common build customization properties, integration with Symbol and Source servers, enhanced build deletion capabilities, and the introduction of a new concept called the *build controller.*

For customers who run their own on-premises Team Foundation Server, the 2012 release of Team Foundation Build was largely a refinement of existing functionality. One of the notable features is the ability to increase the efficiency of the gated check-in process by configuring it to build multiple check-ins at the same time.

For the 2012 release, a lot of effort was put into re-architecting how the build controllers and agents communicate with Team Foundation Server. In previous releases, the Team Foundation Server reached out to the build servers to try and establish a connection and initiate builds. This became a problem when the build server was behind a firewall or otherwise not routable location.

Team Foundation Server 2013 brings additional refinements, such as the inclusion of Server Drop Folders, which allow the build to push the outputs of compilation onto the Team Foundation Server instance rather than to a local file share.

With the introduction of the Visual Studio Online service, the product team needed to allow customers to run their own build servers with the hosted service. This necessitated a move to a polling-based messaging architecture for build server communication. Essentially, the Team Foundation

Server maintains a message queue for each build server, and the build servers poll the queue continuously to keep in sync.

TEAM FOUNDATION BUILD ARCHITECTURE

Figure 18-1 shows several of the logical components that are critical in the Team Foundation Build architecture. A build is defined by a *build definition*, which describes the build in detail, including what should be built, how, and when. More information about build definitions, as well as how to create and manage them, is provided later in this chapter.

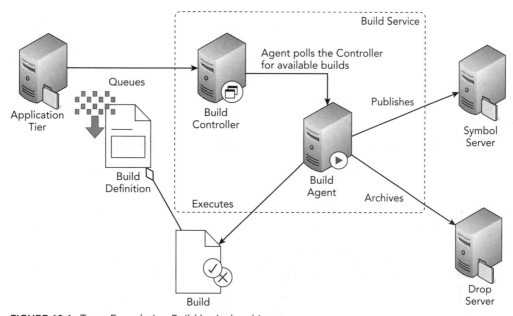

FIGURE 18-1: Team Foundation Build logical architecture

The build definition belongs to a team project in Team Foundation Server. When the application tier determines that a build for the build definition should be performed, it sends a build request message to the queue for that *build controller*.

The build controller then downloads the Windows Workflow–based build process template defined for the build definition and executes it. By default, this causes a build to be queued on the next available *build agent* in the controller's pool of agents. When the selected build agent polls the build controller during the next polling interval, it picks up the build request from its queue.

A build agent is the actual machine that performs the build. Each build agent has a build controller as a parent, but one build controller can have multiple build agents that it can use for the build. Each build controller must be assigned to a single project collection.

The build agent executes the main part of the build process as described in the build definition's process template—including calling MSBuild to perform the actual compilation and test steps.

Once the build agent has successfully executed the build, the default build process template then archives the build results (such as the website, executable files, assemblies, and so on) to a Windows-based file share *or the server drop location*. It will also publish any symbols to the *symbol server* (if configured).

All the information about the resulting build (including the build number, status, and information on the individual build's progress for a particular build definition) are called the *build details*. These details are displayed in a *build report*.

Note that the build controller and build agent processes are hosted by the *build service*. The build controller and build agent may live on the same machine. However, it is recommended that they do not reside on the same machine as the Team Foundation Server application tier in a production configuration. Executing a build is very CPU- and disk I/O-intensive. Therefore, the operation of builds could affect the performance of your application tier if running on the same machine, which could reduce the productivity of your entire development group.

SETTING UP THE TEAM FOUNDATION BUILD SERVICE

This section details how to set up the build service to enable build automation. This is useful for those administering a Team Foundation Server instance. If you already have a build controller for your project collection, you may wish to skip this section and go straight to the section "Working with Builds" to discover how to create new build definitions and manage them.

> **NOTE** *The build service for Team Foundation Server is installed from the Team Foundation Server media. This section briefly touches on installing the build service; but, for the most recent information on how to install and configure the build service, as well as the list of supported hardware and software, see the "Team Foundation Server Installation Guide." The guide is included in the install media for Team Foundation Server, but the latest version is published at* http://aka.ms/tfsInstallGuide. *Microsoft continues to update the "Installation Guide" download to include extra guidance or any new issues that surface. Therefore, it is always worth working from the downloaded version. After you download the "Installation Guide," you cannot view its contents unless you right-click the* .chm *file, click Properties, and then click Unblock. As an alternative, you can double-click the* .chm *file to open the Open File-Security Warning dialog box, clear the "Always ask before opening this file" check box, and then click Open.*

As discussed, for production use, we recommend that you install the build service on a separate machine from the application tier. However, a build machine (any machine running the build service in either the build controller or build agent role—or both) is well-suited to installation in a virtual machine. In the case of a build agent machine, it is particularly important that the virtual machine has fast disk access and plenty of CPU resources allocated.

Hosting the build agent in a virtual machine has several advantages that come along with the technology, such as the ability to rapidly add machines to the available pool of build agents for a controller and manage those agents across the physical hardware hosting them. Because a build process requires access to the machine to run any code that may execute as part of the build and test scripts, running in virtualization also provides for a degree of isolation between build agents to ensure that the actions of one build do not affect the outcome of another. Another benefit of virtualization worth mentioning is that the build agent can easily be restored to a known clean state at any time—again, ensuring a clean build environment.

You must have local administrative permission to install the build controller or agent services on a machine. As part of the installation, you must provide a service account under which the installed services will run. This user is often referred to as the TFSBUILD user.

If standard builds are required, and the policy in your company permits it, it is recommended to use the Network Service account. This will avoid issues encountered when using a real domain user account such as expiring passwords, and so on. The Network Service option is available only when running the build services as a Windows service in a domain environment where the build agent and the application tier machine are in the same domain or have a trusted domain relationship.

If you need to manually add a Network Service account to a group such as the Project Collection Build Service Accounts, the format to use is DOMAIN\MACHINE_NAME$, where DOMAIN is the build server's domain name, and MACHINE_NAME is the machine name of the build server.

If the user performing the installation is also part of the Project Collection Administrators group on the project collection to which you will be attaching the build service, this installation process will automatically add the TFSBUILD user to the appropriate Build Services group in the project collection. Otherwise, you must manually add the TFSBUILD user to the group. (See the "Team Foundation Server Installation Guide http://aka.ms/TFS2013InstallGuide" for more information.)

Just as with the Team Foundation Server installation, setting up the build service is done in two parts: installation followed by configuration.

Installing Team Foundation Build

From the Team Foundation Server installation media, navigate to the tfs_server.exe file and run it. You will then be prompted for the installation directory and to accept the License Terms before you can click Install Now.

The installation will then proceed. Depending on the prerequisites required, you may be forced to do a reboot as part of the installation process. Note that the install will add prerequisites (such as .NET) to do a basic build. However, if you wish to perform more-advanced operations (such as a test impact analysis), you must install a suitable version of Visual Studio (such as Visual Studio Ultimate or Visual Studio Premium) onto the build agent machine as well.

Configuring the Team Foundation Build Service

Once the installation has completed, the Team Foundation Server Configuration Center Wizard will be displayed. If you wish to configure the build service after installation, you can access it by running the Team Foundation Server Administration Console from the Start menu. Click Build Configuration ➪ Configure Installed Features ➪ Configure Team Foundation Build Service, and click Start Wizard.

Regardless of whichever way you get into it, you will be presented with the Welcome screen, which you should read before clicking Start Wizard. After reading the next Welcome screen and opting to send any setup information to Microsoft, click Next to go to the Select a Team Project Collection screen of the wizard, as shown in Figure 18-2.

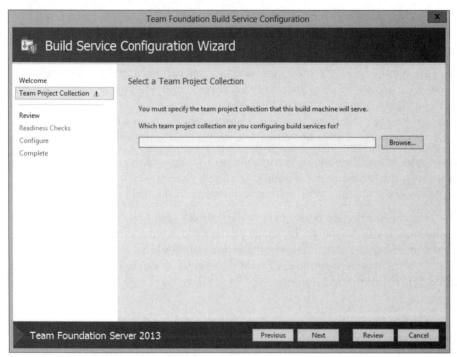

FIGURE 18-2: Build Service Configuration Wizard

Here you must define the project collection to which the build service is bound. Note that this can be one (and only one) project collection per build service instance. If you have many project collections in your organization, but want them to share the same build hardware, you should use virtualization to host several virtual machines running the build controllers for each project collection.

Click the Browse button shown in Figure 18-2 to select the server and project collection. If the server drop-down in the Connect to Team Project Collection dialog box shown in Figure 18-3 is empty, or does not display the server you need to talk to, clicking the Servers button will allow you to add a new server instance first, and then select the project collection.

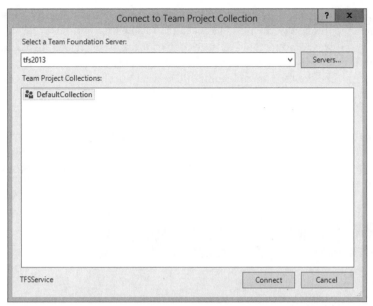

FIGURE 18-3: Connect to Team Project Collection dialog box

Clicking the Connect button in the dialog box shown in Figure 18-3 will then populate the selected project collection in the Build Service Configuration Wizard, and it will allow you to proceed to the Configure Team Foundation Build Service screen shown in Figure 18-4 by clicking Next.

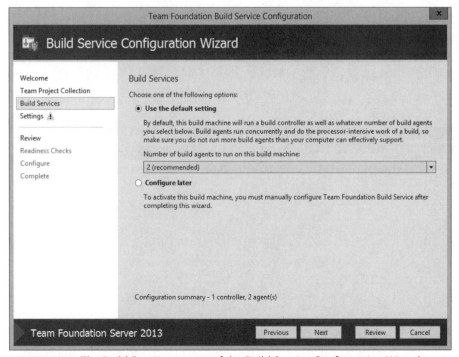

FIGURE 18-4: The Build Services screen of the Build Service Configuration Wizard

Depending on the number of processors that you have available, you may wish to configure multiple build agents to run on the same machine under the build service. This allows for parallel building of projects on the same machine. However, you should be sure that your build server has sufficient CPU resources and fast enough disks to ensure that it can perform adequately in this way. The default setting (and likely most appropriate for a virtualized build server) is to have one build agent per CPU. A dual core virtual machine is shown in Figure 18-4, which is why two agents are shown as the default.

Note that, if you have selected a project collection that already has a build controller, the Configure Team Foundation Build Service screen will look as shown in Figure 18-5. In that instance, if you wanted to add the current machine as a build agent to the selected build controllers pool, you could do so, or you could replace the existing controller with this current machine.

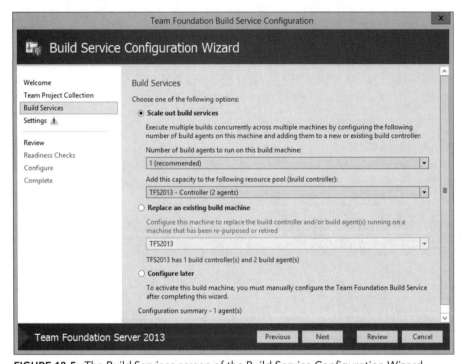

FIGURE 18-5: The Build Services screen of the Build Service Configuration Wizard

Either way, you will now need to provide a build service account (the TFSBUILD user), as shown in Figure 18-6.

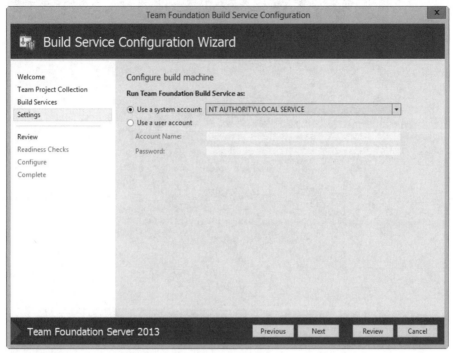

FIGURE 18-6: Configure build machine screen

Click Next to proceed to the review page, where you can check the configuration about to occur. Clicking Next will perform the readiness checks. If you need to correct any errors, do so and then click the link at the bottom of the dialog box that says "Click here to rerun Readiness Checks." Once everything has passed, click Configure to actually begin the build agent configuration process. When this has completed successfully, finish the wizard and your configuration will be complete.

You will now be presented with the Team Foundation Server Administration Console. Viewing the Build Configuration screen shown in Figure 18-7 will allow you to check the status of the build service and the defined controller and agent(s).

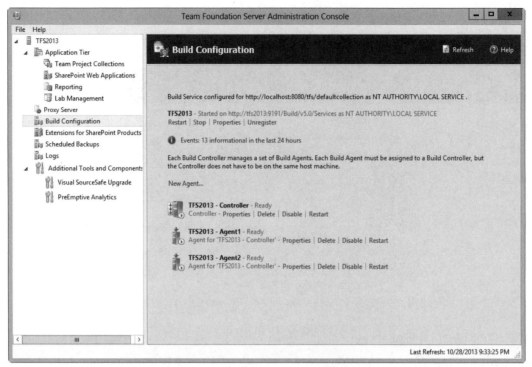

FIGURE 18-7: Build Configuration screen

The top part of the Build Configuration screen shown in Figure 18-7 controls the actual build service hosting the build controller and/or build agent(s). You can control the service from here by starting, stopping, or restarting it. The same could also be done using the usual Windows Services section of Server Manager in Windows Server and selecting the Visual Studio Team Foundation Build Service Host 2013 service, or by issuing the typical `net start "TFSBuildServiceHost.2013"` commands from an Administrative command line. For example, you might need to restart the build service to pick up any changes such as modifications to system environment variables.

More useful is the capability to unregister the build service and adjust the build service properties. Unregistering will remove the build service from the project collection and remove the associated build controller and agents if you wish to decommission the build machine. Once the build service is stopped, clicking the Properties link will display the Build Service Properties dialog box, as shown in Figure 18-8.

In the dialog box, as shown in Figure 18-8, you can change the project collection to which the build services are connected, which is useful if the URL to access the project collection changes because of a move of that collection to a new application tier. You can also specify the web service endpoint for the build services. By clicking Change, you can adjust the configuration to a different port, force SSL, and optionally require client certificate authentication in the instances where you want a cryptographically secure link between the application tier machine and the build service.

The Build Service Properties dialog box also allows you to specify that the build service host process be run as an interactive process, rather than a Windows service, if a session with a desktop login is required (such as when running coded UI tests).

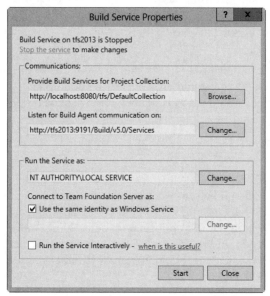

FIGURE 18-8: Build Service Properties dialog box

RUNNING THE BUILD SERVICE HOST AS AN INTERACTIVE PROCESS

It is sometimes necessary to run the build service host as an interactive process with a real domain user account. The most common example is when you require the build agent to interact with a running application through the desktop, such as when you want to run coded UI tests without a full test agent. Several steps are available to ensure this kind of configuration is as reliable as possible.

The first is to configure the build service host to run as an interactive service using the Build Service Properties dialog box, as shown in Figure 18-8.

Next, you should configure the build service user as an auto-logon account for the server. This will ensure that when the machine reboots because of Windows updates requiring restarts or other events, it will go straight to an interactive session for the build user. For more information, see http://aka.ms/KB324737.

You should then ensure that the screen saver is disabled for the build user account to prevent it from locking the session.

Note that all these options degrade the security of the build agent machine because anyone with physical access to the machine would then be able to interact with it as the logged-on build user. Therefore, any build agent configured in this way should be placed in an environment with the appropriate level of physical security.

For more information on coded UI tests and test agents, see Chapter 26.

Additional Software Required on the Build Agent

To perform basic compilation and unit tests of many project types in Visual Studio, no additional software is required on the build agent after installing the build service. However, you must install a suitable Visual Studio edition for other types of projects and activities. For example, to build an ASP.NET Web Application project or a C++ project, you must have Visual Studio 2013 installed on the build agent computer.

Additionally, you may need to install third-party component libraries if they are required to be in the Global Assembly Cache (GAC) by your projects. If your build process requires additional functionality to be present (such as the Build Extensions power tool, along with Java and Ant or Maven to build Java projects), these must also be installed.

WORKING WITH BUILDS

Now that you have configured a build controller and build agent, you can go about automating the build of your project. This section focuses primarily on building Visual Studio projects and managing the build automation from within the Visual Studio IDE. For information on building Ant or Maven projects, see the section "Building Ant and Maven Projects with Team Foundation Server" later in this chapter. Many of the tools and windows are identical (or at least very similar) in Eclipse for Java-based projects, so the following is still relevant.

This discussion assumes that you have a project that cleanly builds in Visual Studio, that you are sharing the source for the build in version control with the rest of your team, and that you want to automate in the build process for that project.

Creating a Build Definition

As previously mentioned, the build definition defines how, what, when, and where to perform your build. You create a new build definition in Visual Studio from the Builds page, and then select New Build Definition or right-click the Builds node in Team Explorer for the team project and select New Build Definition, as shown in Figure 18-9.

This will then show the build definition editor. In Visual Studio, it will show in the main document (see Figure 18-10), and in Eclipse it is a new modal dialog box. The build definition editor is divided into two parts. The area on the left shows the various sections of the build definition, and the area on the right is the form for that section.

FIGURE 18-9: New Build Definition link in Team Explorer

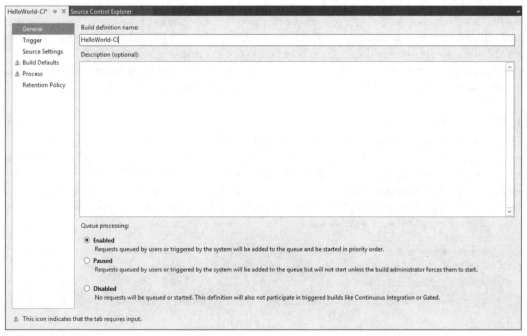

FIGURE 18-10: General section

Note that when you first create the build definition, a number of warning triangles appear on the left-hand side of the dialog box. This is completely normal and just indicates which sections have data that must be filled out before proceeding. However, it is a good practice to go through every section and fill in the relevant data because the defaults are not always what you might want.

> **NOTE** *In Visual Studio, if you have the solution open for which you wish to automate the build, when you create the new build definition, it will default a number of values into the build definition form for you (such as the build definition name, the workspace template, and which solution to build). You can still edit these as you go through the form, but having the solution open before creating the new build definition can save you some time.*

General Section

The General section shown in Figure 18-10 allows you to set the build definition name and description, and you can optionally disable or pause the build definition. It is easy to rename a build definition at any point in the future, so do not worry too much at this point about what naming convention to use if you do not have one already.

For the description of the build, it is a good practice to provide a short (one-line) description of what the build is for, as well as contact details for the build owner or "build master." The first three lines of the build descriptions are displayed in other dialog boxes in Team Foundation Build without scrolling, and they are, therefore, quite useful to add data to in order to make your development system more discoverable and easy to use for new team members.

Trigger Section

The Trigger section controls *when* the build should be run. As shown in Figure 18-11, there are a number of triggers defined that can allow a build to run. Note that these are the only built-in triggers in Team Foundation Server, and they are not extensible. Therefore, if they do not meet your needs, you must create your mechanism for queuing the build using the extensibility APIs for Team Foundation Server. For an example of using the extensibility API to queue a build, see the blog post at http://aka.ms/TfsBuildApiExample.

> **NOTE** *See Chapter 29 for more details on Team Foundation Server extensibility.*

However, the following built-in trigger types are very comprehensive, and they cover the vast majority of build scenarios:

➤ Manual

➤ Continuous Integration

➤ Rolling Builds

➤ Gated Check-in

➤ Schedule

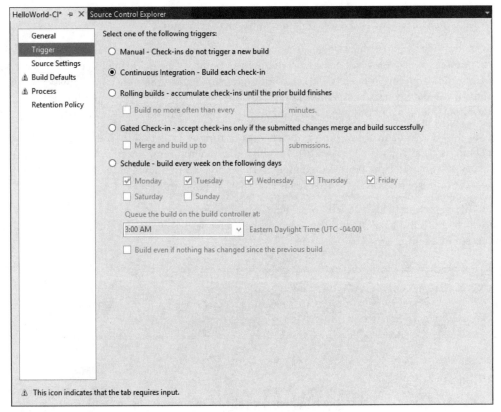

FIGURE 18-11: Trigger section

Manual

The Manual trigger was the only trigger available in Team Foundation Server 2005. When a build is manually triggered, it will be run only when the build is explicitly queued by a user in Visual Studio, Eclipse, by the `tfsbuild.exe` command, or by other code using the extensibility APIs for Team Foundation Server.

Manual builds are useful when first creating the build definition to ensure that everything is working correctly before turning to one of the other triggers. They are also commonly used for a QA build—that is, a build performed when the team wishes to push code to a QA environment. The QA build might perform additional automated tests and documentation activities that take a significant amount of time, and they would be overkill for a standard development build but only necessary when creating a build that may be used in production. Any build definition can always be manually triggered as desired, regardless of the configured trigger type.

Continuous Integration

The Continuous Integration trigger monitors every check-in affecting the build files and causes a new build to be queued. The folders and files that trigger the build are determined by the Workspace definition examined later in this chapter. Because check-ins to Team Foundation Server are denoted by the changeset number as a single atomic transaction, by performing a build for every check-in, it is easy to see which check-in caused a problem ("Who broke the build?").

For systems that have a lot of check-ins, it is essential that the continuous integration build runs as quickly as possible to provide feedback as to whether the build is "good" or not so that the feedback loop is maintained and developers get into the habit of ensuring that their check-ins always result in good builds. If a build agent is busy building the previous check-in, the build controller will look for the next available build agent or keep the builds in a queue until a build agent is available.

The state of the version control repository at the point of time represented by the changeset that triggered the build is what is used when performing the build. Therefore, it doesn't matter if the build for changeset 17 runs after the build for changeset 19 because of build agent availability or build priorities—the builds will represent the state at exactly that point in time.

Because of the precise nature of continuous integration builds—and the clear way in which they indicate which check-in broke the build—they are the preferred trigger to use for a standard development automated build.

> **NOTE** *To prevent a check-in from triggering a build, insert the text* ***NO_ CI*** *anywhere in the comment string. This special string indicates the check-in should be ignored by the build system triggers.*

Rolling Builds

A Rolling Build trigger is similar to the build trigger called Continuous Integration by Team Foundation Server. However, it will group together several check-ins to ensure that the build controller never has a large queue of builds waiting to be processed. Optionally, a time interval can be specified to control the minimum duration that must have passed before a new build is triggered. This is the type of trigger that was first used by the continuous integration build servers such as CruiseControl or CruiseControl.NET.

Rolling builds reduce the number of builds performed and, therefore, can guarantee a time in which the results of a particular check-in will be known. However, the grouping of check-ins from several developers can make it difficult to identify which change was responsible for any build failure.

A build definition with a Rolling Build trigger can also be used in conjunction with a continuous integration build. Both can build the same resources. However, the continuous integration build can be responsible for providing a quick check on quality for the build, whereas the Rolling Build can perform additional activities such as running a full UI automation pass, generating code documentation, packaging the build into MSI installers and ISO images ready for distribution, or even deploying the build into a test environment ready for evaluation.

Gated Check-In

The Gated Check-in trigger was new to Team Foundation Server 2010. It is similar to a Continuous Integration trigger, but with a twist. When a check-in is performed into the area covered by a Gated Check-in build definition, the developer is presented with the dialog box shown in Figure 18-12.

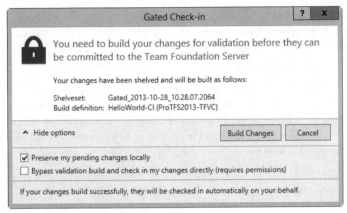

FIGURE 18-12: Gated Check-in dialog box

Any check-ins are first automatically stored as a shelveset. The build server then merges the code as it was before the check-in was attempted with the code stored in the shelveset. Only when the build is successful are the changes then committed to the version control repository by the build controller on behalf of the person performing the check-in (but with the addition of ***NO_CI*** appended to the end of the check-in comment to ensure a subsequent build is not required). If the merge of the shelveset with the latest version of source control is not possible because of a merge conflict, then the build will fail. If the build fails for any reason, then no code is checked in, but the shelveset is kept on the server for remediation.

Team Foundation Server 2012 provided the ability to accumulate gated check-in submissions. This feature is useful if your build server can't keep up with the number of submissions. When this feature is enabled, the server will merge and build a number of submissions as part of a single build execution. However, if a combination of multiple submissions fails, the server will attempt to build them as individual submissions. This allows the valid check-ins to be committed and the invalid check-ins to be rejected without manual intervention.

The user will be notified of the check-in build completion via the build notification tool running in the system notification area on Windows or via the Gated Check-ins view in Eclipse. At this point, the user may *reconcile* his or her workspace—that is, remove the pending changes that were committed as part of the build from the current pending changes list.

If more than one build definition is affected by a gated check-in, the user will be prompted to select the one he or she wishes to use to validate the build in the Gated Check-in warning dialog box shown in Figure 18-12.

Because gated check-ins require the code to be automatically merged as part of the build process, this has two important effects:

➤ The actual code checked in may differ slightly from the code submitted as part of the shelveset.

➤ Even though Team Foundation Server has built-in agent pooling capabilities, only one build of a gated check-in may be executed at a time to prevent merge conflicts.

Gated check-ins are useful in organizations that have very large numbers of developers working in the same codebase where traditional gated continuous integration builds are failing too often because of human error. (Even the best developer might break the build once or twice a year; but, if you have 300 developers checking into the same tree, that means the build breaks at least every day.)

More commonly, gated check-ins are used when organizations wish to ensure that code committed to the main codebase meets certain requirements, such as code quality, test coverage, and so on. These factors can sometimes be determined by deploying custom check-in policies to every developer machine. However, that may require significant overhead and make for a very complex check-in experience. Gated check-ins move all the check-in validation to a centralized server infrastructure.

Schedule

The Schedule trigger can define a time on a weekly schedule that a build is queued—that is, a daily, nightly, or weekly build. Note that only a single time may be provided for each build definition, and that time is used on the chosen days of the week repeated weekly. This time should be selected so that it does not conflict with any ongoing backup or other maintenance jobs in the network, and ideally it should also be selected so that, when the build is due to complete, there are people available to help fix the build if any errors have occurred.

The time in which the build is run is converted to the time zone for the application tier when the build definition is saved, but it is always displayed in the local time zone of the user editing the build definition. Therefore, there can be some confusion around periods when daylight savings is in operation in one of those times zones and not the other.

If a more complex schedule is required (such as every second Thursday or the last Tuesday of the month), it may be preferable to create a build definition using a Manual trigger, and then set up a Windows Scheduled Job to run on the defined schedule that will queue the build using the `tfsbuild.exe` command line.

MANAGING BUILDS FROM THE COMMAND LINE WITH TFSBUILD.EXE

Visual Studio Team Explorer installs a number of command-line tools, one of which is the `tfsbuild.exe` command. The command can be used to perform a limited number of Team Foundation Build tasks and is also useful in scripting scenarios where full access to the Team Foundation extensibility APIs is not required.

For example, to trigger a build, a command similar to the following could be used:

```
tfsbuild start http://vsalm:8080/tfs/DefaultCollection
      AdventureWorks "My Build Definition"
```

In this example, `http://vsalm:8080/tfs/DefaultCollection` is the URL for the team project collection, `AdventureWorks` is the name of the team project, and `My Build Definition` is the name of the build definition for which you wish to queue a build.

For more information on the `tfsbuild` command, open a Developer Command Prompt for VS2013 and type **TFSBuild help**, or visit `http://aka.ms/TfsBuildExe`.

Workspace Section

The Workspace section shown in Figure 18-13 allows you to define the working folder mappings that should be used for your build. This determines not only where the files should be placed on the disk to perform the build, but also which files are relevant to the build definition and, therefore, should be included in any build label or monitored as part of the build trigger.

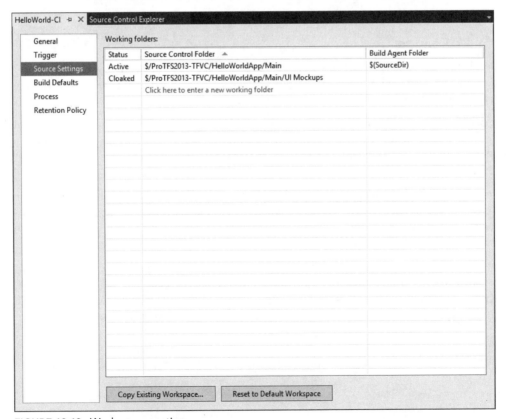

FIGURE 18-13: Workspace section

The default working folder mapping is usually given as the root of the team project (for example, $/AdventureWorks) mapped to the sources directory represented by the environment variable $(SourceDir). This is almost always too broad of a mapping and covers many files that should not be part of your build. It has the effect of triggering builds when they should not be and slowing down the build process (because files outside the area of a source that you are interested in must be downloaded).

The working folder mappings should be altered to include an active mapping with as fine of a granularity as possible (usually the folder containing the solution to be built inside the branch you wish to build, as shown in Figure 18-13). Also, any files or folders that should not trigger a build should be cloaked.

In the example in Figure 18-13, a directory containing a series of UI mockup images is excluded from the build because, while they are checked in alongside the source tree, the files do not make up part of the software being built. (They are for reference by the development team during development and would take a significant amount of time to download in each build because of their large size.)

> **NOTE** *For more information on working folder mappings and cloaked mappings, see Chapter 6.*

Build Defaults Section

In the Build Defaults section shown in Figure 18-14, you select which controller you wish to be responsible for the build definition by default, and select where you want the results of the build to be staged after they have been built (the drop location).

Installing the build service host registers the build controller with the server. If there are no build controllers present in the drop down, you do not have one installed for your current project collection. See the section "Setting Up the Team Foundation Build Service" earlier in this chapter for details on how to do this.

The Description field shows the description assigned to the build controller (useful for conveying information about who owns the controller or what it should be used for), and it is read-only in this section. To edit the description, see the Build Controller Properties dialog box from the Team Foundation Server Administration Console.

The drop location must be a UNC path to a Windows file share on the network. The build agent machine must have network access, and the user running the build service must have permission to write to that location, because files are copied directly from the build agent to the drop location as part of the build. There is a 260-character limit to the full path of all files copied to the drop location, so you should ensure that the server name and path are reasonably short, leaving you the maximum space for your output. However, you should put builds in directories in the drop location that correspond to the build definition to help keep them organized. If your build does not have any output, you can select the first option, which allows the build definition to be valid without filling in a drop location. You can also have the build outputs stored in a special location in Team Foundation Server known as the Server Drop. This feature, new in Team Foundation Server 2013, is handy if you don't have the ability to configure a drop location that can be accessed through a UNC path.

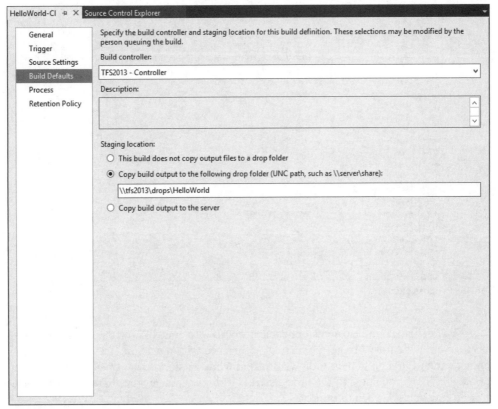

FIGURE 18-14: Build Defaults section

Process Section

The Process section determines which of the registered build process templates should be used for the build definition and what properties should be passed into that Windows Workflow process when it is started, as shown in Figure 18-15.

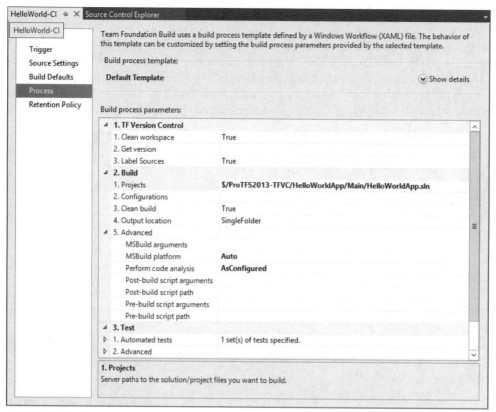

FIGURE 18-15: Process section

Each process can define a number of customizable properties to control how the build behaves. Properties that are mandatory but not populated are marked with a warning triangle when the build definition is created. If the build definition was created while a solution was open in Visual Studio, this solution will be prepopulated in the Projects area. If this occurs, ensure that this is the correct solution or project that you wish to build.

Note that the Process section is one area that differs greatly when creating Java-based builds from Eclipse using Team Explorer Everywhere. For more information, see the section "Building Ant and Maven Projects with Team Foundation Server," later in this chapter.

The build process, along with more details on the various properties used by the main process templates that ship out of the box, is described in more detail later in this chapter in the section "Understanding the Build Process."

Retention Policy Section

The Retention Policy section shown in Figure 18-16 specifies the rules by which builds should be retained automatically and what should be deleted for builds that fall outside of the retention policy.

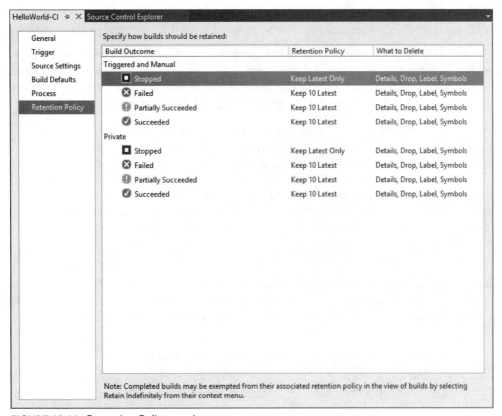

FIGURE 18-16: Retention Policy section

Once you start building on every check-in, the number of builds created by the system can rapidly increase. However, not all of the builds are relevant for very long once the status (passed or failed) is known. Finding the build that you are looking for can get complicated but also the disk space required to store all the build results grows for each build retained.

With Team Foundation Server, a build may finish in one of four states:

➤ **Succeeded**—Everything in the build is good and is what you want to see.

➤ **Partially Succeeded**—This is the default state given to a build that has passed compilation but something else has gone wrong during the build (such as unit tests failing). In the case of unit test failures, it is possible to completely fail the build. (See the section "Build Process Parameters" later in this chapter for more information.)

➤ **Failed**—A Failed build is one that has completely failed for some reason.

➤ **Stopped**—A Stopped build is one that has been terminated manually while it was running.

The retention policy controls how many results you would like to keep by default for each type of build result. At any time, from the context menu of the build details, or from the build report, you can indicate that a particular build should be marked Retain Indefinitely (or Keep Forever). Marking a build as Retain Indefinitely means that it will be excluded from the automatic retention policies.

Separate retention policies are in place for both the team builds triggered (or manually queued) and for the private builds queued by individual developers. More information is given on private builds later in this chapter. Changing the private build retention policy affects all the developers performing private builds for that definition—not just the developer editing the setting.

> **WARNING** *For teams making use of Microsoft Test Manager to record fast-forward test executions, deleting test results will destroy the action recordings required for fast-forwarding. Therefore, be careful with the retention policy settings for build definitions used by your test teams. You may alter the retention policy to exclude test results from the items deleted, as shown in Figure 18-16, or mark any builds used by your test teams as Retain Indefinitely. For more information, see Chapter 26.*

For each retention policy, you can determine what is automatically deleted by selecting the "What to Delete" column. Selecting <Specify What to Delete> displays the dialog box shown in Figure 18-17, which allows a custom setting to be applied when the build is automatically deleted from that point onward.

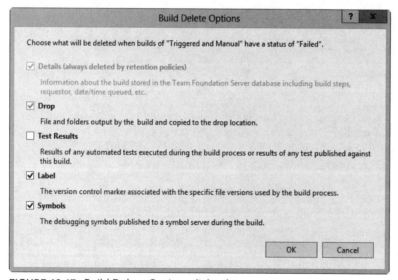

FIGURE 18-17: Build Delete Options dialog box

For more information on what each of the delete options means, see the section "Deleting Builds" later in this chapter.

Saving the Build Definition

Once you are happy with the settings for the build definition, you can save it by clicking the Save button or pressing Ctrl+S. In Eclipse, click OK to save the changes to the server.

Queuing a Build

When you have created a new build definition, you should manually queue the build the first time to ensure that it is working as desired. The latest successful build for a build definition is used to determine which changesets and work items will be associated with the subsequent build, so this first build will be the baseline by which the next triggered build is compared.

To manually queue a build in Visual Studio, go to Build ➪ Queue New Build. Alternatively, in either Eclipse or Visual Studio, you can right-click on the build definition in the `Builds` node of Team Explorer and select Queue New Build.

You will then be presented with the Queue Build dialog box, as shown in Figure 18-18.

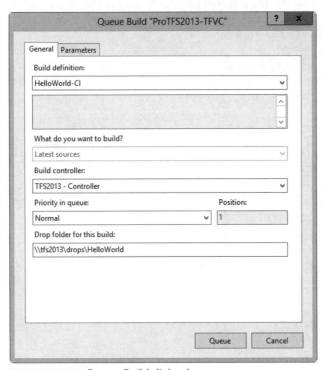

FIGURE 18-18: Queue Build dialog box

Understanding the Queuing Process

When you manually queue a build, you may specify on which controller you would like this to run (overriding the default, which is used for a triggered build). Additionally, you can set the priority of the queued build and get an indication as to where in the queue this priority would put you when submitting the build.

Builds triggered using one of the build definition triggers are done so with a priority of Normal. You can set this to High, Above Normal, Normal, Below Normal, or Low, depending on the priority of your manual build request. Click Queue to trigger the build at this point.

When manually queuing a build, an additional Parameters tab will be displayed. There you will find a customizable list of properties as defined by the build process template, allowing you to alter the value of that property for this single invocation of the build.

For example, if you wanted to manually queue a build of the source tree based on the label `ReadyForTest`, you could manually specify the Get Version property for the build to be `LReadyForTest@$/ProTFS2013-TFVC` (where `L` specifies that this is a Label version specification, and `@$/ProTFS2013-TFVC` specifies that this label was in the scope of a Team Project folder called `$/ProTFS2013-TFVC` in version control), as shown in Figure 18-19.

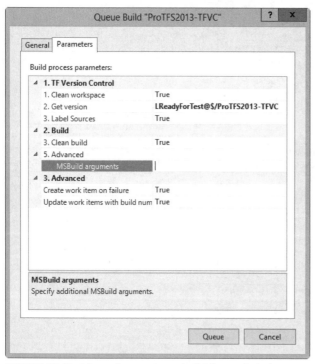

FIGURE 18-19: Manually queuing a build from a Label

Private Builds

A feature of Team Foundation Server is the ability to request that a build be performed using the latest sources merged with a shelveset specified by the developer as a *private build* (sometimes called a *buddy build*). You do this from the Queue Build dialog box when manually queuing a build by changing the "What do you want to build option" to "Latest sources with shelveset," and then specifying the shelveset, as shown in Figure 18-20.

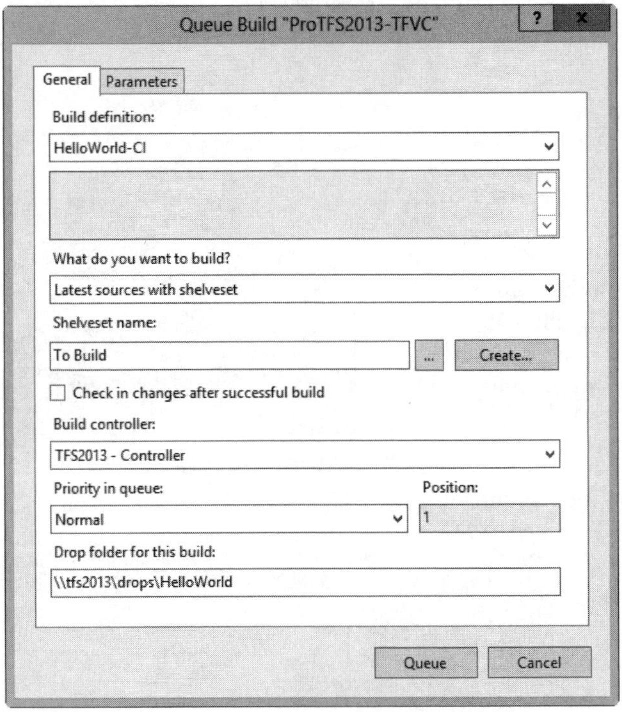

FIGURE 18-20: Manually queuing a private build

Private builds are useful when you want to ensure that you are including all the changes necessary to successfully perform the build on a different machine before committing the changes to the main source repository. They are also very useful when you want to make use of the build process set up on the server to test and create all the build output, but you are not yet sure if the change you are proposing should be included in the codebase.

A private build is similar to a gated check-in, except that the use of shelvesets is not enforced, and checking in of the code in the shelveset after a successful build is optional.

Private builds (those performed without selecting the check-in option) do not follow the same build numbering scheme defined for the regular team builds and have separate retention policies, as discussed earlier in this chapter. The results of the private build are shown to that developer only and are not displayed to the entire team. However, build alerts may notify of private builds depending on their configuration.

Build Notifications and Alerts

Team Foundation Server exposes a powerful eventing model and extensibility APIs that allow for custom integrations of any imaginable application or device for notification of build results, from standard e-mail alerts to lava lamps, confetti-filled leaf blowers, build status screens, and even talking robotic rabbits. However, there are two main notification systems exposed to the developer out of the box:

➤ Build notifications tool on Windows

➤ E-mail alerts

Build Notifications Tool

The notification tool is a small application that runs in the system notification area on Windows. In the 2008 release, this was provided as part of the Team Foundation Server Power Tools but ships with Visual Studio and Visual Studio Team Explorer in the 2010 release and beyond.

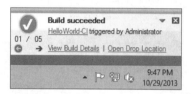

FIGURE 18-21: Notification tool pop-up

Figure 18-21 shows the build notification tool running and displaying a notification to the user as an Outlook style pop-up message in the bottom-right corner of the screen. It can be configured to run on login, but will be run by Visual Studio if a gated check-in is requested. In the case of a gated check-in, if the build is successful, the notification tool will display a dialog box to the users (see Figure 18-22) asking them if they would like to Reconcile their workspaces. The build notification tool works by polling Team Foundation Server at a regular interval, and therefore notifications may take up to two minutes to be displayed to the user after the build has been completed.

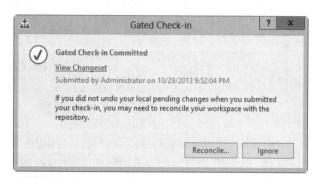

FIGURE 18-22: Notification prompting for reconciliation of workspace

E-mail Alerts

Basic e-mail alerts can be configured from the Team ⇨ Project Alerts menu in Visual Studio once the selected team project has been highlighted in Team Explorer. Using the interface shown in Figure 18-23, e-mail alerts can be enabled when a build quality changes, when any build completes, or when builds are initiated by the developer.

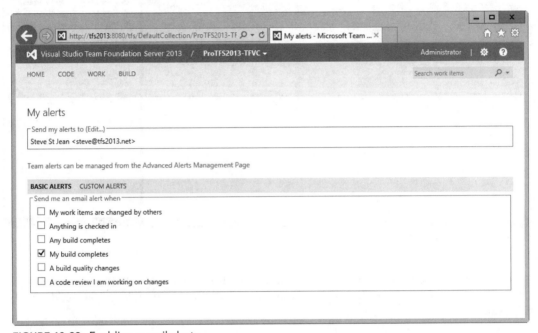

FIGURE 18-23: Enabling e-mail alerts

E-mails can be sent to any e-mail address, including team distribution lists, provided the Team Foundation Server application tier is configured with the correct SMTP server details to send the messages. However, the e-mail alerts belong to the user who created the alert, and that user must delete or edit the alert through the web interface.

On the Team Foundation Server application tier machine, the `BisSubscribe.exe` command is available in the `Team Foundation Server\Tools` folder and can be used to script the creation of project alerts for a team project.

Managing Builds

The main build management activities are performed using the Builds page in Visual Studio or Eclipse, which is accessed by clicking on the Builds link in Team Explorer. Figure 18-24 shows the Build Explorer.

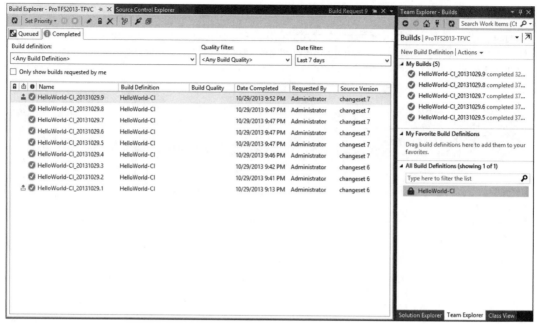

FIGURE 18-24: Build Explorer

All the build definitions for a particular team project are listed under the All Build Definitions section in Team Explorer. Although there is no way to order the builds into folders, the build definitions can be searched and filtered.

Build Explorer

The Build Explorer allows access to builds that the system is aware of, to those that have run, and to those that are running or are waiting to run. The Build Explorer is organized into two tabs as follows:

➤ Queued builds

➤ Completed builds

Queued Builds

From the Queued builds tab shown in Figure 18-25, you can cancel, pause, or change the priority of any build currently waiting to be built. You can also stop builds currently executing. By default, the Queued builds tab will also show you builds that have completed in the past five minutes.

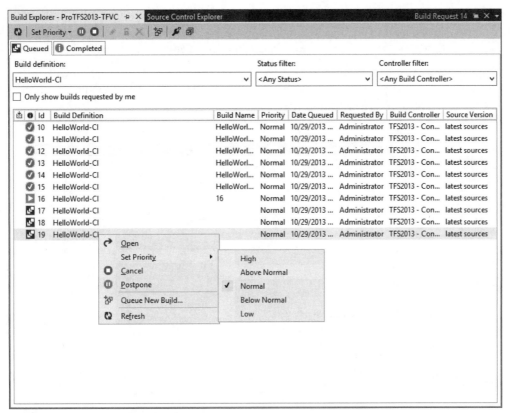

FIGURE 18-25: Queued builds tab

Completed Builds

The Completed builds tab shown in Figure 18-26 displays builds that have completed (have finished execution and are Successful, Partially Successful, Failed, or Stopped). An icon shows the status of the build, with another icon to the left showing the build reason (scheduled build, continuous integration, rolling build, private build, gated check-in, and so on). Hovering over an icon will display a tooltip with a full description.

The builds are filtered by the criteria at the top of the Completed builds tab—by default, showing all builds for that day by everyone on the team. You can constrain the list to show only your builds, or show a greater date range, and so on, by adjusting the options.

The Completed builds tab is where much of the build management is performed for individual build details. You can mark a build to Retain Indefinitely to prevent it from being included in the automatic retention policy rules. You can also delete builds and edit the build quality.

Team Foundation Server 2013 also has the capability of retrying a build. This option will queue the build again with the same parameters as executed in the original build. This functionality is useful if your build fails because of an environmental issue, such as a power failure, rather than a coding issue.

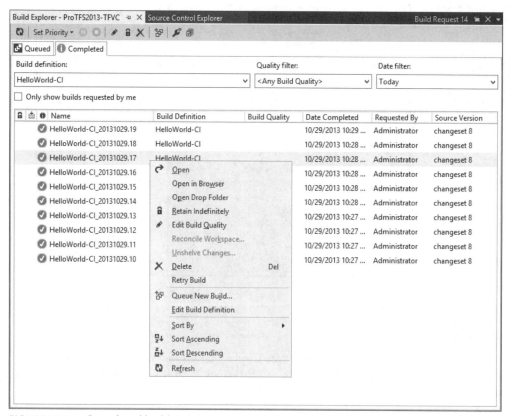

FIGURE 18-26: Completed builds tab

Deleting Builds

If you delete a build, you are presented with the Delete Build dialog box shown in Figure 18-27, which allows you to control the parts of the build you wish to delete.

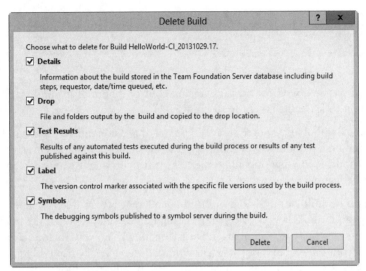

FIGURE 18-27: Delete Build dialog box

You can delete the following:

➤ **Details**—This is the build record in the Team Foundation Server database, and deleting this means that the build no longer shows in the Build Explorer. The build is actually still in the database, just marked as deleted. To completely remove the build record, you must destroy it using the `tfsbuild.exe` command line.

> **NOTE** *For more information about this, as well as what information does and doesn't get deleted and why, see Adam Root's blog post at* `http://aka.ms/ DeletedBuilds`.

➤ **Drop**—These are all the build outputs copied to the network share. These can be very significant in size and, therefore, the most likely thing that you wish to delete. Using this dialog box is a quick way to clean up the drop location without removing the rest of the data for the build.

➤ **Test Results**—This includes all the test results from test runs and any associated test data (including video files and action recordings). Be careful when deleting test data because it may impact testers and developers if there are unresolved bugs with test results.

> **NOTE** *For more information, see Chapter 26.*

➤ **Label**—This is the label associated with the built-in version control. For auditing and tracking purposes, it is common to leave the label for all builds.

➤ **Symbols**—If you are using Symbol and Source servers, you may have configured your build to have symbol files stored on a Symbol server that may take up significant space. However, if you have released this build to anyone (including the test team), you might want to keep the symbols around for debugging purposes.

It is worth noting that the "Found in Build" and "Fixed in Build" fields that are used by some of the process templates in Team Foundation Server work item tracking make use of a global list in the work item system. In previous versions of Team Foundation Server, there was no way to automatically delete these build numbers from the global lists. In Team Foundation Server 2012 and later, there is a maintenance job that runs on a weekly basis to clean up the build number global lists and remove entries that no longer exist.

Build Details View

When you double-click a build in the Build Explorer, you can see a report of the build details, as shown in Figure 18-28. This is known as the Build Details View or the Build Report.

When the build is executing, you will see the build log periodically refreshing to show the latest results of the build. A small bar chart in the top-left corner of the build shows the build duration in comparison with the previous builds to give you an indication of how much longer the build is likely to run.

As the build progresses, more information is added to the build log. If you scroll to the bottom of the build log, the view will maintain that bottom scroll position, and the results will scroll up as the build proceeds further.

The information is displayed in a hierarchical tree, with the duration of each step displayed in the top right-hand side of that node. For steps that create additional log files (such as MSBuild, Ant, or Maven that perform the actual compilation of the code), you can click on the report to download it from the drop location and view it.

Once the build has completed, you will see the build summary view by default (refer to Figure 18-28). This shows all the compilations, test runs, and any unit test results, code coverage, and test impact analysis data. You will also see information regarding the changesets included since the last successful build of that build definition, along with any work items that were associated with those changesets as they were checked in.

In this way, you can see how the full requirement traceability data is being tracked by Team Foundation Server, and why the build automation system completed the feedback loop for the development process. By performing the build, you can see which code was changed, what work items that change was associated with, and what build the changes went into. You can also see which unit tests were run, what the code coverage was, which tests might be impacted by the code that was changed, and so on. All this data is being stored in the Team Foundation Server data warehouse and is available for later analysis.

FIGURE 18-28: Report of the build details

From the Build Details View, you can open the drop location to view the actual outputs of the build (the website or executable files). You can also mark the build to be retained indefinitely and set the build quality. You can even delete the build from this view.

Managing Build Quality Descriptions

For each build, you can set a *build quality* from the Completed builds tab or from the build report. The build quality is a text string that allows the team to tag the build with additional metadata, and it is useful for communicating the quality of the build with the rest of the team. For example, you can easily identify builds that have been released or are ready for testing. Note that, in addition to setting the build quality, you may want to mark the build to be retained indefinitely in those cases.

To manage the options available for the build quality, go to Build ⇨ Manage Build Qualities in Visual Studio. This displays the Edit Build Qualities dialog box shown in Figure 18-29, which you can use to add new entries and remove ones that are not used.

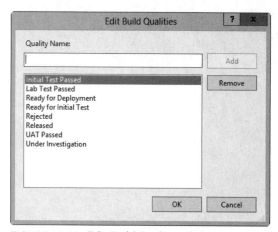

FIGURE 18-29: Edit Build Qualities dialog box

Managing Build Controllers and Build Agents

The build controllers and agents can be managed from the Team Foundation Administration Console on the build controller machine or application tier. However, the controller and agent properties are also available from Visual Studio by going to Build ⇨ Manage Build Controllers, which displays the Manage Build Controllers dialog box. Selecting a build controller and clicking Properties will show you its Properties dialog box (see Figure 18-30), and selecting an agent and clicking Properties will show you its properties (see Figure 18-31).

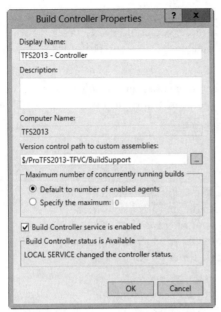

FIGURE 18-30: Build Controller Properties dialog box

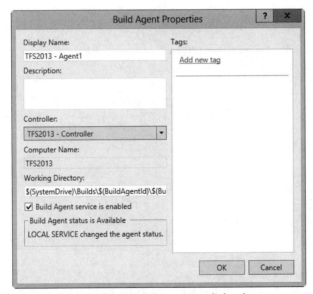

FIGURE 18-31: Build Agent Properties dialog box

From the Build Agent Properties dialog box, you can add a number of tags to the agent to signify capabilities of that agent, as shown in Figure 18-31. For example, you could use CodeSign if you have the project's code signing certificate installed on that machine, DataCenter1 if it is located in your main data center, or Ireland if it is located remotely.

As part of the build process, you can then filter by these tags to ensure that you are allocated a build agent that meets the requirements necessary for the build. For more information on this, see the section "Understanding the Build Process" later in this chapter.

MINIMIZING THE BUILD PATH

Because of limitations in the way that the tools interact with the file system, there is a 260-character limit on the full path of files that make up the build process. In previous versions of Team Foundation Server, the initial working directory for a build agent was in the build service users profile directory, which significantly reduced the number of characters in the path available for your build files.

In Team Foundation Server 2010, the build working folder was reduced to `$(SystemDrive)\Builds\$(BuildAgentId)\$(BuildDefinitionPath)`, which, for a typical build, is something like `C:\Builds\1\Team Project \Build Definition Name\`. While this is much improved, you may still run into issues with build path length and need to reduce it further.

The shortest common build path can be created by setting the build agent working directory to something like `$(SystemDrive)\B\$(BuildAgentId)\ $(BuildDefinitionId)`, which will create a typical build working folder of `C:\B\1\42\`, leaving you with some valuable additional characters if you find yourself pushing the 260-character limit. Using the `BuildDefinitionId` also guarantees that each new working folder created is unique, and it prevents any workspace issues that sometimes happen when deleting and then adding a build definition with the same name for a team project.

> **NOTE** *Both Visual Studio and Team Foundation Server have shifted to a quarterly update cycle. One of the improvements introduced in the first quarterly update for Team Foundation Server 2012 was an increase in the server path limit from 260 to 400 characters.*
>
> *This doesn't completely eliminate the problem, as it is only the server path (for example, `$/Project/Folder/File.cs`), not the local path length.*
>
> *For more information, refer to Brian Harry's blog post at* `http://aka.ms/ Tfs2012FirstUpdate`.

UNDERSTANDING THE BUILD PROCESS

The end-to-end build process performed by a build is defined in a Windows Workflow XAML file stored in the version control repository and in the Team Foundation Server app tier. The initial build process templates available are defined by the overall Team Foundation Server process template and are created as part of the Team Project creation process. In Team Foundation Server 2013 these templates were moved from a folder under each Team Project's node in version control to a storage location inside the App Tier. Locating and downloading these base templates will be discussed in Chapter 19. Any time after the Team Project is created, base build process templates can be downloaded and modified and new build process templates can be created. In both cases, the process template can be registered with Team Foundation Server and stored in version control. Those files can be modified to adjust the behavior of new builds for that particular process template.

The rest of this section focuses on using the process templates that ship in the box with Team Foundation Server. These include the following:

> **NOTE** *For more information on customizing the build process templates, see Chapter 19.*

➤ **DefaultTemplate (TfvcTemplate.12.xaml)**—The default template for all new builds created for Team Foundation Version Control (TFVC) team projects in Team Foundation Server 2013. This is the template that will be the primary focus of discussion in the remainder of this section.

➤ **DefaultTemplate (GitTemplate.12.xaml)**—The default template for all new builds created for Git team projects in Team Foundation Server 2013.

➤ **UpgradeTemplate**—The build template using the MSBuild-wrapped approach from previous versions of Team Foundation Server and also used for non–.NET compilation projects such as VB6, C++, and also Java-based builds with Ant or Maven. The UpgradeTemplate is used by any existing build definitions that existed in a Team Foundation Server 2008 instance upgraded to Team Foundation Server 2010, 2012, or 2013. UpgradeTemplate basically performs some simple housekeeping functionality that used to be hard-coded into the build agent process in earlier versions of Team Foundation Server. It then wraps the call to the MSBuild file called TFSBuild.proj that controls the rest of the MSBuild-based build process.

In addition, the LabDefaultTemplate.11 will also be present for use with the Lab Management functionality described in Chapter 26.

As stated previously, all the base build process templates are stored as XAML files in the Team Foundation Server App Tier. In versions prior to 2013, they lived in a folder called BuildProcessTemplates in the root of the team project ($/TeamProject/BuildProcessTemplates). You can still create this folder in your Team Project, store downloaded templates or create new ones here, and register them with the build system for use. You may also store them inside your team project branching structure so that your build definitions version along with the code they build. You may also store the build process templates alongside your code in version control. In this way your templates version along with the code they build.

DefaultTemplate Process

The `DefaultTemplate (TfvcTemplate.12.xaml)` process (referred to as `DefaultTemplate` for brevity) as defined in the file `TfvcTemplate.12.xaml` is used for all new, un-customized build definitions in Team Foundation Server 2013 for team projects that have a centralized version control repository. The `DefaultTemplate` is greatly simplified from its Team Foundation Server 2012 counterpart. The process is described at a high level in Figure 18-32. To view the process template, you will have to download the process template's XAML file, as described in Chapter 19.

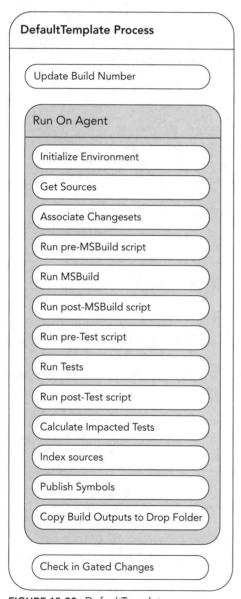

FIGURE 18-32: DefaultTemplate process

> **WARNING** *Chapter 19 describes in more detail how to edit a build process template. However, it is worth noting at this point that, while you can edit the* `DefaultTemplate` *from Visual Studio, the best practice is to create a new process template from the Process section of the Build Definition editor based on the* `DefaultTemplate` *and edit this file. All builds in the team project sharing the same build process template will be affected by a change to that template. Therefore, it is good to leave the standard unedited* `DefaultTemplate.xaml` *file alone in version control to avoid confusing team members who expect the* `DefaultTemplate` *to perform the same between systems using Team Foundation Server.*

Understanding the Process

On the build controller, the BuildDetail object corresponding to this running instance of the build is populated from the Team Foundation Server application tier machine and stored in a variable for later use. Then the build number is created based on a passed build number format (more on that later). If the build requires a drop folder, the next thing to occur is that a folder corresponding to the build number is created in the drop location specified by the build definition. This is the reason why the user running the build service must have write permission to the drop location network share.

The build controller now must determine on which build agent to execute the actual build. It does this by using the Agent Settings property described later in this chapter to determine which build agents to pick from, and then picks the next available build agent. If this is a gated build, only one build may be executed at a time. Otherwise, the build controller will attempt to run as many builds in parallel as it has spare build agents (unless constrained to a maximum number of concurrent builds in the build controller properties shown in Figure 18-30). Once the agent has been determined, execution passes to the build agent.

The build agent determines where the build directory should be located based on the agent working directory property defined in Figure 18-31. It then determines the name of the Team Foundation Server workspace that it should use on the build agent to download the sources into. Then the build agent initializes the workspace and figures out what the root `Sources` directory should be, along with the `Binaries` and `Test Results` folders—creating them if they do not already exist.

Note that if the build requires a clean workspace, the initialization process would have consisted of deleting the old workspace, creating a new one, and setting up the folder structure again. Equally, if incremental builds are not enabled, the `Test Results` and `Binaries` folders will be cleaned of all contents to ensure that binaries are built fresh for every build.

Once the workspace has been initialized as per the working folder template defined in the build definition, a `Get` is performed from version control to download the source files to the build agent. If a shelveset is included with the build (for example, for a gated check-in or for a private build), the contents of the shelveset are automerged with the source code at this point. If a label should be created (the default for most builds), the label name is generated (created based on the version of the source downloaded) and is stored in the build details.

A pre-build script will be run, if configured, once before the compilation occurs. Then, for every project and configuration in the build definition, MSBuild is executed to compile the project. Once all of the compilation is complete, a post-build script will run, if configured.

Once compilation is complete, the system will execute a pre-test script. Then the VS Test Runner will run unit tests after which the post-test script is run. The status of the compilation and test phases of the build are also stored in the build details. At this point, if the build has been defined to treat test failures as build failures, the build will fail here if any failed tests have been detected. By default, a build will carry on from this point regardless of test status. If the build had a successful compilation, but any other phase of the build resulted in an error being thrown, the build will complete with a status of Partially Successful.

The changesets included in the build since the last successful build label was created are recorded. Each of the changesets is analyzed to determine which work items were associated with those changesets. These associated work items are recorded in the build details. If any of the bugs were resolved as a result of one of these changesets, the "Fixed in Build" field for the bug will be updated to inform anyone investigating the resolved work item, which build to test that it was indeed fixed.

Next, the tests impacted by the changes included in the build are determined and stored in with the build details. The sources are indexed, and symbols are published to the Symbol server if specified.

Finally, the binaries generated by the build are copied over to the drop folder created by the build controller. If the build is still successful, then any changes that were being built as part of a gated check-in validation are checked in to version control on the triggering user's behalf.

Build Process Parameters

As you may have noticed already, there are lots of variables in the build process that can control how the build performs. These are stored as workflow parameters that are passed into the build as it is queued, based on the parameters defined in the build definition editor and any parameters modified when manually queuing a build.

Figure 18-33 shows the parameters available when editing the build definition.

Parameters are ordered into groups: TF Version Control, Build, Test, Publish Symbols, and Advanced. For more information on a particular parameter, select it in the build definition editor; the help section at the bottom of the Process section will show more information about that parameter, as shown at the bottom of Figure 18-33.

In the Build section of the `DefaultTemplate`, the items to build are specified. These are made up of the Projects and Configurations.

Configurations

The default Visual Studio build configuration to use is the default build configuration for the selected solution. However, you can override this—for example, if you would like to do a Release build on the build server, but the default in the solution is a Debug build.

To modify the configuration, use the Configurations dialog box displayed when you click the "..." button in the `Configurations` parameter.

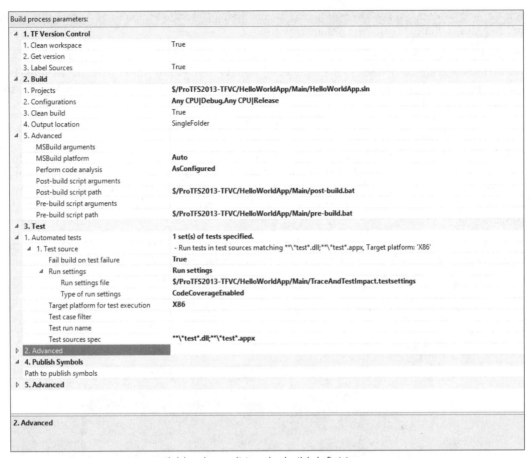

Build process parameters:

▲ **1. TF Version Control**
    1. Clean workspace   True
    2. Get version
    3. Label Sources   True
▲ **2. Build**
    1. Projects $/ProTFS2013-TFVC/HelloWorldApp/Main/HelloWorldApp.sln
    2. Configurations   Any CPU|Debug,Any CPU|Release
    3. Clean build   True
    4. Output location   SingleFolder
▲   5. Advanced
        MSBuild arguments
        MSBuild platform   **Auto**
        Perform code analysis   **AsConfigured**
        Post-build script arguments
        Post-build script path $/ProTFS2013-TFVC/HelloWorldApp/Main/post-build.bat
        Pre-build script arguments
        Pre-build script path $/ProTFS2013-TFVC/HelloWorldApp/Main/pre-build.bat
▲ **3. Test**
▲   1. Automated tests   **1 set(s) of tests specified.**
    ▲   1. Test source   - Run tests in test sources matching ***test*.dll;***test*.appx, Target platform: 'X86'
        Fail build on test failure   **True**
        ▲   Run settings   **Run settings**
            Run settings file   **$/ProTFS2013-TFVC/HelloWorldApp/Main/TraceAndTestImpact.testsettings**
            Type of run settings   **CodeCoverageEnabled**
        Target platform for test execution **X86**
        Test case filter
        Test run name
        Test sources spec   ***test*.dll;***test*.appx
  ▷ 2. Advanced
▲ **4. Publish Symbols**
    Path to publish symbols
▷ **5. Advanced**

2. Advanced

FIGURE 18-33: Parameters available when editing the build definition

> **NOTE** *Team Foundation Build typically deals with solution configurations. These allow you to specify a named collection of project-level platforms and configurations that should be built. For more information on solution configurations, see a blog post by Aaron Hallberg (former lead of the Team Foundation Build team at Microsoft) at* http://aka.ms/TfsBuildSolConf.

Projects

The `Projects` parameter was discussed earlier in this chapter when the build definition was created. This parameter describes which MSBuild project files (`.vbproj` or `.csproj` files) or Visual Studio Solution files (`.sln` files) should be built as part of the build definition.

Projects will be executed in the order they are provided in this property. So, if you wish to call a project after performing the build of the solution (for example, a `.wixproj` file to create an MSI installer using the open source project WiX), specify that second. Clicking the ". . ." button in the

`Projects` parameter displays the Solutions/Projects dialog box, allows you to add other files to the list, and allows you to control the order.

The server paths to the projects to build are provided. These server paths must be mapped by the working folder template defined in the build definition. Otherwise, the build will fail when the build agent attempts to convert the server path of the file to build into a local path on the build agent to use when running the build.

Automated Tests

Under the Test section of the `DefaultTemplate`, the `Automated Tests` parameter provides the tests that will be executed as part of the build. By default, this is set to execute all tests found in an assembly created by the build matching the patterns `*test*.dll` and `*test*.appx`—that is, `HelloWorldTests.dll` would be inspected for tests implemented using the Visual Studio Test Runner.

Clicking the ". . ." button in the `Automated Tests` parameter allows you to specify more tests that should be run, as well as their configuration, as shown in Figure 18-34. When editing a particular set of tests, you can control if the build should fail if those tests fail execution.

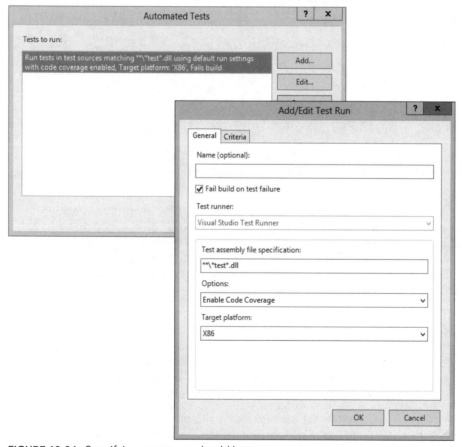

FIGURE 18-34: Specifying more tests should be run

Tests can be filtered based on the test category or test priority using the Criteria/Arguments tab for the test, as shown in Figure 18-35. By categorizing your unit tests, you could set up your build verification tests differently from your coded UI or integration tests. Build verification tests (signified by a category of BVT) could fail the build, whereas failures in integration tests or coded UI tests (which are more prone to failure from external factors) may be recorded and the build marked as Partially Successful. An example of filtering based on category is shown in Figure 18-35.

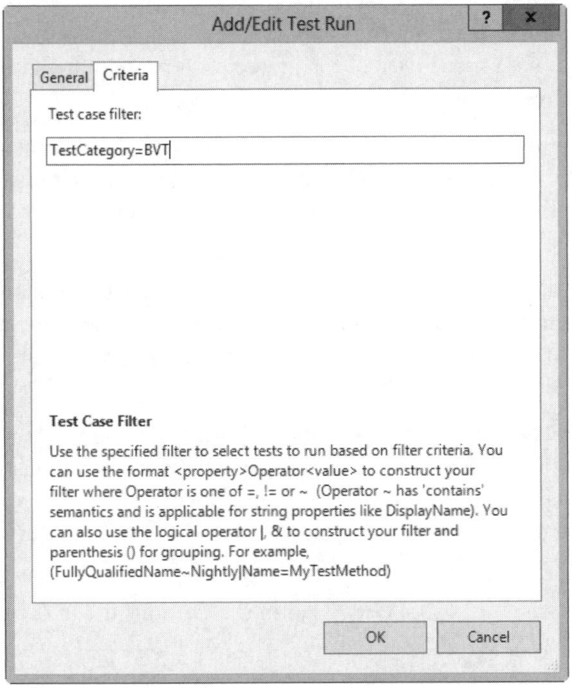

FIGURE 18-35: Criteria/Arguments tab

Another example of using this functionality is that you may set up a build so that all tests with a priority of 1 or less are run as part of the standard continuous integration build, but all tests are run in an additional build definition triggered as a rolling build set to build no more often than once every 30 minutes. That way, the continuous integration build can give rapid feedback on the approximate build quality, but the rolling build can come along later and do a final check that everything is satisfactory.

> **NOTE** *The Automated Tests section also specifies the TestSettings file to be used for a test run. In the example shown in Figure 18-33, this is set to* `$/ ProTFS2013-TFVC/HelloWorldApp/Main/TraceAndTestImpact .testsettings`. *Your Visual Studio solution can contain a number of* `.testsettings` *files to control the behavior of the test environment, and to enable configuration settings such as code coverage and test impact analysis as part of the test run. If you have unit tests executing as part of the build, it may be very useful to enable these.*

> **NOTE** *For more information about running third-party unit testing frameworks, such as xUnit.net, NUnit, MbUnit Chutzpah for QUnit, and Jasmine, see the blog post at* `http://aka.ms/VSUnitTestPlugins`.

Code coverage tracks how much of the application code is being tested by the tests under execution. Test impact analysis determines which tests were affected by the changes since the last successful build—which gives an important indication to your testers about the impact of a particular change and which tests should be revisited first when testing a build.

It is best practice to create a new test settings file specifically for your build server settings. That way, developer test settings used locally by the development team and the actual build server test settings are kept separate but are available to the developer team to validate against locally, if needed.

To create a new server test settings file, open the `Local.testsettings` file in the Solution Items. Then change the name in the General section to `Build Server` and click the Save As button to save the file as `BuildServer.testsettings`. If you do not have a `.testsettings` file, you can right-click the solution and choose Add New Item ⇨ Test Settings file.

In the Data and Diagnostics section of the Test Settings dialog box, check both the Test Impact options, as shown in Figure 18-36. Note that this is also where IntelliTrace can be enabled to get a rich diagnostic trace of any test failures, as well as many other test settings. Once configured, save the test settings file and check-in to version control. Then edit the `TestSettings File` parameter for the test assembly to point to the `BuildServer.testsettings` file.

To get Code Coverage, you will need to select `Enable Code Coverage` in the Options list in the Add/Edit Test Run dialog box, as shown in Figure 18-34.

SPECIFYING WHICH ASSEMBLIES TO MEASURE CODE COVERAGE

In a typical build, you will only want to measure code coverage for your application's assemblies. Unit test assemblies or Framework assemblies tested by other builds would need to be excluded. To tell the build how to exclude these assemblies from measurement, you will need to add a `.runsettings` file to your solution and specify this file in your build's Run settings file parameter. For more information on Run Settings files, see `http://aka.ms/CodeCoverageInBuilds`.

Build Number Format

In the Advanced section of the `DefaultTemplate`, the `Build Number Format` parameter controls the format used when creating the build number at the beginning of the build process. By default, builds are created with the number format of `$(BuildDefinitionName)_ $(Date:yyyyMMdd)$(Rev:.r)`, for example, `HelloWorld_20131104.18`, where this is the 18th build for the HelloWorld build definition on November 4, 2013. Build numbers must be unique across a team project, and, therefore, this format serves as a good default. However, it is common that users wish to customize the build numbering.

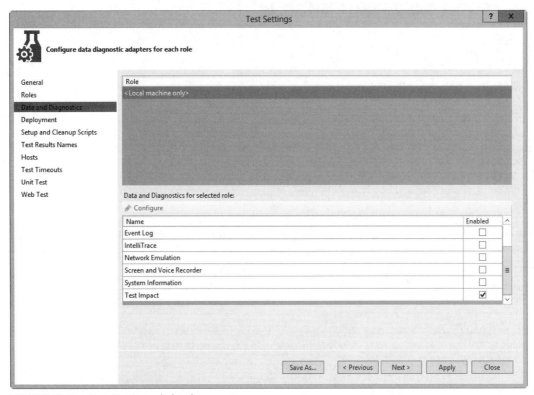

FIGURE 18-36: Test Settings dialog box

In Team Foundation Server 2013, this is simply a matter of editing the build number format by clicking the "..." button to show the BuildNumber Format Editor. Initially, the dialog box shows the current build number format, along with a preview of what a build number generated with this format would look like. Clicking the Macros button expands the dialog box to show a number of available macros, as shown in Figure 18-37.

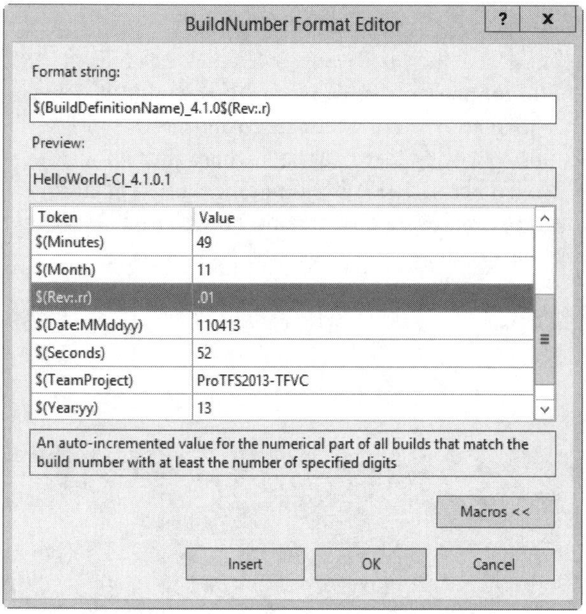

FIGURE 18-37: BuildNumber Format Editor dialog box

A common number format to use is one that matches the version numbers baked into the product assemblies as part of the build. For example, if the build was for version 4.1.0 of the product (where 4 is the major version, 1 is the minor version, and 0 is the servicing version), and the revision number is incremented for each build, the build number format should be set to `$(BuildDefinitionName)_4.1.0$(Rev:.r)`, as shown in Figure 18-37.

> **NOTE** *See Chapter 19 for an example of how to then customize the build process template to add this build number into the assemblies as the build is being performed.*

Clean Workspace

By default, the `Clean Workspace` parameter in the TF Version Control section is set to `True`, meaning that all existing build outputs and sources for that build definition will be deleted at every build. This is the safest option, but it is also the slowest, because it means that all files must be downloaded from version control, and everything built each time, regardless of how little changed between each build.

As discussed in Chapter 6, Team Foundation Server manages workspaces to ensure that files are deleted, moved, and renamed as they are deleted, moved, and renamed in version control, thus ensuring that there are no orphaned files. Therefore, enabling the workspace to be maintained between builds can dramatically improve build performance, especially for continuous integration builds, where the changes between each build are typically small.

If you set the value of the `Clean Workspace` parameter to `False`, neither the sources nor the build outputs will be deleted at the start of a build. Only the files that have been modified in version control will be updated, and only the items that have changed will be recompiled.

In a continuous integration build where the scope of changes between builds is typically small, this setting gives a further performance increase. In addition, it can also be useful for ASP.NET-based websites. In that case, you might only subsequently publish the items that have changed between the build output and your website to minimize the upgrade impact of a new version, thus better facilitating continuous deployment.

> ### CLEAN WORKSPACE SETTING IN VISUAL STUDIO ONLINE
>
> If you are using the Hosted Build Controller provided with your Visual Studio Online account, you will find that this parameter is ignored. By design, you get a new working directory with each build.

Logging Verbosity

In Team Foundation Server 2013, the `Logging Verbosity` parameter was removed and the system was modified to no longer store build log information in the database. Instead, diagnostic-level logging is always performed and the results are stored in the diagnostic log files. For more information on diagnostic logs, see `http://aka.ms/DiagnosticBuildLogs`.

Perform Code Analysis

> **NOTE** *Static code analysis allows you to provide a set of rules that can be checked during a build to ensure that code conventions are being adhered to and common bugs and security issues are avoided. The Managed Code Analysis tool (also known as FxCop) is a tool used by Visual Studio to analyze code against a library of rules. Nearly 200 rules are provided out of the box based on the .NET Framework Design Guidelines. They are organized into a series of rule sets and groups.*

> **NOTE** *For more information about the updated Static Code Analysis features for C++, which arrived in Visual Studio 2012, see the MSDN article at* `http://aka.ms/VS2013CppAnalysis.`

By default, the use of code analysis is set at the project level in Visual Studio. However, the `Perform Code Analysis` parameter in the Build section of the build parameters can set the code analysis to be run `Always`, `Never`, or `AsConfigured` in the Visual Studio project.

If set to `Always`, then code analysis will force all projects in the solution to be analyzed. If a code analysis Rule Set has not been defined for a particular project, then the default Rule Set (Microsoft Minimum Rules) will be used.

> **NOTE** *For more information on using static code analysis with Visual Studio projects, see Chapter 20 of the book Professional Application Lifecycle Management with Visual Studio 2013 (Mickey Gousset, Martin Hinshelwood, Brian A. Randell, Brian Keller, and Martin Woodward, Wiley, 2014).*

Source and Symbol Server Settings

A Symbol server is a file share used to store the symbols or program database (`.pdb`) files for your executable binaries in a defined layout. Visual Studio can then be configured with the details of this server. From then on, when debugging code live or using the advanced historical debugging features (IntelliTrace), Visual Studio is capable of taking you directly to the version of the source code that was used to create the binary being debugged.

The configuration of the Symbol server is performed by providing the Windows file location to be used for the Symbol store in the `Path to Publish Symbols` parameter of the Publish Symbols section of the `DefaultTemplate`.

> **NOTE** *For more information on what every developer should know about symbol files, see the blog post by John Robbins at* `http://aka.ms/PdbFiles.`

Agent Settings

The Agent Settings are located in the Advanced section of the build parameters in the `DefaultTemplate`. In addition to controlling how long a build may execute before being cancelled, and the maximum time a build may wait for an available agent, the Agent Settings provide for a Name and Tag filter. These can be used by the build controller to restrict the selection of agents when determining on which agent the build should execute.

Specifying a full name of a build agent allows you to force it to run on a particular machine. If you adopt a naming convention for your build agents such as `TeamXAgent1`, then using wildcards for the name filter will allow scoping to a particular set of build agents (for example, `TeamX*`).

A more flexible way is to use build agent tagging as shown earlier in this chapter in the "Managing Build Controllers and Build Agents" section. In this way, you can tag a build agent with its capabilities, and then use the Tags filter to specify the tags that you require (such as `BizTalk` to indicate a machine with the BizTalk Server toolkit installed, which is, therefore, suitable for compiling those projects). You can then change the `Tag Comparison Operator` from the default of `MatchExactly` to `MatchAtLeast`, which means that you will accept any build agent that has the `BizTalk` tag, regardless of the other tags it might have.

Analyze Test Impact

If the `.testsettings` file provided for the test run indicates that test impact analysis should be performed, the default setting of `True` for the `Analyze Test Impact` parameter in the Advanced item of the Test section of the `DefaultTemplate` means that the analysis will be performed. Setting this to `False` means that the impact analysis will not be performed, regardless of the `.testsettings`.

Update Work Items with Build Number

By default, the `Update work items with build number` parameter in the Advanced section of the `DefaultTemplate` is set to `True`. This means that the build system will determine which changesets were committed to the build workspace since the last successful run of this build definition by comparing this build's label in version control with the earlier, successful build's label. It will then select all of the work items linked to those changesets. Finally, it will update those work items with the current build number.

This analysis can take a long period of time and can require several server calls, which will impact the performance of your Team Foundation Server instance. Therefore, if you decide that you do not require that functionality for a particular build definition, you can disable it by setting the value to `False`.

Create Work Item on Failure

When a build fails, the default behavior is to create a work item assigned to the person for whom the build was running (the person that checked in files, for example, in the case of a Continuous Integration triggered build definition). Set the `Create Work Item on Failure` parameter in the Advanced section of the `DefaultTemplate` to `False` if you do not require work items to be created automatically.

Disable Tests

By default, the tests specified in the Automated Tests setting will be executed unless the `Disable Tests` parameter in the Advanced section of the `DefaultTemplate` is set to `True`. This is usually selected when you want to perform a manual build that runs without tests. This may be done to temporarily expedite the build process.

Get Version

By default, the Latest version of source is used to perform a build. However, you may wish to create a build definition that always builds the files with a particular label—for example, QARelease in the project MyTeamProject. Setting the Get Version parameter in the TF Version Control section of the DefaultTemplate to LQARelease@$/MyTeamProject would force the build definition to get files only with this label. Because labels can be edited in Team Foundation Server, you can now label the versions and files that make up that QA release and know that they will be included in the build once triggered.

An alternative approach to using Get Version in this way would be to have a branch in version control representing the files that were in QA and merge changes into this branch to be included in that build. For more information on branching, see Chapter 10.

Label Sources

By default, the Label Sources parameter in the TF Version Control section of the DefaultTemplate is set to True, which means that the sources in the workspace of the build are labeled at the start of the build process so that the exact versions included in the build can be easily determined. Set this to False if you do not require a label to be created. However, be warned that this also disables much of the change analysis functionality that relies on the last successful build label to determine the differences between builds.

MSBuild Arguments

Use the MSBuild Arguments parameter in the Advanced item of the Build section of the DefaultTemplate to pass an additional command-line argument to MSBuild.exe whenever it is invoked in the build process.

MSBuild Platform

By default, the MSBuild platform used to execute the build process is auto-detected, based on the current operating system of the build agent. However, this parameter in the Advanced item of the Build section of the DefaultTemplate can be set explicitly to, say, x86 if an explicit platform is required (for example, when the project is calling assemblies that are not x64 compatible so you need to force them to be loaded into the correct version of the CLR).

Pre- and Post-Build Script Arguments

Use the Pre-build script arguments property to specify the command-line arguments to be passed to the script file specified in the Pre-build script path property when it is executed. The Post-build script argument parameter specifies the command-line arguments to pass to the script specified in the Post-build script path parameter. These properties are found in the Advanced item of the Build section of the DefaultTemplate.

Pre- and Post-Build Script Path

Use the Pre-build script path property to specify a batch file or PowerShell script to be run before MSBuild compilation of your source code occurs. The Post-build script path property will specify a script file that will be run after MSBuild compilation. These properties are found in the Advanced item of the Build section of the `DefaultTemplate`.

Pre- and Post-Build Test Arguments

Use the `Pre-test script arguments` property to specify the command-line arguments to be passed to the script file specified in the `Pre-test script path` property when it is executed. The `Post-test script arguments` property specifies the command-line arguments to pass to the script specified in the `Post-test script path` property. These properties are found in the Advanced item of the Test section of the `DefaultTemplate`.

Pre- and Post-Test Script Path

Use the `Pre-test script path` property to specify a batch file or PowerShell script to be run before Visual Studio Test Runner tests your application. The `Post-test script path` property will specify a script file that will be run after the test runner finishes. These properties are found in the Advanced item of the Test section of the `DefaultTemplate`.

Output Location

Use the `Output location` parameter in the Build section of the `DefaultTemplate` to specify where the build system places build outputs. The default value is `SingleFolder`, which will place all of the outputs files together into the drop folder. This is the same default behavior as all previous versions of Team Foundation Server. The `PerProject` setting will put build outputs into folders based on the solution name. The `AsConfigured` setting will leave the binaries in the build's `Sources` folder in the same structure that you see when compiling the code on your local dev machine. This parameter is new in 2013.

> **THE ASCONFIGURED SETTING WILL REQUIRE EXTRA CODING**
>
> If you use the AsConfigured setting in the `Output Location` parameter, Team Foundation Build will not copy your build outputs to the drop folder. You will have to create a post-build script that gathers your outputs and copies them to the location specified by TF_BUILD_BINARIESDIRECTORY so they can be copied to the drop folder.

Building Ant and Maven Projects with Team Foundation Server

A standard build agent may perform basic compilation and test activities for most .NET project types. Visual Studio Ultimate or Visual Studio Premium is required on the build agent to perform advanced .NET builds with features such as code coverage or static code analysis.

It is also possible to execute Java builds from the Team Foundation build agent by installing the Build Extensions Power Tool on the build agent, along with a suitable Java Development Kit (JDK) version as well as Ant and/or Maven. The latest version of the Build Extensions Power Tool can be found at `http://aka.ms/TFS2013BuildExtensions`.

This Power Tool provides a set of Workflow activities and MSBuild tasks that allow a build definition to call Ant or Maven. The results of the build tool are then interpreted and published back to Team Foundation Server by the build agent, along with any JUnit test results. The data for the Java build process is then available in Team Foundation Server in just the same way as Visual Studio builds are.

The easiest way to create a Java-based build definition is to create it from Eclipse using Team Explorer Everywhere. Right-click the `Builds` node in Team Explorer and follow the build definition creation process as outlined earlier in the chapter. The only significant difference is that, instead of the Process section described earlier, the build definition in Eclipse requests that a project file be created.

Click the Create button to display the Create Build Configuration Wizard, and then select the Ant `build.xml` or Maven `pom.xml` file that you wish to use to perform the build.

Note that this creates a build using the `UpgradeTemplate` process template, with all the functionality controlled by a `TFSBuild.proj` file with an MSBuild-based wrapping script. In this way, the build functionality can be easily edited from Eclipse or a cross-platform text editor where a suitable Windows Workflow editor is not easily available.

SUMMARY

This chapter was all about using the build functionality provided by Team Foundation Server. You learned about installation of the build services and about the creation of a build definition. You became familiar with the tools and windows used to manage builds with Team Foundation Server. Finally, the chapter described the build process, provided a detailed examination of the available configuration parameters for the `DefaultTemplate`, and described how to build Java projects (as well as Visual Studio ones) with Team Foundation Server.

Chapter 19 examines customization of the build process in more detail and presents some examples of common build customizations.

19

Customizing the Build Process

WHAT'S IN THIS CHAPTER?

➤ Getting to know build extension points

➤ Creating and configuring script extensions

➤ Reviewing common custom activities

➤ Extending a build with custom activities

➤ Configuring the Build Controller to deploy custom activities automatically

WROX.COM CODE DOWNLOADS FOR THIS CHAPTER

The wrox.com code downloads for this chapter are found at `http://www.wrox.com/go/proftfs2013` on the Download Code tab. The code is in the Chapter 19 download and individually named according to the code filenames noted throughout this chapter.

As you learned in Chapter 18, Team Foundation Server includes a rich set of features for automated builds based on the Windows Workflow Foundation technology included in the .NET Framework. The main functionality for an automated build is included in the default build process template available in the standard process templates. More than likely, however, you will find yourself needing to customize that functionality or add actions for your build process.

In Team Foundation Server 2013, Microsoft has revamped the build system to make it easier to add customizations. In earlier versions, you would have to make changes to the build process template XAML file to customize the process. You can still do this, but now you can also simply hook in your own build scripts (PowerShell or Batch files) to make these customizations.

In this chapter, you learn the fundamentals for working with Windows Workflow Foundation and how to customize the build process template using the workflow designer tools available in Visual Studio 2013. You also learn how to create and call a custom script that can be run during your build.

RUNNING CUSTOM BUILD SCRIPTS DURING YOUR BUILD

Team Foundation Server 2013 introduced a set of scriptable extension points into the default build templates for builds based inside Team Projects that use either TFS Version Control or Git-based source control repositories. These extension points allow you to call your own custom scripts and can pass arguments into those scripts, as shown in Figure 19-1.

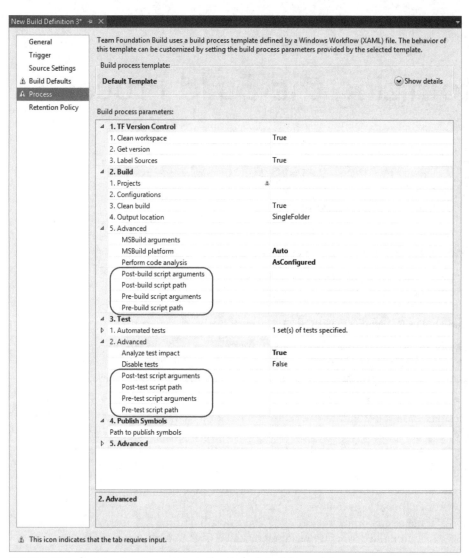

FIGURE 19-1: Script extension points in the Default build template

Extension Points in the Default Build Template

Each extension point is supported by two build process parameters, the Script Path and the Script Arguments. The Script Path is the location of your PowerShell script or batch file in version control. By selecting the file in version control, you get the benefit of having versioned copies of all of the script changes, as well as not having to worry about calling the script from a local path on the build agent. This is handled for you inside the Default Build Template. The Script Arguments parameter lets you pass arguments into your script from the running build process.

The available script extension points are described in Table 19-1.

TABLE 19-1: Script Extension Points in the Default Build Templates

EXTENSION POINT	DESCRIPTION
Pre-build	This script is invoked prior to the compilation of the first solution/configuration pair in your build definition. It is invoked only once per build and not once per solution in the build.
Post-build	This script is invoked after compilation of all of the solutions and configurations in your build.
Pre-test	This script is invoked prior to the first unit test run. It is a good place to set up your test data and configure your test environment.
Post-test	This script is invoked after all of the test runs have completed. It is a good place to perform any cleanup operations you may need after testing.

How to Access Build Information within Your Build Script

When your scripts are invoked, the build system will make all of the build's environment variables available to you. These environment variables are prefixed with TF_BUILD. Some of the commonly used build values are shown in Table 19-2. For a complete list of well-known environment variables, see http://aka.ms/WellKnownEnvVariables.

TABLE 19-2: Common Build Values Available through TF_BUILD Environment Variables

BUILD VALUE	ENVIRONMENT VARIABLE	DESCRIPTION
Binaries Directory	TF_BUILD_BINARIESDIRECTORY	The location where the build will store the outputs of compilation on the Build Agent
Build Definition Name	TF_BUILD_BUILDDEFINITIONNAME	The name of the build definition that is being run

continues

TABLE 19-2: *(continued)*

BUILD VALUE	ENVIRONMENT VARIABLE	DESCRIPTION
Build Number	TF_BUILD_BUILDNUMBER	This is the unique number generated for the build to identify the build.
BuildURI	TF_BUILD_BUILDURI	The address of this build on the TFS Server. Used to query TFS for build information.
Drop Location	TF_BUILD_DROPLOCATION	The location of the Drop folder for this build
Sources Directory	TF_BUILD_SOURCESDIRECTORY	This is the location where the source code for the build was placed on the Build Agent.
Source Get Version	TF_BUILD_SOURCEGETVERSION	The version of the source files retrieved into the build's workspace on the build agent

CUSTOMIZING THE BUILD PROCESS TO STAMP THE VERSION NUMBER INTO YOUR ASSEMBLIES

With the introduction of the script extensions into the Default Build Template, you now have a choice in how you go about extending your builds. You can write a PowerShell script to perform the task or, if it's too complex for a script, you can use a custom build workflow activity. Custom build workflow activities can be acquired from open source projects, as described later in this chapter, or you can create your own in any .NET language.

> **NOTE** *Microsoft has been using Windows Workflow Foundation as the basis for the Team Build system for years now. As with any mature system, a healthy ecosystem of add-ons has emerged. Most of the custom activities you will need for your build have already been built, so you should only have to write your own activities on rare occasions.*
>
> *If you do find that you need to write a custom build activity, then look over Andy Leonard's Customize Your Team Foundation Build process page at* http://aka.ms/CustomizeTFBuild, *MSDN's Customizing the Build Process at* http://aka.ms/CustomizeBuildProcess, *and the Visual Studio Ranger's Build Customization Guide at* http://vsarbuildguide.codeplex.com.

Creating the PowerShell Script

Andy Lewis, a member of the Visual Studio ALM group, has written a couple of blog posts describing how one would go about creating a PowerShell script that can be run during the build to stamp the build number into the AssemblyInfo files for your project. Let's have a look at the script he built as well as how that script is hooked into your build.

> **NOTE** *The entire PowerShell script referenced here can be downloaded from this book's website or from* `http://aka.ms/StampAssemblyInfoPS`.

The `ApplyVersionToAssemblies.ps1` PowerShell script shown in Listing 19-1 reads the current build number from the running Team Build, parses it to extract the version string, and then uses a regular expression to find the version entries within the AssemblyInfo files in the source's directory structure and replaces them with the extracted version string.

LISTING 19-1: PowerShell script to stamp build number into assemblies (code file: ApplyVersionToAssemblies.ps1)

```
##-----------------------------------------------------------------------
## <copyright file="ApplyVersionToAssemblies.ps1">
(c) http://TfsBuildExtensions.codeplex.com/.
This source is subject to the Microsoft Permissive License.
See http://www.microsoft.com/resources/sharedsource
               /licensingbasics/sharedsourcelicenses.mspx.
All other rights reserved.</copyright>
##-----------------------------------------------------------------------
# Look for a 0.0.0.0 pattern in the build number.
# If found use it to version the assemblies.
#
# For example, if the 'Build number format' build process parameter
# $(BuildDefinitionName)_$(Year:yyyy).$(Month).$(DayOfMonth)$(Rev:.r)
# then your build numbers come out like this:
# "Build HelloWorld_2013.07.19.1"
# This script would then apply version 2013.07.19.1 to your assemblies.

# Enable -Verbose option
[CmdletBinding()]

# Disable parameter
# Convenience option so you can debug this script or disable it in
# your build definition without having to remove it from
# the 'Post-build script path' build process parameter.
param([switch]$Disable)
if ($PSBoundParameters.ContainsKey('Disable'))
{
     Write-Verbose "Script disabled; no actions will be taken on the files."
}
```

continues

LISTING 19-1: *(continued)*

```powershell
# Regular expression pattern to find the version in the build number
# and then apply it to the assemblies
$VersionRegex = "\d+\.\d+\.\d+\.\d+"

# If this script is not running on a build server, remind user to
# set environment variables so that this script can be debugged
if(-not $Env:TF_BUILD -and -not ($Env:TF_BUILD_SOURCESDIRECTORY -and
    $Env:TF_BUILD_BUILDNUMBER))
{
    Write-Error "You must set the following environment variables"
    Write-Error "to test this script interactively."
    Write-Host '$Env:TF_BUILD_SOURCESDIRECTORY - For example, enter
something like:'
    Write-Host '$Env:TF_BUILD_SOURCESDIRECTORY =
"C:\code\FabrikamTFVC\HelloWorld"'
    Write-Host '$Env:TF_BUILD_BUILDNUMBER - For example, enter something like:'
    Write-Host '$Env:TF_BUILD_BUILDNUMBER = "Build HelloWorld_0000.00.00.0"'
    exit 1
}

# Make sure path to source code directory is available
if (-not $Env:TF_BUILD_SOURCESDIRECTORY)
{
    Write-Error ("TF_BUILD_SOURCESDIRECTORY environment variable is missing.")
    exit 1
}
elseif (-not (Test-Path $Env:TF_BUILD_SOURCESDIRECTORY))
{
    Write-Error "TF_BUILD_SOURCESDIRECTORY does not exist:
                $Env:TF_BUILD_SOURCESDIRECTORY"
    exit 1
}
Write-Verbose "TF_BUILD_SOURCESDIRECTORY: $Env:TF_BUILD_SOURCESDIRECTORY"

# Make sure there is a build number
if (-not $Env:TF_BUILD_BUILDNUMBER)
{
    Write-Error ("TF_BUILD_BUILDNUMBER environment variable is missing.")
    exit 1
}
Write-Verbose "TF_BUILD_BUILDNUMBER: $Env:TF_BUILD_BUILDNUMBER"

# Get and validate the version data
$VersionData = [regex]::matches($Env:TF_BUILD_BUILDNUMBER,$VersionRegex)
switch($VersionData.Count)
{
   0
     {
        Write-Error "Could not find version number data in TF_BUILD_BUILDNUMBER."
        exit 1
     }
   1 {}
```

```
    default
        {
            Write-Warning "Found more than instance of version data in
                        TF_BUILD_BUILDNUMBER."
            Write-Warning "Will assume first instance is version."
        }
}
$NewVersion = $VersionData[0]
Write-Verbose "Version: $NewVersion"

# Apply the version to the assembly property files
$files = gci $Env:TF_BUILD_SOURCESDIRECTORY -recurse -include "*Properties*",
        "My Project" |
    ?{ $_.PSIsContainer } |
    foreach { gci -Path $_.FullName -Recurse -include AssemblyInfo.* }
if($files)
{
    Write-Verbose "Will apply $NewVersion to $($files.count) files."

    foreach ($file in $files) {


            if(-not $Disable)
            {
                $filecontent = Get-Content($file)
                attrib $file -r
                $filecontent -replace $VersionRegex, $NewVersion | Out-File $file
                Write-Verbose "$file.FullName - version applied"
            }
        }
}
else
{
    Write-Warning "Found no files."
}
```

Once you have this script created, you can check it into version control so that it is available to your builds, as shown in Figure 19-2.

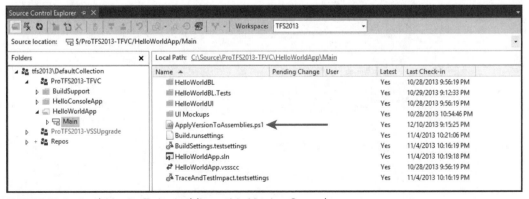

FIGURE 19-2: ApplyVersionToAssemblies.ps1 in Version Control

Configure the Build to Run the Script

You now want to get your build to run the script so that your AssemblyInfo files have their version strings updated prior to compilation. As shown in Table 19-1, the Pre-Build extension point is triggered before compilation occurs, so that is the one you want to use.

To set up the Pre-Build extension point, select your build definition in Team Explorer's Builds pane, right-click on the build definition, and select the Edit Build Definition option. Once the Build Definition Editor opens, select the Process tab and make sure your build is using the Default Template build process template, as shown in Figure 19-3. In the Build process parameters grid, navigate to the 2. Build ➪ Advanced ➪ Pre-build script path parameter. In this parameter field, click the ellipsis button on the right to show the Browse dialog box, as shown in Figure 19-4, to browse your version control repository. Select the location of the `ApplyVersionToAssemblies.ps1` file and click OK to store the version control path in the parameter field.

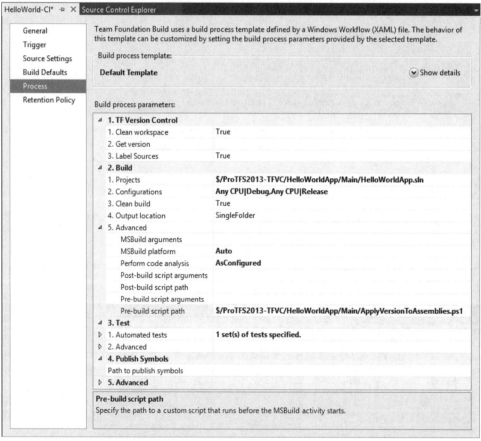

FIGURE 19-3: Build Definition Editor

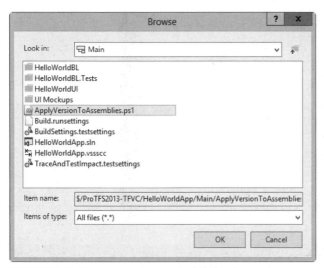

FIGURE 19-4: Browse version control dialog box

You now have the build configured to run the `ApplyVersionToAssemblies.ps1` script on every build. All that's left is to make sure the script has everything it needs to be successful.

> ### PASSING ARGUMENTS FROM THE RUNNING BUILD TO A SCRIPT
>
> As described earlier in this chapter, many of the build details are made available to your script through environment variables. There are times, however, when you may want to explicitly pass arguments (explicit or variables) on the script's command line.
>
> To accomplish this for your Pre-build script, you can use the Pre-build script arguments build parameter in your build definition, as shown in Figure 19-3.
>
> For more information, see `http://aka.ms/PassArgumentsToScripts`.

Configure the Build Number to Work with the Script

Listing 19-2 shows a portion of the `ApplyVersionToAssemblies.ps1` file, which shows that there are some assumptions made by the script as to the format of the build number generated by Team Build.

LISTING 19-2: Assumptions of the ApplyVersionToAssemblies.ps1 script

```
##-------------------------------------------------------------------
# Look for a 0.0.0.0 pattern in the build number.
# If found use it to version the assemblies.
#
# For example, if the 'Build number format' build process parameter
# $(BuildDefinitionName)_$(Year:yyyy).$(Month).$(DayOfMonth)$(Rev:.r)
# then your build numbers come out like this:
# "Build HelloWorld_2013.07.19.1"
# This script would then apply version 2013.07.19.1 to your assemblies.
```

To meet this assumption, you need to look at how Team Build generates its build numbers. The build number pattern is stored in the Process Tab ⇨ Advanced ⇨ Build number format parameter, as shown in Figure 19-5.

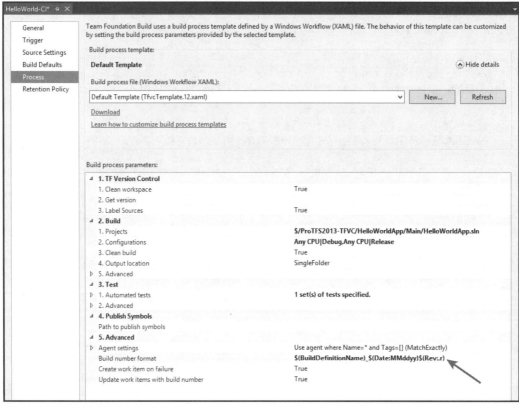

FIGURE 19-5: Initial build number format parameter

The default value for this parameter is $(BuildDefinitionName)_$(Date:yyyyMMdd)$(Rev:.r). The $(BuildDefinitionName) portion represents the name of the build definition, which in this case is `HelloWorld-CI`. The `$(Date:yyyyMMdd)` portion represents the current date formatted in a year, month, day pattern; so if today is December 10, 2013, this portion would return `20131210`. The `$(Rev:.r)` portion represents the Revision, which is the number of times this build definition has been run with the same values in the prior segments; so in this case this number starts at 1 when the build is run for the first time each day and then increments all day long. It will reset to 1 the following day because the date portion of the build number string has changed.

For example, if you have a build called `HelloWorld-CI` that you run for the third time on December 12, 2013, your build number would be `HelloWorld-CI_20131212.3`.

Of course this won't work for the purposes of the `ApplyVersionsToAssemblies` script so you need to change the format to something like `$(BuildDefinitionName)_$1.0.0$(Rev:.r)`, as shown in Figure 19-6. This will give you a build number of `HelloWorld-CI_1.0.0.1` the first time it is run and will increment the revision until someone changes the format string to a new version number.

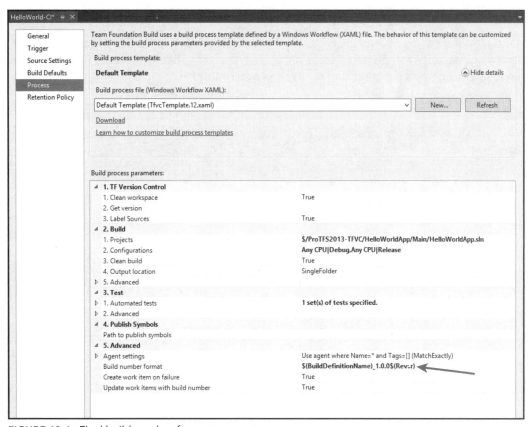

FIGURE 19-6: Final build number format parameter

You can now save your build definition and run it to see the results.

NOTE *For more information on the Build Number Format string and the available macros, see Chapter 18.*

When you run the build, you should note that the build number at the top of the build log now reflects the new build numbering scheme, as shown in Figure 19-7.

✓ **HelloWorld-CI_1.0.0.3 - Build succeeded**

View Summary | View Log - Open Drop Folder | Diagnostics ▼ | <No Quality Assigned> ▼ | Actions ▼

Administrator triggered HelloWorld-CI (ProTFS2013-TFVC) for changeset 36
Ran for 20 seconds (TFS2013 - Controller), completed 3 seconds ago

FIGURE 19-7: Build run using new build number format

You can open the Drop folder and get the properties for each of the compiled assemblies in your build. Looking at the Details tab of each, you can see that they all have the same File Version value, and that value matches the build number, as shown in Figure 19-8.

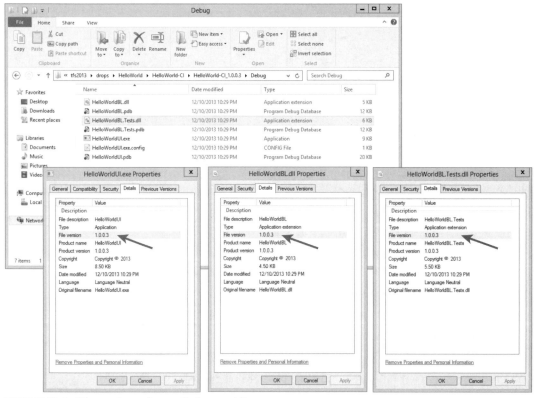

FIGURE 19-8: File versions of compiled assemblies

As you read in Chapter 18, when a build runs, it performs a number of steps. One of these steps is that it creates a label in version control with the build number as its name, which contains all of the file versions that went into the build. You can now look in version control, search for the label, and see its contents, as shown in Figure 19-9.

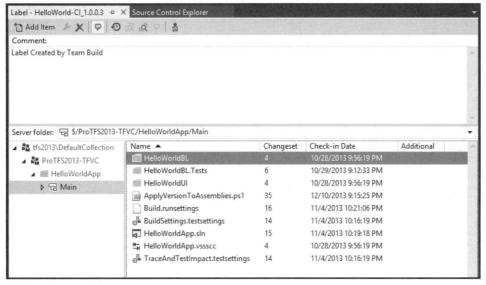

FIGURE 19-9: Build label contents

With this system in place, you can now grab any assembly on your server, get its file version, and trace it back to the label that contains the source code that went into it. You can also trace it back to the build that compiled it, which has references to the changesets and tasks that define the functionality. You can go even further by tracing the tasks back to their User Stories, Requirements, or Product Backlog Items (depending on your process template) to see which features of your application were touched in this build. All in all, you have a very powerful system of traceability implemented with a simple PowerShell script and two build process parameter changes.

AVAILABLE CUSTOM BUILD WORKFLOW ACTIVITIES

A lot of great workflow activities are available in the .NET Framework and provided by Team Foundation Server. However, there may be times when you need to perform a certain functionality and cannot use the standard workflow activities available from Microsoft. Creating custom workflow activities is one of the extensibility points for Team Foundation Server. Over the years, this extension point has been exercised quite a bit by the development community.

One of the most prolific community groups is the Community TFS Build Extensions project on CodePlex. This project is maintained by a dedicated group of Microsoft employees, Visual Studio ALM Rangers, and Microsoft MVPs for Team Foundation Server who have grouped together to provide commonly requested custom workflow activities for Team Foundation Server Build. Some of the build activities currently provided include the items in Table 19-3.

TABLE 19-3: Handy Community TFS Build Extensions Activities

ACTIVITY	DESCRIPTION
AssemblyInfo	An activity to set the build number into the AssemblyInfo files
CatNetScan	Runs the `CATNetCmd.exe` to check for security issues in an assembly
CheckCoverage	Checks Code Coverage and fails build if below a threshold
CodeMetric	Runs code metrics and static analysis (FxCop) against your .NET code during the build and saves the results to a history log
DateAndTime	Performs date-related activities such as date math, checks if a date falls between two others, if a date is later than another, gets the current date, and gets elapsed time from a given date
Email	Sends e-mail to a set of users using a specific SMTP server
Ftp	Used to interact with FTP sites during your build
IIS7	Used to manipulate IIS7 servers during your build
RoboCopy	Used to copy files between locations using RoboCopy
SharePointDeployment	Used to deploy a SharePoint solution to a SharePoint 2010 site via PowerShell commands
SSH	Used to interact with a server using a Secure Shell
SqlExecute	Used to run a SQL script against a SQL Server from your build
TFSVersion	Used to manipulate TFS Version Control during a build
VB6	Used to compile Visual Basic 6 applications
WorkItemTracking	Used to manipulate TFS Work Item Tracking during a build
XML	Used to manipulate XML files
Zip	Used to create and manipulate Zip files

> **NOTE** *The source code for all the activities is available and licensed under the Microsoft Permissive License, which allows you to use the activities for commercial purposes. For more information about the project, to request new custom activities, or to vote on current requests for new activities, visit* `http://tfsbuildextensions.codeplex.com`.

INTEGRATING CUSTOM ACTIVITIES INTO THE BUILD PROCESS TEMPLATE

If you find that the script extensions on the Default Template build template aren't sufficient for your needs, you will have to modify a copy of the build process template and then configure your build definition to use the new template.

For this example, let's assume that you want to take the contents of your Binaries directory and add it to a Zip archive so that only the Zip files are copied to the Drop folder. To implement this, you'll need to use the Zip activity as well as some standard activities provided by Microsoft.

Acquiring a Copy of the Default Template

The first thing you need to do is to get your hands on a copy of the Default Template build template. As noted in Chapter 18, Microsoft moved the out-of-box build process templates from a folder in the version control repository of each team project to a private location inside the Team Foundation Server Application Tier server. This change ensured that Microsoft could easily update the out-of-box templates without having to worry about breaking a customer's build because the upgrade tools didn't notice that the build template was modified. Unfortunately, this change means that you have some extra steps to go through.

1. From the Builds panel in Team Explorer, click the New Build Definition link, as shown in Figure 19-10.

FIGURE 19-10: New Build Definition link in Team Explorer

2. In the Build Definition Editor, click the Process tab to display the build process template parameters, as shown in Figure 19-11.

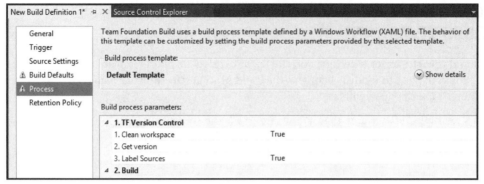

FIGURE 19-11: Process tab in Build Definition Editor

3. Click the Show Details button to expand the Build process template section of the editor.

4. Click the Download button, as shown in Figure 19-12. The Save As dialog box will appear. Navigate to a folder that is mapped into your local workspace and save the build template's XAML file. It's a good idea to change the name of the template file so that it doesn't confuse your team members when they try to make builds after you are done. For this example, we decided to call the template `TfvcTemplate.WithZip.12.xaml` and store it in a folder under the root of our team project called BuildSupport, as shown in Figure 19-13.

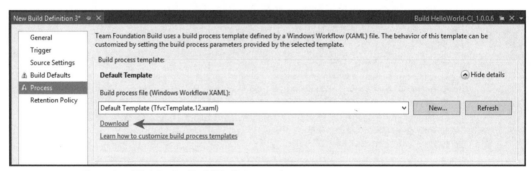

FIGURE 19-12: Download link in the Build Definition editor

5. In Source Control Explorer, select the folder where you saved the build process template and then select the File ➪ Source Control ➪ Add items to folder menu item to launch the Add to Source Control Wizard. Use the wizard to add the XAML file to version control, as shown in Figure 19-14.

6. In the Pending Changes window in Team Explorer, add a check-in comment and click the Checkin button to commit the build process template to version control.

You now have a build process template that you can safely modify for your needs.

FIGURE 19-13: Save As dialog box

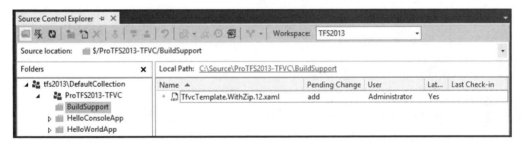

FIGURE 19-14: Build template in version control

Acquiring and Configuring the Community TFS Build Extensions Custom Build Activities

Once you have the build process template, you need to download a copy of the open source TFS Build Extensions custom build activities from CodePlex. After you retrieve the activities you will need to store them in a location that is available to the build controller and agents.

1. Open a browser and navigate to `http://tfsbuildextensions.codeplex.com` and click the big Download button to download the latest version of the extensions, as shown in Figure 19-15. Save the resulting Zip file to your computer.

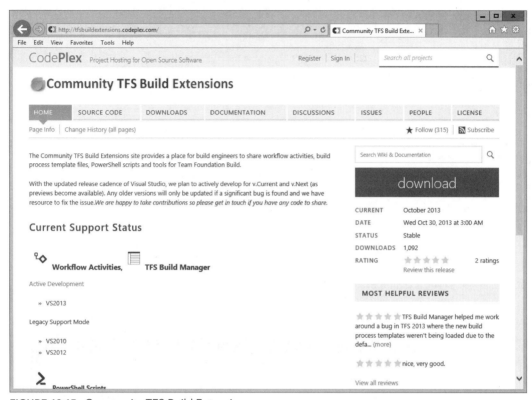

FIGURE 19-15: Community TFS Build Extensions

2. Extract the Zip file contents to your desktop, and then open the folder. Navigate to the
    `TfsBuildExtensions [Month] [Year]\Code Activities\VS2013` folder where
    `[Month] [Year]` represents the release month and year of the activities, as shown in
    Figure 19-16. In our example, the release is October 2013. Find the `TfsBuildExtensions`
    `.Activities.dll` and `Ionic.Zip.dll` files and copy them to the clipboard.

3. In Source Control Explorer, create a new folder under your team project to hold the cus-
    tom activity assemblies. As shown in Figure 19-17, we have created a `Deploy` folder under
    the existing `BuildSupport` folder. Paste the `TfsBuildExtensions.Activities.dll` and
    `Ionic.Zip.dll` files into the new folder and check them into version control.

In the future, any new custom assemblies can be placed into this same folder in version control. In
a later step, you will tell our Build Controller to grab this folder and deploy it to your build agents
before each build.

Creating a Visual Studio Project to Support Editing the Build Template

To edit and debug a build process template, you must create a Visual Studio project so that all of the
assembly references needed by the build template can be found.

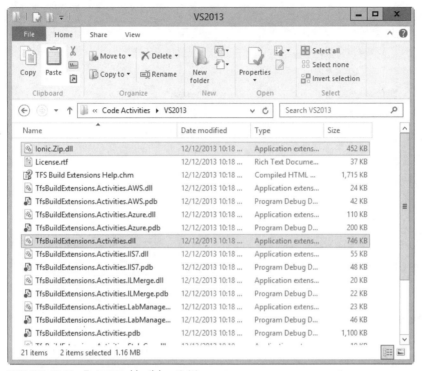

FIGURE 19-16: Extracted build activities

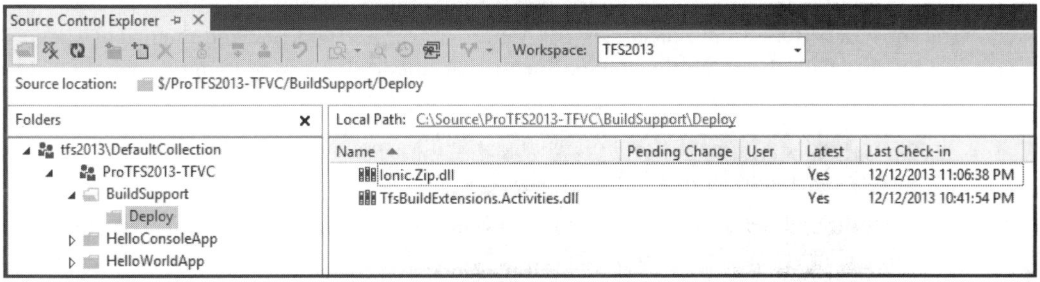

FIGURE 19-17: The custom build activities assembly in version control

Let's walk through the process for getting a Visual Studio project created so that you can use it for editing test versions of the build process templates. Follow these steps:

1. From the Visual Studio menus, click File ⇨ New ⇨ Project to create a new solution and project.

2. At this point, you can choose to use any type of project. However, we're choosing to use a C# Class Library because it has very few default files. Give your class a meaningful name and click OK, as shown in Figure 19-18.

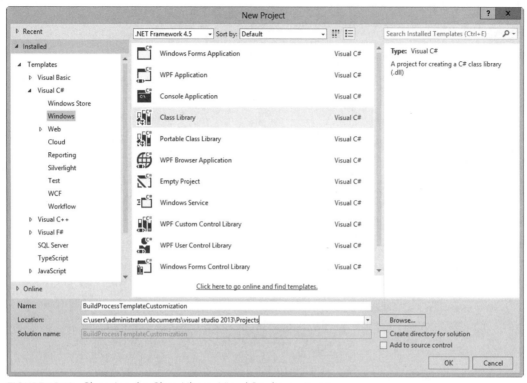

FIGURE 19-18: Choosing the Class Library Visual Studio project type

3. Add the build process template to the new Visual Studio project. You can do that by choosing the new Visual Studio project in the Solution Explorer window and then right-clicking on the project to bring up the context menu. Select Add ⇨ Existing item to open the Add Existing Item dialog box.

4. In the Add Existing Item dialog box, change the file type filter to XAML Files (`*.xaml`, `*.xoml`), as shown in Figure 19-19.

5. Browse to the folder where you stored your build process template and select the template's XAML file, as shown in Figure 19-19.

6. Click the arrow next to the Add button and select the Add as link entry, as shown in Figure 19-19. This will add a link to your project that points to the XAML file without copying the XAML file from its current location to the project's folder, as shown in Figure 19-20. This allows you to use Visual Studio to manage the template while leaving the template XAML file as the only one that needs to be checked into version control.

7. If you were to attempt to compile the solution at this point, you would end up with some compilation errors. This is because, by default, XAML files added to a Visual Studio project

are set to compile. Some walkthroughs available about this topic would instruct you to add the appropriate references to ensure that they compile correctly. However, you can instead instruct MSBuild to ignore the build process template files altogether, and simply copy them to the output directory. You can do this from the Properties window in Visual Studio by setting the Build Action property to None and the Copy to Output Directory property to Copy always, as shown in Figure 19-21.

It has taken a bit to get to this point, but you should be able to compile the entire solution successfully. You can edit process template files from now on by opening the solution and opening the process template file from its location in the Visual Studio project.

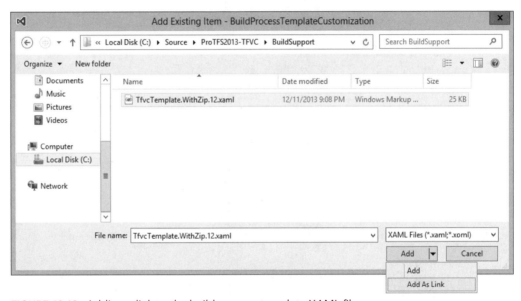

FIGURE 19-19: Adding a link to the build process template XAML file

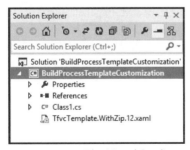

FIGURE 19-20: The Visual Studio project with the XAML file linked

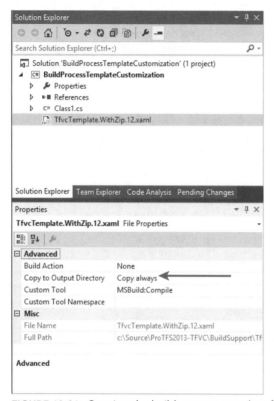

FIGURE 19-21: Copying the build process template files to the output directory

8. Double-click on the process template in Solution Explorer to open the template in the XAML editor.

9. To make the Zip activity available, you need to add a reference to the activity's assembly. In Solution Explorer, right-click on the project's References node and then select Add Reference, as shown in Figure 19-22. This will bring up the Reference Manager dialog box.

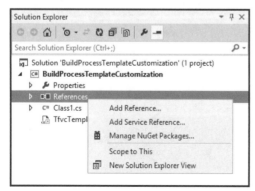

FIGURE 19-22: Add Reference

10. In the Reference Manager, click the Browse button at the bottom of the dialog box. This will bring up the Select the files to reference dialog box. Navigate to the local copy of the `TfsBuildExtensions.Activities.dll` file that you stored in version control, as shown in Figure 19-23. In our case, the path is `C:\Source\ProTFS2013-TFVC\BuildSupport\Deploy`. When you have selected the file, click Add.

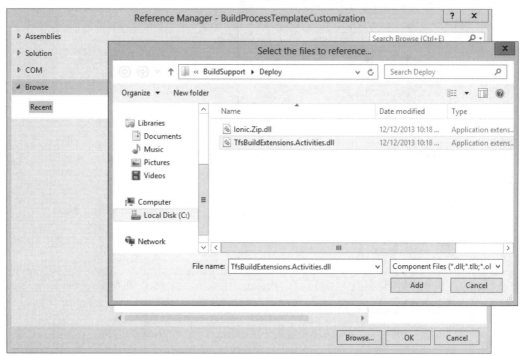

FIGURE 19-23: Browse for Assembly

11. Repeat Step 10 to add the `Ionic.Zip.dll` file.

12. Back in Reference Manager, click Okay to add the references to your project, as shown in Figure 19-24.

13. You need to also add references to the assemblies listed in Table 19-4. Now that you have all of the references set, you need to add the new custom build activities to your toolbox so you can drag them onto the build template's XAML editor canvas.

14. Scroll to the bottom of the Toolbox, right-click on the General section header, and select Choose items, as shown in Figure 19-25.

15. In the Choose Toolbox Items dialog box, click the Browse button.

16. In the Open dialog box, navigate to the location of your custom activities, select the `TfsBuildExtensions.Activities.dll` file, and click Open, as shown in Figure 19-26.

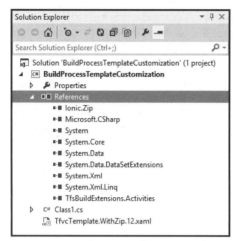

FIGURE 19-24: Correct References in the Project

TABLE 19-4: Additional References Needed to Modify the Build Template

ASSEMBLY	LOCATION
Microsoft.Teamfoundation.Build.Activities	Assemblies\Extensions
Microsoft.TeamFoundation.Build.Client	Assemblies\Extensions
Microsoft.TeamFoundation.Build.Common	Assemblies\Extensions
Microsoft.TeamFoundation.Build Workflow	Assemblies\Extensions
Microsoft.TeamFoundation.Client	Assemblies\Extensions
Microsoft.TeamFoundation.TestImpact .BuildIntegration	Browse to %ProgramFiles%\Microsoft Team Foundation Server 12.0\Tools
Microsoft.TeamFoundation.TestManagement .Client	Assemblies\Extensions
Microsoft.TeamFoundation.VersionControl .Client	Assemblies\Extensions
Microsoft.TeamFoundation.VersionControl .Common	Assemblies\Extensions
Microsoft.VisualBasic	Assemblies\Framework
System	Assemblies\Framework
System.Activities	Assemblies\Framework

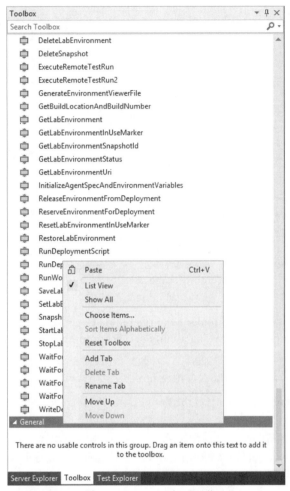

FIGURE 19-25: Choose Items in the Toolbox

17. Scroll down to the bottom of the Choose Toolbox Items dialog box and you should see the Zip activity with a check box next to it along with all of the other build activities in the assembly, as shown in Figure 19-27. Click OK.

18. Scroll down in the toolbox and you will see all of the new custom activities under the General section (see Figure 19-28).

Adding the Zip Activity to the Build Template

Now you are going to add the Zip activity to our build template and wire it up so that you get a Zip file of your application in your Drop folder.

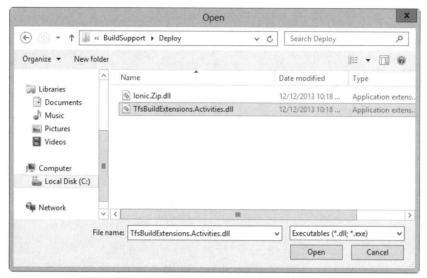

FIGURE 19-26: Select the custom activity assembly for the Toolbox

You first need to grab the location of the Binaries folder from the build. To get this value, you need to create a variable called outDir and populate it using a build activity from the environment variables made available by the build process.

1. Click the Variables tab at the bottom of the XAML editor.

2. Click the Compile, Test and Publish activity in the body of the XAML editor to set your variable's scope.

3. Click the Create variable row in the Variables section to create a new variable. Set the variable name to outDir and the variable type to String. Leave the remaining fields with their defaults, as shown in Figure 19-29.

4. Create a second variable row. Set the variable name to buildNumber and the variable type to String, as shown in Figure 19-29.

5. Find the GetEnvironmentVariable<T> activity in the Team Foundation Build Activities section of the Toolbox and drag it beneath the Publish Symbols activity in the build template, as shown in Figure 19-30. When prompted with the Select Types dialog box, select String.

6. Set the Properties of the GetEnvironmentVariable<String> activity to the values in Table 19-5.

7. Add a second GetEnvironmentVariable<T> activity below the first one. When prompted with the Select Types dialog box, select String.

8. Set the Properties of the second GetEnvironmentVariable<String> activity to the values in Table 19-6.

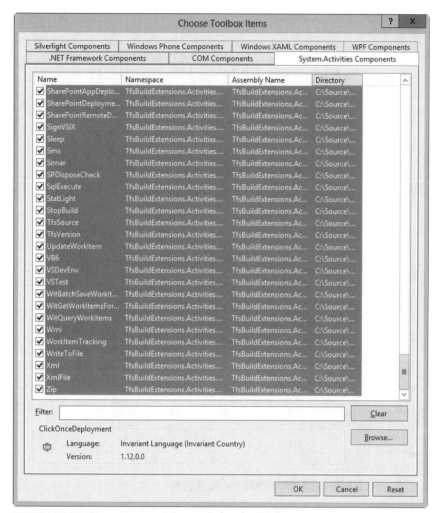

FIGURE 19-27: Zip custom activity ready for the Toolbox

9. Now you need to configure the template to create Zip files. For simplicity's sake, we've configured the Zip activity to collect everything in the Binaries directory and store it in a single Zip file that is named [Build Number].zip where. [Build Number] resolves to the full build number retrieved from the build environment and is based on your build definition's build number format parameter.

Find the Zip activity in the General section of the Toolbox and drag it onto the XAML design surface just after the second GetEnvironmentVariable<String> activity, as shown in Figure 19-31.

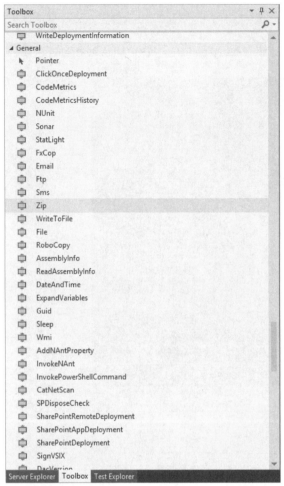

FIGURE 19-28: The custom activities in the Toolbox

10. Right-click on the Zip activity and select Properties from the context menu to display the Properties pane. Set the Zip activity's properties to the values in Table 19-7.

11. Go to the Pending Changes panel in Team Explorer and check in the Build Process Template XAML file.

Configure a Build Definition to Use the New Build Process Template

Once the updated Build Process Template has been checked into version control, you need to register it with the build system. This is a one-time activity that will make it available to all subsequent builds. After it is registered, you will be able to update the HelloWorld-CI build definition to use the new template.

1. Open an existing build definition or create a new one. In this example, we're going to open the HelloWorld-CI build created earlier.

2. Navigate to the Process tab in the Build Definition Editor and click on the Show Details button. The dialog box should look like Figure 19-12.

3. Click New to open the Browse dialog box, as shown in Figure 19-32.

4. Select your Team Project, and then click the Browse button to browse version control for your build process template.

5. Navigate to your custom build process template, select the template, and click OK in both Browse dialog boxes, as shown in Figure 19-32.

FIGURE 19-29: Create the outDir and buildNumber variables.

6. When you return to the Build Definition Editor, you will see that your new build process template is selected, as shown in Figure 19-33.

7. Save your Build Definition.

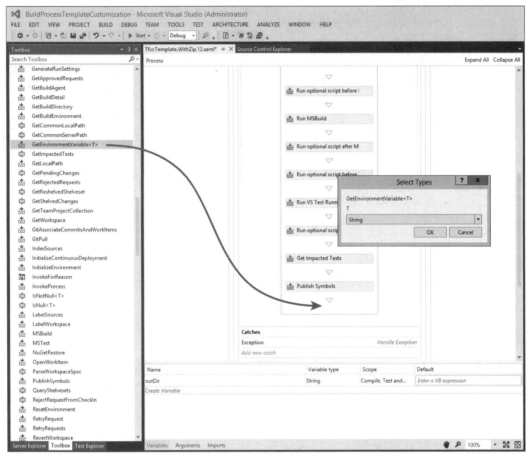

FIGURE 19-30: Add the GetEnvironmentVariable<T> activity.

TABLE 19-5: GetEnvironmentVariable<String> Activity Properties

PROPERTY	VALUE
Name	WellKnownEnvironmentVariables.BinariesDirectory
DisplayName	Get Binaries folder
Result	outDir

TABLE 19-6: GetEnvironmentVariable<String> Activity Properties

PROPERTY	VALUE
Name	WellKnownEnvironmentVariables.BuildNumber
DisplayName	Get Build Number
Result	buildNumber

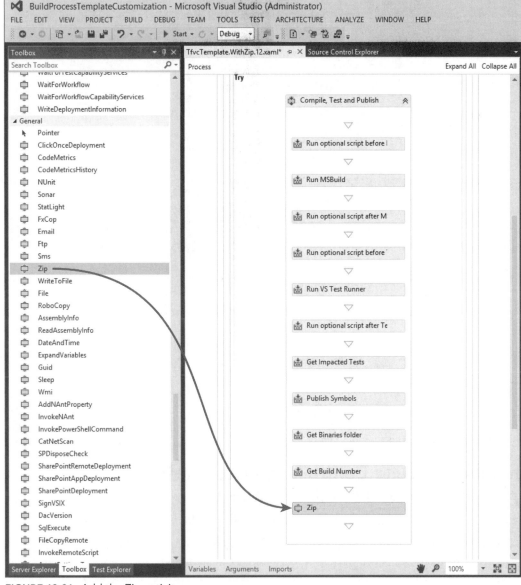

FIGURE 19-31: Add the Zip activity.

TABLE 19-7: Zip Activity Properties

PROPERTY	VALUE
Action	Create
CompressPath	outDir
ZipFileName	String.Format("{0}\\{1}", outDir, WellKnownEnvironmentVariables.BuildNumber & ".zip")

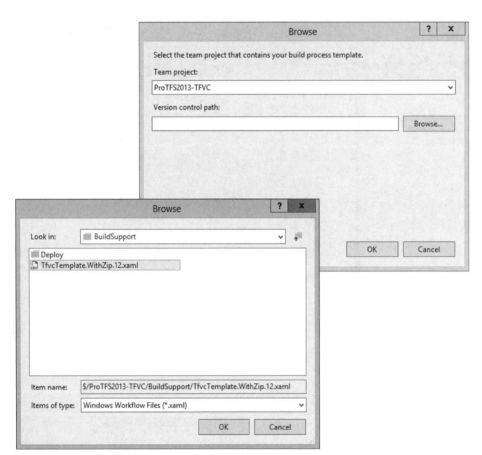

FIGURE 19-32: Register the custom build process template.

Configure the Build Controller to Automatically Deploy Your Custom Build Activities

Before you can run the update build you need to perform one final configuration.

When the build runs, the build process template is sent to the build controller and build agents to orchestrate their actions. When the Zip activity is hit in the build process, the build system will try to find the TfsBuildExtensions.Activities.dll and Ionic.Zip.dll files, which don't exist on your build servers.

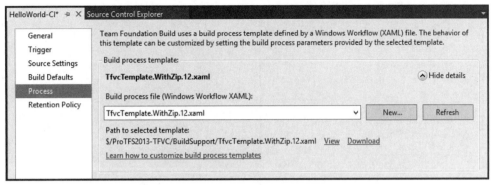

FIGURE 19-33: Custom Build process template selected

To remedy this you could deploy the files to every build machine, but if you create an additional build machine and forget to deploy the files, then any builds that run on that machine will fail.

A better way to handle this is to configure the Build Controller to automatically deploy these files for you every time a build runs. This way, you don't have to remember anything and new build machines get the files the first time they perform a build. You can achieve this by configuring a folder in version control for the build system.

The build controller and the agents managed by the controller will monitor this version control folder and load any appropriate assemblies into the build service for use by build process templates. All you must do to deploy a new version of the custom assemblies is check them into the version control folder. When you check in a new version of the assemblies, the build controllers and agents will restart their services after completing any current builds running by the agents. They then load the new version of the assemblies and continue with any builds currently in the build queue.

This process significantly reduces the complexity of deploying custom assemblies. You can easily add additional build machines to the build farm without having to worry about how to deploy the appropriate custom assemblies to them.

1. In the Build pane of Team Explorer, click the Actions ➪ Manage Build Controllers menu, as shown in Figure 19-34.

2. Select the Build Controller and click the Properties button to show the Build Controller Properties dialog box, as shown in Figure 19-35.

3. Click the ellipsis button next to the Version control path to custom assemblies text box.

4. In the Browse dialog box, select your Team Project. If you have a mix of Team Foundation Version Control and Git-backed Team Projects, changing this selection will change the layout of the dialog box. The following steps are for a Team Foundation Version Control–backed Team Project.

5. Click the Browse button to open the Browse for Folder dialog box.

FIGURE 19-34: Manage Build Controllers menu

6. Navigate to the folder in version control that holds the `TfsBuildExtensions.Activities` `.dll` and `Ionic.Zip.dll` files. Select that folder and click OK.

7. To finish the configuration, click OK, and then OK again, and then Close.

To ensure that assemblies are added into the Deploy directory when they are copied into the local directory on disk, you may want to create a file called `.tfIgnore` in the root of the Deploy folder, the contents of which are shown in Listing 19-3. The single line of `!*.dll` tells Team Foundation Server to include any DLL files that it finds when scanning the local disk, detecting changes that require adding files into version control.

LISTING 19-3: CUSTOMASSEMBLIES .TFIGNORE FILE

```
# Ensure that the custom assembly DLLs are included in version control
!*.dll
```

Run Your Build and Check Your Work

You now have everything in place to test out the build, so queue the update build definition using the default values. When the build completes, switch from the Summary view to the Log view. Toward the bottom of the log, you should see three new entries, Get Binaries folder, Get Build Number, and Zip, as shown in Figure 19-36.

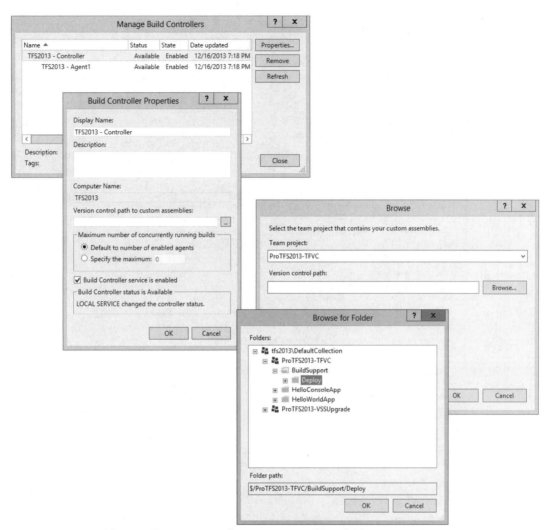

FIGURE 19-35: Build Controller properties for custom assemblies folder

You can now click on the Open Drop Folder link in the build report. The drop folder still contains all of the files and folders that you saw in prior runs, but now it contains a Zip file called `HelloWorld-CI_1.0.0.6.zip`, which is the build number on this build run, as shown in Figure 19-37. Congratulations!

FIGURE 19-36: Build report showing customizations

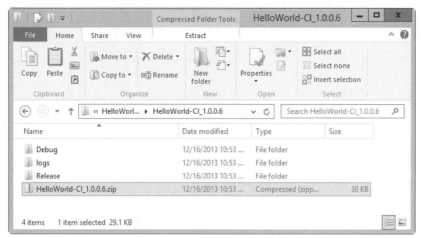

FIGURE 19-37: Drop folder showing Zip file

SUMMARY

In this chapter, you learned how to customize the automated build process by using custom scripting and standard workflow activities available from the .NET Framework, Team Foundation Server, and open source build activity projects. You reviewed the essential functionality from Windows Workflow Foundation (WF) leveraged in Team Foundation Server Build, including creating local workflow variables, setting them from custom activity outputs, and consuming them as custom activity inputs.

You also learned how to configure Build Controllers to automatically deploy dependencies to their Build Agents to support your build process customizations.

In Chapter 20 you learn about the new Release Management tools that can help your team manage the workflow, which supports moving your application from development, to test, and eventually to production.

20

Release Management

WHAT'S IN THIS CHAPTER?

➤ Learning about the new Release Management tool

➤ Installing and configuring Visual Studio Release Management

➤ Planning and managing a release

Team Foundation Server has long supported excellent software development practices, but deployment of built software has traditionally been managed separately. Often, it has involved manual steps at the end of a build, which are prone to human error. Release Management for Visual Studio 2013 provides an integrated and feature-rich deployment tool to ease the release process for developed applications.

A primary goal of any deployment process should be its ability to support frequent releases. If a deployment process is straightforward and relatively hands-off, teams can release more frequently and can respond to change quickly and safely.

Another important consideration, particularly in large enterprises, is transparency and compliance to an established process. It is important to know which version of a project has been released to an environment and who authorized that release.

GETTING STARTED WITH RELEASE MANAGEMENT FOR VISUAL STUDIO 2013

Release Management for Visual Studio 2013 is a set of software applications and components that work with Team Foundation Server to provide an automated deployment solution. It facilitates repeatable and transparent deployment pipelines from Team Foundation Server 2010, 2012, or 2013 to deployment environments right up to production. It also supports managed deployment of packages created outside Team Foundation Server.

Release Management allows complex deployments of builds to client computers, servers, and Windows Azure. It also helps manage release processes by tracking approvals and sign-offs to provide enterprise-level traceability.

Like many Team Foundation Server components, Release Management began its life as a third-party product. In mid-2013, Microsoft acquired InCycle Software's InRelease product and, in November 2013, re-released it as Release Management for Visual Studio 2013.

Components

Release Management for Visual Studio 2013 consists of four main components:

➤   **Release Management Server**—Consists of the database, the workflow controller, and the release dispatcher

➤   **Release Management Client**—Includes two user interfaces: a WPF client that exposes all available functionality; and a lightweight web client for testers, approvers, and managers

➤   **Release Management Deployer**—A service installed on target servers that pulls information from the release management server. This greatly eases deployment as the server does not need security permissions to every target server.

➤   **Deployment Tools**—A set of powerful tools used in deployment steps for installing or uninstalling components, deploying files to specific locations, and starting and stopping services. These tools are embedded in the product and don't require separate installation.

Licensing

You should work with your Microsoft Partner or Microsoft Consulting Services representative to identify your license requirements for Release Management, but the following general licensing guidelines apply:

➤   Each person using the Release Management Client for administration of a release pipeline must be licensed for Visual Studio Ultimate with MSDN, Visual Studio Premium with MSDN, Visual Studio Test Professional with MSDN, or MSDN platforms.

➤   Each person triggering a release must be licensed with a Team Foundation Server CAL.

➤   Each target endpoint to which a release is deployed must be licensed with either Visual Studio Deployment Standard 2013 (one license is included with Visual Studio Ultimate with MSDN) or Visual Studio Deployment Datacenter 2013.

➤   Approval of release stages, or signing off a release, does not require a license.

Hardware and Software Requirements

Prior to installing Release Management for Visual Studio 2013, you should ensure that each server and target machine meets the minimum hardware and software requirements.

The server component should be installed on a single machine. In environments with frequent releases, we recommend provisioning a dedicated physical or virtual machine for this purpose. For teams with relatively basic or infrequent release processes, we recommend installing the server components on the Team Foundation Server Application Tier, and using the SQL Server database on the Team Foundation Server Data Tier. Table 20-1 shows the hardware and software requirements for the server components.

TABLE 20-1: Requirements for Release Management Server

COMPONENT	REQUIREMENTS
CPU	1 GHz Pentium processor or equivalent (minimum) 2 GHz Pentium processor or equivalent (recommended)
RAM	1024MB (minimum) 2048MB (recommended)
Hard disk	Up to 2.2GB of available space may be required for initial installation due to the dependency on .NET. Depending on usage, the database can grow up to 1GB per year.
Database	Microsoft SQL Server 2008 Microsoft SQL Server 2008 R2 Microsoft SQL Server 2012 (recommended)
Operating system	Windows Server 2008 R2 SP1 Windows Server 2012 Windows Server 2012 R2 (recommended)

You have the option of installing the Release Management client application on one or more different servers or client machines. Each machine with the client application installed must meet the minimum requirements shown in Table 20-2.

TABLE 20-2: Requirements for Release Management Client

COMPONENT	REQUIREMENTS
CPU	1 GHz Pentium processor or equivalent (minimum) 2 GHz Pentium processor or equivalent (recommended)
RAM	512MB (minimum) 1024MB (recommended)
Hard disk	Up to 2.2GB of available space may be required for initial installation due to the dependency on .NET.

continues

TABLE 20-2 *(continued)*

COMPONENT	REQUIREMENTS
Operating system	Windows 7 SP1
	Windows 8
	Windows 8.1
	Windows Server 2008 R2 SP1
	Windows Server 2012
	Windows Server 2012 R2 (recommended)

We strongly recommend installing the Release Management Client on the Team Foundation Build Server. Having the Release Management Client on the build server allows it to build release packages directly from Team Foundation Server. This is particularly important for continuous integration scenarios.

Each target computer needs a Microsoft deployment agent installed to enable deployment of software. Software and hardware requirements are more flexible for the deployment agents because of the large number of potential deployment targets. Table 20-3 shows the minimum requirements for a target machine running the deployment agent.

TABLE 20-3: Requirements for Release Management Deployment Agent

COMPONENT	REQUIREMENTS
CPU	400 MHz Pentium processor or equivalent (minimum)
	1 GHz Pentium processor or equivalent (recommended)
RAM	256MB (minimum)
	1024MB (recommended)
Hard disk	Up to 2.2GB of available space may be required for initial installation due to the dependency on .NET.
	You should allow sufficient disk space for the applications you are deploying.
Operating system	Windows Vista (latest service pack)
	Windows 7 SP1
	Windows 8
	Windows 8.1
	Windows Server 2008 R2 SP1
	Windows Server 2012
	Windows Server 2012 R2

Installing Release Management Server

To install Release Management Server, you will need to be logged into the server as a user with local administrator rights. You will also need to have sysadmin rights on the SQL Server you intend to use.

To start installation, run the `rm_Server.exe` file from the package or ISO you downloaded and select a destination folder, as shown in Figure 20-1. In most cases, you should use the default installation directory.

FIGURE 20-1: Release Management Server installation folder

After agreeing to the terms and conditions, click Install to start the installation process. Installation may take several minutes and you may be prompted to restart your machine.

Like Team Foundation Server itself, the installation of each Release Management component is separate from its configuration. After installation, you will be prompted to configure your Release Management server.

In the Identity for Release Management services section, specify the credentials you want to use to run the Release Management Server. The identity you set here will become the owner of the Release Management database, so we recommend using a specific local or domain account rather than the default NetworkService account. You should also make sure the account is a local administrator. For convenience, you may want to use the same service account you use for Team Foundation Server itself.

The Release Management Server settings section lets you set the web service port and the database server details. We recommend using the default port of `1000` unless this will cause problems in your environment. Using a local database instance will improve performance, but you can use any server running SQL Server 2008, SQL Server 2008 R2, or SQL Server 2012. For convenience, you may want to use the existing Team Foundation Server Data Tier for SQL Server.

The configuration dialog box provides useful Test links so you can ensure the credentials you have provided are correct.

When you're confident your settings are correct, click the Apply Settings button to confirm. The setup process will configure the database, web server, and windows services required for Release Management. If there are any issues during configuration, the Configuration summary dialog box will show details and will provide links to the log file for troubleshooting.

Installing Release Management Client

To allow continuous deployment of your projects, the Release Management Client application should be installed on the Build Server of your Team Foundation Server environment. This will allow the build agent to automatically create releases as part of a build.

To install the Release Management Client, run the `rm_Client.exe` file from the package or ISO you downloaded. You will be prompted to choose the installation directory and accept the License Terms and Privacy Policy before clicking Install.

After installation, you will need to configure the client to connect to the web service you set up when installing the server component, as shown in Figure 20-2.

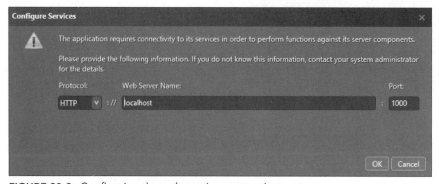

FIGURE 20-2: Configuring the web service connection

Installing Deployment Agents

Deployment agents should be installed on every target machine you want to deploy to. For large projects where you may have to install the agent on a lot of machines, make sure you have a license for each of these services.

To install the deployment agent, run the installer executable from the package or ISO you downloaded. The installer will have a different filename depending on your license model, but the filename will start with `rm_Deployment`. Choose your setup folder and agree to the License Terms and Privacy

Policy before clicking Install. Ensure you run the installation using an account that has local admin privileges.

After installation, you will be prompted to configure the deployment agent, as shown in Figure 20-3.

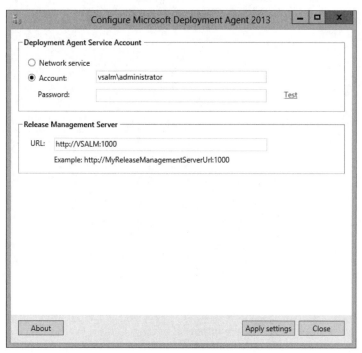

FIGURE 20-3: Configuration of the deployment agent

Because the deployment agent is responsible for installing components on the target server, you should change the default NetworkService account to a specific account that has sufficient permissions to install your application. This account should be set up as a Service User in the server configuration so it doesn't appear as an option in pick lists. We recommend you create a custom domain account for this purpose.

CONFIGURATION

Before you can use Release Management for Visual Studio 2013, you will need to perform some initial configuration steps.

System Settings

Navigate to the Administration ⇨ Settings page to view the system settings and deployer settings for Release Management, as shown in Figure 20-4. Most settings on this page have a help icon you can hover over to learn more.

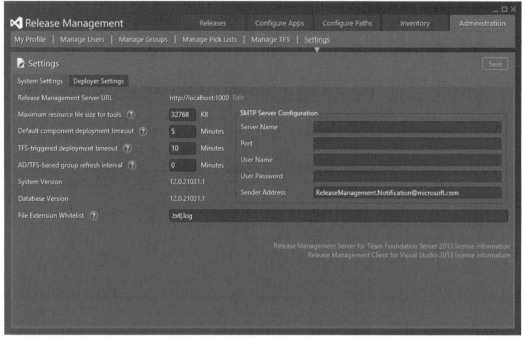

FIGURE 20-4: Release Management system settings

You are likely to leave most of these settings alone at the moment, but you should take the time to set up SMTP settings in this section so that Release Management can send Approval and other notifications to users.

Connecting to Team Foundation Server

One of the first things you will want to configure is the connection to Team Foundation Server. A connection is local to a project collection, but you can configure many connections if you want to manage releases for more than one Team Foundation Server instance or project collection.

> **WARNING** *Release Management currently supports only on-premises installations of Team Foundation Server. If you are using Visual Studio Online, you will be unable to connect with this release of the product.*

Navigate to Administration ➪ Manage TFS and click New to add a connection. Configure the appropriate settings for your Team Foundation Server and click Verify to ensure they are correct. If your Release Management account does not have appropriate permissions, you may need to specify another account in the Connect As section, as shown in Figure 20-5. To avoid having to set individual permissions in Team Foundation Server, we recommend using an account that belongs to the Project Collection Service Accounts in Team Foundation Server.

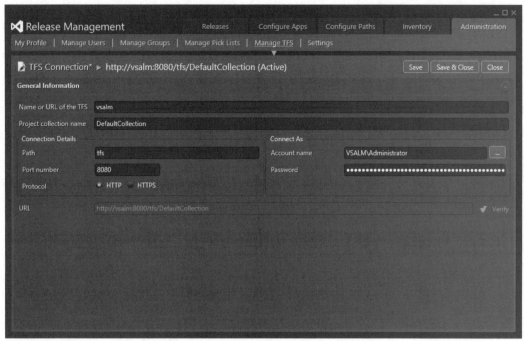

FIGURE 20-5: Configuring the Team Foundation Server Connection

Users and Groups

All users that will interact with Release Management will need to be configured. You can configure individual users from Active Directory as well as import groups from Active Directory or Team Foundation Server.

To configure users, navigate to the Manage Users section in the Administration tab. You will see a list of users currently configured. Click the New button to set up a new user.

Figure 20-6 shows the configuration for a new user. Click the ellipsis button next to the Windows Account field to choose a user and automatically populate the name and e-mail fields. You can configure the user to be a Release Manager and can set e-mail notification settings.

Any Release Management groups the user belongs to will be shown in the Member Of table at the bottom of the page.

> **NOTE** *Any domain accounts used by deployment agents should be set up as Service Users in Release Management.*

To configure groups in Release Management, navigate to Administration ⇨ Manage Groups. You will see all currently configured groups.

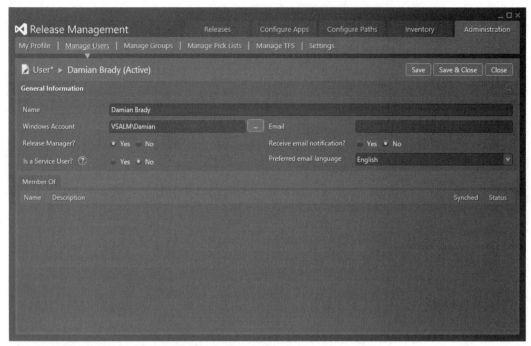

FIGURE 20-6: Configuring Release Management users

Release Management contains a reserved group called "Everyone" that contains every user configured in the system. You can't delete this group, but you can change some of its permissions if you would like to control them manually within other groups.

To create a new group, click the arrow next to the New button on the top right of the screen. You can choose to create a new empty group, import a group from Active Directory, or import a group from Team Foundation Server.

> **NOTE** *Group permissions in Release Management are evaluated to the most permissive for a user. If a user is in more than one group, but only one group has a certain permission, that user will be granted that permission.*

If you add a Team Foundation Server group, you will be given a dialog box allowing you to choose a group from any of your connections and the Team Projects in that project collection. After clicking OK, the group will be automatically created and will be periodically synced with Team Foundation Server. The synchronization interval can be set in the System Settings section described earlier.

Similarly, adding an Active Directory group will show a dialog box asking you to choose an Active Directory group. Active Directory groups will be periodically synced with Active Directory at an interval that can be set in the System Settings section.

> **NOTE** *When you import a Team Foundation Server or Active Directory group, any users in those groups that do not already exist in Release Management will be added. You can see these users in the Manage Users section.*

Choose a group and click the Open button to view the details of the group, as shown in Figure 20-7.

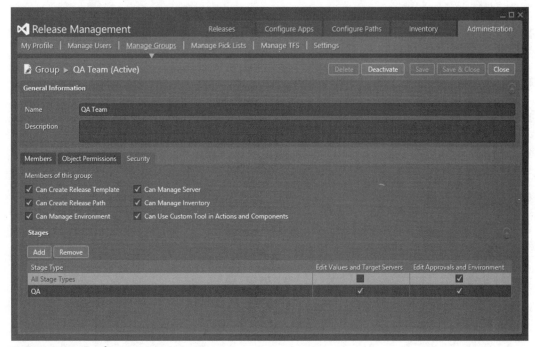

FIGURE 20-7: Configuring groups

On this page, you can delete or deactivate groups and set basic information. The Members tab on this page shows you each member of the group and allows you to create a new user or link an existing user. You can see any permissions set for specific Release Management objects in the Object Permissions tab. If the group is synchronized with Team Foundation Server or Active Directory, you will see an additional tab with information about the synchronization.

The Security tab shown in Figure 20-7 allows you to set permissions for Release Management in general, as well as permissions for configuring individual stages.

Pick Lists

There are two fully configurable pick lists used by Release Management for identifying stages and technology stacks. To configure these lists, navigate to Administration ⇨ Manage Pick Lists.

Stages are used when defining release paths to identify the stages a deployment will transition through. Typically you may have stages such as Development, Staging, QA, and Production. Note that not every release path needs to use every stage.

The Technology Type pick list is used to categorize applications by technology stack. For example, you may have an entry for ASP.NET and another for Windows 8 applications.

Actions and Tools

Actions in Release Management represent steps that can be taken during a release. You will combine and sequence Actions together to create a Release Template. Each Action uses a Tool to perform a particular task.

Out of the box, Release Management comes with 15 Tools and more than 50 Actions you can use to deploy your application.

Navigate to the Inventory tab to see the Actions and Tools currently configured for your Release Management instance. Table 20-4 lists some of the more common Actions you may use to deploy your application. For a complete list of available Actions with detailed descriptions, refer to the Release Management for Visual Studio 2013 User Guide available at `http://aka.ms/ReleaseManagement2013`.

TABLE 20-4: Useful Actions in Release Management

CATEGORY	ACTION(S)
Windows Azure	Start/Stop a Windows Azure VM
IIS	Create/Remove Application Pool
	Start/Stop Application Pool
	Create/Remove Web Site
	Configure Web Site
	Create/Remove Web Application
	Configure Web Application
MS-SQL	Create SQL Database
	Drop SQL Database
	Back up SQL Database
	Restore SQL Database
Windows OS	Copy/Delete/Move/Rename File or Folder
	Create Folder
	Create/Modify/Delete Environment Variable
	Create/Modify/Delete Registry Key
	Run Command Line
	Run Command Line as User
	Kill Windows Process
INI File	Create/Modify/Remove Key and Value
	Modify Section Name

If you have a custom tool you use as part of your deployment, you can add it by navigating to the Tools section and clicking the New button. After giving your tool a name and optional description, set the command to execute as well as the arguments to pass to your tool.

When specifying arguments, you can use tokens to automatically create parameters that can be used by actions to pass information. A token should begin and end with two underscores (__), as shown in the MSI Deployer tool in Figure 20-8.

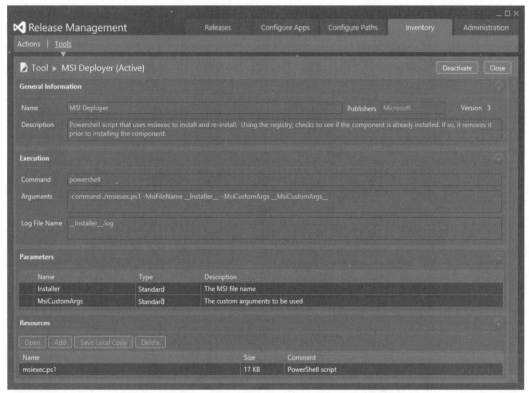

FIGURE 20-8: Tool configuration

You should also specify any additional resources required by your tool in the Resources section. To ensure the deployment agent will be able to find your tool, you might want to include the executable in the Resources list directly.

To create a new Action, click the New button in the Action section of the Inventory tab. Give the Action a name and description and optionally choose a Category. If none of the categories are appropriate, you can create a new one from this page by clicking the New button alongside the dropdown.

For an action to work, it needs to make use of a tool. You can choose an existing tool from the drop-down or click New to create a new one. Depending on the tool you choose, you will be shown the command that will run along with the arguments to be set and any parameters to be passed. You are able to change the default arguments for the tool in this section if you have specific requirements.

Environments and Servers

An Environment is a set of one or more servers used for one or more deployment stages. For example, a "Staging" environment might consist of a web server and a database server used for testing an application prior to final release.

To configure your environments, navigate to Configure Paths ➪ Environments. Clicking the New button will show a page similar to Figure 20-9. You can set the environment name and description as well as an owner for the environment.

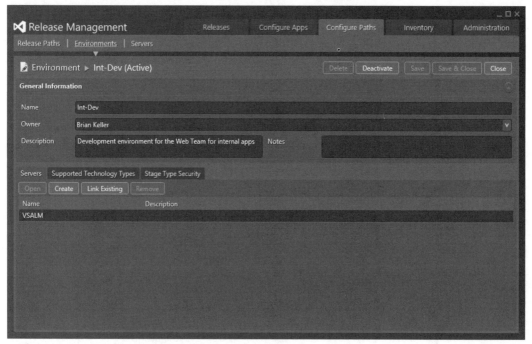

FIGURE 20-9: Configuring environments

The tabs at the bottom of the page show the servers that are part of the environment, the technologies that are supported, and the stages that are able to use this environment. It is good practice to set stage permissions in this section to ensure each stage can only use the appropriate environments. For example, you might want to prevent production environments from being used when deploying a Testing stage.

The Servers tab available in the environment settings allows you to create a new server or link to an existing server. Alternatively, you can navigate to the Configure Paths ➪ Servers section and add servers independently. Figure 20-10 shows this section where you can see all the configured servers as well as their status.

If you have installed the Release Management deployment agent on a server that is not in this list, you can scan for it automatically by clicking on the arrow next to the New button and choosing

Scan for New, as in Figure 20-10. This will search for any unregistered servers running a deployment agent. Figure 20-11 shows a successful scan on a local network.

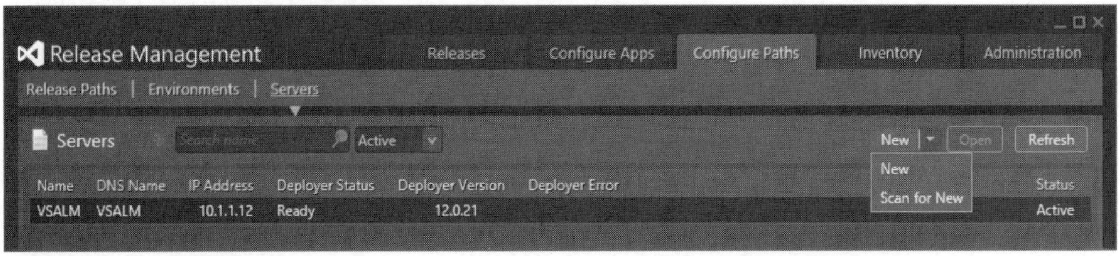

FIGURE 20-10: Setting up Servers

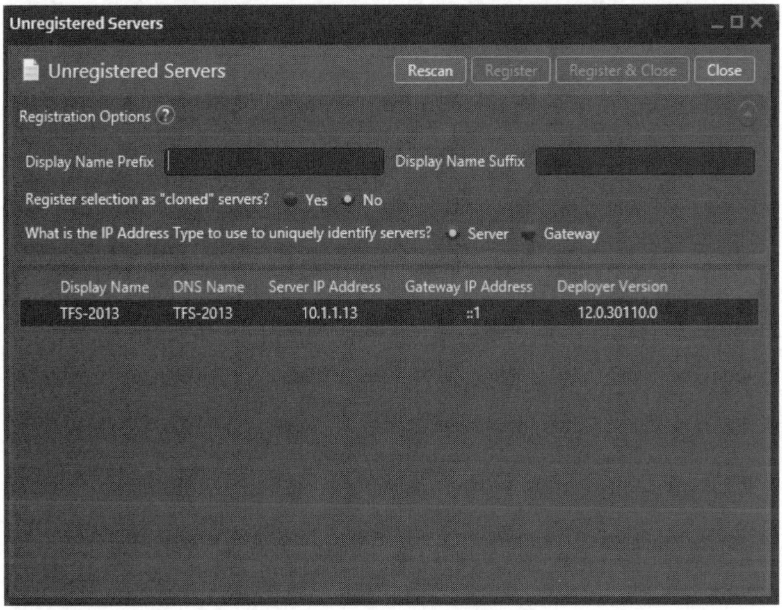

FIGURE 20-11: Scanning for Deployment Servers

You can also add servers by clicking the New button and entering the server details manually, but we strongly recommend adding servers using the Scan for New feature. By using this method, you can avoid typos and be assured the Release Management server can locate the target server.

When defining a server, you will need to specify whether the server is a "cloned" server (refer to Figure 20-11). Cloned servers are effectively identical other than their IP addresses. For this reason, cloned servers must have static IP addresses to allow them to be uniquely identified.

A server can also have a "Server" or "Gateway" type of IP address (again, refer to Figure 20-11). This determines whether the IP address belongs to the actual server or a gateway. The Gateway IP address type is commonly used when the target server is located behind a gateway or firewall with Network Address Translation (NAT).

Choosing a server from the list shown in Figure 20-10 and clicking Open will take you to the server details, as shown in Figure 20-12. The Deployer tab shows the status of the deployment agent and lets you set how files are retrieved by the deployment agent. Using a UNC path will result in faster file transfers to the target servers, but the service account used by the deployment agent requires security access to the drop location. If this is a problem, you can transmit files via the Release Management Server over HTTPS. File transfer rates using this mechanism will be significantly slower, but it can be useful for servers outside the local environment. If you are using HTTPS, the identity of the ReleaseManagementAppPool application pool used by the Release Management web services will need read permissions on the drop location.

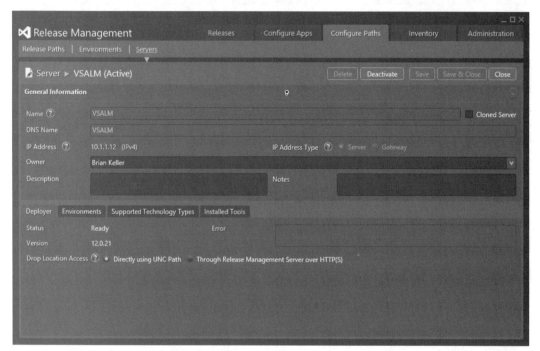

FIGURE 20-12: Deployment Server settings

The Environments tab shows the environments currently using this server and allows you to link to an existing environment. The Supported Technology Types section allows you to specify technology stacks supported by this server, and the Installed Tools tab shows any additional tools you have installed on the server.

Release Paths

A release path is a defined process workflow used to distribute a release in a specific scenario. For example, a standard weekly release might follow a different release path than an emergency patch. A release path defines the stages the release will go through as well as the groups that are allowed to use this release path.

Navigate to Configure Paths ⇨ Release Path to view the release paths configured for your environment. The first time you go to this section, you may see a guide to help you complete any steps you haven't yet finished. These steps are shown in an order that eases configuration. Any steps you have completed will be shown with a check mark, and the next step you should complete will be shown in bold, as in Figure 20-13.

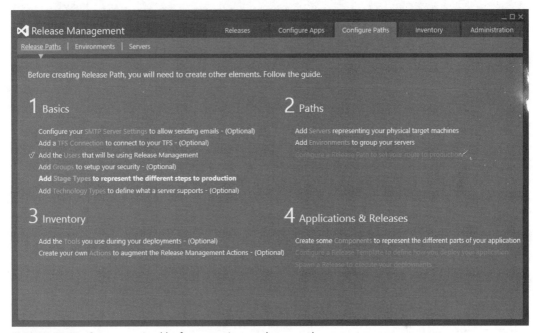

FIGURE 20-13: Steps required before creating a release path

Each release path consists of stages and each stage has settings that must be configured. The Stages tab allows you to add and remove stages in a release path and change the order. Figure 20-14 shows a release path through Dev, QA, and Prod stages.

Each stage must specify an Environment as well as rules for the Acceptance, Deployment, Validation, and Approval steps. For each step, you will need to specify a user or group who is responsible for approving or rejecting progression to the next step. The Acceptance step can be automated such that a deployment is triggered automatically. Similarly, the Validation step can be automated so the release moves straight to approval.

The Deployment and Validation steps can be considered part of the same process. Validation occurs immediately after all components have been deployed successfully and doesn't require any additional interaction.

Finally, one or more users or groups can be listed in the Approval step to approve or reject the release. If no users or groups are specified, the stage is considered to have succeeded.

In the QA stage in Figure 20-14, you can see a deployment to the Int-QA environment with automated Acceptance and Validation steps. The QA group is responsible for all the steps in this stage.

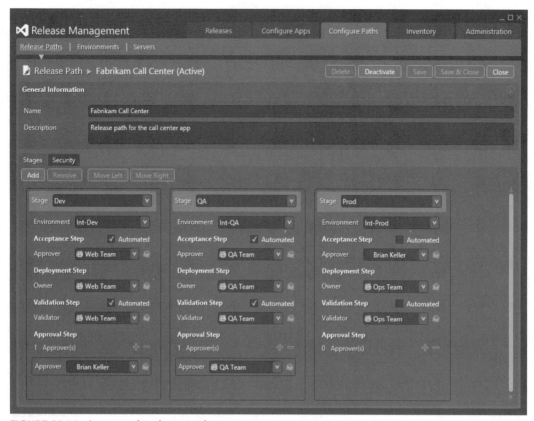

FIGURE 20-14: An example release path

RELEASE TEMPLATES AND COMPONENTS

A Release Template defines a workflow used for releasing an application. It consists of deployment steps to follow for each stage in a specific Release Path. Components represent the details of your software, including the compiled package and how to deploy it. Deployment of one or more components will usually be one of the main steps in your Release Template workflow.

To view your Release Templates, navigate to Configure Apps ⇨ Release Templates. From here you are able to open existing templates and create new templates, either from scratch or by copying existing templates.

When you create a new template or copy an existing one, you will be given a dialog box similar to the one in Figure 20-15.

In addition to setting a name and optional description, you will also have to choose a Release Path to use and, optionally, a Team Project and Build Definition. You are also able to specify whether you can trigger a release directly from the build.

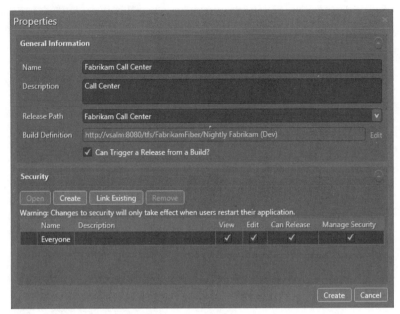

FIGURE 20-15: Creating a new component

The Security tab allows you to set which users are able to manage or use this release template.

> **NOTE** *While you are editing a Release Template, the template will be locked to prevent another user from making changes that overwrite your own. Other users will see a small lock icon to the left of the Release Template and will not be able to edit.*

Deployment Sequence

After setting the basic values of a new Release Template, you will be taken to the Deployment Sequence view. This view consists of a number of sections, as you can see in Figure 20-16.

The top of the screen shows buttons for deleting and deactivating the template, as well as triggering a new release. If you have made any changes to the sequence, buttons to save your changes will be enabled.

Below that are the stages that have been defined by the Release Path in use. Each of these defines a separate Deployment Sequence that can be shown in the main area by clicking on it.

The Toolbox on the left of the screen is organized into categories. There are categories for controlling the workflow, categories representing the servers, and a Components category representing the available components. You learn more about the components in the next section. The remaining categories contain every Action available to you.

The main area of the application is the Deployment Sequence itself. By dragging activities from the Toolbox to the Deployment Sequence window, you can build up your workflow process. This will be familiar to anyone who has worked with the Windows Workflow designer in the past.

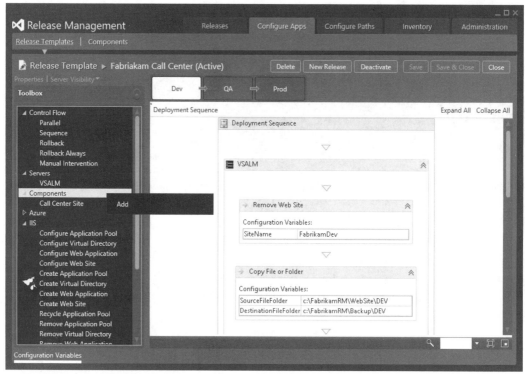

FIGURE 20-16: The Deployment Sequence view

Each Stage has its own Deployment Sequence. Sequences can be copied and pasted between stages by right-clicking on the stage, making it easy to duplicate complex processes. If a specific server is not available for a stage, you will be prompted to provide a server that is available.

Actions and Components can only be added to Server activities, and a Server activity cannot be left blank. Server activities can be organized in sequence or in parallel. That means you can deploy components to multiple servers at the same time.

Components or Actions can be temporarily disabled or skipped by clicking on the activity's icon. This can be useful for deployment sequences that are mostly the same across stages but where one or more activities are inappropriate for an environment.

While many useful Actions are available to you to assist in deployment, your primary aim is to deploy your own software. To do so, you must configure a new Component.

> **NOTE** *The steps required to deploy an application will be very different depending on what software you are deploying.*
>
> *For more information on the actions that might be appropriate for your specific case, see the Actions Catalog appendix in the Release Management for Visual Studio 2013 User Guide available at* `http://aka.ms/ReleaseManagement2013`.

Components

You can set up a new Component in two ways. On the Deployment Sequence view, you can right-click on the Components category in the Toolbox and choose Add, as shown in Figure 20-16. Alternatively, you can add a new component by navigating to Configure Apps ⇨ Components and clicking the New button.

After supplying a name and optional description, open the Source tab to choose one of three methods to get the package to deploy. Each of these options has a help icon you can hover over for more information.

If you select "Builds with application," the build definition is specified automatically from the release template. You must provide a path to the built package, as shown in Figure 20-17.

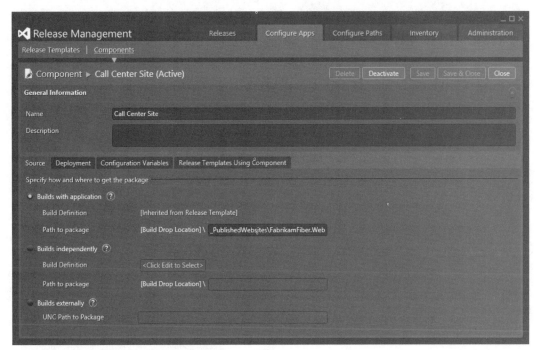

FIGURE 20-17: Configuring a Component

Choosing the "Builds independently" option requires you to additionally select a Team Project and a build definition to use for the component. You will be able to select the build when you release.

If your project is built externally from Team Foundation Server, you should use the "Builds externally option" and provide a UNC path to the base package location.

The Deployment tab allows you to select the Tool that will be used to deploy your component as well as any required command arguments and parameters. In line with the configuration for Actions and Tools, Parameters are created automatically for any arguments that start and end with two underscores (__). You can also set an optional timeout for deployment. This will kill the process if deployment has gone on for too long.

The Configuration Variables tab allows you to set variables to be set during your release. You can use these variables to set properties that may change based on the stage your deployment is up to.

In this tab, you can also define when the configuration variable values will be set during deployment. Different components may require their variables set prior to installation or after installation. Table 20-5 shows the different options and their behavior.

TABLE 20-5: Configuration Variable Replacement Modes

MODE	DESCRIPTION
Only in Command	Only variables specified in command arguments will be replaced.
Before Installation	In addition to arguments, files will be searched for appropriate tokens and changes will be applied prior to running the installation tool.
	You can specify a file extension filter to target a subset of files to modify.
After Installation	In addition to arguments, files will be searched for appropriate tokens, and changes will be applied after running the installation tool.
	This is useful for packages such as MSI files where the target files may not exist until after installation.
	You can specify a file extension filter to target a subset of files to modify.
Before and After Installation	Command arguments and files will be modified both before and after the installation step.
	This can be useful for installation processes that depend on variables in external files and also produce files that need replacements made.

The final tab shows the Release Templates that are using the Component.

Configuration Variables

As you've seen, Actions and Components can be configured with variables, referred to as Configuration Variables. When configuring a Deployment Sequence, these variables can be set with values specific to a stage. When you add a Component or Action to the Deployment Sequence panel, you will see the Configuration Variables you must set for that activity. You saw Configuration Variables for two activities in the Release Template in Figure 20-16.

There are two ways to set configuration variable values when configuring a Release Template. The easiest way is to set them inline simply by choosing the configuration variable in the workflow and typing. Alternatively, you can expand the Configuration Variables panel by clicking the Configuration Variables text under the Toolbox. This will allow you to set the values for all stages at once and makes it easy to compare values between stages.

> **NOTE** *Configuration Variables can be particularly useful for settings in configuration files such as* `web.config` *and* `app.config`*. A single build can be used with a configuration transform file that replaces settings with Release Management tokens. These tokens can then be replaced using Configuration Variables during release.*
>
> *The Build Templates provided with Release Management already contain logic to perform this task.*

Rollback Configuration

The Control Flow category in the Toolbox contains two special containers: Rollback and Rollback Always. During normal execution of a release, the activities in these containers will not be executed. However, if there is an error in execution, the deployment sequence will terminate (parallel activities will finish their execution) and activities in a Rollback or Rollback Always container may be run. Whether or not these activities will run depends on the container, each of which has subtly different behavior.

An activity in a Rollback container will only execute if it follows an activity that may need to be rolled back. In other words, Rollback activities will only run if they are in the deployment sequence before the failed activity, or are the first rollback activity after the failed activity.

An activity in a Rollback Always container will execute if any normal activity fails during execution. In other words, failure of any step in a sequence will cause Rollback Always activities to be run.

FIGURE 20-18: Rollback Container example

Figure 20-18 shows an example process in which the first normal step fails. In this scenario, the activities in the first Rollback container will run while the activities in the second will not. The activities in the final Rollback Always container will run.

RELEASING YOUR APPLICATION

Now that you've set up your Release Template, you can release your application. From a template, you can deploy all the way through a release path until the target stage is reached.

You can view, manage, and create releases by clicking on the Releases tab and navigating to the Releases section. If there are any outstanding configuration steps, you will be shown a similar guide to the one displayed in the Release Template section. You will have to complete these tasks before creating your first release.

Manually Creating a Release

You can manually create a new release by clicking the New button in the Releases view. You will be asked to name your release and select a Release Template and then a target stage. Not every release needs to go all the way to the final stage.

When you have chosen a template and target stage, you may be prompted to provide additional information about the build to use for the release or a location for the package depending on the components you are deploying. For builds from a Team Foundation Server you can click the Latest link to choose the most recent successful build, or you can click Select to choose a specific build.

Figure 20-19 shows an example release with a target stage of QA. This means the release won't be able to progress any further than this stage. The Build definition has been selected using the Latest link.

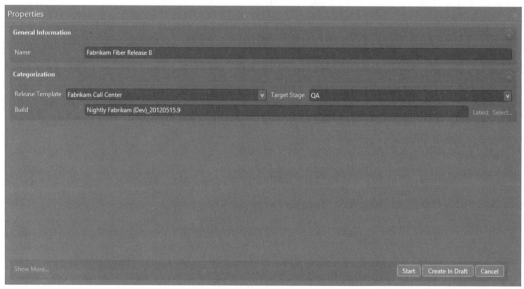

FIGURE 20-19: Creating a release

When you've supplied the required information, you can either start the release immediately by clicking Start or choose Create In Draft to save the release without starting it.

You can also click the Show More link on the bottom left of the window to show all the details of the release.

In the Releases view, you can select a release and click Open to see its details. After creating a new release, you are taken to this screen automatically. You will see the progress of the release through its stages and steps so far. You can check the Include Future Steps option in the bottom left of the screen to show steps that haven't yet been reached. Figure 20-20 shows the progress of a release that is awaiting Approval from a team member. Clicking on any ellipsis button in the Details column will show a log of the actions for that step including any errors that occurred.

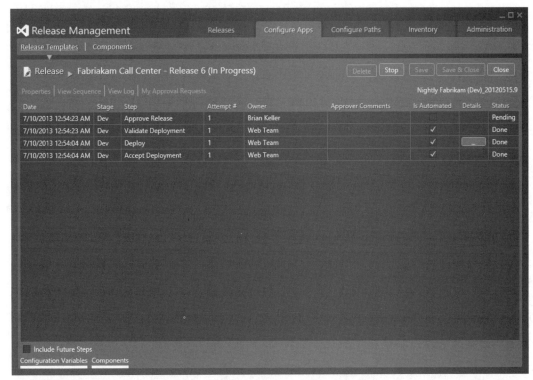

FIGURE 20-20: Viewing the progress of a release

Expanding the Configuration Variables section from the bottom left of the screen allows you to view and change the values for this release. Expanding Components shows you the details of the components being deployed.

You can change your view from the default Log view to the Sequence view by clicking View Sequence above the log entries. This view shows you the Release Template's deployment sequence for each of the stages. The Target Stage for the release is shown with a bulls-eye icon. You can change the target stage for this release by clicking on the Properties link.

If your deployment fails at any stage, you have the ability to retry the failed deployment or restart the stage using the buttons at the top of the screen. This can be useful in cases where file or server permissions have not been set up correctly and are relatively easy to fix. You can make the required changes and try the deployment again without having to run through the complete release process.

While you are using the Release Management Client, you may need to act on an Approval Request. If so, an additional My Approval Requests link will appear next to the Properties, View Sequence, and View Log links, as you can see in Figure 20-20. Clicking this link will show you a list of all pending items awaiting your action. You can approve or reject an item by selecting an entry and clicking Approve or Reject. You can also view all approval requests across multiple releases in the Releases ➪ My Approval Requests section.

Releasing from Team Build

Release Management for Visual Studio 2013 facilitates Continuous Deployment from Team Foundation Server by allowing releases to be triggered from builds.

Prerequisites

A number of conditions must be met to allow a TFS build to trigger a release:

➤ The Release Management Client needs to be installed on the machine(s) running the build agent.

➤ The Release Template must have the Can Trigger a Release from a Build option checked.

➤ All components in the template must be configured with a Team Foundation Server build. If any component has a deployment setting of Builds Independently, it cannot be triggered from a Team Foundation Build.

➤ The Acceptance and Deployment steps must be set to Automated.

➤ The build must be using an appropriate template with logic to trigger a release.

Build Templates

Release Management for Visual Studio 2013 ships with its own set of build templates. The `ReleaseDefaultTemplate.11.1.xaml` template is designed for Team Foundation Server 2012 and 2013, while the `ReleaseDefaultTemplate.xaml` template is for Team Foundation Server 2010.

> **NOTE** *The build templates can be found in the bin folder of the Release Management installation directory. By default, this is located at* `C:\ Program Files (x86)\Microsoft Visual Studio 12.0\Release Management\bin`*.*
>
> *To use a template, you will need to check it into version control in your Team Project and specify it in the Process tab of your build definition.*
>
> *For more information about using Team Foundation Build, see Chapters 18 and 19.*

These build templates contain two important pieces of functionality. They contain steps to trigger a release from a build, and they contain the logic for tokenizing your application configuration files.

To make use of the latter function, you should create a version of your configuration file with a suffix of `.token`, which contains the variable names you want to replace, starting and ending in two underscores (__) as per the parameters set up for Actions and Components. During the build, the templates will replace your `web.config` file (for example) with the `web.config.token` file, allowing Release Management to replace the tokens with Configuration Variable values.

> **NOTE** *It is possible to include the Release Management logic into your existing build template, but we recommend using the provided templates if possible. The Release Management user guide available at* `http://aka.ms/ ReleaseManagement2013` *describes the steps you need to take to add this functionality to your existing build template.*

A build using one of the provided build templates will contain additional arguments for the configurations to release, the target stage, and whether this build should trigger a release at all.

Release Explorer

Release Management for Visual Studio 2013 provides an additional web interface called Release Explorer. This is a lightweight web application designed to be used by approvers to avoid installing the full Release Management Client. Release Explorer exposes the following functions:

➤ Approving and rejecting releases

➤ Reassigning a release

➤ Viewing Components used in a release

➤ Viewing the current stage and step of a release

➤ Viewing the list of Approved and Rejected releases

To access Release Explorer from a browser, use the server name and port you configured for the Release Management web service followed by /ReleaseManagement. On a default installation, the URL will be of the form http://servername:1000/ReleaseManagement.

Figure 20-21 shows the default view with one approval pending. This view shows the current status as well as basic details for the release. Under the required approver's name or group is the number of components being released, and on the far right you can see the stage the release is up to. In Figure 20-21, the current stage of the release contains a single component pending approval at the Dev stage.

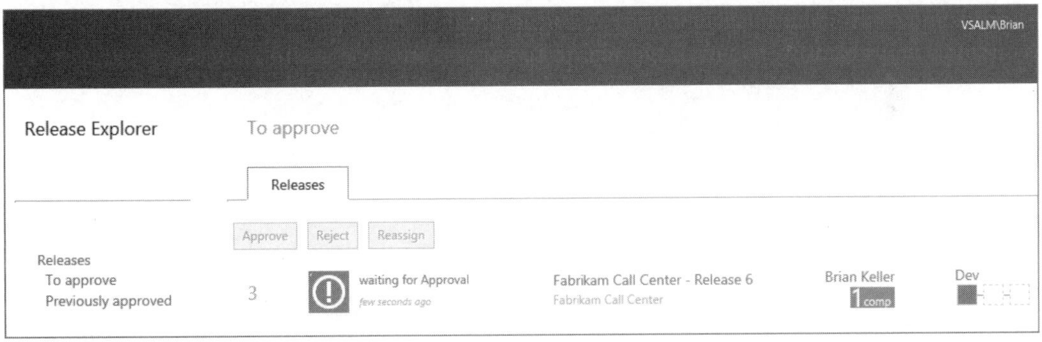

FIGURE 20-21: Release Explorer

You can click on the release to Approve, Reject, or reassign this approval to another user. You will be prompted to confirm an approval or rejection, and you can provide comments if you wish. If you reassign the approval, you will be asked which user or group you wish to assign it to.

Clicking on the shaded box showing the number of components to be deployed will open a window showing details about each component and any related builds. Clicking on the progress diagram on the far right will open a window showing the steps for the current stage as well as their current status. You can use the links in this window to view the next and previous stages in the release.

On the left of the page, you can click the Previously approved link to view historical releases and their status.

SUMMARY

In this chapter, you learned about the new Release Management for Visual Studio 2013 product available with Team Foundation Server 2013. You were introduced to the different components and their responsibilities, as well as how and where to install them. You learned about the concepts and terms used by Release Management and discovered the configuration options required to set up a build.

You learned how to create and configure a Release Template by combining Deployment Sequences, Components, and Actions. You learned how to create a release from that Release Template manually and by way of a Team Foundation Build, and how to help it progress through the approval process required for each stage.

Finally, you were introduced to the lightweight Release Explorer interface available for approvers.

In the final part of the book, you learn about the different topics for administering Team Foundation Server. In Chapter 21, you are introduced to Team Foundation Server administration, including an overview of the different parts of the server, as well as the tools and utilities that will be beneficial for administration.

PART V
Administration

21

Introduction to Team Foundation Server Administration

WHAT'S IN THIS CHAPTER?

➤ Understanding the architecture of the system

➤ Getting to know the administration console

➤ Using the command-line tools

➤ Getting to know other administration tools

Team Foundation Server is a system with lots of moving parts and lots of integration with other systems. For the person (or persons) entrusted with administering all this, it can seem like quite a daunting task at first. For someone not familiar with developer tools, there are lots of new concepts and different things to consider while administering the server.

Don't be discouraged though! As with many products, the administration tools have evolved over time. There was a huge investment in improving the administrative experience for the 2010 and 2012 releases and continued investment with the 2013 release. The biggest improvement for the 2010 release was the streamlined setup and installation experience. These investments also led to the creation of the Team Foundation Server Administration Console, along with the powerful command-line equivalent `TfsConfig.exe`.

In Team Foundation Server 2012, perhaps the biggest change for administrators is the shift of security and permissions management to the web interface, which is covered in detail in Chapter 24.

In Team Foundation Server 2013, the Administration Hub in Team Web Access has been updated to include the permissions needed to manage a Git repository. This is also covered in Chapter 24.

Before you get started with learning about Team Foundation Server administration, it's important to understand the different administrative roles in a Team Foundation Server environment.

ADMINISTRATIVE ROLES

Team Foundation Server has many different administrative roles. Each of these roles has slightly different responsibilities and deals with a different part of the overall system. In smaller organizations, all of these roles may be performed by the same person. In larger organizations with an established IT department, these roles may be performed by many different people and groups.

Infrastructure Administrator

Infrastructure administrators are responsible for anything with a power cord. They manage the physical servers, the networks, and the storage. In some cases, a separate database administrator manages the database servers. In any case, however, the two roles (should) work closely together.

An infrastructure administrator is concerned with reliability, availability, performance, disaster recovery, and security. The infrastructure administrator ensures that the servers are running smoothly and that Team Foundation Server works within the requirements of the organization.

Team Foundation Server Administrator

Team Foundation Server administrators are responsible for configuring and managing the software running on the server. They have the expertise in running software configuration management for the organization, and they often have specialized knowledge about how to operate Team Foundation Server.

This administrator is concerned with the performance of the application and the smooth operation of version control, work item tracking, data warehouse, and any other related applications. Typically, this person acts as a bridge between the development and infrastructure teams. The Team Foundation administrator handles the delicate balance and needs of both groups. Sometimes these administrators coordinate upgrades and patches to the server because it's a critical piece of infrastructure for the teams.

Project Administrator

A server will contain collections that house team projects. For each project, someone who has the ability to change the structure and permissions within that project will perform this role. In some cases, a project administrator might be a project collection administrator who has the ability to create new team projects and manage multiple team projects.

The project administrator role is an important one because it is the closest to the users of the server. People in this role manage groups and permissions for their projects. They have the ability to change the work item type definitions and modify areas and iterations for their projects.

LOGICAL ARCHITECTURE

Before discussing the administration of Team Foundation Server, it's helpful to understand the architecture of the system. As shown in Figure 21-1, Team Foundation Server contains three logical tiers:

➤ Client tier

➤ Application tier (AT)

➤ Data tier (DT)

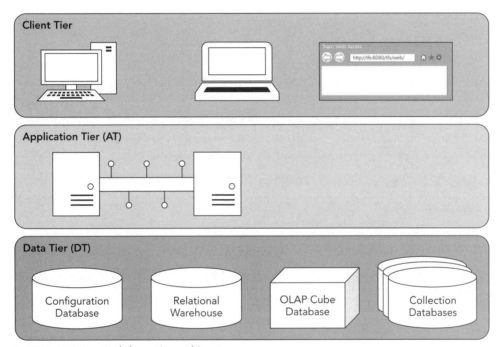

FIGURE 21-1: Logical three-tier architecture

These logical tiers might be deployed across two or more computers.

> **NOTE** *Chapter 22 contains a discussion on the physical architecture for scalability and high availability.*

Client Tier

The client tier is any computer that contains tools for accessing the server. An installed application such as Visual Studio Team Explorer or Team Explorer Everywhere can be used as a client. A web browser and the Team Foundation Server web access interface can also be used. Additionally, any application that uses the Team Foundation Server object model or web services is considered a client of the system.

Application Tier

The application tier is commonly referred to as the "AT." It includes the Team Foundation Server Web Application, which hosts a number of different web services, including the following:

➤ Version control

➤ Work item tracking

➤ Lab management

➤ Framework services

These all run on Windows Server 2008 R2, 2012, or 2012 R2 running Internet Information Services (IIS) and ASP.NET.

The Visual Studio Team Foundation Background Job Agent (or "job agent," for short) is a Windows service that executes Team Foundation Server jobs asynchronously. These jobs implement the `Run` method in `ITeamFoundationJobExtension` and are loaded as plug-ins.

The job agent runs continuously on each application tier using the same service account as the web application. You should not need to manually stop or start this service. It will restart automatically when a server is restarted.

There is no direct configuration required for the job agent. The jobs are defined and scheduled using either the client or server object models and stored in the `Tfs_Configuration` database.

The job agent has direct access to the data tier. Because of this, most of the jobs use the server object model to access the data tier directly, as opposed to using the client object model and making web requests.

Data Tier

The data tier is commonly referred to as the "DT." It includes the databases and data warehouse infrastructure. The data tier runs on SQL Server 2012 with Service Pack 1 or newer and hosts the databases for the system.

Configuration Database

The `Tfs_Configuration` database stores information central to a Team Foundation Server instance, as shown in Table 21-1.

Relational Warehouse and OLAP Cube Database

The `Tfs_Warehouse` database and `Tfs_Analysis` cube are the key stores that support the data warehouse and reporting capabilities of Team Foundation Server. These are discussed in more detail in Chapter 15.

TABLE 21-1: Contents of the Configuration Database

COMPONENT	DESCRIPTION
Team Project Collection connection strings	The SQL connection strings for the collections associated with this instance
Registry	Team Foundation Server has a registry service for storing key and value pairs. This is different from the Windows registry.
Catalog	The catalog is a hierarchical store that describes team projects and all their properties.
Job history	History about when a job was executed and the result of the job is recorded here.
Identity cache	Identities are shared across all team project collections. The identity tables in the configuration database are the master store.
Servicing	Details about the servicing and patching operations are stored in this database.

Team Project Collections

In Team Foundation Server 2008 and earlier, seven different databases made up a server. In Team Foundation Server 2010, these databases were folded together into a single collection database. Note the following key points:

➤ These databases are the main store for all data in Team Foundation Server.

➤ A collection is almost entirely self-contained within a single database.

➤ A server can have one or more collection databases attached to it.

➤ One database contains a group of coupled team projects.

➤ A collection can exist on a different physical SQL server than the configuration database.

BUILT-IN ADMINISTRATION TOOLS

Team Foundation Server has a number of built-in administration tools. This section examines both the Administration Console and the command-line equivalent.

Team Foundation Administration Console

The Team Foundation Administration Console was added in Team Foundation Server 2010. It's the centralized management tool for server administrators. The tool was originally implemented as a Microsoft Management Console (MMC) snap-in. However, there were limitations with what was possible in this implementation, as well as the version of the .NET Framework that the snap-in could use.

Perhaps the biggest limitation of the tool (and most of the built-in administration tools) is that it must be run on the application tier servers themselves. Although you can use Remote Desktop and tools such as PSExec.exe to connect to the server remotely, the tools must still execute locally on the server. After logging on to your application tier server, navigate to the Team Foundation Server Administration Console icon and the administration console will open.

License Information

When previous versions of Team Foundation Server were released, they were first made available to download as a 180-day trial. The final version wasn't available through licensing programs for a few weeks. This meant that a lot of people installed or upgraded using the time-limited version with the plan to enter their license keys before the trial expired.

However, some people got a rude shock when their trial expired and the server suddenly started refusing commands six months later. One of the reasons this occurred was that it wasn't easy to determine whether you were running a trial license, and when that license might expire.

Figure 21-2 shows how you can see your current license type and when it will expire. To see your current license information, open the Team Foundation Server Administration Console from the Start menu. Select your server name in the tree view on the left. You will then see the licensing information on the right. This screen allows you to enter a product key to upgrade to the full version. The Administration Console will also warn you that your trial is about to expire when you open it.

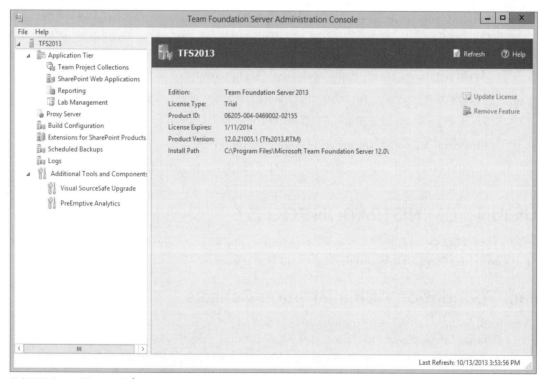

FIGURE 21-2: License information screen

This dialog box will also show you the version number and installation path of Team Foundation Server on this machine. This can be useful for verifying whether you have the latest version installed.

Managing Application Tiers

Possibly the most commonly used dialog box of the Administration Console, the Application Tier section of the console, contains all the configuration settings pertinent to the installation, as shown in Figures 21-3 and 21-4. From this section, you can perform most of the common administrative tasks. Table 21-2 describes each of the settings.

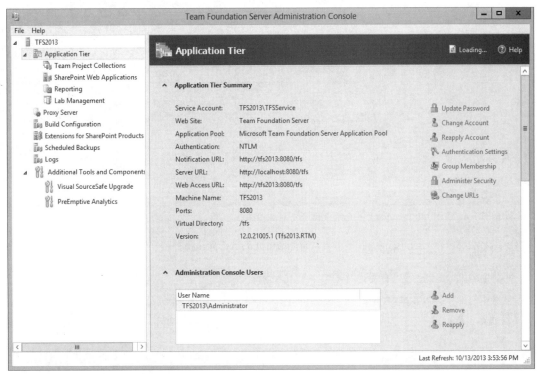

FIGURE 21-3: Application Tier screen

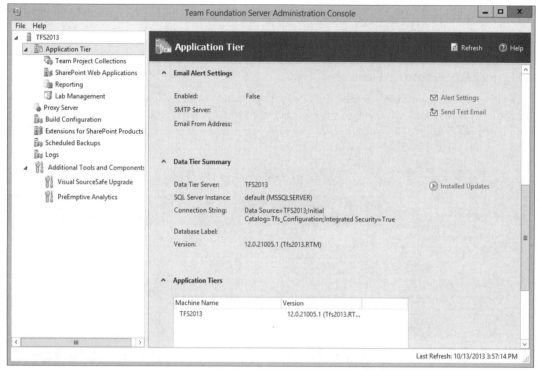

FIGURE 21-4: Continuation of the Application Tier screen

TABLE 21-2: Settings Displayed in the Application Tier Section

SETTING	DESCRIPTION
APPLICATION TIER SUMMARY	
Service Account	The user account under which the application pool and job agent are configured to run
Web Site	The name of the website as it appears in IIS Manager
Application Pool	The name of the application pool as it appears in IIS Manager
Authentication	The current authentication mode. It will be either NTLM (Windows Authentication) or Kerberos.
Notification URL	The URL that users use to connect to the system, and the URL used in the text of e-mail alerts

Server URL	The URL used for server-to-server communication. This is especially important in environments with multiple application tiers. In this case, you don't want one node making requests to another node that the first node could have handled itself. That is why the default is localhost, and it's recommended for most configurations.
Web Access URL	The URL that web access should identify itself as. This is used when the Team Explorer client generates web access links, such as in the Open with Microsoft Office Outlook feature.
Machine Name	The name of the computer that the application tier is running on. Since the Administration Console doesn't allow remote server administration, this is always going to be the same as the computer that the console is open on.
Ports	The TCP port that the application is currently accepting requests on. By default, this will be 8080. However, it may be port 443 for servers configured with secure SSL (HTTPS). Or, it may be changed to another port that is friendlier with your company's firewall policy.
Virtual Directory	This is sometimes referred to as the "vdir." The purpose of adding the virtual directory is to allow other future applications to share the same port and differentiate them by their URLs.
Version	This is a way to identify which version of Team Foundation is running on this server, as well as the current patch level that's installed. This is useful in two scenarios. First, it is an easy way to check whether you have a service pack or hotfix installed. Second, if you are thinking about moving a collection from another server, this is where you can check that the versions match.
E-MAIL ALERT SETTINGS	
Enabled	Show whether TFS will send e-mails when configured alerts are triggered. A value of true means alerts will be e-mailed; false means that they will not be e-mailed.
SMTP Server	The SMTP Server to which e-mail alerts should be directed
E-mail From Address	The address to show on the From: line of the e-mailed alert message

continues

TABLE 21-2 *(continued)*

SETTING	DESCRIPTION
ADMINISTRATION CONSOLE USERS	
User Names	The list of individuals who have been granted administrative access to the Team Foundation Server environment, including SharePoint Services, Reporting Services, and SQL Server databases. You can add and remove administrative users by selecting the Add or Remove links. The Reapply link will re-apply the permissions for those users.
DATA TIER SUMMARY	
Data Tier Server	The SQL Database Server currently running the `Tfs_Configuration` database for this Team Foundation Server environment
SQL Server Instance	SQL Server can have multiple instances running on the same server, differentiated by the instance name. This shows the instance that Team Foundation Server is configured to use.
Connection String	The connection string is the combination of the server name, instance name, and `Tfs_Configuration` database name, which allow the application to connect to the database.
Database Label	Databases from multiple Team Foundation Server environments can be hosted on a single SQL server instance. To avoid database name collisions, the databases can be given a label. For example, `Tfs_ContosoConfiguration` and `Tfs_ContosoDefaultCollection` might represent the databases associated with Contoso's environment on a shared SQL server.
Version	The server has a version of code it is running, and the `Tfs_Configuration` database has a version stamp in the extended properties. This shows what that stamp is, and it must match the application tier version.
APPLICATION TIERS	
Machine List	The list of application tier servers that have ever been associated with this Team Foundation Server environment. If a server has not been active in the last three days, it can be filtered out of the list by selecting the check box. Additionally, if you have an application (not a server plug-in) that uses the server object model, it will show up in this list.

REPORTING SERVICES SUMMARY	
Reporting Services Manager URL	The URL to the root folder of the web-based report manager
Reporting Services Server URL	The URL to the root of the Reporting Services web services
Reader Account	Team Foundation Server uses two reporting data sources, which allow reports to connect to the data warehouse as the account specified here.

Update Service Account Password

Team Foundation Server allows you to use a built-in Windows account as the service account, such as NT AUTHORITY\Network Service or NT AUTHORITY\Local Service. These special built-in accounts don't require manual password changes, and they are good choices to minimize the administrative overhead. However, for an environment with multiple application tiers, using a built-in Windows account is not supported, and you'll have to update the password on the server when it is changed.

Some corporate environments have password policies that require passwords to be changed as frequently as every month. This requirement can make changing passwords for applications a common administrative task.

Fortunately, it's simple to do in Team Foundation Server. After clicking the Update Password link in the Administration Console, you are presented with the dialog box shown in Figure 21-5, which allows you to enter the new password and test it to ensure that it's correct.

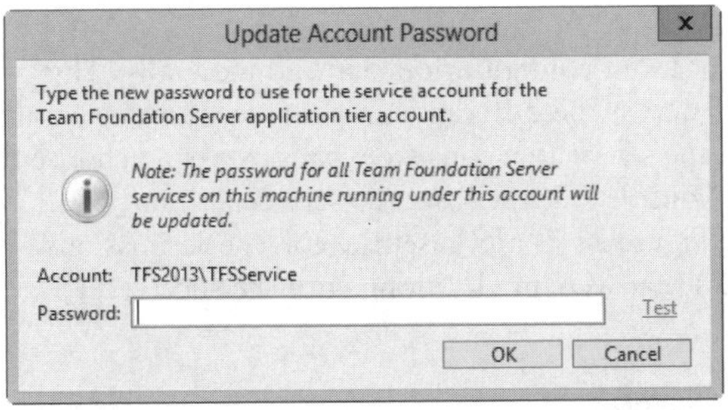

FIGURE 21-5: Update Account Password dialog box

Once you click OK, the password is verified and then the Administration Console changes the password in all the locations where it's used on the current server.

> **NOTE** *For more information, see "Change the Service Account or Password for Team Foundation Server" on MSDN at* `http://aka.ms/Tfs2013ChangePassword`*.*

Change Service Account

Changing the service account that Team Foundation Server runs as is not a common administrative task. Changing it is as simple as clicking the Change Account link in the Administration Console. In the resulting dialog box shown in Figure 21-6, you either select a built-in system account or enter the credentials for a domain account. Similar to changing passwords, it's also possible to verify the credentials before attempting to apply them by clicking the Test link.

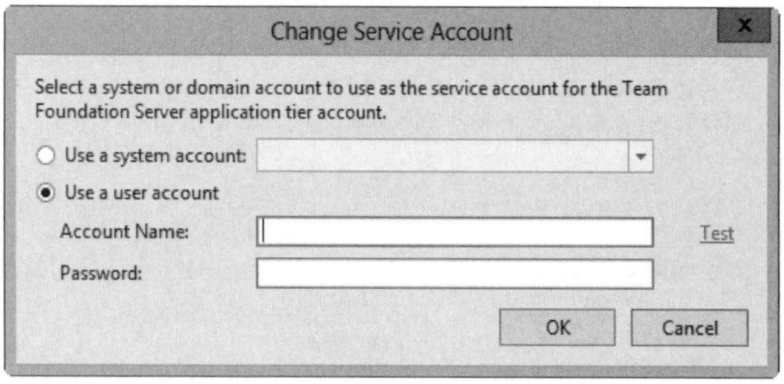

FIGURE 21-6: Change Service Account dialog box

Reapply Service Account

In some cases, a server may have had its service account configuration changed manually. This means that the service accounts might not match across the different components, and this would put the server in an inconsistent state. To return the server to a consistent state, you can choose the Reapply Account link from the Administration Console. This will set the service account of all components to the specified service account (see Figure 21-7) and reset the correct permissions. Similar to Figure 21-8, you should see all changes that were made, along with the successful completion message.

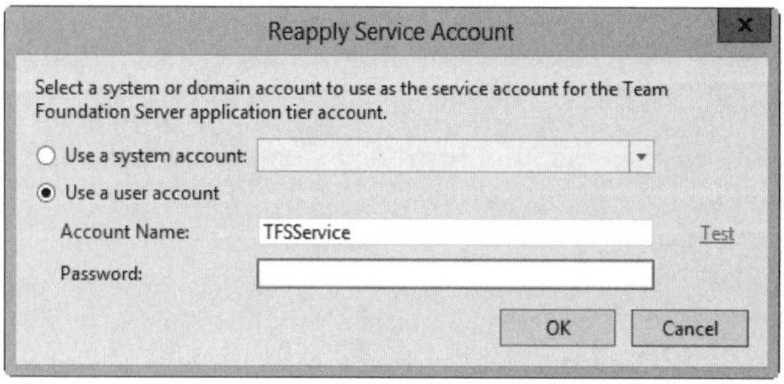

FIGURE 21-7: Reapply Service Account dialog box

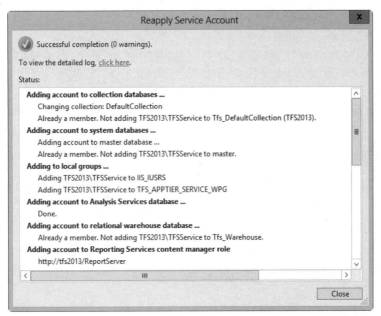

FIGURE 21-8: Reapply Service Account results dialog box

Change URLs

When Team Foundation Server makes requests to itself, it should use localhost. However, if you are using multiple application tiers, or you have a DNS alias configured for your server, then the Server URL setting may need to be changed.

After clicking the Change URLs link in the Administration Console, you see a dialog box similar to Figure 21-9 that allows you to change the two URLs used by the system.

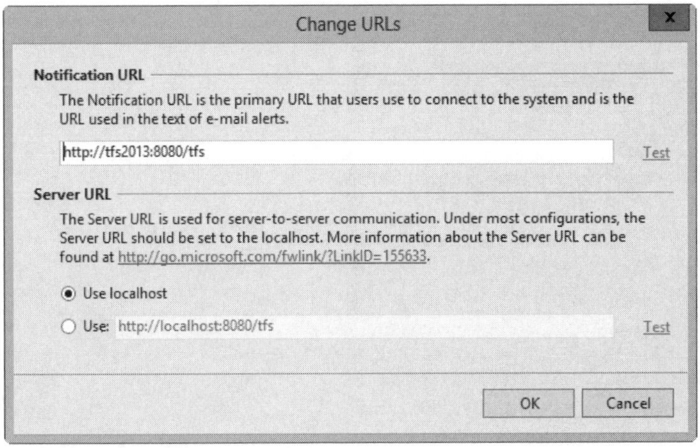

FIGURE 21-9: Change URLs dialog box

Add Team Foundation Server Administration Console User

Users who aren't Team Foundation Server administrators can be given access to open the Administration Console, as well as to create collections and change service accounts. By default, anyone who is an administrator on the server already is a Team Foundation Server administrator.

By clicking the Add link under Administration Console Users, you can give users administrative access in Team Foundation Server. Figure 21-10 shows you the advanced options available to restrict the permissions.

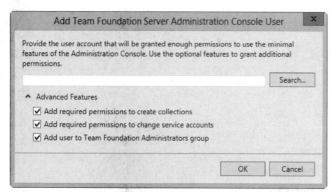

FIGURE 21-10: Add Team Foundation Server Administration Console User dialog box

Installed Updates

The main Administration Console screen will show you the currently installed version of the server. Server patches are cumulative, which means that every new patch includes all the patches released before it. There are some cases where you might want to know each individual patch that has been installed on a server and when it was installed.

By clicking the Installed Updates link in the Administration Console, you can see all the installed patches, as shown in Figure 21-11.

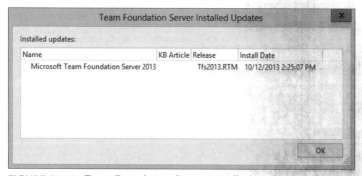

FIGURE 21-11: Team Foundation Server Installed Updates dialog box

Managing Team Project Collections

The Team Project Collections section is perhaps the second-most used section of the Administration Console. This section of the console allows you to perform all tasks that relate to collections. The tasks range from creating new collections to managing security, moving collections, and viewing collection logs.

To get to the Team Project Collections section of the tool, log on to your application tier server and open the Team Foundation Server Administration Console from the Start menu. The tree in the left pane will show Application Tier and then Team Project Collections. As shown in Figure 21-12, you will see a list of the Team Project Collections available in your environment.

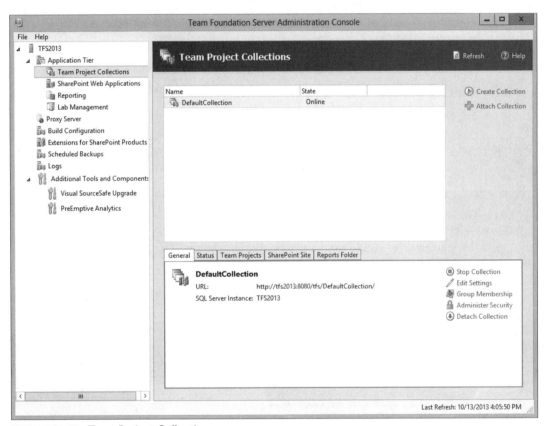

FIGURE 21-12: Team Project Collections

> **NOTE** *If you are using a Basic or Express configuration of Team Foundation Server, or your application tier is running on a client operating system (such as Windows 7 with SP1, Windows 8, or Windows 8.1), the SharePoint and Reporting tabs described in this section won't be available.*

General Tab

The General tab shows the full URL of the collection that can be used to connect from Microsoft Test Manager and Team Explorer Everywhere. Each collection can (but does not have to) reside on a different SQL Server Instance to the `Tfs_Configuration` database. The General tab shows the SQL Server Instance that the current collection is hosted on.

As shown in Figure 21-13, you can also view or edit the description of the collection from the General tab, and administer the group membership and permissions for users and groups in the collection.

FIGURE 21-13: General tab

Stop and Start a Collection

From the General tab of a collection, if a collection is currently running, you can stop it and prevent all new requests by clicking the Stop Collection link. This presents the dialog box shown in Figure 21-14, which allows you to specify a message that users will receive when they attempt to connect to the collection.

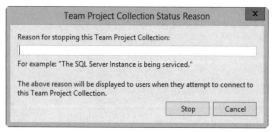

FIGURE 21-14: Team Project Collection Status Reason dialog box

This is useful if you need to perform maintenance on the underlying SQL server, or for any other reason that you need to take a single collection offline. Once the collection is stopped, you can click the Start Collection link to bring the collection back online and start accepting requests again.

Status Tab

As shown in Figure 21-15, the Status tab displays each of the jobs that have been executed for that collection. You can open the log for any of these jobs by double-clicking the entry.

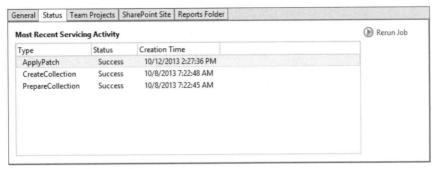

FIGURE 21-15: Status tab

In some circumstances, a job may fail. This can occur because of an interrupted patch installation, a mismatched server and collection version, or a timeout. In these cases, it is possible to attempt the job again by clicking the Rerun Job link. You can view the current progress of a running job by double-clicking the entry.

When you are performing a server upgrade, it's possible to close the upgrade wizard before all the collections have finished upgrading. Additionally, when you are performing a collection import, the import process is command-line only, and it can be difficult to gauge the progress of the import. In these cases, you can also double-click the job to view the current progress of the upgrade or import job.

Team Projects Tab

This tab displays the list of team projects in the collection, along with their descriptions. Because of the existing implementation of the Project Creation Wizard, it's not possible to add new team projects through the Administration Console. You still must use Visual Studio Team Explorer 2013 to create new team projects in a collection.

From the Team Projects tab shown in Figure 21-16, an administrator can delete a team project. Once a project is selected, the Delete link is available.

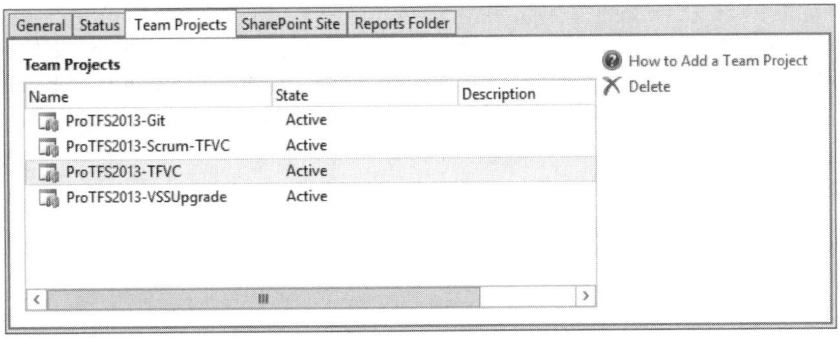

FIGURE 21-16: Team Projects tab

After clicking the Delete link, you can optionally delete lab management, reporting, and build artifacts that relate to the team project. Figure 21-17 shows the dialog box you would use to do this. Additionally, you can optionally delete the version control workspace associated with the project.

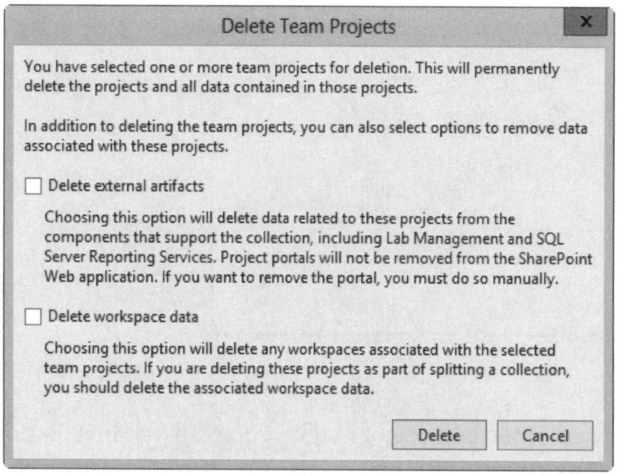

FIGURE 21-17: Delete Team Projects dialog box

DATA MAY REMAIN UNDELETED AFTER DELETING A TEAM PROJECT

Deleting a team project can leave remnants of the team project in the system. For example, the team project data will remain in the data warehouse until it is rebuilt. Work item tracking metadata shared between other team projects is not deleted. Version control shelvesets that contain code from other team projects are also not deleted.

For more information on deleting a team project, see "TFSDeleteProject: Deleting Team Projects" on MSDN at `http://aka.ms/Tfs2013DeleteProject`.

SharePoint Site Tab

Team Foundation Server allows you to configure any SharePoint site for your team project's project portal. As shown in Figure 21-18, this tab shows you the default site location that will be used to create project portals for new team projects. When you create a team project or configure a project portal for an existing team project, this is the URL that will be used by default.

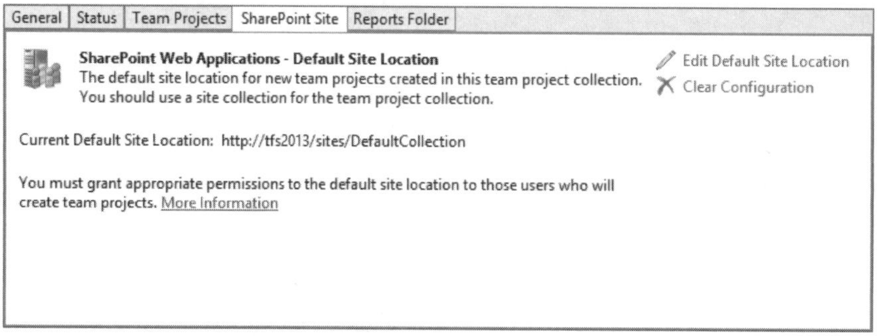

FIGURE 21-18: SharePoint Site tab

If you don't specify a default site location here, then no default will be provided for new or existing team projects when they are created or modified.

Reports Folder Tab

As shown in Figure 21-19, this tab displays the path under which report folders for team projects will be created by default. If you create or modify a team project, you can specify another folder, but this root path will be used as the default.

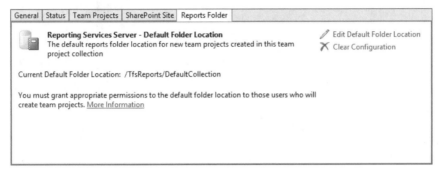

FIGURE 21-19: Reports Folder tab

Create a Team Project Collection

This is also the section where you create new team project collections. To do so, click the Create Collection link as shown on the right side of Figure 21-12. A dialog box is displayed, as shown in Figure 21-20. After you specify a name for the collection and an optional description, a series of readiness checks are run to confirm that a collection can be created on the specified server.

Once the checks pass and you proceed with the wizard, you should see green check marks, as shown in Figure 21-21. In the background, a Create Collection job was queued on the server and the collection was created by the background job agent.

> **NOTE** *For more detailed instructions on this process, see "Create a Team Project Collection" on MSDN at* `http://aka.ms/Tfs2012CreateTPC`*. Although these instructions are for Team Foundation Server 2012, the process is unchanged for 2013.*

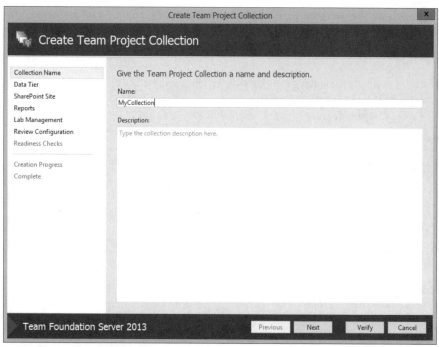

FIGURE 21-20: Create Team Project Collection name and description screen

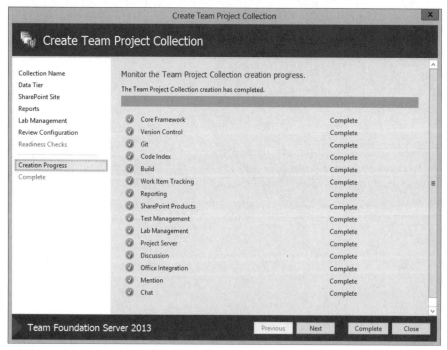

FIGURE 21-21: Successful creation of a Team Project Collection

Move a Team Project Collection

In Team Foundation Server, it's easy to move a team project collection between two servers of matching versions. To detach a collection, click the Detach Collection link shown in Figure 21-13 on the General tab. To attach a collection, click the Attach Collection" link, shown on the right side of Figure 21-12. Following are the two most common scenarios for detaching a collection:

➤ You are a consulting company that has been developing a product for a client, and you want to deliver the code and the collection to the client at the end of the project.

➤ The organizational structure has changed, or the company has been acquired, and you must move the collection to a different Team Foundation Server.

The process is quite safe and relatively straightforward.

> **NOTE** *For more detailed instructions, see "Move a Team Project Collection" on MSDN at* `http://aka.ms/TfsMoveTPC`. *Although these instructions are for Team Foundation Server 2012, the process is unchanged for 2013.*

Detach a Team Project Collection

Each collection has shared information (such as identities) stored in the instance's `Tfs_Configuration` database. Because of this, it's necessary to detach a collection before it can be attached to another server. This detach process copies the shared information into the collection database before disconnecting it from the instance. The database remains online on the SQL server, but it is not associated with the Team Foundation Server anymore.

To start the detach process, click Detach Collection from the General tab for the Team Project Collection node in the Administration Console. For the relatively short duration (typically a few minutes) while the detach operation is in progress, the collection will be offline.

The wizard allows you to optionally specify a message that will be displayed to users who connect during this period, as shown in Figure 21-22. However, once the detach operation finishes, the collection effectively doesn't exist on the server anymore, and this message won't be displayed to users. Instead, they will receive a message indicating that the collection couldn't be found.

Once you proceed with the wizard, the background job agent executes a series of jobs. After a short period, you should receive six green check marks, as shown in Figure 21-23.

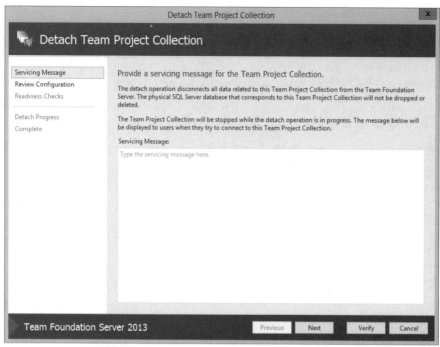

FIGURE 21-22: Detach Team Project Collection servicing message

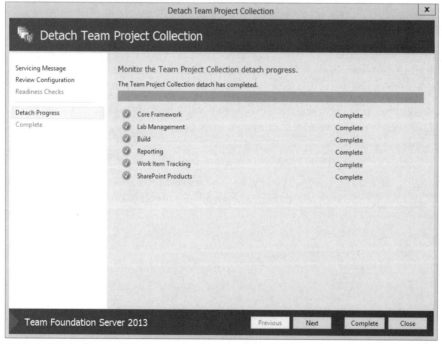

FIGURE 21-23: Successful detach of a Team Project Collection

Once the database is detached, you can use SQL Server Management Studio to back up the collection database and move it to another SQL server, or provide the backup to another person. Remember to treat this backup with care because anyone with access to the file can restore it to Team Foundation Server, and that person will have administrator access to the collection.

> **WARNING** *Detaching a collection requires additional steps beyond just clicking Detach Collection in the Administration Console. To achieve full fidelity, you must save the reports from Reporting Services, delete any Lab Management resources, and rebuild the data warehouse as part of any detach operation.*

Attach a Team Project Collection

Before attaching a previously detached collection, you must have already restored the database backup to the SQL server that you want to use. To start the process, click the Attach Collection link from the Administration Console on the Team Project Collections node, as shown in Figure 21-12, earlier in this section. When the dialog box appears, specify the SQL Server instance and verify that you have a backup of the collection database, as shown in Figure 21-24.

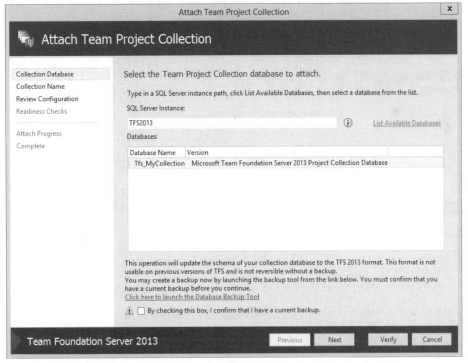

FIGURE 21-24: Specifying a SQL Server instance and database to attach

Once the collection is verified and you proceed with the wizard, a job is executed on the background job agent. This job copies the shared data out of the collection database and places it in the

`Tfs_Configuration` database, for the instance. As shown in Figure 21-25, once the job is completed, the collection is brought online and users can begin accessing it.

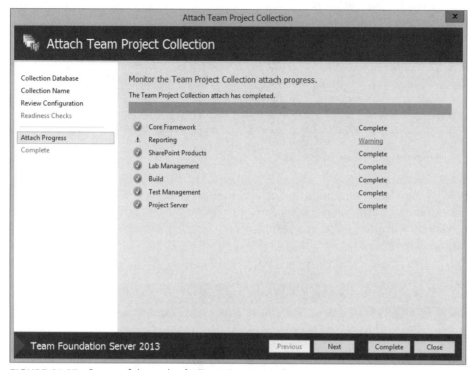

FIGURE 21-25: Successful attach of a Team Project Collection

All Team Foundation Servers and all collections have unique instance IDs. As part of the attach process, the server will check the instance ID of the collection and ensure that it doesn't conflict with an existing collection on the server. If a conflict is detected, then the new collection's instance ID is automatically changed.

Delete a Team Project Collection

To delete a team project collection, click the Detach Collection link from the Administration Console on the Team Project Collections node, as shown in Figure 21-12. Once the collection has been detached, you can then delete the underlying database from SQL Server.

If you would like to delete a team project collection without first detaching it, this is possible using the `TFSConfig.exe` command-line tool. Open a command prompt on an application tier server and run the following command:

```
TFSConfig.exe collection /delete /collectionName:YourCollection
```

The difference between deleting a collection and first detaching a collection is that a deleted collection cannot be reattached to a server.

> **NOTE** *For more details, see "Delete a Team Project Collection" on MSDN at* `http://aka.ms/Tfs2012DeleteTPC`. *Although these instructions are for Team Foundation Server 2012, the process is unchanged for 2013.*

Managing SharePoint Products

As you can see in Figure 21-26, in this section you establish the connection between your Team Foundation Server instance and your SharePoint web applications. If you already have a SharePoint server configured, or you'd like to allow project portals on an additional server, you can add that server here.

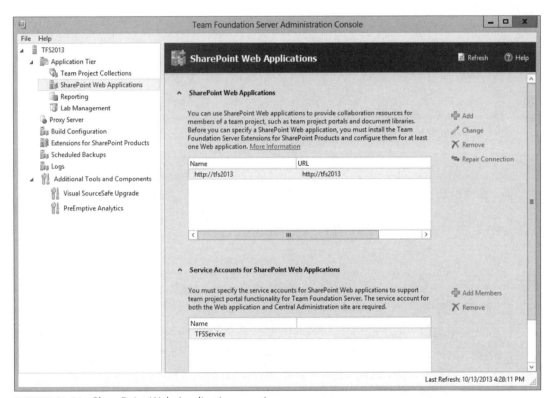

FIGURE 21-26: SharePoint Web Applications section

Managing Reporting

As you can see in Figure 21-27, all the Reporting settings are configured for your Team Foundation Server instance in this section. The main screen shows you the current settings, which you can change by clicking the Edit link.

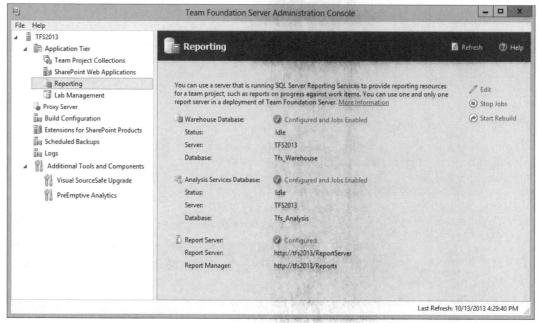

FIGURE 21-27: Reporting section

> **NOTE** *For a more detailed look at the administration aspects of reporting, see Chapter 15.*

> **NOTE** *For details on the other options available in the Administration Console, see the following chapters and sections in this book:*
>
> ➤ "Configuring the Team Foundation Build Service" in Chapter 18.
>
> ➤ "Installing and Configuring Lab Management" in Chapter 26.
>
> ➤ "Team Foundation Server Proxy" in Chapter 28.

Command-Line Configuration Tools

Quite a few command-line configuration tools are available in Team Foundation Server. In Team Foundation Server 2010, a number of disparate administration tools were consolidated into two. For example, the WITImport.exe, WITExport.exe, and WITFields.exe tools are now commands available in the consolidated WITAdmin.exe tool.

Many of the administration tools are examined in other chapters of this book, and you should refer to the following chapters for more details.

➤ **Chapter 13**—WITAdmin.exe

➤ **Chapter 24**—TFSSecurity.exe and TF.exe Permission

➤ **Chapter 28**—TF.exe Proxy

TFSConfig.exe

The TFSConfig.exe tool allows an administrator to perform most server configuration tasks from the command line. When paired with a remote execution tool such as PSExec.exe (which is available at http://aka.ms/PsExec), TFSConfig.exe can help you achieve remote server administration.

Table 21-3 provides an overview of each of the commands available with TFSConfig.exe and what they can be used for.

TABLE 21-3: Commands Available with TFSConfig.exe

COMMAND	DESCRIPTION
Accounts	Allows you to update passwords, change service accounts, add new service accounts, remove service accounts, and reset database ownership
Authentication	Allows you to view or change the current authentication settings (NTLM or Kerberos) for the server
Certificates	Configures how client authentication certificates are used when Team Foundation Server connects to itself using a secure (HTTPS) connection
ChangeServerID	Initializes the Team Foundation Server instance and all of its collections with a new instance ID. This command is required when you restore a copy of your server while the original copy remains online. If you don't change the instance ID of the new server, clients will be confused and will communicate with the original server instead of the new server.
CodeIndex	Manages the Code Indexing Services that support the CodeLens tooling in Visual Studio
Collection	Attaches, detaches, or deletes a team project collection from the server
ConfigureMail	Changes the e-mail From address and the SMTP host used by the server to send notifications
Diagnose	Diagnoses software update problems that might prevent Team Foundation Server from working correctly. This command inspects the system to find any service level (patch) mismatches between the application tier and the collection databases.

continues

TABLE 21-3 *(continued)*

COMMAND	DESCRIPTION
Identities	Lists the status or changes the security identifiers (SIDs) of identities stored by the server. This command is used when you move a server from one domain to another where the user names match, but the SIDs are different.
Import	Imports databases from either a 2005 or 2008 data tier as a new project collection. This command is used when you want to consolidate multiple instances onto a single instance, and don't want to perform an in-place upgrade first.
Jobs	Allows you to retrieve the logs or retry a job on a single, or all, collection(s)
Lab	Configures Lab Management and manages host group and library share assignments for a collection
License	Used to display or modify Team Foundation Server licensing information. Using this command, you can extend your trial period by an additional 30 days.
PrepareClone	Prepares an existing configuration database after cloning. This will reset the SharePoint and Reporting Services URLs to the local machine and create the required SQL roles in the master database.
Proxy	This command can be used to update the Team Foundation Server proxy configuration. For example, you can change the list of servers that the proxy is able to proxy for. The proxy server must be initially configured in either the Team Foundation Server Administration Console or by using the TfsConfig.exe Unattend command.
RebuildWarehouse	Rebuilds the Analysis Services database and the relational database of the warehouse. Unlike the Start Rebuild link in the Administration Console, you can specify the /analysisServices parameter, which will rebuild only the Analysis Services database without rebuilding the relational database.
RegisterDB	Changes the database the application tier uses. This command is usually used when you restore a set of databases and want to connect them to a new application tier.
RemapDBs	Enumerates the databases in the specified SQL instances, and validates that the connection strings match the locations of the found databases

Repair	Re-creates all stored procedures, functions, indexes, constraints, and tables in the configuration and collection databases. It doesn't repair any of the data, only the structure of the databases.
	This command was deprecated in Team Foundation Server 2012 and should not be used.
RepairCollection	As above for `Repair`, however, it operates only on a single collection.
Settings	Manages the notification and server URL settings for the server
Setup	Used for unconfiguring a Team Foundation Server. After running this command, you can open the Administration Console and run the server configuration wizard again.
Unattend	Used for configuring Team Foundation Server using an unattended configuration file. For example, you can use `TfsConfig.exe Unattend /configure /type.basic` to configure a server with the essential development services (Source Control, Work Item Tracking, and Test Case Management).
Updates	Reapplies software updates required to synchronize the service level of the databases for Team Foundation Server to the level of the application tier

> **NOTE** *For more details on this command-line tool, see "Managing Server Configuration with TFSConfig" on MSDN at* `http://aka.ms/TfsConfig2013`.

TFSServiceControl.exe

The `TFSServiceControl.exe` tool is used to stop or start all of the services and application pools that Team Foundation Server uses on a server. If you have multiple application tier servers, you will need to run this command on each server to completely start or stop the environment.

The `quiesce` option will gracefully stop all related services on the server, and the `unquiesce` option will start them. For example, you might want to gracefully stop services when you need to perform maintenance on a server.

OPERATIONAL INTELLIGENCE HUB

Starting in Team Foundation Server 2012, Microsoft provided a "hidden" web-based administration interface that provides insight into the activity within the environment as well as the activities of the Background Job Agent called Operational Intelligence. To access the Operational Intelligence hub, browse to `http://yourServer:8080/tfs/_oi` on your server where you will find the page shown in Figure 21-28. Notice that there are two tabs on this page named Activity Log and Job Monitoring.

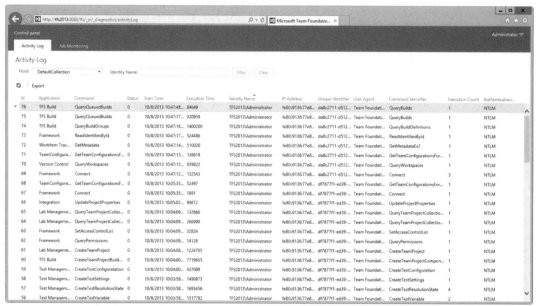

FIGURE 21-28: Activity Log tab in the Operational Intelligence Hub

Activity Log

The Activity Log shows data from the `tbl_Command` table in the `Tfs_Configuration` database and the `tbl_Parameter` table in each Team Project Collection database. These tables keep track of all of the commands from every user that have been executed against the server in the last 14 days.

Table 21-4 provides an overview of each column in the Activity Log and how each is interpreted.

TABLE 21-4: Activity Log Columns

COLUMN	DESCRIPTION
Id	The unique ID of this command execution
Application	The Team Foundation Server component against which this command was executed. Some common applications are TFS Build, Framework, Lab Management, Test Management, and Work Item Tracking.
Command	The name of the command given by the server. These command names are not documented anywhere but they are names similar to their corresponding API calls.

Status	Shows 0 on success, −1 on failure
Start Time	The Date/Time when the command was received by the server
Execution Time	The amount of time it took for the command to run. Expressed in microseconds (1 one-millionth of a second)
Identity Name	The user name of the person or service executing the command
IP Address	The IPv4 or IPv6 address of the machine where the command originated
Unique Identifier	A GUID that is used to correlate multiple server-side requests that are generated by a single client-side request
User Agent	The User-Agent HTTP request header field value from the client. This value gives you the name of the executable making the call if it used the API as well as the version/SKU of the caller.
Command Identifier	The command the user called. If using the tf command-line tool, then this is the sub-command given, i.e., tf get or tf diff.
Execution Count	The number of times this command was executed. If multiple calls are made to the same command, they will not be listed separately, but rather the Execution Count will be incremented for each. In Figure 21-28 you can see that the Connect command at Id 69 was executed three times.
Authentication Type	The authentication method used on this request. Values are NTLM or Kerberos.

You can view additional details for each Activity Log entry by double-clicking on the entry. This opens the Activity Log Entry dialog box shown in Figure 21-29.

Job Monitoring

The Job Monitoring tab shows information about the background jobs that Background Job Agent runs regularly. As shown in Figure 21-30, there are three sub-tabs, which show Job Summary information, the current Job Queue, and Job History.

Job Summary

The Job Summary tab shows three charts that allow you to see the job activity in your system: Total Run Time for Each Job, Result Counts, and Number of Jobs Run.

The Total Run Time for Each Job chart shows the total amount of time that a particular background job took over the time period shown on the bar chart. You can hover your cursor over a bar to see the number of job runs whose time was calculated into the total run time. You can click on a bar to bring up the Job History tab with specific data about that background job.

FIGURE 21-29: Activity Log Entry dialog box

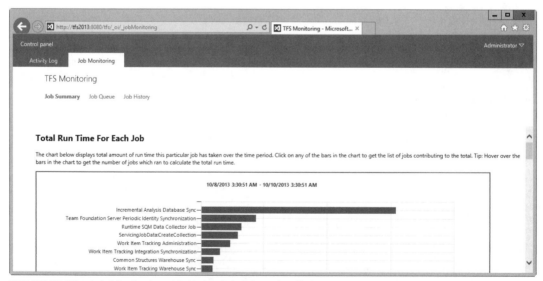

FIGURE 21-30: Job Monitoring tab in the Administration Hub

The Result Counts chart shows a pie chart of the count of the different result types encountered by the background jobs over the period shown in the chart. Some of the result types shown are Succeeded, Failed, and Blocked. Clicking on a result type section of the chart will bring you to the Job History tab filtered to show the jobs with the selected result type.

The Number of Jobs Run chart is a stacked bar chart that shows the number of times a job has run segmented by the result type for that particular job. If the Synchronize Test Cases job ran ten times, of which six were successful and four failed, then the bar for that job would be ten units long—and six units would be green and four red. Hovering over a bar will show a breakdown of the result types for that job. Clicking on any bar will bring you to the Job History tab filtered by the selected job.

Job Queue

The Job Queue tab provides information about the current state of the job queue. The Job Queue Types chart breaks down the queue by queue type to show jobs that are in progress, queued, scheduled, or waiting to run on an offline or dormant application tier server. Clicking on any bar in the chart will populate the Job Queue Details list with the job queue entries for the selected queue type.

Job History

The Job History tab provides information about past performance of background jobs. The Average Run and Queue Time With Total Number of Jobs chart displays the number of jobs run at each hour overlaid with the average time the jobs waited in the queue and the average run time of those jobs. The Job History list shows the detailed job history results over the period shown in the chart. This list excludes successful jobs to make it easier to navigate.

OTHER ADMINISTRATION TOOLS

As with most products, there are gaps in functionality. As with most products, Team Foundation Server 2013 has gaps in functionality. There are many Microsoft-sponsored and non-Microsoft-sponsored utilities available. This section examines the ones released outside Microsoft's normal release cycle, as well as a useful tool developed by another company.

Team Foundation Server Power Tools

Power Tools are extra features developed by Microsoft outside of the normal release cycle. They are always "additive," which means that they are extensions of the shipping product and don't change any core functionality. Typically, they are used to temporarily address customer pain points and adoption blockers. In an ideal world, all the Power Tool features would eventually make it in to the normal product, but that can take some time.

The Power Tools include some useful utilities for administrators, such as the Process Editor (for managing work item types and fields), the Test Attachment Cleaner (`tcmpt.exe`), and the Best Practices Analyzer.

> **NOTE** *The latest version of the Team Foundation Server Power Tools can be downloaded from* `http://aka.ms/TFS2013PowerTools.`

Best Practices Analyzer

Perhaps the most useful Power Tool for administrators is the Best Practices Analyzer (BPA). The BPA is the same tool used by the Microsoft Support team when customers call with a server problem.

The health check scan types have hundreds of rules and alerts built in. These check all the different configuration settings in an environment against expected settings, and generate warnings or errors when something doesn't look correct.

In addition to one other scan that collects statistics of your server, the following are different variations of the health check scan:

- ➤ Team Foundation Server Complete Health Check
- ➤ Team Foundation Server Framework Health Check
- ➤ Team Foundation Server Warehouse Health Check
- ➤ Team Foundation Build Health Check
- ➤ Visual Studio Lab Management Health Check
- ➤ SharePoint Products Health Check
- ➤ Project Server Configuration Health Check
- ➤ Project Server Synchronization Engine Health Check
- ➤ Visual Studio Client Health Check

Team Foundation Server Complete Health Check is the most comprehensive scan, and will take the longest to run. As you can see in Figure 21-31, it enumerates all the servers in an environment (including build agents and lab management components), and it performs the health check scan on them. If you have an environment with more than a few build servers, then this scan type is probably not very useful because it will take a long time to run and scan all your servers.

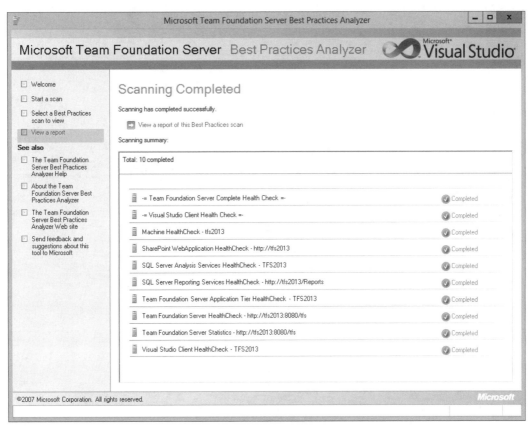

FIGURE 21-31: Microsoft Team Foundation Server Best Practices Analyzer

> **WARNING** *If you have build agents in remote locations that have slow network links, the health check may take a much longer time to complete.*

Additionally, if you are having a problem with a particular component (such as the Warehouse or SharePoint Products), you can just run the health check for those components.

Once the scan completes, you can select each issue and click the "Tell me more about this issue and how to resolve it" link shown toward the bottom of Figure 21-32. This will display the documentation for that particular check and describe the steps to resolve the issue. This is an often overlooked and very valuable resource for diagnosing and troubleshooting Team Foundation Server configuration issues.

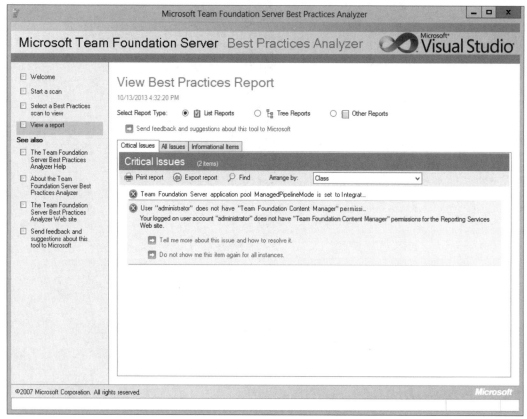

FIGURE 21-32: View Best Practices Report

It's not very well known, but you can actually run the BPA tool from the command line using the TfsBpaCmd.exe tool. With this functionality, you might consider running it once a week as a scheduled task to proactively detect any server configuration issues.

> **NOTE** *Chapter 25 covers the usage of the BPA tool in more detail.*

Team Foundation Server Administration Tool

Team Foundation Server includes integration with SharePoint Products and SQL Reporting Services. However, this integration isn't as great as it could be for project or server administrators. Permissions between Team Foundation Server and these other systems aren't integrated. This means that you have to manage the permissions and group memberships separately through each system's own administration interface.

> **NOTE** *Fortunately, this permission integration issue was identified as an early gap for administrators, and the Team Foundation Server Administration Tool was created. This tool will be discussed further in Chapter 24.*

Team Foundation Sidekicks

As a Team Foundation Server administrator, you may be required to venture beyond SQL servers, application tiers, collections, and team projects. If you must delete old workspaces or unlock files from users who are on vacation, you can use the `tf.exe` command-line tools to do so. For those who are not intimately familiar with the client tools, this can be a little tricky, and you would be much more comfortable in a graphical user interface (GUI).

The Attrice Corporation has created a free suite of tools called the Team Foundation Sidekicks. The tools allow server administrators and advanced users to use a GUI to perform many administrative and advanced version control tasks. Figure 21-33 shows an example of the Workspace sidekick.

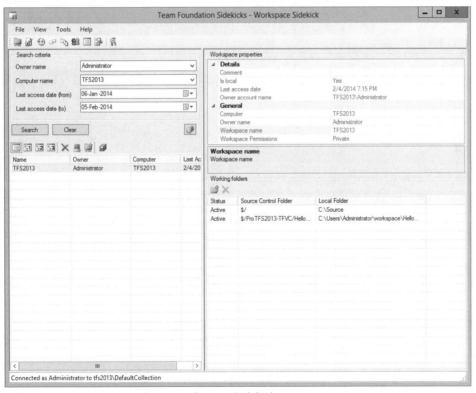

FIGURE 21-33: Team Foundation Workspace Sidekick

The standalone edition of the tool suite provides a GUI for managing different parts of Team Foundation Server. Table 21-5 provides a brief description of each sidekick.

TABLE 21-5: Team Foundation Sidekicks Available in the Standalone Version

SIDEKICK	DESCRIPTION
Workspace Sidekick	View, search, delete, and modify workspaces.
Status Sidekick	View pending changes, and unlock locked files and folders.
History Sidekick	View, search, and compare the history of files and folders, along with their associated branches and merges.
Label Sidekick	View, search, and compare labels, along with any linked changesets and work items.
Shelveset Sidekick	View, delete, compare, and download the contents of a shelveset, along with any linked work items and check-in notes.
Permission Sidekick	View a user's effective global, project-specific, and file permissions.
Users View Sidekick	Display and search all valid users in the system.

These sidekicks are a useful addition to any Team Foundation Server administrator's toolkit and will save plenty of time. To download the Team Foundation Sidekicks, please see the Attrice website at `http://www.attrice.info/cm/tfs/`.

SUMMARY

Along with a brief look at the server architecture, this chapter was all about tools for administrators. The chapter provided a walkthrough of all the different screens and functionality of the Team Foundation Server Administration Console and the new Administration Hub in Team Web Access.

This chapter also provided a brief look at the command-line administration tool `TFSConfig.exe`, and all its different commands. You learned that from this tool, you can change almost any setting in the server.

You also learned about some additional tools that aren't included in the product but are very useful to a server administrator. You learned that the Best Practices Analyzer is great for identifying server misconfigurations. Finally, you learned that the Team Foundation sidekicks allow you to manage workspaces and shelvesets on behalf of other users as well as other administrative and version control focused tasks.

Chapter 22 covers two important topics for server administrators: scalability and high availability. Along with a look at the physical architecture of the system, Chapter 22 includes guidance from and several lessons learned by the Team Foundation Server administrators supporting the Microsoft Developer Division.

22

Scalability and High Availability

WHAT'S IN THIS CHAPTER?

➤ Understanding architectural changes

➤ Understanding scale limitations

➤ Exploring availability solutions

➤ Exploring load balancing

➤ Getting to know configuration best practices

Scalability and high availability are very involved topics, and an entire book could be written on each of them. Every Team Foundation Server environment is unique, and every organization has a different usage pattern and availability requirements.

It's not the purpose or intent of this chapter to provide prescriptive guidance on exact configurations to support your environment or usage pattern. Rather, this chapter is intended to give you insight into the different factors that affect scalability and to offer some solutions to consider in your overall environment design.

> **NOTE** *If you need advice specifically tailored to your organization's needs, your best option is to contact Microsoft Support, Microsoft Services, or a Microsoft Certified Partner in your area. These organizations have deep knowledge, extensive resources, and ample hands-on experience to best meet your individual needs.*

AN EVOLVING ARCHITECTURE

Team Foundation Server 2010 introduced significant architecture and infrastructure changes. On the product team, these product changes were referred to as *Enterprise TFS Management* (ETM). It was a significant and necessary investment of effort to allow the product to handle the future scale demands of enterprises and the Internet.

The full value of these investments is beginning to be realized. With the release of Team Foundation Server 2013 also comes the production release of Visual Studio Online, a cloud-based version of Team Foundation Server. Although the service is running on the Windows Azure Platform, it is built from the same codebase as the on-premises product.

The introduction of team project collections was perhaps the largest architectural change. This innovation took the seven databases that used to make up a server and "folded" them into a single database that represents a collection. This database becomes the unit of isolation, and a collection can be detached and moved between different servers. Collections enable the following:

➤ The consolidation of multiple pre-2010 Team Foundation Server instances onto a single shared instance

➤ The scale-out of a single instance to multiple physical servers

Team Foundation Server 2008 and previous releases included many built-in assumptions about your deployment. For example, you could have only a single application tier. This application tier couldn't be installed on a 64-bit operating system. Analysis Services had to be installed on the same server as SQL Server (although you could move it later if you wanted to). These restrictions made the initial installation and any future configuration changes to the server quite fragile and error-prone.

One of the core deliverables of ETM was to enable configuration flexibility and remove these limitations. Team Foundation Server supports the following features critical to scalability and availability:

➤ Configuration flexibility

➤ Multiple application tiers with load balancing

➤ 64-bit application-tier installation

➤ Stateless application tier and web access

On top of all these infrastructure improvements, there was also a huge investment in the setup, configuration, and administration experiences. All this investment made Team Foundation Server 2010 an exceptionally scalable and robust release.

Because Team Foundation Server 2013 shares the same codebase as the Visual Studio Online, many of the core scalability improvements in the cloud version also flow through to the on-premises version.

An example of these improvements is the memory usage per collection in the environment. For an on-premises server, it would be rare to see more than 100 collections on a single deployment. In the cloud, the target is many thousands of collections. For the server to support this number of collections, a lot of optimization and testing was done around the collection management internals. These changes mean that each collection consumes the least amount of server memory. There are also optimizations such as placing a collection in a dormant state and pausing certain jobs if the collection has not been accessed.

Another significant change that first appeared in Team Foundation Server 2012 is the generalization of the version control content store. Before the 2012 release, Work Item Tracking and Test attachments were stored in their own tables. For the cloud-based service, it is more cost effective to store content in Windows Azure blob storage than inline in Windows Azure SQL Databases. This change also allows the Team Foundation Proxy server to cache additional artifact types.

Much of this chapter is relevant to only the largest Team Foundation Server environments. However, because Team Foundation Server is built on the Microsoft platform, you might find these suggestions also useful for scaling your own applications built on the Microsoft platform.

LIMITING FACTORS

Implementing a system that scales is all about finding the largest bottleneck, removing it, and then finding the next one. A system with as many moving parts as Team Foundation Server has many opportunities for bottlenecks. Even when you manage to remove the largest bottlenecks, you still have some inherent limitations in the architecture to consider.

Microsoft Recommendations

The officially tested and recommended system configurations for deploying Team Foundation Server 2013 are detailed in the Installation Guide at `http://aka.ms/tfsInstallGuide`.

As you can see in Table 22-1 (which information is gathered from the official Installation Guide), the hardware requirements for a small team are quite modest. It's perfectly reasonable to run a server that supports 250 users on a single core machine that has a reasonable hard disk. You should, however, consider these recommendations with respect to your own individual circumstances. In general, the larger your team is, the greater your need will be for a robust hardware configuration.

TABLE 22-1: Recommended Hardware Configurations

NUMBER OF USERS	CONFIGURATION	CPU	MEMORY	HARD DISK
Fewer than 250 users	Single-server (Team Foundation Server and the Database Engine on the same server)	1 single core processor at 2.13 GHz	2GB	1 disk at 7.2 K rpm (125GB)
250 to 500 users	Single-server	1 dual core processor at 2.13 GHz	4GB	1 disk at 10K rpm (300GB)

continues

TABLE 22-1 *(continued)*

NUMBER OF USERS	CONFIGURATION	CPU	MEMORY	HARD DISK
500 to 2,200 users	Dual-server (Team Foundation Server and the Database Engine on different servers)			
	Application tier	1 dual core Intel Xeon processor at 2.13 GHz	4GB	1 disk at 7.2K rpm (500GB)
	Data tier	1 quad core Intel Xeon processor at 2.33 GHz	8GB	SAS disk array at 10K rpm (2TB)
2,200 to 3,600 users	Dual-server			
	Application tier	1 quad core Intel Xeon processor at 2.13 GHz	8GB	1 disk at 7.2K rpm (500GB)
	Data tier	2 quad core Intel Xeon processors at 2.33 GHz	16GB	SAS disk array at 10K rpm (3TB)

As discussed later in this chapter, the number of team project collections and team projects in an environment will also affect the performance of the system. These hardware recommendations don't give an indication of how many collections they can support, only the number of users.

One important distinction for the number of collections is the number of active collections compared to the number of dormant collections. An *active collection* is one that has been accessed in the past five minutes. When a collection is automatically marked as *dormant* in the system, it will be unloaded from memory until another request for that collection is received. Table 22-2 describes the maximum number of active collections per SQL server based upon total available memory.

TABLE 22-2: Recommended Maximum Active Collections per SQL Server

RAM AVAILABLE TO SQL SERVER	ACTIVE COLLECTIONS
2GB	1 to 5
4GB	5 to 10
8GB	30 to 75

16GB	40 to 90
32GB	50 to 125
64GB	75 to 195

For a recommendation of the number of collections per SQL server, you should refer to the "Visual Studio Team Foundation Server Planning Guide" at `http://vsarplanningguide.codeplex.com/`. More specifically, you should refer to the "Capacity Planning" workbook, which is available to download from this site.

This planning workbook lets you enter the maximum expected users and the current number of users for your environment. Using the official hardware recommendations from Table 22-2, the workbook will tell you the recommended configuration for your expected number of users and a maximum number of active collections it can support.

Data Tier

The vast majority of work in Team Foundation Server happens on the data tier. Therefore, it makes sense that the most common bottlenecks are found on the data tier. Team Foundation Server performance is directly proportional to the performance of your SQL server. For a large environment, you must pay the same level of attention that you pay to other critical database applications in your organization, such as your Human Resources, Finance, or Sales databases.

Beware of several opportunities for bottlenecks in the data tier:

➤ Storage performance

➤ SQL query plan cache

➤ SQL buffer cache

Storage Performance

The single biggest factor that contributes to server performance is the storage performance. If your storage isn't matched to the demands of the system, then the performance of everything will suffer. Team Foundation Server makes heavy use of SQL Server's `TempDB` database for large version control commands, which makes that a common source of bottlenecks.

SQL Query Plan Cache

SQL stored procedures have query plans. These plans are precompiled and the server uses them to work out the most efficient way to execute a particular stored procedure. Some commands (such as `Merge`) in Team Foundation Server contain some very complex logic. This makes the query plans quite detailed, and their size adds up. Because each project collection is a separate database, a separate plan is cached in SQL for each stored procedure.

The scalability limitation here is that the plan cache is shared among all databases on the same SQL instance. In SQL Server 2008, the plan cache is sized according to this formula:

➤   75 percent of visible target memory from 0 to 4GB

➤   plus 10 percent of visible target memory from 4GB to 64GB

➤   plus 5 percent of visible target memory greater than 64GB

This means that as you add more collections to a SQL server, there will be more contention for resources in the plan cache. When a stored procedure's plan isn't in the cache, it must be recalculated and recompiled. Although this is not a significant overhead, it's not optimal to be recompiling plan caches all the time.

In Team Foundation Server 2010, most work item tracking queries generated ad hoc SQL and required a new query plan with every execution. In the 2012 release, some optimizations were made to improve caching of work item tracking query plans.

> **NOTE** *For more information on how the SQL plan cache works, see the "Plan Caching in SQL Server 2008" whitepaper from Greg Low at* `http://aka.ms/ SQLPlanCache`.

SQL Buffer Cache

The SQL buffer cache is where recently accessed database pages are kept in memory. Having pages in memory is a good thing because this results in the best performance.

Work item tracking uses a series of tables to store work items with a set of views over those tables. When you run a query from Team Explorer, that query is translated into a SQL query and executed in the database. Because work item tracking is completely customizable and has a dynamic schema, it performs best when all the tables are in the buffer cache.

The buffer cache is shared across all databases on a SQL server. So, if your work item tracking tables are competing in the buffer cache with other tables, then they may get pushed out. When they get pushed out, work item query performance will suffer.

This can be observed as you add more project collections to a server or your collections get bigger. If you look at the SQL Server "Memory Manager\Buffer Cache Hit Ratio" performance counter, it will drop and performance may start to suffer. In particular, when using SQL Express Edition, work item queries that use the `contains` clause will suffer the most noticeable effects because they require a table scan and cannot make use of the SQL Full-Text indexing service. If the pages aren't in the buffer cache, then SQL must fetch them from the disk.

To summarize, the size of the SQL buffer cache (which is calculated based upon total server memory) will limit the size of the project collections that SQL server can support while maintaining reasonable performance.

> **NOTE** *More information on SQL Server Memory Architecture can be found at* `http://aka.ms/SQLMemoryArch`.

Application Tier

You're more likely to encounter bottlenecks in the data tier than the application tier. However, the two main scale limitations that affect the application tier are:

➤ Memory

➤ ASP.NET worker threads configuration

Memory

Access control checks for version control are performed on the application tier. At a high level, this is the way it works:

1. The client makes a `Get` request to the application tier.

2. The application tier runs the `prc_Get` stored procedure on the data tier.

3. The data tier executes the request and returns all the relevant files, regardless of the permissions of the requesting user.

4. The application tier then retrieves the permissions associated with the paths returned. If the permissions are in the cache, then the cached permissions are used. If the permissions are not in the cache, then they are requested from the data tier.

5. The application tier then evaluates the permissions of the requesting user against the path permissions. Any file that the user does not have access to is removed from the response.

6. The application then sends the trimmed response to the client.

What's important here is that each application-tier server keeps a cache of all version control path permissions that it has evaluated. The cache is not persisted and is reset every time the application pool restarts. Cached permissions are also invalidated when the permissions change.

Version control uses Access Control Entries (ACEs) on paths to define which users and groups have access to which files and folders. By default, these permissions are inherited to subdirectories.

However, you can set explicit permissions on subdirectories. Each of these explicit permissions results in an additional ACE that the server must store, evaluate, and cache.

To summarize, if you have many paths, or many paths with explicitly set permissions, then you may run into issues where the cache isn't large enough to be effective. In this scenario, the application tier will be constantly retrieving permissions from the data tier, and this may affect version control performance.

ASP.NET Worker Threads Configuration

ASP.NET 2.0 introduced the `processModel/autoConfig` configuration element, which defines how many worker threads should be running to serve requests. The default configuration setting may not work for everyone because it limits the number of concurrently executing requests per CPU to 12.

This works well for websites with low latency. But in an application like Team Foundation Server, which has longer running requests and higher latency, it may become a bottleneck. If ASP.NET has reached these limits, then users may receive intermittent timeout or "Server does not exist" error messages.

Web Access

Similar to the 2010 release, web access is integrated into the product. However, the 2012 release fully integrated web access with the other web services and it runs in the same application pool. It is not possible to install web access by itself, or separate it from the other web services.

Warehouse

As discussed at the beginning of this chapter, Team Foundation Server 2010 introduced some major architectural changes to support server consolidation and scale-out. One of the commonly requested features from large organizations was the capability to do cross-server (and, therefore, in 2010, cross-collection) reporting. Users wanted the capability to roll up metrics into a company-wide view.

This requirement drove the architectural decision to have a single, shared relational data warehouse and Analysis Services Online Analytical Processing (OLAP) cube per Team Foundation Server instance. This, in itself, is not a big problem. The limitations of the architecture start to emerge when you have multiple project collections attached to an instance that would, by themselves, strain a dedicated data warehouse per collection architecture.

The main limitations with the data warehouse in Team Foundation Server 2013 are:

➤ The relational warehouse has a limit of approximately 1,000 unique reportable fields across all project collections. This is the limit of columns in a SQL Server table, less some overhead.

➤ The time to process the OLAP cube is proportional to the number of reportable fields.

➤ Different field data types will be expanded to more than one dimension in the cube. For example, a `datetime` field is expanded to six dimensions to support the different data slicing requirements of a date: Year Month Date, Year Week Date, Date, Month, Week, and Year.

➤ Analysis Services does not have a scale-out solution for processing a single cube. You can add additional query servers, or process multiple cubes on separate processing servers and swap them in later. But you cannot process a single cube across multiple servers.

In summary, if your SQL Server hardware and application-tier server are not scalability bottlenecks in your environment, some architectural limitations in the data warehouse may affect you.

Team Foundation Proxy

The Team Foundation Proxy is a very effective method of increasing version control performance for users and reducing the load on the application-tier servers. As noted earlier, the 2012 release added support for more than just version control downloads.

The most significant limitations in the performance of the proxy server are:

➤ **Network performance**—Latency and throughput

➤ **Storage performance**—Disk size and throughput

Network Performance

The largest influence on the performance of the proxy server is the network performance between the proxy server and the clients. If the clients are separated from the proxy by a slow link, then the proxy may not provide any benefit at all compared to accessing the application tier directly.

Storage Performance

The amount of disk space available for the file download cache is the next most important influence on the performance of the proxy server. If the cache size isn't large enough then the proxy will be constantly cleaning up and refilling the cache.

Periodically, the cleanup job will scan the entire directory and look for files that have not been accessed recently (more than 14 days by default). The cleanup job will then delete these files. For caches with large numbers of files, the cleanup algorithm can be quite inefficient and can take many hours to identify and clean up stale files. It's important that your disks can handle the normal proxy load in addition to this cleanup load.

To get an estimate of how long this cleanup identification process takes, you can open a command prompt and run a directory listing of your cache directory. To do so, follow these steps:

1. Open a command prompt.

2. Change to your cache directory by typing the following (all on one line):

```
CD /D "C:\Program Files\Microsoft Team Foundation Server 11.0\
    Application Tier\Web Services\_tfs_data"
```

3. Perform a directory listing by typing the following:

```
dir /s > NUL
```

This will retrieve the file descriptors of every file in the cache directory and redirect the output to the NUL device so that it doesn't flood your console. The time it takes for this command to return is roughly the same time it takes for the proxy to identify files for cleanup.

In the case of a cache miss, the proxy server streams the content from the SQL server and writes the stream to the cache drive simultaneously while sending it to the client. In the case of a cache hit, the proxy server streams the content from the disk to the client. This means that the memory and processor demands of the proxy server are relatively moderate. Therefore, if the network speed is not a bottleneck, the throughput of the proxy server is directly proportional to the performance of the disks.

MICROSOFT DEVELOPER DIVISION ADOPTION

The adoption of Team Foundation Server at Microsoft is something that has steadily increased since the early days of the product's development. Brian Harry and others on the product team have been blogging the internal adoption numbers over the years and sharing them with the public. You can see an example of these numbers at http://aka.ms/TfsDogfoodStats.

The Developer Division is the division in which the Team Foundation Server product group works. Until the release of Team Foundation Server 2008, the usage was limited to the product group, and the larger division used the existing Microsoft-only internally developed tools (Product Studio and Source Depot).

Once the division had shipped the 2008 wave of developer tools, there was a huge push to move all the people and systems over to Team Foundation Server. It's fair to say that this was not without its challenges, and the server was constantly patched to meet the scalability demands of the division's 4,000 users and build lab.

These patches made up the majority of the performance-related improvements in Team Foundation Server 2008 Service Pack 1. You can get an overview of these improvements on Brian Harry's blog under the "Performance & Scale" heading at http://aka.ms/Tfs2008Sp1Changes.

Although the use of these systems was painful at times for people in the division and across the company, it has pushed the product team to ensure that the product scales well. The widely varied usage patterns and user base have proven that the product can scale in real-world use far beyond what any load simulation can do.

This internal adoption and usage continued throughout the development of the 2013 release. Perhaps the most important usage though is the usage of the Visual Studio Online service. As scalability and availability issues are found in the service, updates are developed and deployed on at least a weekly basis. By the time Team Foundation Server 2013 was released, the product had been used on a day-to-day basis by many thousands of users.

PRINCIPLES

If you are designing a new Team Foundation Server environment, or if you anticipate having to scale your existing installation, you can generally apply a number of principles. When implemented, these principles will also help you achieve your goals of high availability. These principles are:

➤   Scale out to multiple servers.

➤   Eliminate single points of failure.

➤   Anticipate growth.

➤   Keep it simple.

Scale Out to Multiple Servers

The first principle is to spread out the different components that make up a Team Foundation Server environment over multiple physical or virtual servers. The biggest benefit of doing this is to allow each component to make maximum use of the hardware that it sits on without competing with other components. As bottlenecks develop, the hardware for that single component can be scaled up or scaled out, without touching the other components. It's much easier for users to accept "Reporting won't be available this weekend while we upgrade the reporting server hardware" than it is "The whole server won't be available this weekend while we upgrade the hardware." This reduces overall risk and increases the ability to react to changing usage patterns.

Eliminate Single Points of Failure

The second principle is the well-known formula for achieving high availability. By introducing redundancy in the environment and eliminating single points of failure, you reduce the chances that a failed component will impact the overall availability of the service. Depending on your goals for availability, this can be the most costly principle to implement. However, for some organizations, the impact of a failure greatly outweighs the infrastructure cost to avoid that failure, and it's an easy decision to make.

Anticipate Growth

The third principle can be a difficult one to gauge and plan for. Team Foundation Server is a powerful system with some very compelling features. Without proper planning and preparation, the use of these features can overwhelm the planned capacity of the system. The most common limitation that people encounter in a successful Team Foundation Server environment is the lack of storage space. Once people discover the value of an integrated version control, work item tracking, build, and test case automation system, the storage requirements start to grow rapidly. Without careful growth estimates and foresight in the storage design, this can have a dramatic impact on the stability of the system.

Keep It Simple

The final principle applies not just to Team Foundation Server but also to any system. Keep it simple. Simple things are easy to get right, and they usually cost less to set up and maintain.

SOLUTIONS

Now that the limitations have been covered, it's time to discuss some of the solutions, including:

➤ Data tier

➤ Application tier and web access

➤ Virtualization

This section covers the different components of Team Foundation Server and some strategies to increase their availability and scalability.

Data Tier

If scalability and high availability are important to you, then the data tier is where you will need to invest most of your resources.

High Availability

Availability is not only impacted by unexpected failures but also expected failures or maintenance work. Without a redundant system in place that can respond to requests while the primary system is undergoing maintenance, the system will be unavailable.

When planning for high availability, the most important database is the `Tfs_Configuration` database. Within the current architecture of the system, this is a single point of failure. An issue with this database will cause the entire instance to be unavailable.

SQL Server 2012 introduced a new comprehensive high availability and disaster recovery solution called SQL Server AlwaysOn. These features increase the high availability options for a Team Foundation Server deployment. AlwaysOn offers two core capabilities:

➤ **AlwaysOn Availability Group**—This is a capability that helps protect application databases from both planned and unplanned downtime. The key availability features are failover of a group of databases, multiple secondary copies for improved redundancy, and virtual names for fast application failover.

➤ **AlwaysOn Failover Cluster Instance (FCI)**—This provides protection for the entire instance and is an enhancement to the existing SQL Server Failover Cluster Instance. It includes multi-site clustering across subnets and `TempDB` on a local drive that allows better query performance.

Both of these capabilities rely on the Windows Server Failover Clustering (WSFC) infrastructure, which provides a robust and reliable high-availability platform.

These capabilities can be used by themselves or in combination with each other, depending on your availability needs. AlwaysOn Availability Group is the recommended high availability capability for database availability. It does not require shared storage as each SQL Server in the topology has its own copy of the data and does not need to share. Additionally, the replica can be used as an Active Secondary server for offloading backup operations.

> **NOTE** *For more information on the deployment options, see SQL Server 2012 AlwaysOn High Availability and Disaster Recovery Design Patterns at* `http://aka.ms/SQL2012AlwaysOnHADRPatterns`.

BE CAREFUL OF THE COMPLEXITY

Although a Failover Cluster Instance is a fully supported configuration, it violates the fourth principle of achieving high availability: "Keep it simple." The Developer Division server at Microsoft used to run a two-node, two-instance cluster configuration with the SQL Server instance running on one node and the Analysis Services instance normally running on the other. This worked fine until it came time to upgrade from SQL Server 2005 to SQL Server 2008.

The upgrade wizard supported failover cluster upgrades, but it did not support an online upgrade of a failover cluster with multiple resource groups. In the end, moving Analysis Services out of the cluster and off to its own dedicated hardware kept the configuration simple and allowed the team to use the online upgrade capabilities of the upgrade wizard.

Scalability

Earlier in this chapter, storage performance was identified as the biggest potential bottleneck of Team Foundation Server performance. In general, the same recommendations that generally apply for SQL Server also apply for Team Foundation Server.

You should start with the SQL Server Customer Advisory Team (CAT) "Storage Top 10 Best Practices" at `http://tinyurl.com/SQLServerStorageTop10`. Following are the most important of these 10 best practices:

➤ More or faster spindles are better for performance.

➤ Isolate transaction log files from data files at the physical disk level.

➤ Consider the configuration of the `TempDB` database.

➤ Don't overlook some of SQL Server basics.

➤ Don't overlook storage configuration basics.

Physical disks have physical limitations with the performance they can provide. The only way to increase your storage performance is to have faster spindles or to have more of them to spread the load out onto.

It's fairly common knowledge that SQL transaction logs, data files, and TempDB files should reside on physically separate drives. Because all of these are used at the same time, you don't want contention for resources among them. The aforementioned article includes this advice, along with many other storage configuration best practices.

Your storage is the most critical component of your Team Foundation Server environment. You must collaborate with your storage administrators and vendors to ensure that the storage is optimally configured for your needs.

A STORAGE MISCONFIGURATION

An upgrade of the particularly large Developer Division server at Microsoft occurred during 2008. In the weeks leading up to the upgrade, the storage vendors had identified an issue on the storage array that required a firmware update. This update was supposed to have minimal impact on storage performance, and the team was told that it could be done while the server was online.

Unfortunately, this was not the case. It turns out that the firmware update reset the configuration back to factory defaults. It disabled the write cache setting on the array. It wasn't until halfway through the upgrade that a team member noticed the storage wasn't performing as expected. After some frantic phone calls and support investigations from the vendor, the missed configuration setting was identified and restored. The upgrade still failed for other reasons, but it certainly taught the team to keep the storage administrators close by during critical times.

SQL Server Enterprise Edition

If you separately license the high-end SQL Server edition, Team Foundation Server can use the extra features that it provides. The following features can be used to increase the availability and scalability of the system.

> **NOTE** *For more information on the features available, see "Features Supported by the Editions of SQL Server 2012" at* http://aka.ms/SQL2012Features.

➤ **Online index operations**—Index rebuilds and reorganization will be automatically done using the WITH ONLINE condition as part of the Optimize Databases job. Normally, indexes are taken offline, and operations that rely on those indexes are blocked while they are rebuilt.

➤ **Page compression**—Page compression can yield significant storage savings and increased storage performance. However, compression increases processor use, so be sure that you have enough available capacity. When you create a new collection on a SQL Server Enterprise Edition server, the majority of the version control tables and relational warehouse tables have page compression enabled. With page compression on these tables, storage usage can be reduced by up to a quarter of the uncompressed size. Additionally, the pages remain compressed in the buffer pool, which also results in increased performance.

UPGRADING TO ENTERPRISE EDITION

If you upgrade an existing SQL Server instance that hosts Team Foundation Server databases, compression will not be automatically used for existing collections. Existing collections will need to have compression enabled and their indexes rebuilt to see the benefits of compression. You can do this by running the following script in each of your collection databases:

```
EXEC prc_EnablePrefixCompression @Online = 1, @disable = 0
```

Newly created collections will have compression enabled automatically.

➤ **Table and index partitioning**—On large Team Foundation Server 2010 systems with many files and workspaces, the `tbl_LocalVersion` table can become very large and unwieldy. At Microsoft, this table peaked at five billion rows. This caused all kinds of problems, most notably that it would take more than a week to rebuild the index. If it finished rebuilding, it would need to start again because of the high churn in the table. The obvious solution to this was to implement table partitioning and split the table into more manageable chunks. Because this isn't documented, if you need table partitioning, you must contact Microsoft Support and they will guide you through the process. Team Foundation Server 2013 has a feature enabled by default called *Local Workspaces*. This removes the need to store workspace state on the server and dramatically reduces the size of the `tbl_LocalVersion` table.

➤ **Larger read-ahead buffering**—Enterprise Edition uses 1024KB read-ahead buffering compared to 64KB in Standard Edition. This increased buffering makes some of Team Foundation Server's expensive queries faster.

➤ **Cube perspectives**—A *cube perspective* is a definition that allows users to see the cube in a simpler way. If you are using the Enterprise Edition of Analysis Services, Team Foundation Server defines individual perspectives for work items, builds, and so on, in addition to the `Team System` cube.

NOTE *For more information on cube perspectives, see the article on MSDN at* http://aka.ms/SQL2012CubePerspectives.

Application Tier and Web Access

As discussed at the beginning of this chapter, since the 2008 release there have been some significant changes to the architecture of the system. These changes enable the application tier to be scaled out and meet your scalability and high-availability requirements. With the exception of Web Access, the changes since Team Foundation Server 2010 are minor.

Web Access REST API

The largest limiting factor of web access scalability in Team Foundation Server 2010 was that it used the client object model to access the collections. The client object model was just not designed to operate in a high throughput web application and consumed a large amount of memory.

Therefore, in the 2012 release, the team implemented a lightweight REST API that uses the server object model. This dramatically improves the performance and scalability of web access along with reducing the overall load on the server. They have continued to expand the REST API in the 2013 release.

Stateless

In the 2010 release, aside from the change to support 64-bit architectures, changing web access to be stateless was the biggest change in the application tier from previous versions. Before this change, users would lose their sessions, along with the page they were on or the changes they were making. The lost session was usually triggered by a timeout, an application pool recycle, or by being directed to a different back-end server by a load balancer. This was an extremely frustrating experience for users.

The stateless implementation of web access dehydrates and rehydrates the client's session as required. This eliminates the session timeouts and allows any application tier to serve a user's request.

Load Balancing

Load balancing is an important feature for scalability and high availability. It allows the load to be spread across multiple servers. This increases the number of requests that can be handled by the system, as well as provides protection against planned and unplanned server downtime.

There are many load-balancing options. Whether you use Windows Network Load Balancing, the IIS Application Request Routing (ARR) extension, or a third-party load-balancer device, you need to consider some settings. Table 22-3 provides an overview of these settings and their recommended configurations.

TABLE 22-3: Recommended Load Balancer Configuration Settings

SETTING	DESCRIPTION
Idle Timeout	60 minutes
Affinity, Stickiness, or Persistence	No Affinity
IP Pass Through	Enabled

Idle Timeout

Most load balancers have an idle connection timeout setting. This is because every connection consumes memory, and they want to close the connection if it's idle. The usual default setting of five minutes can cause problems with version control in Team Foundation Server.

If the client sends a request that takes a long time to calculate in SQL Server (such as a large Get), there will be no data transferred over the connection, and it will appear to be idle. If the setting is not long enough, then the load balancer will close the connection and the client will get an error like "The connection was forcibly closed by the remote server." In this scenario, you want to match the idle timeout setting of the load balancer with the request timeout setting of Team Foundation Server, which is 60 minutes.

Team Explorer 2013 and the forward-compatibility patches for earlier versions will send TCP Keep-Alive packets after a connection is idle for 30 seconds. This is enough to keep most load balancers from closing the connection. However, if your connection to the remote server relies on an intermediate proxy server (Microsoft Forefront Threat Management Gateway, for example), then the TCP Keep-Alive packets may not propagate to the destination server. In this situation, you may continue to have problems with long-running commands.

HTTP KEEP-ALIVE AND TCP KEEP-ALIVE EXPLAINED

When people talk about Keep-Alive settings in the context of a web application, they normally mean *HTTP Keep-Alive*. HTTP Keep-Alive is a feature of the HTTP 1.1 protocol that instructs the server to keep the client's connection open after it has responded to a request. This avoids the cost of connection handshaking and is very useful for when web browsers open web pages with many images. Instead of opening and closing connections for every single image, connections are reused.

TCP Keep-Alive operates at a level below the HTTP traffic. It periodically sends a benign packet to the server over an existing connection, which then sends an acknowledgement response. This all happens without interfering with the client's HTTP conversation with the server.

Affinity

Affinity is the setting that determines if a client should be routed to the same back-end server for successive requests. Depending on the load balancer implementation, it is sometimes referred to as *persistence* or *stickiness*.

Some operations in Team Foundation Server can take a long time to process. Some operations (such as downloading version control file content) will use multiple threads. If you have affinity enabled, then it's possible that the load won't be evenly distributed between your back-end servers. In the case of a two-server, load-balanced instance, it's possible for one server to be overloaded processing most of the requests while the other server is sitting idle. For this reason, you may want to disable connection affinity.

Unfortunately, some load-balancing technologies don't handle authentication well. Users may receive generic authentication errors if they were authenticated against one back-end server, but then are load-balanced to another back-end server. In this scenario, you will need to fix the authentication issues or enable affinity.

IP Pass Through

One of the useful diagnostic tools in Team Foundation Server is the activity log. (See Chapter 25 and the Operational Intelligence Hub in Chapter 21 for more information on this.) The activity log records the IP address of each request in the system. The use of a load balancer can mask the actual IP address of the client. In this case, the activity log will show that the load balancer is the only client of the system.

To avoid this masking, you will want to enable the IP pass-through setting or some equivalent setting. If the load balancer sets the `X-Forwarded-For` HTTP header with the actual client IP address, then the activity log will show this address.

ASP.NET Worker Threads

As discussed earlier, the default configuration of ASP.NET limits the number of concurrently executing requests per CPU to 12. You can check to see if you are reaching this limit by monitoring the ASP.NET Applications\Requests in the Application Queue performance counter. If this is a non-zero value, then it means you definitely have a performance problem.

To enable increased concurrency, you can follow the guidance in the KB821268 article at `http://aka.ms/KB821268`. This describes the steps to change the `maxWorkerThreads` and `maxIoThreads` settings.

If your bottleneck is the throughput of your SQL server, then the majority of the concurrent requests will be sitting idle waiting for a response from the data tier. In this scenario, you can safely increase the settings to allow more concurrent connections.

Resource Governor

Similar to the Resource Governor feature available in SQL Server, Team Foundation Server also includes its own resource governor. Every command in the system is assigned a cost based on how resource intensive it is. Once the total cost of all the commands currently executing hits a configurable limit, subsequent requests are queued until sufficient resources are available. Each individual command can have a limit on its concurrency as well.

This resource governor prevents the server from becoming overwhelmed with a large number of requests and overloading the SQL server.

RESOURCE GOVERNOR AT MICROSOFT

While running the internal servers for the Developer Division at Microsoft, the team constantly battled to keep the server performance ahead of user demand. It seemed that no matter how many optimizations and hardware upgrades they did, the gains were quickly eroded. This was usually because of the sheer growth of data in the system or, more commonly, a misbehaving tool.

This problem was tackled in two ways. The first approach was to do some analysis on the server's activity logs and identify the tools or users generating the most load. In one case, a single user was responsible for more than 50 percent of the load on the system. Once identified, the team worked with the tool owners to understand their requirements and made suggestions for using the object model more efficiently.

This effort yielded some great results but left the team vulnerable and waiting for the next rogue tool to hit the system.

Toward the end of the 2010 release, the team implemented a resource governor with a default policy.

As an example, the (recursive) Merge command is assigned a cost of VeryHigh (5). The default limit for a server is 200. This means that, by default, each application tier will allow only 40 Merge operations to execute concurrently. Table 22-4 includes a listing of common commands and their costs.

TABLE 22-4: Resource Governor Command Costs

METHOD NAME	ESTIMATED METHOD COST
CancelRequest	Free (0)
CheckIn	High (4)
CreateBranch	High (4)
DeleteCollection	High (4)
Destroy	VeryHigh (5)
Get (non-recursive)	Low (2)
Get (recursive)	Moderate (3)
LabelItem	High (4)

continues

TABLE 22-4 *(continued)*

METHOD NAME	ESTIMATED METHOD COST
Merge (non-recursive)	Low (2)
Merge (recursive)	VeryHigh (5)
MethodologyUpload	High (4)
QueryHistory	Moderate (3)
ReadIdentityFromSource	Moderate (3)
VCDownloadHandler	VeryLow (1)

Configuration of the resource governor is performed within the Team Foundation Server registry (not the Windows Registry). The configuration isn't documented by Microsoft, so if you have a specific need to change the default configuration, you will need to contact Microsoft Support, and they will be able to guide you through.

Team Foundation Server 2013 has additions to the Windows performance counters and event logging. These changes help you identify if you are reaching a scalability limit and need to configure the resource governor. More information on these changes can be found in Chapter 25.

> **NOTE** *Although the configuration isn't documented by Microsoft, if you are experienced with modifying the server registry, you can use the following information to change the configuration:*
>
> ➤ By default, the resource governor is always enabled. You can disable it by setting the following registry key:
>
> ```
> /Service/ResourceGovernor/Settings/Enabled = false
> ```
>
> ➤ To limit the number of Merge commands that can execute concurrently, create and set a key that specifies the total cost limit. For example:
>
> ```
> /Service/ResourceGovernor/Method/Merge = 10
> ```
>
> ➤ To limit the total resources an individual user can consume, you will need to create and set a key that specifies the total cost limit for that user. The key name is the unique Team Foundation Identity of the user. This is different than the Windows SID and can be found by querying the `tf_id` column in the `tbl_security_identity_cache` table of the `Tfs_Configuration` database. The following example limits a particular user to executing commands with a total cost of 10:
>
> ```
> /Service/ResourceGovernor/User/<tf id> = 10
> /Service/ResourceGovernor/User/
> 0DA27F4C-61CB-4F18-B30A-3F65E62899CD = 10
> ```

File Download Cache Directory

If you have a large or busy server, the file download cache directory is going to be important for you. Previously, this cache directory was used only for version control content, but it now includes Work Item Tracking and Test attachments. By default, it lives in the `\Web Services\_tfs_data` directory where Team Foundation Server is installed. Depending on the usage patterns of your server, this directory can become very large, very quickly, and you should consider moving it to its own dedicated disk drive. You can move this directory in two ways:

Option 1—The first option doesn't require any Team Foundation Server configuration changes. You can use the Disk Management administrative tools and use a mount point to mount the additional drive to the `_tfs_data` path.

Option 2—The second option is to follow these steps:

1. On the application-tier server, create a cache folder.

2. Right-click the folder, and click Properties. The Properties dialog box for the folder opens.

3. Click the Security tab, and click Add.

4. Add the local group `TFS_APPTIER_SERVICE_WPG`, and click OK.

5. Select both the Read and Write check boxes, clear all other check boxes, and then click OK.

6. Open Windows Explorer, and browse to `C:\Program Files\ Microsoft Team Foundation Server 11.0\Application Tier\Web Services`.

7. Open the `Web.config` file in a text or XML editor, and locate the `<appSettings>` section.

8. Add a new line within the `<appSettings>` section and change the value to match the new location:

   `<add key="dataDirectory" value="D:\Cache" />`

9. Save and close the `Web.config` file. The application pool will be recycled automatically. The next time a file is downloaded from the application tier, it will be cached to this new location.

10. If the old cache folder has files in it, you should delete it to free up disk space on the server.

> **NOTE** *An alternative (and possibly better) way to configure the file download cache directory is to use a setting in the Team Foundation Server registry. The benefit of using the registry is that the configuration is maintained after a server upgrade and when additional application-tier servers are added to an environment. To configure the cache directory location, you will need to set the following Team Foundation Server registry key:*
>
> ```
> /Configuration/Application/DataDirectory = "D:\Cache"
> ```
>
> *When you use this key, it is automatically applied to any new application tiers that you configure. If the specified drive or directory does not exist on that server then that server will have an invalid cache configuration. This will impact performance until rectified by creating the specified directory with the correct permissions. The invalid configuration will manifest itself through errors in the Application Event Log on the server.*
>
> *If you set the* dataDirectory *key in the* Web.config *file, that setting will override any registry settings.*

Team Foundation Proxy

The proxy server is completely stateless and has always supported being in a load-balanced configuration. If your proxy server is overloaded, the simplest solution is to set up an additional server and configure network load balancing.

When designing a proxy server for scalability, you should prioritize the following:

1. Proximity to build servers and users
2. Storage size
3. Storage performance

If your application tier is in another building or another city, then having a proxy server in the same building as your biggest group of users is important. You want to keep the latency low for the most benefit.

Given the choice of storage size or storage speed, you should prioritize for storage size. For example, there's no point in having high-performance, solid-state drives for your proxy if they're not big enough to hold a day's worth of files.

The more storage that the proxy server can use, the more files and versions of files it can store. This increases the chance of a cache hit and decreases the number of times a file must be downloaded from the main server.

Like the application tier, you should also change the version control cache directory for the proxy server to be a dedicated drive.

> **NOTE** *For more information, see "How to: Change Cache Settings for Team Foundation Server Proxy" at* `http://aka.ms/TfsProxySettings`.

Virtualization

Virtualization can be a great solution for achieving your high-availability goals. You can configure your application tier and data tier servers as virtual machine guests on a highly available host machine. If the underlying host requires planned or unplanned maintenance, you can perform a quick migration of the guest machines to another host without interruption.

> **NOTE** *This configuration is beyond the scope of this chapter, and you should refer to the article "Reference Architecture for Private Cloud" at* `http://aka.ms/PrivateCloudRefArch`.

Microsoft supports virtualization of Team Foundation Server in supported virtualization environments. For more information, see the following pages on the Microsoft website:

➤ Microsoft server software and supported virtualization environments at `http://aka.ms/VirtSupport1`

➤ Support policy for Microsoft software running in non-Microsoft hardware virtualization software at `http://aka.ms/VirtSupport2`

➤ Support partners for non-Microsoft hardware virtualization software at `http://aka.ms/VirtSupport3`

➤ Server Virtualization (officially supported products) at `http://aka.ms/VirtSupport4`

You should also read the best practices and performance recommendations on "Running SQL Server 2008 in a Hyper-V Environment" at `http://aka.ms/SQLHyperV` along with "Running SQL Server with Hyper-V Dynamic Memory" at `http://aka.ms/SQLHyperVDM`. Regardless of your virtualization technology, the tests and recommendations are very relevant.

SUMMARY

This chapter explored some of the scalability and availability limitations of Team Foundation Server, as well as the issues faced by large and busy environments. You learned that the performance of Team Foundation Server is tied directly to the performance of SQL Server. Finally, solutions and best practices were discussed for overcoming these limitations to meet your scalability and high-availability goals.

Chapter 23 discusses another important aspect of Team Foundation Server administration—disaster recovery.

23
Disaster Recovery

WHAT'S IN THIS CHAPTER?

➤ Using the backup-and-restore wizard

➤ Walking through step-by-step examples of how to back up and restore your Team Foundation Server environment

➤ Learning about backup plan considerations

Disaster recovery is an important topic, but it is too broad to cover in a single chapter. The purpose of this chapter is to prompt you to think about what your disaster-recovery plan is and how it relates to Team Foundation Server.

> **NOTE** *For more information, see "Proven SQL Server Architectures for High Availability and Disaster Recovery" at* `http://tinyurl.com/SQLHADR`.

BUSINESS CONTINUITY AND RECOVERY GOALS

Before discussing disaster recovery in detail, let's establish some goals. You should consult with the team that will be using Team Foundation Server and ask some important questions. The answer to each question has an effect on the cost and complexity of your solution. Following are examples of some questions to ask:

➤ In the event of a hardware failure (for example, a hard drive crash or a network outage), how quickly must service be restored?

➤ In the event of a major disaster (for example, a hurricane or an earthquake), how quickly must service be restored?

➤ If the service is unavailable for a period of time, what is the cost to the business?

➤ What is an acceptable level of data loss (for example, 15 minutes or 15 hours)?

➤ How long and how often should backup copies be kept (for example, seven days, seven weeks, or seven years)?

➤ When can backup media be overwritten? When should backup media be retired? How is backup media retired?

➤ Where are backups kept (for example, on-site, in another building, another city, or another continent)?

➤ Who should have access to the backups? Are they encrypted?

The answers to these questions will be different for every organization. At one end of the scale will be the highly regulated financial and engineering industries. At the other end will likely be the small companies and individuals. With different needs and requirements, the costs will be very different depending on the chosen solution.

DEFINING RESPONSIBILITIES

Having a robust and reliable disaster-recovery plan is an important responsibility of any Team Foundation Server administrator. In large organizations, this responsibility may fall on a central business continuity team or maybe the database administration team.

As the Team Foundation Server administrator, it is your responsibility to ensure that the implementation of the plan is supported by Team Foundation Server. Backups that were not taken correctly, or that cannot be restored, are a risk to the business and effectively useless. For this reason, it's important to not only have a backup plan but also to regularly test that plan to ensure that it's working for when you need it.

BACKING UP TEAM FOUNDATION SERVER

Team Foundation Server includes many components. There's the data tier, application tier(s), SQL Reporting Services, SharePoint server, Lab Management environments, file shares for build drops and symbol server repositories, test controllers and agents, and Team Build.

The most important components to back up are the databases on the data tier. These are the "crown jewels" of Team Foundation Server, where the majority of the information is kept. If you are unable to recover at least these databases in the event of a disaster, it's time to look for a new job.

For example, if you are able to recover a collection database, the relational warehouse and Online Analytical Processing (OLAP) cube can be rebuilt from the original data. It takes time, but it's possible. As another example, if you can restore the source control data, then you can re-create a build from that source.

Components to Back Up

Table 23-1 provides an overview of the different components that should be backed up.

TABLE 23-1: Components to Back Up

COMPONENT	ARTIFACTS
Data tier	Configuration database, collection databases, warehouse database, Reporting Services databases
Application tier	Configuration settings, user names and passwords, custom controls, SQL Reporting Services encryption key, configuration settings for third-party tools
SharePoint	SharePoint products configuration databases, site content databases, site collection custom controls, encryption keys, databases
Lab Management	System Center Virtual Machine Manager (SCVMM) configuration, virtual machines, lab environments, environment and VM templates
Team Build	Server configurations, custom activities, build-drops file share, symbol server file share
Clients	No client-side backups required, although you might want to use shelvesets for saving in-progress work to the server

SharePoint Products

For the officially supported procedures to back up SharePoint products associated with a Team Foundation Server, you should refer to "Overview of backup and recovery in SharePoint 2013" at `http://tinyurl.com/SharePointBackup`. In particular, if you have any customizations to SharePoint products, you must also back those up so they can be reproduced on a new server.

SQL Reporting Services Encryption Key

SQL Reporting Services uses an encryption key to encrypt data source connection strings, report credentials, and shared data source credentials. You should include the encryption key backup and the associated password to restore the key in your backup plan.

Chapter 11 discussed a method of using a team project designed for administering artifacts for Team Foundation Server, including storing the reporting services encryption key in version control. The team project collection databases are likely to be backed up and restored, so this is a great location for always ensuring that the encryption key is backed up appropriately.

> **NOTE** *For more information, see "Back Up the SQL Reporting Services Encryption Key" at* `http://aka.ms/BackupReportingServicesKey`. *This link points to a Team Foundation Server 2010 article which is applicable to Team Foundation Server 2013.*

YOU LOST THE REPORTING SERVICES ENCRYPTION KEY?

An encryption key? That must be important, right? Have you ever wondered what would happen if you didn't back it up and you lost it? Or, even worse, what if you did back it up, but you don't know the password to restore it?

It turns out that it's not the end of the world. If you are unable to restore the encryption key, you will have to use the Reporting Services Configuration Manager to delete the encrypted data. After you delete the encrypted content, you must create the encrypted data again.

Without re-creating the deleted data, the following will happen:

➤ Connection strings in shared data sources are deleted. Users who run reports get the error, "The `ConnectionString` property has not been initialized."

➤ Stored credentials are deleted. Reports and shared data sources are reconfigured to use prompted credentials.

➤ Reports based on models (and require shared data sources configured with stored or no credentials) will not run.

➤ Subscriptions are deactivated.

For more information, see the "Deleting and Re-creating Encryption Keys" article on MSDN at `http://aka.ms/RecreateRSEncryptionKey`.

Lab Management

If you are using Lab Management in your Team Foundation Server environment, you will need to include backups of your SCVMM environment. You will also want to be sure that any SCVMM Library file shares are included in normal backups because they will contain the environment and virtual machine templates as well as stored environments that your engineering teams will need to get back up and running.

> **NOTE** *For more information, see "Backing Up and Restoring the VMM Database" at* `http://aka.ms/BackupSCVMM`.

Types of Database Backups

SQL Server has the following recovery modes, which are set on a per-database basis:

➤ **FULL recovery mode**—In this mode, each transaction is kept in the transaction log until the log is backed up and a checkpoint is set.

➤ **SIMPLE recovery mode**—In this mode, each transaction is written to the transaction log, but it can be overwritten at a later time.

The default recovery mode used by SQL Server for all user databases is FULL. The recovery mode of a database can be changed at any time without impacting currently running commands.

TRANSACTION LOG GROWING OUT OF CONTROL?

In FULL recovery mode, without transaction log backups, the log will continue to grow until it reaches the configured limit. If the log is set to AUTOGROW, it will continue growing until the disk is full if no limit is set. When either the database or transaction log is full, users will receive a "Database is full" message when performing operations in Team Foundation Server.

If your database recovery targets are met without doing transaction log backups, then you may want to change your databases to SIMPLE recovery mode. This means that the transaction logs will grow only to the size of your largest transaction.

Full Database Backups

At least one full database backup is required to restore a database. A full database backup includes the entire contents of the database at the time the database backup finished. It does not include any uncommitted transactions. Typically, full backups are performed once a month or once a week, depending on the rate of data change.

> **NOTE** *For more information, see "Full Database Backups" on MSDN at* `http://aka.ms/FullSQLDatabaseBackups`.

DATABASE EDITIONS AND VERSIONS

When you use the built-in native SQL Server backup and restore functions, you should be aware of the version compatibility. For example, a database backup from SQL Server 2012 cannot be restored to a server with a down-level version, such as SQL Server 2008 R2.

Additionally, if you create a backup with compression enabled, it can be restored only on a server that also has compression available. This can be a problem when moving a database from a SQL Server Enterprise instance to a SQL Server Standard instance.

Differential Database Backups

A *differential backup* includes everything that has changed since the last full backup. This is sometimes referred to as a "diff" or *incremental backup*. Because a differential backup is only recording differences, it usually takes less time and uses less storage than a full backup.

Over time, as more data changes in the database since the last full backup, the differential backup will become larger. At some point, the differential backup may become larger than the original full backup, and it will be more efficient to run a new full backup. Typically, differential backups are performed once per day.

> **NOTE** *For more information, see "Differential Database Backups" at* http://
> aka.ms/DifferentialSQLDatabaseBackups.

Transaction Log Backups

When a database is in FULL recovery mode, the transaction log contains all the data changes in the database. By performing transaction log backups (along with full and differential backups), you can later restore a database to a point in time or a specific transaction. Typically, transaction log backups are performed anywhere from every 5 minutes to every 60 minutes, depending on data recovery goals.

> **NOTE** *For more information, see "Working with Transaction Log Backups" at*
> http://aka.ms/SQLTransactionLogBackups.

Important Considerations

Team Foundation Server has two types of databases: the Tfs_Configuration database and the collection databases. Users who have access to Team Foundation Server have their name, e-mail, and group memberships synchronized with Active Directory. Rather than synchronizing this information with each individual collection, it is stored in the configuration database.

Because of this dependency between the databases, it is vital that the configuration database and collection databases are backed up in a way that they can be restored to a common point in time. Achieving this can become more difficult when your configuration database is on a different server or instance than your collection databases.

If this synchronization between the databases is not maintained, then it is possible that an identity is referenced in a collection database that doesn't exist in the configuration database. Team Foundation Server does not handle this scenario well, and the databases will be in an inconsistent state. Users may lose their permissions to their projects, and other data inconsistencies may be seen.

> **NOTE** *If you do find yourself in the situation where your configuration and collection backups are out of sync, you should contact Microsoft Support* (http://support.microsoft.com). *In some cases, the identity data can be reconstructed to overcome the inconsistencies. However, you should design your backup plan to avoid this situation.*

SQL Marked Transactions

The SQL Server solution to ensure synchronization across databases and database servers is to use marked transactions. Establishing a transaction that spans all the databases in the environment provides a common point that can be restored to and ensure synchronization.

New Collections

Each time a new collection is created on a Team Foundation Server instance, a new database will be created. You must ensure that this database is added to your backup plan. It's best if new databases are backed up automatically by your backup scripts so that they aren't accidentally excluded.

Virtualization and Backups

If you are virtualizing your data tier, you can back up the entire virtual machine that your SQL server is running in. But you should consider SQL database backups as well. Not all virtual backup technologies ensure transactional consistency within the database. If transactional consistency is not maintained, then it is not safe to restore from your virtual machine backups, and you may encounter data loss.

In an environment with multiple SQL servers, it's impossible to keep the database backups synchronized without using marked transactions. Additionally, transaction log backups can be run much more frequently than a backup of a virtual machine, and they allow a much finer-grained recovery point.

Also, when using a virtualized SQL Server, avoid using the snapshot features of many virtualization technologies while the server is turned on. Take snapshots only when the system has been shut down completely. Virtualization snapshots that are taken while a server is turned on with SQL Server instances are not supported.

Data Security

One of the most common breaches of data security is mishandled backup media. After you have defined how you are going to run your SQL backups, you must define how you are going to store them to meet your retention and off-site backup requirements.

Because a database backup contains all of your data, it would be a big problem if it weren't adequately protected and an untrusted person was able to restore it. This person could restore the data to another server and use his or her own administrative credentials to access the contents of the databases.

For this reason, it's important to consider the security of your backups in the same way you consider the security of your server itself. Consider using encryption as well as secure transport, handling, and storage of your backups.

Software Versions, Installation Media, and License Keys

In the event of a major disaster or a hardware failure, the backups by themselves are not usually enough to bring the server back online. You will also need software installed to restore those backups to. You should consider the following software in your backup plan:

➤ Windows installation media and product keys

➤ Drivers for the server and storage hardware

➤ Team Foundation Server installation media and product key

➤ SQL Server installation media and product keys

➤ Third-party backup software (if you are not using SQL Server backups)

➤ Service Packs and Updates for Windows, SQL Server, and Team Foundation Server

SQL Server 2012 AlwaysOn Technology

Team Foundation Server 2012 introduced support for the new high-availability feature *AlwaysOn* in SQL Server 2012. This can be particularly useful in a disaster recovery and high-availability strategy for Team Foundation Server. It enhances the existing SQL Server features of database mirroring and clustering. To find out more information about SQL Server 2012 AlwaysOn, visit http://aka.ms/SQLAlwaysOn. Team Foundation Server has some special steps required if you intend to use a SQL AlwaysOn instance, which are documented at: http://aka.ms/SQLAlwaysOnTFSConfig.

CREATING A BACKUP PLAN

Creating a reliable backup plan can be quite a daunting task. Fortunately, the Team Foundation Server team has made it simple by making a backup-and-restore wizard available in the Scheduled Backups section of the Team Foundation Server Administration Console.

The Team Foundation Server backup-and-restore wizard takes care of two of the important backup considerations discussed earlier:

➤ It configures and uses SQL-marked transactions to keep the databases in sync.

➤ It automatically adds new collections to the backup plan so that they don't miss out on backups.

To access the Scheduled Backups Wizard, open the Team Foundation Server Administration Console. As shown in Figure 23-1, when you select the Scheduled Backups option for the first time, you get a link to create a scheduled backup and one to restore backed up databases.

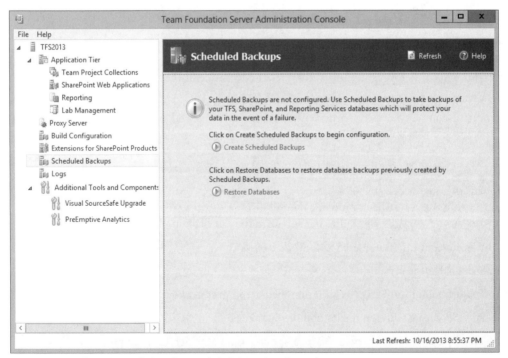

FIGURE 23-1: Team Foundation Server Administration Console

Once you click the Create Scheduled Backups link, the Scheduled Backups Wizard appears. Figure 23-2, shows that the wizard is very similar to the configuration wizard that you used to configure Team Foundation Server the first time. The left pane shows each of the wizard pages, and the wizard ends with a Review screen before making any changes.

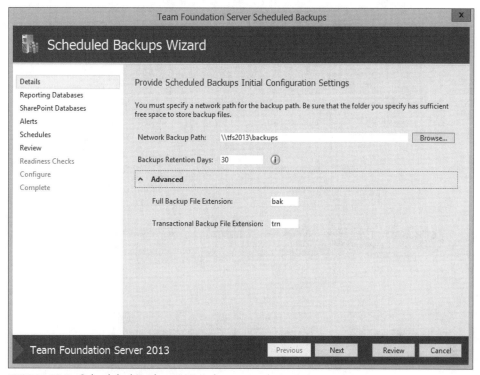

FIGURE 23-2: Scheduled Backups Wizard

The first step of the wizard allows you to specify a location to store the backups. This is specified as a UNC network path, which means that the share must already exist. When you specify the backup account later in the wizard, it will be given read-and-write access to the share.

Even though the wizard asks for a Network Backup Path, it is possible to back up to the local machine. To do this, you must create a share that is accessible by the backup account, and then specify the local machine as a backup path. For example, in Figure 23-2, the path specified refers to the name of the Team Foundation Server machine itself.

It is also possible to specify the backup retention period. Each time the backup runs, it will delete any backups that are older than this number of days. The default retention period is 30 days. If you expand the Advanced section, you can configure the database and transaction log backup file extensions to match your corporate standards.

If you have Team Foundation Server installed on a server operating system and you are not using the "Basic" configuration of the server, you will have the option to back up the Reporting Services database, as shown in Figure 23-3. This database may be located on the same SQL server as your Team Foundation Server, or on a remote instance.

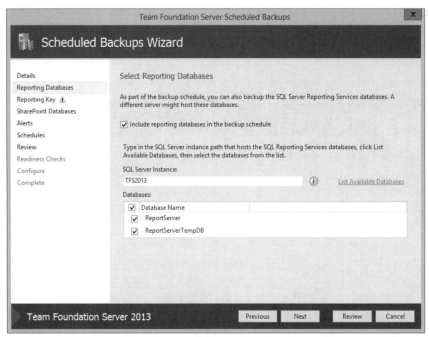

FIGURE 23-3: Reporting instance database backup

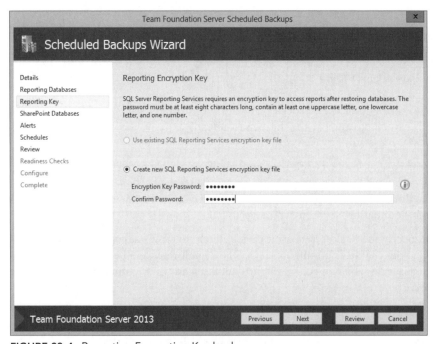

FIGURE 23-4: Reporting Encryption Key backup

The backup plan will also automatically back up the SQL Reporting Services encryption key so this screen prompts for a password to use for the key backup file, as shown in Figure 23-4. As with Reporting Services, if you have SharePoint installed, you will have the option to back up the SharePoint databases, as shown in Figure 23-5.

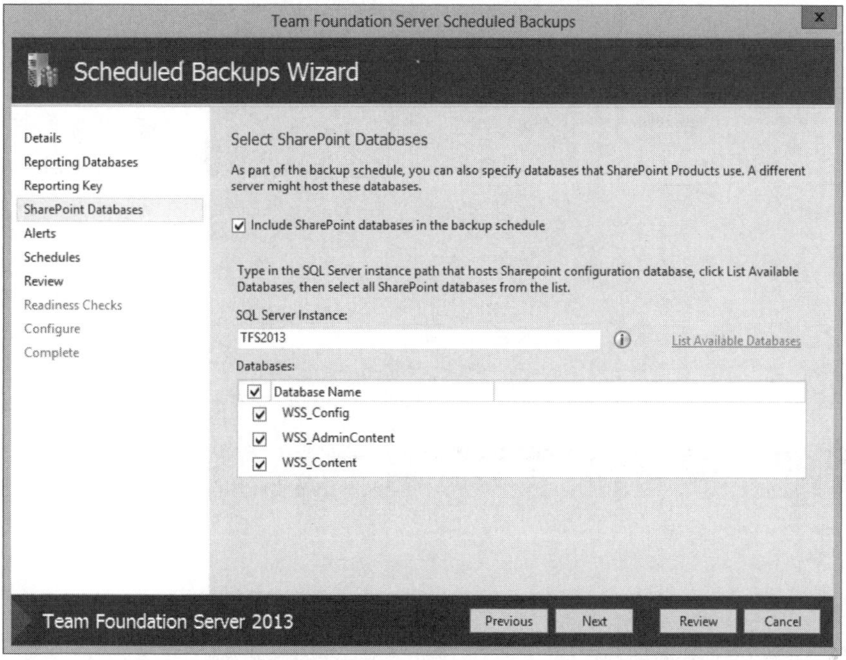

FIGURE 23-5: SharePoint database backup

As an administrator, you will want to know when the backup fails so you can investigate and fix it. The Alerts page of the wizard (shown in Figure 23-6) allows you to specify whether you receive an e-mail on success, failure, both, or neither. Because the Scheduled Backups Wizard has access to the Team Foundation Server configuration database, it retrieves the e-mail server settings from the instance. If you want to change the e-mail server or the From address, then you must change it in the Team Foundation Server Administration Console before starting the Scheduled Backups Wizard.

The Backup Schedule page allows you to set the schedule and backup types. As discussed earlier in this chapter, there are three different types of SQL Server backups. You can choose one of these three options from the Scheduled Backups Wizard dialog box shown in Figure 23-7:

➤ If it's acceptable to your business to lose up to a day's worth of data and your database is not very big, the Nightly Full Backups schedule is the simplest option to choose. This will schedule a full database backup to happen once every day.

➤ If you don't use the server very often, or you don't have any need for a regularly scheduled backup, you can choose the Manual Backup Only option.

➤ If you want the backups to run automatically, but need the flexibility to specify a mix of settings, then select the Custom Schedule option. This option allows you to configure any mix of Full, Differential, and Transactional backup at different times on different or overlapping days.

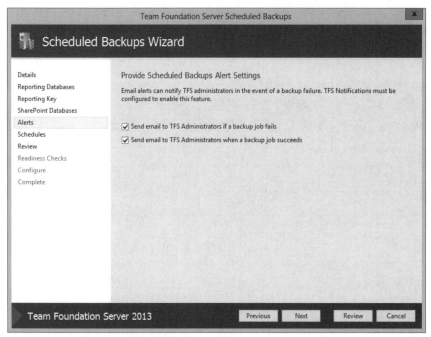

FIGURE 23-6: Alert configuration screen

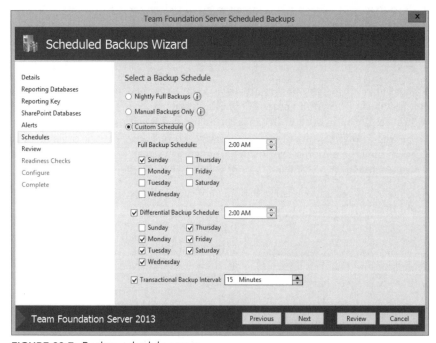

FIGURE 23-7: Backup schedule screen

Similar to the Server Configuration Wizard, the Scheduled Backups Wizard allows you to review and confirm your settings (see Figure 23-8) before any changes are made to your server. Review the settings and, if they are correct, click Verify to start the verification process.

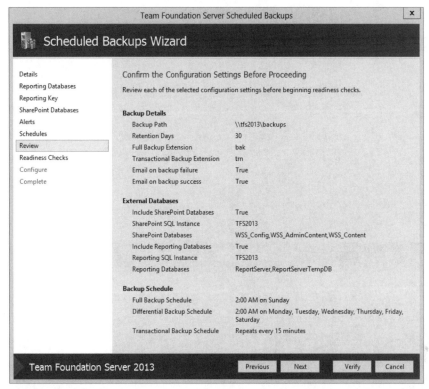

FIGURE 23-8: Review screen

Without making any changes to the system, the Readiness Checks screen shown in Figure 23-9 verifies that the configuration changes can be made and the backup plan can be set up without any problems. If any of the checks don't pass, then you must address them before you can continue. When you are ready to create the backup plan, click Create Plan.

In the final stage of the wizard (shown in Figure 23-10), you set server permissions, create the tables for marked transactions, and create the scheduled tasks.

The Team Foundation Server backup plan runs as a scheduled task on the application tier that you ran the wizard from. As part of setting up the backup plan, the wizard will add a table to each database included in the plan. This table is required to establish a marked transaction that spans multiple databases.

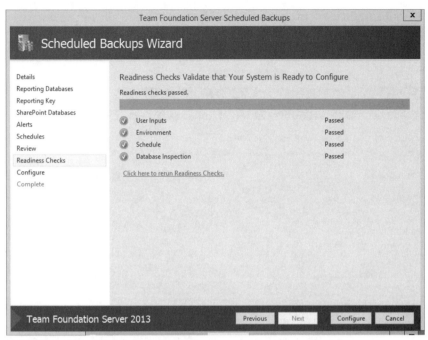

FIGURE 23-9: Readiness Checks screen

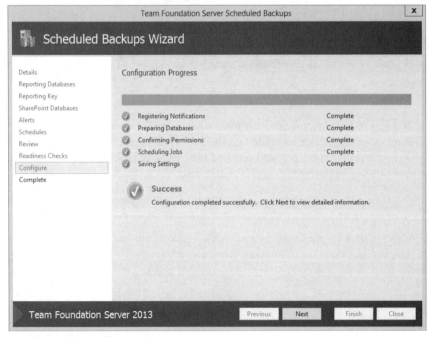

FIGURE 23-10: Configuration Progress screen

Team Foundation Server Backup Plan Details

Once you have configured a backup plan, the Scheduled Backups tab in the Team Foundation Server Administration Console will show the details of the backup plan. The details screen in Figure 23-11 shows configuration settings such as the path that backups are being sent to, along with the databases and SQL servers included in the backup plan.

As shown in Figure 23-11, the lower half of the Backup Plan Details screen shows you the scheduled tasks information. This is the same information you will see if you open Task Scheduler from the control panel in Windows. It shows you each of the scheduled tasks that were created as part of the plan, when they are scheduled to run, and when they last ran.

Take Full Backup Now

Once you've created a backup plan, regardless of which schedule option you chose, you can manually take a full database backup at any time. This is done by clicking "Take Full Backup Now" in the Backup Plan Details pane. Once you select it, a dialog box similar to Figure 23-12 will allow you to monitor the progress of the backup. As discussed earlier, for a valid backup, it's required to have a marked transaction that spans all databases in the backup. After completing the full backup, the backup engine will automatically create a marked transaction and perform a transaction log backup that includes the marked transaction.

Restoring a Backup to the Original Server

Even with the backup-and-restore wizards, there are a lot of steps to follow when restoring database backups. To restore a backup of Team Foundation Server, you should refer to the official documentation, "Back Up and Restore TFS," on MSDN at `http://aka.ms/TFS2013BackupRestore`.

At a high level, following are the steps from the official documentation that you will need to perform to successfully restore your deployment from a database backup:

1.   Stop services that Team Foundation Server uses.

2.   Restore Team Foundation databases.

3.   Clear the version control cache.

4.   Update all service accounts.

5.   Rebuild the warehouse.

6.   Restart services that Team Foundation server uses.

Stop Services That Team Foundation Server Uses

Team Foundation Server has an application pool and a job agent. If you restore a backup while either of these is running, the restore may fail or you may end up in an inconsistent state.

To safely stop the services, you should use the `TFSServiceControl.exe` command with the `quiesce` option in the Tools directory of each application tier. This utility stops the application pool and the job agent. You must run it on every application tier in your Team Foundation Server farm if you have multiple application tier servers.

> **NOTE** *For more information, see "TFSServiceControl Command" at* `http://` `aka.ms/TFSServiceControl.`

QUIESCE COMMAND FAILED?

In certain situations in Team Foundation Server, the `quiesce` command may fail. If the application pool takes too long to stop, then the `TFSServiceControl.exe` command may time out and display an error message. Additionally, if the Team Foundation job agent is currently executing a long-running job, the command may also time out.

In either of these situations, you should try to run the `quiesce` command a second time. If that does not work correctly, then you can run `IISReset` and use Task Manager to end the `TFSJobAgent.exe` process.

Restore Team Foundation Databases Using the Restore Wizard

Once you have stopped the Team Foundation services, it's time to restore the databases from backups. The Restore Wizard will not let you overwrite an existing database, so you will need to delete it or move it out of the way first.

> **NOTE** *If you have SQL Server Management Studio installed, you can use it. For more information, see "How to: Delete a Database" at* `http://aka.ms/` `DeleteSQLDatabase.` *If you are using SQL Server Express, then you will need to download and install SQL Server Management Studio Express from* `http://` `aka.ms/SQLManagementStudio` *before you can delete the database.*

To start the wizard, follow these steps:

1. Log on to your Team Foundation Server application tier.
2. Start the Team Foundation Server Administration Console from the Start menu.
3. Select Team Foundation Server Backups.
4. Select the Restore Databases link from the Backup Details pane.

When the wizard starts, as shown in Figure 23-13, you'll see that it has a similar look and feel to the Server Configuration Wizard and the Scheduled Backups Wizard.

The first page of the Restore Wizard allows you to select a UNC network backup path and a backup set to restore. By default, the backup path is the same as the one that the backup plan is configured for. You may choose a different path if you have a backup stored elsewhere that you want to use. When you select the List Backups link, the wizard will look on the share for any backup sets and display them in the list, as shown in Figure 23-13. Once you have selected the backup set from the date that you want to restore to, click Next.

On the Select Databases to Restore screen shown in Figure 23-14, you can select which databases you want to restore and which SQL server you want to restore them to. By default, the SQL Server field for each database will be the original server that the backup was taken on. If you want to restore a database to a different SQL server, you should enter its name before clicking Next.

Just like the other wizards in Team Foundation Server, the review screen shown in Figure 23-15 allows you to confirm all the configuration settings before making any changes to your server. When you click the Verify button, the wizard will start performing readiness checks.

If the destination databases already exist, or the destination SQL server is not accessible, then the readiness checks will fail. You will need to address the errors and rerun the readiness checks.

Once the readiness checks pass and the configuration details are verified, as shown in Figure 23-16, you can click the Restore button to begin the database restore process.

Depending on the size of your backup and the speed of your hardware, the restore process may take some time. Once the restore is completed, as shown in Figure 23-17, you can close the wizard and continue with the other steps required to restore your Team Foundation Server.

Clear the Version Control Cache

Each application tier and Team Foundation Proxy server includes a version control cache. The version control cache keeps a copy of every file requested by a user. Each version of each file has a unique FileID assigned when the file is checked in the first time. The version control cache uses this FileID to store the files. If you restore a backup from a different Team Foundation Server or from a previous point in time, it's likely that the FileID of the files in the cache will be different from the ones in the database.

It's very important that you purge each version control cache before starting the server again. If you don't, then users will unknowingly download incorrect files and versions.

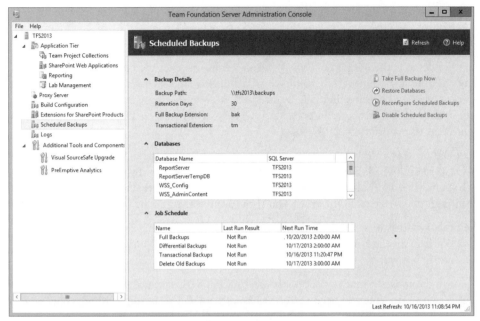

FIGURE 23-11: Scheduled Backup details

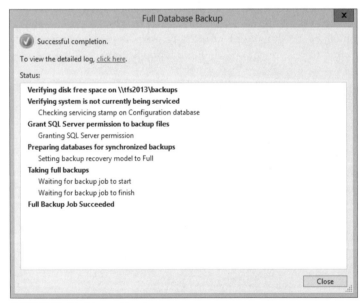

FIGURE 23-12: Manual backup progress screen

> **NOTE** *For more information on the procedure, you should refer to the KB2025763 article at* `http://aka.ms/TFSPurgeVersionControlCache`. *Essentially, it involves deleting the contents of the version control cache directory on each application tier and proxy server.*

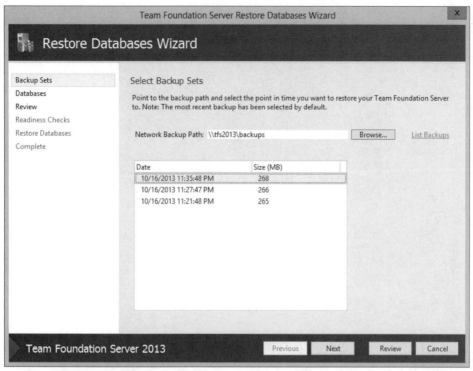

FIGURE 23-13: Select Backup Sets screen

PURGING LARGE VERSION CONTROL CACHES

On application tiers and proxy servers with a large drive for the version control cache, there will be a large number of cached files. Deleting all of these files individually will take a considerable amount of time and will increase the time it takes to bring the server back online.

There are two ways to mitigate this and allow you to bring the server back online sooner:

➤ **Format the drive**—If you have configured the cache directory on a separate partition or a separate drive, the fastest way is to perform a Quick Format of the drive. After formatting the drive, you will need to re-create the top-level cache directory and configure the correct permissions.

➤ **Rename the cache directory**—By moving the cache directory out of the way, it allows the server to start with an empty directory. Because renaming a directory is a metadata-only operation on a single folder, it will be done almost instantly. Then you can start deleting the old directory in the background after bringing the server back online.

FIGURE 23-14: Select Databases to Restore screen

Update All Service Accounts

Once you restore Team Foundation Server databases, you must ensure that the current Team Foundation Server service accounts have the required access and permissions on the databases. This is done by using the TfsConfig.exe command, which is found in the Tools directory of your application tier.

> **NOTE** *For more information on this procedure, refer to the "Restore Data to the Same Location" article on MSDN at* http://aka.ms/ TFSRestoreSameLocation.

Rebuild the Warehouse

If you restored the Tfs_Warehouse relational database to the same point in time as your other databases, then it should be in sync already. The only remaining step is to re-create the Tfs_Analysis analysis services database. You can do this by following these steps:

1. Log on to one of your application tier servers.

2. Open a command prompt.

3. Change directories to \Program Files\Microsoft Team Foundation Server\Tools.

4. Type the following command:

```
TfsConfig rebuildwarehouse /analysisServices
```

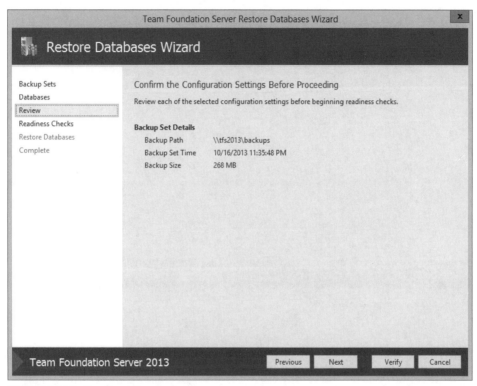

FIGURE 23-15: Configuration review screen

This will drop the Analysis Services database if it exists and create a new one from the operational store. This is slightly different than selecting the Start Rebuild link from the Reporting view in the Administration Console. That link will drop the relational warehouse as well as the Analysis Services Cube, and your rebuild will take much longer.

> **NOTE** *For more information, see "Manually Process the Data Warehouse and Analysis Services Cube for Team Foundation Server" at* http://aka.ms/ TFSWarehouseManualUpdate.

Restart Services That Team Foundation Server Uses

The last step to bring the server back online is to restart the application pool and job agent. Using a similar procedure to when you stopped the services, you can do this by running the TFSServiceControl .exe command with the unquiesce option on each application tier server in your deployment.

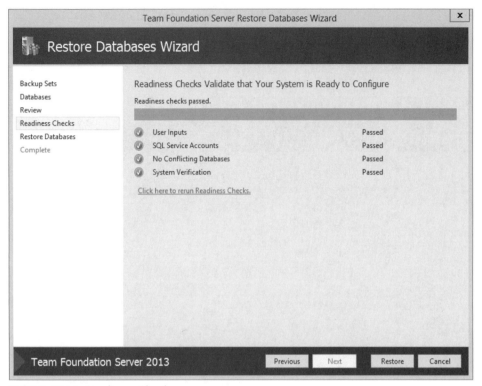

FIGURE 23-16: Readiness Checks screen

> **NOTE** *For more information, see "TFSServiceControl Command" at* `http://aka.ms/TFSServiceControl`.

Restoring to Different Hardware

If you have suffered a hardware failure, or you just want to move to a new server, you will need to restore backups to the new server. The steps for restoring data to different hardware are not the same as the steps to restore to the same hardware.

For the officially supported procedures, you should refer to the following documents:

➤ "Restore a Single-Server Deployment to New Hardware" at `http://aka.ms/TFSRestoreNewHardware`

➤ "Restore Data to a Different Server or Instance" at `http://aka.ms/TFSRestoreDifferentServer`

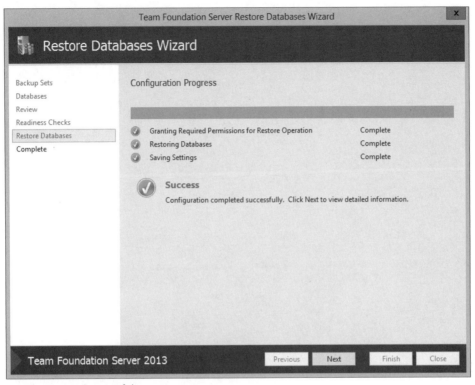

FIGURE 23-17: Successful restore screen

SUMMARY

This chapter started with the important questions to ask when defining your disaster-recovery plan. It highlighted that it is the responsibility of a Team Foundation Server administrator to make sure that the server is correctly backed up.

The main part of the chapter covered a walk-through with screen-by-screen examples of how to back up and restore your Team Foundation Server environment. It also discussed the important considerations that your backup plan must take into account, such as the use of SQL-marked transactions to synchronize backups.

Chapter 24 examines all things related to security and permissions in Team Foundation Server. The chapter will take a look at all the different places that security can be set, along with some best practices for avoiding a permissions mess.

24

Security and Privileges

WHAT'S IN THIS CHAPTER?

➤ Getting to know the different types of users and groups

➤ Understanding the new and interesting permissions

➤ Using tips for managing security

➤ Learning about useful tools

When you first start looking at security, groups, and permissions in Team Foundation Server, you might find it very daunting. This is a large system with many different features. A large part of the customer base also demands fine-grained controls in order to meet compliance goals. Combined, these two features make managing security a sometimes tricky task.

However, by understanding some basic principles and avoiding some of the traps, Team Foundation Server security can be corralled to achieve your security objectives. This chapter examines those principles and provides the information you'll need to avoid common pitfalls.

SECURITY WHEN USING VISUAL STUDIO ONLINE

The Visual Studio Online service provides the same core Team Foundation Server capabilities as does its on-premises counterpart. Where it diverges is in the security realm. As you will see later in this chapter, Team Foundation Server can work with Domain and Workgroup user accounts. The problem encountered with a cloud-based service is that there is no common Domain or Workgroup that can be called upon to provide authentication. To resolve this, Microsoft built the service's security model around the Microsoft account system (formerly Windows Live ID). This means that anyone that wishes to use Visual Studio Online must have a Windows account. Fortunately, if you use an e-mail address and a password to sign in to

Hotmail, Outlook.com, OneDrive, Windows Phone, Xbox LIVE, or other Microsoft services, you already have a Microsoft account.

Authorization using a Microsoft account isn't ideal in some situations because it requires an interactive web page login. When using non-browser–based tools such as the Team Explorer Everywhere command line, this becomes an issue. To mitigate this, Microsoft added the ability to log in with alternate credentials.

Basic Authentication for Visual Studio Online

Basic Authentication in Visual Studio Online is provided through a standard HTTP basic authentication implementation. If you need to access the system from a tool that works outside a browser, enable basic authentication by creating alternate credentials for your account.

To create alternate credentials, log in to Visual Studio Online, click on your name, and then select My Profile to open your User Profile dialog box. Now click on the Credentials tab and click the Enable alternate credentials link. You will see the e-mail address used in your Microsoft account as the primary user name along with a location to enter a password. You can simply set a password here and click the Save Changes button. This does not change your Microsoft account password, but rather, gives you a second password to use for basic authentication. Once you save these changes, you can log in with your e-mail address and basic authentication password when using applications that work outside a browser.

> **HAVING TROUBLE WITH THAT E-MAIL ADDRESS?**
>
> Some programs that use basic authentication have difficulty with special characters such as the @ sign, which makes it difficult to use an e-mail address as your user name. If you encounter this problem, you can set a secondary user name on the Credentials tab, which can be used in place of your e-mail address during login.

USERS

A key concept to understand in Team Foundation Server security is that there are different types of users, including the following:

➤ Domain users

➤ Local users

Domain Users

A *domain* in a Windows network usually means an Active Directory (AD) domain. AD is a directory and authentication service that comes with Windows Server. User accounts created in the directory are called *domain users*. In the directory, each user object has a set of properties, including a unique identifier (called a security ID, or SID), a display name, and an e-mail address.

> **NOTE** *Currently, the Visual Studio Online service is using Microsoft Accounts as its mechanism for authentication and identity management. However, because the product team is implementing identity using the Windows Azure Access Control Service, it could potentially support other identity providers in the future, such as Active Directory federation, with on-premises AD servers, Google ID, Yahoo, Facebook, and so on. This chapter primarily focuses on the on-premises version of Team Foundation Server and may not be completely applicable to the Visual Studio Online Service.*

Service Accounts

A *service account* is nothing more than just another domain user. The main difference is that a domain user is usually a real person. A service account is a domain account created and used specifically to run a Windows service or other application.

It's generally considered a bad practice to run services as accounts that real people use for their day-to-day work. A service account usually has elevated privileges compared to a normal user. For this reason, the service account passwords are often randomly generated strong passwords, and they are kept a closely guarded secret by the owners.

Machine Accounts

Three accounts are built into a Windows computer:

➤ `Local System`

➤ `Local Service`

➤ `Network Service`

The first two accounts cannot be used to authenticate to other computers. `Local System` is an administrator on the system. `Local Service` has limited privileges, and it is designed for running Windows services. Similarly, `Network Service` has limited local privileges. However, it is capable of connecting to other computers on the domain.

When a computer is joined to a domain, a trust relationship is established between the computer and the domain. Once this trust is established, the computer is essentially under the control of the domain. This allows domain policies to be applied and enforced from the central directory service.

When the domain join occurs, a special domain account called a *machine account* is created with an automatically generated password. As long as the computer remains in contact with the domain, this password will change periodically, and the trust relationship will remain. If the computer does not connect to the domain controller for a period of time, the account will be disabled, and the trust relationship will be voided.

A machine account is represented as a domain user followed by $ in its account name, as shown in the following example:

```
MYDOMAIN\MYCOMPUTER$
```

To give the `Network Service` account permissions on the machine itself, you can use either the `Network Service` account or the machine account. To give the `Network Service` account permissions on a remote resource, you must use the machine account.

Local Users

If you install Team Foundation Server on a computer that isn't joined to a domain, it is considered to be running in *workgroup mode*. In workgroup mode, there is no domain, so the only users that exist are users on that local computer. These users are called *local users*.

Even if your computer is installed on a domain, you can still have local users. However, these local users cannot be added to domain groups or used for authenticating to other computers in the domain.

> **SHADOW ACCOUNTS**
>
> If you have computers in different domains, or computers that are not part of any domain, there are cases where you want to be able to authenticate between them. When connecting to a remote machine, normally you must provide a user name and password to an account on that machine.
>
> There is a trick called "shadow accounts" that you can use to avoid being prompted for credentials. To use shadow accounts, you establish a local account on both machines with a matching user name and password. When the user from one machine tries to connect to the other machine, the account first tries to connect using the current user name and password. Because the user names and passwords match on both machines, this works without prompting for credentials.

Identity Synchronization

Team Foundation Server synchronizes some properties of every user that is a member of a group in the system. This is so that domain group membership changes are reflected in the system, and other property changes (such as display names and e-mail addresses) are kept up to date.

Identity Synchronization Job

The Team Foundation Background job agent on each application tier server periodically executes the Identity Synchronization job. By default, it runs once per hour, and it is also triggered when a new domain group is added to Team Foundation Server.

The job agent runs as the Team Foundation Server service account. This will be either a domain user, `Network Service`, or a local user (in the case of a server running in workgroup mode).

Domains and Trusts

Because the Identity Synchronization job runs on the job agent, it accesses Active Directory using these credentials. If the appropriate domain trusts aren't in place, or the account doesn't have permissions to list users in the directory, those users will not be able to access Team Foundation Server. There are lots of different permutations on domain topologies, firewalls, and trust relationships.

> **NOTE** *For more information on what is supported by Team Foundation Server, see "Trusts and Forests Considerations for Team Foundation Server" at* `http://aka.ms/TFSADTrusts.`

Handling Display Name Changes

One of the big changes introduced in Team Foundation Server 2010 was server updates to your display name when it changed in AD. This is a fairly common scenario, similar to when people get married and change their names from their maiden names to married names.

In Team Foundation Server 2008, even though the change was made in AD, Team Foundation Server would keep using the old name. In all Team Foundation Server versions after 2008, the change is detected as part of the identity synchronization job and updated throughout the environment.

Display Name Disambiguation

Another change introduced in Team Foundation Server 2010 was something called *display name disambiguation*. In the 2008 version, if you had two different user accounts with the same display name, that display name would show only once in people fields such as the "Assigned To" field. There was no way to distinguish which user account was actually being referred to. Some people tried to solve this by changing the display name of one of the users in AD, but without the previously mentioned display name changes detection feature, this did not solve the problem.

With the disambiguation feature, if two user accounts with the same display name exist within the same team project collection, the identity synchronization job will append the domain and account name to the end. For example, imagine two users that have the same display name John Smith. One user's account is MYDOMAIN\JSmith, and the other user's account is MYDOMAIN\JohnS. Team Foundation Server 2013 will disambiguate these and show them as two separate entries in the "Assigned To" field, as shown here:

➤ John Smith (MYDOMAIN\JSmith)

➤ John Smith (MYDOMAIN\JohnS)

In a large organization where you have many domains and trusts, sometimes a user will be moved to or re-created in a different domain. Think of the example where someone moves from a position in Australia to a position in Seattle, and the organization has an AD domain for each region.

If both users still exist (whether disabled or not) and continue to be members of a group in Team Foundation Server, this will also be disambiguated to the following:

➤   John Smith (AUSTRALIA\JSmith)

➤   John Smith (USA\JSmith)

If you want to remove this artifact of disambiguation in the display name, you have two options:

➤   Change the display name of one of the users in AD.

➤   Remove one of the users from all groups in that team project collection and remove all of the individual security access grants that exist in each of the team project collection(s).

> **NOTE** *If you find yourself in the latter situation, it may be helpful to open a Microsoft product support case to assist with finding all of the artifacts and security permission entries that Team Foundation Server is using to keep the account active in its identity cache. The product support team can assist with removing everything that would cause the disambiguation to occur.*

Customizing Display Name Options and Alias Mode

Some organizations don't set the display name field in AD to a useful value. Instead, they use it to store an employee ID or something like that. In these environments, it's not very easy to run a work item tracking query looking for bugs assigned to `Grant Holliday` when you have to specify it as assigned to `GH31337`. Additionally, this becomes more important in Team Foundation Server 2012 because the display name is used in additional locations such as in the build system and in version control.

Fortunately, there are two options for customizing the user's display name. The first and preferred option is that each team member can log in to Team Web Access and customize their display name, e-mail address, and other preferences in the Manage Profile dialog box available by clicking on the user's name in the upper-right corner of any Team Web Access page. This is actually the primary method for display name updates when using the Team Foundation Service because the Identity Synchronization service does not import a display name with Windows Live ID accounts.

The second option is a privately supported feature called *alias mode*. When this feature is enabled, Team Foundation Server will use the user name for the "Assigned To" field instead of the display name. Of course, this is not useful if your account name is also meaningless, but it is useful in some environments. To enable alias mode, you will need to contact Microsoft Support. It also must be done before you install Team Foundation Server for the first time.

GROUPS

Another Team Foundation Server security concept that you should be familiar with involves the use of different types of groups. These include:

- ➤ Domain groups
- ➤ Distribution groups
- ➤ Local groups
- ➤ Team Foundation Server groups

Domain Groups

Like domain users, *domain groups* are groups that exist in AD. Sometimes they are also referred to as *security groups*. They can contain other domain users, groups, and machine accounts.

Distribution Groups

In an AD environment that also has Microsoft Exchange mail configured, you can create *distribution groups*. These distribution groups can be used to send mail to a list of recipients.

Distribution groups cannot be used to secure resources; only domain groups can be used for that. If you want a group that can be used to secure resources as well as receive mail, you can have a *mail-enabled security group*.

Local Groups

Like local users, *local groups* exist only on a single machine. These can be used only to secure resources that exist on that machine. One feature of local groups is that they can contain domain users and groups as members.

This is useful, for example, if you want to allow administrative access to your machine to members of a domain group. You can add a domain group called MYDOMAIN\MyGroup to the BUILTIN\ Administrators local group on your computer.

Team Foundation Server Groups

Team Foundation Server also has its own application group structure. There are groups at three different levels within the system:

- ➤ Server groups
- ➤ Team project collection groups
- ➤ Team project groups

Server Groups

The default server groups (as shown in Table 24-1) have hard-coded names that cannot be changed or removed from the server. To modify the group memberships or permissions of server groups, you will need to use the Team Foundation Server Administration Console or the TFSSecurity.exe command-line tool.

TABLE 24-1: Built-In Team Foundation Server Groups

GROUP NAME	GROUP DESCRIPTION	GROUP MEMBERS
Team Foundation Administrators	Members of this group can perform all operations on the Team Foundation Application Instance.	By default, this group contains the Local Administrators group (`BUILTIN\ Administrators`) for any server that hosts the application services for Team Foundation Server. This group also contains the members of the Service Accounts server group.
Team Foundation Proxy Service Accounts	This group should include only service accounts used by Team Foundation Server Proxy.	No group members included by default
Team Foundation Service Accounts	Members of this group have service-level permissions for the Team Foundation Application Instance. This is for service accounts only.	This group contains the service account that the server is currently running as. If you find that this group includes personal user accounts, you should remove them because those users will have a degraded experience in Team Foundation Server 2013 in areas such as e-mail alerts management/ownership. If you need to remove user accounts, you can use this blog post for instructions: `http://aka.ms/ TFSRemoveFromServiceAccountGroup.`
Team Foundation Valid Users	Members of this group have access to the Team Foundation Application Instance.	Members of this group have access to Team Foundation Server. This group automatically contains all users and groups that have been added anywhere within Team Foundation Server. You cannot modify the membership of this group.
SharePoint Web Application Services	This application group should contain service accounts only for SharePoint web applications.	If your Team Foundation Server is configured for integration with SharePoint Products, the SharePoint Web Application service account will be a member.
Project Server Integration Service Accounts	Members of this group have service-level permissions for Project Server Integration. It is for service accounts only.	No group members included by default

Team Project Collection Groups

The default team project collection groups are created as part of the collection-creation process. Table 24-2 shows each of the groups and their members.

TABLE 24-2: Default Team Project Collection Groups

GROUP NAME	GROUP DESCRIPTION	GROUP MEMBERS
Project Collection Administrators	Members of this application group can perform all privileged operations on the team project collection.	By default, this group contains the Team Foundation Administrators server group. It also contains the Project Collection Service Accounts group and the user who created the team project collection.
Project Collection Build Administrators	Members of this group should include accounts for people to able to administer the build resources.	No group members included by default
Project Collection Build Service Accounts	Members of this group should include the service accounts used by the build services set up for this project collection.	No group members included by default
Project Collection Proxy Service Accounts	This group should include only service accounts used by proxies set up for this team project collection.	This group contains the Team Foundation Proxy Service Accounts server group. This allows a proxy server access to all collections in an environment. If you find that this group includes personal user accounts, you should remove them because those users will have a degraded experience in Team Foundation Server 2013 in areas such as e-mail alerts management and ownership. If you need to remove user accounts, you can use this blog post for instructions: `http://aka.ms / TFSRemoveFromServiceAccountGroup`.
Project Collection Service Accounts	This application group contains Team Project Collection service accounts.	This group contains the Team Foundation Service Accounts server group.

continues

TABLE 24-2 *(continued)*

GROUP NAME	GROUP DESCRIPTION	GROUP MEMBERS
Project Collection Test Service Accounts	Members of this group should include the service accounts used by the test controllers set up for this project collection.	
Project Collection Valid Users	This application group contains all users and groups that have access to the team project collection.	This group automatically contains all users and groups that have been added anywhere within the team project collection. You cannot modify the membership of this group.

To modify a team project collection group's memberships or permissions, you can use the Team Foundation Server Administration Console, Visual Studio Team Web Access, or the TFSSecurity .exe command-line tool.

Team Project Groups

Team project groups are initially defined in the process template and created as part of the team project creation wizard. Table 24-3 shows the default groups included with the Microsoft Solutions Framework (MSF) for Agile Software Development and MSF for Capability Maturity Model Integration (CMMI) Process Improvement process templates. You may additionally create security groups or use the team project groups created when defining teams to further define security inside a team project.

TABLE 22-3: Default Team Project Groups

GROUP NAME	GROUP DESCRIPTION	GROUP MEMBERS
Builder Administrators	Members of this group can create, modify, and delete build definitions, as well as manage queued and completed builds.	No group members included by default
Contributors	Members of this group can add, modify, and delete items within the team project.	No group members included by default
Project Administrators	Members of this group can perform all operations in the team project.	The user who created the team project
Readers	Members of this group have access to the team project.	No group members included by default

PERMISSIONS

Rather than providing a listing of the more than 80 different permissions available in Team Foundation Server, this section focuses on the permissions that are new in the 2013 version, or are otherwise ambiguous or interesting. In particular, this discussion examines the following:

➤ Server permissions

➤ Team project collection permissions

➤ Team project permissions

➤ Team Room permissions

> **NOTE** *For a comprehensive list of all the permissions available, refer to "Team Foundation Server Default Groups, Permissions, and Roles" at* `http://aka.ms/ TFSDefaultSecurity`.

Server Permissions

The Team Foundation Administrators group, along with the Team Foundation Service Accounts group, has hard-coded permissions. This is to prevent an administrator from being inadvertently locked out of the system. Table 24-4 shows some of the interesting server-level permissions.

TABLE 24-4: Server Permissions

PERMISSION NAME	COMMAND-LINE NAME	DESCRIPTION
Make requests on behalf of others	Impersonate	Users who have this permission can perform operations on behalf of other users or services.
Edit instance-level information	GENERIC _WRITE	Users with this permission can start and stop a collection, edit the description, manage the group memberships, and manage the permissions for users and groups in a collection. It's a powerful permission.
Use full Web Access features	FullAccess	Users who have this permission can use all of the features of Team Web Access. If this permission is set to Deny, the user will see only those features permitted for the Limited group in Team Web. A Deny will override any implicit Allow, even for accounts that are members of administrative groups such as Team Foundation Administrators.
View instance-level information	GENERIC _READ	Users who have this permission can view server-level group membership and the permissions of those users.

Team Project Collection Permissions

Most of the permissions that used to be at the server level in Team Foundation Server 2008 have been moved to the team project collection level in Team Foundation Server 2010 to 2013. This is useful when you have many collections running on a single consolidated and shared server instance. In this kind of environment, you can delegate permissions that allow someone to create team projects within a collection without having to grant them full server administrator rights.

Table 24-5 shows some of the permissions available at the collection level.

TABLE 24-5: Team Project Collection Permissions

PERMISSION NAME	COMMAND-LINE NAME	DESCRIPTION
Edit collection-level information	GENERIC_WRITE	Users who have this permission can edit collection-level permissions for users and groups in the team project collection. They can add or remove collection-level Team Foundation Server application groups from the collection.
View collection-level information	GENERIC_READ	Users who have this permission can view collection-level group membership and the permissions of those users.
Manage build resources	ManageBuildResources	Users who have this permission can manage the build computers, build agents, and build controllers for the team project collection. These users can also grant or deny the "View build resources" and "Use build resources" permissions for other users.
Use build resources	UseBuildResources	Users who have this permission can reserve and allocate build agents. This permission should be assigned only to service accounts for build services.
View build resources	ViewBuildResources	Users who have this permission can view build controllers and build agents configured for the collection. To use these resources, you need additional permissions.

Manage test controllers	MANAGE_TEST_CONTROLLERS	Users who have this permission can register and de-register test controllers for the team project collection.
Manage work item link types	WORK_ITEM_WRITE	Users who have this permission can add, remove, and change the types of links for work items.
Administer Project Server integration	AdministerProjectserver	Users who have this permission can configure the integration of Team Foundation Server with Project Server to support synchronization between the two server products.
Alter trace settings	DIAGNOSTIC_TRACE	Users who have this permission can change the trace settings for gathering more detailed diagnostic information about Web Services for Team Foundation Server.

The `ManageBuildResources` permission can cause some angst for organizations using Team Foundation Build. There are three problems with this permission:

➤ It is very broad and powerful.

➤ It is required to be able to connect a build agent to a collection.

➤ When you configure a build server, if you do not have the "Edit collection-level information" permission, configuration will fail.

These three problems work against each other when you want to allow people to run their own build agents without making everybody a project collection administrator.

Fortunately, there is a reasonable solution. Before anyone runs the Team Foundation Build configuration wizard, the service account they want to run the build service as can be added to the Project Collection Build Services group. This avoids the second and third problems.

If you force people to use `Network Service` or a service account as the account for their build service, you can avoid the problem of having normal user accounts as project collection administrators.

Team Project Permissions

As shown in Table 24-6, Team Foundation Server 2010 introduced several new team project level permissions that control access to some of the Microsoft Test Manager assets.

TABLE 24-6: Team Project Permissions

PERMISSION NAME	COMMAND-LINE NAME	DESCRIPTION
Create test runs	PUBLISH_TEST_RESULTS	Users who have this permission can add and remove test results, as well as add or modify test runs for the team project.
Delete test runs	DELETE_TEST_RESULTS	Users who have this permission can delete a scheduled test for this team project.
Manage test configurations	MANAGE_TEST_CONFIGURATIONS	Users who have this permission can create and delete test configurations for this team project.
Manage test environments	MANAGE_TEST_ENVIRONMENTS	Users who have this permission can create and delete test environments for this team project.
View test runs	VIEW_TEST_RESULTS	Users who have this permission can view test plans in this node.
Delete team project	DELETE	Users who have this permission can delete from Team Foundation Server the project for which they have this permission.
Edit project-level information	GENERIC_WRITE	Users who have this permission can edit project-level permissions for users and groups on Team Foundation Server.
View project-level information	GENERIC_READ	Users who have this permission can view project-level group membership and the permissions of those project users.

Let's take a closer look at a couple of these permissions.

View Project-Level Information

When users have the "View project-level information" permission, they are able to see that the project exists in the collection, as well as list the project's group memberships and permissions. Before Team Foundation Server 2010, the Valid Users group was given this permission for every team project by default. This meant that users could see all the projects that existed on a server. It also made the list of projects in the team project connect dialog box quite long on a server with many projects.

Starting in the 2010 version, this was no longer the case. However, if your server was upgraded from an earlier version, these permissions will still exist. If you want to trim down the projects that users see when they connect to the server, you can remove this permission for them.

Edit Project-Level Information

The "Edit project-level information" permission is also very generic, and it's not very clear from the name what a user with this permission can do. To clarify, a user with this permission can do the following:

➤ Edit areas and iterations.

➤ Change the version control check-in policies enabled for a project.

➤ Create and modify team queries, team query folders (discussed later in this chapter), and the team query folder permissions.

➤ Modify group memberships and project-level permissions.

Work Item Tracking

Within the work item tracking components of Team Foundation Server are three different sets of permissions that can be managed. There are permissions on the following:

➤ Areas

➤ Iterations

➤ Team query folders

Areas

Area path permissions can be applied to any node in the tree. The permissions on a parent node can be inherited by the child nodes if inheritance is enabled. The available permissions fall into two categories:

➤ Permissions to modify work items *in* area paths

➤ Permissions to modify the area paths *themselves*

The permissions shown in Table 24-7 are particularly interesting because they can be used to hide or lock down parts of the tree for different sets of users.

TABLE 24-7: Selected Area Level Permissions

PERMISSION NAME	COMMAND-LINE NAME	DESCRIPTION
Edit work items in this node	WORK_ITEM_WRITE	Users who have this permission can edit work items in this area node.
View work items in this node	WORK_ITEM_READ	Users who have this permission can view, but not change, work items in this area node.

For example, say you had a large team project that your whole organization or product engineering department shared. You might do this if you wanted to do all work with one set of work items, instead of having projects in silos. If there was a super-secret product that a team was working on, and you didn't want anyone else in the organization to see those work items, you could remove the "View work items in this node" permission.

Another example might be a change request area path. Your team could have a set of area paths, and one of those area paths could be called \Change Requests. You could configure the permissions so that anyone on the server could create a work item in just that area path.

Iterations

The permissions for iterations are much the same as those for area paths. The notable difference though is the lack of the "View work items in this node" and "Edit work items in this node" permissions. This means that you cannot control who can move work items into iteration paths. You can control modifications only to the iteration path structure itself.

Team Query Folders

Team query folders is a new feature introduced in Team Foundation Server 2010. Before these folders, you could have only a flat list of queries. Some people tried to work around this by coming up with elaborate naming schemes. Others used a SharePoint document library with folders and *.WIQ files in each folder to achieve the same thing.

Team query folders were actually available before 2010 on an internal release of Team Foundation Server built especially for the Windows and Office organizations at Microsoft. The feedback from teams using the folders was that there needed to be permissions on them. Because of this feedback, the team added the permissions shown in Table 24-8 before including the feature in the final Team Foundation Server 2010 release.

TABLE 24-8: Team Query Folder Permissions

PERMISSION NAME	DESCRIPTION
Read	View this folder and its contents.
Contribute	View and edit this folder and its contents.
Delete	View, edit, and delete this folder and its contents.
Manage Permissions	Manage permissions for this folder and its contents.

Team Web Access and Licensing Access Levels

The legacy Work Item Only View (WIOV) feature allows users in your organization to create and view work items *that they created* in Team Web Access without having a client access license (CAL). This is useful if you want to allow others to log bugs or feature requests for your product directly into Team Foundation Server.

> **NOTE** *For more information, see the latest version of the "Visual Studio Licensing White Paper" at* http://aka.ms/VisualStudioLicensing. *This licensing white paper is updated regularly.*

BYPASS RULES AND THE FORCING ROLLBACK ERROR

Team Foundation Server has a `ClientService.asmx` web service. This is the same web service that the Team Foundation object model uses.

If you are migrating work items from another system, you will likely need to save work items with invalid values. Team Foundation Server provides a mechanism for doing this, which is commonly called *Bypass Rules*.

By calling the web service directly from your own code (which is not recommended), you can set the `BypassRules` flag and submit an XML package that includes the values that you want to set. Only members of the Project Collection Service Accounts group are able to use this functionality because it can put a work item into an invalid state.

If you try to use this functionality and the account is not in the correct group, you'll receive a very cryptic `SoapException`:

```
Forcing rollback ---> Forcing rollback ---> Forcing rollback
```

This indicates that SQL was trying to apply your changes but found that you didn't have the required permissions.

There is an administration page in Team Web Access that was introduced in Team Foundation Server 2012 to help assist with the management of different features available to end users in Team Web Access, as shown in Figure 24-1. This tab is labeled "Access Levels." Users can be a member of the following groups:

➤ Limited

➤ Standard

➤ Full

The *Limited* access level allows user access similar to the legacy Work Item Only View feature. It allows them to view work items and is perfect for those users who do not have a CAL for Team Foundation Server. However, it does not provide them with the security rights necessary to perform these activities, so be sure to also add these users to either the Contributors default security group for projects or enable the "View work items in this node" and "Edit work items in this node" permissions. This access level also enables users to submit feedback using the new Feedback Client, as you learned in Chapter 14.

The great thing about this Limited access level is that you can create a linked work item from a bug submitted by an end user. The end user cannot see the linked work item and the discussion that happens for that linked bug. When the work is complete and the original bug is resolved, the end user can see that his or her feedback was addressed.

The *Standard* access level is designed for those users who have an individual Team Foundation Server CAL or for Visual Studio Professional with MSDN users. The members of this group will additionally have the standard Web Access features as well as the Agile Task Boards, Backlog and Sprint planning tools, and Chart viewing available to them. For upgraded or brand new instances of Team Foundation Server 2013, this is the default group for all users, as shown in Figure 24-1.

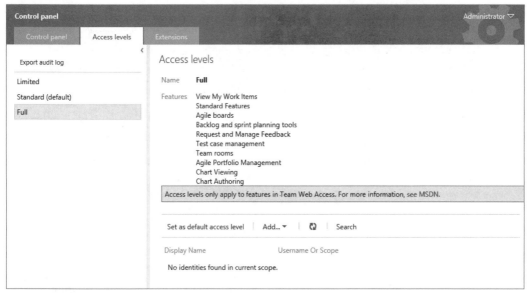

FIGURE 24-1: New feature access administration page.

The *Full* access level is designed for those users that have any of the higher editions of Visual Studio such as the following:

➤ Visual Studio Test Professional 2013 with MSDN

➤ Visual Studio Premium 2013 with MSDN

➤ Visual Studio Ultimate 2013 with MSDN

The members of the Full access level receive all of the features in the Limited and Standard groups but are also able to use the web-based Test Management features, Team rooms, and Agile Portfolio Management tools, and will be able to create Charts for their teams.

Because the *Standard* access level is the default group, you will want to be sure to add any users with a higher edition of the Visual Studio products to the Full group because they will not see the advanced features of Team Web Access until that happens.

To assist organizations with ensuring license compliance, there is also an Export Audit Log feature from this page that will allow you to generate an Excel workbook that contains all of the users and their relevant licensing access to features.

Version Control Permissions

When we discuss Version Control Permissions here, we are talking about the centralized version control system that has been part of the system since Team Foundation Server 2005. These permissions haven't changed significantly since Team Foundation Server 2010, when the branching and merging permissions were separated from the check-in permission. This can be seen in Table 24-9. The Git (distributed version control) permissions will be discussed in the section "Managing Git Repository Security."

TABLE 24-9: New and Interesting Version Control Permissions

PERMISSION NAME	COMMAND-LINE NAME	DESCRIPTION
Merge	tf: Merge	Users who have this permission for a given path can merge changes into this path.
Manage branch	tf: ManageBranch	Users who have this permission for a given path can convert any folder under that path into a branch. Users with this permission can also take the following actions on a branch: Edit its properties, re-parent it, and convert it to a folder. Users who have this permission can branch this only if they also have the Merge permission for the target path. Users cannot create branches from a branch for which they do not have the "Manage branch" permission.
Check in other users' changes	tf: CheckinOther	Users who have this permission can check in changes that were made by other users. Pending changes will be committed at check-in.

When your server is upgraded from the 2008 version to the 2010 or higher versions, folders that were branches are detected and automatically converted to real branches. If you previously had `Read` and `CheckIn` permissions on that folder, you are grandfathered in and given the `Merge` and `ManageBranch` permissions.

CHECK-IN ON BEHALF OF ANOTHER USER

In some scenarios, you may want to check in some changes using one account but record that another user actually made the changes. An example of this is a shared workstation used for generating hotfixes. Each user would log on to the machine and access the server using a shared user name. Then, after the user makes the fix, he or she checks it in and specifies that his or her user name is the actual author of the change.

To do this, you must specify the `/author` flag on the `TF.exe checkin` command line:

```
C:\Code\MyProject> tf checkin * /author:jsmith
Checking in add: MyFolder

Changeset #11 checked in.
```

If you want to see who checked in a changeset on behalf of another user, unfortunately, you will have to use the command-line tools. To do this, specify the `/noprompt` flag on the `TF.exe changeset` command:

```
C:\Code\MyProject> tf changeset 11 /noprompt
Changeset: 11
User: jsmith
Checked in by: Administrator
```

Check-In Policies

The check-in policy settings for a team project are stored as a version control annotation. Annotations aren't part of the public API and, in Team Foundation Server 2013, are superseded by the Properties API. Annotations are like properties in that they are extra metadata attached to a particular path in version control.

Because the annotation is on the root version control folder for each team project, users will need at least Read permissions on that folder. Without this permission, they will get an error message similar to "$/MyProject does not exist or you don't have access to it." This can be quite confusing when the user is trying to check in to some other path that the user actually does have permission to.

Branching and Permissions

When you branch a folder, the permissions from the source folder are copied to the target. In most cases, this is acceptable. However, there are other cases (such as when creating a maintenance or release branch) that you don't want to copy the permissions to. In these cases, you'll have to lock down the permissions after creating the branch. Then, as people need to check in patches, you can grant them the PendChange and Checkin permissions.

The reverse is also true. For example, your Main branch might have very restrictive permissions to prevent people from making changes directly. When you create a branch of Main, those restrictive permissions will also be copied. In this case, you'll have to add the extra permissions after creating the branch.

HOW TO UNDO CHANGES FROM ANOTHER USER

A very common question on the support forums and e-mail lists concerns when someone has a set of files checked out and locked, and the person goes on vacation or is otherwise unavailable. Until these locks are removed, no one else can check in these files.

Fortunately, it's fairly simple for someone with the "Administer workspaces" permission to undo changes for another user.

One option is to use the TF.exe command-line tool, as shown here:

```
tf undo "$/MyProject/VersionX/Utils/file.cs"
     /workspace:MyWorkspace;Domain\User
     /collection:http://server:8080/tfs/Collection
     /recursive
```

Another option is to use the Team Foundation Power Tools. Follow these steps:

1. Open Source Control Explorer.

2. Right-click the item on which check-out is to be undone (or a parent folder of multiple files to be undone).

3. Select Find in Source Control ⇨ Status.

4. In the Find in Source Control dialog box, leave the Status check box selected.

5. Optionally, enter a value for the Wildcard text box.

6. Optionally, enter a user name in the "Display files checked out to" text box and select that radio button.

7. Click Find. This will result in a list of files.

8. Select the items to undo.

9. Right-click and select Undo.

10. Click Yes when prompted with "Undo all selected changes?"

Destroy

When you delete a file in version control, it is just a "soft" delete. The file contents and all the previous revisions still exist, and anyone with Read permissions can still retrieve the file or undelete it.

To permanently delete a file from version control and remove all previous versions of it, you can use the TF.exe destroy command. Because this is a potentially very destructive operation, you must be a member of the Team Foundation Administrators server group.

Once a file is destroyed, the only way to recover it is to restore a backup of your server to a previous point in time. Each time a file is destroyed, a message is logged to the Application event log on the application tier that the destroy command ran on.

Managing Git Repository Security

Team Foundation Server 2013 introduced the ability to use the Git distributed version control repository instead of the standard centralized version control repository that has shipped with every version of the product. Git does not define any access control whatsoever but relies on third-party add-ins or the underlying storage and transport mechanisms to enforce read-only or read-write permissions.

The Visual Studio team has had a goal of providing an enterprise-grade Git solution. To support that goal, the team has provided a permission set that is specific to Git repositories hosted in Team Foundation Server.

The most notable permissions are around branch-level permissions. These give you the ability to control who has the capability to push certain branches to the server. With this model, team members still have full control over their local Git repositories while providing the Team Foundation Server administrators with a level of control over the central server.

Table 24-10 lists the permissions available when using a Git version control repository with Team Foundation Server.

TABLE 24-10: Git Repository Permissions

PERMISSION NAME	COMMAND-LINE NAME	DESCRIPTION
Contribute to the Git repository	CONTRIBUTE	Enables users to push their changes to the repository
Allow force pushes in the Git repository	FORCE	Enables users to force an update, which can overwrite or discard commits from any user. Deleting commits changes the history. Without this permission, users cannot discard their own changes. Allow Force is also required to delete a branch
Administer the Git repository	ADMINISTER	Enables users to rename or delete the repository, add additional repositories, and verify the database
Read the Git Repository	READ	Enables users to clone, fetch, pull, and explore the contents of the repository, but cannot push any changes they make to the repository
Branch Creation	BRANCH	Enables users to create branches in the repository
Note Management	NOTE	Enables users to append additional messages to existing commits without changing the original commit message or checksum
Tag Creation	TAG	Enables users to apply tags to points in the Git repository history

When you compare the permission set for a Git repository against the permission set for a standard, centralized version control repository, you can see that the Visual Studio team wanted to provide enough control over the "central" Git repository that enterprises need without impeding the usage patterns that Git users have come to rely on.

> **NOTE** *Be aware that the Allow Force pushes in the Git repository permission will allow users to change the history or remove a commit from history. Any users given this permission will be able to delete a change and its history from the server. They can also modify the commit history of the server repository.*

Build Permissions

Teams are also able to provide for permissions at the build definition level. Some of the more interesting permissions available are listed in Table 24-11.

TABLE 24-11: New and Interesting Build Permissions

PERMISSION NAME	COMMAND-LINE NAME	DESCRIPTION
Retain indefinitely	RetainIndefinitely	Users who have this permission can mark a build so that it will not be automatically deleted by any applicable retention policy.
Delete builds	DeleteBuilds	Users who have this permission can delete a completed build.
Queue build	QueueBuilds	Users who have this permission can put a build in the queue through the interface for Team Foundation Build (Web Access or Team Explorer) or at a command prompt. They can also stop the builds that they have queued.
Edit build definition	EditBuildDefinition	Users who have this permission can create and modify specific build definitions for this project.
Override check-in validation by build	OverrideBuildCheckInValidation	Users who have this permission can commit a changeset that affects a gated build definition without triggering the system to shelve and build their changes first.

Reporting

By default, users do not have access to query the relational warehouse database or the Analysis Services cube. If you want to allow users to use the Excel reporting features of Team Foundation Server, you must grant them access to at least the Analysis Services cube.

The Analysis Services cube contains aggregated and summarized data from all team projects in all team project collections in an environment. There is no security filtering based on your permissions within Team Foundation Server. If a user has Read access to the cube, then that user can query the summarized data from all projects. If this is a concern for you, you may want to consider limiting the users who have access to the cube and its data.

If you have a more relaxed security policy, and all users can see all work items, you should consider giving all users access to the warehouse and cube. This will allow them to leverage the useful metrics that the data warehouse provides. To do this, you must add the users (or a security group) to the roles shown in Table 24-12.

TABLE 24-12: Team Foundation Server Reporting Roles

COMPONENT	DATABASE NAME	ROLE
Relational warehouse database	Tfs_Warehouse	TfsWarehouseDataReader
Analysis Services cube	Tfs_Analysis	TfsWarehouseDataReader

For more information, see the following articles on MSDN:

➤ "Grant Access to the Databases of the Data Warehouse for Visual Studio ALM" at `http://aka.ms/TFSGrantWarehouseAccess`

➤ "Assigning Permissions to View and Manage Reports for Visual Studio ALM" at `http://aka.ms/TFSReportsPermissions`

SECURITY MANAGEMENT

If you ever have to manage security and permissions in a Team Foundation Server environment, you'll want to follow a few general principles.

Deny, Allow, and Unset Permissions

A deny permission takes precedence over all other permission settings, including an allow permission. Consider the example where a user is a member of two groups. One group has a permission set to deny, and the other group has the same permission set to allow. In this case, the user will be denied that permission.

Because the deny permission takes precedence, a common practice is to not set any explicit permissions. If permissions are neither set to allow nor deny, an implicit permission of deny is applied. This setting is referred to as "unset." This allows the user to gain that permission by inclusion in another group that has an allow for that permission.

> **NOTE** *For more information, see "Team Foundation Server Permissions" at* `http://aka.ms/TFSPermissions`.

Use Active Directory Groups

Before Team Foundation Server is introduced into an organization, there is usually a process (whether formal or informal) whereby people can be given access to different network resources. The easiest way to manage this is by creating security groups in AD and applying the permissions to the group.

Some organizations have self-service tools with built-in approval processes that allow users to join groups. One such example of a product that provides this service is Microsoft Forefront Identity Manager.

Some organizations have Help Desk processes that allow people to join groups. The Help Desk staff has training in the AD tools, and it can move users in and out of groups.

As discussed earlier, Team Foundation Server has its own concept of groups and tools for managing those groups. A lot of organizations keep the Team Foundation Server groups very simple and put a single AD group in each of them. This allows the existing group management processes to be used without having to train people on how Team Foundation Server groups work.

Avoid Granting Individual User Permissions

To make permission and security management easier, you should avoid setting explicit user permissions. Instead, identify the role of the user and create a group for that role. Then apply permissions to the role.

With this process, it's much easier to give other people the same permissions. For example, when someone changes roles within the organization or gets a promotion, that person can easily be added to the "Branch Admins" or "Build Masters" group to provide the required access for his or her new responsibilities.

With that said, though, you want to avoid a proliferation of groups and nesting of groups. If you want to find out how a user has access to a file, you don't want to be hunting through five different nested groups. Keep the nesting shallow.

Additionally, the teams you create in Team Foundation Server 2013 can also serve as team project groups for granting and managing security access.

Use Inheritance

Where possible, you should set permissions at a high level, and enable inheritance for the sub-items. This is especially true for version control because the files in every command must have their security permissions checked.

If you have many individually set permissions throughout your version control tree, that means lots of work for the application tier to validate them and trim the results. You will see increased CPU load on your application tiers and sometimes poor response times. By setting permissions higher in the tree, they can be cached and files can be transferred with very little overhead. You will see similar performance degradation each time you break the inheritance lower in the tree or when you use deny grants.

TOOLS

People use a few tools to manage permissions in Team Foundation Server. Visual Studio Team Explorer and the Team Foundation Server Administration Console are the most common. If you do a lot of security management in Team Foundation Server, you will want to become familiar with the command-line tools.

`TFSSecurity.exe` is included with a Visual Studio Team Explorer installation. If you're comfortable with the command line, you'll find it to be a very powerful tool that is much faster than clicking through menus and dialog boxes in Visual Studio.

Perhaps the most useful application of this tool is the `/imx` command. Using this option, you can list the expanded group memberships of any user or group within the system. This is great for working out how a user is nested in a group.

To run the command, you must specify a server to run it against and a user or group to look up.

```
TFSSecurity.exe /collection:http://server:8080/tfs/Collection
    /imx n:DOMAIN\user
```

You can also use the tool with the `/g+` command to add team project groups to server groups, which is something that you cannot do through Visual Studio.

> **NOTE** *For more information, see "Changing Groups and Permissions with TFSSecurity" at* `http://aka.ms/TFSSecurityTool`*.*

`TFSSecurity.exe` is not the only tool. Table 24-13 shows some other included command-line tools.

TABLE 24-13: Other Command-Line Tools

TOOL NAME	MORE INFORMATION
TF.exe Permission	`http://aka.ms/TFPermission`
TFSLabConfig.exe Permissions	`http://aka.ms/TFSLabConfigPermissions`

SUMMARY

This chapter started with an overview of the security model used in Visual Studio Online as well as different types of users and groups that you'll encounter when managing a Team Foundation Server 2013 environment. Following this, you caught a glimpse into some of the new and interesting permissions available in Team Foundation Server. Some ambiguous permissions purposes were also clarified.

After taking a look at the different parts that make up security, the rest of the chapter covered some tips for managing security, along with some tools to make things easier, such as the Team Foundation Server Administration Tool.

Chapter 25 covers all things related to monitoring the server health and reporting on the performance of Team Foundation Server. The chapter will introduce you to the Best Practices Analyzer and the System Center Operations Manager management pack. It will also cover some of the rich activity logging details that the server collects over time.

25
Monitoring Server Health and Performance

WHAT'S IN THIS CHAPTER?

➤ Understanding factors that affect Team Foundation Server health

➤ Monitoring SQL Server health

➤ Learning useful queries for investigating SQL Server performance

➤ Learning about data sources available for monitoring Team Foundation Server

➤ New diagnostics and monitoring functionality in Team Foundation Server 2013

➤ Using valuable tools and reports

The health of a Team Foundation Server can be broken down into three components:

➤ System health

➤ SQL Server health

➤ Team Foundation Server health

The health and performance of Team Foundation Server is largely dependent upon the health and performance of the underlying components. For example, if the storage subsystem is not performing well, then SQL Server performance will likely suffer and, in turn, affect the performance of Team Foundation Server commands.

This chapter provides an overview of how you can monitor the health and performance of Team Foundation Server.

> **NOTE** *While Team Foundation Server was being developed, the entire Developer Division at Microsoft (approximately 3,000 users) started using the server as its primary source control and bug-tracking system. This onboarding process continued through the 2008 release, and the overall size and usage of the server increased. As more teams were moved onto the server, performance issues with the application were identified and fixed.*
>
> *Because of this aggressive internal usage over an extended time period, the 2010 release was highly tuned based upon real-world usage, rather than synthetic load tests. In the 2012 release cycle, the Visual Studio Online service was brought online. Additional performance bottlenecks were identified and fixed through its preview period. This level of tuning continued throughout the development of the 2013 release and it means that, in most cases, the cause of a performance problem in the server is likely to be a configuration or hardware problem in the underlying systems, rather than in Team Foundation Server itself.*

SYSTEM HEALTH

Server health refers to the health of the operating system and the underlying hardware. The easiest and most reliable way to monitor and measure server health is through the use of Windows performance counters.

Performance counters are generally considered an accurate representation of system performance. Performance counters are understood across different disciplines (development, testing, and operations) and across different groups (customers, vendors, and product teams). This makes them very useful for understanding the performance of a system.

If you don't already have a system (such as System Center Operations Manager) for collecting and analyzing performance counters, it's fairly easy to get started without one. You can configure a performance counter log to capture a core set of counters, once a minute, to a circular log file on each server. This will prove invaluable when you get the inevitable phone call asking, "Why is the server slow?"

> **NOTE** *To configure a performance counter log in Windows Server, see the article "Create a Data Collector Set from a Template" at* `http://aka.ms/ DataCollectorSet.`

The next thing to look at is *storage health.* In large applications and database applications, the most common source of slow system performance or high application response times is the performance of the storage system. To determine if you are having an issue with storage latency, you should use the following performance counters:

➤ **Object**—`Physical Disk` or `Logical Disk`

➤ **Counter**—`Avg. Disk Sec/Transfer`

➤ **Instance**—Ideally, you should collect this for individual disks. However, you may also use _Total to identify general issues. If _Total is high, then further collections can be taken to isolate the specific disks affected.

➤ **Collection interval**—Ideally, you should collect at least every one minute (but no more than every 15 seconds). The collection should be run for a significant period of time to show it is an ongoing issue, and not just a transient spike. The minimum suggested interval is 15 minutes.

When looking at the results, the following are the thresholds (in seconds) that you should consider:

➤ `< 0.030`—This is normal, and no storage latency issues are apparent.

➤ `> 0.030 to 0.050`—You may be somewhat concerned. Continue to collect and analyze data. Try to correlate application performance issues to these spikes.

➤ `> 0.050 to 0.100`—You should be concerned, and you should escalate to your storage provider with your data and analysis. Correlate spikes to application performance concerns.

➤ `> 0.100`—You should be very concerned, and you should escalate to your storage provider. Correlate spikes to application performance concerns.

With this data and these thresholds, you should be able to confidently identify a storage issue and work with either your server administrators or storage providers to get the issue resolved.

In large organizations, the storage will usually be provided by a Storage Area Network (SAN). SAN administrators usually work with the SAN vendors to ensure optimal configuration and performance. The administrators have many knobs they can tweak, and quite often it's just a matter of allocating more bandwidth and processing power from the SAN controller to your server. Sometimes, however, there just may not be enough disks available to meet the performance demands. If this is the case, it will often require a redesign and data migration to new SAN drives.

SQL SERVER

The majority of the Team Foundation Server application logic is implemented in SQL Server as stored procedures. The application tier itself is responsible for very little processing. For source control, the application tier performs caching and security checks. For work item tracking, the majority of the requests are passed directly to SQL Server. Because of this, the health of Team Foundation Server can largely be determined using the tools and functions provided by SQL Server.

Dynamic Management Views

Dynamic management views (DMVs) return server state information that can be used to monitor the health of a server instance, diagnose problems, and tune performance. To use them, you must have the VIEW SERVER STATE permission on the SQL server, or be a member of the sysadmins database role.

If DMVs are new to you, the easiest way to get started is to download the sample script from Jimmy May's blog at http://aka.ms/SQLDMVAllStars. Following are the five examples included in this script:

➤ Expensive Queries (CPU, reads, frequency, and so on)

➤ Wait Stats

➤ Virtual File Stats (including calculations for virtual file latency)

➤ Plan Cache

➤ Blocking (real time)

Each of these queries has a series of commented-out WHERE and ORDER BY clauses that can be uncommented to surface different information.

> **NOTE** *For more information and examples, see "Dynamic Management Views and Functions (Transact-SQL)" at* http://aka.ms/SQL2012DMV.

Currently Running Processes

The query examined here is perhaps the single most useful query for identifying performance problems within SQL Server. It uses a combination of the dm_exec_requests, dm_exec_sql_text, and dm_exec_query_memory_grants DMVs to discover problems in real time. This query is not specific to Team Foundation Server, and it can be used on any SQL server to see what SQL is doing.

As shown here, the query will return interesting details (explained in Table 25-1) about all non-system processes. It also excludes the process running the query, and it sorts all the processes with the longest-running ones at the top.

```
SELECT
@@SERVERNAME as ServerName,
a.session_id,
datediff(ss, a.Start_Time, getdate()) as seconds,
a.wait_type,
a.wait_time,
m.requested_memory_kb / 1024 as requestedMB,
a.granted_query_memory,
m.dop,
a.command,
d.Name as DBName,
a.blocking_session_id as blockedby,
LTRIM(b.text) as sproc,
substring(b.text, a.statement_start_offset / 2,
CASE WHEN
  (a.statement_end_offset - a.statement_start_offset) / 2 > 0
  THEN
    (a.statement_end_offset - a.statement_start_offset) / 2
  ELSE 1
END) as stmt,
a.last_wait_type,
a.wait_resource,
a.reads,
a.writes,
a.logical_reads,
a.cpu_time
```

```
FROM
  sys.dm_exec_requests a with (NOLOCK)
OUTER APPLY sys.dm_exec_sql_text(a.sql_handle) b
LEFT JOIN
  sys.dm_exec_query_memory_grants m (NOLOCK)
  on m.session_id = a.session_id
  and m.request_id = a.request_id
LEFT JOIN
  sys.databases d
  ON d.database_id = a.database_id
WHERE
  a.session_id > 50
  AND a.session_id <> @@spid
ORDER BY
  datediff(ss, a.Start_Time, getdate()) DESC
```

TABLE 25-1: Description of the Columns Returned by the Currently Running Processes Query

COLUMN	DESCRIPTION
ServerName	The name of the server that the query was executed on. When using SQL Server Management Studio to connect to multiple servers, this column is useful to verify that the query was executed against the correct server.
session_id	The ID of the SQL process. This is commonly referred to as a SPID, as in a *SQL Process ID*. It is unique while the process is running, and it can be reused by another process later.
Seconds	Total seconds since the query was started.
wait_type	See the section "SQL Wait Types" later in this chapter.
requestedMB	Memory requested by the query.
granted_query_memory	Memory allocated to the query.
Dop	The degree of parallelism (DOP). This indicates how many CPU cores this process is using.
Command	Command that the query is running (for example, SELECT, INSERT, UPDATE, DELETE, or BACKUP DATABASE).
DBName	Name of the database that the query is running on.
Blockedby	The ID of the process that this process is blocked by or waiting for.
Sproc	The text of the currently running query.
Stmt	The currently executing statement within the currently running query.

continues

TABLE 25-1 *(continued)*

COLUMN	DESCRIPTION
last_wait_type	The wait type that the process was previously waiting for
wait_resource	The resource that the process is currently blocked by or waiting for
Reads	Physical read operations of the process
Writes	Physical write operations of the process
logical_reads	Logical read operations of the process
cpu_time	CPU time (in milliseconds) that is used by the process

The detailed information provided by this query can be used to identify many common SQL Server issues.

Long-Running Processes

The `seconds` column will tell you how long a process has been running. Team Foundation Server has a default SQL time-out setting of one hour (3,600 seconds). If there are processes running against the `Tfs_Configuration` or the `Tfs_Collection` databases that are anywhere near 3,600 seconds, then you likely have a problem.

Once a Team Foundation Server process runs for 3,600 seconds in SQL, it will be cancelled on the application tier, and clients will receive an error message. The exception to this is queries executed by the Team Foundation Server Background Job Agent. These queries usually have a much longer time-out.

> **NOTE** *There may be processes that did not originate from Team Foundation Server that run for longer than one hour. An example is a SQL backup or other database maintenance task.*

High Memory Usage

The `granted_query_memory` column tells you how much memory SQL has allocated to a specific process. Each process will require different amounts of memory to perform its work.

In general, the commonly executed Team Foundation Server commands use less than 4GB of memory, and anything consistently higher is worth further investigation. If a process is using large amounts of memory, it can mean that SQL has chosen an inefficient query plan. If the total of the column is close to the total physical memory of the server, you may want to consider adding more memory.

UPGRADES AND SQL QUERY PLANS

When SQL compiles a stored procedure, it uses the query optimizer engine to generate a query plan. Upon execution, the query plan is used to determine the most efficient way to run the query. Based upon index statistics, data histograms, and other metrics, it determines things like whether it is more efficient to use a scan (iterate through all rows) or a seek (skip to a specific location based upon an index). As a SQL developer, you can set query hints in your stored procedure that force the query optimizer to choose a specific plan.

Although the SQL team strives to ensure that query plans remain stable, many things can cause SQL to pick a new query plan. During the development of Team Foundation Server 2010, there were a couple of events that caused query plan instability on the busy internal servers. The first was a hardware and operating system upgrade. The SQL server was moved from a 32-bit to a 64-bit machine with more capable storage.

The second change was an upgrade from SQL Server 2005 to SQL Server 2008. Changes in the query optimization engine caused SQL to overestimate memory for some of the important commands. For example, `Get` commands started consuming 10GB of memory each. `Get` was the most commonly executed command, and there was only 64GB of memory available on the server. This meant that everything ground to a halt until the inefficient query plan was identified and a query hint was added to force the old behavior.

Sometimes other changes such as index fragmentation and growing data sizes will cause a query plan to be inefficient over time. Fortunately, most of these types of issues have been flushed out through Microsoft's own internal usage, and you are unlikely to encounter them on your own server. In other cases, a restart of SQL server or `DBCC FREEPROCCACHE` will cause the query plans to be flushed and regenerated.

For much more detailed information on how SQL Server allocates memory for plan caching, see the "Plan Caching in SQL Server 2008" white paper by Greg Low at `http://aka.ms/SQLPlanCache`.

High Processor Usage

The `dop` column indicates the degree of parallelism for a query. A value of `0` indicates that the process is running in parallel on all processors. SQL Server has a setting for the maximum degree of parallelism (referred to as `MAXDOP`). This controls how many processors any individual process can use. The default setting is zero, meaning all processors.

If a process is using all processors, it means that it is making the most of the CPU hardware available. This is great. However, it also reduces the concurrency of the system and will block other processes from running until it is finished.

On busy servers, you may want to reduce the MAXDOP setting to allow increased concurrency. For example, do you want one large Merge command to block all the smaller commands while it executes? Or, could you live with a slightly slower Merge command that doesn't block all the other smaller commands?

> **NOTE** *For more information, see the article "max degree of parallelism Option" at* http://aka.ms/MAXDOP.

Performance Problems in a Specific Collection Database

The DBName column indicates in which database the process is currently executing. If you are experiencing a performance problem for a particular team project collection, this column will help you identify what commands are currently running for that collection.

Blocking Processes

The blockedby column indicates the ID of the process for which this process is waiting. If one process has a lock on a table or an index, and another process requires that same lock, it will be blocked until the first process releases the lock.

An example of this is a check-in lock. Because all check-ins are serialized, there must be a lock until SQL has committed the changes. If a check-in is large and requires lots of processing, it can hold the lock for a period of time. This can frustrate users who are just trying to check in a single file.

Another example is a lock in the tbl_LocalVersion table. If a user has a large workspace with many files, a DeleteWorkspace command may cause blocking of other commands such as a Get. This is because SQL Server does lock escalation. Team Foundation Server will request row locks (which lock only the affected rows), but SQL may determine that a page lock (which affects all rows on the same page) or a table lock (which affects all rows in the table) is more efficient.

Locking (and, therefore, blocking) was a significant problem during the internal usage of Team Foundation Server 2008 and 2010. The 2010 release eliminated the most common causes of blocking (for example, undo, edit, and check-in commands), which results in a much improved user experience.

Resource Contention

The wait_resource column is an identifier for what resource the process is waiting for. If the wait_type is PAGIOLATCH_*, this value will likely be a set of three colon-separated numbers such as 6:1:35162 in which:

➤ The first number is the database ID.

➤ The second number is the physical file ID.

➤ The third number is the page number.

You can look up the name of the database from the database ID by running the following query:

```
SELECT database_id, name FROM sys.databases
```

You can look up the physical file path by running the following query:

```
USE [Database_Name]
GO
SELECT file_id, type_desc, name, physical_name
FROM sys.database_files
```

> **WARNING** *For large operations, Team Foundation Server makes heavy use of SQL's* TempDB. *The database ID of* TempDB *is usually* 2. *If you see processes waiting on* TempDB *as a resource, this may indicate that you have a storage throughput problem. The general scalability recommendation for* TempDB *is that you should have one equal-sized data file per CPU.*

SQL Wait Types

A SQL process will be either running or waiting. When the process is waiting, SQL will record the wait type and wait time. Specific wait types and times can indicate bottlenecks or hot spots within the server.

The wait_type column of the currently running requests query will indicate what each process is waiting for (if anything). If you see many processes with the same value, this may indicate a system-wide bottleneck.

If it's not clear from the list of processes, you can also use the dm_os_wait_stats DMV, which collects cumulative wait statistics since the server was last restarted (or the statistics were reset). The following command will give you an output similar to Table 25-2:

```
-- What is SQL waiting for the most?
SELECT TOP 5 wait_type, wait_time_ms
FROM sys.dm_os_wait_stats
ORDER BY wait_time_ms DESC
```

TABLE 25-2: Sample Output from dm_os_wait_stats

WAIT_TYPE	WAIT_TIME_MS
FT_IFTS_SCHEDULER_IDLE_WAIT	2669883
DISPATCHER_QUEUE_SEMAPHORE	2316915
BACKUPBUFFER	2029392
CXPACKET	1292475
XE_TIMER_EVENT	932119

You can also manually reset the wait statistics for a server by running the following command:

```
-- Clear wait stats for this instance
DBCC SQLPERF ('sys.dm_os_wait_stats', CLEAR)
```

By looking at the results of the `dm_os_wait_stats` DMV, you can determine the most likely bottleneck in the system. Table 25-3 describes the common wait types.

TABLE 25-3: Common Wait Types

WAIT TYPE	DESCRIPTION
CXPACKET	Indicates time spent waiting for multiple processors to synchronize work. You may consider lowering the degree of parallelism or increasing the number of processors if contention on this wait type becomes a problem.
PAGEIOLATCH_*	Indicates time spent waiting for storage operations to complete. You may have a storage throughput problem if this is consistently high.
LOGBUFFER	Indicates time spent waiting for the transaction log. Consistently high values may indicate that the transaction log devices cannot keep up with the amount of logging being generated by the server. You will also see this wait type if your transaction log is full and has triggered an auto-grow. In this case, you should check that your transaction log backups are working and correctly truncating the log files.

> **NOTE** *For more information and a description of each of the wait types, see "sys.dm_os_wait_stats" at* `http://aka.ms/SQL2012WaitTypes`.

Storage Health

SQL Server provides the `dm_io_virtual_file_stats` DMV for keeping track of various storage metrics. The following query will list each of the physical database files in descending latency order:

```
SELECT
    --virtual file latency
    vLatency
      = CASE WHEN (num_of_reads = 0 AND num_of_writes = 0)
            THEN 0 ELSE (io_stall/(num_of_reads + num_of_writes)) END
, vReadLatency
      = CASE WHEN num_of_reads = 0
              THEN 0 ELSE (io_stall_read_ms/num_of_reads) END
, vWriteLatency
      = CASE WHEN num_of_writes = 0
            THEN 0 ELSE (io_stall_write_ms/num_of_writes) END
--avg bytes per IOP
, BytesperRead
      = CASE WHEN num_of_reads = 0
```

```
                THEN 0 ELSE (num_of_bytes_read/num_of_reads) END
, BytesperWrite
    = CASE WHEN num_of_writes = 0
              THEN 0 ELSE (num_of_bytes_written/num_of_writes) END
, BytesperTransfer
    = CASE WHEN (num_of_reads = 0 AND num_of_writes = 0)
              THEN 0 ELSE (
                (num_of_bytes_read+num_of_bytes_written)/
                (num_of_reads + num_of_writes)) END

, LEFT(mf.physical_name,2) as Drive
, DB_NAME(vfs.database_id) as DB
, vfs.*
, mf.physical_name
FROM sys.dm_io_virtual_file_stats(NULL,NULL) as vfs
  JOIN sys.master_files as mf
  ON vfs.database_id = mf.database_id AND vfs.file_id = mf.file_id
ORDER BY vLatency DESC
```

In the results of this query, you should pay particular attention to the vLatency and physical_name columns. The vLatency column indicates the combined average read and write latency for a file (in milliseconds). The physical_name column indicates which database file the results are for.

Following are some general points to consider when looking at these results:

➤   A latency of more than 30 milliseconds is something worth investigating for large databases with lots of activity.

➤   Latency in TempDB will affect overall server performance.

➤   High write latency (greater than 50 milliseconds) may be an indication that write caching is disabled or not working correctly. If this is the case, you will need to work with either your server administrators or storage providers to get the issue resolved.

Memory Contention

SQL Server (and, therefore, Team Foundation Server) performs best when the data pages that it requires are in memory. SQL Server maintains a buffer pool of pages. You can see how much of each database is available in the buffer pool by using the dm_os_buffer_descriptors DMV. If your database is not in the buffer pool, or if it is lower than you expect, you may need to add more memory to your SQL Server. As another option, you could move the database to a new SQL Server.

The following query produces an output similar to Table 25-4:

```
-- How much of the databases are in memory?
SELECT
db_name(database_id) as dbName,
COUNT(*)*8/1024 as BufferPoolMB
FROM sys.dm_os_buffer_descriptors
GROUP BY db_name(database_id)
ORDER BY 2 DESC
```

TABLE 25-4: Example Output of dm_os_buffer_descriptors

DBNAME	BUFFERPOOLMB
Tfs_Collection1	92251
Tfs_Collection2	15252
Tempdb	2914
Tfs_Warehouse	1175
Tfs_Configuration	231
Tfs_Collection3	129
ReportServer	27
Master	2
ReportServerTempDB	2
Model	0

TEAM FOUNDATION SERVER

Ever since the very first release of Team Foundation Server, the server has included rich command logging and tracing functionality. This level of logging and tracing is invaluable in identifying and measuring server performance.

With the release of the Visual Studio Online service, built on the Windows Azure platform, the monitoring and diagnostics functionality of the product has been enhanced. Because the product team members are responsible for the smooth operation of the service, it is in their best interest for the product to be easy to monitor and diagnose. These new responsibilities lead to new tracing infrastructures and enhancements to how the Windows Event Log is used in the on-premises version as well.

Command Log

The application tier keeps track of who executed what command at what time. It logs information such as the user name, IP address, user agent, execution time, and execution count for each request. In Team Foundation Server 2013, the command log also shows activity performed using the Web Access interface.

> **NOTE** *The command log data is also presented in Team Web Access through the Operational Intelligence Hub. For more information see the Operational Intelligence Hub section of Chapter 21.*

In the 2005 and 2008 versions, this data was recorded in the `TfsActivityLogging` database. In Team Foundation Server 2010, the tables were moved into the `Tfs_Configuration` and Team Project Collection databases. Following are the two tables used to record this data:

➤ `tbl_Command`

➤ `tbl_Parameter`

Approximately every 30 seconds, the application tier flushes recent requests to the command log tables in the database, where they can be queried. There is also an internal job that trims the command log to the past 14 days of data.

To show all the commands run by a particular user in the past 24 hours, you can run the following query:

```
-- Recent commands from a particular user
USE [Tfs_DefaultCollection]
GO
SELECT *
FROM [dbo].[tbl_Command] WITH (NOLOCK)
WHERE StartTime > DATEADD(HOUR, -24, GETUTCDATE())
AND IdentityName = 'DOMAIN\Username'
ORDER BY StartTime DESC
```

For commands that run longer than 30 seconds, or commands that fail, the parameters are also logged to `tbl_Parameter`. This is useful to identify if the user is trying to do something unreasonable. One such example is a `QueryHistory` call of the root folder (`$/`) with the `Recursive` flag set. To retrieve the parameters for the command, you must join or filter on the `CommandId` column, as shown in the following example:

```
-- Parameters for a particular CommandId
USE [Tfs_DefaultCollection]
GO
SELECT *
FROM tbl_Parameter WITH (NOLOCK)
WHERE CommandId = 12345678
ORDER BY ParameterIndex
```

The data in the command log is useful for seeing how many users actively use the server. For example, if you want to know how many distinct users have actively used the server in the past seven days, you can run the following query:

```
-- Recent active users
USE [Tfs_DefaultCollection]
GO
SELECT
  COUNT(DISTINCT IdentityName) as DistinctUsers,
  SUM(ExecutionCount) as TotalExecutionCount
FROM [dbo].[tbl_Command] WITH (NOLOCK)
WHERE StartTime > DATEADD(DAY, -7, GETUTCDATE())
AND Command IN
  ('UpdateLocalVersion', 'PendChanges', 'Get', 'CheckIn', 'Update', 'GetWorkItem')
```

This will include any user who has refreshed his or her workspace, checked out a file, saved a work item, or opened a work item. For measuring active users, it's important to filter based upon the command. Otherwise, if a user happens to select a collection in the "Connect to Team Foundation Server" dialog box, he or she will be included in the count, even though that user is not actively using that collection. This can lead to inflated numbers.

> **NOTE** *With the introduction of the "Local Workspaces" feature in Team Foundation Server 2012, it is no longer necessary for clients to contact the server to update their workspace and check out files. As such, the activity log may not accurately reflect all the active users of the system. You can read more about Local Workspaces in Chapter 6.*

The command log is incredibly useful for identifying performance problems for particular commands. For example, you can use the ExecutionTime and ExecutionCount columns to determine the average response time for each command. So, if you want to know the top ten slowest commands for the past seven days, you can run the following query:

```
-- Top 10 commands with the highest average response time
USE [Tfs_DefaultCollection]
GO
SELECT TOP 10
  Application,
  Command,
  ROUND(SUM(Cast(ExecutionTime AS float) / 1000000) / SUM(ExecutionCount),3)
    AS ResponseTimeSeconds
FROM [dbo].[tbl_Command] WITH (NOLOCK)
WHERE StartTime > DATEADD(DAY, -7, GETUTCDATE())
GROUP BY Application, Command
ORDER BY
  SUM(Cast(ExecutionTime AS Float) / 1000000) / SUM(ExecutionCount) DESC
```

Using the information within the command log, you can help determine whether user complaints of slow performance are widespread on the client side or specific to a particular user.

> **NOTE** *The ExecutionTime in the command log starts when the server receives the first byte of the request. It finishes when the server starts transmitting the last packet of the response to the client.*
>
> *Because of this, it only shows the server's view of the request, and there may be additional time spent on the client to complete processing of a request. For a more accurate view from a particular client, you can use client-side tracing. An example of this behavior is the GetMetadataEx command. This command is called when Team Explorer connects to a Team Project Collection for the first time. When connecting to a collection with a large number of Team Projects, the metadata will be relatively large (sometimes hundreds of megabytes). Once the server has processed the request and sent it to the client, the client will spend some time processing the response. This processing time won't be reflected in the command log.*

Active Server Requests

Team Foundation Server provides a web service that lists the currently executing requests on an application tier server. This web service can be used to see real-time blocking, as well as which users are currently using the server. The Team Foundation Server URL for the web service is `http://localhost:8080/tfs/TeamFoundation/Administration/v3.0/AdministrationService.asmx`.

> **WARNING** *If you have multiple application tiers in a network load-balancing configuration, you will need to query each server. The active requests are local to each server and are not aggregated between servers.*

No tools are provided with Team Foundation Server for calling this web service. You will need to write your own, or use another method. The simplest (but not necessarily the prettiest) way to view the requests is to use Windows PowerShell.

The following script will dynamically generate a web service proxy object, execute the request, retrieve the results, and print them out (as shown in Figure 25-1).

```
$tfsadmin = New-WebServiceProxy -UseDefaultCredential
    -URI http://tfsserver:8080/tfs/TeamFoundation/administration
    /v3.0/AdministrationService.asmx?WSDL
$tfsadmin.QueryActiveRequests($null, "False") | %{ $_.ActiveRequests } |
    sort StartTime | ft StartTime,UserName,MethodName,RemoteComputer
```

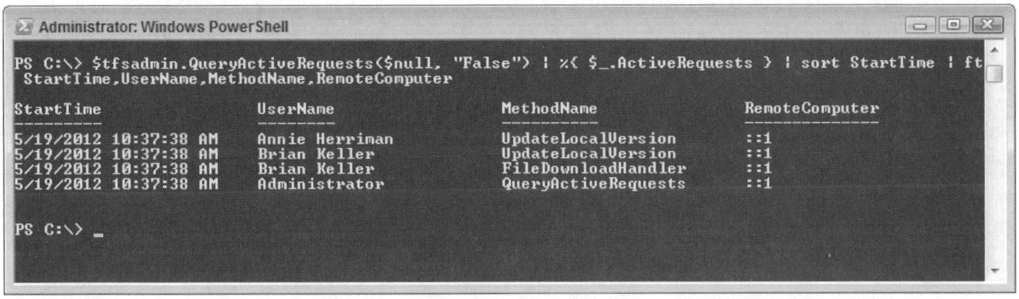

FIGURE 25-1: Example output from PowerShell script

If you are not a member of the Team Foundation Server Administrators security group, you will see only your own requests. Otherwise, you will see the requests for all users in all collections.

Health Monitoring Events

Querying the active requests list periodically is a very effective way to identify blocking and other problems in real time. In Team Foundation Server 2013, an internal task exists that identifies long-running requests. By default, it runs every 30 seconds and looks for the following:

➤ Requests that have been queued for longer than 15 seconds

➤ When there are more than 10 requests in the queue

➤ Requests that have been executing for longer than 60 seconds

If any of these conditions are met, a warning event with ID 7005 is logged to the Windows Application Event log indicating the condition. This then allows monitoring systems (such as System Center) to alert on the fact. The event text will look something like this:

```
Detailed Message: A request for service host DefaultCollection
   has been executing for 34 seconds, exceeding the warning
   threshold of 30.
     Request details: Request Context Details
     Url: /tfs/DefaultCollection/VersionControl/v1.0/repository.asmx
     Method: QueryHistory
     Parameters: itemSpec = $/ (Full)
versionItem = T
maxCount = 256
includeFiles = False
slotMode = True
generateDownloadUrls = False
sortAscending = False
     User Name: VSALM\Administrator
     User Agent: Team Foundation (TF.exe, 11.0.50727.1, Other, SKU:9)
     Unique Id: af139ed8-3526-422a-a9ee-16fa084ba5c6
```

One of the problems often encountered with monitoring systems is that alerts fire too often, are never closed, and eventually are deemed too noisy and disabled. In Team Foundation Server 2013, once the condition has passed, an additional event is logged with ID 7006. This allows the monitoring system to be intelligent and auto-resolve the alert. The event text will look something like this:

```
Detailed Message: There are no active requests for service host DefaultCollection
that exceed the warning threshold of 30.
```

The default thresholds are designed to be reasonable for most environments. However, in some environments, it might be perfectly reasonable for many commands to run longer than 60 seconds. These thresholds can be overridden under the path /Configuration/ServiceHostMonitor/ in the following Team Foundation Server registry keys:

➤ QueuedRequestElapsedThreshold = 15

➤ QueuedRequestThreshold = 10

➤ TotalExecutionElapsedThreshold = 60

Performance Counters

All versions of Team Foundation Server have included performance counters that allow administrators to monitor various aspects of the system. The release of Visual Studio Online forced the product team to add additional performance counters so that they can monitor the behavior of the system. Unlike an on-premises server, it is not possible to view the SQL performance counters with SQL Azure. This necessitated the addition of the following performance counters in the \TFS Services category:

➤ Average SQL Connect Time

➤ Current SQL Connection Failures/Sec

➤ Current SQL Connection Retries/Sec

➤   `Current SQL Execution Retries/Sec`

➤   `Current SQL Executions/Sec`

➤   `Current SQL Notification Queries/Sec`

These counters can be used to diagnose connectivity and transient errors with the SQL Server environment being used by Team Foundation Server.

Server Tracing

Team Foundation Server also includes low-level tracing for diagnosing complex server problems. Typically, this is used only by Microsoft support personnel when investigating a bug or strange behavior.

With the introduction of Visual Studio Online, the product team required a more detailed and flexible tracing mechanism. Because the service shares the same codebase, this tracing infrastructure is available in the on-premises product as well. However, because it requires an intimate knowledge of how the product works, it should be used only under the direction of Microsoft support personnel.

TRACING AT INTERNET SCALE

To move an application from an on-premises product to an Internet-scale service often requires design changes. One such example of this is the server tracing in Team Foundation Server.

For Team Foundation Server 2010 and prior versions, tracing was pretty much an "all or nothing" approach. You could turn it on for a subsystem (for example, Work Item Tracking), but then everything within that subsystem produced reams of tracing data. Additionally, the tracing was scoped to a single application tier in a load-balanced environment.

For Visual Studio Online, the team needed more flexibility and much finer grained central control. Some of the scenarios that were considered were:

➤   A single user is having problems checking in a file to his or her project.

➤   Many users are having problems with a particular part of the system.

➤   One of the jobs is not completing successfully but doesn't log enough information in the job result message.

➤   A very small number of executions of a particular command over a period of time are failing and it's not known why.

➤   Some users of a particular version of a particular client are experiencing a performance problem.

With these scenarios, the team came up with a flexible solution driven by the `prc_CreateTrace` and `prc_QueryTraces` stored procedures in the `Tfs_Configuration` database. Additionally, thousands of trace messages are spread throughout the code, each with unique `TracePoint` identifiers. They all remain dormant until enabled in the central database configuration.

continues

> *continued*
>
> This solution allows support personnel to enable tracing for specific code
> `TracePoints` within a method, whole methods, individual users, and specific user
> agents. It is also possible to enable tracing for whole layers of the system, such as
> `BusinessLogic` and with areas, such as `CheckIn` and `CreateWorkspace`.
>
> The output of this tracing infrastructure is logged to an Event Tracing for Windows
> (ETW) session. By default, an Event Log trace listener is available in the Windows
> Event Viewer under `\Applications and Services Logs\`
> `Microsoft-Team Foundation Server\Debug`.

Client Performance Tracing

Similar to server tracing, tracing is also available in the client object model.

> **NOTE** *For more information on enabling client-side tracing, see the*
> *"Team Foundation Server Client Tracing" blog post at* `http://aka.ms/`
> `TfsClientTracing`.

If you want a convenient way to see the web service calls your Team Foundation Server clients are
making to the server, you can enable the `PerfTraceListener` trace listener on your client. This is
done by adding the following configuration in the appropriate `app.config` file:

```
<configuration>
  <appSettings>
      <add key="TFTrace.Writer" value="true" />
      <add key="TFTrace.DirectoryName" value="C:\Temp" />
      <add key="VersionControl.EnableSoapTracing" value="true" />
  </appSettings>
  <system.diagnostics>
    <switches>
      <add name="TeamFoundationSoapProxy" value="4" />
      <add name="VersionControl" value="4" />
      <add name="Download" value="2" />
      <add name="LocalWorkspaces" value="4" />
    </switches>
    <trace autoflush="true" indentsize="3">
      <listeners>
        <add name="perfListener"
type="Microsoft.TeamFoundation.Client.PerfTraceListener,
Microsoft.TeamFoundation.Client,
Version=11.0.0.0, Culture=neutral,
PublicKeyToken=b03f5f7f11d50a3a"
        />
      </listeners>
    </trace>
  </system.diagnostics>
<configuration>
```

Once the trace listener is enabled and the application is started, a dialog box will appear, as shown in Figure 25-2. In the dialog box, you'll see how long each call takes (in milliseconds), the number of calls made, and the average time for each call.

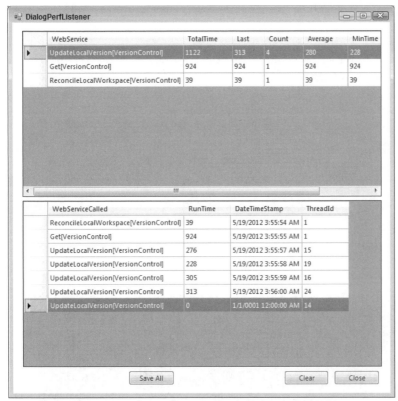

FIGURE 25-2: Example of the performance trace listener dialog box

The top section of the dialog box shows the aggregated information. The bottom section shows the list of web service methods in the order in which they were called, the elapsed time in milliseconds, and the time of day when the method completed execution. If the method has not completed, it will display Running for the completion time. If you move the mouse over the entries in the bottom section, a tooltip will show you the stack trace, so you can see what part of the application made the call.

> **NOTE** *For more information on how to interpret the results of the dialog box, see Buck Hodges's blog post, "How to see the TFS server calls made by the client,"* at http://aka.ms/TfsPerfListener.

Job History

Team Foundation Server 2013 includes a background job agent, just as the previous versions did. Jobs are defined in the configuration and in each collection database. The history for each of these jobs is stored in the configuration database. The supported way of accessing this history is through the object model.

> **NOTE** *The background job data is also presented in Team Web Access through the Operational Intelligence Hub. For more information, see the Job Monitoring topic in the Operational Intelligence Hub section of Chapter 21.*

To list the currently defined jobs for a server, you can use the following PowerShell script. The output will be similar to that shown in Figure 25-3:

```
$ErrorActionPreference = "Stop";
[void] [Reflection.Assembly]::Load("Microsoft.TeamFoundation.Client,
    Version=11.0.0.0, Culture=neutral, PublicKeyToken=b03f5f7f11d50a3a");

# Modify the collection URL as necessary.
$tpc = new-object Microsoft.TeamFoundation.Client.TfsTeamProjectCollection
    "http://localhost:8080/tfs/DefaultCollection"

$jobService = $tpc.GetService([Microsoft.TeamFoundation
    .Framework.Client.ITeamFoundationJobService])

# List all the jobs and their JobIds
$jobService.QueryJobs() | sort Name | select JobId, Name | ft -a
```

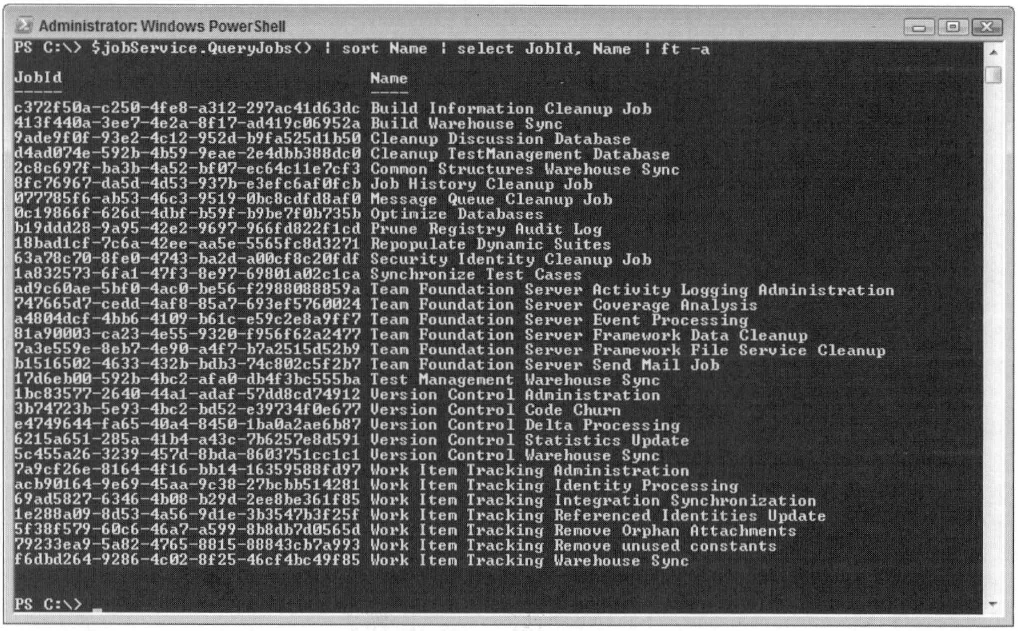

FIGURE 25-3: PowerShell example of currently defined jobs

To get the recent execution history of a job, as shown in Figure 25-4, you can use the following PowerShell command after running the previous one:

```
# Get the 20 latest execution results for a particular JobId
$jobService.QueryJobHistory([Guid[]] @('a4804dcf-4bb6-4109-b61c-e59c2e8a9ff7'))
    | select -last 20 | ft ExecutionStartTime,Result,ResultMessage
```

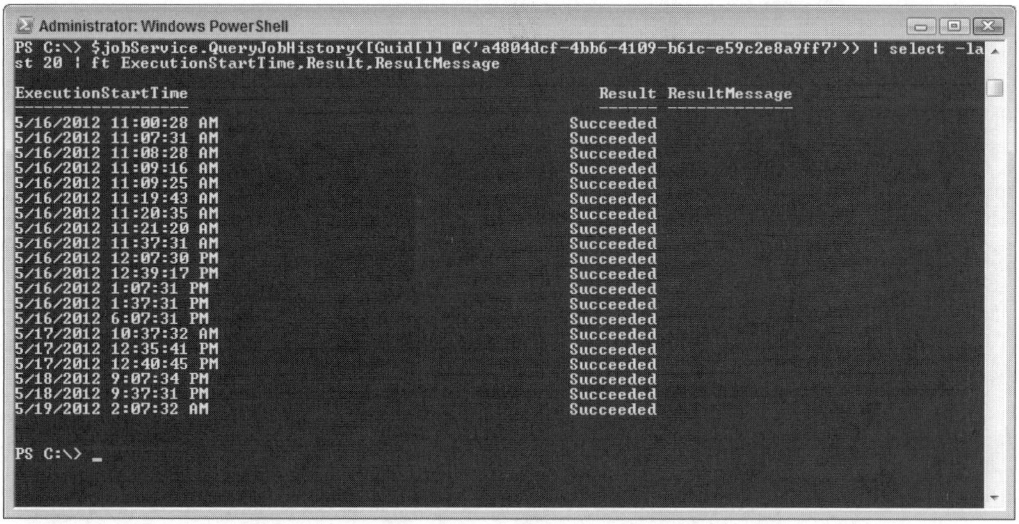

FIGURE 25-4: PowerShell example of recent job history

> **NOTE** *For more information, see Chris Sidi's blog post, "TFS 2010: Introducing the TFS Background Job Agent and Service,"* at http://aka.ms/ TfsJobAgent.

Storage Usage

With a system like Team Foundation Server, it's not uncommon for the storage usage to grow rapidly as people discover the value of the system and start using it for more things. As a Team Foundation administrator, you may want to know what is causing your databases to grow. Because all Team Foundation Server data is stored in SQL Server, you can use the SQL sp_spaceused stored procedure to identify where the data growth is occurring.

The following script will list the total database size and the top 10 largest tables. You will need to run it for each collection database.

```
-- Database total space used
EXEC sp_spaceused

-- Table rows and data sizes
CREATE TABLE #t (
    [name] NVARCHAR(128),
    [rows] CHAR(11),
    reserved VARCHAR(18),
    data VARCHAR(18),
```

```
      index_size VARCHAR(18),
      unused VARCHAR(18)
)
INSERT #t
EXEC [sys].[sp_MSforeachtable] 'EXEC sp_spaceused ''?'''
SELECT TOP 10
   name as TableName,
   Rows,
   ROUND(CAST(REPLACE(reserved, ' KB', '') as float) / 1024,2) as ReservedMB,
   ROUND(CAST(REPLACE(data, ' KB', '') as float) / 1024,2) as DataMB,
   ROUND(CAST(REPLACE(index_size, ' KB', '') as float) / 1024,2) as IndexMB,
   ROUND(CAST(REPLACE(unused, ' KB', '') as float) / 1024,2) as UnusedMB
FROM #t
ORDER BY CAST(REPLACE(reserved, ' KB', '') as float) DESC

DROP TABLE #t
```

You can then use the information in Table 25-5 to match table names to their purposes, and implement strategies to reduce the storage used and control the growth.

TABLE 25-5: Largest Tables within a Collection Database

TABLE NAME	USED FOR	HOW TO REDUCE
tbl_Content	All blob content, including: version control files, test attachments, and work item tracking attachments	Destroy version control content, delete team projects, or run the Test Attachment Cleanup tool.
tbl_LocalVersion	Version control workspaces	Switch users to Local Workspaces; delete workspaces or reduce the number of folders for which they have mappings; upgrade to a SQL Server edition that supports data compression.
tbl_PropertyValue	Version control code churn metrics	Upgrade to a SQL Server edition that supports data compression.
WorkItemsWere	Work item tracking historical revisions	Destroy work items.
WorkItemLongTexts	Work item tracking long text field data	Destroy work items.
WorkItemsLatest	Work item tracking latest revisions	Destroy work items.
WorkItemsAre	Work item tracking latest revisions	Destroy work items.
tbl_tmpLobParameter	Temporary storage for large in-progress check-ins	N/A

> **NOTE** *In Team Foundation Server 2013, the Work Item Tracking Attachments and Test Attachments are contained in the* `tbl_Content` *table that Version Control also uses.*

Data Warehouse

One of the key components of Team Foundation Server is the data warehouse. In general, people don't have a problem with the performance or operation of the data warehouse. However, there are two classes of problems that you're more likely to run into as your servers grow larger:

➤ **Processing time**—As the number of reportable fields increases, the number of dimensions that Analysis Services must process also increases. This increases the time it takes to process the cube and, therefore, the latency of the data is higher.

➤ **Schema conflicts**—In the simple case, when there are two fields in different collections (for example, `Priority`) with the same name, but a different type (for example, `String` versus `Integer`), this results in a schema conflict. That project collection is then blocked from processing warehouse updates, and the data in the relational warehouse and cube become stale.

You can use two reports ("Cube Status" and "Blocked Fields") to monitor the health and performance of the Team Foundation Server data warehouse. They display the following information:

➤ Recent processing times

➤ Current status (whether the cube is processing now and, if not, when it is scheduled to process next)

➤ Schema conflicts

➤ Most recent time that each warehouse adapter successfully ran

> **NOTE** *For more information on how to download, install, and interpret the reports, see "Administrative Report Pack for Team Foundation Server 2010 and 2012" at* `http://aka.ms/TfsWarehouseReports` *and "Monitoring the TFS Data Warehouse—FAQ" at* `http://aka.ms/WarehouseReportsFAQ`. *The same reports continue to work for Team Foundation Server 2013 without modifications.*

TOOLS

A few tools are useful for monitoring server health and performance. Some are specific to Team Foundation Server, and some are not.

Performance Analysis of Logs Tool

The Performance Analysis of Logs (PAL) tool knows how to analyze a performance counter log file, look for threshold violations, and produce a server health report. It is not specific to Team Foundation Server, and it can identify SQL Server issues.

The tool encapsulates the collective wisdom of Microsoft engineers and other experts to identify possible problems with your servers. Figure 25-5 shows an example of a CPU utilization threshold violation. You can use this report to identify potential problems that might need to be looked at on the server or deeper in SQL Server and Team Foundation Server.

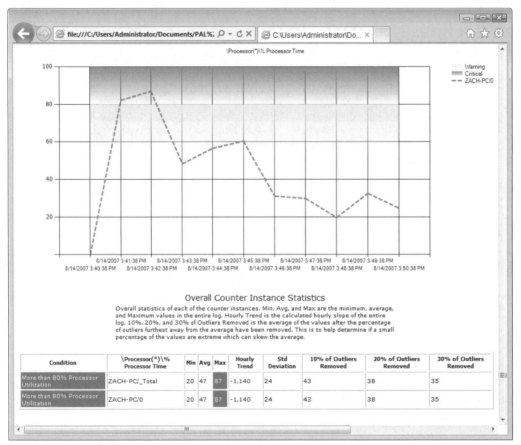

FIGURE 25-5: Example PAL report

> **NOTE** *For more information and to download the tool, see the PAL project site on CodePlex at* `http://pal.codeplex.com/`.

Team Foundation Server Best Practices Analyzer

The Team Foundation Server Best Practices Analyzer (BPA) is a tool used by Microsoft support personnel to help diagnose customer issues. When executed, the BPA tool will connect to your Team Foundation Server, download the event logs and command logs, and run queries against the database. With each Power Tool release, the tool is updated to include rules that detect the causes of common support requests.

For the most complete results, you should run the tool as an administrator on one of your application tier servers. It can also be run remotely if you are an administrator and remote administration is enabled for Windows and SQL Server.

> **NOTE** *To run the BPA tool, you must download and install the latest Team Foundation Server Power Tools from* `http://aka.ms/TFS2013PowerTools`.

Once it has finished collecting the data, it will parse it and run a series of rules that look for known problems. It displays a report similar to Figure 25-6. Each of the rules has an expected result and a help topic that describes how to rectify an unexpected result.

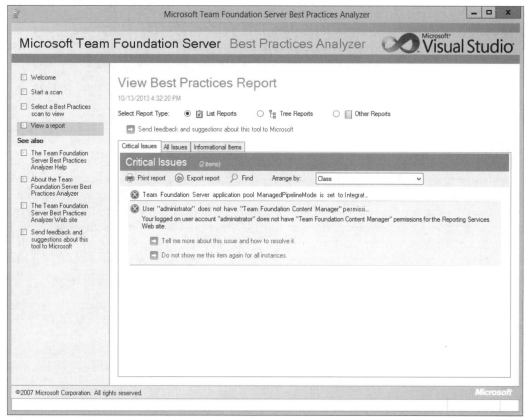

FIGURE 25-6: Best Practices Analyzer scan report

Team Foundation Server Management Pack for System Center Operations Manager

System Center Operations Manager (SCOM) is an enterprise-level monitoring product from Microsoft. A management pack defines monitors and rules for monitoring specific applications.

The Team Foundation Server 2012 management pack provides both proactive and reactive monitoring of Team Foundation Server 2012. It monitors application tier servers, team project collections, build servers, and proxy servers.

You can download the management pack from `http://aka.ms/TFS2013SCOM`. Once you have downloaded the management pack, you should review the `MPGuide_TFS2013.docx` document. This document includes important information on how to set up and use the management pack.

> **NOTE** *You will need to create a* `Run As Profile` *and an associated* `Run As Account` *that has administrative access within Team Foundation Server to be able to use the management pack. Refer to the installation guide.*

If everything is configured correctly, the management pack will automatically discover Team Foundation Server instances and start monitoring them. It has a series of rules and monitors that look for problems in the event log and check the health of the system.

When the Best Practices Analyzer tool is installed, you can also initiate a BPA scan from the Operator Console.

SUMMARY

In this chapter, you learned about the factors that influence the health of Team Foundation Server. You learned that Windows performance counters are a useful way to record system health, and you learned how to use the built-in SQL Server Dynamic Management Views to understand many aspects of SQL Server Performance. You also learned about the different data sources available within Team Foundation Server, along with some useful queries and reports for determining the health of the system. Additionally, you looked at the tracing and Windows Events available in Team Foundation Server 2013. Finally, this chapter covered three useful tools for monitoring server health and performance.

Chapter 26 takes a look at the new Testing and Lab Management features, and how they can be used to build high-quality software.

26

Testing and Lab Management

WHAT'S IN THIS CHAPTER?

➤ Learning about the testing capabilities of Visual Studio 2013

➤ Understanding the architecture of the software testing components of Visual Studio 2013

➤ Planning for and administering your Team Foundation Server deployment when used for software testing

Across the Visual Studio 2013 family of products, Microsoft has made significant investments to better support software testing activities. This is arguably the single biggest investment Microsoft made for application lifecycle management since the Visual Studio 2010 release, and many software development and testing organizations have already shown great results by embracing these capabilities.

While many of these enhancements include tooling features outside the scope of a book about Team Foundation Server, there are several testing technologies and workflows that, in one way or another, involve Team Foundation Server. In this chapter, you will become more familiar with the testing capabilities of the Visual Studio product line and the impact that adopting these technologies will have as you plan, implement, and manage your Team Foundation Server deployment.

As you will see in this chapter, there is a high potential for complexity as you begin embracing Visual Studio as your software testing solution. Many factors will influence the complexity of your specific environment, such as which capabilities you want to use, how much you wish to automate, and your organization's network topology. For this reason, every effort has been made in this chapter to provide you with a broad overview of the topics you will need to consider, with links to supporting documentation and blog posts that provide detailed guidance.

WHAT'S NEW IN SOFTWARE TESTING?

The Team Foundation Server 2013 and Visual Studio Online releases have introduced a number of advancements in the software testing area, including a load testing service hosted in Windows Azure which allows for quick test ramp-up and near infinite scaling of your load. They have also introduced improvements to the Test Case Management features in Web Access.

New Cloud-Based Load Testing Service

With the release of Visual Studio Online and Visual Studio 2013, Microsoft unveiled Cloud-based Load Testing as an additional service. With this service, you can create a relatively infinite scale load by taking existing load tests created with Visual Studio 2010 or later and running them on the service. You no longer have to worry about acquiring hardware or virtual machines, setting up test controllers or agents, deploying your tests or running your tests. You simply need to connect Visual Studio 2013 to a Visual Studio Online account, open the .testsettings file in your solution, and select the new Run tests using the Visual Studio Team Foundation Service option for the Test run location on the General tab, as shown in Figure 26-1.

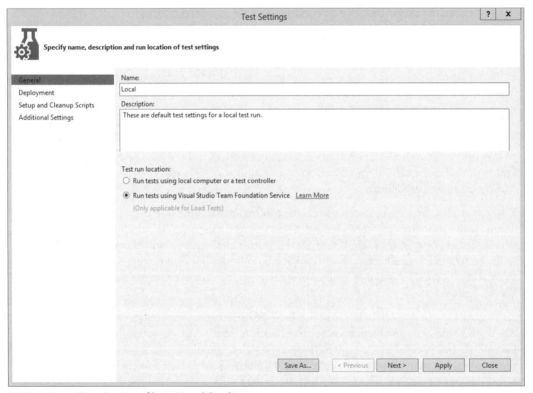

FIGURE 26-1: Test Settings file in Visual Studio

For more information on Microsoft's Cloud-based Load Testing, please see the Getting Started page at Visual Studio Online, which can be found at http://aka.ms/CloudLoadTesting.

Web-Based Test Case Management

Team Foundation Server 2013 and Visual Studio Online have also added the capability to manage existing Test Plans from within the Web Access user interface. From the new Web Test Manager, you can create edit, delete, move, and rename Test Suites as well as create, edit, delete, and run Test Cases all without the need to install any software locally. We will discuss the features of Web Test Manager later in this chapter.

SOFTWARE TESTING

> **NOTE** *For more information about how to use the specific testing technologies included across the Visual Studio 2013 family of products, see the companion book* Professional Application Lifecycle Management with Visual Studio 2013 *by Mickey Gousset, Martin Hinshelwood, Brian A. Randell, Brian Keller, and Martin Woodward (Wiley 2014). Part VI of that book is dedicated to detailing the different testing tools and technologies that can be found throughout the Visual Studio 2013 product line. The book is available at* `http://aka.ms/ALM2013Book`*.*

It should go without saying that the role of software testing in any development process is to ensure a high level of quality for any software by the time it is released to end users. Numerous studies suggest that software defects discovered in production are exponentially more expensive to identify and correct than if those same defects had been discovered and fixed during the development or testing phases of a project, before release. Hence, it stands to reason that most investments in software testing will more than pay for themselves in the long run.

> **NOTE** *Steve McConnell's* Code Complete, Second Edition *(Microsoft Press, 2004) cites data from several interesting studies that exhibit the high cost of quality issues once they are discovered downstream. See Chapter 3, "Measure Twice, Cut Once: Upstream Prerequisites," for examples. You can find this book at* `http://aka.ms/CodeCompleteBook`*.*

Many approaches to software testing have been developed over the years to address the variety of defects that can be found in software. The field of software testing can be divided into areas such as functional testing, regression testing, scalability testing, acceptance testing, security testing, and so on. But, in your role as a Team Foundation Server administrator, there are generally two major categorizations of software testing you should be familiar with:

➤ Manual testing is by far the most common type of testing employed across the software testing field. As the name implies, manual testing involves human labor testers interacting with software, usually in the same way as the end user is expected to, with the purpose of validating functionality and filing bugs for any defects they discover. This can be either with planned test cases or through new Agile techniques and tools such as exploratory testing.

➤ Automated testing involves writing and running software, which, in turn, inspects the software you are testing. The obvious advantage of automated tests is that they can run quickly, frequently, and involve little or no human interaction. But an investment is usually required to author and maintain automated tests.

It may seem counterintuitive that the software industry—which has a reputation for automating everything from banking to automobile assembly—would rely so heavily on manual testing. But the reality is that early on, as a software project is evolving and undergoing a heavy degree of churn, manual testing provides the flexibility required to adapt to rapid changes. Keeping automated tests up to date under these conditions may be cost-prohibitive.

Manual and exploratory testing also provides the added insurance policy of a set of human eyes analyzing an application and spotting defects that an automated test may not be programmed to look for. Investment in automated tests usually becomes attractive only after an application or set of functionality has matured and stabilized.

Later in this chapter, you will learn more about how the Visual Studio 2013 family of products addresses both manual and automated testing.

Test Case Management

Test case management is a discipline of software engineering much like requirements management, project management, or change management. Effective test case management ensures that the right sets of tests are designed and executed in order to validate that an application behaves as it should. This is based on the explicit set of requirements that have been defined by, or on behalf of, its users. Test case management should also account for implicit requirements—those requirements that may not have been stated up front by a user, but are understood to be important (such as making sure that the user interface is easy to read, text is spelled properly, and the application doesn't crash when Daylight Savings Time goes into effect).

Test case management was a new feature introduced in Team Foundation Server 2010, expanded in Team Foundation Server 2012, and extended to the browser in Team Foundation 2013 and Visual Studio Online. Test plans and their associated artifacts (which you will learn about later in this chapter) can be stored in Team Foundation Server or Visual Studio Online and linked to other artifacts, such as requirements and builds. By centralizing all of these artifacts, Team Foundation Server allows you to track your test plans alongside your implementation.

For any given feature, you can already ask, "How long before this feature is done being coded?" With the addition of test case management to Team Foundation Server, you can now ask questions such as, "How many tests have we written? For last night's build, how many tests have been run? Did those tests pass or fail? For the tests that failed, what types of bugs did we generate?"

Visual Studio 2010 introduced a new product family member—Microsoft Test Manager—which can be used by testers and test leads to manage and execute test plans. You learn more about Microsoft Test Manager later in this chapter.

Team Foundation Server 2013 and Visual Studio Online introduce Web Test Management in Team Web Access. This is a new interface that provides the main set of testing tools from Microsoft Test Manager (MTM) through a web interface.

Lab Management

Gone are the days when the typical installation procedure for an application was to "xcopy deploy" it to the system and launch an executable. Nowadays, most applications require an increasingly complex installation procedure that could involve deploying software packages across multiple machines and requires a long list of prerequisite software.

Conversely, removing a piece of software from a machine isn't always straightforward, and commonly leaves behind unwanted artifacts, making it difficult to clean a test machine for subsequent deployments. This complicates the process of effectively testing your software, especially when this deployment procedure must be repeated to accommodate daily (or even hourly) changes being checked in by your development team.

Advances to virtualization technology have helped to alleviate this problem. Virtualization provides an easy mechanism for staging test environments, creating snapshots of them at some known state (such as when the latest updates and prerequisites have been applied), and restoring them to that known state to prepare to deploy a new build. Although virtualization solves some of these problems today, orchestrating an automated workflow for building, deploying, and testing your software across these virtual environments often requires a great deal of manual effort or expensive automation investment.

Lab Management is designed to address this problem. Lab Management was another new capability introduced in Team Foundation Server 2010 that you will learn about in this chapter. Lab Management provides an out-of-the-box solution for automating a build-deploy-test workflow for your software project with your existing environments or with virtualized environments created during the development and testing life cycle.

Imagine having your software automatically built and deployed to one or more virtual environments, each environment consisting of one or more virtual machines. The deployment could include not only configuring your application, but also deploying the latest database schema and a clean baseline data set used by your manual and automated tests. Each virtual environment might represent a different configuration under which your software needs to be tested. Automated tests are run, defects are noted, and environments are readied for use by manual testers to complete the test pass and scour for additional defects. As bugs are found, snapshots of a virtual environment can be created again so that developers can instantly see a bug for themselves without having to re-create it in their own environments. Testers and developers can even create dedicated temporary environments designed to be used individually and then shut down and deleted when they are no longer needed. The Lab Management capabilities of Visual Studio and Team Foundation Server make all of this possible.

TESTING ARCHITECTURE

In Part I of this book, you learned about the possible configurations for installing and configuring Team Foundation Server. In Part IV, you learned about how build controllers and build agents can be used to provide build automation capabilities to Team Foundation Server. If you intend to use the software testing capabilities covered in this chapter, there are a few other components you should begin to familiarize yourself with. Figure 26-2 shows an example of a topology that uses all of the software testing capabilities covered in this chapter.

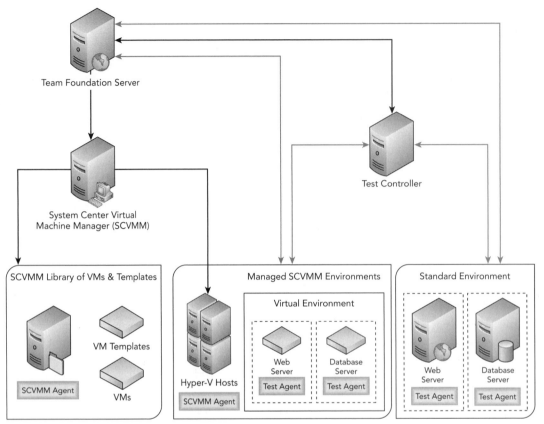

FIGURE 26-2: Testing architecture in TFS

The first thing to notice is that (not surprisingly) Team Foundation Server is at the heart of this solution. Team Foundation Server is ultimately responsible for orchestrating such activities as test automation, lab deployments, and test result collection, although it does get some help from other servers and services that facilitate these tasks.

The remaining components in the test architecture are as follows:

➤ A test controller is responsible for orchestrating one or more test agents in order to execute automated tests. A test controller also collects test result data from test agents after a test run has finished. This data can then be stored in Team Foundation Server for reporting and diagnosis purposes.

➤ System Center Virtual Machine Manager (SCVMM) is required to orchestrate virtual machine (VM) operations (such as deployment, provisioning, snapshots, and state management) across one or more physical Hyper-V host machines. An SCVMM server is required in order to configure SCVMM virtual environments with Lab Management in Team Foundation Server.

➤ An SCVMM library server is used by SCVMM to store VMs and virtual machine templates (VM templates). Once a VM or VM template is available in a VM library, it can be deployed as a running instance to a physical Hyper-V host. You will learn more about VMs and VM templates later in this chapter.

➤ An SCVMM virtual environment is a collection of one or more deployed VMs. Lab Management treats a managed environment as a single entity that can be deployed, snapshotted, or rolled back together as a single collection of machines. An SCVMM environment can be used to simulate a real environment, which might contain a web server, a database server, and a client machine with a web browser. SCVMM environments are deployed to physical Hyper-V host servers, which are, in turn, managed and monitored by SCVMM. An SCVMM agent is automatically installed on the Hyper-V hosts, enabling that physical machine to act as a VM host and to communicate with the SCVMM server.

➤ A standard environment can also play an important role in your testing architecture, especially when virtualization or Hyper-V is not an option (such as to support tests that require special hardware not accessible from a virtual machine). You can create standard environments using the existing machines in your current environments that you are using today. Although standard environments are the quickest way to get started with Lab Management in Team Foundation Server 2013, you will learn more about the capabilities and limitations of standard environments as compared to SCVMM virtual environments later in this chapter.

One important limitation to be aware of in this architecture is that a test controller can be bound to just one team project collection. If your Team Foundation Server deployment includes multiple team project collections that need test controllers, you must install those test controllers on separate servers.

If you are familiar with the test architecture from Team Foundation Server 2010, you will notice there are several simplifications in the architecture for Team Foundation Server 2012. For example, build controllers and build agents are no longer needed for the deployment functionality. Deployment is now handled through the test controller and test agents. In Team Foundation Server 2013, Test Agent deployment was simplified. When you create a Standard or SCVMM environment using Test Manager, any machines running Windows Vista or higher will automatically have Test Agents installed and configured.

Also, there is no longer a separate lab agent needed if you choose to use the network isolation feature with SCVMM virtual environments. Network isolation allows you to establish virtual environments with their own private virtual network, without fear of machine name conflicts or IP address collisions. Each machine in a network-isolated environment is accessible through a special and unique DNS name and is still able to access network resources outside of the environment. This network isolation functionality that used to be in the lab agent has now merged into the consolidated test agent.

> **NOTE** *Detailed instructions for installing and configuring test controllers and test agents can be found at* `http://aka.ms/ConfiguringTestControllerAndAgents`.

MICROSOFT TEST MANAGER

Microsoft Test Manager (MTM) was first introduced in the Visual Studio 2010 release. It was built from the ground up to provide software testers and test leads with a dedicated tool for managing and executing test plans. These test plans and associated artifacts are stored in Team Foundation Server. Figure 26-3 shows Microsoft Test Manager, which is included with Visual Studio Premium 2013, Visual Studio Ultimate 2013, and Visual Studio Test Professional 2013 editions.

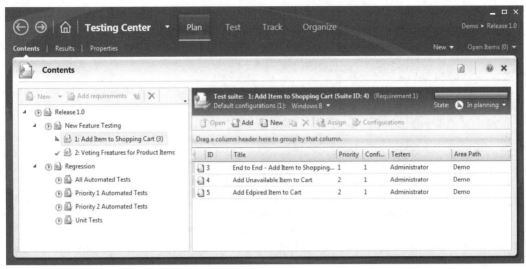

FIGURE 26-3: Microsoft Test Manager

> **NOTE** *If you are confused about the differences between the Visual Studio Test Professional product and Microsoft Test Manager, you are not alone. There are more details about the differences available at this blog post:* `http://aka.ms/ MTMvsVSTestPro.`

Team Foundation Server 2013 and Visual Studio Online have extended the Web Access portal to include some of the functionality found in MTM, as shown in Figure 26-4. These new testing features are gathered under the Web Test Management umbrella and will be discussed throughout this chapter.

This section provides a brief overview of the terminology and artifacts used by Microsoft Test Manager and Web Test Management, along with a few key settings that you should be aware of as a Team Foundation Server administrator. The term "Test Manager" will be used to refer to both Microsoft Test Manager and Web Test Manager features. If there is a difference in functionality between the tools, it will be noted.

> **NOTE** *You can learn much more about Microsoft Test Manager and Web Test Manager from Part VI of* Professional Application Lifecycle Management with Visual Studio 2013 (*John Wiley & Sons, 2014*), *available at* `http:// aka.ms/ALM2013Book` *and from the MSDN Library at* `http://aka.ms/ VisualStudioTesting.`

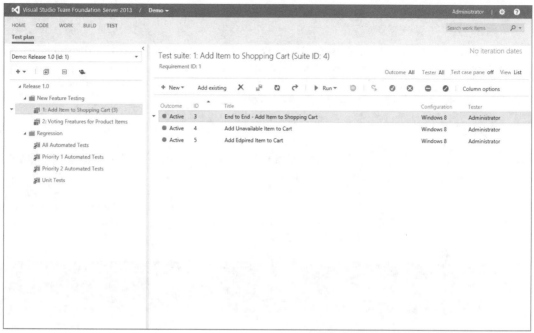

FIGURE 26-4: Web Test Manager

Test Plans

A test plan is used by Test Manager to define and track everything being tested for a given software release. A testing team will usually create a test plan that corresponds to each development iteration or release. This is so that the tests they are designing and running ensure that the features the development team is implementing work as expected.

Test plans can be created and managed in both Microsoft Test Manager and Web Test Manager.

Test Suites

Test suites are used to organize your test cases. There are three types of test suites in Test Manager:

➤ **Requirements-based test suite**—This includes any test cases linked to requirement work items via a "Tests" relationship. For any given iteration of an application's development, you will usually want to start by adding to your test plan all of the requirements being implemented in that iteration. By linking test cases with requirements, you can later report against an individual requirement to determine whether it is working as expected.

➤ **Query-based test suite**—This allows you to specify a dynamic work item query for selecting test cases. For example, you might want to include all test cases with a priority of 1, even if they are for requirements that were implemented and already tested in earlier iterations.

This can help ensure that critical functionality that was working doesn't break (or regress) as development progresses.

➤ **Static test suite**—This is a list of test cases that can be added manually to the suite. A static test suite can also be used as a container for other test suites, giving you an option to hierarchically organize your tests. It is the only test suite type that can contain other test suites and can be used to organize a test suite hierarchy in the test plan.

Test Cases

A test case is used to describe a set of actions a tester should perform to validate that an application is working as expected. For example, a simple test case might confirm that a user can visit a web page and create a new user account using a strong password. Likewise, another test case may validate that, if a user tries to create a new account with a weak password, the application prevents the user from doing so. Figure 26-5 shows an example test case in Microsoft Test Manager. For comparison, Figure 26-6 shows the same test case in Web Test Manager.

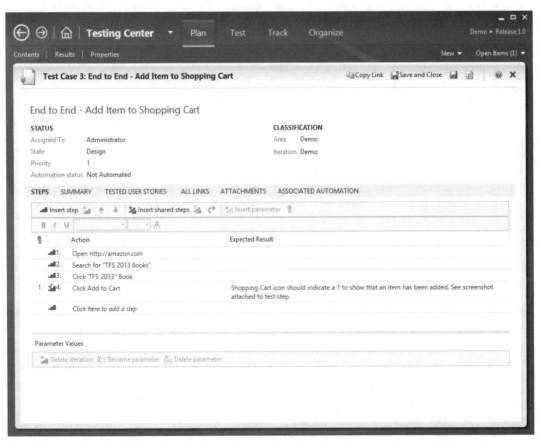

FIGURE 26-5: Test case work item in Microsoft Test Manager

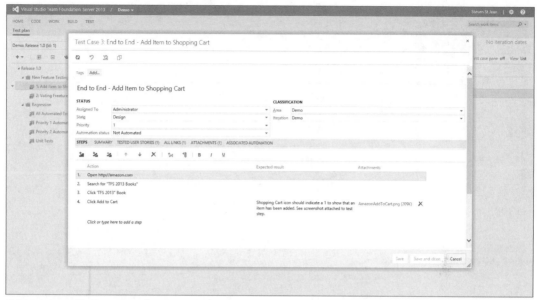

FIGURE 26-6: Test case work item in Web Test Manager

The structure of a test case should look familiar to you. A test case is stored as a work item in Team Foundation Server. It contains all of the core work item fields (Title, Iteration, Area, Assigned To, and so on). But a test case also has a Steps tab that contains the individual test steps testers should perform when they exercise this test case. A major advantage of a test case being represented as a work item within Team Foundation Server is that it can be linked to other work items (such as the relationship with requirements described earlier) and reported on. The downside to using the work item engine to store test cases is that you do not have the ability to branch a test case when your code branches. In this case you will need to create a copy of the test case if you need to have both the old and new versions of the test case available to support the old and new versions of your application.

A shared step is another work item type that can be used to consolidate a series of test steps that may be shared across multiple test cases. Shared steps allow you to centrally manage changes to commonly used parts of your application (such as user sign-in, account creation, and so on).

Test Runs

Test Manager provides testers with the ability to run test cases from a test plan using the local Test Runner or Web Test Runner. It will guide testers, step by step, through test case execution, alerting them about what they should expect to see in order to validate an application's intended behavior. Testers can even file bugs directly from this interface. Figure 26-7 shows a test case being run in Test Runner, and Figure 26-8 shows the same test in Web Test Runner.

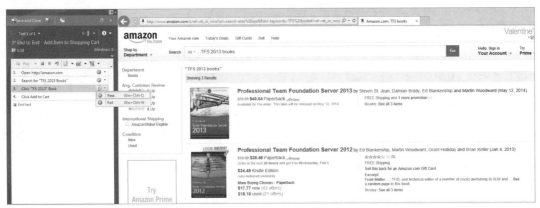

FIGURE 26-7: Test case execution in Test Runner

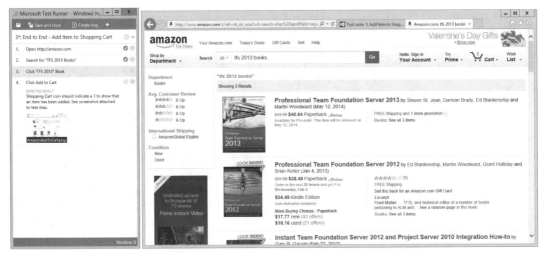

FIGURE 26-8: Test case execution in Web Test Runner

Exploratory Testing

Agile teams perform a type of testing, called exploratory testing, and do not typically start out with formal manual test cases. The exploratory testing tools, first available in Microsoft Test Manager 2012, allow you to start an exploratory testing session without having test cases defined. Testers are able to track what they are doing and provide comments as they perform ad hoc testing.

The nice thing is that the tester can also create formal test cases during the exploratory testing session because the test runner has recorded the actions that were taken. Additionally, if a bug is found, the tester is able to file rich actionable bugs from the exploratory test runner using those recorded action steps. You will find out more about filing rich actionable bugs using the test runner in the next section.

Exploratory testing features are only available in Microsoft Test Manager.

Actionable Bugs

Many software projects fall prey to an all-too-common scenario in which the tester finds and documents a defect, but the developer is unable to reproduce it. This is known as the "No Repro" scenario, and it is the source of the adage, "It works on my machine." To address this problem, Microsoft's test architecture is capable of capturing rich data about a test run from each of the machines in the environment being tested, including the local machine. This happens automatically, without any additional work required by testers. When testers file a bug, Microsoft Test Manager can automatically include rich details such as system information (operating system, service pack level, total memory, available memory, and so on), action logs, event logs, and even a video recording that shows exactly what testers did as they ran a test case.

Even if a developer can't reproduce the same problem on his or her machine, the developer can at least get proof that a defect exists, along with a set of data used to look for clues about why the problem occurred in the tester's environment. The set of data that is collected during a test run is configured by test settings.

The collectors that are used to capture this rich data must be installed on the client machine where the tests are running. As such, this rich data is unavailable when using the Web Test Runner.

Test Settings

Test settings can be configured per test plan to describe what information should be collected while a tester is running a test. Collecting the right set of information can be invaluable for developers as they analyze bugs to determine why a problem occurred.

However, as a Team Foundation Server administrator, you should also be aware that test settings have the potential to occupy a lot of disk space. Figure 26-9 shows the test settings configuration dialog box from within Microsoft Test Manager, along with a list of diagnostic data adapters that can be enabled and configured to collect a variety of details from a test run.

You can specify the types of diagnostic data adapters to run for each machine in your environment. Some diagnostic data adapters make more sense than others for different machine roles. For example, collecting a video recording on your database server may lead to a pretty boring video.

There is a temptation to want to collect everything, all of the time, from every test run, to avoid missing key pieces of information if a bug is discovered. However, this can impact test run performance, and it could quickly consume all of the available disk space on your Team Foundation Server instance.

Therefore, it's important for test leads and development leads to work together to construct test settings that thoughtfully capture the right information. You can also have multiple test settings, such as one called "Full Diagnostics" and another called "Lightweight Diagnostics." Testers can run with the Lightweight Diagnostics test settings for the majority of their work, and, if they encounter a bug, they can re-run a test with the Full Diagnostics and add the additional details to the same bug.

The exact amount of disk space required per test setting will vary based on the length of your test runs, the complexity of the application being tested, and the number of machines in a test environment from which you are gathering information. But, generally speaking, from a resource perspective, the two diagnostic data adapters to pay special attention to are IntelliTrace and Video Recorder.

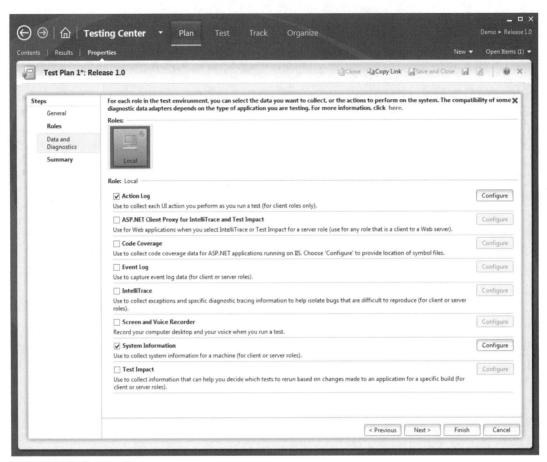

FIGURE 26-9: Test settings

IntelliTrace can provide extremely rich, historical debugging data about .NET applications, which can help developers understand exactly what was happening during the execution of an application. Developers can analyze IntelliTrace files using Visual Studio 2013 Ultimate edition, but testers running Microsoft Test Manager can capture IntelliTrace files during test execution.

> **NOTE** *You can read more about using IntelliTrace at* `http://aka.ms/ IntelliTrace2013.`

Left unchecked, the IntelliTrace files themselves can quickly consume tens or even hundreds of megabytes of disk space. The good news is that the maximum size of an IntelliTrace file can be limited by configuring that particular diagnostic data adapter; and for successful test runs (where a test case passes), IntelliTrace files will be discarded. But, from a resource perspective, this is the most important diagnostic data adapter to pay attention to.

Video recordings can also consume about a megabyte of disk space per minute of test execution. If enabled, video recordings will always be attached to test results if a test case fails. You can optionally configure video recordings to be saved even if a test case passes. This can be useful for auditing third-party testing organizations, to ensure that they are running test cases properly. It can also be useful for capturing ad hoc video "documentation" of your application, which can easily be shared with business stakeholders to show them the progress of your development.

Test settings configuration is only available within Microsoft Test Manager.

> **NOTE** *You can learn more about configuring test settings at* `http://aka.ms/` `Configuring2013TestSettings.`

Test Attachments Cleaner

If you are making effective use of the diagnostic data adapters to collect rich, actionable information about your test runs, eventually you will probably want to clean up old test run data in order to reclaim disk space. Microsoft has created the Test Attachments Cleaner to aid with this process. This is a command-line tool that you can configure to clean up test attachments based on age, size, attachment type (such as IntelliTrace files or video files), and so on.

Team Foundation Server administrators can work with their development and test teams to figure out the appropriate retention, and then create a scheduled task to run the test attachment cleaner on a regular basis.

Be careful and realize that, if you do remove a test attachment, any bugs that were created that link to those attachments will no longer have access to the original attachment. For example, if you decide that IntelliTrace and video recordings older than 180 days should be removed, then someone opening a bug after it has been removed using the cleaner will no longer have access to those attachments.

> **NOTE** *The Test Attachments Cleaner is included with the Team Foundation Server Power Tools available at* `http://aka.ms/TFS2013PowerTools.`

Assigning a Build to a Test Plan

Another challenging aspect of any test team's job is determining which builds they should test. A development team will likely produce several builds during the course of a week, and perhaps even multiple builds during a given day, especially if it is embracing continuous integration. It is usually impractical to expect that a test team will install and test every build. Microsoft Test Manager can help test teams with this process.

Because Team Foundation Server already contains rich information about builds and the work items that have been incorporated into each build (such as which bugs are fixed or which requirements are implemented), this information can be used by a test team to determine which builds are worth testing. Figure 26-10 shows the Assign Build dialog box within Microsoft Test Manager.

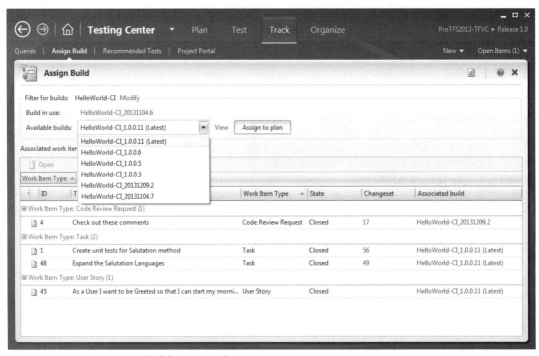

FIGURE 26-10: Assigning a build to a test plan

Assigning the build can be done from the Test Plan properties window and is typically done by a test lead to indicate to the team which build should be used to test. It is used as the default when testers start a new manual or automated test run but can be overridden for an individual test run as well.

The build currently in use can be compared with newer builds to determine what has changed in a given build and to help determine whether a newer build is worth adopting. For example, maybe a bug has been resolved by a developer but must be validated by a tester. Or, maybe a requirement has been coded and is ready for testing.

> **NOTE** *The cadence of your builds is something you should think about when configuring your test plans. For example, you probably don't want every single continuous integration build to show up in the list of available builds. Instead, you might consider creating a dedicated build definition that produces nightly or rolling builds, and choose that build definition as the filter for your test plan. If the test team needs a new build before the next scheduled build, it is able to manually queue a new build for that build definition as well. Having a consolidated number of builds on a predictable cadence will also make your build quality reports easier to read.*

Analyzing Impacted Tests

Test impact analysis is a powerful feature that can help improve the productivity of testers by allowing them to quickly identify tests to re-run based on changes to code. Test impact analysis can be enabled to run in the background while tests are being executed. This feature records which methods of code are executed while each test is run. These can be automated tests (for example, unit tests, load tests, or coded UI tests), as well as manual tests, but the code you are analyzing must be managed code (that is, based on .NET Framework 2.0 and above).

Microsoft Test Manager can provide testers with a list of impacted tests whenever they select a new build. In order to support this capability, you must be running tests with Microsoft Test Manager's Test Runner, using the Test Impact diagnostic data adapter during your test runs (as configured by your test settings), and your build definition must be configured with test impact analysis enabled as described in Part IV of this book. Test impact analysis data is not captured when testing from the Web Test Runner.

Build Retention

In Part IV of this book, you learned how to define build definitions, trigger a build, delete builds, and set build retention policy. Most of the time, accidentally deleting a build (or inadvertently losing a build because of an aggressive retention policy) does not create much of a problem for a software development team because you can just re-create a build based on an older changeset. But if you are conducting manual testing with Test Manager, improperly deleting a build can cause you to lose the test results run against that build.

When test runs are stored in Team Foundation Server, they are stored along with the associated build they were run against. This can include artifacts such as video recordings, IntelliTrace files, or action recordings (which can be used to partially or fully automate test execution). If a developer needs any of this information to diagnose a problem, and the build was deleted along with the test results, he or she may lose valuable information to help reproduce and debug a problem. Likewise, if testers are using action recordings to fast-forward test execution (a feature of Microsoft Test Manager), deleting test results will destroy the action recordings required for fast-forwarding. These same action recordings can be used to create fully automated, coded UI regression tests as well.

To avoid this problem, be very careful when deleting builds that may have been used by your test team. This is another good reason to follow the build cadence described earlier for the builds you will test with.

You can periodically clean up your irregular continuous integration builds without jeopardizing the test results from the builds that your testing team may have used. You should then disable the retention policy from deleting builds from your testing build definition, or at least configure the retention policy to preserve test results when builds are deleted.

If disk space becomes scarce, you can then use the Test Attachments Cleaner to selectively delete old testing artifacts (such as video recordings and IntelliTrace files) without jeopardizing important test results that may still be useful. Keep in mind that action recordings may be useful long after a feature is considered "done" because a test team may occasionally re-test older features to ensure that nothing has regressed in a recent build.

Custom Work Item Types

You have seen how Microsoft Test Manager uses requirements, test cases, shared steps, and bugs, all of which are stored in Team Foundation Server as work items. But if you want to customize your process template, or use a third-party process template, how does Test Manager know which work item type is the equivalent of a "requirement" or a "bug" and so on? The answer is to use categories to define the roles for each of your work item types in Team Foundation Server.

> **NOTE** *More information on using categories to define work item roles can be found at* `http://aka.ms/MTMWITCategories`. *More information on customizing your process template can be found in Chapter 13.*

TEST AUTOMATION

This chapter has mostly dealt with manual testing, but Visual Studio and Microsoft Test Manager also provide support for automated tests. As mentioned previously, automated tests are beneficial because they have the ability to run quickly and repeatedly, without human interaction, in order to surface regressions that indicate to a development team that (for example) the last change they made to the code broke a feature that was working in last night's build.

Table 26-1 shows several types of automated test types supported by Visual Studio 2013.

TABLE 26-1: Automated Test Types

TEST	DESCRIPTION
Coded UI	This test provides the ability to author tests that automatically interact with the user interface of an application and verify some expected result, and file bugs if an error is encountered. Coded UI tests typically evolve from test cases that were previously run manually, once the application's user interface (UI) has mostly stabilized. You can even use action recordings from manual test runs as the basis for creating new coded UI tests.
Unit	These low-level tests verify that target application code functions as the developer expects.
Web performance	This test is used primarily to test performance of a web application. For example, you may create a web performance test capturing the web requests that occur when a user shops for items on your website. This web performance test could be one of a suite of web performance tests that you run periodically to verify that your website is performing as expected.

Load	These tests verify that a target application will perform and scale as necessary. A target system is stressed by repeatedly executing a variety of tests. Visual Studio records details of the target system's performance and automatically generates reports from the data. Load tests are frequently based on sets of web performance tests. However, even non-web applications can be tested by defining a set of unit tests or database unit tests to execute.
Generic	These tests enable calling of alternative external testing systems, such as an existing suite of tests leveraging a third-party testing package. Results of those tests can be automatically parsed to determine success. This could range from something as simple as the result code from a console application to parsing the XML document exported from an external testing package.
Ordered	Essentially containers of other tests, these establish a specific order in which tests are executed, and they enable the same test to be included more than once.

Each of these test types is described in detail in Parts V and VI of the companion book *Professional Application Lifecycle Management with Visual Studio 2013* (John Wiley & Sons, 2014). As a Team Foundation Server administrator, you should familiarize yourself with how automated tests can be run as part of a build definition, which was described in Part IV of this book. You should also familiarize yourself with test controllers and agents, introduced earlier in this chapter (see the section, "Testing Architecture"). When configuring test agents, some test types (such as coded UI tests) will require you to configure the test agent to run as an interactive process so that it has access to the desktop.

Automated tests can also be run as part of an automated test run or a build-deploy-test workflow in a Lab Management environment. You will learn about Lab Management in the next section.

If you would like to run an automated test through Microsoft Test Manager or in a Lab Management environment, then you need to make sure that the test case work items that represent those automated tests understand which test is the automation for them. Associating the automation with the test case work item is the key step, and you can find out more on how to do this here at `http://aka.ms/TestCaseAssociatedAutomation2013`.

> **NOTE** *If you want to run large numbers of tests, such as unit tests, and would like to automate the process of creating and updating the associated automation for a lot of tests, you can use the* `tcm.exe testcase import` *command-line utility. Running this command will create test cases and automatically associate unit tests or other coded tests with those test cases. Subsequent runs of this command-line utility will update existing test cases and create new test cases based on any new tests that are found. More information about this functionality is available here at* `http://aka.ms/ImportTestCasesFromTestAssembly`.

VISUAL STUDIO LAB MANAGEMENT

Visual Studio Lab Management is a powerful capability of Team Foundation Server that allows you to orchestrate physical and virtual test labs, empower developers and testers to self-provision needed environments, automate build-deploy-test workflows, and enhance developer-tester collaboration. Some Lab Management features are not to users of Visual Studio Online. This section provides an overview of the components required to enable Lab Management, along with their associated capabilities.

This section also provides you with a starting point as you plan your adoption of Lab Management, considerations for maintaining your testing environment, and troubleshooting tips. Several URLs have been provided throughout this section, as well as links to supporting documentation, all of which dive deeper into these topics.

> ### CHALLENGES OF CONFIGURING LAB MANAGEMENT
>
> It should be stated up-front that configuring the virtual lab aspect of Visual Studio Lab Management (especially for the first time) can be overwhelming and even frustrating at times. While the Lab Management technology is capable of doing a lot of heavy lifting for you, there are always going to be areas that you must customize for your own environment, to suit your individual process, and to meet the requirements of your existing IT infrastructure. Stick with it because the benefits of Lab Management often far outweigh the initial investment. You can read about some teams that have already adopted Lab Management and their results at `http://aka.ms/LabManagementCaseStudies`.
>
> Configuring Lab Management also requires a mixture of disciplines across development, build engineering, testing, and IT. So be prepared to immerse yourself in the documentation, and then buy some doughnuts and assemble a virtual team with the right level of expertise.

What's New for Lab Management in Team Foundation Server 2013?

There are several improvements in Lab Management since its introduction in Team Foundation Server 2010. This section begins by helping you get acquainted with what's new.

Standard Environments

Standard environments were introduced in Team Foundation Server 2012 to replace the concept of "physical environments" that existed in Team Foundation Server 2010. Standard environments, as opposed to SCVMM environments, allow you to use any machine (whether it is virtual or physical) as an environment in Visual Studio, Team Foundation Server, and Microsoft Test Manager. You are able to take advantage of manual testing and collecting data with the standard environment as well.

Standard environments do have certain drawbacks though—because they are not managed by SCVMM, you are not able to provision machines with Microsoft Test Manager and rollback/snapshot, or perform operations like start and stop with standard environments.

However, creating standard environments out of your current environments are by far the easiest way to get started immediately with Lab Management. You only need to set up a test controller before creating your first standard environment and you are ready to go. This is a great first step for those looking to immediately gain benefits from what is provided in Lab Management. Standard environments are available from Team Foundation Server and Visual Studio Online. You can find out more about how to create a standard environment by visiting `http://aka.ms/CreatingStandardEnvironments2013`.

System Center Virtual Machine Manager 2012

In addition to support for System Center Virtual Machine Manager 2008 R2, Team Foundation Server 2013 also supports System Center Virtual Machine Manager 2012. There are quite a few improvements included in SCVMM 2012 that are out of scope for this book, but Lab Management will now support clustered host groups, highly available virtual machines in environments, and the new `.VHDx` hard drive file format. One item to note is that even though Lab Management supports clustered host groups, network-isolated environments must still reside on a single Hyper-V host.

Consolidation of Agents

One of the simplifications that has been made is the need for only one agent: a test agent. Previously, three agents were required for Lab Management: build agent, test agent, and lab agent. All of the functionality from the previous agents have now been consolidated into the single agent install.

Auto-Installation of Agents

Another improvement introduced in Lab Management for Team Foundation Server 2013 was that you no longer need to worry about installing and configuring the test agent on the individual machines that make up an environment. Whenever you create a new standard environment or an SCVMM environment, Lab Management will automatically handle the installation and configuration for you. When new updates are released for the agents, Lab Management will also handle uninstalling and installing the new version of the agents for you. This can dramatically reduce the amount of maintenance required for using Lab Management. For the auto-update of agents, you will want to make sure that your test controller(s) are updated as each new periodic update is released for Visual Studio.

Repairing Environments

Environments and machines can end up in states where they are unreachable or have issues at times. Lab Management now includes several troubleshooting wizards as well as "repair" tools, which attempt to resolve the most common problems that end up occurring.

Installing and Configuring Lab Management

Earlier in this chapter (in the section, "Testing Architecture"), you learned about the components that make up a testing environment that uses standard and SCVMM virtual environments. A solid understanding of these components and how they integrate with one another is important for configuring and administering Lab Management.

When you are ready to move toward enabling SCVMM virtual environments for your own Team Foundation Server setup, you should start with the MSDN Library documentation at `http://aka .ms/ConfiguringLabManagement2013`. This help topic provides step-by-step instructions for configuring your environment for the first time. Read the documentation end to end before getting started, and be prepared for this to take several hours.

When you are finished, you will have added the Lab Management capability to Team Foundation Server and have configured an SCVMM server, along with a VM library share and one or more VM hosts. You are then ready to begin preparing virtual machines, defining virtual environments, and configuring build definitions to support build-deploy-test workflows.

The remainder of this section covers additional considerations you may need to account for in your environment as well as optimizations and best practices to be aware of, which can save you time and enhance the quality of your Lab Management deployment.

Ports and Protocols

Unless you are the system administrator for your organization's IT department, you may need to request that certain ports and protocols be enabled to support your testing architecture. This becomes especially important if your solution will span multiple networks, such as if your existing test lab infrastructure is separate from your Team Foundation Server instance.

> **NOTE** *A detailed description of the ports and protocols required to support the testing architecture described in this chapter can be found at* `http://aka.ms/ TFSPorts2013`.

Capacity Planning

Many factors will affect the hardware requirements in order for your team to use Lab Management capabilities. These factors include variables such as the following:

➤ At any given time, how many testers will need access to their own individual virtual environments to run tests?

➤ At any given time, how many developers will need access to virtual environments (for analyzing bugs reported by testers or initial testing and debugging of new builds)?

➤ How many VMs are required in each virtual environment? In other words, can the tiers in your software run on a single server, or will your tests involve multiple servers?

➤ What are the system requirements of each VM in your virtual environments (disk space, memory usage, processing power)?

➤ How often will you run your build-deploy-test workflow, and how long will you need to retain historical snapshots containing older builds?

➤ How many VMs and VM templates do you need to store in your VM library, and what is the size of those files?

➤ Do you need multiple testing environments in order to support geographically distributed teams?

The answers to these questions will begin to form the hardware requirements of your testing environment. This will allow you to calculate the answers to questions such as the following:

➤ How many VM physical host servers do I need?

➤ What kinds of servers should I buy?

➤ How much storage capacity do I need?

> **NOTE** *The Lab Management product team has compiled guidelines to help you answer these questions. You can access these guidelines at* http://aka .ms/LabManagementCapacityPlanning. *The Visual Studio ALM Rangers also have included a capacity planning workbook in their Lab Management guidance available on CodePlex:* http://aka.ms/ALMRangersLabManagementGuidance.

Managing Host Groups and Library Shares

The basic infrastructure of any Lab Management deployment will consist of an SCVMM server, one or more library shares, and one or more physical host servers running Hyper-V (which are organized along with other VM hosts into host groups). The SCVMM server coordinates the deployment of VMs from a library share to a Hyper-V host by examining the available resources on each Hyper-V host within a host group to determine to which host server a VM should be deployed.

There are several techniques you can use to optimize the performance of your Lab Management deployment. For example, ensuring that your library share is on the same network switch as your VM hosts can substantially reduce the amount of time required to deploy VMs to hosts. Another technique is to allow unencrypted file transfers between your library share and the VM hosts.

> **NOTE** *The Lab Management team has compiled guidelines to help you better understand the way SCVMM host groups and libraries interact with Team Foundation Server's Lab Management capability. These guidelines also provide best practices for optimizing your host groups and library shares. You can find the guidelines at* http://aka.ms/LabManagementHostsAndLibraries.

Creating VMs and VM Templates

Creating VMs and VM templates for your SCVMM library can be a time-consuming (but important) step in building out your Lab Management environment. Depending on the requirements of the software you are testing, you may need to create multiple VM templates that correspond to different operating system editions, languages, browser versions, and so on. You no longer need to pre-install the test agent into the VM template, but it can save on provisioning time when the environments are created using that VM template. Be sure to keep the template up to date with the most recent version of the test agent (and any periodic Visual Studio updates that are released from Microsoft) if you do decide to pre-install the agents. Otherwise, as mentioned earlier in the chapter, Lab Management will now automatically install and configure the agents when an environment is created.

CHOOSING BETWEEN A VM AND VM TEMPLATE

You may be wondering what the difference is between a VM and a VM template, and when you should use each.

A VM can be stored in an SCVMM library by starting with a running VM, shutting it down, saving it to the SCVMM library share, and registering it with the SCVMM server. When it is later deployed from the library to a VM host, it will have the same machine name and other configuration properties as it did when it was originally saved to the library. The obvious downside with this approach is that if you deploy this VM more than once, you may experience machine name conflicts on your Lab Management network. The solution to this is to use VM templates.

A VM template has gone through a `sysprep` step to essentially remove its machine name, domain memberships, and other uniquely identifying properties. When a VM template is later deployed from the library to a VM host, you can specify its machine name (or use a randomly chosen GUID), domain memberships, and so on. This provides you with protection from machine name collisions, and even allows you to use the same VM template more than once in a given virtual environment.

Generally speaking, you should use VM templates whenever you can. The major exception to this rule is if your test environments require software that is not supported with `sysprep`. For example, SQL Server 2008 did not support `sysprepping`. SQL Server 2008 R2 supports `sysprepping` of some features and SQL Server 2012 supports `sysprepping` of all features. If you are forced to use VMs, be sure to create virtual environments that use network isolation in Lab Management. This won't prevent machine name collisions within a virtual environment (you will have problems if you have two VMs with the same name in the same virtual environment), but it will provide isolation between different SCVMM virtual environments.

A very good walkthrough is kept up to date on MSDN with information on how to create a virtual machine template for Lab Management and making it available for your developers and testers to use in their environments available here: `http://aka.ms/CreatingVirtualMachineTemplates2013`.

Working with Virtual Environments

After you have populated your SCVMM library with VMs and/or VM templates, you can use Microsoft Test Manager to define an SCVMM virtual environment. An SCVMM environment consists of one or more VMs or VM templates, and you can use the same VM template twice within a given SCVMM environment. (This will customize the VM template twice, creating two instances of running VMs from the same template.) After you have defined your SCVMM environments, you can then deploy those to SCVMM host groups.

> **NOTE** *For more information on creating Lab environments, see* `http://aka.ms/CreatingLabEnvironments`.

DETERMINING VIRTUAL MACHINE RAM

When you are configuring and deploying virtual environments, you can decide how much RAM to assign to each VM within each virtual environment. Remember that the more RAM you assign to each VM, the more RAM will be required by your VM host groups.

If you multiply the number of VMs in each virtual environment by the number of simultaneous virtual environments you need to support, you may discover that trimming even a few hundred megabytes of RAM off of each VM can represent a substantial resource savings for your environment. Therefore, it's important to understand what the minimum RAM requirements can be for the VMs in your test environments without sacrificing the performance or accuracy of your testing efforts.

If you are using machines based on Windows 7 SP1, Windows Server 2008 R2 SP1, Windows 8, and Windows Server 2012, be sure to take advantage of the Hyper-V feature called dynamic memory to support more virtual machines in your virtual lab. Dynamic memory allows you to specify a minimum and maximum amount of memory available for a VM and will provide the VM with more memory as it needs it instead of keeping it static. It can greatly increase your VM density ratio for your Hyper-V host servers.

Defining a Build-Deploy-Test Workflow

Although you can choose to use Lab Management purely for managing a lab of VMs to conduct manual testing, the real power of Lab Management is unlocked when you begin to take advantage of the automation support for building your software, deploying it to an environment, and running your automated tests in that environment. This is known as a build-deploy-test workflow.

Imagine the benefits of this workflow by considering the following hypothetical scenario. The software you create consists of a website, powered by a database, which needs to be accessed by people running multiple supported web browsers. Your web application needs to work with Internet Information Services (IIS) 7 and IIS 8, and you support both SQL Server and Oracle for the database tier.

Just deploying the dozens of machines required to support each of these configurations alone can be time-consuming. After the machines are ready, you must deploy the software, and then run your tests. Now, consider repeating this process every night in order to support the daily changes coming from the development team.

Of course, some organizations have already invested heavily in scripts to automate some or all of this workflow, but the cost of doing so can be quite high. Development and testing teams should not be in the business of maintaining this type of infrastructure—they should be spending their time building and testing great software.

Once you have installed and configured your Lab Management infrastructure, you can easily create a new build definition using Team Build, which allows you to establish a build-deploy-test work-flow. You can create multiple definitions to support multiple environments. (For example, you might create one workflow to test a SQL Server deployment with IIS 7 and a separate workflow to test an

Oracle deployment with IIS 8.) Imagine arriving to work in the morning and being able to instantly discover that last night's build caused a failure in the account authorization logic, which only occurs with SQL Server 2008 R2 SP2.

This is the type of rapid, iterative feedback that can allow teams to identify and fix bugs well before a release is ever distributed to customers. Figure 26-11 shows an example of a typical build-deploy-test workflow enabled by Lab Management. This workflow can be customized and extended to suit your specific requirements.

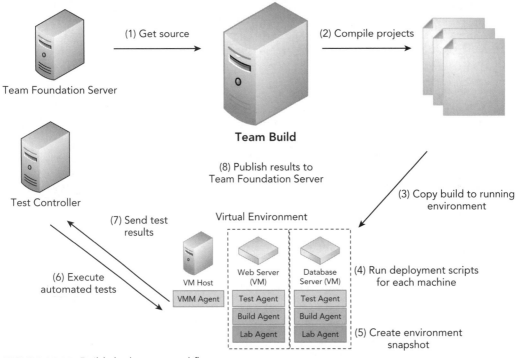

FIGURE 26-11: Build-deploy-test workflow

> **NOTE** *To get step-by-step instructions for configuring a build-deploy-test workflow with Team Build and Lab Management, visit* `http://aka.ms/BuildDeployTestWorkflow2013`.

Note that, in order to run automated tests as part of a build-deploy-test workflow, you must create automated tests (such as coded UI tests or unit tests), store these tests in Team Foundation Server Version Control, include them in your application's automated build, and associate these tests with test case work items. These test case work items must, in turn, be part of a test plan. Admittedly this will require a bit of up-front work to create these associations, but the end result is that you will get rich reporting data that links your builds with your test plans, test cases, and, ultimately, the requirements being tested.

> **NOTE** *To learn how to associate automated tests with test cases, visit* `http://aka.ms/TestCaseAssociatedAutomation2013`.

Remember also that the build-deploy-test workflow build process template can help you with manual testing scenarios where you want to deploy out only a new chosen build. Testers or developers can always queue a new build manually and perform only the build and deployment portion of the workflow, which gets their environment ready with a fresh deployment of their chosen build.

Lab Management Permissions

There are several permissions to be aware of when you are configuring Lab Management. You may want to consider using these permissions to govern, for example, who has the ability to modify virtual environment definitions. Because your build-deploy-test workflow will depend on these definitions, it is important that users change them only if they understand the implications of their changes.

> **NOTE** *To learn about the granular permissions you can assign related to Lab Management activities, visit* `http://aka.ms/LabManagementPermissions2013`.

Geographically Distributed Teams

You may have geographically distributed teams that need to work with Lab Management. But the size of Lab Management artifacts such as VMs can put a heavy strain on wide area networks (WANs).

You should consider co-locating VM hosts and corresponding library shares with the testing teams who need them. If you have multiple teams that need access, consider naming virtual environments appropriately to indicate to users which ones they should be using. (For example, you might prepend your Chicago-based virtual environments with "CHI," New York-based virtual environments with "NYC," and so on.) You can even regulate this more tightly by using permissions.

The best way to handle this situation is to create multiple host groups in SCVMM for each location. You can then place the Hyper-V host servers in that location into the SCVMM host group that corresponds with it. You can then expose each of the host groups in Lab Management, and developers and testers are able to choose the location's host group they want to provision their environment in.

You may also want to create additional library servers that exist in each location for use by the host groups. This helps by not copying large files (like VM templates) across the WAN and allows them to be available in each location for the corresponding host group.

VMware

VMware is a popular virtualization technology, and a common query centers on whether the Lab Management infrastructure supports VMware images. The answer is, "It depends on what you want it to do."

Out of the box, Lab Management capabilities for SCVMM environments will work only with Microsoft's Hyper-V virtualization technology. However, you can create a standard environment out of the machines hosted by VMware, which will let you take advantage of the automated build-deploy-test workflow and use the environment with manual test runs.

However, despite VMware being a virtualization technology, the Lab Management standard environment does not provide any workflow activities for accessing VMware snapshotting capabilities. It is possible to author these activities and integrate them with Team Build's build-deploy-test workflow; but, as of this writing, there are no community projects to support this so you would be faced with writing these activities yourself. Alternatively, there are several free tools available that can be used to help you convert existing VMware images that you might be using into Hyper-V images.

> **NOTE** *Microsoft has provided more details about the level of support for standard environments with Lab Management at* `http://aka.ms/CreatingStandardEnvironments`.

Advanced Topologies

Your existing IT infrastructure requirements (such as whether you have multiple domains), your Team Foundation Server topology (such as whether you have a single AT/DT server, or a scale-out infrastructure), and other factors can have an impact on how you configure your Lab Management infrastructure. If you believe that your implementation might be nonstandard, you should read about the advanced topologies with which Lab Management has been tested and documented. This is available as a four-part blog series at the following locations:

- ➤ `http://aka.ms/LabTopology1`
- ➤ `http://aka.ms/LabTopology2`
- ➤ `http://aka.ms/LabTopology3`
- ➤ `http://aka.ms/LabTopology4`

Maintaining a Healthy Test Lab

An effective Lab Management infrastructure can be a powerful tool for development and testing teams alike to automate the delivery of their iterative software changes into environments that can be tested and, if defects are discovered, debugged. But this environment will require some level of administration to ensure that it remains healthy and that resources are used effectively. This section highlights a few things to consider as your test lab starts to light up with activity.

Instilling Good Citizenship

Lab Management allows testers to easily deploy multiple virtual environments, often consisting of multiple VMs, across numerous physical VM hosts, with just a few clicks of their mouse. But Lab Management does not have a mechanism to enforce that testers shut down environments they are no longer using. Left unchecked, you may find that your VM hosts are running out of disk space, processing power, or (most likely) RAM. There is no substitute for educating testers about the resource constraints of the environment and instructing them to power down environments that they aren't actively using. If an environment is obsolete, it should be deleted.

Lab Management allows you to pause an environment, which will prevent that environment from consuming any CPU cycles on its VM hosts. But this will not free allocated RAM. If testers wish to retain the state of VMs that they aren't actively using, a better approach is to create a snapshot of the environment. After a snapshot is taken, the environment can be powered off completely. When testers are once again ready to resume working with that SCVMM virtual environment, they can restore it to the previous snapshot, and it will be restored to the state it was in before being powered off.

Finally, Lab Management allows testers to mark an environment as "In Use" to signal that they are actively working with it, or planning on working with it soon. This indicates to other testers that they should not try to connect to that environment. Administrators will then know that running environments not marked "In Use" can probably be powered off if they need to reclaim VM host resources. Of course, testers should also be instructed to unmark environments that they are no longer using. If you notice that a tester has an unusually high number of environments in use, then this may indicate that he or she is claiming more resources than should be necessary.

Managing Snapshots

Snapshots are a great benefit of virtualization that allow you to easily store the state of a VM at any point in time and easily restore that state in the future. Snapshots have several uses in a Lab Management environment.

You can use snapshots to capture the baseline system state of an SCVMM environment before deploying your builds. You can again use snapshots to capture the state of the SCVMM environment after the build has been deployed, but before any of your tests have been run. Finally, if you find a defect, a tester can create a snapshot of an entire SCVMM environment and share a pointer to that snapshot when he or she creates a bug. This way, a developer can easily restore an environment back to the state it was in when the tester found the bug.

> **NOTE** *You can learn more about using snapshots within Microsoft Test Manager at* `http://aka.ms/LabManagementSnapshots`.

But snapshots also have the capability of consuming hefty amounts of disk space on your Hyper-V host servers. Additionally, Lab Management does not have a built-in retention policy to prune older snapshots—this will need to be done manually. Even if you set a retention policy in your build definition using Team Build, the process of deleting a build from here will not modify any SCVMM environments. Obsolete snapshots will need to be managed by the testers using the environments or by a lab administrator.

> **NOTE** *Another reason to prune your snapshots is that Hyper-V has a built-in limitation of 50 snapshots per VM. Depending on how you use Lab Management, this limitation could be something to watch for, especially if you build and deploy multiple times per day to the same environment.*

While it is possible to manage snapshots via the SCVMM Administration Console, this is not recommended. SCVMM is aware of only individual VMs. It doesn't understand the composition of VMs in entire SCVMM environments because this level of organization is maintained by Lab Management. Therefore, it is best to manage snapshots using Lab Management via the Microsoft Test Manager interface.

Another important consideration regarding snapshots is that of password expiration. Because snapshots can date back many months, password expiration policies can cause authentication to fail if appropriate precautions are not taken to prevent this from happening. The documentation at http://aka.ms/LabManagementSnapshots provides a detailed explanation of this process, along with preventative measures to keep it from impacting your SCVMM environments.

Workflow Customizations

The default build-deploy-test workflow provided with Lab Management is a powerful workflow, but there may be times when you want to customize this to add new activities, or change existing ones. Because the Lab Management workflows are built on Team Build, and Team Build in this release uses Windows Workflow, there are endless possibilities for extending and customizing the built-in workflows.

> **NOTE** *To read more about customizing the built-in Lab Management workflow, see* http://aka.ms/CustomizingLabManagementWorkflow2013. *This article also details the Lab Management activities provided out of the box and can easily be added to existing workflows with very little additional work. Also, a blog post at* http://aka.ms/LabManagementBDTSnapshot *details how to use the Lab Management activities to automatically create a snapshot to reference from a bug if part of a build-deploy-test workflow fails.*

Patching of VMs and VM Templates

Many of the snapshots you create as part of your experience using Lab Management will be short-lived. Snapshots are commonly created when a new build is deployed or when a bug is discovered. But a week or two later, older snapshots may be cleaned up in favor of newer builds and as bugs are resolved. However, some VM artifacts—such as the VMs and VM templates in your VM library, or the baseline snapshots of SCVMM virtual environments that you use as part of your build-deploy-test workflows—may last for months, or even years. Usually, you will want to keep these artifacts up to date with the latest security updates and other patches from Windows Update, but manually maintaining all of the VMs in your environment may prove to be very painstaking.

The recommended solution to this is to use the Virtual Machine Servicing Tool available at http://aka.ms/VMServicingTool. This tool can be scheduled to automatically patch your VMs and VM templates with the latest updates from Windows Update. The use of this tool will require that you host and maintain Windows Server Update Services (WSUS) locally. This is a free download from Microsoft that allows you to specify which patches you wish to incorporate into your environments.

Windows Activation

One of the other Windows technologies you may need to become familiar with is Windows Activation. If your developers and testers each have MSDN subscriptions, then you are probably familiar with the benefits of being able to use software included in the MSDN subscription for development and test use, which includes the operating system software. (See `http://aka.ms/VisualStudioLicensing`). It's a great benefit of MSDN and is important for development and testing environments like those used in Lab Management. However, you will still need to deal with Windows Activation even though each of the MSDN subscribers is licensed for usage.

A couple of decision points are recommended. If you are using virtual machine templates, after the machines are created from those templates the trial period will begin all over. Therefore, if you are using an environment for less than the operating system evaluation period (180 days for some), we recommend that you not activate the machines in an environment and leverage the trial functionality. In this case, you will want to use the Key Management Server (KMS) Client product keys available at `http://aka.ms/KMSClientKeys`. These special product keys will put Windows in a trial state and force Windows to look for a KMS server if one is available, which will be discussed shortly.

If you need to use environments longer than the operating system evaluation period, then you will want to activate the software. If you happen to be a volume license customer, then you can set up a special kind of activation server within your company, called a Key Management Server (KMS), for use by Lab Management environments. You will need special product keys for the KMS server that are available from the Volume Licensing Service Center at `http://aka.ms/VolumeLicensingServiceCenter`. To learn more about setting up an internal KMS server, you can read more at `http://aka.ms/UnderstandingKMS`.

Troubleshooting

As you have seen in this chapter, using the software testing capabilities of Visual Studio and Team Foundation Server 2013 can involve many moving parts, long-running workflows, complex topologies, and many stakeholders from across your development and testing teams. The Lab Management product team diligently manages a list of evolving troubleshooting techniques, along with an active forum, on MSDN at `http://aka.ms/TroubleshootingLabManagement`.

SUMMARY

In this chapter, you learned about the testing capabilities of Visual Studio 2013 and Visual Studio Online as well as the impact that adopting these tools can have on your Team Foundation Server planning and administration. We covered the new Cloud-based Load Testing Service in Visual Studio Online. You also learned about the architecture of Team Foundation Server when configured in concert with test controllers and agents, SCVMM, Hyper-V host servers, VM libraries, and both standard and SCVMM environments. Finally, you learned some key areas to consider as you build and scale out your Lab Management environment, as well as some tips to maintain this environment over time.

In Chapter 27, you will learn about upgrading from earlier editions of Team Foundation Server to Team Foundation Server 2013.

27

Upgrading Team Foundation Server

Instead of installing a brand-new Team Foundation Server 2013 instance, you may have an earlier version of Team Foundation Server internally and want to upgrade to Team Foundation Server 2013. Thankfully, Microsoft has provided the means to upgrade an existing server to the latest version. However, as a Team Foundation Server administrator, you will actually have several additional tasks to complete to ensure that end users are able to leverage the new features.

The upgrade wizard in Team Foundation Server 2013 allows a full-fidelity data upgrade from the following legacy versions:

➤ Team Foundation Server 2010

➤ Team Foundation Server 2010 with Service Pack 1

➤ Team Foundation Server 2012 Beta or Release Candidate

➤ Team Foundation Server 2012

➤ Team Foundation Server 2012 with Updates 1, 2, or 3

➤ Team Foundation Server 2013 Preview or Release Candidate

You may notice that Team Foundation Server 2005 and 2008 are not listed. If you still have a Team Foundation Server 2005 instance, then you will want to upgrade first to Team Foundation Server 2010 with Service Pack 1, and then you can perform the upgrade to Team Foundation Server 2013. If you still have a Team Foundation Server 2008 instance, you will want to upgrade first to Team Foundation Server 2012, and then upgrade to Team Foundation Server 2013.

In this chapter, you learn about the different approaches to take for upgrading from an earlier version of Team Foundation Server, as well as what is involved with performing an upgrade for each part.

OVERVIEW

Upgrading the software and database schema from earlier versions to Team Foundation Server 2013 could not be easier. However, you will discover that the upgraded Team Foundation Server 2013 environment containing legacy team projects will essentially work as though it were a Team Foundation Server 2010 or 2012 instance running in Team Foundation Server 2013. This is so that the upgrade itself will limit the impact on how teams have been working to continue to be productive immediately after the upgrade. It will be your job to enable, at a schedule convenient for the teams in your organization, any new features that you desire for the legacy team projects that exist before upgrade.

There are several aspects of an upgrade to take into consideration. In this section, you learn about some of those aspects to ensure that your team can go through a smooth upgrade experience.

In-Place Upgrades versus Migrating to New Hardware

The first major decision is whether you want to perform an in-place upgrade on the current hardware where Team Foundation Server is installed or move to new hardware (including any environment topology changes, such as splitting to a dual-tier configuration).

The upgrade wizard in the configuration utility enables you to connect to a set of Team Foundation Server 2010 or 2012 databases and upgrade the schema and data appropriately.

During an in-place upgrade, the former versions of the software are uninstalled, and then Team Foundation Server 2013 is installed in addition to the latest updates. You will be able to then use the upgrade wizard and input the connection information for the existing database server, and the database schema is upgraded in place.

For a hardware migration-based upgrade, the legacy databases are fully backed up and then restored to the new hardware environment. The upgrade wizard is then pointed to the new database server instance with a copy of the latest database backups restored. It will discover the legacy version of those databases and appropriately upgrade the database schema to Team Foundation Server 2013.

DIFFERENCE BETWEEN MIGRATIONS AND UPGRADES

Moving to new hardware is considered a *hardware migration-based upgrade*, which should not be confused with another option that some may describe as "migrating to Team Foundation Server 2013." Note that despite having a similar name, a migration-based upgrade is *not* a migration.

The approach that others have described (not recommended) would involve setting up a brand-new Team Foundation Server 2013 environment with new databases, creating new team projects, and then migrating the source code and work items using a tool such as the Team Foundation Server Integration platform.

That approach will lead to many side effects. It is considered a *low-fidelity data transfer* because the data has changed (such as changeset, dates, and work item ID numbers), and because this approach doesn't move over other data, such as reporting, security privileges, and build information. By taking the actual upgrade route (described in this chapter), the configuration wizard will upgrade the database schema and keep all of the data as it existed from the earlier Team Foundation Server environment. For that reason, this is considered a *high-fidelity upgrade*.

For more about these differences, you can read Matt Mitrik's articles about this topic at the following sites:

➤ http://aka.ms/TFSMigrationDefinition

➤ http://aka.ms/TFSUpgradeDefinition

There are several advantages and disadvantages to both an in-place upgrade and a hardware migration-based upgrade. The main disadvantage to performing a hardware migration is that you will need to acquire new hardware (whether physical or virtual machines). The nice thing, though, is that, after the upgrade is completed and verified, you will be able to retire the legacy hardware and repurpose it for some other use or completely discard any virtual machines previously used. After personally being involved with a very large number of upgrades over several years, we would overwhelmingly recommend the hardware migration-based upgrade.

Following are the advantages of performing a hardware migration-based upgrade:

➤ **Testing the upgrade**—Having a separate Team Foundation Server environment allows you to perform the upgrade steps while the production environment is still running. This allows you to perform the upgrade to test it before going through with the final upgrade run.

➤ **Having a rollback plan**—One of the main advantages of performing a hardware migration-based upgrade is that you have a rollback plan already in place in case the upgrade is not successful, or in case it cannot be verified. By keeping up the legacy hardware environment, you can have users continue to connect to the old environment (if needed) while researching any upgrade issues in the new hardware environment.

➤ **Taking advantage of new operating system versions**—If the legacy environment is using Windows Server 2008 R2 with SP1, you can take advantage of newer operating system versions (such as Windows Server 2012) by ensuring that the new hardware has the latest versions installed. Otherwise, the final upgrade plan would require you to upgrade the operating system as well, which can affect your rollback plan.

➤ **Taking advantage of a 64-bit application tier**—Earlier versions of the Team Foundation Server application tier software supported installation only on 32-bit operating systems. If you are planning to use a Windows Server operating system, then Team Foundation Server 2013 supports only 64-bit versions.

➤ **Installing new copies of prerequisite software**—As discussed later in this chapter, you will end up needing to ensure that SQL Server and SharePoint are upgraded to newer versions for Team Foundation Server 2013. Acquiring new hardware allows you to install each prerequisite software fresh, instead of worrying about having to upgrade the software during the final upgrade.

➤ **New built-in backup and restore functionality**—You do not even have to worry about performing the database backup and restoration in a separate tool. To make the process easier for moving to new hardware during the upgrade, Team Foundation Server 2013 introduces two new utilities to help ease with the process: `TFSBackup.exe` and `TFSRestore.exe`.

Planning Upgrades

There are additional considerations to account for with the upgrade process that are different from a fresh Team Foundation Server 2013 installation. Let's take a look at a few of those.

Connection URL

Let's hope that the person setting up the earlier version of Team Foundation Server used fully qualified, friendly DNS names for each of the subsystems of Team Foundation Server, as described in Chapter 2. After the upgrade is complete, you should ensure that the friendly DNS entries are changed to point to the new hardware environment. When users start connecting to the Team Foundation Server environment using the friendly DNS entries, they will automatically be pointing to the new environment fully upgraded without having to make any additional changes. The Visual Studio and other clients will continue to work without any additional changes.

If friendly DNS names were not used in the previous setup, then we recommend that you use the concepts described in Chapter 2 to allow for smoother upgrades in the future. Future Team Foundation Server administrators and your team members will thank you for it. A blog post about using friendly DNS names in a Team Foundation Server environment is available at `http://aka.ms/FriendlyDNSTFS`.

Also, remember that some legacy versions of Visual Studio clients and other tools that connect to Team Foundation Server 2013 may need to include the Project Collection name and the virtual directory in the connection URL. Chapters 4 and 21 provide more information about these changes.

Other Servers in the Team Foundation Server Environment

Remember that there might be other servers that should be upgraded before they can be fully used. For example, all of the build servers will need to be upgraded to the latest version, as well as proxy servers, test controllers, and test agents.

Update 2 of Team Foundation Server 2012 added support for Team Foundation Server 2010 build servers, and that support has carried over to Team Foundation Server 2013. You can safely connect Team Foundation Server 2010 and 2012 build servers to Team Foundation Server 2013.

After testing the upgrade in a separate environment, you will want to establish downtime for the Team Foundation Server environment to be unavailable to end users while the upgrade wizard is upgrading the schema for the databases. The amount of time necessary depends on the amount of data currently stored in the legacy databases as well as the version of the database schema in the legacy databases. For example, if you are upgrading from Team Foundation Server 2010, then the upgrade process will take more time because there are more schema upgrade steps necessary. The amount of time is also extremely variable and dependent on hardware, disk speed, available memory, and so on. This is also another great reason for doing a hardware migration-based upgrade.

When the predetermined cutoff time for your team arrives, make sure that users are no longer using the environment and take a full backup of the database. Any changes made to the legacy environment after the full backup occurs will not be available on the upgraded server.

After the upgrade has been successfully completed, a different set of databases will be used by the Team Foundation Server 2013 environment, if you were upgrading from Team Foundation Server 2010. Legacy SQL Server backup plans may be looking for the legacy database names, so you will want to ensure that any relevant backup plans are reviewed and modified accordingly.

> **NOTE** *Chapter 23 provides more information about disaster recovery with Team Foundation Server.*

UPGRADING PREREQUISITES

Team Foundation Server 2013 drops support for several pieces of prerequisite software formerly supported with earlier versions of Team Foundation Server. Before running the upgrade wizard, you will want to ensure that all prerequisite software has been upgraded to the supported versions because the upgrade wizard will block you from continuing if those conditions have not been met.

Like Team Foundation Server 2012, Team Foundation Server 2013 does not support 32-bit Windows Server operating systems. The following Windows Server operating system versions are supported with Team Foundation Server 2013:

➤ 64-bit version of Windows Server 2008 R2 with SP1 (Standard, Enterprise, or Datacenter editions)

➤ Windows Small Business Server 2011 with SP1 (Standard, Essentials, or Premium Add-on editions)

➤ 64-bit versions of Windows Server 2012 (Essentials, Standard, or Datacenter editions)

➤ 64-bit versions of Windows Server 2012 R2 (Essentials, Standard, or Datacenter editions)

Additionally, Team Foundation Server 2013 supports installing Windows client operating systems, although the reporting and SharePoint integration features will be disabled if you install on any of the supported client operating systems. You will also be unable to run a TFS proxy if you are using a client operating system. The following versions of the Windows client operating systems are supported with Team Foundation Server 2013:

➤ 64-bit or 32-bit versions of Windows 7 with SP1 (Home Premium, Professional, Enterprise, or Ultimate editions)

➤ 64-bit or 32-bit versions of Windows 8 (Basic, Pro, or Enterprise editions)

➤ 64-bit or 32-bit versions of Windows 8.1 (Basic, Pro, or Enterprise editions)

SQL Server

Several changes were made in this release for the requirements for SQL Server. The following versions of SQL Server are supported with Team Foundation Server 2013:

➤ SQL Server 2012 with SP1 (Express, Standard, or Enterprise editions)

➤ SQL Server 2014 (Express, Standard or Enterprise editions)

You will notice that SQL Server 2008 is no longer supported with Team Foundation Server 2012. You will also notice that Microsoft has confirmed support for the next version of SQL Server. This is unusual, but is helpful to know for teams who always want to be using the latest and greatest versions of software.

Team Foundation Server 2013 supports using the Express version of SQL Server 2012, if you would like to take advantage of a lighter-weight version of SQL. The Reporting Services and Analysis Services features are not available if you use SQL Express. This configuration is common if you choose to use the Basic configuration wizard or use Team Foundation Server Express. However, if you are upgrading a server, you will be using the Upgrade configuration wizard.

> **WARNING** *Despite offering only a single (current) option for SQL Server support, there are some caveats and warnings to be aware of. These include choosing the correct collation settings, installing updates in certain cases, and being aware of feature availability for different editions.*
>
> *We recommend that you familiarize yourself with these details to ensure your upgrade succeeds. You can find these details at* `http://tinyurl.com/ SQLTFS2013.`

> **WARNING** *Virtualization of the server that has SQL Server installed is not recommended without the proper hardware and disk performance outputs because it can lead to data loss and severe performance problems. If you choose to use virtualization of the SQL Server machine, be sure to configure the virtual machine for top performance when working with Team Foundation Server. See the discussion about virtualization in Chapters 2 and 21 for more information.*

SharePoint

Team Foundation Server 2008 supported Windows SharePoint Services 2.0 for the team project portal sites. Unfortunately, if you are still using Windows SharePoint Services 2.0, you must upgrade to one of the following versions of SharePoint products and technologies supported by Team Foundation Server 2013:

➤ Windows SharePoint Services 3.0 (no licensing cost)

➤ Microsoft Office SharePoint Server 2007

➤ SharePoint 2010 Foundation (no licensing cost)

➤ Office SharePoint 2010 Server

➤ Office SharePoint 2013 Server

> **NOTE** *For more information about upgrading the SharePoint products and technologies for a Team Foundation Server 2010 environment, see the related information and step-by-step instructions available on MSDN at* `http://aka .ms/TFSUpgradingSharePoint`.

Project Server

If you integrated with a Project Server instance in Team Foundation Server 2010, then you will not need to worry about upgrading the Project Server software before upgrading your Team Foundation Server instance. The following versions of Project Server are supported with Team Foundation Server 2013:

➤ Project Server 2010 with SP1

➤ Project Server 2013

System Center

If you have set up the Lab Management functionality in Team Foundation Server 2010 with System Center Virtual Machine Manager, then you do not need to make any changes to your System Center 2008 R2 instance. That version is still supported in Team Foundation Server 2013. You can later upgrade that instance to use System Center Virtual Machine Manager 2012 with SP1, but that does not need to occur during the upgrade. If you are going to install System Center 2012, be sure to also install Service Pack 1 which adds support for Windows 8 and Windows Server 2012.

USING THE CONFIGURATION UTILITY

The latest version of the *Team Foundation Server 2012 Installation Guide* and the MSDN Library have step-by-step lists of instructions and checklists that detail how to upgrade using either upgrade approach (in-place upgrade or hardware migration-based upgrade). You will want to make sure that you follow each part of the checklist to ensure the smoothest upgrade possible. The latest version of the step-by-step walkthroughs and checklists are always available on the MSDN library at `http:// aka.ms/UpgradeTFS`.

If you are following the hardware migration-based upgrade approach, you will essentially back up the databases on the old database server instance and then restore them on the new database server instance. Once you have upgraded all of the prerequisite software and restored a full backup of all of the Team Foundation Server databases as listed in the *Installation Guide*, you are ready to go through the Team Foundation Server upgrade wizard.

As mentioned in Chapter 3, the setup configuration process is split into two parts. There is an installation phase that puts all of the necessary software on the application tier server. You will also want to make sure that you have installed the latest Team Foundation Server 2013 update released from Microsoft before moving forward.

Once the software and updates are installed, you configure them with a separate configuration utility. This segmented approach resolves the legacy issue introduced in earlier versions of Team Foundation Server (an installation that was successful but whose configuration failed). In those cases, all of the software was removed from the server, even though it was correctly placed. Now you are able to get everything installed, and a rich user interface (UI) can let you know if there are any problems during the configuration phase, instead of it occurring inside of an installer.

Interestingly, another benefit of this two-phase approach is that Microsoft can release service packs and updates that will easily fix problems with the configuration utility. This became particularly important starting with Team Foundation Server 2012 because Microsoft has committed to providing more frequent updates that include new features along with performance and bug fixes. The faster release cadence means you can expect three or four major updates every year for Team Foundation Server.

Upgrade Wizard

Instead of installing a new server as described in Chapter 3, you will need to run the upgrade wizard once to get the database schema upgraded to the version used by Team Foundation Server 2013. The Upgrade wizard option is available in the configuration utility, as shown in Figure 27-1.

If you will be including multiple application tier servers in a Team Foundation Server application tier farm, you must run the Upgrade wizard only once for the first application tier server. You can then use the Application-Tier Only wizard for each additional application tier server to connect them to the already upgraded databases.

> **NOTE** *Chapter 22 provides more information about scalability options for Team Foundation Server using network load balancing to create a Team Foundation Server application tier farm.*

Follow each of the upgrade wizard pages at this point and enter the information requested. The latest version of the *Installation Guide*, or the MSDN Library upgrade articles mentioned earlier, has step-by-step directions and information about each option displayed within the upgrade wizard.

Before the upgrade process begins, all of the options and information that you input will be validated to ensure that there are no issues. If you see any errors listed, you must resolve them before continuing. For several errors that may occur, you are able to restart the verification process without leaving the wizard.

FIGURE 27-1: Upgrade wizard option

Once you are ready, you can begin the upgrade process. This will kick off several upgrade jobs that will run through the upgrade steps necessary for each subsystem of Team Foundation Server. The upgrade wizard will show you the progress of each set of upgrade jobs, the configuration instance, and each of the project collections.

Verification of Upgrade

After all of the upgrade jobs have completed for project collections, you will get a confirmation. If there were any issues, you can restart the job using the Team Foundation Server Administration utility. If you did receive a successful confirmation that the upgrade has completed, you can try out any or all of the following verification items to ensure everything is working properly:

➤ Check to ensure that any existing version control workspaces still exist and are configured the same as before the upgrade.

➤ Open the version control repository and check to make sure shelvesets and pending changes for your workspace still exist.

➤ Check the maximum changeset in the version control repository and ensure that it is the latest expected changeset that occurred before the cutoff time and the full backup.

➤ Open and create work items.

➤ Run work item queries to check that all of the expected work items are returned.

➤ View existing builds and queue new builds with legacy build definitions.

➤ Navigate and open SQL Reporting Services reports. (It may take several hours before the new warehouse has been populated with data.)

➤ Ensure that you can navigate to the SharePoint team portal sites and that the Documents node shows all document libraries from the associated team portal sites.

➤ Navigate to the Team Web Access site to verify that it loads successfully and displays the correct information.

➤ Ensure that test plans and test cases can be accessed through Microsoft Test Manager.

➤ Check to make sure that environments created using Lab Management are listed in the Lab Center of Microsoft Test Manager.

Additionally, to ensure that the entire environment is healthy, you should run the Best Practices Analyzer for Team Foundation Server 2013 (as introduced in Chapter 21), available in the latest version of the Team Foundation Server 2013 Power Tools. This will run a full set of rules to check the entire environment to make sure everything is working as expected. You can also start monitoring the environment using the techniques you learned in Chapter 25.

UPGRADING LEGACY TEAM PROJECTS

Now that you have a working Team Foundation Server 2013 instance based on the upgraded legacy version of the databases, you will notice that the legacy team projects will be working exactly the way they did in the earlier versions of Team Foundation Server. This means that several of the new features introduced in Team Foundation Server 2013 will not be available for team members. This will also be the case for some features introduced in Team Foundation Server 2012, if you were upgrading from Team Foundation Server 2010.

One way that you can start using the new features is to create new team projects that use the latest version of the process templates included with Team Foundation Server 2013, then to perform a version control move operation into the new team project.

However, existing build definitions and work item tracking do not have standard tools available for moving to the new team project. For work item tracking, you could potentially use the Team Foundation Server Integration Platform tools; but, again, this would be a low-fidelity data transfer, as previously discussed.

The upcoming sections primarily focus on the steps necessary to enable Team Foundation Server 2013 features for team projects created using the standard process templates available in Team Foundation Server 2010 or Team Foundation Server 2012.

Feature Enablement

One of the exciting improvements that was introduced in Team Foundation Server 2012 was the new Configure Features Wizard. The Configure Features Wizard helps you enable the new features available in Team Foundation Server for team projects created using one of the standard process templates available in earlier versions.

To clarify, the Configure Features Wizard will not change the process template or upgrade those team projects to new versions of the corresponding process templates, but it will help by enabling some of the new Team Foundation Server 2012 and 2013 features. This is primarily to save you time that would normally be needed to perform manual steps. The features that can be enabled by the Configure Features Wizard are:

➤ Portfolio backlogs (including Feature work item type and Category)

➤ Code Reviews

➤ Stakeholder Feedback

➤ My Work

➤ Planning tools (product backlog, Iteration planning, and task boards)

➤ Storyboard integration

➤ Hidden Types work item category

The first time that you navigate to the Team Project administration section in Team Web Access, you will see a message indicating that features are available for that team project, but they must be configured before they can be used, as shown in Figure 27-2.

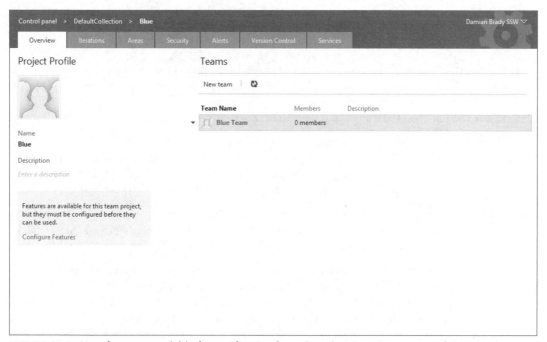

FIGURE 27-2: New features available for notification from the administration section of Team Web Access

By clicking on the link in that message, you can start the Configure Features Wizard for this team project, as shown in Figure 27-3.

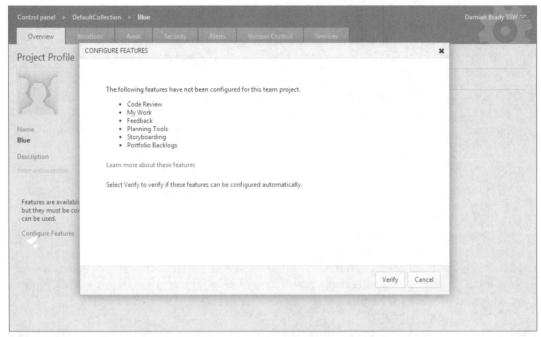

FIGURE 27-3: Configure Features Wizard

The Configure Features Wizard will attempt to inspect the process template currently being used by that team project and see if it can detect a newer version that can be partially applied. If it is not able to detect the appropriate process template, it may allow you to manually choose a new Team Foundation Server 2013–based process template registered with the server.

If you are satisfied with the choice, you can click Configure and the wizard will enable as many features as possible. A confirmation page that lists any additional steps that you need to take will appear. If the process does not complete successfully, you must either manually update the team project or attempt to run the Configure Features Wizard again after updating a registered process template.

You can find out more about the Configure Features Wizard, as well as other manual methods for enabling the features introduced in Team Foundation Server 2013, by visiting this MSDN article: http://tinyurl.com/EnableTFS2013Features.

If you have a team project created from a heavily customized process template, manual instructions that you can follow to enable the features introduced in Team Foundation Server 2013 are available at http://aka.ms/UpdateCustomTFSProcess. One of the options for those with customized process templates is the ability to manually add the necessary functionality to your custom process template and upload and register the compatible process template. You can then run the Configure Features Wizard and use your updated custom process template. This can be extremely beneficial if you have several team projects to update.

CONFIGURING FEATURES FOR MANY TEAM PROJECTS

If you need to configure features for several team projects at once, running through the wizard for all of your projects one at a time can be very time consuming. With Team Foundation Server 2013, you have the ability to programmatically configure features.

Ewald Hofman has a great blog post that walks readers through the process of automating this configuration. The post relates to Team Foundation Server 2012, but with some minor changes it will work with Team Foundation Server 2013. You can find it at `http://tinyurl.com/MultipleTFS2013Features`.

Allowing Access to Premium Features

As previously discussed in Chapter 24, Team Foundation Server 2013 includes premium features in Team Web Access that should be available to use only by team members with certain editions of Visual Studio licensed to them. Those Visual Studio editions are as follows:

➤   Visual Studio 2013 Premium with MSDN

➤   Visual Studio 2013 Ultimate with MSDN

➤   Visual Studio 2013 Test Professional with MSDN

You control this access by setting the licenses for users in the Team Web Access Administration pages. Three types of license groups are available for Team Foundation Server 2013, which enable certain features:

➤   **Limited**—Can include all users in your organization who need the ability to create work items. Does not require a Team Foundation Server CAL.

➤   **Standard**—Includes all users that have a Team Foundation Server CAL or Visual Studio Professional with MSDN.

➤   **Full**—Includes all users with one of the Visual Studio editions mentioned previously that have access to all of the features in Team Web Access.

LICENSING GROUPS AND PERMISSIONS

Adding a user or security group to one of the Licensing groups mentioned in this section does not give those users the permissions required. Those users still need to be granted the appropriate permissions necessary to use the features that are enabled for each team project. More information about security and permissions can be found in Chapter 24.

After you upgrade to Team Foundation Server 2013, the default licensing group is set to Standard, which would include administrative users such as your account. When navigating to a team site in Team Web Access, you will see a notification similar to Figure 27-4 that indicates that some features are not visible to you.

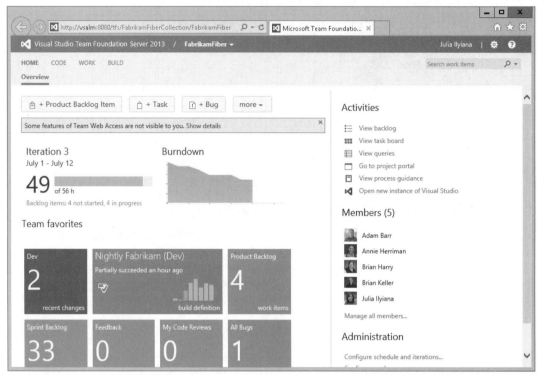

FIGURE 27-4: Features Not Visible notification from Team Web Access

To enable the full set of features for users that have a license to access them, you should go to the Team Web Access Administration site for managing the license groups, as shown in Figure 27-5. You can find that site by opening an Internet browser and navigating to the URL for your Team Web Access site in the format of `http://yourtfsservername:8080/tfs/_admin/_licenses` and replacing it with the appropriate settings for your Team Foundation Server instance.

Add the appropriate users or security groups to the Full licensing group, or if you know that all users who will be accessing this Team Foundation Server instance will be licensed appropriately, you can set the Full licensing group as the default web access licensing group for all users.

Automated Builds

Build definitions that existed in Team Foundation Server 2010 before upgrading that used the default workflow-based build process template will continue to work after the upgrade. If you have an opportunity, especially if you do not have any build process template customizations, you can switch your build definitions over to using the new default build process template that was added to each of the team projects during the upgrade process. This will ensure that you are using all of the latest updates included in the latest version.

If you had any custom build process templates that included custom build workflow activities, you will need to take an additional step: Update the references to the latest version before recompiling your customer workflow activities and making them available for deployment to the build controller and agents, as explained in Chapter 19.

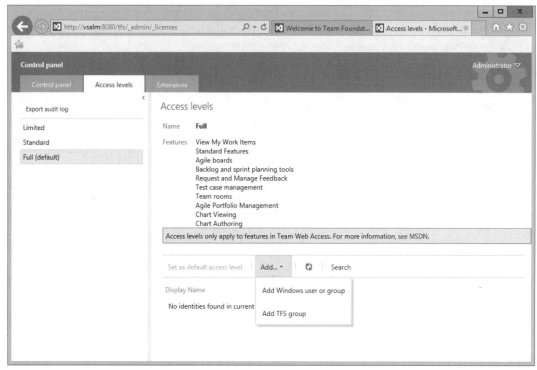

FIGURE 27-5: Managing the licensing groups

We highly recommend taking the new default build process template from Team Foundation Server 2013 and applying all of your customizations appropriately so that you can take advantage of all of the new features included in the new version of the build process template. You can then use that newly customized build process template going forward.

> **NOTE** *Chapter 19 includes more information about how to customize the build process and create custom build workflow activities.*

Enable Local Workspaces

Local Workspaces, which you learned about in Chapter 6, are one of the features that make developers more productive. For new Team Foundation Server 2013 installs, Local Workspaces (as opposed to server workspaces) are enabled by default for any new workspaces that are created. However, for backwards compatibility reasons and because it is a new paradigm shift for those that might have worked with Visual SourceSafe or earlier versions of Team Foundation Server in the past, the default remains set to server workspaces whenever you upgrade from an earlier version of Team Foundation Server.

We highly recommend that after your server is upgraded you change the default to Local Workspaces. The next time one of your developers connects to the server, she will even get an option to "upgrade" her legacy workspace into a Local Workspace. That notification to the developer is only shown if the default is changed in the server settings. A step-by-step walkthrough is available for how to update the default at `http://aka.ms/SetTFSWorkspacesDefault`.

Deploying New Reports

The data warehouse schema for Team Foundation Server 2013 has been updated and no longer works with the reports included in Team Foundation Server 2008 or earlier. If your migration involved an upgrade from Team Foundation Server 2008 (via either Team Foundation Server 2010 or 2012), you can deploy a new set of reports using the new process templates (assuming you have performed all of the "morphing" steps to get your team project up to the latest process template version) by using a tool available from the latest version of Team Foundation Server Power Tools. It is available from the command line by using the following:

```
tfpt.exe addprojectreports /collection:http://tfs:8080/tfs/
    DefaultCollection /teamproject:LegacyTeamProject /
    processtemplate:"MSF for Agile Software Development 2013" /force
```

This command will download the specified process template and deploy all of the reports included in the process template appropriately to the reporting site associated with the specified team project. The `/force` option allows you to overwrite what already exists if there is a report with the same name. You can modify the reports, upload the updated process template, and repeat this process as necessary.

Deploying New SharePoint Team Portal Site

Team portal sites that exist in legacy team projects do not take advantage of all of the SharePoint dashboard features as described in Chapter 15. This is one of the toughest options because there is no way to convert an existing site and enable the dashboards on a portal site template.

In this case, the best option would be to archive the document library content from the legacy team portal site, create a new team portal site using the latest process template, and then add the archived document library content. There may be other types of features that were used that may not be able to migrate over successfully. You will have to weigh the options appropriately.

The latest version of the Team Foundation Server Power Tools also includes a command-line tool for creating a new team portal site and associating it with a team project. The following example command could be used to perform this step:

```
tfpt.exe addprojectportal /collection:http://tfs:8080/tfs/
    DefaultCollection /teamproject:LegacyTeamProject /
    processtemplate:"MSF for Agile Software Development 2013"
```

You can specify additional options if you want the team portal site to be created in a different location from the default location specified for the team project collection.

Upgrading Lab Management Environments

You need to make sure that you upgrade any test controllers that you have configured for your Team Foundation Server instance to the Visual Studio 2013 version of the test controller software. Be sure to also install any of the relevant updates that might be available for the Visual Studio 2013 test controllers.

After upgrading from Team Foundation Server 2010, all of the environments created using Lab Management (available from the Lab Center in Microsoft Test Manager) will be marked as needing to be upgraded before they can be used again. The Visual Studio agents installed in each of the machines in the environment need to be updated.

Thankfully, you can leverage the agent auto-install and auto-configure features in Team Foundation Server 2013. These will automatically uninstall the old agents and install and configure the new test agent software for you. Be sure that you have installed any of the latest updates for the Test Controllers so that the most up-to-date version of the Visual Studio 2013 Agents is installed.

If you do decide to also upgrade to System Center Virtual Machine Manager 2012, be sure to also upgrade the System Center Virtual Machine Manager 2012 Administration Console software on each of the application tier servers. You will also likely be prompted with an informational message that indicates that Team Foundation Server has detected a newer version of System Center, similar to Figure 27-6.

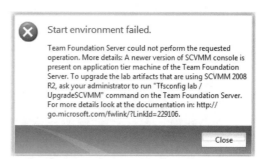

FIGURE 27-6: New System Center version detected

You will want to perform the step indicated in that informational message, which is running this one-time command on any of the Team Foundation Server 2013 application tier servers:

```
TFSConfig.exe Lab /UpgradeSCVMM
```

SUMMARY

As you learned in this chapter, the upgrade wizard will allow you to move all of your data from a legacy version of Team Foundation Server to Team Foundation Server 2013, using a high-fidelity upgrade method. In this chapter, you learned about the two types of upgrades—an in-place upgrade and a hardware migrated-based upgrade.

Additionally, you learned about the preparation steps necessary for a successful upgrade, including taking care of any prerequisite software. Finally, you learned about the features not available on legacy team projects until they are enabled in Team Foundation Server 2013.

Chapter 28 introduces the issues that come up whenever you have geographically separated teams that need to use the Team Foundation Server environment. The chapter explores the different options available to resolve those issues, and it provides methods for ensuring a smoothly operating worldwide environment for all of the geographically separated teams.

28

Working with Geographically Distributed Teams

WHAT'S IN THIS CHAPTER?

➤ Understanding the difficulties of a distributed development environment

➤ Getting to know Team Foundation Server Proxy

➤ Learning techniques for working with remote teams

➤ Dealing with build servers in a distributed environment

➤ Introducing Team Foundation Server Integration Tools

➤ Understanding how to be effective when the server is not available

The development of software by distributed teams is a growing trend. People are working in a global economy with greater competition and choice. There are many reasons you may be working with a distributed team, including the following:

➤ Your company has grown and expanded, and it has several field offices.

➤ Your company contracts out portions of development to third parties.

➤ Your company merged with another company and both companies must work interactively over great distances.

Even if you don't work in a distributed team, you may work in an environment whereby your server infrastructure is located at a different physical location. Following are a few examples:

➤ Your IT infrastructure is outsourced to another company—for example, using the Visual Studio Online hosted by Microsoft.

➤ Your development team is located in a different city from the main office to take advantage of skilled workers in that area.

➤ You have a mobile workforce that moves between offices and has no main office.

When you work with Team Foundation Server 2013 in this environment, there are a number of challenges that you will face and specific issues you are more likely to encounter as a result of having physically separated teams. This chapter explores those challenges and ways that you can overcome them.

Team Foundation Server 2013 was built with these geographical challenges in mind. In this chapter, you'll learn about the capabilities of Team Foundation Server that allow you to overcome these boundaries and collaborate as a cohesive team, whether separated by feet or by oceans.

IDENTIFYING THE CHALLENGES

You face a number of challenges when working with geographically distributed teams. This chapter walks you through the challenges most relevant to your Team Foundation Server environment.

Latency over the Wide Area Network

Perhaps the biggest technical challenge that distributed teams will face is the network connection that separates them and the server. Network connectivity can be affected by many different factors. However, the biggest factor is latency.

Latency is the time that it takes for packets of data to travel between two points. Think of when you connect a garden hose to a tap and then turn it on. There is a delay between when you turn on the tap and when water starts pouring out the other end. This delay is called latency. Latency in a networking context can be "one-way" or "round-trip." *Round-trip latency* is the time it takes data to travel from the client to the server and back again. It is usually measured by running the ping command against a server.

On a local area network (LAN), typical round-trip latency is less than five milliseconds. Between two computers within the same continent, typical round-trip latency is less than 100 milliseconds.

What's important to realize is that regardless of the speed of your Internet connection, your latency can never beat the speed of light. The speed of light in fiber-optic cable is roughly 35 percent slower than in a vacuum. As an example, the shortest distance between Sydney, Australia, and Seattle, Washington, is about 8,000 miles, or 12,000 kilometers. Therefore, the absolute minimum one-way latency is 60 milliseconds, and the round-trip latency is 120 milliseconds. In reality, though, the cables don't run directly between two points, so the latency is higher because of this and intermediate network equipment.

Another aspect of latency is that it isn't always symmetric. Latency could be greater in one direction compared to the other. This can be seen when using a one-way satellite Internet connection. The upstream data is sent using a landline, and the downstream data is received via a satellite dish. Because the data must travel from the Internet to a base station, to the satellite, and then back down to the receiving dish, typical round-trip latency is 300 milliseconds.

Microsoft recommends that a server running Team Foundation Server should have a reliable network connection with a minimum bandwidth of 1 Mbps and a maximum latency of 350 milliseconds.

Sources of Network Traffic

Many different sources of network traffic exist within the components of a Team Foundation Server environment. Table 28-1 details the contribution of each component, which will vary in each environment. In most environments, version control and work item tracking are typically the biggest contributors. Depending on your configuration, virtual machine deployments from Lab Management can be a large contributor.

TABLE 28-1: Network Traffic Associated with Each Component

COMPONENT	TRAFFIC
Version control	Source files and operations
Work item tracking	Work items, operations, metadata cache, and attachments
Web access	Web pages, images, scripts, style sheets, attachments, and source files
Reporting	Reports, database queries, and Analysis Services queries
SharePoint products (including dashboards)	Web pages, documents, work items, and reports
Team Foundation Build	Build logs and build outputs
Lab Management	Commands, System Center Virtual Machine Manager (SCVMM) traffic, lab environments, and templates

Version Control

Version control in a Team Foundation Server environment will almost always be the largest contributor to network traffic. There are two sources of traffic:

➤ User commands

➤ File content downloads

Whenever a client performs a `Get` (if using Team Foundation Version Control) or a `Pull` (if using Git), the server will send the entire contents of any file that has changed to the client. The more clients you have, the more traffic there is. The amount of traffic is also proportional to the number, frequency, and size of files that change in the repository.

Work Item Tracking

Work item tracking has three main sources of traffic:

➤ User commands (queries, opens, saves, and bulk updates)

➤ Metadata Cache downloads

➤ Attachment downloads and uploads

The biggest contributor of these three is usually the Metadata Cache.

Every team project has a set of metadata that includes work item rules, global lists, form layouts, and other project settings. The more team projects that you have and that people have access to, the more metadata that needs to be potentially sent to each of the clients. There is a linear relationship in the metadata size increase and the number of team projects even if each of the team projects uses the same process template.

Whenever a client communicates with the server to perform a work item–related query, it tells the server what version of the metadata it is using. The server then sends back all the metadata that it doesn't know about yet, along with the data the client was actually asking for. This is called a *Metadata Refresh*. There are two types of Metadata Refreshes: *incremental* and *full*.

In Team Foundation Server 2008, certain administrative operations such as deleting a field caused the Metadata Cache to be invalidated. All clients would then download the full Metadata Cache the next time they performed a query.

In Team Foundation Server 2010, 2012, and 2013, almost all operations that invalidate the cache will use an incremental update. This means that not only the load on the server (in the form of memory pressure and metadata requests) is greatly reduced, but also the overall network traffic to the client is reduced.

> **NOTE** *To measure the work item tracking Metadata Cache size, on any client computer, locate the* `C:\Users\<user>\AppData\Local\Microsoft\Team Foundation\5.0\Cache` *folder. Right-click a subdirectory that has a GUID as the name, select Properties, and read the size in the Properties dialog box. Remember that the Metadata Cache is likely to be compressed when it travels over the network, so you might have to use a network traffic sniffer such as* `NetMon` *to see the actual network transfer size, rather than looking at the folder size.*

PROBLEMS WITH METADATA CACHE REFRESHES AT MICROSOFT

Because of the level of process template customization by various teams at Microsoft, there were a lot of unique fields, rules, and work items on the internal servers. In an effort to clean up some of the fields and consolidate them, the project administrators started to delete the unused fields.

This field deletion caused the Metadata Cache to be invalidated and forced all clients to perform a full Metadata Cache refresh. The combination of a large Metadata Cache and a large number of clients effectively took the server offline by consuming all the memory available, and all available connections, while the clients refreshed their caches.

As a brute-force work-around before metadata filtering was available, the team renamed the stored procedure that invalidated the cache to prevent the problem from happening during business hours. Then, if there was a need to delete the fields and invalidate the cache, the team would rename it back and run the command on a weekend. The cache refreshes would then be staggered as people arrived at work on Monday and connected to the server.

Visual Studio 2010, 2012, and 2013 clients perform an incremental update if a field is deleted on the server, so this is no longer a problem.

SOLUTIONS

You have a number of different ways to overcome the challenges of working with geographically distributed teams. Each of these solutions can be used by itself or combined with others to fit your needs.

Using Visual Studio Online Geographically Distributed

Using the Microsoft-hosted Visual Studio Online is the easiest way to offload a large portion of the infrastructure required by Team Foundation Server. A scalable cloud infrastructure greatly simplifies deployment and is a great way to avoid worrying about increased server load when your team grows.

There are drawbacks for some distributed teams, however. Because the service is hosted in the cloud, all communication happens via the Internet. This can result in significantly greater latency than you would find with a server deployed on a local network. If most of your team is in one office and only a few users need access from another geographic location, this solution may not be appropriate.

In some organizations, it is not acceptable for any intellectual property to be hosted on third-party infrastructure. This is especially true in highly regulated environments such as governmental, defense, and financial industries. In this case, a hosted solution such as Visual Studio Online may be immediately ruled out.

The benefits of using hosted server infrastructure can be substantial for teams that are distributed across the globe. It is certainly the simplest solution for providing access to anyone in any location, but it may come with increased latency for some or all of your users.

Central Server with Remote Proxy Servers

The Team Foundation Server Proxy is a server that is capable of caching downloads of files from version control and test result attachments. It is discussed later in this chapter. This is the recommended and simplest environment to configure and maintain. It is the best choice when your users are working from branch offices that can host remote proxy servers.

However, the drawback is that if your users are evenly spread around the world, then there is no central place to locate the server, and latency will be a problem for everybody. You will want to place proxy servers in each of the remote locations.

Multiple Distributed Servers

If your distributed teams are working on different products that can be developed in isolation of each other, then running multiple servers may be an option. This has the benefit of allowing people to work with a local server on their projects. The drawback, of course, is that there are now multiple servers to maintain, along with codebases in different repositories. Additionally, reporting and managing software releases and resources across multiple Team Foundation Server instances becomes quite challenging.

The remote team could host its own Team Foundation Server and maintain a dedicated team project collection. Then, when it comes time to hand off the product to the in-house maintenance team, the collection can be detached from the remote server, backed up, and then attached to the local server.

> **NOTE** *For more information on this procedure, see the "Move a Team Project Collection" page on MSDN at* `http://aka.ms/TFSMoveTPC.`

Mirroring

If your development cannot be partitioned between the different remote sites, then one option is to use the Team Foundation Server Integration Tools to mirror source code and work items between the different Team Foundation Server environments. This may sound like the silver bullet that can solve all of your problems, but it is not without a large cost.

Every mirror that you set up has overhead associated with it. When people are depending upon the mirror, its operation and maintenance must be taken just as seriously as running the Team Foundation Server environments themselves. This topic will be looked at in more detail later in this chapter.

Remote Desktops

As mentioned earlier, in some environments, it is not acceptable to have intellectual property stored on remote machines outside the IT department's control.

One solution for these environments is to maintain a central Team Foundation Server along with Remote Desktop Services (RDS) or other Virtual Desktop Infrastructure (VDI) for clients. Essentially, a remote user will connect to a virtual desktop on the same network as the central server. The only traffic that must travel across the network is the keyboard and mouse input and the video output. However, depending on your usage of Team Foundation Server, this may require more bandwidth than not using Remote Desktops.

Internet-Connected "Extranet" Server

Virtual Private Networks (VPNs) and other remote access technologies can become a bottleneck compared to accessing servers directly over the Internet. If you have teams clustered at remote sites, the site(s) will often have a dedicated VPN that has less overall overhead and usually a better network connection. However, if you have mobile workers spread around the world, they will often be able to get a better Internet connection from their local ISP than connecting to the corporate network.

By exposing your server directly on the Internet, you allow people to connect directly to it without having the overhead of encapsulating their traffic in a VPN tunnel. If you decide to connect your Team Foundation Server to the Internet, you should consider enabling and requiring the HTTP over SSL (HTTPS) protocol to encrypt the traffic to and from the server. The hosted Visual Studio Online by Microsoft uses this approach.

Metadata Filtering

As mentioned earlier in this chapter, the Metadata Cache has the potential to become a huge source of network traffic. When metadata filtering is enabled, the server will send the minimum amount of metadata required for the project that you are connecting to. This can reduce the network traffic if people generally connect to only one team project.

The downside is that the Metadata Cache is invalidated each time you connect to a new server. This can especially be a hindrance if people connect to more than one team project on the server. In this case, the server will be sending some of the same metadata each time they connect. It would be more efficient to download the full metadata for all team projects just once.

> **NOTE** *More information on how metadata filtering works and how to enable it can be found on Martin Woodward's blog at* `http://aka.ms/ TFSMetadataFiltering`.

BUILD SERVERS

When you work in a geographically distributed team, the availability of nightly builds to your testers can be an important decision point. You have a few different options available, and each has different benefits and trade-offs.

Local Build Server Farm

This is the most common scenario for small to midsized teams, where the build server farm is in the same location as the Team Foundation Server environment itself. In this scenario, the speed of the build isn't affected by the speed of the WAN. If you are using the hosted Visual Studio Online, a hosted build controller is available to you.

The downside of this approach is that it will take time and use WAN bandwidth for remote teams to get the build outputs. Additionally, unless you use some other caching technology, or set up a script to copy build outputs to remote sites, then everyone at the remote sites will be transferring the same files over the WAN multiple times. This is slow and can be expensive if you are charged for WAN traffic.

Alternately, useful features are available in Windows Server 2008 R2 and Windows Server 2012 for hosting a file share that can be cached or distributed appropriately for this scenario. For example, you could use Distributed File System (DFS) or BranchCache to expose the same UNC path but have Active Directory locate the closest file server with the actual file content. If you do take this approach, be sure to use the UNC path in the build definition that has DFS or BranchCache enabled instead of a UNC path that contains a hard-coded server name in it. Friendly DNS names as described in Chapter 2 would be a perfect choice for both the Build Drops and Symbol Server file shares.

Remote Build Server Farm

In this scenario, you would situate build servers at your remote locations. Combining this with a Team Foundation Server Proxy at each remote site, you get a good solution. The build servers have access to a local cache as facilitated by the proxy server, and the developers have access to local build outputs. However, if multiple teams need the ability to access the same build drops and Symbol Server store, then you may want to consider the options for caching/synchronizing file shares as mentioned in the previous section.

> **NOTE** *Team Foundation Server Builds are discussed in detail in Part IV of this book.*

TEAM FOUNDATION SERVER PROXY

The Team Foundation Server Proxy is a server capable of caching downloads of files from version control. Additionally, the Team Foundation Server Proxy for the 2012 release has introduced the ability to also cache test result attachments, which can be quite large. Types of test result attachments are those that come from the different diagnostic data adapters that are run during test runs such as IntelliTrace, video recorder, code coverage, and so on. Even if you don't have a geographically distributed team, there are features that will be useful to all teams that use version control, including for local build server farms and local teams.

How the Team Foundation Server Proxy Works

The Team Foundation Server Proxy server is used purely for Team Foundation Version Control downloads and caching test result attachments. It is not yet used for work item tracking attachments or other functions in Team Foundation Server. Typically, the proxy server is used at remote offices to improve the performance of version control downloads and test result attachments. However, it can (and should) be a part of any reasonably busy Team Foundation Server environment topology.

> **NOTE** *For more detailed information on how the Team Foundation Server Proxy works, refer to* `http://tinyurl.com/HowTFSProxyWorks`*. This article was written for the Team Foundation Server 2008 product but still applies for version control downloads.*

Compatibility

The 2008, 2010, 2012, and 2013 proxy servers can act as proxies for Team Foundation Server 2008, 2010, 2012, and 2013. Each of those versions can proxy for multiple Team Foundation Server instances and team project collections. When a 2010, 2012, or 2013 proxy server is configured and given access to a Team Foundation Server 2010, 2012, or 2013 server instance, it automatically proxies requests for all team project collections on that instance. This is useful when you add new collections to a server, because you don't need to do anything special to set up the proxy to be available for those collections.

It is important to note that only Team Foundation Server 2012 and 2013 proxy servers have the ability to cache test result attachments from a Team Foundation Server 2012 or 2013 environment. This is true with the different clients available such as Visual Studio 2013 and Microsoft Test Manager 2013. The earlier versions of the clients and proxy servers will not have the necessary functionality to cache test result attachments since it was newly introduced in the 2012 release.

Configuring Proxies

A proxy server doesn't necessarily have to be registered with the Team Foundation Server to be used. The only requirement is that the service account under which the proxy server runs must have the "View collection-level information" permission for each project collection.

The easiest way to set this up is to add the proxy service account to the built-in server-level group:

```
[TEAM FOUNDATION]\Team Foundation Proxy Service Accounts
```

Each team project collection has its own group that the server-level group is a member of:

```
[DefaultCollection]\Project Collection Proxy Service Accounts
```

If you are setting up a proxy server for use by all users at a particular remote location, you'll want to do these three things:

➤ Run the proxy as the built-in `Network Service` account so that you don't have to update the service account password every time it changes.

➤ Add the proxy service account to the server-level group on each server that you want it to proxy for.

➤ Register the proxy server with the server, and set it as the default for the Active Directory site(s) that the proxy server is located in or should serve as the proxy server for other locations. There are additional details on how to accomplish this later in this chapter.

> **NOTE** *To register a proxy server, substitute your own Active Directory site and TFS environment friendly DNS names when you use the following command from any client with appropriate permissions:*
>
> ```
> tf proxy
>     /add http://ProxyFriendlyDNS:8081/VersionControlProxy
>     /site:US-WA-REDMOND /default:site
>     /collection:http://ServerFriendlyDNS:8080/tfs/DefaultCollection
> ```

Proxy Cleanup Settings

A proxy server will perform best when it has a copy of the files that people most often request. In reality, that's easier said than done because it's difficult to predict which version of which files people are going to want before they actually request them. To deal with this, the proxy will keep a copy in its cache of every version of every file that is requested. Without any cleanup, the cache directory will eventually fill to capacity.

The proxy has a built-in cleanup job designed to delete older files and make space available for more recently requested files. You can express the cache limit in many ways, including as a percentage of disk space. For example, the proxy cache with the following configuration can take up only 75 percent of your hard drive space.

```
<PercentageBasedPolicy>75</PercentageBasedPolicy>
```

You can also express your cache limit as a fixed number of megabytes, as shown here:

```
<FixedSizeBasedPolicy>1000</FixedSizeBasedPolicy>
```

The cleanup will trigger when the cache size exceeds the threshold.

> **NOTE** *For more information on these cache settings and how to change them, see "How to: Change Cache Settings for Team Foundation Server Proxy" at* `http://aka.ms/TFSProxyCacheSettings.`

Automatically Detecting the Proxy Settings

A feature in Team Foundation Server, introduced in Team Foundation Server 2010, allows a proxy server to be registered with the collection. This means that users don't have to know which proxy server they should be using. In addition to the `tf proxy /configure` command, the Visual Studio IDE will automatically query and set a default proxy server if one is registered on the server. This is achieved through the `GetBestProxies` method in the version control object model.

Active Directory Sites

The physical structure of a Windows network is defined in Active Directory as a site. A site contains one or more subnet objects. Typically, a remote office will have its own subnet and will be defined as a separate site.

Team Foundation Server leverages this infrastructure and allows you to define a default proxy server for each site in Active Directory. As an example, the Team Foundation Server and Visual Studio ALM product teams are split between Raleigh, North Carolina; Hyderabad, India; and Redmond, Washington. The corporate network has the Raleigh and Hyderabad offices configured as a

separate Active Directory site to the Redmond office. When a developer travels from one office to the other, and connects to the office network, the Visual Studio client automatically detects the new site and reconfigures itself to use the default proxy for that site.

You will likely need to work with your Active Directory administrators in the IT department to work out which sites should be used. You can see what is configured for your network as well if you have the Remote Server Administration Tools for Windows features installed on your local Windows machine. Open the Active Directory Sites and Services utility from the Start ➪ Administration Tools folder and you will see each of the sites defined in Active Directory for your Windows network. A sample set of Active Directory sites is shown in Figure 28-1.

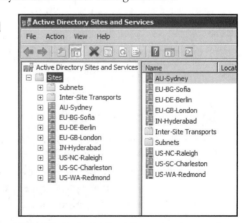

FIGURE 28-1: Active Directory sites and services

Setting a Proxy

The version control proxy settings are a per-user and per-machine setting. To force your client to configure the default proxy for the site, you can run the following commands:

```
tf.exe proxy /configure
tf.exe proxy /enabled:true
```

You can query registry keys to see if you have a proxy configured by running the following commands:

```
reg.exe query HKEY_CURRENT_USER\Software\Microsoft\VisualStudio\12.0\
    TeamFoundation\SourceControl\Proxy /v Enabled
reg.exe query HKEY_CURRENT_USER\Software\Microsoft\VisualStudio\12.0\
    TeamFoundation\SourceControl\Proxy /v Url
```

You can also set registry keys to enable a proxy server without using `tf.exe` by running the following commands (replacing the proxy server name with your own):

```
reg.exe add HKEY_CURRENT_USER\Software\Microsoft\VisualStudio\12.0\
    TeamFoundation\SourceControl\Proxy /v Enabled /d True /f
reg.exe reg add HKEY_CURRENT_USER\Software\Microsoft\VisualStudio\12.0\
    TeamFoundation\SourceControl\Proxy
    /v Url /d http://redmond.proxy.tfs.contoso.local:8081 /f
```

Although it's not documented or officially supported, you can also set the TFSPROXY environment variable, and any client that uses the version control object model will use the proxy.

```
set TFSPROXY=http://redmond.proxy.tfs.contoso.local:8081
```

Seeding Proxies

As mentioned earlier in this chapter, the proxy server will cache a copy of a file only if someone requests it. Because of this, you may want to implement a process that will seed the proxy with the most commonly used files in an off-peak period, or after a period of high churn.

As an example, for the Team Foundation Server product team at Microsoft, the main servers are located in Washington on the West Coast. The other half of the team is in North Carolina on the East Coast. The nightly build checks in some of the build outputs to source control. These binary files can be quite large, and the bandwidth at the remote site is often strained during the day.

The team implemented a scheduled task at the remote site that requests the latest versions from the main server after the build has completed. Because the proxy server doesn't have these versions, it then downloads them and caches a copy. This means that the first person who needs those files the following day doesn't have to wait for the lengthy download, and that person gets sent the cached copy from the proxy server.

Using scheduled tasks is one approach to this problem. Another approach is to set up a build server at the remote site. The first part of a build is generally to create a workspace and get the latest version of the source code. If this build is set up to run nightly, or build every check-in (in other words, a continuous integration build), then it will keep the contents of the proxy fresh for other users of that code.

Personal Proxies

A personal proxy server is useful if you do not have a remote office with a proxy server near you. By setting up your own personal proxy server, you will have to download a file's contents only once.

One of the changes, introduced in the 2010 release, in the Team Foundation Server license agreement, is that each MSDN subscription provides a license to deploy one instance of Team Foundation Server into production on one device. Since Team Foundation Server Proxy is just a different configuration of the product, this means that each user with an MSDN subscription could run a personal proxy server or use the production license for a remote office proxy server.

> **NOTE** *For the full details, see the "Visual Studio Licensing" whitepaper at* `http://aka.ms/VisualStudioLicensing` *and your applicable licensing agreements.*

MIRRORING WITH THE TEAM FOUNDATION SERVER INTEGRATION TOOLS

In the past, there was a download available on CodePlex called the "TFS Migration Synchronization Toolkit." The intention of the toolkit was to allow people to build custom tools that enabled migration and synchronization with other version control and work-tracking systems. The original release of the toolkit received a lot of negative feedback, and not many people were able to successfully use it.

In 2008, the product team made a decision to invest in an effort to address the feedback from the previous version and build a solid platform that enabled synchronization with other systems. The result of this effort is Team Foundation Server Integration Tools, which was released in the Visual Studio Gallery at `http://aka.ms/TFSIntegrationPlatform`. The Integration Tools are fully supported by Microsoft Support, and they are the same tools that Microsoft uses internally to keep data synchronized between different Team Foundation Server instances.

The platform uses adapter architecture, and it ships with a Software Development Kit (SDK) that allows others to implement the interfaces and leverage all the capabilities of the platform. The first adapters written were the work item tracking and version control adapters for Team Foundation Server 2008 and 2010. The selfish reason the product group invested in the platform was that they had a desire to start using early builds of Team Foundation Server 2010 for day-to-day usage. The problem with this was that the server code was not yet stable enough to risk upgrading the entire developer division's main Team Foundation Server environment. This prompted the team to set up a second server and run a two-way synchronization of work items and source code between them.

This not only allowed the team to be confident in the quality of Team Foundation Server 2010 before shipping it, but it also allowed the Integration Tools team to test drive their solution to drive features and improvements into the product. The end result is a proven and versatile tool for migration and synchronization of other systems with Team Foundation Server.

> **WARNING** *If you choose to use the Team Foundation Integration Tools, be aware that it is not often an easy path to take. Microsoft uses the tools internally with the latest versions of Team Foundation Server, so you can be relatively confident the tool will work in most cases, but there is likely to be a lot of handholding to ensure mirroring happens smoothly.*
>
> *Unless absolutely required, we advise you avoid mirroring entirely.*

Capabilities

In the first release, the built-in Team Foundation Server 2008 and 2010 adapters had the following capabilities:

> **Synchronization**—This included unidirectional or bidirectional synchronization.

> **Version control**—This included the migration of all files and folders and support for preserving changeset contents. The following change types are currently supported: add, edit, rename, delete, branch, merge, and type.

> **Work item tracking**—This included the migration of all work item revisions, fields, attachments, areas and iterations, and links (including links to changesets).

> **Context synchronization**—The tool can synchronize work item types, group memberships, and global lists.

Field Maps, Value Maps, and User Maps

When synchronizing two different systems, you are almost guaranteed that the configuration will be different between the two endpoints. This is where mappings are useful. As an example, you might have a `Priority` field with values `1`, `2`, and `3` on one side and values `A`, `B`, and `C` on the other. By defining a *field map* and associating it with a *value map*, the tool can seamlessly translate values back and forth when updates occur.

Another powerful capability is *user maps*. As an example, this is useful when you are synchronizing Team Foundation Server (which uses Active Directory for authentication) with a system that uses its own store of built-in user names. The user-mapping functionality allows you to map one system to the other.

Intelligent Conflict Resolution

In any type of synchronization, there will always be problems that you can't anticipate and automatically handle. Following are some examples:

> Someone changes the same field on both sides at the same time (an "edit/edit conflict").

> One endpoint encounters an error and the update can't be saved.

> Permissions are insufficient for making an update.

> An attachment from one side is larger than the limit on the other side.

> A field can't be renamed because the new name already exists.

In all of these cases, the tool will raise a conflict that requires manual intervention. Depending on the type of conflict, the tool may stop processing more changes, or if the changes don't depend on each other, it will continue processing others.

The conflict-resolution process allows you to resolve conflicts and give the resolution a "scope." For example, you can say, "Whenever an edit/edit conflict occurs, always choose the changes from the left endpoint." Over time, the system is given rules, and the number of new conflicts to resolve is reduced.

Health Monitoring

When you install the Team Foundation Server Integration Tools, two reports get copied to your machine. To make use of these reports, you can follow the included instructions on how to set up the data sources and upload the reports. Once they are running, they will show you two things:

➤   Latency

➤   Conflicts

If people depend on synchronization for their day-to-day work, then you will want to make the reports available to users. You can also set up a data-driven subscription to e-mail you the report when latency exceeds a specific threshold. For example, at Microsoft, each of the synchronizations has a data-driven subscription that checks every 30 minutes to see if any endpoint is more than 30 minutes out of date. When one of them is, then it e-mails that report to the synchronization owner to alert him or her of the situation.

Following are the three most common reasons that an endpoint will be out of date:

➤   Someone has made a bulk update to hundreds of work items, and the mirror is still synchronizing the backlog.

➤   In version control, a conflict will block the processing of future changes, because it's not valid to skip mirroring a changeset and continue on.

➤   The mirror is not running for some reason. This can happen if the service stops, the machine running the service loses connectivity, or the password changes.

Each of these conditions can be detected by a subscription to the latency report and the conflicts report.

Examples

Team Foundation Server Integration Tools include a number of templates to get started, but the following are some of the most common uses.

Version Control Two-Way Synchronization to a Second Server

Take a look at the following snippet from a version control session configuration:

```
<FilterPair>
  <FilterItem MigrationSourceUniqueId="1f87ff05-2e09-49c8-9e9b-0ac6db9dd595"
          FilterString="$/Project1/Main"
          MergeScope="$/Project1/Main" />
  <FilterItem MigrationSourceUniqueId="8c85d8eb-f3b3-4f05-b8dc-c0ab823f1a44"
          FilterString="$/Project1/Main"
          MergeScope="$/Project1/Main" />
</FilterPair>
```

In this scenario, you configure a left and right migration source and provide two version control paths that you want to keep synchronized. It is possible to provide multiple paths, as well as different paths. The tool will translate the paths between the two endpoints.

You should always choose the smallest mapping possible because the more changes that must be processed the more likely it is to fall behind and get out of sync. If people are working on the same code in the two different locations, it's often a good idea to mirror into a branch of the code. That way, you can control when and how the changes from the remote server get merged into the main branch on the other side.

Work Item Synchronization to a Different Process Template

An outsourced development team may use a different process template than the in-house development team. This will cause a mismatch in the fields and values used to describe bugs, tasks, and other work items. Both organizations may have very valid reasons for using their own templates, and that's fine.

To accommodate this mismatch, the Team Foundation Server Integration Tools can be configured to map the different types to their closest equivalents. The following snippet from a session configuration file shows how a field can be mapped using a value map:

```
<WITSessionCustomSetting >
  <Settings />
  <WorkItemTypes>
    <WorkItemType LeftWorkItemTypeName="Bug"
                  RightWorkItemTypeName="Defect"
                  fieldMap="BugToDefectFieldMap" />
  </WorkItemTypes>
  <FieldMaps>
    <FieldMap name="BugToDefectFieldMap">
      <MappedFields>
        <MappedField MapFromSide="Left"
                     LeftName="*"
                     RightName="*" />
        <MappedField MapFromSide="Left"
                     LeftName="Microsoft.VSTS.Common.Priority"
                     RightName="Company.Priority"
                     valueMap="PriorityValueMap" />
      </MappedFields>
    </FieldMap>
  </FieldMaps>
  <ValueMaps>
    <ValueMap name="PriorityValueMap">
      <Value LeftValue="1" RightValue="A" />
      <Value LeftValue="2" RightValue="B" />
      <Value LeftValue="3" RightValue="C" />
    </ValueMap>
  </ValueMaps>
</WITSessionCustomSetting>
```

WORKING OFFLINE

In a geographically distributed team, you sometimes need to work offline. There may be connectivity problems between your client and the server, or the server could just be offline for maintenance. In any case, you can take measures to stay productive while you are working offline.

Version Control

If your solution file is bound to Team Foundation Server using Team Foundation Version Control, Visual Studio 2008, 2010, 2012, and 2013 will attempt to connect to the server when you attempt to open the solution. If the server is unavailable for some reason, the solution will be opened in "offline mode." This allows you to continue working on your code while you are disconnected from the server.

Team Foundation Server 2012 introduced the concept of Local Workspaces, as discussed in Chapter 6. This feature better supports working offline and disconnection from the server because the items in your workspace are not marked with the read-only flag. You can continue to work with most operations, even undo pending changes, without needing to be connected to the server. Once the server is available, each of the pending changes is discovered automatically on the next file scan.

However, if you are using the legacy server workspaces or an earlier version of Visual Studio, a Visual Studio solution will remain offline until it is explicitly taken online. Once the server is available again, you can click Go Online in Solution Explorer and the connection with the server will be attempted again. Alternatively, you can open the solution and, when the server is available, go online.

With server workspaces, when you go online again, Visual Studio will scan your workspace for writable files, and then check out the files and pend the changes that you made while you were working offline. If you don't do this, and you perform a "Get Latest," there is a chance you may overwrite your offline work, because the server doesn't know which changes you made while you were offline.

If you are planning to use this functionality in server workspaces, you must follow very specific instructions:

➤   When in offline mode, remove the read-only flag on the files you want to edit. You will need to do this from within Windows Explorer, not within Visual Studio. When you try to save a file that you haven't yet checked out, the file will be read-only, and Visual Studio will prompt you to see if you want to overwrite the file. This will unset the read-only flag and overwrite the contents.

➤   Don't rename files while offline. Team Foundation Server will not know the difference between a renamed file and a new file.

➤   When you are ready to connect to the server again, before doing anything else, run the online tool and check in the pending changes that it generates. That way, there will be no confusion between the new online work you will be doing and your offline work. If you don't do this, and you perform a "Get Latest," there is a chance you may overwrite your offline work because the server doesn't know which changes you made.

For these reasons, we highly recommend that you consider using Local Workspaces instead of the traditional server workspaces, and that you use Visual Studio 2013 or Team Explorer Everywhere 2013.

Forcing Offline

If the connection to the server is slow or unreliable, it may be desirable to mark the Team Foundation Server as offline and disable auto reconnect on startup, so that you don't have to wait for it to time out. To do this, you need to have the Team Foundation Server Power Tools installed. Once you have them installed, you can follow these steps:

1. Open a Developer Command Prompt for Visual Studio 2013.

2. Type the following:

   `tfpt.exe connections`

3. Once the TFS Connections dialog box is displayed, as shown in Figure 28-2, select your server, expand the node, and select the collection.

4. Click Edit.

5. Clear the "Automatically reconnect to last server on startup" check box.

6. Select the Server Is Offline check box.

7. Click OK.

8. Close the dialog box.

Now, when you open your solution, it will be marked offline until you click the Go Online button and connect to Team Foundation Server.

FIGURE 28-2: TFS Connections dialog box

Work Items

The intended way to work offline with work items is to use the Microsoft Office Excel and Microsoft Office Project integration installed with the Team Explorer client. With this integration, work items can be exported into a worksheet and saved to your machine for working offline. When you are ready to connect to the server again, the changes can be published back to the server. There is a limitation while working offline that prevents you from creating links to work items and creating attachments.

Additionally, the third-party tool, TeamCompanion from Ekobit, provides an Outlook add-in that also caches work item query results and allows for viewing and editing that data while offline.

> **NOTE** *For more information, see the "Work Offline and Reconnect to Team Foundation Server" article on MSDN at* `http://aka.ms/TFSWorkOffline`.

OTHER CONSIDERATIONS

Several other considerations can make the experience of working with geographically distributed teams better.

Maintenance Windows and Time Zones

The default Team Foundation Server installation will schedule optimization and cleanup jobs to start at 3 a.m. UTC time. This time means that these jobs run in the evening in North America, early morning in Europe, and in the middle of the day in Asia.

One of the benefits of Team Foundation Server is that you typically don't need the expertise of a database administrator or any extra SQL maintenance plans (beyond backups) to keep it reasonably healthy. To see how some jobs are affected, and perhaps change their schedules accordingly, see Table 28-2.

TABLE 28-2: Built-In Server and Collection-Level Jobs

JOB NAME	DESCRIPTION	FREQUENCY
Optimize Databases (server-level job)	Operates on the relational warehouse database. It reorganizes fragmented indexes and updates table statistics.	Daily
Full Analysis Database Sync	Triggers a full process of the Analysis Services Online Analytical Processing (OLAP) cube	Daily
Incremental Analysis Database Sync	Triggers an incremental process of the Analysis Services OLAP cube	Every 2 hours
Job History Cleanup Job	Removes the internal job history log records that are older than 31 days	Daily
Team Foundation Server Activity Logging Administration	Removes command history older than 14 days	Daily
Optimize Databases (collection-level job)	Operates on the version control tables. It reorganizes and rebuilds fragmented indexes and updates table statistics.	Daily
Version Control Administration	Removes content in the database that has been previously destroyed. Also, it removes content that gets staged to a temporary table as part of a large check-in.	Daily
Work Item Tracking Administration	Operates on the Work Item Tracking tables. It reorganizes fragmented indexes and updates table statistics. It also deletes work items and attachments no longer used by the system. It will also delete orphaned attachments because saving a work item and uploading an attachment are two separate transactions, and one can succeed without the other.	Daily

> **NOTE** *For a full list of jobs that run across the configuration and collection databases and their schedules, see Grant Holliday's post at* `http://tinyurl.com/TFSJobSchedule`.

Online Index Operations with SQL Server Enterprise

When the `Optimize Databases` job is running for each collection, it may cause blocking and slow performance for some version control commands. If you have users around the world, and you have large indexes, there may be no ideal time for this job to run. In this case, you may want to consider upgrading SQL Server to an edition that supports online index operations.

The full version of Team Foundation Server 2013 includes a restricted-use license for SQL Server 2013 Standard Edition. Team Foundation Server 2013 Express includes SQL 2012 Express. If you license the Enterprise or Data Center edition separately for your data tier server, then Team Foundation Server will automatically make use of the online index operations available in these editions, which will prevent the blocking and slow performance that is typical with indexing operations that are not online.

Distributed Application Tiers

In Team Foundation Server 2008, it was possible to install Team System Web Access on a separate server than your main application tier. In Team Foundation Server 2010, 2012, and 2013, this is no longer possible because Web Access is now integrated into the server itself.

In the 2012 and 2013 versions, it is not supported and highly not recommended to have application tiers distributed away from your data tier servers. They should be on the same server (for a single-server installation) or in the same data center (for a multiple-server installation).

For version control operations, the architecture of the system is such that the application tier will request all the data that the user specified and then discard the results that it doesn't need or that the user doesn't have access to. This is because permission evaluation is done on the application tier.

These are just some of the reasons why Team Foundation Server 2013 does not support having application tiers distributed away from data tiers. It is very important to follow this advice because customers have experienced major issues with non-supported configurations and topologies by not following this guidance.

If your goal is for higher availability and spreading out the load across multiple application tiers, you can refer to Chapter 22, which discusses scalability and high availability.

SQL Mirroring

SQL mirroring involves synchronizing the data on one server with a copy of that data on another server. The limitation of mirroring is that it allows only one server (the principal) to be active at a time. The mirrored server cannot be used until the mirror is failed over, and the application tiers are configured to use the new principal server.

Because of this limitation, mirroring and technologies such as SQL AlwaysOn are useful only in a disaster-recovery or high-availability situation, rather than a geographically distributed team situation.

SUMMARY

This chapter explored what it means to work with a geographically distributed team using Team Foundation Server 2013. You learned about some challenges, and then explored some of the solutions to overcome those challenges. You looked at Team Foundation Server Proxy in detail, and you learned about the potential of mirroring between servers with the Team Foundation Server Integration Tools. Finally, you looked at strategies for working offline while disconnected from the server.

Chapter 29 describes extensibility best practices, as well as all the different ways that Team Foundation Server can be extended through custom plug-ins and tools.

29

Extending Team Foundation Server

WHAT'S IN THIS CHAPTER?

➤ Getting started with the client object model

➤ Exploring the server object model

➤ Building server plug-ins

➤ Exploring other extension options

WROX.COM CODE DOWNLOADS FOR THIS CHAPTER

The wrox.com code downloads for this chapter are found at http://www.wrox.com/go/proftfs2013 on the Download Code tab. The code is in the Chapter 29 download and individually named according to the code filenames noted throughout this chapter.

From the very start, Team Foundation Server was built to be extended. Microsoft acknowledged that it would never be able to build all the different features and functionality that customers would want. The philosophy was that Microsoft's own features should be built upon the same API that customers and partners can use to build additional features.

This proved to be a very wise design choice and has led to a thriving ecosystem of products and extensions. Following are some examples of this ecosystem:

➤ Microsoft partners have built products that provide rich integration with products such as Outlook and Word.

➤ Competing and complementary Application Lifecycle Management (ALM) products have been built to integrate with Team Foundation Server.

➤ Consultants have leveraged the APIs to fill gaps to meet their client's very specific requirements.

➤ The community has built and shared useful tools and utilities for performing common tasks.

➤ The Visual Studio ALM Ranger community builds tools and solutions that address common adoption blockers and pain points.

➤ Microsoft itself builds the Team Foundation Server Power Tools to address gaps within the product outside the normal release cycle.

Perhaps the two most successful examples of the extensibility model (and people leveraging it) were the products formerly known as TeamPlain and Teamprise:

➤ **TeamPlain**—was a product built on the client object model to provide web browser-based access to Team Foundation Server. When it was first released, it was a "must-have" extension for organizations adopting Team Foundation Server. It allowed non-technical users to access the server and participate in the software development life cycle.

➤ **Teamprise**—was a fully featured, cross-platform client implemented in native Java. It allowed Mac, Linux, and Java users to access Team Foundation Server from their native environments.

Ultimately, both of these products and their development teams were acquired by Microsoft, and the products now ship as a standard part of Team Foundation Server. TeamPlain is now incorporated as *Web Access*, and Teamprise is available as *Team Explorer Everywhere*. However, the fact that these once-partner products were integrated so tightly into the shipping Team Foundation Server release also gives you a clue to how the team develops the product. The same APIs, events, and protocols available for different parts of the product to talk to each other are made public and are available as extension points for you to integrate with Team Foundation Server.

EXTENSIBILITY POINTS

When people talk about Team Foundation Server extensibility, they are likely referring to building something that leverages the *client object model* or the *TFS SDK for Java*. The client object model assemblies are installed with Visual Studio Team Explorer. It is the main .NET API used by products, tools, and utilities that interact with Team Foundation Server. The TFS SDK for Java is a very similar client API implemented entirely in Java and used by the Team Explorer Everywhere clients to talk to Team Foundation Server. The TFS SDK for Java is also available as a standalone download and can be redistributed with your applications.

All of the client interaction with the server is performed through web services. Although it is possible to invoke the web services directly, they are not documented, and their use is discouraged. Microsoft reserves the right to change the web service interfaces in any future release, and it maintains only backward compatibility via the client object model.

On the application tier, the web services then interact with services provided by the *server object model*. The server object model then accesses the internal SQL tables and stored procedures. Figure 29-1 shows how these different components interact.

Additionally, the server provides other extensibility points, such as the following:

➤ Simple Object Access Protocol (SOAP) event subscription notifications

➤ In-process server events

➤ Request filters

➤ Server jobs

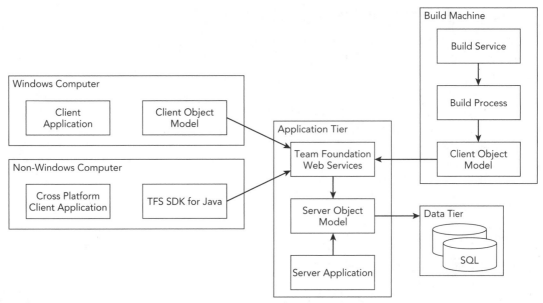

FIGURE 29-1: Team Foundation Server extensibility architecture

The functionality provided within Team Explorer and Excel clients also can be extended. As you can see, just about everything Microsoft ships as part of Team Foundation Server can be extended and built upon to suit your own needs and requirements.

> **NOTE** *Not all of the extensibility points are available to you if your Team Foundation Server instance is hosted on Visual Studio Online. The Client Object Model, SOAP Event Subscriptions, and Visual Studio extensibility points are all available for both on-premises and Visual Studio Online instances. However, due to the installation requirements, the Server Object Model is available to you only if you have an on-premises installation.*

.NET CLIENT OBJECT MODEL

The client object model is the most commonly used way to programmatically interact with Team Foundation Server. It is the same API that Team Explorer and all .NET-based client-side applications use to access the server.

> **NOTE** *This chapter only briefly covers the client object model. For more detailed instructions and plenty of examples on how to use the .NET client object model, you should refer to the Team Foundation Server 2013 SDK at* `http://aka.ms/TFS2013SDK`*.*

Connecting to the Server

Depending on what you want to do, to get connected to the server, you must use one of the following classes defined in the `Microsoft.TeamFoundation.Client.dll` assembly:

➤   `TfsConnection`

➤   `TfsConfigurationServer`

➤   `TfsTeamProjectCollection`

The following code will connect to the server and retrieve the latest changeset (code file: `ClientObjectModelSample.cs`).

```
using System;
using Microsoft.TeamFoundation.Client;
using Microsoft.TeamFoundation.VersionControl.Client;

namespace ClientObjectModelSample
{
  class Program
  {
    static void Main(string[] args)
    {
      TfsTeamProjectCollection tfs =
        new TfsTeamProjectCollection(
          new Uri("http://localhost:8080/tfs/DefaultCollection"),
          new TfsClientCredentials());

      VersionControlServer vcs = tfs.GetService<VersionControlServer>();
      int latestChangesetId = vcs.GetLatestChangesetId();
      Console.WriteLine("Latest Changeset = {0}", latestChangesetId);
    }
  }
}
```

For this example to work, you will need to add a reference to both `Microsoft.TeamFoundation.Client.dll` and `Microsoft.TeamFoundation.VersionControl.Client.dll` in the references section of your project.

In this example, you create a connection to the collection using the collection URL. Then, you get the `VersionControlServer` service using `GetService<T>`. You then use it to retrieve the ID of the most recent changeset on the collection. It's that simple!

TEAM FOUNDATION SERVER IMPERSONATION

Team Foundation Server Impersonation allows a privileged user to execute commands as if the execution had been done by another user. In short, by using the constructor overloads available on the `TeamProjectCollection` and `TfsConfigurationServer` classes, you can pass in the identity of a user to impersonate.

For more information, see "Introducing TFS Impersonation" at `http://tinyurl.com/TFSImpersonation`. Note that while the article is for Team Foundation Server 2010, this part of the API has not changed.

For another example, see "Using TFS Impersonation with the Version Control Client APIs" at `http://tinyurl.com/TFSImpersonationVC`.

Team Project Selection Dialog Box

Although you can enumerate the collections and team projects using the client object model, you can also leverage the `TeamProjectPicker` dialog box. This is the same dialog box that Visual Studio uses and is prepopulated with servers that the user has previously connected to.

The following snippet shows how to create a `TeamProjectPicker` that allows the user to select a server, collection, and multiple projects (code file: `ProjectPicker.cs`):

```
using (TeamProjectPicker tpp = new
       TeamProjectPicker(TeamProjectPickerMode.MultiProject,
       false))
{
    DialogResult result = tpp.ShowDialog();
    if (result == DialogResult.OK)
    {
        // tpp.SelectedTeamProjectCollection.Uri
        foreach(ProjectInfo projectInfo in tpp.SelectedProjects)
        {
            // projectInfo.Name
        }
    }
}
```

> **NOTE** *For more information, see "Using the TeamProjectPicker API" at* `http://tinyurl.com/TeamProjectPicker`.

Handling Multiple API Versions

If you are building an extension using the client object model, you may want to ensure that it works against different server versions. There is no single, definitive way to do this. You can infer the server version by looking at the features and services provided by the server.

The following is an example that does this against the Version Control Service using a PowerShell script that retrieves the `VersionControlServer.WebServiceLevel`. Then the `VersionControlServer.SupportedFeatures` property that can be used to infer what the server version is as follows (code file: `MultipleApiVersions.ps1`):

```
#
# TFS2013 VersionControl has a WebServiceLevel that gives
# an idea of the version of the server you are talking to
#
# Tfs2012_1     Team Foundation Server 2012 Beta
# Tfs2012_2     Team Foundation Server 2012 RC
# Tfs2012_3     Team Foundation Server 2012 RTM
# Tfs2012_QU1   Team Foundation Server 2012 Update 1
# Tfs2012_QU1_1 Team Foundation Server 2012 Update 1 with Hotfix
# Tfs2013       Team Foundation Server 2013
#
# Prior to TFS 2012, VersionControlServer.SupportedFeatures
# is an indicator of what server version you are talking to
#
# 7     Team Foundation Server 2008 RTM
# 31    Team Foundation Server 2008 SP1
```

```
# 895   Team Foundation Server 2010 RTM
# 1919  Team Foundation Server 2010 SP1
#

# Halt on errors
$ErrorActionPreference = "Stop"

$Uri = $args[0]

if ([String]::IsNullOrEmpty($Uri))
{
    $Uri = "http://localhost:8080/tfs/DefaultCollection"
}

Add-Type -LiteralPath "C:\Program Files (x86)\Microsoft Visual Studio 12.0\Common7\
IDE\ReferenceAssemblies\v2.0\Microsoft.TeamFoundation.Client.dll"
Add-Type -
LiteralPath "C:\Program Files (x86)\Microsoft Visual Studio 12.0\Common7\IDE\
ReferenceAssemblies\v2.0\Microsoft.TeamFoundation.Common.dll"
Add-Type -LiteralPath
 "C:\Program Files (x86)\Microsoft Visual Studio
12.0\Common7\IDE\ReferenceAssemblies\v2.0\Microsoft.TeamFoundation.VersionControl.
Client.dll"
Add-Type -LiteralPath "C:\Program Files (x86)\Microsoft Visual Studio
12.0\Common7\IDE\ReferenceAssemblies\v2.0\Microsoft.TeamFoundation.VersionControl.
Common.dll"

$Tpc = New-Object Microsoft.TeamFoundation.Client.TfsTeamProjectCollection -
ArgumentList $Uri
$vcs = $Tpc.GetService(
        [Microsoft.TeamFoundation.VersionControl.Client.VersionControlServer])

if ($vcs.WebServiceLevel -eq $WebServiceLevel.PreTfs2010)
{
  switch ($vcs.SupportedFeatures)
  {
     7   {"Tfs2008_RTM"}
     31  {"Tfs2008_SP1"}
     default {"Tfs2005"}
  }
}
elseif ($vcs.WebServiceLevel -eq $WebServiceLevel.Tfs2010)
{
  switch ($vcs.SupportedFeatures)
  {
     895  {"Tfs2010_RTM"}
     1919 {"Tfs2010_SP1"}
     default {"Tfs2010"}
  }
}
else
{
  $vcs.WebServiceLevel
}
```

> **NOTE** *This approach is necessary only to determine programmatically what features a server you are talking to has from the client side. If you are an administrator looking to see exactly what service level your Team Foundation Server instance is running at, then you can easily see this from the Team Foundation Server Administration Console from a Team Foundation Server Application Tier machine.*

Distributing the Client Object Model

Once you have built an application, you will probably want to make it available for others to use. Your application will have a dependency on the client object model assemblies that you are not allowed to redistribute with your application.

The general recommendation is that any client that requires the object model should have Visual Studio Team Explorer installed already; however, there is a standalone installer for the TFS Object Model available at `http://aka.ms/TFS2013OM`.

SOAP EVENT SUBSCRIPTIONS

All versions of Team Foundation Server include SOAP event subscriptions. You can subscribe to work item changes, check-ins, and other events. In the subscription definition, you specify the event type to subscribe to and the SOAP endpoint that should be called. When an event is triggered, Team Foundation Server calls the `Notify` web method on your endpoint, and that code is executed.

A great example for the use of SOAP subscriptions came from the Team Foundation Server 2005 release. The product lacked continuous integration build functionality. The community responded by building a service that subscribed to the `CheckinEvent`. Then, when someone checked in a file to a particular path, the service would start a build on that path.

While there were significant improvements to the way that e-mail alerts were managed in Team Foundation Server 2012, SOAP event subscriptions have remained largely unchanged since the 2010 release. A few new events were added in the 2012 release, and a small number were added in the 2013 release as well. For SOAP event subscribers coming from a version of Team Foundation Server before 2012, two important things should be considered:

- ➤ There can be a delay of up to two minutes for event delivery. SOAP event subscriptions are delivered using a job agent job. The default schedule of this job is to run every two minutes.

- ➤ The protocol version is now SOAP 1.2. This means the `content-type` of the request is now `text/xml` instead of `application/soap+xml` as in versions of Team Foundation Server before 2010. If you're using Windows Communication Foundation (WCF), you must change your bindings from `BasicHttpBinding` to `WSHttpBinding`.

There are two limitations of SOAP event subscriptions that you will want to consider before using them:

➤ SOAP event subscriptions allow you to react only after the fact. You cannot prevent an event from further execution. Team Foundation Server requests the endpoint asynchronously after the event has happened. This means that they are not very well-suited to "enforcement" activities. They can only send an alert or run further code to change the item back to its previous values.

➤ Delivery of SOAP event subscriptions is not guaranteed. If your endpoint is unavailable, or if it has a problem processing the event, that event can be missed. If missed events are a problem for you, you will need to periodically run a task that reconciles missed events.

> **WARNING** *For more information, see "Does TFS guarantee event subscription delivery?" at* `http://tinyurl.com/TFSGuaranteedEvents.`

Available Event Types

To retrieve a list of all the SOAP events available for subscription, you can use the `IRegistration` service with the following PowerShell script (code file: `AvailableEventTypes.ps1`):

```
# Halt on errors
$ErrorActionPreference = "Stop"

$Uri = $args[0]

if ([String]::IsNullOrEmpty($Uri))
{
    $Uri = "http://localhost:8080/tfs/DefaultCollection"
}

Add-Type -LiteralPath "C:\Program Files (x86)\Microsoft Visual Studio 12.0\Common7\
IDE\ReferenceAssemblies\v2.0\Microsoft.TeamFoundation.Client.dll"

$Tpc = New-Object Microsoft.TeamFoundation.Client.TfsTeamProjectCollection
  -ArgumentList $Uri
$reg = $Tpc.GetService([Microsoft.TeamFoundation.Server.IRegistration])

$reg.GetRegistrationEntries($null) | fl Type, EventType
```

This script calls the `GetRegistrationEntries` method and outputs the results. Table 29-1 lists the event types available in Team Foundation Server 2013.

> **NOTE** *GitPushEvent is a new event in Team Foundation Server 2013. Its purpose is fairly self-explanatory, but it serves to show that distributed source control is fully integrated into the product.*

TABLE 29-1: Available SOAP Event Types

COMPONENT	EVENT TYPE
Build	BuildCompletionEvent
	BuildCompletionEvent2
	BuildCompletedEvent
	BuildStatusChangeEvent
	BuildDefinitionChangedEvent
	BuildDefinitionUpgradeCompletionEvent
	BuildResourceChangedEvent
Version Control	CheckinEvent
	ShelvesetEvent
vstfs	BranchMovedEvent
	DataChangedEvent
	NodeCreatedEvent
	NodePropertiesChangedEvent
	NodeRenamedEvent
	NodesDeletedEvent
	ProjectCreatedEvent
	ProjectDeletedEvent
Git	GitPushEvent
Work Item Tracking	WorkItemChangedEvent
	WITAdapterSchemaConflictEvent
Test Management	TestRunCompletedEvent
	TestRunStartedEvent
Discussion	CodeReviewChangeEvent

Building an Endpoint

The easiest way to host an endpoint is to build a Windows Service and use WCF with `WSHttpBinding` bindings. Alternatively, you can deploy it as a website in IIS.

> **NOTE** *For more information on creating a SOAP event subscription handler, see Ewald Hofman's blog post, "How to use WCF to subscribe to the TFS Event Service," at* `http://tinyurl.com/TFSEventSubWCF`*. This post is targeted at Team Foundation Server 2010 so you will need to change file paths where appropriate.*

Adding the Subscription

Once you have a subscription handler, you must add the subscription to Team Foundation Server. The usual way of doing this in a scriptable form is by running the `BisSubscribe.exe` tool from `C:\ Program Files\Microsoft Team Foundation Server 12.0\Tools\` on any of your application tier servers. You can also copy this program to a local machine if you don't want to log on to the server for adding new subscriptions.

In Team Foundation Server 2013, you can also create new Alerts from the same Alerts web pages that you use to create e-mail alerts. Simply change the format of the message to be a SOAP message and specify the web service endpoint in the Send To field, as shown in Figure 29-2.

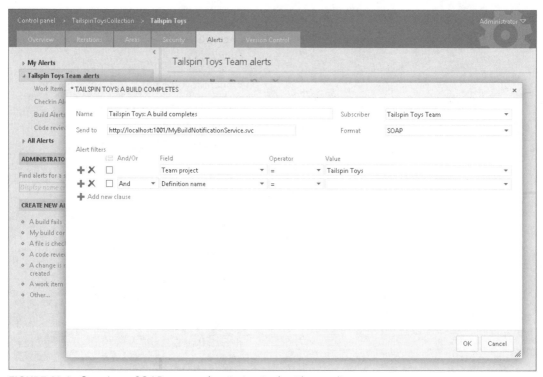

FIGURE 29-2: Creating a SOAP event subscription in the Alerts editor

> **WARNING** *Project Collection Administrator permissions are required to add SOAP subscriptions.*

Listing All Event Subscriptions

If you are a project collection administrator, you may want to see what subscriptions are configured for your collection for all users. This is not possible through `BisSubscribe.exe` or Alerts Explorer.

You can do this by using the following PowerShell script that calls the `GetAllEventSubscriptions` method on the `IEventService` service (code file: `ListEventSubscriptions.ps1`):

```
# Get all event subscriptions
#
# Halt on errors
$ErrorActionPreference = "Stop"

$Uri = $args[0]

if ([String]::IsNullOrEmpty($Uri))
{
    $Uri = "http://localhost:8080/tfs/DefaultCollection"
}

Add-Type -LiteralPath "C:\Program Files (x86)\Microsoft Visual Studio 12.0\Common7\
IDE\ReferenceAssemblies\v2.0\Microsoft.TeamFoundation.Client.dll"

$Tpc = New-Object Microsoft.TeamFoundation.Client.TfsTeamProjectCollection
    -ArgumentList $Uri
$event = $Tpc.GetService([Microsoft.TeamFoundation.Framework.Client.IEventService])

$event.GetAllEventSubscriptions() | fl ID,EventType,ConditionString
```

If there are subscriptions that you'd like to remove, you can use `BisSubscribe.exe /unsubscribe`, or use the following PowerShell line after running the previous script:

```
# Unsubscribe an event
$event.UnsubscribeEvent(<id here>)
```

> **NOTE** *SOAP subscriptions can be a convenient way to respond to events with Team Foundation Server, but SOAP is a fairly legacy technology. Additionally, notifications are not guaranteed. If the event is important, you should consider using a server plug-in.*

SERVER OBJECT MODEL

With all the architectural changes in Team Foundation Server to support multiple collections, the server object model is now more accessible.

> **NOTE** *For more information on the server object model, see "Extending Team Foundation" on MSDN at* `http://aka.ms/TFS2013ServerOM`.

Server Extensibility Interfaces

Although many of the interfaces in the server object model are marked `public`, some are more suitable for customization and extending than others. Table 29-2 describes the interfaces and their suitability according to the following guide:

➤ **Suitable**—This is intended for third-party extensions. This is used by Team Foundation Server internally for extensibility.

➤ **Limited**—Some extension is expected by tool providers, though in a limited fashion.

➤ **Not Suitable**—This is dangerous or not really intended for third-party extensions.

TABLE 29-2: Server Extensibility Interfaces and Their Suitability

INTERFACE	DESCRIPTION	SUITABILITY
ISubscriber	The in-process event system is described later in this chapter.	Suitable
ITeamFoundationRequestFilter	This is intended to allow the extension to inspect and manage all incoming requests. It is described later in this chapter.	Suitable
ISecurityChangedEventHandler	A notification useful for reacting to security changes. The most common use would be to write an auditor of security changes to tie in to your needs. However, you would normally use an ISubscriber, because all security changes are published through events.	Limited
ITeamFoundationHostStateValidator	Used to prevent a collection from being started. If a customer wants to implement custom online/offline semantics, this would allow it.	Limited
ICatalogResourceTypeRuleSet	If you are going to extend the catalog with custom objects, and you want to implement some rules to enforce that your catalog objects conform to a specific set of rules, this is the interface you would implement. This is not a real high-profile interface, and there should not be many extensions in this area.	Limited
IStepPerformer	This is the servicing engine's API. Servicing is a method for performing a set of actions within the job agent scripted through an XML document. This is very similar to a workflow. You can add behaviors to a servicing job by writing IStepPerformers.	Limited

IServicingStepGroupExecutionHandler	These are hooks in the servicing engine that allow you to alter the set of steps executed, or change the state of the execution engine before and after a step group.	Limited
ISecurityNamespaceExtension	This allows you to override behaviors within an existing security namespace. This one is particularly dangerous. If you wanted to implement custom security rules for a given dataset, this will allow you to do it.	Not Suitable
ILinkingConsumer, ILinkingProvider	The linking interfaces are used to extend the artifact system. This system is not currently used extensively throughout the server, and isn't a great place for third parties to add extensions.	Not Suitable
ISubscriptionPersistence	This is used when eventing subscriptions are read and written. This allows subscriptions to be stored in a canonical form, and then they are expanded at evaluation time. There is very little value here for third parties.	Not Suitable
ITeamFoundationSystemHostStateValidator	This interface is internal and not intended for public use. See ITeamFoundationHostStateValidator.	Not Suitable
IIdentityProvider	This interface is to support other Identity types. Team Foundation Server has two identity types built in, which are used in on-premises installations: WindowsIdentity and TeamFoundationIdentity. This interface is what allows the overall support of other Identity types such as ASP.NET Membership, Live ID, custom, and so on. However, some services (such as Work Item Tracking) support only the built-in types. This may be available in a future release for extensions.	Not Suitable

> **WARNING** *Extending many of these interfaces can have negative effects on the performance and stability of your servers. The server will also disable any plug-ins that throw exceptions. If you don't want your plug-in disabled, you can catch* `System.Exception` *and log it so that you can diagnose failure conditions.*

Server Plug-Ins

Team Foundation Server includes the concept of *server plug-ins*. These plug-ins are relatively straightforward to write and very easy to deploy. Because they are deployed on the server, they don't require any client-side changes to be effective. These attributes make them a great candidate for extending and controlling Team Foundation Server.

Two interfaces are suitable for extending:

➤   `ISubscriber`—Used to define real-time, in-process event subscriptions.

➤   `ITeamFoundationRequestFilter`—Implementations can inspect all requests.

To use these interfaces, you must add a reference to the `Microsoft.TeamFoundation.Framework` `.Server.dll` assembly from the `\Application Tier\Web Services\bin` directory of your application tier. You will also need a reference to the assemblies that contain the events that you want to subscribe to.

> **WARNING** *If you have multiple application tiers, your server plug-ins and job extensions must be deployed to all of them. If the plug-in is not available on a particular application tier, requests to that application tier will not trigger the plug-in.*

ISubscriber: In-Process Eventing

This is the most common place for third parties to use extensions. Team Foundation Server 2013 fires events to all `ISubscribers` that sign up for events. Almost all major events on the server publish events.

There are two different types of events that you can subscribe to:

➤   `DecisionPoint`—You can prevent something from happening.

➤   `Notification`—You receive an event as soon as something happens.

In most (but not all) cases, a `DecisionPoint` and a `Notification` event will be fired, as shown in Table 29-3. This means that you must check the `NotificationType` in your event handler; otherwise, your code may run twice when you were expecting it to run only once.

> **NOTE** *For the ISubscriber Interface definition, see* `http://aka.ms/` `ISubscriber`.

Decision Points

`DecisionPoint` events are triggered before the action is committed and can be used to prevent the action from occurring. Most actions do not allow you to change the values, just accept or deny the request.

TABLE 29-3: Available Notification Events

COMPONENT	SERVER OBJECT MODEL ASSEMBLY	EVENT	NOTIFICATION TYPE
Version Control	Microsoft .TeamFoundation .VersionControl .Server.dll	CheckinNotification	Decision, Notification
		PendChangesNotification	Decision, Notification
		UndoPendingChangesNotification	Decision, Notification
		ShelvesetNotification	Decision, Notification
		WorkspaceNotification	Decision, Notification
		LabelNotification	Notification
		CodeChurnCompletedNotification	Notification
Git	Microsoft .TeamFoundation .Git.Server.dll	PushNotification	Notification, Decision
		RefUpdateNotification	Notification, Decision
Build	Microsoft .TeamFoundation .Build.Server.dll	BuildCompletionNotificationEvent	Notification
		BuildQualityChangedNotificationEvent	Notification
Work Item Tracking	Microsoft .TeamFoundation .WorkItemTracking .Server .DataAccessLayer .dll	WorkItemChangedEvent	Notification
		WorkItemMetadataChangedNotification	Notification (minimal)
		WorkItemsDestroyedNotification	Notification (minimal)
Test Management	Microosft .TeamFoundation .TestManagement .Server.dll	TestSuiteChangedNotification	Notification
		TestRunChangedNotification	Notification
		TestPlanChangedNotification	Notification
		TestCaseResultChangedNotification	Notification
		TestPointChangedNotification	Notification
		TestRunCoverageUpdatedNotification	Notification
		BuildCoverageUpdatedNotification	Notification
		TestConfigurationChangedNotification	Notification

continues

TABLE 29-3 *(continued)*

COMPONENT	SERVER OBJECT MODEL ASSEMBLY	EVENT	NOTIFICATION TYPE
Framework	Microsoft .TeamFoundation .Server.dll	StructureChangedNotification	Notification
		AuthorizationChangedNotification	Notification
Framework	Microsoft .TeamFoundation .Framework .Server.dll	IdentityChangedNotification	Notification
		SecurityChangedNotification	Decision, Notification
		SendEmailNotification	Decision
		HostReadyEvent	Notification
Chat	Microsoft .TeamFoundation .Chat.Server	MessageSentEvent	Notification
		MessageDeletedEvent	Notification
		MessageUpdatedEvent	Notification
		GetMessagesEvent	Notification
		RoomCreatedEvent	Notification
		RoomDeletedEvent	Notification
		RoomUpdatedEvent	Notification
		MemberEvent	Notification
		MemberAddedEvent	Notification
		MemberRemovedEvent	Notification
		MemberEnteredEvent	Notification
		MemberLeftEvent	Notification
		ClientEvent	Notification
		ClientCreatedEvent	Notification
		ClientDeletedEvent	Notification

> **WARNING** *These are handled on the request processing thread and, therefore, they should be lightweight and execute quickly. Otherwise, they will impact any caller that triggers the event.*

For a `DecisionPoint` notification, your `ProcessEvent` call will be called before the change occurs. If you deny the request, you can set a message that will be shown to the user. The change will be aborted, and the processing will not continue.

The following code sample shows a simple `ISubscriber` plug-in that subscribes to the `CheckinNotification` event and `DecisionPoint` notification type (code file: `DecisionPointSubscriber.cs`):

```csharp
using System;
using Microsoft.TeamFoundation.Common;
using Microsoft.TeamFoundation.Framework.Server;
using Microsoft.TeamFoundation.VersionControl.Server;

namespace DecisionPointSubscriber
{
    /// <summary>
    /// This plugin will reject any checkins that have comments
    /// containing the word 'foobar'
    /// </summary>
    public class DecisionPointSubscriber : ISubscriber
    {
        public string Name
        {
            get { return "Sample DecisionPoint Subscriber"; }
        }

        public SubscriberPriority Priority
        {
            get { return SubscriberPriority.Low; }
        }

        public Type[] SubscribedTypes()
        {
            return new Type[] {
                typeof(CheckinNotification)
            };
        }

        public EventNotificationStatus ProcessEvent(TeamFoundationRequestContext
            requestContext, NotificationType notificationType,
            object notificationEventArgs, out int statusCode,
            out string statusMessage, out ExceptionPropertyCollection
            properties)
        {
            statusCode = 0;
            properties = null;
            statusMessage = string.Empty;

            if (notificationType == NotificationType.DecisionPoint)
            {
                try
                {
                    if (notificationEventArgs is CheckinNotification)
```

```
                    {
                        CheckinNotification notification =
                            notificationEventArgs as CheckinNotification;

                        // Logic goes here
                        if (notification.Comment.Contains("foobar"))
                        {
                            statusMessage = "Sorry, your checkin was rejected.
                                The word 'foobar' cannot be used in
                                checkin comments";
                            return EventNotificationStatus.ActionDenied;
                        }
                    }
                }
                catch (Exception exception)
                {
                    // Our plugin cannot throw any exception or it will
                    // get disabled by TFS. Log it and eat it.
                    TeamFoundationApplicationCore.LogException("DecisionPoint
                        plugin encountered the following error
                        while processing events", exception);
                }
            }
            return EventNotificationStatus.ActionPermitted;
        }
    }
}
```

Inside the `ProcessEvent` method, the plug-in checks whether the check-in comment contains the string `foobar`. If it does, a custom error message is set, and the return value is `ActionDenied`.

The other possible return values are as follows:

➤ `ActionDenied`—Action denied; do not notify other subscribers.

➤ `ActionPermitted`—Action permitted; continue with subscriber notification.

➤ `ActionApproved`—Similar to `ActionPermitted`, but do not notify other subscribers.

Notifications

For a `Notification` event, no return values are expected, and the publication serves as a notification of the occurrence of an event. `Notification` events are performed asynchronously and, therefore, do not have an impact on the caller. You should still take care to not consume too many resources here.

The following code sample shows a simple `ISubscriber` plug-in that subscribes to the `LabelNotification` event:

```
using System;
using System.Text;
using Microsoft.TeamFoundation.Common;
using Microsoft.TeamFoundation.Framework.Server;
```

```csharp
using Microsoft.TeamFoundation.VersionControl.Server;

namespace NotificationSubscriber
{
    /// <summary>
    /// This request filter will log an event to the Application
    /// event log whenever TFS labels are changed
    /// </summary>
    public class NotificationSubscriber : ISubscriber
    {
        public string Name
        {
            get { return "Sample Notification Subscriber"; }
        }

        public SubscriberPriority Priority
        {
            get { return SubscriberPriority.Low; }
        }

        public Type[] SubscribedTypes()
        {
            return new Type[] {
                typeof(LabelNotification)
            };
        }

        public EventNotificationStatus ProcessEvent(TeamFoundationRequestContext
            requestContext, NotificationType notificationType,
            object notificationEventArgs, out int statusCode,
            out string statusMessage, out ExceptionPropertyCollection properties)
        {
            statusCode = 0;
            properties = null;
            statusMessage = string.Empty;

            if (notificationType == NotificationType.Notification)
            {
                try
                {
                    if (notificationEventArgs is LabelNotification)
                    {
                        LabelNotification notification = notificationEventArgs
                            as LabelNotification;

                        StringBuilder sb = new StringBuilder();
                        sb.AppendLine(string.Format("Labels changed by {0}",
                            notification.UserName));

                        foreach (LabelResult label in notification.AffectedLabels)
                        {
                            sb.AppendLine(string.Format("{0}: {1}@{2}",
                                label.Status, label.Label, label.Scope));
                        }

                        TeamFoundationApplicationCore.Log(sb.ToString(), 0,
                            System.Diagnostics.EventLogEntryType.Information);
```

```
                }
            }
            catch (Exception exception)
            {
                // Our plugin cannot throw any exception or it will get
                // disabled by TFS. Log it and eat it.
                TeamFoundationApplicationCore.LogException("Notification plugin
                    encountered the following error while
                    processing events", exception);
            }
        }
        return EventNotificationStatus.ActionPermitted;
    }
  }
}
```

Inside the `ProcessEvent` method, the plug-in extracts the user who changed the label, along with the label details. It then uses `TeamFoundationApplicationCore.Log` to send the details to the Application event log.

```
Log Name:      Application
Source:        TFS Services
Date:          1/1/2011 12:00:00 AM
Event ID:      0
Task Category: None
Level:         Information
Keywords:      Classic
User:          N/A
Computer:      WIN-GS9GMUJITS8
Description:

Labels changed by WIN-GS9GMUJITS8\Administrator
Created: MyLabel@$/TestAgile

Application Domain: /LM/W3SVC/8080/ROOT/tfs-2-129366296712694768
```

Rather than writing to the event log, this plug-in could be easily modified to send an e-mail notification or call another web service with the label change details.

ITeamFoundationRequestFilter: Inspecting Requests

This interface is intended to allow the plug-in to inspect and manage all incoming requests. Team Foundation Server 2013 includes a number of built-in request filters. These filters perform tasks such as logging, collecting performance metrics, controlling the number of requests that can run concurrently, checking for disabled features, and checking the requests that are being made by compatible clients.

> **NOTE** *For the ITeamFoundationRequestFilter Interface definition, see* http://aka.ms/ITeamFoundationRequestFilter.

Because request filters don't rely on any particular events being implemented in the server, they are a way to inspect any and all server requests. Table 29-4 describes each of the methods in ITeamFoundationRequestFilter and when they are called in the request pipeline.

TABLE 29-4: ITeamFoundationRequestFilter Interface Methods

METHOD	DESCRIPTION
BeginRequest	BeginRequest is called after the server has determined which site or host the request is targeting and verified that it is processing requests. A call to BeginRequest is not guaranteed for all requests. An ITeamFoundationRequestFilter can throw a RequestFilterException in BeginRequest to cause the request to be completed early and an error message to be returned to the caller.
RequestReady	RequestReady is called once the request has completed authentication and is about to begin execution. At this point, the requestContext .UserContext property will contain the authenticated user information. An ITeamFoundationRequestFilter can throw a RequestFilterException in RequestReady to cause the request to be completed early and an error message to be returned to the caller.
EnterMethod	EnterMethod is called once the method being executed on this request is declared. At the time EnterMethod is called, the basic method information will be available. This includes method name, type, and the list of input parameters. This information will be available in requestContext.Method. An ITeamFoundationRequestFilter can throw a RequestFilterException in EnterMethod to cause the request to be completed early and an error message to be returned to the caller.
LeaveMethod	LeaveMethod is called once the method is complete. Once EnterMethod is called, LeaveMethod should always be called as well. Exceptions are ignored because the request is now complete.
EndRequest	EndRequest is called once the request is complete. All requests with a BeginRequest will have a matching EndRequest call. Exceptions are ignored because the request is now complete.

The following code sample shows a simple ITeamFoundationRequestFilter plug-in that only implements EnterMethod (code file: RequestFilter.cs):

```
using System;
using System.Diagnostics;
using System.Text;
using System.Text.RegularExpressions;
using Microsoft.TeamFoundation.Framework.Common;
```

```csharp
using Microsoft.TeamFoundation.Framework.Server;
using Microsoft.TeamFoundation.Server.Core;

namespace RequestFilter
{
    /// <summary>
    /// This request filter will log an event to the Application event log
    /// whenever TFS group memberships are changed
    /// </summary>
    public class RequestFilter : ITeamFoundationRequestFilter
    {
        public void EnterMethod(TeamFoundationRequestContext requestContext)
        {
            switch (requestContext.Method.Name)
            {
                case "AddMemberToApplicationGroup":
                case "RemoveMemberFromApplicationGroup":
                    try
                    {
                        StringBuilder sb = new StringBuilder();
                        sb.AppendLine(string.Format("TFS group memberships have
                            been changed by {0}",
                            requestContext.AuthenticatedUserName));
                        sb.AppendLine(string.Format("{0}",
                            requestContext.Method.Name));

                        Regex regex = new Regex(@"^IdentityDescriptor
                            \(IdentityType: (?<IdentityType>[\w\.]+);
                            Identifier: (?<Identifier>[S\d\-]+)\)?",
                            RegexOptions.Compiled);
                        foreach (string parameterKey in
                            requestContext.Method.Parameters.AllKeys)
                        {
                            string parameterValue =
                                requestContext.Method.Parameters
                                [parameterKey];

                            if (regex.IsMatch(parameterValue))
                            {
                                // If the parameter is an identity descriptor,
                                // resolve the SID to a display name using IMS
                                string identityType =
                                    regex.Match(parameterValue).Groups
                                    ["IdentityType"].Value;
                                string identifier =
                                    regex.Match(parameterValue).Groups
                                    ["Identifier"].Value;
                                IdentityDescriptor identityDescriptor = new
                                    IdentityDescriptor(identityType,
                                        identifier);
                                TeamFoundationIdentityService ims =
                                    requestContext.GetService
                                    <TeamFoundationIdentityService>();
                                TeamFoundationIdentity identity =
                                    ims.ReadIdentity(requestContext,
                                    identityDescriptor, MembershipQuery.None,
```

```
                                            ReadIdentityOptions.None);

                            sb.AppendLine(string.Format("{0}: {1}",
                                parameterKey, identity.DisplayName));
                        }
                        else
                        {
                            // Log other parameters, if any
                            sb.AppendLine(string.Format("{0}: {1}",
                                parameterKey, parameterValue));
                        }
                    }

                    TeamFoundationApplicationCore.Log(sb.ToString(), 0,
                        EventLogEntryType.Information);
                }
                catch (Exception exception)
                {
                    // Our plugin cannot throw any exception or it will get
                    // disabled by TFS. Log it and eat it.
                    TeamFoundationApplicationCore.LogException("DecisionPoint
                        plugin encountered the following error while
                        processing events", exception);
                }

                break;
        }
    }

    public void BeginRequest(TeamFoundationRequestContext requestContext)
    {
    }

    public void EndRequest(TeamFoundationRequestContext requestContext)
    {
    }

    public void LeaveMethod(TeamFoundationRequestContext requestContext)
    {
    }

    public void RequestReady(TeamFoundationRequestContext requestContext)
    {
    }
    }
}
```

In this example, if the method name matches AddMemberToApplicationGroup or RemoveMember FromApplicationGroup, the plug-in logs a message. It uses the IdentityManagementService from the server object model to resolve the SID from the method parameters to a display name. It then logs a message to the Application event log, indicating that the application group memberships have been modified.

Job Extensions

All jobs in Team Foundation Server are plug-ins that implement the ITeamFoundationJobExtension interface. This is an example of the product using its own extensibility interfaces.

> **NOTE** *For the ITeamFoundationJobExtension interface definition, see* http://aka.ms/ITeamFoundationJobExtension.

In addition to how they are invoked, the main difference between ISubscriber plug-ins and job extensions is how they're deployed:

➤ Jobs are deployed by copying the assembly into the \Application Tier\TFSJobAgent\PlugIns directory, rather than the Web Services\bin\PlugIns directory.

➤ If a job plug-in is already loaded, and the job agent is currently running, you must stop the job agent before you can replace the plug-in assembly. This releases the file handle.

➤ Along with having the assembly deployed, a job must be either scheduled to run or manually queued using the job service API.

The following code sample shows a simple ITeamFoundationJobExtension plug-in that implements the Run method (code file: JobExtension.cs):

```csharp
using System;
using System.Diagnostics;
using Microsoft.TeamFoundation.Framework.Server;
using Microsoft.TeamFoundation.VersionControl.Server;

namespace JobExtension
{
    /// <summary>
    /// This job will log an event to the Application event log with the
    /// current number of workspaces that have not been accessed in 30 days
    /// </summary>
    public class JobExtension : ITeamFoundationJobExtension
    {
        public TeamFoundationJobExecutionResult Run(
            TeamFoundationRequestContext requestContext,
            TeamFoundationJobDefinition jobDefinition, DateTime queueTime,
            out string resultMessage)
        {
            resultMessage = null;
            int warningDays = 30;
            int oldWorkspaces = 0;

            try
            {
                // Get all workspaces in the collection
                foreach (Workspace workspace in
                    requestContext.GetService
```

```
            <TeamFoundationVersionControlService>
            ().QueryWorkspaces(requestContext, null, null, 0))
        {
            if (workspace.LastAccessDate <= DateTime.Now.Subtract(new
                TimeSpan(warningDays, 0, 0, 0)))
            {
                oldWorkspaces++;
            }
        }

        TeamFoundationApplicationCore.Log(string.Format("There are {0}
            workspaces that have not been accessed in the last {1}
            days", oldWorkspaces, warningDays), 0,
            EventLogEntryType.Information);
        return TeamFoundationJobExecutionResult.Succeeded;
    }
    catch (RequestCanceledException)
    {
        resultMessage = null;
        return TeamFoundationJobExecutionResult.Stopped;
    }
    catch (Exception exception)
    {
        resultMessage = exception.ToString();
        return TeamFoundationJobExecutionResult.Failed;
    }
        }
    }
}
```

When this job is executed, it uses `TeamFoundationVersionControlService` from the server object model to enumerate all workspaces in the collection. It then checks whether the workspace has been accessed in the past 30 days. If it has not been accessed, a counter is incremented.

Finally, the job logs a message to the Application event log, indicating how many workspaces are stale and have not been accessed in the past month.

Job Deployment

The most difficult part of custom job extensions is deployment. It's easy enough to define a single job for a single collection. However, if you want to have your job defined and scheduled for all new collections, there's not an easy way to do that.

> **NOTE** *The built-in jobs are scheduled using servicing steps that are part of the built-in project collection creation scripts. Unfortunately, these servicing steps are replaced with each patch of Team Foundation Server. So, if you customized them, they would get overwritten the next time you upgraded. A creative solution would be to build an* ISubscriber Notification *plug-in that subscribes to the* HostReadyEvent. *Each time the server starts, it could check if the job is scheduled for all project collections, and schedule it if it isn't.*

The following PowerShell script demonstrates how to use `ITeamFoundationJobService` from the client object model to define and schedule a job for a single collection (code file: `Install-JobExtension.ps1`):

```
# Install-JobExtension.ps1
# Usage: Install-JobExtension <TfsCollectionUri>
# Example: Install-JobExtension http://yourserver:8080/tfs/yourcollection
#
# Before running this, you will need to copy the assembly containing the
# class that implements ITeamFoundationJobExtension to the following directory
# on all Application Tier servers:
# C:\Program Files\Microsoft Team Foundation Server 12.0\Application
# Tier\TFSJobAgent\plugins
#
# This will use the TFS client object model to register and schedule the job
# By default the job will be scheduled to run at 5 AM daily.

# Halt on errors
$ErrorActionPreference = "Stop"

$Uri = $args[0]

if ([String]::IsNullOrEmpty($Uri))
{
    $Uri = "http://localhost:8080/tfs"
}

# Define your own well-known GUIDs for your job
$JobDefinitionGuid = New-Object System.Guid -ArgumentList
    "E2B88C7A-7745-4E49-9442-5A6851190242"

Add-Type -LiteralPath "C:\Program Files (x86)\Microsoft Visual Studio 12.0\Common7\
IDE\ReferenceAssemblies\v2.0\Microsoft.TeamFoundation.Common.dll"
Add-Type -LiteralPath "C:\Program Files (x86)\Microsoft Visual Studio 12.0\Common7\
IDE\ReferenceAssemblies\v2.0\Microsoft.TeamFoundation.Client.dll"


# Get the job service for the collection.
$Tpc = New-Object Microsoft.TeamFoundation.Client.TfsTeamProjectCollection
    -ArgumentList $Uri
$JobService = $Tpc.GetService([Microsoft.TeamFoundation.
    Framework.Client.ITeamFoundationJobService])

# Define the job agent job
$JobDefinition = New-Object Microsoft.TeamFoundation.
    Framework.Client.TeamFoundationJobDefinition                `
                                -ArgumentList $JobDefinitionGuid,            `
                                              "Sample Job Extension",        `
                                              "JobExtension.JobExtension",   `
                                              $null

# Schedule the job to run at 5 AM every day, starting tomorrow.
$TomorrowFiveAM = [DateTime]::Today.AddDays(1).AddHours(5).ToUniversalTime()
$JobSchedule = New-Object Microsoft.TeamFoundation.
    Framework.Client.TeamFoundationJobSchedule `
```

```
                              -ArgumentList $TomorrowFiveAM, 86400

$JobDefinition.Schedule.Add($JobSchedule)

# Save the job definition to the collection's job service.
$JobService.UpdateJob($JobDefinition)
```

This script connects to the specified collection or the default collection if none is specified. It then creates a `TeamFoundationJobDefinition` object for the job extension and then creates a `TeamFoundationJobSchedule` for the job that schedules it to be run every 24 hours (86400 seconds) starting at 5 a.m. tomorrow, UTC time.

Once the job and its schedule are defined, it is saved to the server using `ITeamFoundation JobService.UpdateJob()`.

To invoke the job manually, and to see if your job extension works, you can run the following PowerShell command:

```
# Run the job now manually
$jobService.QueueJobNow($JobDefinition, $false)
```

VISUAL STUDIO EXTENSIBILITY

You can extend Visual Studio by using macros, add-ins, `VSPackages`, and Managed Extensibility Framework (MEF) extensions, and you can deploy them in a number of ways, including VSIX and custom extension galleries.

By leveraging Visual Studio extensibility, it's also possible to automate and extend some of the Team Foundation Server windows, dialog boxes, and events. Figure 29-3 shows a sample add-in that interacts with Source Control Explorer. Be warned, however, that not all of the dialog boxes are extensible without getting deep into reflection, and if you do so, it is very likely that an update to Visual Studio may break your integration.

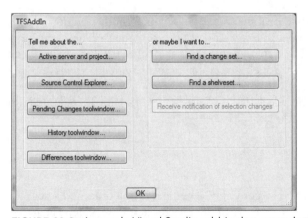

FIGURE 29-3: A sample Visual Studio add-in that extends the Source Control Explorer

> **NOTE** *For an example of extending Source Control Explorer, see* `http://tinyurl.com/TFSExtendingSCE`. *For an example of extending the work item tracking context menu, see* `http://tinyurl.com/TFSExtendingWITMenu`. *For general information on Visual Studio extensibility, see "Customizing, Automating, and Extending the Development Environment" at* `http://aka.ms/VSExtensions`.

One area of the Team Foundation Server UI that was designed for extensibility inside Visual Studio is the Team Explorer view and all the controls that it hosts. For example, it is possible to extend the pending changes page by adding new sections to it. Table 29-5 describes the possible Team Explorer extensibility points.

TABLE 29-5: Team Explorer Extensibility

EXTENSIBILITY TYPE	DESCRIPTION
Team Explorer Page	Team Explorer consists of multiple pages (for example, the Pending Changes view is a page). You can create your own pages or add sections to existing ones.
Team Explorer Section	A page is made up of sections.
Team Explorer Navigation Item	Team Explorer allows shortcuts to pages to appear in the drop-down menu at the top of Team Explorer. These are defined at Navigation Items.
Team Explorer Navigation Link	Sections can contain links that navigate to other pages in Team Explorer.

The Team Explorer control is a WPF based-control that makes use of extensibility points defined in the `Microsoft.TeamFoundation.VersionControl.Extensibility` namespace. The ALM Rangers released a great article on extending the Team Explorer view in Visual Studio 2012, which you can read at `http://aka.ms/ExtendTE`. The walkthrough is very comprehensive, but there have been some changes in the Team Foundation Server 2013 release. Tarun Arora, a Microsoft MVP, has an excellent blog post explaining how to upgrade a 2012 extension to work with Team Foundation Server 2013 at `http://aka.ms/UpgradingVISXExtensions`.

OTHER RESOURCES

Team Foundation Server is very extensible, and, accordingly, a number of solutions and resources are available to assist you. These resources can have useful samples for getting started. The partners can also be engaged to build custom solutions for your needs.

Table 29-6 shows a breakdown of some available resources.

TABLE 29-6: Available Resources

RESOURCE	DESCRIPTION	NOTES
Visual Studio ALM Rangers	This delivers out-of-band solutions for missing features or for guidance. Periodically, they take nominations for new projects, vote for them, develop them, and then release them on CodePlex.	For more information, refer to the Visual Studio ALM Ranger page on MSDN at `http://aka.ms/AlmRangers`.
Visual Studio Industry Partners (VSIP)	This provides technical resources, business insight, and extensive co-marketing to partners who sell products that integrate with and extend Visual Studio.	To learn about existing VSIP partners, see `http://aka.ms/vsip`.
Microsoft Partner Program: ALM Competency	The Application Lifecycle Management (ALM) Competency in the Microsoft Partner Program enables partners to demonstrate their expertise in providing training and consultation for, or deploying, Microsoft Visual Studio tools.	To find partners who have achieved the ALM Competency, see Microsoft Pinpoint at `http://aka.ms/AlmPartners`.
CodePlex	This is Microsoft's Open Source project hosting website. You can download and use many projects on CodePlex that extend Team Foundation Server. You can also use CodePlex to share your own extensions with the world.	For Open Source projects that extend Team Foundation Server, see `http://www.codeplex.com/site/search?query=tfs`.
Visual Studio Gallery	This provides quick access to tools, controls, and templates to help you get the most out of Visual Studio.	For a list of Visual Studio tools and extensions, see `http://tinyurl.com/VSGalleryTFS`.
MSDN Code Gallery	This is a site where you may download and share applications, code snippets, and other resources with the developer community.	For a list of code snippets, see `http://tinyurl.com/MSDNGalleryTFS`.

SUMMARY

This chapter began with an overview of the high-level architecture of the extensibility available within Team Foundation Server. You learned how to get started with the client object model as well as some useful tips for working with it. SOAP event subscriptions were then discussed, along with the available event types that can be subscribed to.

The server object model was examined, and examples of server plug-ins were provided. This included plug-ins that send real-time notifications and plug-ins that can change the flow of a command. Finally, other resources were discussed that can help you leverage the extensibility available in Team Foundation Server.

INDEX

M

S